The Industrial Composition of Income and Product

NATIONAL BUREAU OF ECONOMIC RESEARCH

CONFERENCE ON RESEARCH IN INCOME AND WEALTH

The Industrial Composition of Income and Product

JOHN W. KENDRICK, *editor*
THE GEORGE WASHINGTON UNIVERSITY

Studies in Income and Wealth
VOLUME THIRTY-TWO
by the Conference on Research in Income and Wealth

NATIONAL BUREAU OF ECONOMIC RESEARCH
NEW YORK

Distributed by COLUMBIA UNIVERSITY PRESS
NEW YORK AND LONDON 1968

Relation of National Bureau Directors to
Publications Reporting Conference Proceedings

Since the present volume is a record of conference proceedings, it has been exempted from the rules governing submission of manuscripts to, and critical review by, the Board of Directors of the National Bureau. It has, however, been reviewed and accepted for publication by the Director of Research.

Resolution adopted July 6, 1948,
as revised November 21, 1949

L. C. Card: 67-29642
Printed in the United States of America

NATIONAL BUREAU OF ECONOMIC RESEARCH
1967

Prefatory Note

This volume of Studies in Income and Wealth contains the papers presented at the Conference on the Industrial Composition of Income and Product held on December 1–2, 1966, at the Brookings Institution in Washington, D.C. The Program Committee consisted of John W. Kendrick, chairman, Jack Alterman, Martin Marimont, Milton Moss, and John P. Powelson. We are indebted to Gerald R. Paul for preparation of the manuscript for press and to H. Irving Forman for drawing the charts.

Executive Committee, 1967–68

Robert Eisner, *Chairman*
Evsey D. Domar
Graeme S. Dorrance
Morris R. Goldman
Zvi Griliches
F. Thomas Juster
Irving B. Kravis
Milton Moss
Malcolm C. Urquhart
Harold W. Watts
Mildred E. Courtney, *Secretary*

Contents

The Industrial Composition of Income and Product

Introduction

JOHN W. KENDRICK
THE GEORGE WASHINGTON UNIVERSITY

The gradual refinement and elaboration of national income and product accounts in the United States and Canada since the 1930's have made possible increasingly sophisticated quantitative analyses of these economies. There have been important advances in econometric models explaining changes in aggregate demand by major categories of final product, and these new techniques are now useful tools for short-term forecasting. The income and product accounts in current and constant prices also serve as the basis for analyses of economic growth and as background for reasonably accurate long-term aggregate projections.

Until recently, however, the basic estimates were not at hand for adequate analysis of changes in the industrial structure of the economy. For many years estimates of national income by industry and type of income have been available, but not until 1962 in the United States and 1963 in Canada did official estimates of national product by industry in current and constant dollars become available. Then, in 1964 and 1965, input–output tables for the United States economy were published on a consistent basis with the income and product accounts, making possible a linkage between final demand and industry product.

It was against this background of statistical developments that a conference on the industrial composition of income and product was planned. The date of this conference was delayed until December 1966, however, to enable the authors of the papers on the U.S. economy to take advantage of revisions of the industry product estimates which were made available on an unpublished basis in May 1966 and subsequently published for broad industry groupings in the April 1967 *Survey of Current Business.*

The structure of the program can be described briefly, although each of the papers is summarized in the next section for those who wish a more detailed guide. Three of the conference papers (in Part III) describe the U.S. and Canadian estimates of industry product, discuss the conceptual and statistical problems encountered in their preparation, and point to directions for further improvement. The other papers make use of the new estimates for analytical purposes. The two papers of Part I discuss the uses of input–output tables in providing a bridge between expenditures for, and prices of, final products and real product and prices by industry. The three papers of Part II are concerned with explaining industry changes in labor and nonlabor costs (total and per unit of real product) and in factor shares by industry. Unit costs are decomposed into the productivity and factor price components. Relative changes in factor prices and inputs are used to explain changes in the functional distribution of gross income by industry.

The conference papers thus make a definite statistical and analytical contribution to understanding economic structure. The thorough description and critical appraisal of the industry estimates of income and product will be of value to both users and producers of the numbers for some time to come.

The papers by Jack Gottsegen and Richard C. Ziemer, Gordon Garston and David Worton, Clayton Gehman and Cornelia Motheral, and their several discussants, will serve as reference documents for continuing efforts to improve the estimates and for further analytical work. In particular, the comparisons of the real industry product estimates for the United States with the other important body of industrial production measures—those of the Federal Reserve Board—provide a systematic appraisal of the conceptual and statistical differences between the series. It is to be hoped that the conference has provided both an impetus to, and an agenda for, further efforts to refine the two sets of estimates and to reconcile them while preserving the distinctive features and advantages of each for their somewhat different analytical uses.

The authors of the analytical papers addressed themselves to key elements in the changing industry structure of income and product. Their substantive findings enhance our understanding of this important area of economics, and their methodological innovations will facilitate future work. The papers do not, nor were they intended to, provide a comprehensive analysis of changing economic structure. Yet the future authors of the systematic models that may eventually be built will have to link changes in final demand and in the technical coefficients of input–output matrixes to change in industry products, as done by Beatrice Vaccara and Nancy Simon. They will have to translate changes in final-product prices into changes in industry prices, as done by Jack Alterman, before the interaction of factor markets and product markets can be understood. They will have to decompose changes in labor and property costs into price and quantity components, and unit factor costs into price and productivity components, as done by Leon Greenberg, Jerome Mark, and John Kendrick, as a prerequisite for further analysis of the factor markets. They will have to examine relative changes in quantities and prices of labor and property in order to explain factor substitutions, whether by the approach suggested by Alvin Egbert or Ta-Chung Liu, as an element in the production and pricing of products as well as in the functional distribution of income.

Obviously, much further analytical work will be necessary before we understand the process of change in the mutually determined sets of prices and quantities of factors and products which result in alterations in economic structure, as revealed by the industry income and product estimates. In a concluding section of the introduction, I suggest some possible avenues for further work; this indication of the needs and possibilities for further analysis attests to the importance of the present set of papers as a contribution to understanding changes in the structure of the economy. The following section attempts to summarize in somewhat greater detail the chief points covered by the authors and their discussants.

Summaries of the Papers and Discussions

In his introductory paper, "A Framework for Analysis of the Industrial Origin of Income, Product, Costs and Prices," Jack Alterman discusses various analytical uses of the industry income and product estimates in current and constant prices, both separately and in conjunction with input-output information. Alterman's summary sections provide a useful background for other papers in the volume. In addition, he develops in some depth the use of input–output tables for tracing the industrial origin of changes in prices of final goods and services and for decomposing price changes into specific factor and nonfactor cost elements. The analysis is performed with respect to changes in costs and prices of final expenditures between 1958 and 1964 for forty-two industry groups.

As background for his analysis, Alterman had to convert the conventional input–output total-requirements table, which shows *total* output generated in each industry per dollar of final expenditures, into one showing the value-added content of final-expenditure categories, which could be further distributed into types of primary inputs. These distributions are of interest in their own right, but particularly as they contribute to his analysis of the industrial origin of changes in prices of consumer goods and services for 1958–64 (see his Table 7). Here, the industry value-added content of 1958 consumption is used to weight the changes in industry unit value added (net price) to derive the 1958–64 change in price of total personal consumption expenditures. The results suggest many things. For example, of the 7.2 per cent over-all increase in prices of consumer products, 2.5 percentage points were contributed by business and personal services. This was 34 per cent of the over-all price rise, while the industry's share of the value-added content of personal consumption outlays was 12 per cent. With respect to the primary-input content of the 7.2 per cent price change, change in unit labor cost, for example, corresponded to 4.1 percentage points, or 57 per cent of the increase, although employee compensation comprised 48.5 per cent of value added in 1958. Unit gross property compensation also is seen to have contributed more than proportionately, with unit proprietor and rental income contributing less than proportionately.

As Alterman and his discussant Richard Ruggles emphasize, the analysis does not explain price behavior, and causality should not be imputed to the "contributing" factors. Ruggles further notes that the use of unit value-added indexes has serious limitations in price analysis, since consolidation of the accounts to exclude intermediate materials and services obscures important behavioral relationships. Nevertheless, Ruggles states that the papers make a real contribution in analyzing price and unit cost changes by industry and type, in contrast to ". . . the simplistic view which suggests that the price change taking place in the economy represents over-all demand and cost situations which permeate all sectors of the economy in much the same degree."

In "Factors Affecting the Postwar Industrial Composition of Real

Product," Beatrice Vaccara and Nancy Simon of the Office of Business Economics start by noting the sizable dispersion among industry groups in rates of growth of real product. They set themselves the task of explaining the industry growth differentials in terms of two factors: changes in the level and composition of final demand and changes in the technical coefficients revealed by input–output studies that relate the outputs of industries to final demand generally. The input-output technique is essential since it enables the analyst to measure the impact on a given industry's gross and net output not only of changes in the final demand for the products of that industry but also the indirect requirements due to changes in the final demand for outputs of all other industries.

Building on previous work, Vaccara and Simon were able to develop a 1947 input–output table reasonably consistent with the published OBE table for 1958 and thus with the national income and product accounts. They were then able to obtain alternative estimates of the relative importance of the two factors in explaining industry output changes between 1947 and 1958, depending on whether they applied the fixed technical coefficients of the initial or terminal year. Since there were marked differences between the alternative measures of the relative importance of the two factors, they averaged the results in order to obtain single measures.

The authors' interesting findings are presented in some detail in the tables and text. They conclude that the changing level and pattern of final demand were somewhat more important in explaining relative changes in industry real product from 1947 to 1958 than were changes in the technical coefficients. They found further that the two elements of change generally reinforced one another, especially in cases of marked relative changes in output. Estimates of relative importance of the two factors using both 1958 and 1963 technical coefficients will have to await completion of the OBE input–output matrix for the latter year.

Vaccara and Simon recognize various difficulties in their approach. In particular, they point out that changes in the technical coefficients reflect not only technological change, but also changes in product mix both at the final-demand and intermediate-input levels; nonproportionalities due to scale effects and changes in capacity utilization; and errors of observation, estimation, and computation. Their discussant, Gary Fromm, puts additional heavy stress on the index number problems. He argues that the averaging of Paasche and Laspeyres indicators gives "a bastard measure." He would also like to see the analysis cast in terms of partial as well as total derivatives. Finally, he would have welcomed clues as to why output and coefficient shifts took place—including analysis of reactions to altered relative prices, capital-labor substitutions, degree of embodiment of technical progress, effects of changing average age of capital, and other aspects of the underlying production functions.

To examine "Sector Changes in Unit Labor Costs," Leon Greenberg and Jerome Mark of the Bureau of Labor Statistics first calculate the quotients of index numbers of employee compensation and of real product, using the OBE nonfarm industry sector estimates. They then "explain" the changes and trends in unit labor cost for the several sectors in terms of the two components, average hourly labor compensation and real product per man-hour. The man-hour estimates used as the denominators for compensation and real product were based primarily on the BLS employment and average hours estimates obtained from establishments in the various industries, supplemented by additional data on average hours of nonproduction workers (and for proprietors and unpaid family workers in the case of farming and the total private economy).

Each industry group had its own pattern of changes in unit labor costs, viewed as a quotient of average hourly earnings and output per man-hour as depicted in the charts accompanying the Greenberg-Mark paper. In general, the authors found a marked deceleration in the rate of increase in unit labor costs during the period 1960–64 compared with the earlier period 1947–60. This was the combined result of some deceleration in the rates of increase in hourly compensation and acceleration of the gains in output per man-hour, with the productivity element generally the more important. Also, year-to-year fluctuations in unit labor costs were greater in the earlier period than in the later one. The chief exceptions to their generalizations are to be found in the construction and service sectors, for which the authors believe the product estimates to be less reliable. Their discussant, Albert Rees, points out that it would not be difficult to improve the construction estimates substantially.

Greenberg and Mark have also developed estimates of total labor cost, including an imputation for proprietors, both for the farm sector and the total private economy. The trends and relationships for the latter are quite similar to those obtained by using employee costs alone. The authors also calculate the effects of interindustry production shifts on unit labor costs, hourly compensation, and output per man-hour. They find the shift effect to be relatively small—averaging 0.3 of a percentage point a year or less—on the proportionate changes in each of the three variables.

Albert Rees comments that the deceleration of the rise in average earnings and unit labor costs from 1960 to 1964 was associated with a higher average unemployment rate than prevailed in the earlier period. The relevance of his remark is apparent when it is further noted that in the subsequent period, 1965–67, rising labor costs experienced a resumed acceleration as unemployment fell to a low level.

My own paper "Industry Changes in Nonlabor Costs," complements the one by Greenberg and Mark. The analysis was confined to changes between average values for the two three-year periods 1948–50 and 1961–63. First, there is some discussion of industry changes in direct business taxes, total and per unit of output, to clear the way for analysis of the major nonlabor cost, gross property compensation. Not only did indirect business taxes per unit of product in the domestic business economy rise substantially more than unit factor costs and product prices but there was more dispersion in rates of change among industries. Assuming that Commerce Department allocations of the taxes among industries are reasonably accurate, the differential effect of indirect business taxes on prices and resource allocation among industries is obviously a prime subject for further investigation.

Changes in industry shares of gross property compensation (GPC) are broken down into their components: relative changes in real product and in GPC per unit of product. Paralleling the work of Greenberg and Mark, relative industry changes in GPC per unit were analyzed in terms of relative changes in the two components: capital productivity and the price of capital. A significant negative correlation shows up between these variables, as is to be expected for reasons adduced. Relative industry changes in capital (and labor) productivity also appear to be significantly correlated with relative changes in output.

I also consider changes in the property share of gross factor income. The share declined somewhat in the domestic business economy and in about two-thirds of the industry groupings. That is, in these industries and in the sector as a whole, unit GPC rose less than total factor cost per unit of product. To put it differently, the declining capital share was associated with a proportionate increase in the quantity of capital input relative to total factor input. Estimates of these variables are given in the tables; the associated historical elasticities of substitution are less than unity in twenty-five of the thirty-five industry groups and for the domestic business economy as a whole. In the concluding section of the paper, I suggest the reasons for the apparent general tendency towards a declining property share and the basic variables that would have to be explored to account for industry variations in, and exceptions to, the general pattern.

The discussant, Dale Jorgenson, concentrated on developing a concept of capital input alternative to mine, which assumes that capital services parallel the movement of the stock of capital. Under certain conditions, estimates of capital input under the two concepts would show the same movements, but economy-wide estimates prepared by Jorgenson and Griliches show a significantly larger increase than mine for the postwar period, and thus the associated capital- and total-productivity estimates (and presumably capital prices) show a lesser increase. The effects of the higher growth in quantities of capital inputs and the lesser increase in prices would tend to be offsetting as regards the calculated elasticities of substitution, however.

The paper by Alvin Egbert of the U.S. Department of Agriculture, "Changing Factor Shares by Industry: Factor Prices and Factor Substitutions" covers a challenging topic. After pointing out the limitations of an aggregate production function approach, Egbert develops several equations explaining factor shares of a firm, which he then relates to industry income accounts. Basically, he explains the profit share of gross (or net) income in relation to the proportions of gross income absorbed by the other major cost elements, which in turn are viewed generally as the product of quantities and prices of inputs. He discusses qualitatively the elements, such as market structure and the technological changes, that would affect ratios of profits and costs to sales or value added. But due to lack of data on nonlabor inputs and prices, Egbert is unable to statistically implement his complete model. Rather, he turns to an analysis of changes in labor shares of national product by industry.

He points out that employee compensation as a percentage of GNP has increased moderately since World War II, mainly between 1947 and 1957. There has been considerable dispersion among industries in the trend of the labor share, with some industries showing marked declines, and there has been variation in movement over subperiods. In general, he finds that the industries in which the labor share has declined are either high-growth or declining industries. Egbert then "explains" statistically the changing industry labor shares by subperiod in terms of the relative changes in four variables: man-hours, average hourly compensation, net output, and the implicit price deflator. He speculates as to the more fundamental dynamic causal forces behind the changes in demand for, and supply of, outputs and inputs, whose interplay is reflected in the factor shares. As he points out, the first step in specifying the relevant behavioral relations within and between industries is obtaining adequate data, particularly on nonlabor inputs and their prices.

In his comments, Ta-Chung Liu notes that the usefulness of Egbert's formal approach is similar to that of the quantity theory of money in that it identifies components of change without providing a theoretical explanation. Further, Egbert's four components are not the result of the working of mutually exclusive forces. Liu enumerates five basic parameters, each of which, with one exception—the speed of adjustment towards equilibrium in the labor market—affects at least two of the terms in Egbert's identity. Liu finds the paper a useful contribution, but advocates constructing a dynamic theoretical model that would include all basic parameters. He believes the difficulties raised by Egbert could be largely overcome except for the problem of aggregation.

The final group of three papers is devoted largely to a discussion of the basic estimates. The paper by Gottsegen and Ziemer of the Office of Business Economics describes in detail the underlying concept and methods used to estimate gross product originating in the various industries. The authors' chief purpose is to compare the OBE estimates in constant prices with the other widely used production measures for manufacturing—those of the FRB. Both sets of measures for the broad categories of total manufacturing, durables and nondurables, show much the same patterns of change over the period 1948–64, although the FRB indexes may be interpreted as having a somewhat higher growth rate. But measures for some of the two-digit industry groups exhibit considerable divergence.

Gottsegen and Ziemer point out that the differences are of three main types. First, the concepts differ in that the OBE estimates are true net output measures, in which the real intermediate product costs are, in effect, deducted from the real gross value of production by the "double deflation" method, while the FRB extrapolates base-period value added by gross production indexes. The second source of divergence is methodological; in particular, the FRB uses Census gross value-added weights, while the OBE weights are net value added, gross of excise taxes and depreciation. Third, there are statistical differences: OBE uses a price-deflation approach, while FRB uses primarily physical volume measures, or proxies for them, particularly productivity-adjusted man-hours following the most recent Census bench mark. At the time of the comparisons, the FRB had not yet adjusted its indexes to the 1958 and 1963 Census production index numbers, so as Gehman and Motheral point out in their comments, the Gottsegen-Ziemer comparisons are more meaningful for the 1947–54 period. The authors provide comparisons annually by two-digit industries for the period 1947–64.

Commenting on the Gottsegen-Ziemer paper, Vivian Spencer is impressed by the striking similarities of the FRB and OBE series, considering the differences of concept and methodology. She points out that the deflated Census value-added series usually fall between the other two, but closer to the OBE series. Marked divergencies in a few groups, however, underscore the need for further study. The availability in 1967 of the Census bench-mark production indexes for 1958 and 1963 will facilitate reconciliation work. Even before completion of this work, Spencer is able to note that the BLS price indexes used by OBE for deflation tend to show more increase than the Census unit value indexes. She suggests this may be a major factor accounting for the slightly lower growth rate indicated by the OBE estimates.

Frank Garfield stresses the sensitivity to errors in either the output- or input-price indexes of the OBE estimates based on the double deflation procedure. He calls for further investigation of these problems and suggests that for some industries alternative approaches are desirable. He also implies that the net output approach is unlikely to be satisfactory for monthly and possibly for quarterly measures.

Milton Moss contributes a comprehensive critique entitled "Eliminating Disparity in the U.S. Measures of Output in Constant Prices." He points to the specific areas in which reconciliation is to be sought;

for example, reconciling Census value added and gross product originating, and the detailed gross output indexes which should be identical in both systems. Moss hopes that the discussion here will provide the necessary push to get the work done. He calls for making bench marks of the FRB indexes more frequently. He also suggests that eventually the OBE should publish its estimates of gross output and intermediate inputs, and the underlying industry detail, at least for special analyses. Moss sees a continuing role for both the OBE- and FRB-type measures.

In the paper "Measures of Industrial Production and Final Demand," Clayton Gehman and Cornelia Motheral describe the FRB index numbers of production by particular market groupings—consumer goods, equipment, and materials—by various categories of each. Their primary interest is in explaining how these series, first published in 1959 and subsequently expanded and refined, are of value in current economic analysis. For example, comparisons of the end-product measures with those for the related materials provide indications of inventory change prior to the availability of the direct inventory measures. Further, the subdivisions of the end-product measures add interesting dimensions to analysis of fluctuations not provided by the final-expenditure estimates.

The authors also compare their end-product measures with roughly comparable segments of the OBE's real final-product estimates. They do not attempt to reconcile the two sets of measures by estimating distributive margins and inventory changes, and adjusting for scope, weights, and other statistical differences. But they do find some puzzling discrepancies, which call for further investigation, between the two sets of measures. In fact, their paper suggests much regarding areas for further substantive and statistical research. They also propose new FRB measures of farm output, commodity transportation and distribution, and foreign merchandise trade in order to provide a complete system of monthly indexes for the goods and construction sectors of the economy.

Michael Godfrey comments on the Gehman-Motheral paper in the context of theoretical and policy considerations. Commenting on both the OBE and FRB papers, Stanley Sigel expresses the belief that a detailed reconciliation between the two data systems should now be possible and regrets that both papers contained only partial elements of a comprehensive comparison. Sigel specifies the framework he would use for a systematic reconciliation. Certainly, the analytical and policy uses of output measures are of sufficient importance to warrant a major effort to improve and reconcile both major sets of estimates.

Gordon Garston and David Worton, in their paper, "Problems in the Estimation of Industry Output in Current and Constant Dollars in Canada," state their primary purposes as being ". . . to describe the progress already achieved in the development of industry-of-origin domestic product measures . . . , to indicate the remaining major conceptual and statistical problems which stand in the way of fully consistent and integrated industry-of-origin data, and to present some statistical results and analytical uses." The Canadian industry product estimates were first published in 1963, although industry income estimates became available in 1951 on a net basis, and on a gross domestic basis in 1958.

The Canadian paper is a useful supplement to the one by the OBE representatives in that Garston and Worton discuss in some detail various conceptual problems that pertain to the U.S. as well as the Canadian estimates. For example, the authors opt for the real-net-national-product-at-factor-cost concept vs. gross product at market price. Although the Canadian measures are now gross and only partially exclude indirect business taxes by industry, the authors discuss the problems involved in estimating the remaining business taxes and in obtaining current-value depreciation estimates by industry through further development of perpetual-inventory series. They also would treat interest and rent payments as nonfactor costs, rather than as part of income originating in given industries.

Garston and Worton consider the convention of measuring the product of noncommercial sectors at cost (generally labor cost, without allowance for rental values of capital assets), and the inadequacy of the corresponding real-product measures which do not reflect productivity change. They likewise note the inadequacy of some of the service industry measures, and they suggest a new approach to the financial sector.

The authors report progress in development of industry price indexes for production and intermediate purchases. They hope for increasing reliance on the double deflation approach to real-product estimates, rather than extrapolation of base-period product by physical-quantity indexes. On the thorny issue of quality change, the authors propose a partial adjustment for it to the extent that it is reflected in changes in real costs per unit.

The paper's discussant, Michael Gort, argues that if carried to its logical extreme, the proposed approach to quality change would result in the measurement of real output in terms of real input. Gort also argues in favor of the concept of industry product at market values, which he believes will give better deflated estimates for comparisons over time. Gort disagrees with Garston and Worton's proposed treatment of income and product originating in the finance and real estate sectors; and he believes the problem of discrepancy between company- and establishment-based data is smaller for most industries than they imply.

Estimation problems aside, Garston and Worton provide illustrations of an impressive array of uses for industry product estimates—as a check on the final-expenditure estimates, for business cycle or current business analysis, for analysis of aggregate growth and structural changes, and as a framework for projections which could serve as background for policy decisions. They look forward to the development of Canadian income estimates on a consistent industry basis to make possible the analysis of cost-price interrelations of the sort done for the U.S. in some of the other papers here.

All in all, the conference papers represent important progress reports on the continuing efforts of economists to better understand the process of changing economic structure. It will be evident to the reader that, as noted earlier, various forces affecting economic structure were not covered, nor could they have been in the space of a two-day conference. In concluding this introduction, I shall point out some of the areas which must be covered in other investigations before we can hope to construct a comprehensive model of the changing industry composition of national income and product.

The papers of Part I took as given the changes in the composition of consumption expenditures. Yet relative changes in quantities purchased can be explained with reference to changes in relative prices, differential income elasticities, and shifts in preferences. Even the shifts in preferences might be explained in terms of other variables, such as outlays for new product development and advertising.

The papers of Part II took as given the relative industry changes in factor productivities. Yet these, as well as the changes in technical coefficients, might be explained in terms of the forces behind cost-reducing innovations, such as research and development, scale, cyclical variation of output, and other industry variables. The factor substitutions by industry, which also affect partial productivity ratios, could be explained in terms of changes in relative factor prices and the nature of industry innovations.

To explain relative changes in the prices of the factors, it will be necessary to investigate the forces behind changing factor supplies which interact with the changing factor demands as influenced by product demands and factor productivities. The influence on prices of differing market structures is also relevant, as is the problem of time lags in the adjustment of factor supplies and prices to changes in demand.

Not only is additional analytical work called for, given the existing body of estimates, but additional data will be needed if a comprehensive structural model is to be developed. In particular, better and more detailed estimates of industry stocks and inputs of capital, and prices of capital services will be needed. In addition to the real industry product estimates and implicit price deflators, it will be helpful if the OBE also publishes the companion estimates of gross outputs and their prices and the intermediate inputs and their prices. Estimates of research, development, training, advertising, and other explanatory variables on an industry basis will also be of use in the correlations suggested above. Finally, there is the perennial question of the advisability of further industry disaggregation of income and product and of the interindustry sales and purchases matrix. Additional detail will add to the usefulness of analyses, but the benefits must be weighed against the costs of greater complexity.

Regardless of the direction of future work, we are fortunate that industry income and product and input–output estimates are firmly embedded in the national economic accounting framework. This ensures that structural analyses will be consistent with aggregate models and that future improvements in the accounts will benefit both.

Part I

Changes in Final Demand, Industry Product, and Prices

Factors Affecting the Postwar Industrial Composition of Real Product

BEATRICE N. VACCARA
NANCY W. SIMON
OFFICE OF BUSINESS ECONOMICS

The period since the end of World War II has been characterized by an ever rising level of real gross national product. The sizable postwar increase in real product has not, however, been shared equally by all industry groups in the economy.[1] While real GNP increased by 84 per cent between 1947 and 1964, for some industry groups the increase was over 250 per cent, and for others less than 10 per cent. (Real product in one industry group actually declined during this period of over-all growth.) More than one-fourth of the industry groups analyzed had increases in real product 50 per cent above the average, and one-third had increases of 50 per cent less than the average. What factors explain the sizable differences among industry groups in the extent to which they shared in the over-all postwar expansion of GNP? This paper utilizes the input–output technique to explain industry differences in the postwar growth of real product in terms of two factors—changes in the level and composition of final demand, and changes in the coefficients, which reflect, among other things, the basic technological processes of producing a given basket of final goods.

[1] See "GNP by Major Industries" by Martin L. Marimont in the *Survey of Current Business,* October 1962, and "Comparison of Federal Reserve and OBE Measures of Real Manufacturing Output, 1947–64" by Jack J. Gottsegen and Richard C. Ziemer in this volume.

NOTE: The term real product is used in this paper as a shortcut for the more accurate label, gross national product originating in an industry expressed in constant (1958) prices. The term net product or value added is used to refer to gross national product originating in an industry in current dollars.

Industry Indexes of Real Product and Direct Sales to Final Demand

The wide dispersion by industry in the postwar movement of real product is evident from Table 1, which presents indexes of real product (1958 = 100) for three points in time (1947, 1958, and 1964) for forty-two industrial groups in the economy.[2] (In general, this industrial grouping corresponds to the two-digit level of the standard industrial classification. In some cases, however, it was necessary to combine two-digit SIC groups, because the classification level of the input–output table was more aggregative than the two-digit level.)

It is interesting to examine the extent to which industry differences in the postwar growth of real product are related to differences among industries in the degree to which they participated in the over-all growth of final demand between 1947 and 1958, and 1958 and 1964. For example, if consumer, government, investment, and foreign demand for the products of a given industry increased at a much slower rate than total final demand, one would expect the increase in production, and consequently value added and real product in this industry, to be slower than average, and vice versa. Indeed this is the case in the food products industry and other industries which sell a large proportion of their total output directly to final users. However, many industry groups sell only a small proportion of their total output directly to final users; for such industries it is unlikely that changes in real product would be highly correlated with changes in direct sales to final users.

For the purpose of systematically examining the relationship between changes in real product and changes in direct final demand, indexes of final demand (in constant 1958 prices) were computed for each of the forty-two industry groups in the economy for the two periods 1947–58 and 1958–64. The individual industry indexes for real product

[2] For the period 1947–58 the industrial distribution of real product upon which this table is based is that derived from input–output data, and as such differs somewhat from that which emerges from OBE's work in real product. In general, these differences are due to various definitional differences in coverage of an industry. For example, in the input–output table, the construction industry is defined to cover all construction activity wherever performed, including both private and public force account activity; in the national accounts the construction industry covers only contract construction. There are numerous other differences of this sort, but it is not essential for the purpose of this paper to catalogue them.

TABLE 1

Indexes of Real Product by Industry Group 1947, 1958, 1964
(1958=100)

SIC No.[a]	Title	1947[b]	1964[c]
All Industries		70.4	129.7
01, 02	Farms	80.1	105.8
07-9	Ag. services, forestry, and fisheries	92.7	106.4
10	Metal mining	91.0	123.2
11, 12	Coal mining	175.9	114.7
13	Crude petroleum and natural gas	83.2	115.0
14	Nonmetallic minerals mining	58.6	123.1
15-17	Construction[d]	59.9	109.8
20	Food and kindred products	82.9	117.1
21	Tobacco manufacturers	71.8	119.0
22	Textile mill products	96.9	130.1
23	Apparel and related products	76.0	128.1
24	Lumber and wood products	121.8	128.9
25	Furniture and fixtures	72.5	128.7
26	Paper and allied products	69.7	140.0
27	Printing and publishing	77.8	125.7
28	Chemicals and allied products	42.6	152.0
29	Petroleum refining and related industries	45.1	144.3
30	Rubber and misc. plastics products	83.2	163.4
31	Leather and leather products	102.3	108.9
32	Stone, clay, and glass products	65.8	131.2
33	Primary metal industries	113.7	130.2
34	Fabricated metal products	74.1	135.2
35	Machinery, except electrical	87.9	153.3
36	Electrical machinery	55.5	167.3
37, 19	Transportation equip. and ordnance	56.0	163.6
38	Instruments and related products	55.2	139.6
39	Miscellaneous manufacturing	81.0	119.3
40-47	Transportation	108.7	127.7
48	Communication	43.4	149.4
49	Electric, gas, and sanitary services	41.0	143.9
50-59	Wholesale and retail trade	69.1	131.6
60-64, 66, 67	Finance and insurance	76.4	119.0
65	Real estate	53.5	136.2
70, 72, 76	Hotels, personal, and repair services	85.4	119.7

(continued)

TABLE 1 (concluded)

SIC No.[a]	Title	1947[b]	1964[c]
73, 80-89 (except 88)	Business, medical, etc., services	56.5	133.2
75	Auto repair, etc.	92.4	160.6
78, 79	Amusements	104.2	121.4
--	Federal government enterprises	54.8	145.1
--	State and local government enterprises	77.9	142.9
--	Government industry	68.9	116.8
--	Rest of world	52.7	193.8
88	Household	90.1	118.6

[a]For more complete industry titles and the 1958 Input-Output (I.O.) industry composition of each, see Appendix Table A.

[b]The real-product indexes for 1947 are based on value data from the reworked 1947 input-output table and the 1958 input-output table. The 1947 value-added data were converted to 1958 prices by the use of value-added deflators developed in connection with OBE's work on real product.

[c]The indexes of real product for 1964 are not strictly comparable to those for 1947 since they were derived directly from OBE's real-product data without any adjustments for differences between input-output and real product in industry definitions. These 1964 indexes are preliminary.

[d]The 1947 index includes public and private force account construction as well as contract construction activities. The index for 1964 reflects contract construction activity only.

(from Table 1) and for final demand were then ranked from the lowest to the highest, and a coefficient of rank correlation computed.[3] The coefficient of rank correlation was .705 for the 1947 indexes, and .601 for the 1964 indexes. Thus, even such a crude measure as *rank* correlation does not indicate a marked degree of association between changes in an industry's direct sales to final users and changes in its real product.

It is thus evident that the explanation of industry differences in the movement of real product cannot rest solely upon an examination of changes in an industry's *direct sales* to final users. One must also

[3] Three industries, rest of the world, household, and government—all industries in which value added and final demand are equal by definition—were omitted from the calculation of rank correlation.

examine an industry's *indirect* sales to final users: sales via the utilization of its products in the production of other goods and services which then go directly or indirectly into the satisfaction of final demands. Such an analysis must utilize the input–output technique, for this technique enables one to measure the impact on a given industry's gross output and net output (or value added) not only of changes in the final demand for the products of that industry but of changes in final demand for the output of all other industries as well. Thus, for example, by using an input–output matrix, one can measure the impact on output and value added in the steel industry not only of changes in final demand for steel itself (primarily net export demand) but also of changes in the final demand for motor vehicles, machinery, and all other products which directly or indirectly utilize steel in their production process.[4]

Methodology for Factoring Causes of Change in Industry Real Product

To better understand the methodology used in this paper to factor the causes of change in industry real product, it is helpful to view the industrial distribution of gross national product in any given year as the direct result of a combination of two basic sets of relationships. One set is the level and pattern of industry final demands that prevailed during

[4] Of necessity, it is assumed that the reader of this paper is fairly familiar with input–output analysis and no attempt is made to describe in detail the nature of this technique. Should the reader wish to familiarize himself further, it may interest him to consult the following sources:

1. Wassily W. Leontief, *The Structure of the American Economy, 1919–39,* Oxford, 1951, 2nd ed.
2. Duane Evans and Marvin Hoffenberg, "The Interindustry Relations Study for 1947," *Review of Economics and Statistics,* May 1952.
3. *Input–Output Analysis: An Appraisal,* Studies in Income and Wealth, 18, Princeton University Press for The National Bureau of Economic Research, 1955.
4. Chenery and Clark, *Interindustry Economics,* New York, 1959.

The reader may also wish to consult the three comprehensive input–output bibliographies listed below:

1. V. Riley and R. L. Allen, *Bibliography of Interindustry Economic Studies,* Operations Research Office, Johns Hopkins University, March 1955.
2. Charlotte Taskier, *Input–Output Bibliography, 1955–60,* Harvard Economic Research Project, United Nations, New York 1961.
3. United Nations, *Input–Output Bibliography, 1960–63,* Selected Papers Series M, No. 39, New York, 1964.

the year, and the other is the prevailing technical relationships between individual industry final demands and the gross output and net output (or value added) of each industry. Indeed, the 1958 input–output table prepared by the Office of Business Economics describes the economy in just these terms.[5]

If, in any given year, either the set of industry final demands or the set of technical relationships between final demand and gross and net output had differed from what they actually were, a different set of industry net outputs would have resulted. Thus, for example, if one multiplied a set of 1964 industry final demands (expressed in 1958 prices) by OBE's 1958 input–output inverse matrix, he would derive industry estimates of 1964 gross and net output (in 1958 prices) if 1958, rather than 1964, technical relationships had prevailed. If these *derived* 1964 real-product estimates are then compared with actual real product in 1958, one derives a measure of the change between 1958 and 1964 in real product by industry which is attributable solely to changes in final demand. Further, if these derived estimates of real product in 1964 are compared to actual 1964 real-product estimates, one derives a measure of the amount of change in real product between 1964 and 1958 which is due solely to changes in technical coefficients. (These two sources of change, of course, exhaust the total 1958–64 difference in an industry's real product.) [6]

Likewise, if one multiplied a set of 1947 final demands by industry (in 1958 prices) by the 1958 input–output inverse, he would derive estimates of 1947 real product if 1958 rather than 1947 technical relationships had prevailed. By comparing these derived estimates of 1947 real product to actual real product in 1958, one could measure the amount of change in industry real product which is attributable solely to changing final demand. Similarly, by comparing these derived estimates of 1947 real product by industry with actual 1947 real product

[5] See "The Interindustry Structure of the United States," by Morris R. Goldman, Martin L. Marimont, and Beatrice N. Vaccara in the *Survey of Current Business,* November 1964; also "The Transactions Table of the 1958 Input–Output Study," *Survey of Current Business,* September 1965.

[6] The two sources of change exhaust the total change in real product only under the particular procedure just described. This procedure in effect employs 1964 weights for the measurement of the technological change factor and 1958 weights for the measurement of the final-demand factor. A procedure which employed the same set of weights for each factor would leave a residual or "interaction" factor. See Appendix Table E. For further discussion of this point see references cited in footnote 7.

by industry, one could derive a measure of the 1947–58 change in real product which is due to changing technical relationships. Thus by the procedures described it is possible to divide the postwar changes in real product, for two periods 1947–58 and 1958–64, into two components, that which is due to changes in technical coefficients, and that due to changes in the level and structure of final demand.

It is also theoretically possible, however, to factor the causes of postwar change in an industry's real product by alternative methods. For example, the change between 1947 and 1958 in real product by industry can be separated into its two components by a procedure which involves multiplying the 1958 final demands by fixed 1947 technical relationships. This process would yield industry estimates of real product in 1958 if 1947 technical relationships prevailed. When these derived estimates of 1958 real product are compared to actual 1958 measures of real product by industry, one would get another estimate of the amount of change in real product between 1947 and 1958 which is attributable to changing technical relationships. Likewise, if these derived estimates of 1958 real product by industry are compared to actual 1947 industry data on real product, one derives an alternative measure of the amount of change in real product between 1947 and 1958 that is attributable to changing final demand. These measures would, in all likelihood, not be the same as those which were derived by the use of fixed *1958* technical coefficients.[7] (Similarly, one could explain the 1958–64 changes in real product by industry by a procedure which involved assuming fixed 1964 rather than 1958 technical relationships for both the 1964 and 1958 final demand.)

It thus becomes obvious that for each subperiod there is no single correct method of measuring the relative importance of the two factors—final demand and technical coefficients—which explain the postwar changes in real product. The best measure of the relative im-

[7] This phenomenon is attributable to the "interaction" factor and occurs whenever one attempts to factor out "causes of change" when alternative weighting schemes are available. For further discussion of this point see comments by Edward F. Denison on the paper by Frank A. Hanna, "Analysis of Interstate Income Differentials: Theory and Practice" in *Regional Income,* Studies in Income and Wealth 21; Princeton for NBER, 1957; *Concepts and Measurement of Production and Productivity* by Irving H. Siegel, pp. 86–92 (a working paper of the BLS); and the Technical Appendix to "Corporate Profits Since World War II" by Harlow D. Osborne and Joseph B. Epstein in the *Survey of Current Business,* January 1956.

portance of the two factors would be an average of the answers that result from the two alternative procedures available for each subperiod, i.e., assuming the fixed technical coefficients of the terminal year and the fixed technical coefficients of the initial year.

In actual practice, however, we were not faced with the immediate possibility of applying the two alternative procedures for the two subperiods 1947–58 and 1958–64. There is, as yet, no input–output inverse matrix for 1964 (the Office of Business Economics is currently working on an input–output table for the year 1963), and the 1947 input–output matrix constructed by the BLS was not conceptually or statistically consistent with the 1958 input–output table or the national accounts estimates of the total and component categories of final demand.

Some progress had been made, however, towards adjusting the 1947 input–output table to the 1958 basis. The Harvard Economic Research Project, under contract to the Interagency Growth Project, had already performed the extremely difficult task of reconciling the 1945 Standard Industrial Classification with the completely revised 1957 Standard Industrial Classification and had collapsed the 1947 table to the more aggregative basis of the 1958 table. It had also converted the 1947 table to a 1958 valuation basis. In addition, considerable work had been done at OBE to make the 1947 estimates of personal consumption expenditures by industry consistent with the 1958 table.[8] It was decided to build upon this work and to develop a 1947 input–output table as far as possible conceptually consistent with the 1958 table and the national income and product accounts.[9] In this way, we would have the necessary working tool for applying two alternative methods of factoring out causes of change in industry real product between 1947 and 1958.

The present unavailability of an input–output table for the mid-1960's meant that for the period 1958–64 only one of the two alternative methods could be applied. Since results for the period 1947–58 indicated that there was a marked difference in the measures of the

[8] See "Personal Consumption Expenditures in the 1958 Input–Output Study" by Nancy W. Simon in the October 1965 issue of the *Survey of Current Business*.

[9] This paper does not examine any of the many complicated statistical and conceptual problems which arose in the reworking of 1947 input–output table to make it conceptually consistent with the 1958 table. It is hoped that at some later date the authors can write a paper explaining these procedures.

relative importance of the two factors, depending upon whether one assumed the fixed technical coefficients of the initial or the terminal year, it was believed that the use of a single method for the period 1958–64 would not yield a true measure of the relative importance of the two factors. It was therefore decided to confine this paper to an analysis of the factors affecting real product in the postwar period 1947–58.

The work plan thus calls for an averaging of the two methods of factoring the total change in industry real product between 1947 and 1958—one method involving the application of a 1958 set of final demands to a 1947 input–output inverse matrix, and the other the application of 1947 final demands to a 1958 input–output inverse matrix.[10] The output totals which result from these matrix multiplications will then be converted to estimates of value added by the application of industry value-added/output ratios which are consistent with the given year's input–output table. Where necessary these value-added estimates will be converted to real-product estimates by the use of value-added price indexes (1958 = 100).[11]

Let us now turn to an analysis of the results obtained by applying the methodology just described.

Influence of Changes in Final Demand on Real Product by Industry

During the period 1947–58, total final demand in constant prices (and its counterpart, total real product) increased by 42 per cent. As indicated earlier, this rising level of final demand did not affect all industry groups in the economy to the same extent. For some industry groups, the direct and indirect effect of the over-all increase in final demand was a slight lowering in the level of real product, while for other

[10] See Appendix Tables C and D for the separate results of each of these two methods. Appendix Table E combines the results obtained from both these procedures and presents alternative measures of each of the two factors which do not exhaust the total change in real product and thus permit the measurement of the "interaction" effect as a separate factor.

[11] The reworked 1947 table has not yet been repriced in 1958 dollars. The methodology of this paper required only the deflation of final demand (1947 and 1958, each in the other year's prices) and 1947 value added. The actual step-by-step procedures for deriving the alternative value-added estimates, together with the necessary data on value-added/output ratios, final-demand deflators, and implicit value-added deflators are presented in Appendix Tables A and B.

industry groups the direct and indirect effect was an increase of more than double the over-all percentage. These facts become clear from an examination of Table 2, which shows the total change in real product (1947–58) for each of forty-two industry groups in the economy and distributes this total change between its two components, final-demand change and change in technical coefficients. Column 6 of this table shows the actual 1958 industry indexes of real product, while column 8 indicates what the 1958 indexes of real product would have been had there been no change in the technical coefficients but merely a change in final demand.

An examination of column 8 shows a wide range in the indexes for individual industry groups—from a low of 90.8 in the amusements group to a high of 206.7 in the electricity and gas group. This range of almost 116 index points is, however, considerably smaller than the range of 187 points in the total indexes of real product shown in column 6. Thus, if only final demand had changed between 1947 and 1958 (while the technical relationships had remained constant), there would have been a considerable narrowing of the extent to which individual industry indexes of real product differed from the average index. For example, the index of real product for the coal mining industry would have been 98.0 rather than the actual index of 56.8 while, at the other extreme, the index for electricity and gas would have been 206.7 instead of 244.2. This narrowing of the difference between individual industry indexes of real product and the average index, if one considers indexes based only on final demand change rather than indexes based on total change, is almost universal and not just the case for the extremes of the array. In thirty-two cases, the index in column 8 is closer to the average index of 142 than is its counterpart index in column 6, and in only seven cases is it further from the average than its counterpart. (For three industries, those where gross product and final demand are equal by definition, the indexes in column 6 and column 8 are identical.) The differences between the various individual industry indexes of real product and the over-all index are shown in Table 3. For the total indexes of real product the differences between individual industry indexes and the over-all index average 34.3 points, for the indexes of real product which assume that only final demand changed, these differences average 20.8 points.

The fact that the range and average variation of the individual in-

TABLE 2

Change in Real Product by Industry Group, 1947 to 1958, Distributed by Cause of Change

(millions of 1958 dollars)

SIC No.[a]	Title	Real Product		Change in Real Product, 1947–1958			Index of Change in Real Product (1947=100)		
		1947[b]	1958[c]	Total	Due to Coefficient Changes	Due to Final-Demand Changes	Total Col. 2 ÷ 1	Coefficient Cols. 1 + 4 ÷ 1	Final Demand Cols. 1 + 5 ÷ 1
		(1)	(2)	(3)	(4)	(5)	(6)	(7)	(8)
01, 02	Farms	16,698	20,846	4,148	-1,461	5,609	124.8	91.2	133.6
07-9	Ag. services, forestry, and fisheries	1,172	1,264	92	-240	332	107.8	79.5	128.3
10	Metal mining	832	914	82	-100	182	109.9	88.0	121.9
11, 12	Coal mining	2,822	1,604	-1,218	-1,161	- 57	56.8	58.8	98.0
13	Crude petroleum and natural gas	5,548	6,671	1,123	-1,412	2,535	120.2	74.5	145.7
14	Nonmetallic minerals mining	719	1,226	507	80	427	170.5	111.1	159.4
15-17	Construction[d]	17,322	28,937	11,615	-226	11,841	167.1	98.7	168.4
20	Food and kindred products	13,734	16,630	2,896	-880	3,776	121.1	93.6	127.5
21	Tobacco manufacturers	2,050	2,854	804	333	471	139.2	116.2	123.0
22	Textile mill products	3,285	3,389	104	2	102	103.2	100.1	103.1

(continued)

TABLE 2 (continued)

SIC No.[a]	Title	Real Product		Change in Real Product, 1947–1958			Index of Change in Real Product (1947=100)		
		1947[b]	1958[c]	Total	Due to Coefficient Changes	Due to Final-Demand Changes	Total Col. 2 ÷ 1	Coefficient Cols. 1 + 4 ÷ 1	Final Demand Cols. 1 + 5 ÷ 1
		(1)	(2)	(3)	(4)	(5)	(6)	(7)	(8)
23	Apparel & related products	4,593	6,042	1,449	-113	1,562	131.5	97.5	134.0
24	Lumber and wood products	3,509	2,880	-629	-1,398	769	82.1	60.2	121.9
25	Furniture and fixtures	1,481	2,042	561	15	546	137.9	101.0	136.9
26	Paper and allied products	3,501	5,020	1,519	38	1,481	143.4	101.0	142.3
27	Printing and publishing	4,646	5,974	1,328	-167	1,495	128.6	96.4	132.2
28	Chemicals and allied products	4,178	9,811	5,633	2,736	2,897	234.8	165.5	169.3
29	Petroleum refining and related industries	1,628	3,608	1,980	767	1,213	221.6	147.1	174.5
30	Rubber and misc. plastics products	2,605	3,131	526	-31	557	120.2	98.8	121.4
31	Leather and leather products	1,693	1,655	-38	-42	4	97.8	97.5	100.2
32	Stone, clay, and glass products	3,225	4,900	1,675	424	1,251	151.9	113.1	138.8
33	Primary metal industries	11,951	10,510	-1,441	-3,892	2,451	87.9	67.4	120.5

(continued)

TABLE 2 (continued)

SIC No.[a]	Title	Real Product		Change in Real Product, 1947–1958			Index of Change in Real Product (1947=100)		
		1947[b]	1958[c]	Total	Due to Coefficient Changes	Due to Final-Demand Changes	Total Col. 2 ÷ 1	Coefficient Cols. 1 + 4 ÷ 1	Final Demand Cols. 1 + 5 ÷ 1
		(1)	(2)	(3)	(4)	(5)	(6)	(7)	(8)
34	Fabricated metal products	6,099	8,231	2,132	154	1,987	135.0	102.5	132.4
35	Machinery, except electrical	9,767	11,112	1,345	78	1,267	113.8	100.8	113.0
36	Electrical machinery	5,327	9,602	4,275	1,760	2,515	180.3	133.0	147.2
37, 19	Transportation equip. and ordnance	8,883	15,868	6,985	110	6,875	178.6	101.2	177.4
38	Instruments and related products	1,372	2,484	1,112	353	759	181.0	125.7	155.3
39	Miscellaneous manufacturing	1,805	2,229	424	-32	456	123.5	98.2	125.3
40-47	Transportation	22,386	20,600	-1,786	-4,141	2,355	92.0	81.5	110.5
48	Communication	3,821	8,800	4,979	2,016	2,963	230.3	152.8	177.5
49	Electric, gas, and sanitary services	4,060	9,914	5,854	1,522	4,332	244.2	137.5	206.7
50-59	Wholesale and retail trade	47,658	69,006	21,348	2,531	18,817	144.8	105.3	139.5
60-64, 66, 67	Finance and insurance	11,338	14,831	3,493	-1,728	5,221	130.8	84.8	146.0
65	Real estate	23,998	44,821	20,823	4,287	16,536	186.8	117.9	168.9
70, 72, 76	Hotels, personal, and repair services	6,321	7,402	1,081	-568	1,649	117.1	91.0	126.1

(continued)

TABLE 2 (concluded)

		Real Product		Change in Real Product, 1947–1958			Index of Change in Real Product (1947=100)		
SIC No.[a]	Title	1947[b]	1958[c]	Total	Due to Coeffi-cient Changes	Due to Final-Demand Changes	Total Col. 2 ÷ 1	Coeffi-cient Cols. 1 + 4 ÷ 1	Final Demand Cols. 1 + 5 ÷ 1
		(1)	(2)	(3)	(4)	(5)	(6)	(7)	(8)
73, 80-89 (except 88)	Business, medical, etc. services	15,288	27,082	11,794	1,814	9,980	177.1	111.9	165.3
75	Auto repair, etc.	3,519	3,808	289	-1,274	1,563	108.2	63.8	144.4
78, 79	Amusements	3,116	2,989	-127	158	-285	95.9	105.1	90.8
--	Federal government enterprises	980	1,788	808	238	570	182.4	124.3	158.2
--	State and local government enterprises	2,028	2,604	576	-550	1,126	128.4	72.9	155.5
--	Government industry	26,889	39,029	12,140	0	12,140	145.1	100.0	145.1
--	Rest of world	1,069	2,030	961	0	961	189.9	100.0	189.9
88	Household	3,156	3,503	347	0	347	111.0	100.0	111.0
	IVA[e]	-944	-311	633	0	633	n.a.	n.a.	n.a.
All industries		315,128[f]	447,330	132,202	0	132,202	142.0	100.0	142.0

Notes to Table 2

n.a. not applicable.

[a]For more complete industry titles and the 1958 Input-Output (I.O.) industry composition of each, see Appendix Table A.

[b]The real-product estimates shown in this column are based on value-added data from the reworked 1947 input-output table. These value-added figures were converted to 1958 prices by the use, with some slight modifications, of the two-digit value-added deflators developed in connection with OBE's work on real product.

[c]These data are derived from the published 1958 input-output flow table. See *Survey of Current Business,* September 1965.

[d]In addition to contract construction activity this industry group includes public and private force account construction.

[e]This is not an actual industry but rather a balancing entry required by the fact that in the 1958 input-output table the inventory valuation adjustment was made in total only—not industry by industry as in the national income accounts. In computing inventory change for the original 1947 input-output table a mixture of procedures was employed. For some industries, notably trade, inventory change was computed on a revalued basis, for others, inventory change was computed before revaluation. The information which was required to redo the 1947 inventory change data on a basis consistent with the 1958 input-output table was not available. Thus, the 1947 entry for the inventory valuation adjustment is not the total of this adjustment in the national accounts but only that portion of the total which was not taken account of in the original 1947 procedure for calculating inventory change by industry.

[f]The grand total for real product shown in this table is slightly different from the published 1947 GNP in constant prices of $314.4 billion. In reworking the 1947 BLS input-output table it was not possible to agree precisely with the published figures on GNP because minor statistical revisions in the basic data were not taken account of in the reworking of the 1947 table.

dustry indexes of real product is considerably narrowed when one constructs indexes which reflect solely changes in final demand indicates that during the period 1947 and 1958 the influence of changing technical coefficients was to increase the variability of the actual industry indexes of real product. This would thus imply that, in general, those industries which had above average increases in final demand (direct and indirect) were also faced with increasing demand for their product because of changing technical requirements, while those industries

TABLE 3

Divergence of Industry Indexes of Real Product From Average Index for All Industries

(1947=100)

SIC No.	Index of Real Product[a]		
	Total	Final-Demand Change Only	Coefficient Change Only
01, 02	-17.2	-8.4	-8.8
07-9	-34.2	-13.7	-20.5
10	-32.1	-20.1	-12.0
11, 12	-85.2	-44.0	-41.2
13	-21.8	3.7	-25.5
14	28.5	17.4	11.1
15-17	25.1	26.4	-1.3
20	-20.9	-14.5	-6.4
21	-2.8	-19.0	16.2
22	-38.8	-38.9	.1
23	-10.5	-8.0	-2.5
24	-59.9	-20.1	-39.8
25	-4.1	-5.1	1.0
26	1.4	.3	1.1
27	-13.4	-9.8	-3.6
28	92.8	27.3	65.5
29	79.6	32.5	47.1
30	-21.8	-20.6	-1.2
31	-44.2	-41.8	-2.5
32	9.9	-3.2	13.1
33	-54.1	-21.5	-32.6
34	-7.0	-9.6	2.5
35	-28.2	-29.0	.8
36	38.3	5.2	33.0
37, 19	36.6	35.4	1.2
38	39.0	13.3	25.7
39	-18.5	-16.7	-1.8
40-47	-50 .0	-31.5	-18.5
48	88.3	35.5	52.8
49	102.2	64.7	37.5
50-59	2.8	-2.5	5.3
60-64, 66, 67	-11.2	4.0	-15.2
65	44.8	26.9	17.9
70, 72, 76	-24.9	-15.9	9.0
73, 80-89 (except 88)	35.1	23.3	11.9
75	-33.8	2.4	-36.2
78, 79	-46.1	-51.2	5.1
Fed. gov't enterprises	40.4	16.2	24.3
State and local gov't enterprises	-13.6	13.5	-27.1
Gov't industry	3.1	3.1	0
Rest of world	47.9	47.9	0
Household	-31.0	-31.0	0
All industries average[b]	34.3	20.8	16.2

[a]Based on indexes shown in columns 6-8 of Table 2.

[b]Signs ignored in computation of this average.

which experienced below average increases, or actual decreases, in final demand were also industries whose output was in lessened demand because of changes in the technical requirements of production. (These facts will become clear in a later section in which we examine the interrelationship between changing technical requirements and changing final demand.)

Influence of Changing Technical Requirements on Real Product by Industry

The amount of change in each industry's real product (1947–58) which is attributable solely to changes in the technical relationships reflected in the input–output matrices for the two years 1947 and 1958 is shown in column 4 of Table 2. Within the fixed column total of zero,[12] there is a wide range in the individual entries from large positives to large negatives, with the number of cases of negative values about equal to the number of positive cases. Perhaps a more interesting way to analyze the impact of changing technical relationships is to examine the indexes in column 7 of Table 2. The entries in this column show what the 1958 industry indexes of real product (1947 = 100) would have been had there been no change in final demand during the period but only a change in the technical relationships reflected in the input–output tables. An index of 100 indicates that there was a neutral effect of technical change, an index of under 100 indicates that there was a decline between 1947 and 1958 in the output and real product of a given industry that would be required in order to produce a given basket of final goods, and an index of over 100 indicates an increase between 1947 and 1958 in the output requirements from a given industry to produce a fixed basket of final goods.

Before we proceed with a detailed examination of the changing technical relationships, it should be pointed out that the changes in technical requirements reflected in columns 4 and 7 cannot be equated with *technological change*. Changing technology is only one of the many possible causes of change between two periods in the technical coefficients reflected in an input–output table. One of the important

[12] Since the total final demand is always equal to the total value added, no matter what the technical relationships, changing technical relationships can only affect the industry distribution of real product, not its total.

factors that could cause a difference between any two periods in the technical coefficients for a given industry is changing product mix. In such a highly aggregative picture of the U.S. economy as is reflected in the eighty-five-order classification system of the 1958 input–output table, an individual industry cannot represent a single or even a homogeneous set of commodities. Shifts between 1947 and 1958 in the product composition of an individual industry could thus affect the 1947–58 comparison of the technical relationship for that industry. Over a time span as long as eleven years, changing product mix could be an important cause of change in the technical relationships.

Another factor which could contribute to changes in technical relationships between two time periods is the divergence of actual technical relationships from a linear-homogeneous function. For some inputs, particularly those which reflect overhead-type costs, there undoubtedly is not a strictly proportional relationship between changes in outputs and changes in inputs. Thus the 1947 coefficients for a given industry might differ from those of 1958 merely because the scale of operation or degree of capacity utilization was much greater in 1958 than 1947 (or vice versa).

The problem of nonproportionality of some, if not most, inputs could be particularly important in the present analysis since we are comparing technical relationships in two years which reflect different phases of the business cycle. The year 1947 was generally one of over-all expansion of the business economy while the year 1958 was a year of a business cycle trough. Hence, for some industries, the two time periods would reflect markedly different degrees of capacity utilization—a phenomenon which could seriously influence the comparison of technical coefficients in the two years.

Finally, it should be pointed out that some of the difference in technical coefficients may reflect random factors such as differences between the two input–output tables in the statistical methods of estimating the technical relationships, as well as some errors that may have cropped up in our work in revising the 1947 BLS table to make it conceptually consistent with the 1958 table. Thus we note several factors which could contribute to changes between 1947 and 1958 in the technical coefficients which are not related to changes in the technological requirements for producing a fixed basket of final goods.

It may be noted from Table 2 that the greatest positive impact of coefficient change occurred in the chemicals and allied products industry (SIC 28) where the increase in real product between 1947 and 1958 (based solely on coefficient change) was 65.5 per cent. A strong positive influence of changing technical relationships was also evident in the communications industry (SIC 48) and in the petroleum refining industry (SIC 29) with indexes of real product of 152.8 and 147.1 respectively. The largest negative impact on real product occurs in the coal mining industry (SIC 11 and 12) where there was a 41 per cent decline in real product between 1947 and 1958 due solely to changes in the technical coefficients. Large negative impacts of changes in technical coefficients also occur in the lumber and wood products (SIC 24) and primary metal (SIC 33) industries where there are reductions in real product of 40 and 33 per cent, respectively.

It may be noted (from Table 3) that the average industry impact on real product of changes between 1947 and 1958 in the technical coefficients was 16.2 per cent (ignoring sign), a somewhat smaller average impact than that of changes in final demand. Moreover, in only five industries did the absolute magnitude of the impact on real product of changes in technical coefficients exceed that of changes in final demand. In thirty-four industry groups the change in real product attributable to changes in final demand exceeded that which was attributable to changes in technical coefficients. (In three industries, by definition, the entire change in real product is attributable solely to changes in final demand.) Thus for the period 1947–58 the changing level and pattern of final demand was a somewhat more important factor than changes in technical coefficients in explaining industry changes in real product.

Interrelationship Between Changes in Final Demand and Technical Coefficients

It may be noted from the tables presented that in most cases the individual industry indexes of real product which reflect changes in *both* final demand and technical coefficients vary from the average index to a considerably greater extent than do either of the corresponding indexes which consider solely changes in final demand or technical coefficients. There is thus an indication that, in general, the two elements of change in an industry's real product reinforced rather than offset one another. This is especially true of the extremes in the array of indexes of total change in real product. The industries with the largest increase in final demand are generally those with the largest increase in technical coefficients and correspondingly the industries with the smallest increase in final demand are generally those which also show a negative influence of coefficient change.

In an attempt to systematically study the interrelationships between the various industry indexes of real product—total real product, final demand, and technical coefficients—the individual industry indexes of total real product have been cross-classified by their corresponding indexes for the two separate factors. These relationships are displayed in Table 4 in the form of a frequency distribution where the various individual industry indexes of total real product have been combined into five groups. Each of these groups is then distributed according to whether the indexes of real product based solely on final demand or technical coefficient were average, above, or below average. A final-demand index of real product was considered below average if it was below 128.0 and above average if it exceeded 155.9. An index of real product for technical coefficients was classed as below average if it was under 90.0, and above average if it exceeded 110.0.

It may be noted from Table 4 that all six industries which had the lowest indexes of total real product were in the group with below average final-demand indexes, and that four of these six had below average technical coefficient indexes as well. Of the twelve industries which had total-real-product indexes in the below average range, none were included in the group with above average final-demand indexes, and eight were in the group with below average final-demand indexes. Furthermore, all of these twelve industries had average or below average technical coefficient indexes. Within the group of eleven industries with average indexes of total real product, seven had average indexes for *both* final-demand and technical coefficients. There was only one industry in the average group (SIC 21—tobacco manufactures) which had offsetting indexes, below average final demand and above average technical coefficients. All but two of the seven industries in the subgroup with above average indexes of total real product were industries with above average indexes of final demand and none of these industries had below average indexes of technical coefficients. Five of the six industries with the highest indexes of total real product fell into

TABLE 4

Frequency Distribution of 1958 Industry Indexes of Total Real Product Cross-Classified by Separate Factor Indexes[a]

(1947=100)

Total Index of Real Product	No.	Final-Demand Index – Above Average: Technical Coefficients			Final-Demand Index – Average: Technical Coefficients			Final-Demand Index – Below Average: Technical Coefficients		
		Above	Average	Below	Above	Average	Below	Above	Average	Below
Lowest (Under 100.0)	6	--	--	--	--	--	--	--	2	4
Below average (100.0 – 127.9)	12	--	--	--	--	1	3	--	7	1
Average (128.0 – 155.9)	11	--	--	--	1	7	2	1	--	--
Above average (156.0 – 183.9)	7	3	2	--	2	--	--	--	--	--
Highest (184.0 and above)	6	5	1	--	--	--	--	--	--	--
Total	42	8	3	0	3	8	5	1	9	5

[a]The index of real product based solely on technical coefficient change was considered *above average* if it exceeded 111.0, *average* if it was between 90.0 and 110.0, inclusive, and *below average* if it was less than 90.0. The index of real product based solely on final demand change was considered *above average* if it exceeded 155.9, *average* if it was between 128.0 and 155.9 inclusive, and *below average* if it was less than 128.0.

the category of above average indexes for both final demand and technical coefficients. Thus, a fairly regular pattern of relationships between the component indexes of an industry's real product and its total index seems to emerge.

The fact that the two factors, technical coefficient change and final demand change, tended to reinforce one another makes it seem likely that there are some basic underlying trends which influenced both these movements in the same direction. For example, in the chemicals industry (SIC 28) the above average real-product indexes for both final-demand and technical coefficients may be regarded as a reflection of the growing importance of chemicals in all aspects of our modern day life. Similarly, the below average indexes for technical coefficients and final demand in the coal industry are indications of the declining importance of coal as both an industrial and residential fuel. One would logically expect such strong tendencies to continue beyond 1958.

If these observed trends were to continue, one would expect a fair degree of success in predicting the 1964 pattern of individual industry indexes of real product based on the pattern evidenced during the 1947–58 period. Thus we would expect the six industries that had above average real-product indexes in the 1947–58 period to be the industries with above average indexes of total real product in the 1958–64 period. This should be particularly true for the five industries in this group which had above average indexes for *both* final demand and technical coefficients. Correspondingly, we would expect the four industries with 1958 indexes below average, both for final demand and for technical coefficients, to be in the group with below average 1964 indexes of total real product.

Relationship Between 1958 and 1964 Indexes of Total Real Product

In this section we examine the relationship between individual industry indexes of real product in the 1947–58 period and the 1958–64 period. This relationship can be observed from Table 5, which distributes the various industries according to both their 1958 and 1964 indexes of total real product. This table is in the form of a two-way frequency distribution in which the total array of real-product indexes are divided into five broad categories for each time period.

TABLE 5

1958 Industry Indexes of Total Real Product (1947 = 100), Distributed by 1964 Indexes of Total Real Product (1958 = 100)[a]

1958 Index (1947 = 100)	No.	1964 Indexes of Total Real Product (1958 = 100)[b]: Lowest (110 and under)	Below Average (110.1-123.1)	Average (123.2-136.2)	Above Average (136.3-149.3)	Highest (149.4 and over)
Highest (184.0 and over)	6			65 (1)	29,49 (2)	28,48,R of W(3)
Above average (156.0-183.9)	7	15 (1)	14 (1)	73 (1)	38, fed. enterprises (2)	36,37 (2)
Average (128.0-155.9)	11		21,60,gov't (3)	23,25,27,32, 34,50 (6)	26, state & local enterprises (2)	
Below average (100.0-127.9)	12	01,07(2)	13,20,39,70,88(5)	10,22 (2)		30,35,75 (3)
Lowest (under 100)	6	31 (1)	11,78 (2)	24,33,40 (3)		
Total number	42	4	11	13	6	8

[a]The entries (except those in the "Total" row) identify the industry by the first SIC number associated with it; the numbers in parenthesis opposite the SIC numbers are the total number of industries in question. Numbers in the "Total" row are the sum of industries in each column.

[b]Because the over-all range of the 1964 real-product indexes was considerably smaller than that of the 1958 indexes, the same absolute class intervals could not be used for the two distributions. The class intervals for the 1964 indexes were designed to represent approximately the same *percentage deviation* from the average index as the 1958 class intervals.

It can be noted from this table that there is some positive correlation between the relative standing of an industry index in 1958 and in 1964, but the correlation is not as marked as one might expect. Though none of the industries which were in the lowest group in 1958 can be found in the highest group for 1964, and vice versa, there is nevertheless fairly wide dispersion.[13]

Of the six industries which were in the lowest group in the 1947–58 period only one was in the lowest group in the 1958–64 period; two were in the below average group; and three were in the group with average change in the second period. What is more surprising is that the three industries which diverged most from their expected position in the frequency distribution had below average indexes for both final demand and technical coefficients in the 1947–58 period. However, for some of them, particularly the primary metals industry (SIC 33), cyclical rather than trend factors may have caused the 1947–58 final-demand indexes to be below average. (The year 1947 was a period of expanding activity, while 1958 was a year of diminished growth and low demand for durable goods.) It would not be expected that these cyclical influences would continue into the 1960's.

Of the twelve industries which showed below average growth in real product in the earlier period, only five were in the corresponding class in the 1958–64 period. Contrary to expectations, three of the twelve industries (SIC's 30, 35, and 75) were in the highest group in the 1958–64 period. However, since these were industries where there was mixed influence of technical coefficients and final demand in the earlier period, one might expect the 1958–64 index of change to be less predictable. The automobile repair industry (SIC 75) had an average final-demand index but a below average coefficient index in the 1947–58 period, while the two others, rubber and miscellaneous plastics (SIC 30) and machinery, except electrical (SIC 35), had below average final-demand indexes and average coefficient indexes. For at least one of these, the machinery industry, the low level of invest-

[13] One possible explanation for this dispersion may be that the indexes of real product for 1964 are not strictly comparable to those for 1947 since they were derived directly from OBE's real-product data without any adjustments for differences between input–output and real product in industry definitions. In addition, all of the 1964 indexes are preliminary in the sense that they have not benefitted from a bench-mark revision.

ment demand in 1958 might have contributed to the low final-demand index in the 1947–58 comparison.

Towards the other end of the scale in Table 5, only two of the seven industries which showed above average increases in the 1947–58 period were in the corresponding class in 1958–64. Two industries differed markedly from their expected position in the table, construction (SIC 15–17), which had one of the lowest indexes, and nonmetallic minerals mining (SIC 14), which showed a below average increase in the latter period. For construction, the failure to include force account activity in the 1958–64 indexes may have influenced the comparison of the two periods. For nonmetallic minerals mining, there is no apparent reason for its different relative standing in the two periods, particularly since this industry falls in the above average groups of Table 4 on both counts, technical coefficients and final demand. Here is a case where one would have expected the above average increase to have continued into the 1958–64 period.

Of the six industries in the group with the highest increases from 1947 to 1958, only one, real estate (SIC 65), differed considerably from what one might expect. It showed only an average increase in the 1958–64 period, despite the fact that it had above average indexes for both final-demand effect and technical coefficient effect in the 1947–58 period. The above average 1958 indexes for final demand, however, may have reflected cyclical rather than longer-range factors since consumer rental payments are not as sensitive to cyclical changes in the level of economic activity as is the demand for other goods and services. Similarly, rent is a production cost which is likely to be nonproportional and, consequently, to show a higher ratio to total costs in times of reduced activity than in times of expanding activity, thus explaining the above average position of the 1958 technical coefficient index for the real estate and rental industry.

A varied picture thus emerges from Table 5. Only seventeen industry groups were in their expected positions in the array of indexes for the 1958–64 period, sixteen industry groups differed slightly from their expected positions, and nine differed markedly. In some cases, these differences may be explained in terms of cyclical influences on the component factor indexes. In other cases, random factors or statistical noncomparabilities may have affected the comparison of indexes of real product for the two periods. When the 1963 OBE input–output table becomes available and it becomes possible to factor out the causes of change in real product for the period 1958–64, one can then determine to what extent the tendencies which operate in the 1947–58 period have continued into the latter period.

Appendix: Step by Step Procedure for Factoring Change in Real Product by Industry Group (1947–58)

I. *Compute total change in real product 1947–58.*

   A. Combine industry estimates of value added from 1958 input–output table to two-digit level.

   B. Combine industry estimates of value added from reworked 1947 input–output table to two-digit level.

   C. Convert 1947 value added to 1958 prices by use of implicit value added deflators.

   D. Subtract 1947 real product from 1958 real product.

II. *Compute 1958 real product if 1947 technical coefficients and 1958 final demand had prevailed.*

   A. Convert 1958 final demand to 1947 prices by use of special final-demand deflators for each industry developed for this paper.

   B. Apply 1958 final demand to 1947 inverse to yield 1958 output in 1947 prices.

   C. Multiply derived 1958 outputs by value added/output ratios from reworked 1947 I.O. Table to yield 1958 value added in 1947 prices—combine to two-digit level.

   D. Convert estimated 1958 value added in 1947 prices to 1958 prices by use of implicit deflator for value added.

III. *Factor total change in real product 1947–58 (fixed 1947 coefficient method).*

   A. For each industry group, subtract derived 1958 real product (from Step II, D above) from the actual 1958 input–output estimate of real product—to yield amount of real product difference (1947–58) which is due to changes in coefficients.

   B. For each industry group, subtract actual 1947 real product from derived 1958 real product (from Step II, D above) to yield amount of real product change (1947–58) which is due to changing final demand.

IV. *Compute 1947 real product if 1958 technical coefficients and 1947 final demand had prevailed.*

A. Convert 1947 final demand to 1958 prices by use of special final-demand deflators by industry developed for this paper.

B. Apply 1947 final demand to 1958 inverse to yield 1947 output in 1958 prices.

C. Apply 1958 value added/output ratios from 1958 I.O. Table to yield 1947 value added in 1958 prices (real product)—combine to two-digit level.

V. *Factor total change in real product, 1947–58 (fixed 1958 coefficient method).*

A. For each industry group, subtract derived 1947 real product (from Step IV, C, above) from actual 1958 input–output estimate of real product to yield amount of real product difference (1947–58) which is due to changing final demands.

B. For each industry group, subtract actual 1947 input–output real product from derived 1947 real product (from Step IV, C, above) to yield amount of real product change (1947–58) which is due to change in coefficients.

VI. *Averaging of factor shares—two methods.*

A. For each industry group, average values obtained in Step III, A, and Step V, B, to yield amount of real product change (1947–58) due to coefficient changes.

B. For each industry group, average values obtained in Step III, B, and V, A, to yield amount of real product change (1947–58) due to final demand changes.

TABLE A

Standard Industrial Classification Groups and Their 1958 Input-Output Industry Composition

SIC Number	1958 Input-Output Industry Number	Title
01, 02	1, 2	Farms
07-9	3, 4	Agricultural services, hunting and trapping, forestry and fisheries[a]
10	5, 6	Metal mining
11, 12	7	Coal mining
13	8	Crude petroleum and natural gas[b]
14	9, 10	Mining and quarrying of nonmetallic minerals, except fuels
15-17	11, 12	Construction[bc]
20	14	Food and kindred products
21	15	Tobacco manufactures
22	16, 17	Textile mill products[d]
23	18, 19	Apparel and related products[de]
24	20, 21	Lumber and wood products, except furniture
25	22, 23	Furniture and fixtures
26	24, 25	Paper and allied products
27	26	Printing and publishing
28	27-30	Chemicals and allied products[f]
29	31	Petroleum and related industries
30	32	Rubber and miscellaneous plastics products
31	33, 34	Leather and leather products
32	35, 36	Stone, clay, and glass products
33	37, 38	Primary metal industries[f]
34	39-42	Fabricated metal products
35	43-52	Machinery, except electrical
36	53-58	Electrical machinery
37, 19	13, 59-61	Transportantion equipment and ordnance
38	62-63	Instruments and related products
39	64	Miscellaneous manufacturing[e]
40-47	65	Transportation
48	66, 67	Communication

(continued)

TABLE A (concluded)

SIC Number	1958 Input-Output Industry Number	Title
49	68	Electric, gas, and sanitary services
50-59	69	Wholesale and retail trade
60-64, 66, 67	70	Finance and insurance
65	71	Real estate[g]
70, 72, 76	72	Hotels, personal, and repair services, except auto repair[h]
73, 80-89 (except 88)	73, 74, 77	Business, medical, professional, and educational services, and nonprofit organizations[agh]
75	75	Auto repair, auto services, and garages
78, 79	76	Amusements
--	78	Federal government enterprises[i]
--	79	State and local government enterprises[i]
--	84	Government industry[j]
--	85	Rest of the world industry[k]
88	86	Household industry[l]

[a]SIC 0722 – Offices of veterinatians and animal hospitals is included with SIC 80, medical and other health services.

[b]SIC 138, oil and gas field services is included with SIC 15-17, construction.

[c]In addition to contract construction activity, as specified by the SIC, this industry group includes public and private force account construction.

[d]SIC 225, knitting mills is included with SIC 23, apparel and related products.

[e]SIC 3922, furs, dressed and dyed, is included with SIC 23, apparel.

[f]Alumina, part of SIC 2819, is included with SIC 33, primary metal industries.

[g]SIC 6541, title abstract companies is included with SIC 73, business services.

[h]SIC 7694, armature rewinding shops and SIC 7699, repair shops nec are included with SIC 73, business services.

[i]This industry includes those activities of government agencies, with separate accounting records, that cover over half of their current operating costs by the sale of goods and services to the general public.

[j]Value added in this industry is measured by employee compensation of federal, state, and local government employees.

[k]Value added in this industry reflects income originating in the rest of the world.

[l]Value added in this industry reflects employee compensation of domestic servants.

TABLE B

Basic Data on Final Demand, Prices, and Value Added
by Input Output Industry, 1947 and 1958

I.O. Industry	Final Demand (current dollars thousands)[a]		1947 Final–Demand Price Deflator (1958=100)	Value-Added/Output Ratio (current dollars)		1947 Value–Added Deflator (1958=100)
	1947	1958		1947	1958	
1	1,668,613	2,526,740	151.4[b]	.29011	.34531	120.8 (1–2)
2	3,668,957	5,419,010	89.4[b]	.60268	.51155	
3	8,765	-108,116	46.3	.39281	.49260	63.1 (3–4)
4	-36,272	233	65.9	.48184	.44629	
5	-93,932	-431,180	60.9	.72607	.55276	77.9 (5–6)
6	-150,698	-124,816	79.8	.75320	.45975	
7	1,092,808	628,220	71.0	.78629	.58348	85.8
8	-93,121	-1,195,846	62.2	.73358	.68994	55.7
9	-92,879	-74,969	60.6	.67503	.61671	80.5 (9–10)
10	32,317	-1,640	67.3	.78606	.61284	
11	20,329,109	52,416,000	68.7	.39339	.35493	69.5 (11–12)
12	1,712,959	4,419,828	61.3	.44987	.61233	
13	131,914	2,520,411	59.7	.56641	.34837	(inc. with 59–61)
14	32,629,360	46,328,371	89.1	.25401	.26039	83.9
15	2,873,862	4,633,996	75.1	.42491	.48226	82.3
16	2,160,725	624,212	113.5	.33004	.26117	127.7 (16–17)
17	607,086	489,152	83.9	.40051	.28086	

(continued)

TABLE B (continued)

I.O. Industry	Final Demand (current dollars thousands)[a]		1947 Final–Demand Price Deflator (1958=100)	Value-Added/Output Ratio (current dollars)		1947 Value–Added Deflator (1958=100)
	1947	1958		1947	1958	
18	9,184,971	11,280,502	108.6	.38407	.38666	98.1
19	841,488	1,213,233	111.1	.23141	.23094	
20	651,088	-188,800	79.2	.47881	.34258	81.8
21	77,862	-9,728	82.5	.36340	.36854	
22	1,574,737	2,634,185	79.2	.41039	.41606	72.0
23	529,150	1,098,951	61.6	.37521	.44749	
24	-207,291	252,148	69.2	.39388	.38383	69.8
25	196,770	56,859	77.7	.34243	.37452	
26	1,676,748	2,892,509	63.6	.50920	.47364	70.9
27	532,115	1,511,692	84.5	.36341	.39711	91.8
28	2,776	271,675	77.6	.40023	.39830	
29	2,158,877	4,357,513	105.8	.32295	.41990	
30	178,588	42,239	81.0	.29489	.36446	
31	3,146,938	8,181,243	76.0	.18788	.20804	92.2
32	1,142,087	1,700,449	68.0	.43172	.45761	58.2
33	33,919	-11,442	103.4	.29533	.32577	70.5
34	2,247,308	2,689,431	82.3	.32626	.44072	
35	255,628	133,591	57.8	.49973	.57063	61.6
36	328,781	248,890	67.1	.47267	.48961	
37	972,616	224,824	50.2	.37961	.40100	48.8
38	64,895	-269,861	50.6	.24986	.30994	

(continued)

TABLE B (continued)

I.O. Industry	Final Demand (current dollars thousands)[a] 1947	1958	1947 Final–Demand Price Deflator (1958=100)	Value–Added/Output Ratio (current dollars) 1947	1958	1947 Value–Added Deflator (1958=100)
39	70,799	66,359	57.2	.27699	.33556	
40	716,161	916,163	73.3	.42792	.38482	70.8
41	393,131	279,975	60.3	.43862	.44276	
42	621,868	803,101	59.7	.48398	.43540	
43	364,746	1,089,086	57.2	.35579	.42364	
44	1,177,004	1,739,853	63.2	.36597	.37679	
45	1,216,990	2,055,234	56.4	.39482	.44131	
46	378,937	575,135	56.1	.43621	.37188	
47	931,573	1,522,695	52.9	.56017	.51144	62.1
48	1,591,900	1,788,388	61.0	.50318	.44560	
49	859,653	1,438,877	58.1	.47684	.43590	
50	45,274	64,197	60.9	.53176	.53623	
51	579,389	1,317,570	75.0	.63453	.57375	
52	760,137	1,382,725	76.3	.39842	.34193	
53	1,310,068	1,909,886	62.3	.48363	.49755	
54	2,087,847	2,628,806	86.2	.37985	.37257	
55	393,300	387,939	61.5	.46218	.46874	80.7
56	1,480,101	3,919,141	90.5	.44969	.44607	
57	344,366	450,667	80.1	.44517	.49717	
58	329,241	492,752	64.4	.40988	.42699	

(continued)

TABLE B (continued)

I.O. Industry	Final Demand (current dollars thousands)[a] 1947	Final Demand (current dollars thousands)[a] 1958	1947 Final-Demand Price Deflator (1958=100)	Value-Added/Output Ratio (current dollars) 1947	Value-Added/Output Ratio (current dollars) 1958	1947 Value-Added Deflator (1958=100)
59	7,538,200	13,276,432	65.1	.32658	.29839	
60	920,361	7,123,289	59.7	.46245	.47223	(inc. 13) 65.8
61	1,949,741	2,761,445	62.0	.41127	.38625	
62	782,879	1,577,675	67.1	.41394	.46941	67.2
63	378,256	803,314	75.2	.53335	.54604	
64	2,073,105	2,962,099	84.5	.49232	.42009	89.1
65	10,083,936	13,480,940	61.8	.67341	.61880	65.4
66	1,886,468	4,693,956	78.0	.79313	.85159	77.3
67	8,839	9,000	75.6	.58104	.57263	
68	3,085,278	8,892,883	92.0	.55638	.48951	87.9
69	41,011,501	68,258,759	82.7	.75029	.72447	84.3
70	4,513,923	12,073,809	57.8	.54948	.56042	51.0
71	16,487,886	41,771,742	70.6	.65591	.72401	70.3
72	5,470,319	9,787,904	69.2	.65572	.60817	73.1
73	1,331,935	3,183,596	53.6	.47395	.45866	(inc. 77) 62.6
74	365,261	5,177,000	59.9	--	.07679	
75	1,858,589	4,598,596	67.3	.60244	.48123	68.0
76	2,915,899	3,516,158	71.8	.58780	.53185	72.6
77	7,877,617	20,880,011	66.3	.66192	.68106	(inc. with 73 & 74)
78	340,901	816,554	69.6	.68308	.43557	127.3
79	72,662	434,213	100.0	.70063	.54431	48.6

(continued)

TABLE B (concluded)

I.O. Industry	Final Demand (current dollars thousands)[a]		1947 Final–Demand Price Deflator (1958=100)	Value-Added/Output Ratio (current dollars)		1947 Value–Added Deflator (1958=100)
	1947	1958		1947	1958	
80	-2,164,565	-3,369,362	76.8	--	1.00000	--
81	--	-160,000	--	--	0	--
82	--	0	--	--	0	--
83	-1,251,870	-669,714	110.5	--	1.00000	--
84	15,730,000	39,029,000	58.5	1.00000	1.00000	58.5
85	824,000	2,030,000	77.1	1.00000	1.00000	77.1
86	2,348,000	3,503,000	74.4	1.00000	1.00000	74.4
87	-763,965	-311,000	80.9	1.00000	1.00000	80.9

[a]The final demands for both 1947 and 1958 are designed to be used with an input-output table with gross *domestic* output for each industry as the base for the input coefficients. They therefore incorporate imports, at domestic port value, as a negative final-demand column. The 1958 final demand differs in this respect from the flow table published September 1965, which showed competitive imports destined for intermediate use transferred into their domestic counterpart industry. The 1958 final-demand column also differs from the published input-output table in that the demand for office supplies is shown as demands on the various industries which produce these products instead of a single demand on the office supply dummy industry.

[b]The deflators shown here were used to put 1947 final demands in 1958 prices. In converting 1958 final demands to 1947 prices, different deflators were used for these industries because of extreme differences in product mix. For this latter conversion, the price index for industry 1 is 116.3, and for industry 2, 108.1.

TABLE C

Factoring of Total Change in Real Product 1947–1958, Fixed 1958 Coefficient Method
(millions of 1958 dollars)

SIC No.	Actual 1958 Real Product (1)	Derived 1947 Real Product (2)	Change Due To Final Demand (col. 1 – col. 2) (3)	Actual 1947 Real Product (4)	Change Due To Coefficients[a] (col. 2 – col. 4) (5)
All Industries	447,330	315,857	131,473	315,128	729
01, 02	20,846	15,561	5,285	16,698	-1,137
07-9	1,264	1,003	261	1,172	-169
10	914	811	103	832	-21
11, 12	1,604	1,905	-301	2,822	-917
13	6,671	4,482	2,189	5,548	-1,066
14	1,226	772	454	719	53
15-17	28,937	17,295	11,642	17,322	-27
20	16,630	13,018	3,612	13,734	-716
21	2,854	2,349	505	2,050	299
22	3,389	3,283	106	3,285	-2
23	6,042	4,497	1,545	4,593	-96
24	2,880	2,377	503	3,509	-1,132
25	2,042	1,492	550	1,481	11
26	5,020	3,616	1,404	3,501	115
27	5,974	4,546	1,428	4,646	-100
28	9,811	6,487	3,324	4,178	2,309
29	3,608	2,233	1,375	1,628	605
30	3,131	2,531	600	2,605	-74
31	1,655	1,666	-11	1,693	-27
32	4,900	3,585	1,315	3,225	360
33	10,510	8,840	1,670	11,951	-3,111
34	8,231	6,245	1,986	6,099	146

(continued)

TABLE C (concluded)

SIC No.	Actual 1958 Real Product (1)	Derived 1947 Real Product (2)	Change Due To Final Demand (col. 1 – col. 2) (3)	Actual 1947 Real Product (4)	Change Due To Coefficients[a] (col. 2 – col. 4) (5)
35	11,112	9,680	1,432	9,767	-87
36	9,602	6,631	2,971	5,327	1,304
37, 19	15,868	8,927	6,941	8,883	44
38	2,484	1,618	866	1,372	246
39	2,229	1,772	457	1,805	-33
40-47	20,600	19,212	1,388	22,386	-3,174
48	8,800	5,509	3,291	3,821	1,688
49	9,914	5,370	4,544	4,060	1,310
50-59	69,006	49,846	19,160	47,658	2,188
60-64, 66, 67	14,831	10,011	4,820	11,338	-1,327
65	44,821	27,371	17,450	23,998	3,373
70, 72, 76	7,402	5,862	1,540	6,321	-459
73, 80-89 (except 88)	27,082	16,780	10,302	15,288	1,492
75	3,808	2,543	1,265	3,519	-976
78, 79	2,989	3,202	-213	3,116	86
Fed. gov't enterprises	1,788	1,203	585	980	223
State and local gov't enterprises	2,604	1,556	1,048	2,028	-472
Gov't industry	39,029	26,889	12,140	26,889	--
Rest of world	2,030	1,069	961	1,069	--
Household	3,503	3,156	347	3,156	--
IVA	-311	-944	633	-944	--

[a]Theoretically the sum of this column should be zero but it is not precisely zero because of rounding errors and a slight discrepancy which arises in connection with the scrap and by-product adjustment.

TABLE D

Factoring of Total Change in Real Product 1947–1958, Fixed 1947 Coefficient Method
(millions of 1958 dollars)

SIC No.	Actual 1958 Real Product (1)	Derived 1958 Real Product (2)	Change Due To Coefficients[a] (col. 1 – col. 2) (3)	Actual 1947 Real Product (4)	Change Due To Final Demand (col. 2 – col. 4) (5)
All Industries	447,330	448,059	-729	315,128	132,931
01, 02	20,846	22,631	-1,785	16,698	5,933
07-9	1,264	1,576	-312	1,172	404
10	914	1,092	-178	832	260
11, 12	1,604	3,009	-1,405	2,822	187
13	6,671	8,429	-1,758	5,548	2,881
14	1,226	1,119	107	719	400
15-17	28,937	29,362	-425	17,322	12,040
20	16,630	17,674	-1,044	13,734	3,940
21	2,854	2,487	367	2,050	437
22	3,389	3,383	6	3,285	93
23	6,042	6,172	-130	4,593	1,579
24	2,880	4,544	-1,664	3,509	1,035
25	2,042	2,023	19	1,481	542
26	5,020	5,058	-38	3,501	1,557
27	5,974	6,208	-234	4,646	1,562
28	9,811	6,647	3,164	4,178	2,469
29	3,608	2,679	929	1,628	1,051
30	3,131	3,119	12	2,605	514
31	1,655	1,711	-56	1,693	18
32	4,900	4,412	488	3,225	1,187
33	10,510	15,183	-4,673	11,951	3,232
34	8,231	8,069	162	6,099	1,970

(continued)

TABLE D (concluded)

SIC No.	Actual 1958 Real Product (1)	Derived 1958 Real Product (2)	Change Due To Coefficients[a] (col. 1 – col. 2) (3)	Actual 1947 Real Product (4)	Change Due To Final Demand (col. 2 – col. 4) (6)
35	11,112	10,869	243	9,767	1,102
36	9,602	7,385	2,217	5,327	2,058
37, 19	15,868	15,692	176	8,883	6,809
38	2,484	2,025	459	1,372	653
39	2,229	2,261	-32	1,805	456
40-47	20,600	25,709	-5,109	22,386	3,323
48	8,800	6,456	2,344	3,821	2,635
49	9,914	8,179	1,735	4,060	4,119
50-59	69,006	66,132	2,874	47,658	18,474
60-64, 66, 67	14,831	16,961	-2,130	11,338	5,623
65	44,821	39,621	5,200	23,998	15,623
70, 72, 76	7,402	8,079	-677	6,321	1,758
73, 80-89 (except 88)	27,082	24,946	2,136	15,288	9,658
75	3,808	5,381	-1,573	3,519	1,862
78, 79	2,989	2,759	230	3,116	-357
Fed. gov't enterprises	1,788	1,535	253	980	555
State and local gov't enterprises	2,604	3,231	-627	2,028	1,203
Gov't industry	39,029	39,029	0	26,889	12,140
Rest of world	2,030	2,030	0	1,069	961
Household	3,503	3,503	0	3,156	347
IVA	-311	-311	0	-944	633

[a]Theoretically the sum of this column should be zero but it is not precisely zero because of rounding errors and a slight discrepancy which arises in connection with the scrap and by-product adjustment.

TABLE E

Computation of "Interaction" Effect by Use of 1947 and 1958 Weights
(millions of 1958 dollars)

	Total Difference in Real Product (col. 1 minus col. 4, Table C) (1)	1947 Weights Change due to: Final Demand (col. 5, Table D) (2)	Coefficients (col. 5, Table C) (3)	Interaction (col. 1 minus cols. 2 + 3) (4)	1958 Weights Change due to: Final Demand (col. 3, Table C) (5)	Coefficients (col. 3, Table D) (6)	Interaction (col. 1 minus cols. 5 + 6) (7)
All industries	132,202	132,931	729	-1458	131,473	-729	1458
01,02	4,148	5,933	-1,137	-648	5,285	-1,785	648
07-9	92	404	-169	-143	261	-312	143
10	82	260	-21	-157	103	-178	157
11, 12	-1,218	187	-917	-488	-301	-1,405	488
13	1,123	2,881	-1,066	-692	2,189	-1,758	692
14	507	400	53	54	454	107	-54
15-17	11,615	12,040	-27	-398	11,642	-425	398
20	2,896	3,940	-716	-328	3,612	-1,044	328
21	804	437	299	68	505	367	-68
22	104	98	-2	8	106	6	-8
23	1,449	1,579	-96	-34	1,545	-130	34
24	-629	1,035	-1,132	-532	503	-1,664	532
25	561	542	11	8	550	19	-8
26	1,519	1,557	115	-153	1,404	-38	153
27	1,328	1,562	-100	-134	1,428	-234	134
28	5,633	2,469	2,309	855	3,324	3,164	-855
29	1,980	1,051	605	324	1,375	929	-324
30	526	514	-74	86	600	12	-86
31	-38	18	-27	-29	-11	-56	29

(continued)

TABLE E (concluded)

	Total Difference in Real Product (col. 1 minus col. 4, Table C) (1)	1947 Weights, Change due to: Final Demand (col. 5, Table D) (2)	Coefficients (col. 5, Table C) (3)	Interaction (col. 1 minus cols. 2 + 3) (4)	1958 Weights, Change due to: Final Demand (col. 3, Table C) (5)	Coefficients (col. 3, Table D) (6)	Interaction (col. 1 minus cols. 5 + 6) (7)
32	1,675	1,187	360	128	1,315	488	-128
33	-1,441	3,232	-3,111	-1562	1,670	-4,673	1562
34	2,132	1,970	146	16	1,986	162	-16
35	1,345	1,102	-87	330	1,432	243	-330
36	4,275	2,058	1,304	913	2,971	2,217	-913
37, 19	6,985	6,809	44	132	6,941	176	-132
38	1,112	653	246	213	866	459	-213
39	424	456	-33	1	457	-32	-1
40-47	-1,786	3,323	-3,174	-1935	1,388	-5,109	1935
48	4,979	2,635	1,688	656	3,291	2,344	-656
49	5,854	4,119	1,310	425	4,544	1,735	-425
50-59	21,348	18,474	2,188	686	19,160	2,874	-686
60-64, 66, 67	3,493	5,623	-1,327	-803	4,820	-2,130	803
65	20,823	15,623	3,373	1827	17,450	5,200	-1827
70, 72, 76	1,081	1,758	-459	-218	1,540	-677	218
73, 80-89 (except 38)	11,794	9,658	1,492	644	10,302	2,136	-644
75	289	1,862	-976	-597	1,265	-1,573	597
78, 79	-127	-357	86	144	-213	230	-144
Fed. gov't enterprises	808	555	223	30	585	253	-30
State & local gov't enterprises	576	1,203	-472	-155	1,048	-627	155
Gov't industry	12,140	12,140	--	0	12,140	--	0
Rest of world	961	961	--	0	961	--	0
Household	347	347	--	0	347	--	0
IVA	633	633	--	0	633	--	0

COMMENT

GARY FROMM, The Brookings Institution

It is always delightful to read a paper by Bea Vaccara. Her papers are neat, direct, methodical, and meticulous. The procedures employed are stated explicitly, and one can be sure that the calculations have been carried out with great care. This paper by Vaccara and Simon is no exception.

The idea involved is a simple one. The authors present it in verbal form; for additional clarity, I shall restate it mathematically and diagrammatically. They begin with the basic input–output relation:

$$F = (I - A)S \tag{1}$$

where F = an n component column vector of industry final demands;
I = an $n \times n$ identity matrix;
A = an $n \times n$ matrix of coefficients with elements a_{ij} which are the dollars of input from industry i required to produce a dollar of gross output of industry j;
S = an n component column vector of gross industry output.

Then, a substitution is made for S:

$$S = CX \tag{2}$$

where C = an $n \times n$ diagonal matrix whose elements are the dollars of gross output of industry i per dollar of real product (value added) of that industry;
X = an n component column vector of industry real product.

Therefore,

$$F = (I - A)CX \tag{3}$$

and

$$X = C^{-1}(I - A)^{-1}F$$

A time subscript can be attached to the X and F vectors. They must, however, be measured in the same prices as C and A, although then they can be transformed into quantities with prices of other periods. Thus,

$$P_X{}^{58}{}_{1947}^{-1} X^{47}{}_{1958} = P_X{}^{58}{}_{1947}^{-1} C^{-1}(I - A)^{-1}{}_{1947} P_F{}^{58}{}_{1947} F^{58}{}_{1958} \tag{4}$$

where *superscripts* are the base year of price indexes or the constant dollars in which monetary flows are measured; *subscripts* are the period of observation. The price variables are defined as follows:

$P_X{}^{58}$ = an $n \times n$ diagonal matrix of indexes of current-dollar value added per constant dollar of real product, 1958 = 1.00

$P_F{}^{58}$ = an $n \times n$ diagonal matrix of indexes of prices of industry gross output, 1958 = 1.00.

Now, call the left hand variable $\hat{X}^{58}{}_{1958,1947}$, or "estimated output originating measured in superscript (1958) dollars in year i (1958) using input-output matrix for year j (1947)." That is:

$$\hat{X}^{58}{}_{1958,1947} = P_X{}^{58}{}^{-1}_{1947}\, X^{47}{}_{1958}$$

Vaccara and Simon use this quantity to divide the total change in gross product originating in each industry into two components: (a) that due to changes in final demand of *all* industries; and (b) that due to shifts in input-output coefficients of *all* industries. That is:

$$\text{Total change} = X^{58}{}_{1958} - X^{58}{}_{1947}$$

(5) Due to change in coefficients $= X^{58}{}_{1958} - \hat{X}^{58}{}_{1958,1947}$

(6) Due to change in final demand $= \hat{X}^{58}{}_{1958,1947} - X^{58}{}_{1947}$

Similarly, it is possible to derive the estimated output originating in 1947, measured in 1958 dollars, using the input-output matrix for 1958, i.e., $\hat{X}^{58}{}_{1947,1958}$. Then an alternative set of change measures is

$$\text{Total change} = X^{58}{}_{1958} - X^{58}{}_{1947}$$

(7) Due to change in final demand $= X^{58}{}_{1958} - \hat{X}^{58}{}_{1947,1958}$

(8) Due to change in coefficients $= \hat{X}^{58}{}_{1947,1958} - X^{58}{}_{1947}$

While the total change is the same for either measure, the distribution of the output difference between that due to a change in coefficients or a change in final demand is not likely to be identical. Therefore, Vaccara and Simon take the simple arithmetic average as their indicator, or:

Average change in final demand =
$$\tfrac{1}{2}[(X^{58}{}_{1958} - X^{58}{}_{1947}) + (\hat{X}^{58}{}_{1958,1947} - \hat{X}^{58}{}_{1947,1958})]$$

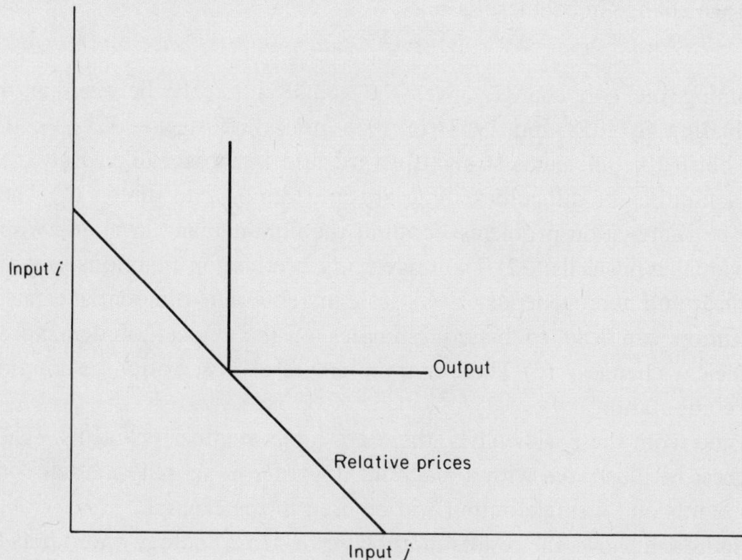

FIGURE 1-a
1947 Production

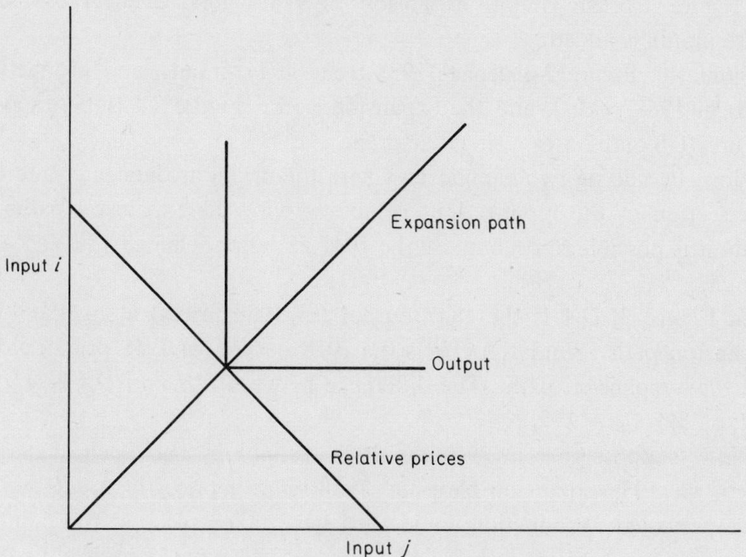

FIGURE 1-b
1947 Technology Expansion Path

Average change in coefficients =

$$\tfrac{1}{2}[(X^{58}{}_{1958} - X^{58}{}_{1947}) + (\hat{X}^{58}{}_{1947,1958} - \hat{X}^{58}{}_{1958,1947})]$$

Summing the two changes gives the actual difference between output originating in 1958 and 1947 (in 1958 prices), $X^{58}{}_{1958} - X^{58}{}_{1947}$. On first blush this all seems straightforward and irreproachable. But, there are a number of difficulties. Vaccara and Simon cite three: (1) There may be aggregation problems—both at the final-demand level and within individual input cells. (2) The underlying production functions may not be linear and homogeneous. Ergo, scale increases and differential capacity utilization can lead to biased estimates of the impact of demand vs. coefficient changes. (3) There may be errors of observation, estimation, and computation.

Aside from these difficulties, there are index number problems. These can best be illustrated with a diagram. In order to simplify matters, only two inputs and a single output will be used in the example.

Figure 1-a shows the results of applying 1947 technology and inputs (in 1958 prices) for the production of actual 1947 final demand. The isoquant depicted is that of a fixed proportion, linear, homogeneous production function, i.e., the type implicit in the input-output assumptions above. In Figure 1-b, an output expansion ray showing the effect of using more inputs is added.

Similarly, Figure 2-a depicts 1958 technology, inputs, and production (also in 1958 prices), and the expansion path. Figure 2-b superimposes Figures 1-b and 2-a in a single diagram.

Now, by adding two circular arcs with the origin as the center and the intersection of the input-output isoquants with the expansion paths as radii, it is possible to decompose the 1947-58 output change à la Vaccara-Simon.

In Figure 3, *OA* is the 1947 output (in 1958 prices) along the 1947 expansion path. Similarly, *OH* is the 1958 output (in 1958 prices) along the 1958 expansion path. The difference between *OH* and *OA* is *AD* = *EH*, or $X^{58}{}_{1958} - X^{58}{}_{1947}$.

Now, suppose that in 1947 the 1958 technology had been available. Then, the 1958 expansion path and 1958 relative prices of inputs would have prevailed. Production could then have taken place at the point *G* on the 1958 expansion path (*aa′* is a line through point *A* parallel to 1958 prices at point *H*). Output (in 1958 dollars) would be *OG*. Actual 1947 output (in 1958 dollars) was *OA* and, scribing off the same distance on the

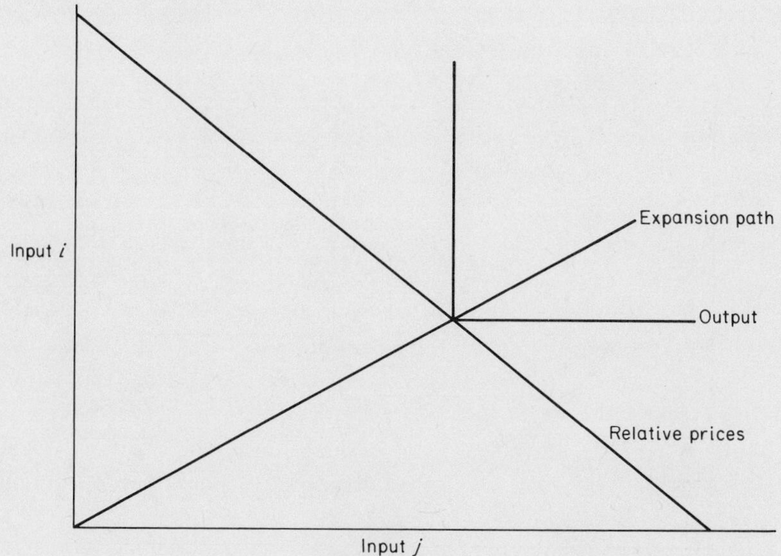

FIGURE 2-a
1958 Production

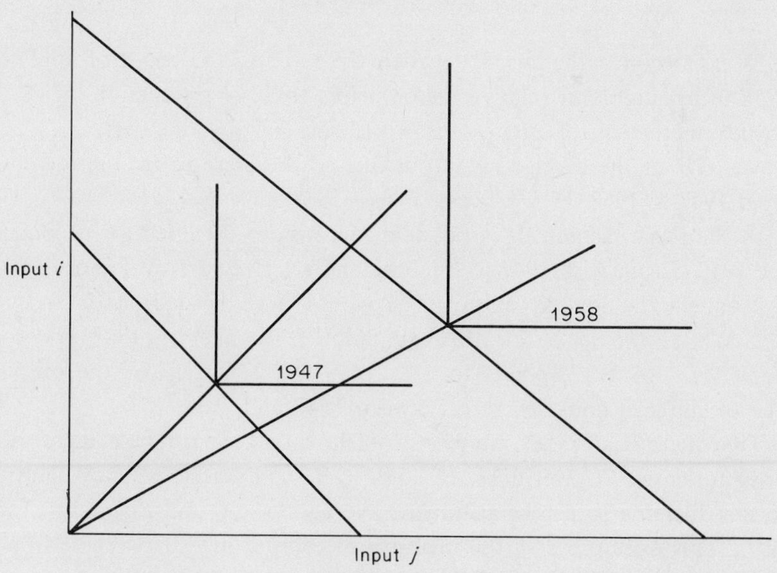

FIGURE 2-b
1947 and 1958 Technology Expansion Paths

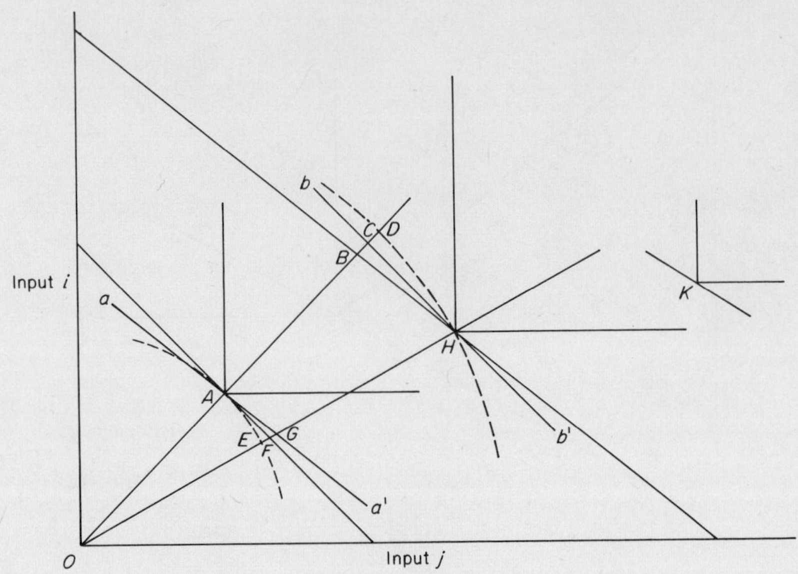

FIGURE 3
Derivation of Final Demand and Technology Contributions to Output Increments

1958 expansion path, this is equal to *OE*.[1] Thus, the result of applying 1958 technology and relative factor prices to 1947 production yields an output increment of $OG - OE = EG$, or $\hat{X}^{58}{}_{1947,1958} - \hat{X}_{1947}$. This leaves *GH* as the change in output due to the increase in final demand from 1947 to 1958, or $X^{58}{}_{1958} - \hat{X}^{58}{}_{1947,1958}$.

In the same fashion, it is possible to consider the effect of producing the 1958 output with 1947 technology and relative costs of factor inputs. *CD* equals the loss in output that would have ensued, or $X^{58}{}_{1958} - \hat{X}^{58}{}_{1958,1947}$ (*bb'* is a line through point *H* parallel to 1947 prices at point *A*). *AC* corresponds to $\hat{X}^{58}{}_{1958,1947} - X^{58}{}_{1947}$, i.e., the outputs due to shifts in final demands between 1947 and 1958.

That there is an index number problem should clearly be evident. *CD* does not equal *EG*, nor does *AC* equal *GH*. The Vaccara-Simon solution to this dilemma is to take arithmetic averages of *CD* and *EG* and *AC* and *GH*. This does preserve the measure of total change between 1947 and 1958, but it does little else.

[1] Stated alternatively, *A* is an interior point in the 1958 production possibility set. To get the same output as *A*, at lower cost, production would have taken place at *E*.

The distance *EG* is essentially a Paasche indicator of the effects of technological change between the end points of the period while *CD* is a Laspeyres indicator.[2] Averaging the two gives a bastard measure of beginning- and end-point quantities and prices.

Moreover, when a third year, say 1964, is added, matters become even worse. Then, assuming further relative price and technological shifts, using the Vaccara-Simon technique leads to extremely ambiguous results. If, for example, 1964 production took place at point *K* in Figure 3, it would turn out that the sum of their coefficient change measures for 1947–58 and 1958–64 would not equal their measure for 1947–64.

There are other ramifications of the index number problem. The impact of applying 1958 technology to the production of 1947 final demands was calculated assuming 1958 relative input prices. It could just as well have been done with 1947 price relatives, yielding the measure of coefficient change *EF*. (Again, this does not necessarily equal *CD*.) Similarly, the loss of output from applying 1947 technology to 1958 production could have been computed with 1958 instead of 1947 relative input prices. This gives the output amount due to technical progress and coefficient shifts *BD* (instead of *CD*).

Finally, outputs are measured in 1958 prices using 1958 relative importance weights. The answers would be different if the weights employed were for 1947 or some other year.

Thus, for all these reasons, the need for explicitly confronting the index number problem should be clear. It should not be casually left in a gray area of implicit ignorance.

There are further issues. First, there is the minor point that Vaccara and Simon cast their analysis in terms of total rather than partial derivatives. They compute the change in output of an industry due to *all* coefficient changes and *all* final demand shifts. In order to better understand what actually took place, it would seem desirable to compute and show two triangular matrices: (1) a set of partial derivatives of output with respect to changes in final demand of each industry (this might also be put in the form of total increments over the period); and (2) a set of partial derivatives of output with respect to shifts in coefficients of each industry.

[2] The term technological change here and above encompasses both the output increment due to improvement in production processes and that due to choice of inputs in response to shifting relative prices.

More importantly, the Vaccara-Simon computations give no clue as to why output and coefficient shifts have taken place. They do not reveal to what extent the changes are due to technical progress or to reactions to altered relative prices. No information is gained as to whether the technical progress is capital or labor augmenting, whether it is embodied or disembodied, or whether it is merely the consequence of younger average vintages of equipment or labor education. Nothing is learned about capital-labor substitutions or their consequences. These, of course, are all questions revolving about knowledge of production functions. Unfortunately, the input–output assumptions of Vaccara and Simon preclude acquiring any insights in that regard. Nevertheless, their paper is an interesting, although simplistic, initial attempt to provide first approximations of the output changes associated with shifting technical coefficients and final demands. It is hoped that the authors will continue their study and make it more powerful and definitive.

A Framework for Analysis of the Industrial Origin of Income, Product, Costs, and Prices

JACK ALTERMAN
BUREAU OF LABOR STATISTICS
U.S. DEPARTMENT OF LABOR

Introduction

In the long history of meetings sponsored by the Conference on Research in Income and Wealth, this is the first meeting to be entirely devoted to the subject of the industrial composition of income and product. This delay has not been due to a lack of interest in the subject matter but rather to a lack of data which could be used for such an analysis. Estimates of the industrial composition of national income have, of course, been available for almost as long a period as the aggregate estimates of national income. However, such estimates represent only one element of a comprehensive and systematic body of data needed for the analysis of the industrial composition of income and product. In the past few years, the data "gap" has been narrowed considerably with the broadening of the national accounts to include estimates of current- and constant-dollar gross product on an industry basis,[1] and an input–output table [2] which is consistent with the national income and product accounts.

[1] Jack J. Gottsegen, *Revised Data on GNP by Major Industries,* Office of Business Economics, U.S. Department of Commerce, May 1966. This is a working paper containing unpublished estimates of current- and constant-dollar GNP and price indexes, by industry. The estimates incorporate revisions to the measures previously published by OBE and provide additional industry detail. (See *Survey of Current Business,* October 1962 and September 1964.) The working paper by Gottsegen as well as additional worksheet detail have been made available by OBE to the authors of the papers for this conference. The OBE estimates of in-

NOTE: The major assistance of Mrs. Eva E. Jacobs in the preparation of this paper is gratefully acknowledged.

There are two complementary approaches to the analysis of the industrial origin of income and product (and implicit costs and prices). One approach starts with the measures of aggregate gross national income (charges against gross national product) and product as the sum of income and product originating in each sector in the economy. The analysis flowing from this approach is concerned with the various producing industries' contribution to the level and change in aggregate gross national income, product, costs, and prices, and the factors underlying such changes.[3] The OBE estimates of industry current- and constant-dollar product and implicit price indexes are basic to such an analysis.

An alternative approach starts with the expenditure side of the national accounts and traces through for total final demand and each component, i.e., consumption, investment, government expenditures for goods and services, and net exports, the contribution (value added) of each industry to the detailed final-demand expenditures and the proportionate share of the industry's gross income payments, costs, and prices, "embodied" in the various components of final demand. This approach requires the use of both industry income and product data, and input–output information.

Much of the recent empirical work on the industrial origin of income and product has been largely concerned with the first approach.

---

dustry real product are based, in part, on the earlier work by Alterman and Jacobs in a paper given at the twenty-fifth meeting sponsored by the Conference on Research in Income and Wealth. See Jack Alterman and Eva E. Jacobs, "Estimates of Real Product in the United States by Industrial Sector, 1947–55," *Output, Input, and Productivity Measurement,* Studies in Income and Wealth 25, Princeton for NBER, 1961.

[2] Morris R. Goldman, Martin L. Marimont, and Beatrice Vaccara, "The Interindustry Structure of the United States, A Report on the 1958 Input–Output Study," *Survey of Current Business,* November 1964; also, National Economics Division staff, "The Transactions Table of the 1958 Input–Output Study and Revised Direct and Total Requirements Data," *Survey of Current Business,* September 1965.

[3] The framework for the analysis of costs, prices, and output within a consistent structure of industry and national income and real product measures is based, to a considerable extent, on the work of Charles L. Schultze. Schultze's work was initially developed as an extended comment on the Alterman-Jacobs paper at the 1958 meeting of the Conference on Research in Income and Wealth (Studies in Income and Wealth 25). The approach was further developed and expanded by Schultze in "Prices, Costs and Output, 1947–57," Committee for Economic Development, 1960. Also, see Charles L. Schultze and Joseph Tryon, "Prices and Costs in Manufacturing Industries," Study Paper No. 17, Study of Employment, Growth and Price Levels, U.S. Joint Economic Committee, 1960.

This paper, after a brief review of this approach, is primarily devoted to a discussion of how the estimates of industry current- and constant-dollar gross product can be used, along with input–output information, to provide a link between final demand and industry income, product, costs, and prices.

Industrial Origin of Aggregate Income and Product

As background for the discussion which follows, it may be useful here to review the conceptual basis for the measures of GNP by industry. Since much of this may be familiar to members of the conference, only the main elements will be noted. Further detailed information may be found in the OBE working paper and articles in the *Survey of Current Business,* and in the studies by Schultze.

In the conventional income and product accounts, GNP is derived by two alternative methods. As a measure of the market value of all final goods and services produced by the economy, it is derived as the sum of expenditures for consumption, investment (including change in business inventories), government services, and net exports. GNP is also derived as the sum of income payments to the factors of production (labor compensation, profits, proprietors' income, rent, interest) plus nonfactor charges (indirect business taxes, depreciation, etc.). The two measures are identical in concept, but because they are derived independently they may differ because of a statistical discrepancy.

As a measure of the market value of final goods and services, GNP may be affected by the change in prices as well as changes in physical volume of goods and services purchased by final users. For analytical purposes and in order to derive a measure of "real" growth in the economy, the current-dollar estimates of GNP are deflated in considerable detail in order to obtain a measure of constant-dollar GNP. Dividing the index of current-dollar GNP by the constant-dollar index yields an implicit price index.

Gross national product can also be derived as the sum of each industry's contribution to the nation's total output of goods and services. Because an industry's gross product or value added represents its unduplicated contribution to total output, it may be measured as the value of production less the contribution to its production made by other industries, i.e., materials and services purchased on current account from other industries.

The industry's contribution to GNP may also be derived by summing its factor payments and nonfactor costs of production, which is comparable to the measure of total GNP obtained from the income side of the accounts. The sum of the industries' gross products—measured by either method—is equal to total GNP.

The current-dollar measure of an industry's gross product derived as the sum of its factor payments and nonfactor costs is not directly convertible to a constant-dollar measure because the components (employee compensation, profits, interest, etc.) cannot be expressed in quantity and unit price suitable for this purpose.

The alternative definition of industry gross product as the difference between output and input of materials, business services, and other current account items is therefore used as the basis for deriving estimates of industry real product. Each industry's current-dollar sales (including inventory change) and purchases of intermediate materials and services are deflated separately and the difference between the estimates of constant-dollar production and cost of materials, etc., is constant-dollar industry gross product. In practice, it is not always possible to develop industry-real-product measures by this conceptually correct method and various alternative methods are used. The methods actually used are described in the OBE working paper on GNP, by industry, and statement on concepts and methodology.

The industry measures of current- and constant-dollar gross product provide the basis for the analysis of the industrial composition of aggregate gross national income and product. Estimates of the contribution of each industry to the change in current- and constant-dollar GNP can be derived by weighting the change in each industry with its relative contribution to GNP in the base period.

The change in the factor and nonfactor composition of aggregate current-dollar GNP, developed from the income side of the national accounts, can be further analyzed to determine how much of the changing composition of gross income is due to shifts within industries and how much to changes in the relative importance of industries.

On the real-product side of the accounts, measures of output per man-hour can be derived by developing man-hour data in each industry consistent with the real-product measure. The gain in industry and national real output can then be factored into increases in man-hours and increases in labor productivity (output per man-hour). Further, the over-all gain in productivity can be analyzed to determine how much of the increase is attributable to increases in each industry and how much to the shift in relative importance of industries between low- and high-productivity industries.

The industry current- and constant-dollar gross product measures also lend themselves to an analysis of the industrial origin of the over-all change in unit costs and prices. The division of the current- by the constant-dollar estimates of industry gross product yields a price index of gross product. This price index differs from the usual concept of price of a particular commodity or service. The ordinary price index reflects all costs and not just those originating within the industry in question. The price index of industry value added or gross product is equal to the market price of the industry's product minus the unit cost of purchased raw materials, supplies, services, etc.

The development of price and real-product measures for each industry makes it possible to determine how much of the change in current-dollar gross product, at both the industry and total economy level, is due to the real-product increase and how much to price change.

In addition, since the price index is obtained by dividing current-dollar by constant-dollar gross product and since current-dollar gross product is the sum of all costs (broadly defined to include profits) originating in the industry, the price index can be distributed into the various cost elements of which it is composed—employee compensation, profits, capital consumption allowances, etc. This is done by dividing the index for each cost element by the real-gross product index.

Having derived price indexes for each industry, it is possible to weight the indexes by the relative importance of the industries in the total economy and construct a general price index for the entire economy or major subgroups. The general price index can then be distributed into elements representing the contribution of each industry, and into the various cost components.

The analysis can be broadened by using measures of man-hours and capital stock consistent with the industry income and real product estimates. The use of man-hour estimates to derive output per man-hour measures has been indicated previously. The man-hour estimates can also be used, along with measures of labor compensation, to derive industry indexes of labor compensation per man-hour. The change in unit labor costs at the industry level and for the economy as a whole can then be analyzed in terms of the increase in compensation per man-hour relative to the increase in labor productivity. The change in aggregate unit labor costs, earnings, and labor productivity can be further analyzed to determine how much of the over-all change is due to changes at the industry level and how much to the change in the relative importance of industries—the shift effect.[4]

A similar analysis can be developed to distribute the change in property income per unit into the change in property income per dollar of capital stock (constant dollars) and the capital-output ratio. The aggregate change in property income per unit can also be analyzed from the viewpoint of changes at the industry level and the effect of interindustry shifts on the aggregate ratio.[5]

There are several problem areas in the analysis of the industry income and real-product estimates which should be mentioned. These will be noted only briefly since some of them are discussed in other papers in this volume. These include the problems of allocating income of proprietors between labor compensation and property income, the incomparability of the time series on capital consumption and profits because of the effect of changing accounting methods and tax legislation on depreciation, and finally the problems of interpreting implicit price deflators and the appropriate weights required to partition the change in an aggregate measure among the component elements.

The need for allocating proprietor income between labor compensation and property income is a perennial problem in the analysis of changes in income shares and the relationship of labor and nonlabor unit costs to price change. The problem arises because a relative decline in the proportion of self-employed in the labor force and the corresponding relative increase in wage and salary employees would result in an increase in unit labor cost even though there may be no change in compensation per man-hour or in the productivity of all workers. There is no consensus among economists as to the appropriate method of splitting proprietors' income between labor and property

[4] See the paper by Leon Greenberg and Jerome A. Mark, "Industry Changes in Labor Costs," in this volume.

[5] See the paper by John W. Kendrick, "Industry Changes in Nonlabor Costs," in this volume.

income. The problem is mentioned in this paper, not to suggest a particular method of allocation but to emphasize the need to take this factor into account, either qualitatively or quantitatively, in the analysis of the industrial origin of income, product, costs, and prices.

Another area in which the data, as published, may lead to misinterpretation is the estimate of the capital consumption allowance and its effect on profits. Depreciation, the major component of the capital consumption allowance, is in concept the allowance for replacing the capital "used up" in the course of production. In practice, it is affected by the changing accounting procedures and tax laws, including various forms of accelerated depreciation. As a result, the estimates of depreciation do not reflect a consistent concept or method and it is difficult to interpret the unadjusted data in unambiguous terms. The lack of consistent depreciation estimates also affects the data on profits since profits are derived as the residual component of income. Consistent estimates of depreciation have been developed by OBE, based on various alternative assumptions regarding depreciation methods and these estimates are being revised as part of the continuing work of OBE in the capital investment area.[6] Here again, the comment on the particular problem area serves to point up the need to qualify or adjust the results to take this factor into account, rather than suggesting a specific method or set of depreciation rates for handling the problem.

Regarding the interpretation of the implicit GNP deflator, it is well known that such a price index has changing weights and technically can only be used to measure the change in price between the base year and a given year. Comparisons between given years reflect the change in product mix as well as the change in price. In practice, the GNP deflator is interpreted as though it were a fixed-weight price index, on the assumption that the effect on prices of the change in output mix is relatively minor.

The industry price deflators derived at the industry level by dividing the current-dollar by the constant-dollar GNP measures also are Paasche-type price indexes, i.e., changing-quantity weights. They can, however, be combined with fixed weights to provide partial information on the extent to which the over-all price index may be affected by changing weights. Such an index has been developed for this

[6] Murray Brown, "Depreciation and Corporate Profits," *Survey of Current Business,* October 1963, pp. 5–12.

paper. The changing-weight industry price deflators have been combined with 1958 gross-output weights to derive a partial fixed-weight (Laspeyres) price index.

The partial fixed-1958-weight price index cannot be compared directly with the published GNP deflator because the sum of the industry current- and constant-dollar measures developed by OBE does not correspond exactly to the published GNP estimates. The sum of industry current-dollar GNP is, of course, equal to aggregate factor and nonfactor payments for the economy as a whole. This differs from the total GNP by the amount of the statistical discrepancy. On the real-product side of the accounts, the industry estimates are developed independently, and since no industry estimate is derived as a residual, the sum of the industry real-product estimates does not necessarily agree with the published constant-dollar GNP total. As a result of the differences between the sum of industry GNP and published GNP, the implicit deflators may also differ. In order to make a direct comparison with the fixed-weight price index developed for this comparison, a modified GNP deflator has been derived which adjusts for the differences noted above and is consistent with the sum of the industry current- and constant-dollar GNP estimates.[7]

A comparison of the GNP price change for the 1947–58 and 1958–64 subperiods, based on the various indexes, is shown in Table 1 below. The various measures have been arranged to determine whether the "earlier" or "later" period for the weights affects the price change.

The comparison does indicate that the difference between published GNP and the sum of industry current- and constant-dollar GNP can affect the resulting price comparison. A more meaningful analysis would therefore limit the comparison to the measures which are consistent with industry GNP. The differences between the fixed- and changing-weight indexes are quite small—about one-tenth of 1 per cent per year, on the average.

If one analyzes the two derived measures in terms of earlier versus later year weights, the changes are consistent with the expectation that price changes based on weights of the earlier period would show relatively higher rates of increase. This corresponds to the assumption that output is inversely related to price and that industries with less (more)

[7] The modified changing-weight price index was developed solely for comparison with the fixed-weight price index and is not to be considered as a substitute for the published GNP deflator.

TABLE 1

Comparison of GNP Price Changes, Measures of Price Change Arranged in Terms of Earlier and Later Period Weights, 1947–58, 1958–64

	1947–58	
Earlier period weights		
Published	implicit 1947 weights	34.0
Derived	implicit 1947 weights	37.2
Later period weights		
Derived	explicit 1958 industry weights	36.2
	1958–64	
Earlier period weights		
Derived	1958 fixed weights	9.1
Later period weights		
Derived	implicit 1964 weights	8.5
Published	implicit 1964 weights	8.9

Note: Derived estimates consistent with industry GNP measures.

than average increases in output would also have more (less) than average increases in price.

A further analysis of the two measures on an annual basis indicates reasonably close correspondence, except for the 1950–51 period, which was affected by the Korean War and related inflation. It should be noted that the fixed-weight price index developed for this comparison is only a partial fixed-weight measure and reflects changing weights within industries. With expansion of industry detail it may be possible to develop a more conceptually correct Laspeyres price index.

Finally, there is the problem of determining the appropriate weights to be used in the statistical analysis of the industrial origin of income, product, costs, and prices so that the component elements are additive and can be used to measure how much each component "contributed" to the change in the aggregate measure. Specifically, what are the appropriate weights for determining how much of the change in total current-dollar GNP is due to the increase in real product of the component industries and how much to the change in price of industry gross product? As noted earlier, the usual price index derived by dividing current-dollar GNP by the constant-dollar GNP measure yields a price index which has opposite weights from that of the production index. As a result, the variables which are held constant in the production and price indexes refer to different time periods. In the published real-GNP estimates and implicit deflators, the real-GNP estimates are based on holding 1958 prices constant, the price deflators have changing weights. The deflators therefore measure the change in price between the base period and the given year, of the given year's mix of final goods and services. Conceptually, the change in production and price derived from these indexes cannot be added to explain the change in total current-dollar GNP. In order to be able to answer the question of how much each component has contributed to the change in a particular aggregate, the weights for each component should be based on the same time period.

As a practical matter, failure to use appropriate weights for the purpose of apportioning a change to contributing factors will distort the results only if the change in the relative importance of the weights is substantial. Testing for the significance of changing weights provides the information required to partition the change into components which can be added to "explain" the total.

Even with weights for each component based on the same time period, the components may not add to the total because of the contribution of the "interaction" among the components to the aggregate change. The need to explicitly estimate the "interaction" effect and the various methods of then allocating the contribution of the "interaction" effect among the components is discussed in various articles and studies and need not be treated here in detail.[8]

Industry Income and Real-Product Origin of Final-Demand Expenditures

The OBE estimates of current- and constant-dollar GNP, by industry, provide a major body of comprehensive and consistent information basic to an analysis of the industry composition of aggregate level and change in gross national income, product, costs, and prices.

[8] Irving H. Siegel, *Concepts and Measurement of Production and Productivity*, Bureau of Labor Statistics, U.S. Department of Labor, 1952, pp. 86–92; Harlowe Osborne and Joseph B. Epstein, "Corporate Profits Since World War II," *Survey of Current Business*, January 1956, p. 20.

The industry income and product estimates, however, are limited to the supply side of the accounts—there is no direct link to the detailed final-demand side of the national accounts. The analysis of the relationship between the industrial structure of production and the changing composition of final demand requires information from another part of the expanded national accounts—the input–output tables. The input–output tables also provide the means for tracing through the industrial origin of changes in costs and prices of final goods and services.

Input–output tables provide information on what each industry in the economy buys from other industries, as well as from itself, to produce its own output. The total-requirements form of the input–output table links together the interindustry sales-purchase relationships (input–output coefficients) to show how much output (direct and indirect) is generated in each industry to meet the final demand for a dollar's worth of expenditures for the products of each industry. Given information on (a) the changing composition of final-demand components and detailed expenditures for consumption, investment, etc., consistent with the industry classification system and definitions of the input–output table and (b) input–output relationships which link final-demand expenditures and industry output, it is possible to analyze the changing industrial structure of real output in the economy in terms of how much is due to the changing composition of final demand and how much to the change in input–output relationships. Such an analysis is hampered, however, by lack of consistent detailed information, classified by input–output categories, on changes in the structure of final demand and input–output relationships. The paper by Beatrice N. Vaccara and Nancy W. Simon, "Factors Affecting the Postwar Industrial Composition of Real Product-Final Demand and Technical Coefficients," in this volume, helps narrow this data gap and analyzes the factors underlying the changing industrial structure of real product, based on a reconciliation and comparison of the 1947 and 1958 input–output tables. The publication in the near future by OBE of a 1961 input–output table should provide additional information to broaden the time horizon for this type of analysis.

The input–output information can also be used, along with the industry income and real-product estimates, to analyze the industrial origin of final-demand prices. Although this approach is implicit in input–output price models, it has not been developed empirically in a comprehensive and systematic manner.[9] The remainder of this paper is devoted to a discussion of the methodology involved and a presentation of the results of exploratory work based on this approach.

The approach can be stated rather simply. If information is available on how much each industry contributes, in terms of value added (gross product), to final goods and services, and information is also available on the change in price of industry gross product, then it follows that the industrial origin of the change in price of goods and services purchased for consumption, investment, etc., can be determined. Since the price change for each industry can be further distributed into specific cost elements, e.g., unit labor costs, unit depreciation costs, it is also possible to analyze how much of the change in price of final goods and services is contributed by each category of factor and nonfactor costs.

This approach has been used to analyze the industrial origin of the change in costs and prices of final-demand expenditures between 1958 and 1964. The availability of an input–output table for 1958 was the reason for selecting 1958 as the base period. The year 1964 was chosen simply because it was the latest year covered by the OBE estimates of industry income, real product, and prices. The 1958–64 period was selected as the basis for the analysis due to availability of data and convenience rather than because it represents a "normal" period for the analysis of costs and prices. It should be noted, however, that the price change for the period was quite modest—about 1.5 per cent per year.

Because the data from the two sources of information used differ in industry detail, they have been aggregated to a common grouping of industries. There are forty-two industry groups in all, representing a consolidation of the more detailed manufacturing industries in the input–output table to two-digit SIC industry groups generally, and some consolidation of the industry GNP estimates in the nonmanufacturing area.

The common classification system derived for this purpose is shown in Table 2, along with SIC codes and input–output industry numbers. It should be noted that a comparison of the industry "value added"

[9] For further information on input–output price models see Wassily Leontief, *Input–Output Economics,* 1966, Sections 3 and 7.7; also, United Nations, *Problems of Input–Output Tables and Analysis,* Studies in Methods, Series F, No. 14, 1966, pp. 17–21, 89–102.

TABLE 2

Industrial Classification Used for Analysis of Industrial Origin of Final Demand

Industry Number and Title	SIC	Input-Output Number
1 Farms	01, 02	1, 2
2 Agricultural, forestry, & fishery services	07-09	3, 4
3 Metal mining	10	5, 6
4 Coal mining	11, 12	7
5 Crude petroleum and natural gas	13	8
6 Nonmetallic mining	14	9, 10
7 Contract construction	15-17	11, 12
8 Food	20	14
9 Tobacco	21	15
10 Textile mill products	22	16, 17, 19
11 Apparel	23	18
12 Paper	26	24, 25
13 Printing and publishing	27	26
14 Chemicals	28	27-30
15 Petroleum refining	29	31
16 Rubber and misc. plastics	30	32
17 Leather	31	33, 34
18 Lumber and products	24	20, 21
19 Furniture	25	22, 23
20 Stone, clay, and glass	32	35, 36
21 Primary metals	33	37, 38
22 Fabricated metal products	34	39-42
23 Machinery, except electrical	35	43-52
24 Electrical machinery	36	53-58
25 Transportation equipment, except motor vehicles	37 (-371), 19	60, 61, 13
26 Motor vehicles	371	59
27 Instruments	38	62, 63
28 Misc. manufacturing	39	64
29 Transportation	40-42, 45-47	65
30 Communication, except radio and TV	48 (-483)	66
31 Radio and TV	483	67
32 Electricity, gas, and sanitary services	49	68
33 Trade	50, 52-59	69
34 Finance and insurance	60-64, 66, 67	70
35 Real estate	65	71
36 Services	70, 73, 75, 76	72-77
37 Federal gov't enterprises		78
38 State and local gov't enterprises		79
39 Imports		80
40 General gov't employee compensation		84
41 Rest of the world		85
42 Domestics		86

shown in the input–output table does not correspond exactly with value added for the corresponding industry derived from the industry GNP estimates. There are a number of reasons for these differences, but the largest differences are due to the modification in the input–output system of construction, from an industry basis (contract construction) to an activity basis. The transfer of force account construction from the industries where the work is done to the construction activity category has the effect of increasing the value added in construction and reducing it in the original industries. The effect on the aggregate price change of using unit cost and price indexes derived from the industry GNP estimates, with weights derived from the input–output tables is discussed later in the paper.

The conventional input–output total-requirements table, as previously indicated, shows the total output generated in each industry per dollar of final-demand expenditures. The sum of total transactions generated is, of course, larger than the initial final-demand expenditure because it reflects the duplication of the value of materials and the value of products made from these materials, rather than just the value added by each industry. The first stage in the methodology, therefore, is to convert industry output in the total-requirements table from a gross duplicated output to a value-added basis.

Expenditures for final goods may exceed the aggregate "value added" contributed by the various industries to the final product, if part of final demand for the product is met from imports, e.g., automobiles, or some of the materials used to make the final product are imported, e.g., steel.

In order to trace the industrial origin of the value of final goods and services, the modified form of the total-requirements table shows the total value added (direct and indirect) generated in each industry, plus imports, per dollar of final-demand expenditures for the products of each industry.

The difference between the original and modified total-requirements tables is illustrated in Table 3, which compares total output and value added generated in each industry per $1,000 (producers' value) of final-demand expenditures for the products of the motor vehicle industry. The value of imports is the same in both tables, but the value of production (sales, including inventory change) and value added differ considerably, depending on whether an industry's output consists largely of its own contribution (value added) or whether pur-

TABLE 3

Comparison of Total Output (Direct and Indirect) and Value Added Generated in Each Industry Per 1,000 Dollars of Final-Demand Expenditures for Products of Motor Vehicle Industry, 1958

Industry Number	Total Output	Value Added
1	$ 10.37	$ 4.56
2	1.21	.50
3	17.58	6.13
4	9.66	5.65
5	9.43	5.89
6	3.06	1.69
7	14.75	9.04
8	8.62	2.17
9	.42	.20
10	39.58	9.76
11	1.91	.74
12	27.62	10.09
13	18.99	8.89
14	51.12	20.15
15	14.69	2.94
16	48.10	21.88
17	.96	.52
18	6.97	2.27
19	1.11	.47
20	29.16	15.48
21	253.66	98.37
22	119.81	50.75
23	68.55	31.97
24	55.61	24.72
25	7.36	3.04
26	1,427.08	406.72
27	9.01	4.07
28	4.52	1.80
29	66.08	39.77
30	9.38	7.98
31	3.43	1.96
32	26.36	12.92
33	80.93	58.72
34	20.51	11.49
35	24.20	17.48
36	69.16	32.90
37	6.74	2.94
38	5.89	3.21
39	60.00	60.00
40		
41		
42		
Total	$2,633.59	$1,000.00

chased materials, parts, services, etc. represent the major part of the value of the industry's output, and the value added is relatively small.

The gross duplicated transactions, covering all industries generated by an initial expenditure for motor vehicles is about 2.6 times as large as the initial expenditure. This compares to an average of almost two to one for the economy as a whole. The latter figure is derived by dividing the grand total of industry output (sales, including inventory change) by value added (GNP) for the economy as a whole. For the motor vehicle industry (Industry 26), the value of gross duplicated output of the industry, including motor vehicle parts produced and consumed within the industry, is about 3.5 times the value added of the industry.

Given information on the value-added content by industry of specific categories of final goods and services, and detailed estimates of final-demand expenditures (bill of goods) classified by industry, estimates of how much each industry has contributed to total final demand and major components can be derived.

Using the data on final-demand expenditures from the 1958 input–output table and the total-requirements–value-added table, estimates of the value-added content by industry of final-demand expenditures have been developed for personal consumption expenditures and other major components of final demand. The distribution of the industrial origin of personal consumption expenditures is shown in Table 4 and compared to the industrial composition of consumption based on the industry of final production. The latter distribution is derived from the published estimates of consumption, classified by producing industry, as shown in the 1958 table.

Before discussing the composition of personal consumption expenditures, based on the final-value and value-added concepts, some explanation of the conventions of the input–output system is required. In the input–output system, trade is considered a marginal industry with purchasers buying goods and services directly from producers. Output of goods and services is stated in producers' prices. Expenditures, therefore, consists of three components—(a) value of product purchased at producers' prices, (b) value of "purchases" by the consumer of the services of trade, and (c) transportation. The latter two items represent the gap between producers' and purchasers' value.

Consistent with the input–output conventions, the largest "purchase" shown in Table 4 is from trade (Industry 33), covering the trade

TABLE 4

Comparison of Industrial Composition of Personal Consumption Expenditures, Final-Value (Producers' Prices), and Value-Added Content, 1958

Industry Number	Final Value (Producers' Prices) (1)	Value-Added Content (2)	Col. 2 Minus Col. 1 (3)
1	1.57	5.92	4.35
2	.10	.32	.22
3	--	.09	.09
4	.09	.30	.21
5	--	1.69	1.69
6	.01	.13	.12
7	--	2.16	2.16
8	15.76	5.31	-10.45
9	1.47	.89	-.58
10	.88	1.17	.29
11	3.85	1.85	-2.00
12	.31	1.24	.93
13	.84	1.49	.65
14	1.36	2.17	.81
15	2.50	.88	-1.62
16	.45	.68	.23
17	.90	.61	-.29
18	.05	.30	.25
19	.88	.40	-.48
20	.12	.55	.43
21	.01	1.16	1.15
22	.24	.99	.75
23	.17	.66	.49
24	1.56	1.19	-.37
25	.31	.27	-.04
26	3.17	1.49	-1.68
27	.28	.34	.06
28	.87	.57	-.30
29	2.99	4.38	1.39
30	1.35	2.09	.74
31	--	.20	.20
32	2.78	2.72	-.06
33	21.21	19.20	-2.01
34	4.07	4.43	.36
35	13.78	13.78	--
36	13.60	11.99	-1.61
37	.22	.47	.25
38	.11	.69	.58
39	1.33	4.41	3.08
40	--	--	--
41	-.40	-.40	--
42	1.21	1.21	--
Total	100.00	100.00	--

Note: Detail may not add to total due to rounding.

margins on all goods purchased by consumers. The contribution of the trade industry, defined as trade margins, to personal consumption expenditures amounted to over 21 per cent of the total in 1958. It is somewhat lower when the contribution of trade to personal consumption expenditures is measured in terms of value added.

The differences between the two concepts of the industrial composition of final demand are perhaps best illustrated by reference to the contribution of food processing (Industry 8) and farms (Industry 1) to personal consumption expenditures.

Most food purchased for consumption is processed food, and only a relatively small proportion represents direct purchases from the farm, e.g., fresh fruits and vegetables. Considered from the viewpoint of what the consumer buys directly from final producers (at producers' prices), almost 16 per cent of the consumers' dollar goes for processed food products. Direct purchase of farm products accounts for less than 2 per cent. However, in terms of the value-added content of consumption expenditures, the distribution is modified considerably. The percentage of the consumer's dollar accounted for by food processing is reduced to slightly more than 5 per cent and the percentage accounted for by agriculture is increased to almost 6 per cent. The increase in the latter figure is, of course, due to taking account of the value-added content of farm products processed by the food products industry, as well as the agricultural products, e.g., cotton, which are raw materials for the textile industry, and are embodied ultimately in apparel purchased by consumers.

Estimates of the value-added content of final-demand expenditures by industry have also been developed for the other major components of final demand and for the total "bill of goods." These estimates are shown in Table 5. Inventory change is not shown separately, but is included in total final-demand expenditures.

The treatment of imports in the table requires some clarification. The estimates for the separate components of final demand include an estimate for the import content of final expenditures. "Import content" covers items which are purchased directly as imports, e.g., food, automobiles; and imported materials such as steel and crude oil, which are refined or processed and used to make the final products. Since GNP measures the sum of domestic value added plus net income from abroad, the import content of the separate components of final demand should

TABLE 5

Industrial Origin (Value-Added Content) of Final-Demand Expenditures, 1958
(percentage distribution)

Industry Number	Total	Personal Consumption Expenditures	Fixed Investment	Fed. Gov't	State & Local Gov't	Gross Exports
1	4.66	5.92	.73	1.50	.57	6.88
2	.28	.32	.27	.03	.08	.36
3	.20	.09	.46	.44	.18	.44
4	.36	.30	.38	.19	.30	1.33
5	1.49	1.69	.97	.98	.97	1.96
6	.27	.13	.74	.21	.44	.44
7	6.46	2.16	21.72	4.09	16.29	1.15
8	3.72	5.31	.26	.20	.35	2.06
9	.64	.89	.02	.01	.01	1.14
10	.87	1.17	.26	.27	.15	.77
11	1.23	1.85	.05	.07	.13	.33
12	1.12	1.24	1.03	.61	.67	1.46
13	1.33	1.49	.96	.66	1.00	1.01
14	2.19	2.17	1.56	1.88	1.60	4.73
15	.81	.88	.53	.54	.53	1.08
16	.70	.68	.80	.56	.41	.98
17	.37	.61	.04	.05	.02	.21
18	.64	.30	1.97	.36	1.08	.50
19	.46	.40	.99	.16	.36	.11
20	1.09	.55	3.24	.72	1.76	.95
21	2.35	1.16	6.57	3.17	2.44	4.83

(continued)

TABLE 5 (concluded)

Industry Number	Total	Personal Consumption Expenditures	Fixed Investment	Fed. Gov't	State & Local Gov't	Gross Exports
22	1.84	.99	4.99	1.60	2.19	2.24
23	2.48	.66	9.42	2.81	1.12	6.46
24	2.15	1.19	4.61	4.38	.97	2.88
25	2.02	.27	1.46	12.87	.15	2.35
26	1.52	1.49	2.58	.58	.53	1.86
27	.55	.34	.88	1.15	.27	.78
28	.50	.57	.38	.16	.32	.35
29	4.60	4.38	4.44	3.40	2.69	8.95
30	1.77	2.09	1.37	.78	.86	.97
31	.20	.20	.22	.11	.16	.19
32	2.21	2.72	1.17	1.04	1.29	1.12
33	15.42	19.21	12.08	3.83	4.50	8.27
34	3.31	4.43	1.42	.68	1.05	1.25
35	10.01	13.79	3.70	1.60	1.72	3.58
36	9.22	11.99	3.74	3.90	3.24	3.76
37	.40	.47	.26	.19	.22	.34
38	.58	.69	.34	.36	.28	.40
39	--	4.41	3.37	7.09	1.68	4.04
40	8.72	--	--	37.31	47.43	--
41	.45	-.40	--	-.57	--	17.48
42	.78	1.21	--	--	--	--
Total	100.00	100.00	100.00	100.00	100.00	100.00

Note: Inventory change, by industry, is not shown separately but included in total column. Imports are not shown separately but are reflected in the total column as an offset to the import content of final-demand components. Detail may not add to totals due to rounding.

be excluded from total GNP. In the GNP accounts, this is done by subtracting total imports from total exports to derive the net export figure. In Table 5, exports are shown on a gross basis, before deduction of imports. Imports are not shown separately in the table as an offset to exports, but are excluded from the total "bill of goods" to be consistent with the measure of GNP.

A comparison of the value-added content, by industry, of the various components of final demand indicates substantial variation among the components. The contribution of agriculture to final demand is important for personal consumption expenditures and exports, but not for investment and government expenditures. Conversely, construction constitutes a substantial portion of fixed-investment expenditures and state and local government expenditures for goods and services, but obviously it is not a major item of consumption expenditures. Transportation equipment (excluding motor vehicles) and ordnance represents the largest single component, after the direct government payroll, of federal government expenditures for goods and services, but it does not represent a major portion of expenditures for any other category of final demand.

As previously indicated, industry value added is also the sum of industry factor payment and nonfactor costs. Given information on the distribution of industry value added by income shares, capital consumption allowances, and indirect business taxes, the value-added content of final-demand expenditures can be further distributed into these primary inputs. Primary inputs are defined to cover the factor and nonfactor payments plus imports.

The OBE estimates of the distribution of industry current-dollar GNP by income shares and nonfactor costs have been used to distribute the industry-value-added content of final-demand expenditures into primary-input content. The results for personal consumption expenditures in 1958 are shown in Table 6. The estimates show how much of the consumer's dollar is ultimately paid out in the form of employee compensation, profits, depreciation, etc. Further, they show how much of the aggregate payment to employees, for example, is in the motor vehicle industry, the food products industry, trade, etc. Similar distributions are provided for each category of income payment and nonfactor costs. Imports are shown as a single item.

Similar estimates of primary-input content have been developed for

TABLE 6

Primary-Input Content (Gross Income, Indirect Business Taxes, and Imports) of Personal Consumption Expenditures, by Industrial Origin, 1958

(percentage distribution)

Industry Number	Total Primary Inputs	Employee Compensation	Net Interest	Capital Consumption Allowance	Indirect Business Taxes	Profits	Proprietors' Income	Rent Income & Subsidies	Imports
1	5.92	.74	.24	1.08	.31	.02	3.81	-.28	--
2	.32	.15	*	.04	.01	*	.12	--	--
3	.09	.05	-*	.01	*	.03	*	--	--
4	.30	.22	*	.03	.01	.04	*	--	--
5	1.69	.38	*	.43	.11	.71	.06	--	--
6	.13	.08	*	.03	*	.02	*	--	--
7	2.16	1.56	*	.13	.05	.08	.34	--	--
8	5.31	3.08	.02	.35	1.07	.69	.10	--	--
9	.89	.13	.01	.01	.59	.15	*	--	--
10	1.17	.94	.01	.08	.02	.11	.01	--	--
11	1.85	1.59	-*	.04	.02	.11	.09	--	--
12	1.24	.80	.01	.13	.03	.26	.01	--	--
13	1.49	1.16	-*	.07	.03	.17	.06	--	--
14	2.17	1.23	.01	.27	.05	.60	.01	--	--
15	.88	.55	-*	.13	.50	-.30	*	--	--
16	.68	.46	*	.05	.08	.08	.01	--	--
17	.61	.54	*	.02	.01	.03	.01	--	--
18	.30	.20	*	.03	.01	.04	.02	--	--
19	.40	.33	*	.02	.01	.03	.01	--	--
20	.55	.35	-*	.06	.01	.12	.01	--	--

(continued)

TABLE 6 (concluded)

Industry Number	Total Primary Inputs	Employee Compensation	Net Interest	Capital Consumption Allowance	Indirect Business Taxes	Profits	Proprietors' Income	Rent Income & Subsidies	Imports
21	1.16	.79	.01	.14	.03	.19	*	--	--
22	.99	.78	*	.06	.02	.11	.02	--	--
23	.66	.50	*	.05	.02	.08	.01	--	--
24	1.19	.90	*	.05	.06	.18	*	--	--
25	.27	.23	*	.01	*	.03	*	--	--
26	1.49	.96	-.01	.13	.28	.13	*	--	--
27	.34	.26	*	.02	.01	.05	*	--	--
28	.57	.43	*	.03	.02	.07	.02	--	--
29	4.38	3.03	.09	.55	.40	.18	.17	-.04	--
30	2.09	1.01	.06	.19	.32	.51	*	--	--
31	.20	.14	*	.02	*	.04	*	--	--
32	2.72	.95	.23	.53	.31	.68	.02	--	--
33	19.20	10.72	.04	1.09	3.03	1.36	2.96	--	--
34	4.43	3.04	-1.47	.20	.34	1.89	.43	--	--
35	13.78	.63	2.45	2.58	2.55	.28	.59	4.70	--
36	11.99	7.22	.08	.90	.37	.20	3.22	--	--
37	.47	.82	--	--	.01	--	--	-.36	--
38	.69	.32	--	--	--	--	--	.37	--
39	4.41	--	--	--	--	--	--	--	4.41
40	--	--	--	--	--	--	--	--	--
41	-.40	-*	-.06	--	--	-.34	--	--	--
42	1.21	1.21	--	--	--	--	--	--	--
Total	100.00	48.48	1.72	9.56	10.69	8.63	12.11	4.39	4.41

Notes to Table 6

Note: Employee compensation consists of wages, salaries and supplements. Net interest is the net interest component of national income. Capital consumption allowances consist of depreciation and accidental damage to fixed business property. Indirect business taxes consist of indirect business tax and nontax liability and business transfer payments. Profits are corporate profits after inventory valuation adjustment. Proprietors' income is self-explanatory. Rental income and subsidies consist of rental income of persons and surplus of government enterprises, less subsidies. Imports are the import content of final demand expenditures. Individual final demand components have estimates of import content; total reflects negative entry in GNP for imports (not shown separately) and therefore has no import content.
*Less than .005. Detail may not add to total due to rounding.

each major component of final demand and the results are summarized in Table 7. The distribution of primary inputs by type is compared for each major component of final demand and total final demand. Again, imports appear in the distribution of individual final-demand components but not in the distribution of the total. Here, too, the distribution varies considerably among the individual components. The employee compensation content of state and local government expenditures for goods and services is 80 per cent of the total but less than 50 per cent of personal consumption expenditures. Capital consumption allowances represent a higher proportion of the primary-input content of personal consumption expenditures than of fixed investment or government expenditures. Profits constitute a major component of gross exports, but this is due to the fact that it includes income from rest of the world.

The detailed information developed on the value-added and primary-input content of final-demand expenditures, classified by industry, provides the basis for an analysis of the origin of the change in costs and prices of final-demand expenditures. These data can be used as weights, along with the estimates of industry unit costs and prices derived from the OBE current- and constant-dollar GNP estimates, including the worksheet detail, to develop estimates of the change in price for each component of final demand and total final demand. Since the price change is derived as a weighted average of the change in price of component industries, the aggregate price change can, in turn, be analyzed in terms of its industrial origin. A similar analysis can be developed in terms of primary-input content.

TABLE 7

Primary-Input Content (Gross Income, Indirect Taxes, and Imports) of Final-Demand Expenditures, 1958
(percentage distribution)

Item	Total	Personal Consumption Expenditures	Fixed Investment	Federal Government	State and Local Government	Gross Exports
Employee compensation	58.4	48.5	62.9	75.0	80.0	45.3
Net interest	1.5	1.7	.7	.4	.3	3.3
Capital consumption allowance	8.6	9.6	7.9	4.5	4.4	8.1
Indirect business taxes	8.9	10.7	6.3	3.2	3.1	6.9
Profits	9.0	8.6	9.5	5.5	4.9	23.4
Proprietors' income	10.4	12.1	8.1	3.8	5.1	8.2
Rent and subsidies	3.2	4.4	1.2	.5	.5	.8
Imports	--	4.4	3.4	7.1	1.7	4.0
Total	100.0	100.0	100.0	100.0	100.0	100.0

Note: Inventory change is not shown separately but included in total column. Imports not shown separately but reflected in total column as an offset to import content of final-demand components.

Based on this approach, estimates of the industrial origin of the change in price of final-demand expenditures have been developed for each major final-demand category. The estimates for personal consumption expenditures are shown in Table 8. The value-added content of 1958 consumption, classified by industry, is used as weights, along with the change in price of industry value added, to derive the change in price between 1958 and 1964 of total consumption expenditures. The derived increase in price over this period is 7.2 per cent. This is exactly the same figure as that shown in the OBE published deflators for major components of final-demand expenditures. It should be noted that the derived personal consumption expenditure price change has 1958 weights; the published deflator has implicit 1964 weights. It is reassuring, however, to find that, at least at the aggregate level, the difference in weights and the difference in method of derivation have not yielded different results.

The over-all change in price of the 1958 mix of consumer goods and services can be distributed according to industry of origin, using the industry value-added weights and the change in price of industry value added. The weighted contribution of each industry to the total price change in consumer goods and services is also shown in Table 8. Of the 7.2 per cent increase, about 2.5 percentage points were contributed by the increased price of business and personal services; another 1.2 percentage points by the real estate industry (rent) and about 1 percentage point by trade. The remaining 2.5 percentage points were distributed broadly among the other industries. It should be noted that the reduction in the price of value added in agriculture contributed to a decline of about .5 in the price index, which meant that the gross increase in the rest of the increase accounted for 3 percentage points of the total increase.

The weighted contribution of each industry can also be analyzed to determine whether an industry contributed more or less than its proportionate share of the total increase. This is done by converting the weighted contribution of each industry to the total price change into a percentage distribution. The percentage share of each industry in the total price change (which is taken as 100 per cent), can then be compared to its relative contribution to total consumption expenditures in the base period 1958. For example, business, personal, and professional services accounted for 12 per cent, in terms of value added, of

TABLE 8

Industrial Origin of the Change in Prices of Personal Consumption Expenditures, 1958–64

Industry Number	Value-Added Content 1958 % Distribution	% Change Implicit Deflator 1958–64	Weighted Contribution to Change in Personal Consumption Expenditures and Price	% Distribution of Contribution to Price Change
1	5.92	-1.5	-.52	-7.18
2	.32	14.6	.05	.69
3	.09	-.6	.00	--
4	.30	-3.2	-.05	-.69
5	1.69	.3	.01	.14
6	.13	14.8	.02	.28
7	2.16	26.3	.57	7.87
8	5.31	9.1	.48	6.63
9	.89	3.6	.03	.41
10	1.17	3.6	.04	.55
11	1.85	7.2	.13	1.80
12	1.24	-.5	-.04	-.55
13	1.49	12.8	.19	2.62
14	2.17	-.5	-.07	-.97
15	.88	18.9	.17	2.35
16	.68	-1.6	-.06	-.83
17	.61	12.8	.08	1.10
18	.30	3.8	.01	.14
19	.40	10.6	.04	.55
20	.55	.7	.00	--
21	1.16	7.4	.09	1.24
22	.99	5.9	.06	.83
23	.66	7.5	.05	.69
24	1.19	-1.8	-.12	-1.66
25	.27	7.7	.02	.28
26	1.49	-.8	-.07	-.97
27	.34	6.1	.02	.28
28	.57	3.3	.02	.28
29	4.38	-.1	-.02	-.28
30	2.09	2.7	.06	.83
31	.20	27.9	.06	.83
32	2.72	2.5	.07	.97
33	19.21	5.0	.96	13.26
34	4.43	17.0	.75	10.36
35	13.79	8.9	1.23	16.99
36	11.99	20.6	2.47	34.12
37	.47	12.1	.06	.83
38	.69	16.7	.12	1.66
39	4.41	1.9	.08	1.10
40	--	--	--	--
41	-.40	1.9	-.01	-.14
42	1.21	21.2	.26	3.59
Total	100.00	7.2	7.24	100.00

Note: Detail may not add to totals due to rounding.

total consumption expenditures in 1958, but contributed about 34 per cent of the total price change. Similarly, real estate accounted for about 14 per cent in 1958 and contributed about 17 per cent of the over-all price change. Trade had a 19 per cent weight but contributed only 13 per cent of the price increase. Agriculture contributed less than its share to the price change; a minus 7 per cent compared to its contribution of 6 per cent to total consumption expenditures in 1958.

In the same way that the value-added content of final-demand expenditures can be further distributed into employee compensation and other components of value added, the industrial origin of the change in price can be further analyzed in terms of unit labor costs and other elements of costs originating in each industry. These can then be combined with the base-year weights, to determine how much of the aggregate price change reflects increased unit labor costs, unit profits, etc.[10]

Using the estimates of primary-input content, by industry, of personal consumption expenditures shown in Table 6 and the unit cost changes derived from the OBE industry GNP data, estimates of the primary-input content of the 1958–64 change in price of consumer goods and services have been derived. The changes in factor and nonfactor costs, initially developed at the industry level, have been summarized for total consumption expenditures and are shown in Table 9. The same method is used, as in the previous table, to analyze how much of the 7.2 per cent increase during the 1958–64 period was contributed by each item of cost.

The results indicate that unit costs for interest, indirect business taxes, and profits increased substantially more than the over-all increase in price. Unit employee compensation, and capital consumption costs also increased more than price, but by a smaller margin. Proprietors' income and rental income per unit actually declined. However, the decline in proprietors' income per unit may be due to the shift, within industries of the composition of employment from proprietors to wage and salary employees.[11] This might also account for part of the increase in unit labor costs relative to price. The effect on unit labor costs of the

[10] Given information on the change in industry output per man-hour and compensation per man-hour, the aggregate change in unit labor costs of final goods and services can be factored into the two components.

[11] Shifts among industries are not a factor because the relative importance of industries is held constant with 1958 weights.

TABLE 9

Primary Input Content of the Change in Price of Personal Consumption Expenditures, 1958–64

Item	Primary Inputs 1958 (% Dist.)	% Change Unit Costs 1958–64	Weighted Contribution to Change in Price	% Distribution of Contribution to Price Change
Employee compensation	48.5	8.4	4.1	56.6
Net interest	1.7	50.3	.9	12.1
Capital consumption allowance	9.6	10.3	1.0	13.6
Indirect business taxes	10.7	14.8	1.6	22.0
Profits	8.6	18.6	1.6	22.4
Proprietors' income	12.1	-9.9	-1.2	-16.7
Rent and subsidies	4.4	-18.1	-.8	-11.1
Imports	4.4	1.9	.1	1.1
Total	100.0	7.2	7.2	100.0

shift in composition of employment is discussed in the paper by Greenberg and Mark in this volume.

The relative changes in unit costs are combined with base-year weights, to indicate how much each component has contributed to the price change. For example, increased employee compensation costs per unit accounted for 4.1 percentage points of the 7.2 per cent price increase. Profits contributed 1.6 percentage points. The contribution to the price change is put in different perspective if the increase is compared to the relative importance of the cost item in the base period. Employee compensation constituted 49 per cent of the primary-input content of consumer expenditures in 1958 and accounted for 57 per cent of the price increase. Profits represented slightly less than 9 per cent of primary inputs in 1958, but accounted for 22 per cent of the price change. Net interest was 1.7 per cent in the base period, but contributed 12 per cent of the price increase. The more than proportionate increases for most of the primary-input components are offset by the actual declines in proprietor and rental income.

Similar estimates have been prepared for fixed investment and total final demand showing how much each category of factor and nonfactor costs has contributed to the price change of final goods and services.

Finally, to determine whether the derived price changes for total final demand and major components are approximately in line with the published implicit deflators for these components, the derived price changes for the 1958–64 period are summarized in Table 10, along with the change derived from the published deflators. The comparison can only be approximate for various reasons. As indicated in the first section of the paper, the GNP deflator, based on the industry GNP estimates, differs from the published deflator because of the statistical discrepancy on the income side of the accounts and the gap, on the real-product side of the accounts, between constant-dollar GNP and the sum of industry real gross product. The two estimates show approximately the same change, 8.9 per cent, based on the published deflator, and 8.5 per cent derived on the basis of the industry GNP estimates. Further, the implicit deflators have 1964 weights, the derived price indexes have 1958 weights. At the aggregate level, the industry implicit price indexes, combined with 1958 industry gross product weights, showed an increase of 9.1 per cent compared to the 8.5 per cent increase, based on 1964 weights.

TABLE 10

Comparison of Published[a] and Derived Final-Demand Price Changes, 1958–64

Item	Published Implicit Expenditures Wts.	Derived Industry Gross Product Wts.		Input-Output Value-Added Wts.
	1964	1964	1958	1958
Total	8.9	8.5	9.1	9.5
Personal consumption expenditures	7.2	--	--	7.2
Fixed investment	7.8	--	--	9.3
Federal expenditures for goods and services	12.9	--	--	13.3
State and local expenditures for goods and services	19.3	--	--	20.4
Gross exports	1.5	--	--	3.1

Note: Price change for business inventory change and imports is not shown separately but included in total.

[a]*Survey of Current Business*, August 1965, Table 17, p. 52.

There is one other factor which affects the comparison. The industry value-added estimates used to derive the price change of final demand expenditures were based on the 1958 input–output value added estimates. As previously noted, these do not correspond exactly with the industry gross product estimates in the OBE working paper on industry GNP. The major difference is in construction, but this has one of the largest implicit price changes. The difference in industry gross-product and value-added weights results in a higher GNP price index, based on the 1958 input–output value-added weights; 9.5 per cent compared to the 9.1 per cent with industry GNP weights.

Keeping these differences in mind, the resulting comparison shows a reasonably close correspondence between the published deflators and the derived price indexes. The derived estimates are roughly in the right order of magnitude and in all cases are either the same as the published deflator or slightly higher. The difference in the price change for fixed investment is due to the high implicit deflator for construction, which raises some question as to the reasonableness of the current- and constant-dollar GNP estimates for this industry.

Limitations and Comment

In interpreting the results of this exploratory study, a number of limitations must be taken into account. The derivation of the basic industry real-product estimates by OBE presents particularly difficult problems for those industries where the "double deflation" method was actually used. The separate deflation of output and total intermediate input to derive a residual—real net output—means that the residual may be affected by errors in both the real-gross-output and input estimates. The validity and "reasonableness" of the industry-real-gross-product estimates are discussed in the paper by Gottsegen and Ziemer, "Reconciling Industry Real Product and Industrial Production" in this volume.

The estimates of current-dollar GNP, by industry, and its distribution among the various factor and nonfactor costs also present some problems. Perhaps the most difficult problem is that of adjusting the various items, such as profits and capital consumption allowances, which are initially on a company basis, to an establishment basis to be consistent with the industry output measure. This adjustment is made in the OBE estimates, but the lack of detailed information needed for this purpose may affect the distribution of gross income and the related estimates of unit costs for specific industries.

The detail provided by the new industry GNP estimates is substantially greater than that previously published, but it still represents quite broad industry groups, particularly in manufacturing. This puts some limitations on their use in the analysis of the industrial origin of income, products, costs, and prices. The primary metals group, for example, combines steel, aluminum, copper, and other primary metals in one group. The price change for the group is a weighted average of the differential price changes of the various primary metals. The primary metals value-added content in the individual components of final demand may have different "mixes" of ferrous and nonferrous metals, but the primary metals implicit price index is weighted by the total industry mix. The application of the same implicit price index to the primary metals value-added content for each final-demand component may, therefore, lead to some error.

The use, in the analysis, of the same industry price index for each component of final demand may be another source of error if the price change varies depending, for example, on whether the product is sold to domestic consumers or is exported.

Finally, the statistical analysis of how much each industry and its component cost elements have "contributed" to the change in price of final goods and services should not be interpreted to imply cause and effect relationships. Prices in a given industry, and during a particular period may rise because costs rise, but it is equally possible that costs may rise because prices are going up. The phrase, "contributed to the price increase," should therefore be interpreted as a statement of statistical relationship, not a causal relationship.

With these limitations in mind, it is hoped that the framework provided in this paper for the analysis of the interrelationship among industry income, product, costs and prices, and final-demand expenditures and prices may provide the basis for further exploration and improvement.

COMMENT

Richard Ruggles, Yale University

Alterman's paper represents a significant and very useful effort to analyze the relation of implicit price changes in different industrial sectors to the final uses of output. The basic technique involves the creation of constant-price output measures for each industrial sector based on deflating the cost of inputs and outputs separately, and then dividing this derived constant-price measure into the current value of gross product in order to obtain an implicit price deflator for each industrial sector. Weighting this set of implicit price deflators by the relative importance of the different industries yields an average implicit price deflator for the economy as a whole. Thus, the contribution of each industry to the over-all price change in the economy as a whole can be analyzed, as well as the implicit price effect of each industry on the different categories of final-output prices, by taking into account through input–output relations the contribution of each industry to the various categories of final output.

Several of Alterman's results are very interesting indeed. First, it is very comforting that he finds the difference between the Paasche and Laspeyres weighting schemes over a period of eight years or so not to be highly significant. Although this conclusion is not new, it is reassuring to have it borne out in connection with the development of implicit price indicators. Second, I was very much impressed with the closeness of the published OBE end-use implicit price indexes and those obtained by Alterman which were estimated on an input–output basis using industry-originating implicit price deflators. Such comparisons give one a little more faith in the consistency of the price observations for final products and for intermediate products.

However, there are also some elements of the results which are quite disturbing. According to Alterman's results, over 80 per cent of the price increase which occurred between 1958 and 1964 was accounted for by the price behavior of five industries: contract construction, trade, finance and insurance, real estate, and services. These are, of course, precisely the industries where the measurement of prices is weakest and least meaningful. In some of these industries it is necessary to assume that output prices move directly with input prices, with zero productivity change over time. One cannot help but wonder, therefore, whether much of our empirical measurement of prices may not result from our theoretical deficiencies, and whether the measurement of the price behavior of the different sectors, and in fact of the economy as a whole, may not be based upon assumptions which are grossly invalid, rather than upon meaningful data. These observations, however, are not directly related to Alterman's techniques. He, like everyone else, has merely assumed that the basic price information which is reported is meaningful.

There are, however, some methodological questions which can be raised regarding Alterman's approach. He is attempting to bridge the gap between the price behavior of the economic system seen as a whole and the more disaggregated implicit price behavior of specific industries. Although he cautions against using his results to impute causality to the contributing factors, there is a general tendency to use the results from such an analysis as an explanation of price behavior in the economy. Alterman's technique has serious limitations for this purpose. The method of deriving constant-price product originating and its relation to current-price product originating yields a price index which is the net result of many different elements buried in the data. Value theory has in the past been based upon a consideration of the *total* output of the firm and the various costs incurred in the production of such *total* output. The theory of the firm does not apply if output is defined as value added rather than total value of product. Producers are in fact sensitive to raw material prices and changes in technology which alter raw material inputs. Consolidating the accounts to exclude raw materials obscures important behavior relationships. Basing the analysis of price behavior on value added is not dissimilar in concept to analyzing the net exports of a country without taking into account separately the behavior of imports and the behavior of exports. In order to understand and explain price behavior in any ultimate sense, it will be necessary to analyze how the individual production units respond to different kinds of change, such as changes in the level of demand, changes in costs, changes in productivity, etc. The price behavior of the economy as a whole will of course be the combined result of the different kinds of price behavior at the microeconomic level and the manner in which the aggregation of such price behavior affects the economy. In this connection the use of input–output is of course essential. Though consolidated implicit price behavior may be derived for each industrial sector and for the final uses of output, the result is a consolidated aggregate of "micro-behavior" and the aggregation process, not an explanation of micro-behavior.

Nevertheless, Alterman's analysis does raise a large number of interesting and provocative questions and provides material for further investigation. He is to be congratulated for tackling the problem of the price behavior of the economy as a whole. This approach is a considerable improvement over the simplistic view which suggests that the price change taking place in the economy represents over-all demand and cost situations which permeate all sectors of the economy in much the same degree.

Part II

Changing Factor Costs and Shares of Gross Income by Industry

Sector Changes in Unit Labor Costs

LEON GREENBERG
JEROME A. MARK
BUREAU OF LABOR STATISTICS
U.S. DEPARTMENT OF LABOR

Introduction

The subject of unit costs, including labor costs, at one time aroused sporadic interest, which tended to be highly correlated with the occurrence, or the threat of inflation. The promulgation of wage-price guideposts by the Council of Economic Advisers in January 1962 [1] and the increasing role they have played as policy instruments has fostered a more frequent and regular examination of unit cost trends and tended to bring the subject to the attention of a wider audience, particularly outside the economic profession. With or without the guideposts, the analysis of unit labor-cost trends has included intensive examination of two major determinants of cost—productivity and wages.

Analysis of these trends has been aided by the availability of annual indexes of productivity, compensation per man-hour, and compensation per unit of output for employees in the nonfarm sector of the economy, which have been published regularly by the Bureau of Labor Statistics since 1957. More recently, the Bureau has developed and published a similar range of estimates for employment costs in the total private economy, including both the farm and nonfarm sectors.[2] There are some questions about the meaningfulness of these over-all measures—about which more will be said later.

[1] *Economic Report of the President,* January 1962.
[2] *Economic Report of the President,* January 1966.

NOTE: This paper was prepared with the assistance of Nicholas K. Bruck of the Office of Productivity, Technology, and Growth of the Bureau of Labor Statistics.

The recent availability of sector output measures consistent with the concept of gross national product has made it possible to develop new estimates of sector output per man-hour, compensation per man-hour, and unit employment costs (Table 1).[3] These sector ratios are useful not only for tracing the individual sector trends but also for "explaining" the trends of the total private economy.[4]

The purpose of this paper is to examine the trends in the sector ratios, the determinants of variation in sector unit labor-cost trends, and the effect of sector trends on the over-all figures for the private economy. The paper also examines the extent to which the trends in unit labor costs, hourly compensation, and output per man-hour for the nonfarm economy and for the private economy are affected by shifts among sectors.

Limitations, Qualifications, and Definitions

The analysis of the trends in the private economy and its component sectors and their interrelationships has encountered some difficult problems arising out of (1) limitations or inadequacies in the basic data and (2) the difficulty of defining conceptual issues sharply and clearly.

The sector output measures are gross output originating in the respective sectors, in constant (1958) dollars. When these sector output measures are summed they equal total private gross national product. The availability of this detail makes it easier to scrutinize the composition of GNP, and computing the various ratios makes it easier to evaluate the "reasonableness" of some of the trends.

To be sure, this evaluation often tends to be influenced by intuitive judgments. Nevertheless, the productivity trends derived for some of the sectors do not appear reasonable. For example, those for the construction sector show a decline in productivity in the last few years—a trend which does not accord with other information available for this important activity. In this case, the deflator for construction volume

[3] The sector data from the Office of Business Economics cover the period 1947–64 and are not yet consistent with the most recent revised estimates of total gross national product and are being revised. It is hoped that the revised sector estimates will not yield significantly different results from those appearing in this paper. Meanwhile, these estimates are tentative and not to be regarded as official BLS estimates of either productivity or unit labor costs.

[4] The general government sector is excluded from these calculations. Its output is measured by wages and salaries moved by the trend in employment.

TABLE 1

Indexes of Unit Labor Costs, Hourly Compensation, and Output Per Man-Hour for Employees in the Private Nonfarm Economy and Major Sectors, 1947–64

(1947 = 100)

	Private Nonfarm Economy[a]			Mining			Construction			Manufacturing		
Years	Unit Labor Costs[b]	Hourly Compen-sation	Output Per Man-Hour	Unit Labor Costs[b]	Hourly Compen-sation	Output Per Man-Hour	Unit Labor Costs[b]	Hourly Compen-sation	Output Per Man-Hour	Unit Labor Costs[b]	Hourly Compen-sation	Output Per Man-Hour
1948	107.3	108.7	103.0	106.5	114.3	104.8	112.8	111.6	100.3	106.2	109.4	104.9
1949	104.9	111.9	107.9	106.5	117.5	108.5	106.4	111.0	105.8	106.2	114.4	108.4
1950	104.9	118.3	114.1	106.5	127.9	119.5	110.6	118.7	109.2	104.2	120.1	115.7
1951	112.2	128.6	115.8	109.7	139.6	125.8	121.3	129.7	108.3	112.5	132.4	118.5
1952	117.1	135.7	116.8	112.9	146.1	128.6	131.9	136.8	105.2	120.8	141.0	118.9
1953	122.0	143.7	119.7	112.9	155.2	137.2	134.0	147.7	111.9	122.9	148.9	122.0
1954	122.0	148.4	122.7	106.5	156.5	145.9	134.0	154.2	116.8	127.1	155.4	124.1
1955	122.0	153.2	127.6	103.2	161.0	152.5	134.0	154.8	117.4	125.0	161.2	131.1
1956	129.3	162.7	127.0	109.7	173.4	154.7	140.4	159.4	114.1	133.3	171.9	129.7
1957	134.1	172.2	129.9	112.9	180.5	156.1	151.1	171.0	115.0	139.6	182.0	132.2
1958	134.1	178.6	133.6	112.9	183.8	161.8	153.2	181.3	119.0	145.8	189.9	132.2
1959	136.6	186.5	137.2	109.7	185.1	165.8	157.4	185.2	119.3	143.7	197.8	139.5
1960	141.5	193.7	139.1	109.7	191.6	174.8	163.8	196.8	120.8	147.9	205.8	142.0
1961	141.5	200.0	143.4	106.5	198.7	186.5	170.2	205.2	121.1	147.9	212.2	145.5
1962	141.5	207.9	149.0	103.2	205.8	195.4	178.7	211.0	119.0	145.8	220.9	154.2
1963	141.5	215.1	153.0	103.2	209.1	201.8	189.4	218.7	116.2	143.7	228.8	160.1
1964	143.9	225.4	158.2	103.2	215.6	207.0	200.0	231.6	116.8	143.7	238.8	167.5

(continued)

TABLE 1 (continued)

Years	Transportation			Communications			Public Utilities			Trade		
	Unit Labor Costs[b]	Hourly Compen-sation	Output Per Man-Hour	Unit Labor Costs[b]	Hourly Compen-sation	Output Per Man-Hour	Unit Labor Costs[b]	Hourly Compen-sation	Output Per Man-Hour	Unit Labor Costs[b]	Hourly Compen-sation	Output Per Man-Hour
1948	108.7	109.5	100.7	104.3	107.1	102.7	100.0	109.0	109.0	107.0	106.8	99.6
1949	117.4	117.5	99.0	104.3	115.7	110.7	100.0	115.2	117.0	104.7	108.5	101.4
1950	115.2	127.0	110.1	102.1	122.1	118.1	100.0	121.4	123.4	102.3	114.5	109.4
1951	119.6	137.2	113.8	102.1	129.3	126.4	94.4	131.7	138.7	111.6	121.4	107.2
1952	128.3	145.3	112.4	106.4	140.0	129.8	97.2	141.4	146.9	114.0	125.6	108.3
1953	134.8	152.6	113.1	108.5	147.1	135.1	97.2	150.3	154.6	118.6	131.6	110.1
1954	137.0	157.7	115.8	112.8	154.3	137.5	94.4	158.6	169.6	120.9	135.9	111.6
1955	132.6	162.8	123.5	108.5	160.0	145.8	94.4	165.5	178.8	116.3	141.0	118.8
1956	137.0	173.7	126.2	112.8	165.7	147.5	94.4	175.2	187.8	123.3	149.6	119.6
1957	145.7	184.7	126.5	110.6	175.0	157.2	94.4	184.1	196.5	127.9	159.0	122.8
1958	150.0	194.2	129.5	106.4	184.3	171.6	97.2	199.3	205.7	130.2	164.1	124.6
1959	152.2	202.2	133.6	104.3	196.4	186.3	94.4	210.3	222.2	130.2	170.9	129.3
1960	154.3	210.9	136.2	104.3	204.3	194.3	94.4	218.6	234.9	134.9	177.8	127.9
1961	154.3	216.1	140.6	102.1	215.7	209.0	94.4	230.3	246.9	137.2	183.8	132.2
1962	152.2	223.4	147.7	100.0	224.3	224.1	91.7	239.3	261.3	134.9	190.6	138.4
1963	147.8	229.9	155.7	95.7	232.9	239.8	91.7	249.0	270.3	137.2	198.3	142.0
1964	147.8	238.0	161.7	97.9	245.7	250.8	94.4	261.4	281.8	139.5	206.8	146.7

(continued)

TABLE 1 (concluded)

Years	Finance, Insurance, and Real Estate			Services			Government Enterprises		
	Unit Labor Costs[b]	Hourly Compen-sation	Output Per Man-Hour	Unit Labor Costs[b]	Hourly Compen-sation	Output Per Man-Hour	Unit Labor Costs[b]	Hourly Compen-sation	Output Per Man-Hour
1948	115.4	106.9	98.5	102.5	108.1	104.6	101.9	106.3	105.1
1949	115.4	110.8	100.8	105.0	112.8	105.5	101.9	112.6	110.6
1950	115.4	119.2	105.8	107.5	114.0	104.6	111.1	119.7	107.7
1951	123.1	126.2	106.9	115.0	123.3	105.5	111.1	126.8	114.5
1952	123.1	131.5	106.8	120.0	130.2	106.0	116.7	135.4	115.3
1953	130.8	138.5	108.1	127.5	137.2	106.4	120.4	139.4	116.2
1954	138.5	145.4	110.9	132.5	143.0	106.9	127.8	140.9	110.2
1955	138.5	150.8	112.1	135.0	146.5	108.3	140.7	148.8	106.4
1956	146.2	161.5	114.2	140.0	155.8	110.1	159.3	155.1	97.4
1957	146.2	170.8	117.8	145.0	166.3	112.8	161.1	162.2	100.4
1958	153.8	178.5	118.9	150.0	174.4	114.7	172.2	174.8	102.1
1959	161.5	187.7	119.8	155.5	183.7	117.4	174.1	178.7	103.0
1960	161.5	195.4	121.4	162.5	191.9	117.4	181.5	190.6	104.7
1961	169.2	206.9	125.1	165.0	198.8	119.3	172.2	190.6	110.6
1962	169.2	210.0	127.7	170.0	208.1	121.1	172.2	200.0	116.2
1963	169.2	216.2	128.9	175.0	216.3	121.1	183.3	210.2	114.9
1964	176.9	225.4	132.3	185.0	230.2	122.9	174.1	217.3	124.7

Source: Output and compensation data are from the U.S. Department of Commerce, Office of Business Economics. Man-hour data are from U.S. Department of Labor, Bureau of Labor Statistics.

[a]Excludes general government and farm.

[b]Employee compensation per unit of output.

appears suspect. In other sectors where the changes in the volume of output are largely determined by the trend in wages and salaries, the output measure has limitations similar to that of the government sector —the output and productivity trends may be understated and the resultant unit labor-cost trends overstated.

The concept or definition of unit labor costs may be a bit troublesome depending on the objective and uses of the measures. One may be interested in determining whether, for the total private economy, there has been an imbalance in the trends of productivity and compensation and whether, as a result, unit labor costs have been declining or rising. An economy-wide measure may, however, not be useful in examining cost-price relationships because of the variable impact of costs upon prices among different sectors of the economy.

Compensation (or wages) per man-hour and unit labor costs are usually derived—although not explicitly spelled out—in the context of all employee costs. However, unit labor costs are often mentally translated as relating to production workers, or blue-collar workers, although they include administrative, supervisory, clerical, and other employees.

In deriving unit labor cost estimates by relating productivity to compensation per man-hour, one has to take account of the fact that the productivity figures are usually based on output per man-hour of all persons engaged, including employees, self-employed, and unpaid family workers. A compatible compensation per man-hour figure would also have to include all persons. However, wage (or salary, or compensation) statistics are not available for the self-employed. The income reported for this group is total income (of proprietors), which includes, implicitly, wage payments, return on investment, interest, etc. So it is necessary to estimate compensation per man-hour for the self-employed (i.e., the wage return to proprietors) for comparison with output per man-hour of all persons in the total private economy.

In sectors such as manufacturing, finance, mining, and transportation, where there is relatively very little self-employment, trends in output per man-hour of all persons or of employees would be virtually the same. For sectors such as trade and construction, where self-employment is rather important, a change in the ratio of self-employed to the total could have a significant effect on productivity trends. In the farm sector, where only one-third of the persons engaged are employees, an output per employee figure would have little meaning.

Alternative compensation and cost estimates are, therefore, presented in this paper. One estimate, for the total private economy, is based on all persons, including the self-employed. Another estimate, for the nonfarm sector, includes employees only, and omits the self-employed. Unit labor-cost estimates for the nonfarm sector are probably more appropriate for wage-cost-price analysis than those for the total private economy since prices of farm output are largely determined by factors other than labor costs.

Compensation, as used in this paper, reflects payments by an employer directly to employees (wages and salaries) and to Social Security and private welfare and pension plans. There is another concept of employment costs which embraces a group of indirect employment costs such as maintenance of a cafeteria, recreational facilities and first aid unit, payments for workmen's compensation, and others. These costs are not included in the compensation and unit labor-cost estimates.

The man-hour estimates used in the hourly compensation and productivity measures were developed primarily from published estimates of employment and hours obtained by the Bureau of Labor Statistics from establishments in the various industries throughout the economy. These BLS establishment estimates provided data on employment for all sectors of the private nonfarm economy, but average-hours data were available only for production workers in manufacturing and mining and nonsupervisory workers in certain nonmanufacturing industries. As a result, the BLS establishment data had to be supplemented with data from other sources and in some cases imputations had to be made.

Major supplements included the following: (a) average hours for nonsupervisory workers in some sectors for which no establishment information was available, (b) average hours of nonproduction workers and supervisory workers for all sectors, and (c) numbers and average hours of self-employed and unpaid family workers by sector. For the most part, data for (a) were based on unpublished estimates from the household (labor force) surveys conducted by the Bureau of the Census for the BLS. These data were adjusted to make them as consistent as possible in concept with the hours from the establishment survey. Estimates for (b), the average hours of nonproduction workers, were based either on information on scheduled hours of professional, technical, clerical, and administrative workers derived from the BLS surveys of supplementary payments and community wage surveys or by imputing the average hours of nonsupervisory workers for each sector to those of supervisory workers. Data for (c) were developed from OBE information on the number of proprietors as derived from the *Survey of Current Business* and on BLS Labor Force estimates of weekly hours.

Finally, this analysis is focused primarily on the question of costs. It is important, however, not to overlook the income implications of the wage-productivity relationship. Unit labor costs may remain stable, but if consumer prices increase, the increase in money wages does not measure the change in purchasing power of the worker. In order to examine the extent to which workers are sharing the economy's productivity growth, it would be necessary to compare changes in *real* compensation per man-hour with the trend in output per man-hour for the economy. Since this paper is to deal specifically with costs, the real-wage–productivity relationship is not explored, but it should not be ignored in any analysis of the income-sharing potential of productivity growth.

Employee Unit Labor Costs in the Nonfarm Economy

The analysis will first be focused on unit labor costs for employees in the private nonfarm economy—employees only because employee man-hours represent over 85 per cent of the total man-hours of persons engaged in nonfarm activities and employee compensation is the largest single element of the value of production—the nonfarm economy because of the important role of unit labor costs in relation to price movements. In contrast, farm price movements are largely determined by elements other than employee unit labor costs. Moreover, employees comprise less than a third of the work force in the farm sector;[5] cost estimates based on compensation of employees only would exclude payment for the bulk of labor activities involved in the farm production process.

[5] In 1947 the man-hours of proprietors and unpaid family workers represented 81 per cent of total man-hours. In 1964 they were 71 per cent.

CHART 1

Indexes of Unit Labor Costs: Hourly Compensation and Output per Man-Hour for Employees in the Private Nonfarm Economy, 1947–64 (1947 = 100)

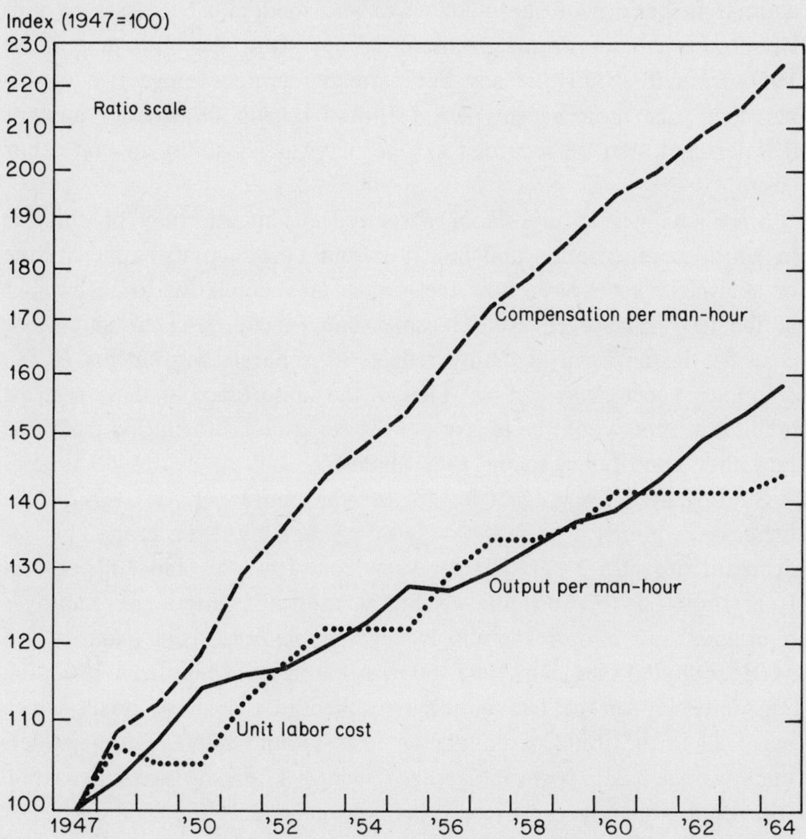

OVER-ALL SECTOR TRENDS

Over the entire postwar period 1947–64 employee compensation per unit of output in the private nonfarm economy (unit labor costs) rose 2.2 per cent per year.[6] This growth was not uniform, however, as can be seen in Chart 1. A pattern of sharp increases from 1947–60, interrupted briefly for two two-year periods, was followed by a pattern of relatively small increases in the 1960's.

[6] This rate and all rates in this paper were derived from the least squares trend of the logarithms of the index numbers.

The figures present the common problem of showing different trends depending on which terminal years are selected for analysis. But they do seem to indicate two periods with different patterns of change within the 1947–60 period. First, the period 1947–56 which included alternating periods of sharp increases and moderate decreases in unit labor costs for an average gain of 2.7 per cent. Second, the period 1956–60 with a fairly steady but more moderate average rise of 1.9 per cent. The more recent period 1960–64, with an average gain of 0.5 per cent, can be regarded as one of virtual stability in unit labor costs.

Since changes in unit labor costs reflect the interplay of changes in hourly compensation and hourly output (productivity), one avenue of analysis is to explore how these have moved relative to each other at the aggregate level. At the same time, since trends in unit labor costs in the nonfarm economy reflect the separate movements of the component sectors as well as shifts in the importance of these sectors, another avenue would be to explore the separate sector movements and how they contributed to the total change.

Starting at the aggregate level, over the entire period 1947–64 the increase in hourly compensation was 4.8 per cent per year. This reflected a rise of 5.2 per cent per year from 1947–60 and 3.8 per cent from 1960–64—a substantial decline in the rate. Output per employee man-hour had a correspondingly reverse pattern, rising from a 2.5 per cent annual rate from 1947–60 to a 3.3 per cent rate from 1960–64. The interplay of the two patterns resulted in the sharp break which occurred in the trend of unit labor costs around 1960. Thus, greater-than-average (i.e., postwar average) increases in hourly compensation with approximately average productivity gains resulted in the 2.6 per cent annual increase in unit labor costs in the first part of the period (1947–60). Less-than-average increases in hourly compensation and greater-than-average gains in output per man-hour provided the small 0.5 per cent rate for the later years.

Annual and cyclical variations in the movement of unit labor costs also seem to have undergone some change. The years 1947–60 were characterized by brief periods of rapid increases and decreases in unit labor costs and the magnitude of these changes was substantial. In contrast, the 1960–64 period has been marked by smaller year-to-year fluctuations. As can be seen in Chart 1, these short-term changes in unit labor costs in the early part of the period are primarily reflections of changes in the movements of productivity.

INDIVIDUAL SECTORS

Table 2 presents the average annual rates of growth of unit labor costs, hourly compensation, and output per man-hour for each of the separate sectors which comprise the nonfarm economy. They are listed in order of unit labor-cost increases from the smallest to the highest. It is evident that the over-all rate reflects a wide dispersion of individual sector rates, ranging from an actual decline of 0.4 per cent per year for public utilities to a rise of 4.2 per cent for government enterprises.[7] The degree of dispersion as measured by the coefficient of variation [8] of the various sector rates about the nonfarm rate is a very high 74 per cent.

What is also evident from the table is that the dispersion in the changes in unit labor-cost rates among the various sectors is almost entirely a reflection of the variation in the rates of productivity growth. The coefficient of variation of the rates of productivity change among the sectors was 79 per cent, whereas the coefficient for hourly compensation was only 10 per cent.

These findings are consistent with those found in earlier studies of the relationship of movements in hourly compensation, productivity, and unit labor costs. For example, in their examination of costs in manufacturing industries covering the period 1948–56, Schultze and Tryon found that there was substantial variation among different industries in the percentage rise in unit labor costs (Chart 2) and that differences in productivity behavior (Chart 4) were more important than wage and salary changes (Chart 3) in producing the variation in unit labor-cost changes.[9]

[7] Too much emphasis should not be placed on the actual level of the increases for some of the sectors. The adequacy of the separate sector output and man-hour measures vary considerably. While these measures are useful as general indicators, they do have limitations.

[8] The coefficient of variation, the standard deviation as a percentage of the weighted mean change, measures the extent to which indicated changes for the individual sectors are clustered about the mean percentage change for the nonfarm economy.

[9] Charles L. Schultze and Joseph I. Tryon, "Prices and Costs in Manufacturing Industries," Study Paper No. 17. Materials prepared in connection with the Study of Employment Growth and Price Levels, Joint Economic Committee, Congress of the United States, January 1960.

TABLE 2

Average Annual Rates of Change[a] in Unit Labor Costs, Hourly Compensation, and Output per Man-Hour for Employees in the Private Nonfarm Economy and Major Sectors, Selected Periods, 1947–64, in Percentages

Sector	1947–64			1947–60			1960–64		
	Unit Labor Costs	Output Per Man-Hour	Hourly Compensation	Unit Labor Costs	Output Per Man-Hour	Hourly Compensation	Unit Labor Costs	Output Per Man-Hour	Hourly Compensation
Private nonfarm economy[b]	2.2	2.5	4.8	2.6	2.5	5.2	0.5	3.3	3.8
Public utilities	-0.4	6.3	5.8	-0.5	6.7	6.2	-0.3	4.7	4.5
Communications	-0.2	5.5	5.3	0.4	5.0	5.5	-1.9	6.7	4.6
Mining	-0.0	4.3	4.2	0.5	4.4	4.9	-1.5	4.3	2.9
Trade	2.0	2.3	4.4	2,3	2.1	4.5	0.7	3.5	3.9
Transportation	2.3	2.8	5.1	3.1	2.5	5.7	-1.3	4.6	3.1
Manufacturing	2.5	2.7	5.2	3.2	2.5	5.7	-0.9	4.4	3.8
Finance, insurance, and real estate	3.1	1.7	5.0	3.5	1.6	5.3	1.8	2.0	3.4
Services	3.7	1.2	4.9	3.9	1.1	5.1	3.2	1.1	4.6
Construction	3.8	1.0	4.9	3.7	1.4	5.1	5.2	-1.1	4.0
Government enterprises	4.2	0.4	4.6	5.3	-0.4	4.8	-0.2	4.0	3.7

Source: Output and compensation data are from the U.S. Department of Commerce, Office of Business Economics. Man-hours data are from the U.S. Department of Labor, Bureau of Labor Statistics.

[a] All rates computed from the least squares trend of the logarithms of the index numbers.

[b] Excludes general government and farm.

CHART 2

Indexes of Unit Labor Costs for Employees in Nonfarm Sectors, 1947–64

(1947 = 100)

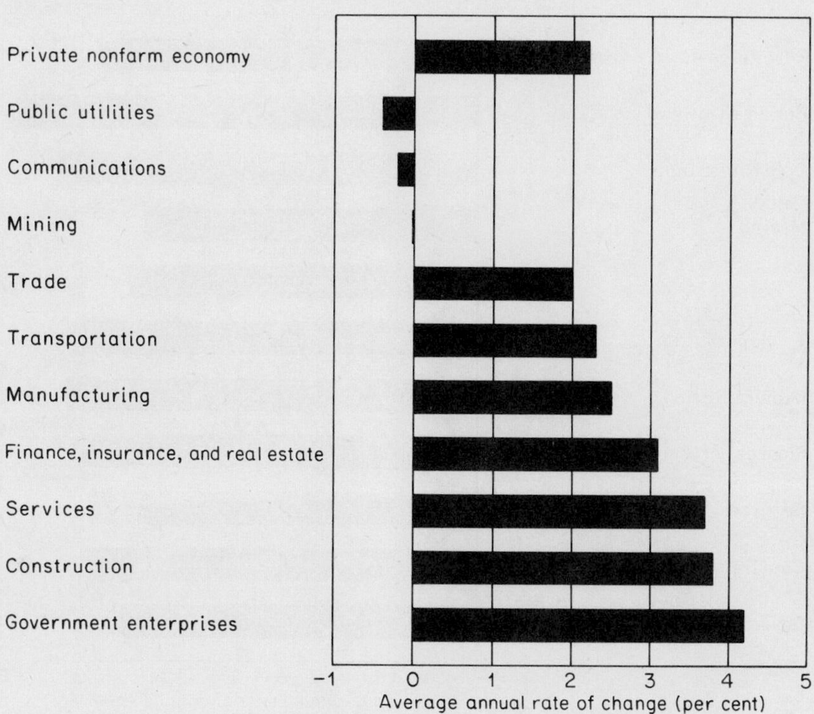

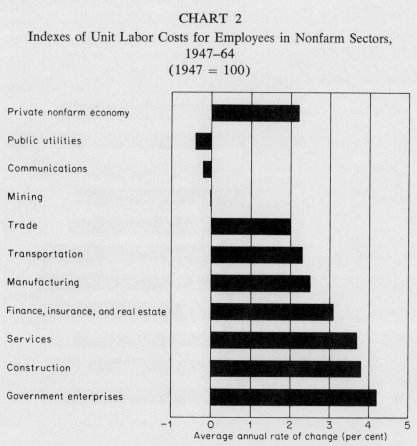

Apparently, this wide dispersion of unit labor-cost movements and their close relationship to differences in productivity changes rather than differences in hourly compensation movements was true for subperiods within the postwar period.

Not only did each of the separate sectors show differences in their average annual rates over the entire period but their patterns of movement varied. For example, the over-all decline in unit labor costs for the public utilities sector and the communications sector are the result of two distinctly different patterns of change over the period. The following section describes in somewhat repetitive detail the movements of unit labor costs and the related productivity and hourly compensation behavior for each of the major sectors. No attempt was made

CHART 3

Indexes of Hourly Compensation for Employees in Nonfarm Sectors, 1947–64
(1947 = 100)

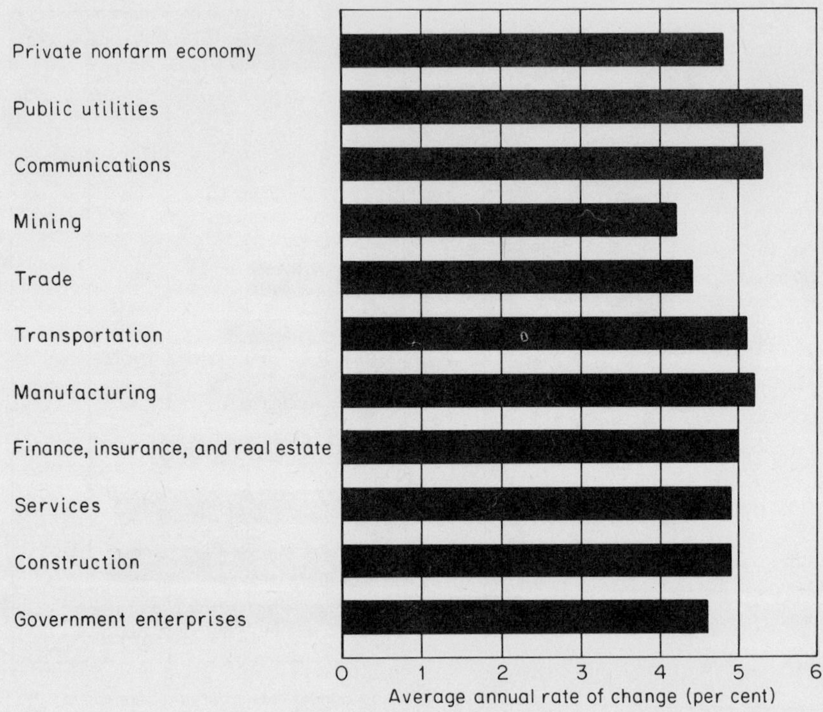

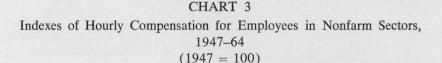

to explain differences in movements or underlying factors contributing to the pattern primarily because of data limitations as well as a desire to minimize the speculation which would have been required.

Public Utilities

This sector comprises electrical, gas, and sanitary enterprises. In 1964 it produced approximately 3 per cent of the output in the nonfarm sector and its employee man-hours accounted for 1.3 per cent of nonfarm man-hours.

Unit labor costs for this sector show the greatest decline of all nonfarm sectors in the entire postwar period. The average annual rate of decline was 0.4 per cent per year. This sector also experienced the

CHART 4

Indexes of Output per Man-Hour for Employees in Nonfarm Sectors, 1947–64 (1947 = 100)

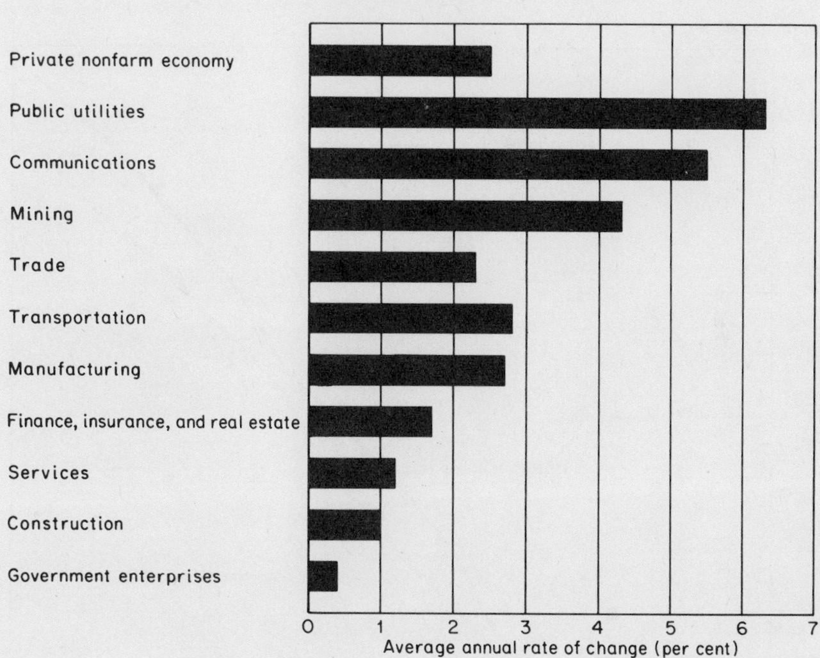

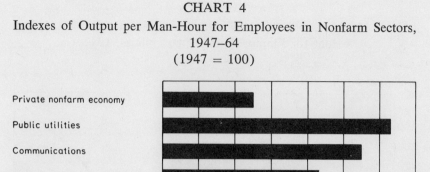

greatest increase in hourly compensation for all sectors (5.8 per cent per year). Despite the high wage cost increase, the decline in unit labor costs occurred because the productivity increase was a substantial 6.3 per cent per year, the highest increase of all sectors.

The over-all decline in unit labor costs was not uniform, however, and resulted from numerous reversals in the trend within the period. There were, in fact, three annual increases in unit labor costs, two years with no change, and twelve annual declines with as many as six turning points. However, within the period, three general patterns of trend movement seem to emerge from examination of Chart 5. From 1947 to 1955 there was an irregular but still over-all decline, followed by a gradual rise and sharp gain in the recession year 1958, after which the decline continued. It has been modified in the last few years and, in fact, from 1959 the long-run rate of change has been virtually stable.

CHART 5

Indexes of Unit Labor Costs: Hourly Compensation and Output per Man-Hour for Employees in Public Utilities, 1947–64
(1947 = 100)

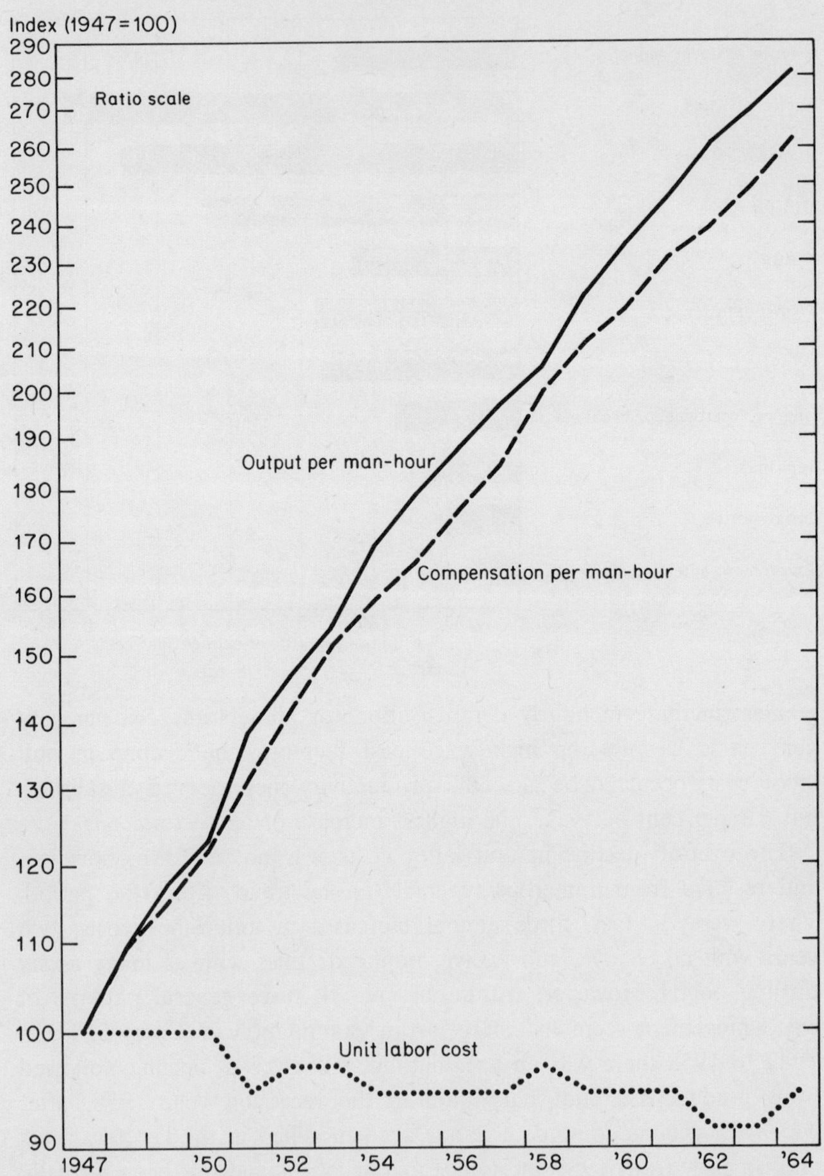

The year-to-year variability in unit labor-cost movements was primarily a reflection of the variability in the productivity movements. Productivity in this sector was very sensitive to output changes and the over-all trend corresponded very closely to the movement of output.

Communications

This sector comprises the telephone, telegraph, and radio and television industries, representing approximately 2 and one-half per cent of the output in the nonfarm sector and 1.7 per cent of the man-hours. It also experienced an over-all decline in the trend of unit labor costs over the entire period, although the decline was small (0.2 per cent per year). Again, both the increases in productivity and in hourly compensation were substantial (5.5 and 5.3 per cent per year, respectively).

The over-all slight decline in unit labor costs resulted from a very distinctly different pattern of movement from that of public utilities. Here, a period of increases was followed by a period of steady declines (Chart 6). With the exception of small declines in 1950 and 1951, from 1947 through the middle 1950's the pattern was rising unit labor costs averaging 1.3 per cent per year, which was primarily a reflection of very substantial increases in hourly compensation. Since 1956, with the exception of 1964, there was a rather steady decline in unit labor costs, averaging 1.9 per cent for the period 1956–64.

The decline since 1956 has resulted from the very high productivity gains with the somewhat less than average increases in hourly compensation. The high productivity gains in turn were associated with large output increases. Since 1956, communications was the leading growth sector in the private nonfarm economy. Its output grew at a rate of 6.5 per cent during this period and its productivity gains averaged 7.0 per cent.

Mining

This sector comprises metal mining, coal mining, crude petroleum and natural gas production, and the mining and quarrying of nonmetallic minerals. It accounted for approximately 3 per cent of the output in 1964 and 1.3 per cent of the total man-hours. Its importance within the nonfarm sector has declined very substantially since 1947.

Despite a low output growth rate (2.1 per cent per year, which was

CHART 6

Indexes of Unit Labor Costs: Hourly Compensation and Output per Man-Hour for Employees in Communications, 1947–64
(1947 = 100)

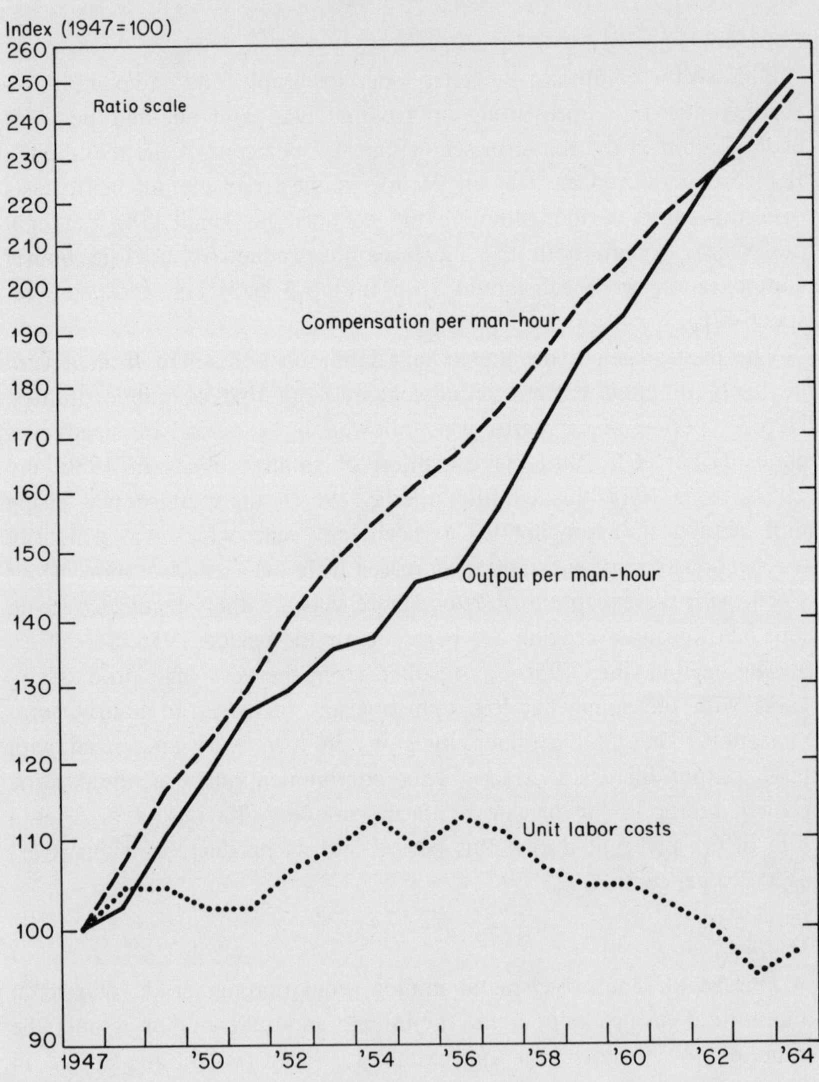

next to the lowest for the individual sectors), mining maintained a high and stable rate of productivity gains (4.3 per cent per year). Its gain exceeded those for all sectors with the exception of public utilities and communications. The high productivity rate had the effect of keeping unit labor costs almost stable. For the entire period, they showed an insignificant decrease of less than one-tenth of a per cent per year and for the seven years 1957–64 there was a substantial decline, averaging 1.5 per cent annually (Chart 7).

CHART 7

Indexes of Unit Labor Costs: Hourly Compensation and Output per Man-Hour for Employees in Mining, 1947–64
(1947 = 100)

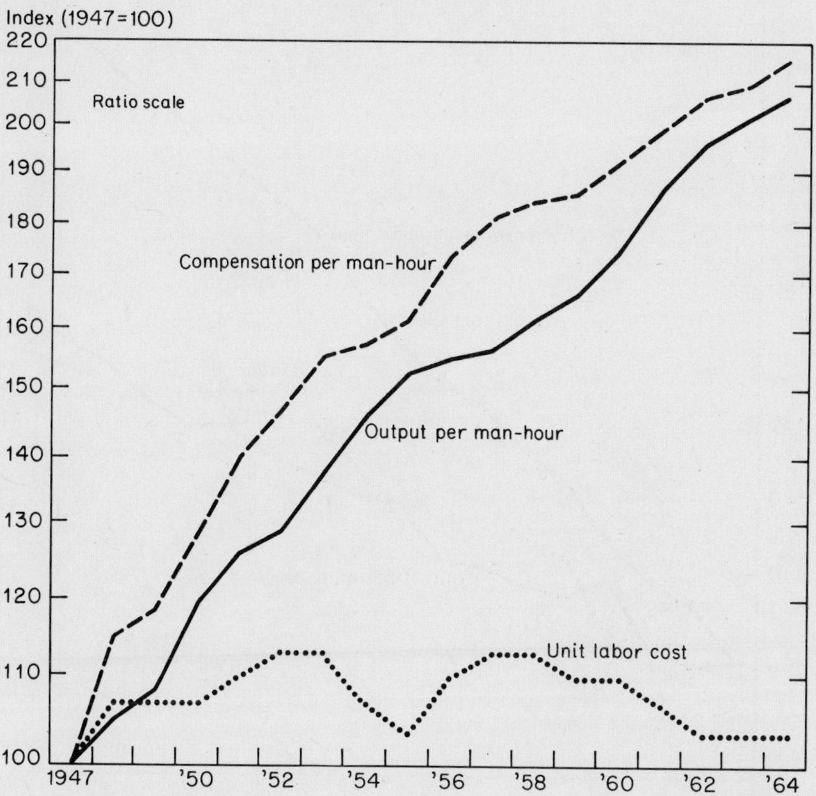

Within the period, unit labor costs displayed two distinct patterns—from 1947–57, an over-all increase in unit labor costs with relatively large year-to-year alternative increases and decreases; from 1957–64, steadily declining unit labor costs and small year-to-year fluctuations. The smaller fluctuations during the latter part of the period are primarily a reflection of the relatively steady trends which occurred in both productivity and hourly compensation.

CHART 8

Indexes of Unit Labor Costs: Hourly Compensation and Output per Man-Hour for Employees in Trade, 1947–64
(1947 = 100)

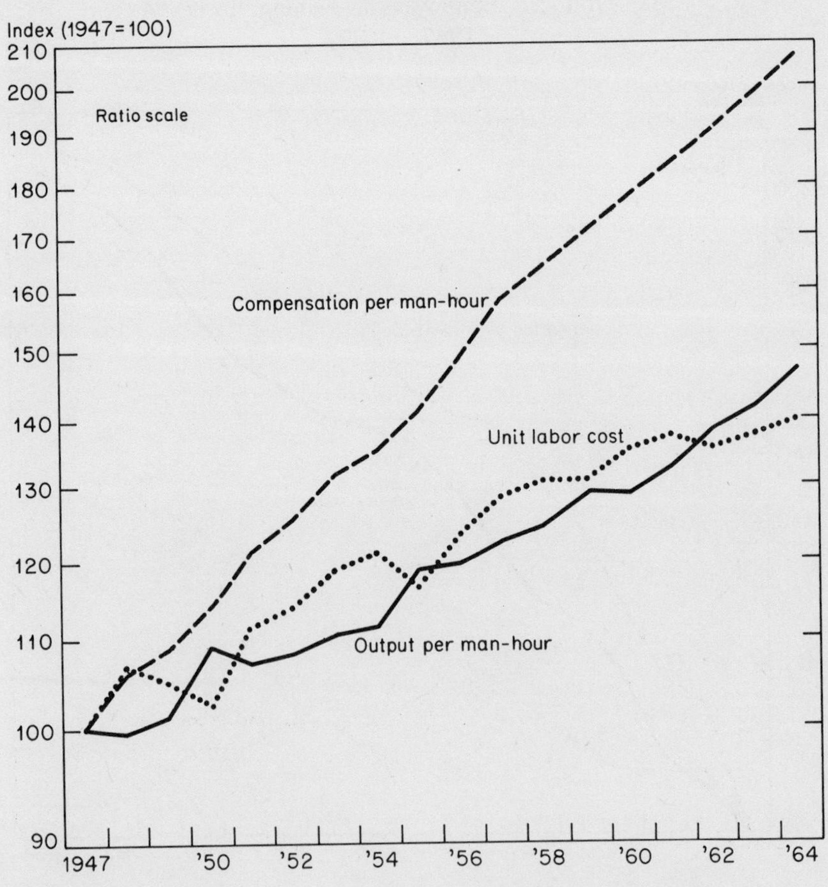

Trade

This sector includes wholesale and retail trade establishments. It ranks second in importance in the private nonfarm economy (after manufacturing), accounting for approximately one-fifth of private nonfarm output and 23 per cent of the man-hours throughout the period.

Unit labor costs for trade increased at about the same rate as the average for the entire nonfarm sector. However, this was the result of a slightly lower than average rate of gain in productivity (2.3 per cent) combined with a below average increase in compensation—in fact the latter showed the smallest increase (4.4 per cent) of all the sectors (Chart 8).

The pattern of change in unit labor costs was slightly different from that of the nonfarm sector as a whole—large fluctuations with rising costs for 1947–60; smaller fluctuations and continuing, though smaller, increases during 1960–64. These changes in turn are very sensitive to, and directly related to, output changes which took place.

Manufacturing

Manufacturing accounts for more than a third of the output generated in the private nonfarm economy and over 35 per cent of the man-hours. It represents, by far, the most important sector of the economy. In many ways its trends in labor costs dominate those for the private nonfarm economy. Until 1961, the revenue share of manufacturing had been declining, but since then the rate of output growth has been above the average rate for the nonfarm economy as a whole, resulting in a small increase in its revenue share.

Unit labor costs rose over the whole period at a rate of 2.5 per cent a year—this is above the increase for the private nonfarm economy as a whole. Also, the productivity gains in manufacturing and the hourly compensation gains exceeded those for the nonfarm sector as a whole. Over the whole period, productivity rose 2.7 per cent per year and hourly compensation 5.2 per cent (Chart 9).

A very significant change occurred in the pattern of movement within the postwar period. From 1947 to 1960, the average annual increase in unit labor costs in manufacturing was very high—3.2 per cent. Since that time, however, virtual stability has occurred with a

CHART 9

Indexes of Unit Labor Costs: Hourly Compensation and Output per Man-Hour for Employees in Manufacturing, 1947–64

(1947 = 100)

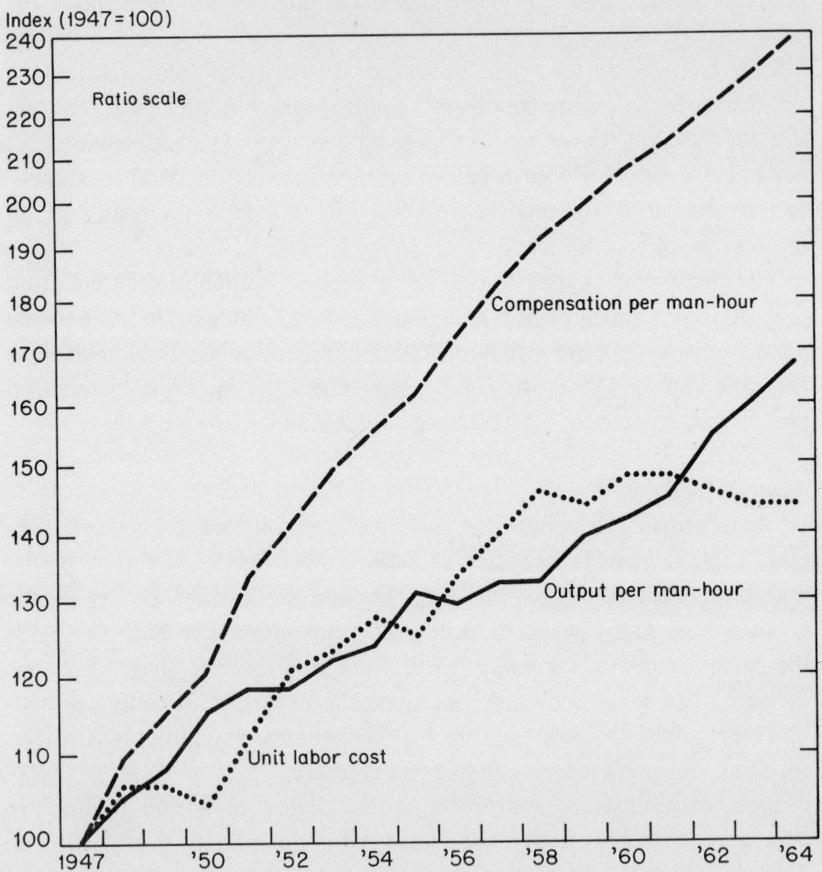

slight decline in recent years. The change in direction was primarily the reflection of the sharp increases in manufacturing productivity which occurred in the latter part of the period. From 1960–64, productivity rose to 4.4 per cent a year in contrast to the earlier gain of 2.5 per cent. While the hourly compensation increase was also somewhat small in the latter part of the period in contrast to the earlier part, the difference was far less than that for productivity.

Transportation

This sector covers rail, water, bus, motor freight, air, and pipeline transportation establishments and accounts for approximately 5 per cent of the goods and services produced by the private nonfarm economy. It had the lowest rate of output growth for any sector (1.4 per cent annually), and, consequently, its share within the nonfarm economy declined from 8 per cent in 1947. Man-hours of this sector also declined from 8 per cent of the total nonfarm man-hours in 1947 to 5 per cent in 1964.

Over the entire period, unit labor costs in transportation increased 2.3 per cent per year—slightly higher than the average for all nonfarm sectors. As in the case of other sectors, the over-all rate reflected a substantially higher rate in the earlier part of the period followed by a decline over the last four years. Although there were two declines in 1950 and 1955, the over-all annual increase from 1947–60 was 3.1 per cent in contrast to the decline of 1.3 per cent per year after 1960. Again, yearly fluctuations were much greater in the earlier period than in recent years (Chart 10).

The change in direction in unit labor costs reflected to some extent the decline in the growth rate of hourly compensation but, more importantly, the very sharp increase in the productivity rate. In the latter part of the period, the productivity rate almost doubled. The sharp increase in the productivity rate was also associated with a relatively higher increase in output in the latter part of the period.

Finance, Insurance, and Real Estate

In 1947 this sector accounted for 13.5 per cent of total nonfarm output and approximately 4 per cent of nonfarm man-hours. By 1964, these proportions had increased to 16 per cent and almost 6 per cent (Chart 11).

Unit labor costs in the sector rose at a substantial rate of 3.1 per cent per year over the entire period. This increase was fairly uniform and, although there was some decline in the rate of increase after 1960 (from 3.5 per cent 1947–60 to 1.8 per cent), the rate for the latter part was still higher than that for all other sectors with the exception of services, construction, and government enterprises. Moreover, in contrast to almost all other sectors, the year-to-year fluctuations were not much different in the later years from the earlier part of the period.

CHART 10

Indexes of Unit Labor Costs: Hourly Compensation and Output per Man-Hour for Employees in Transportation, 1947–64
(1947 = 100)

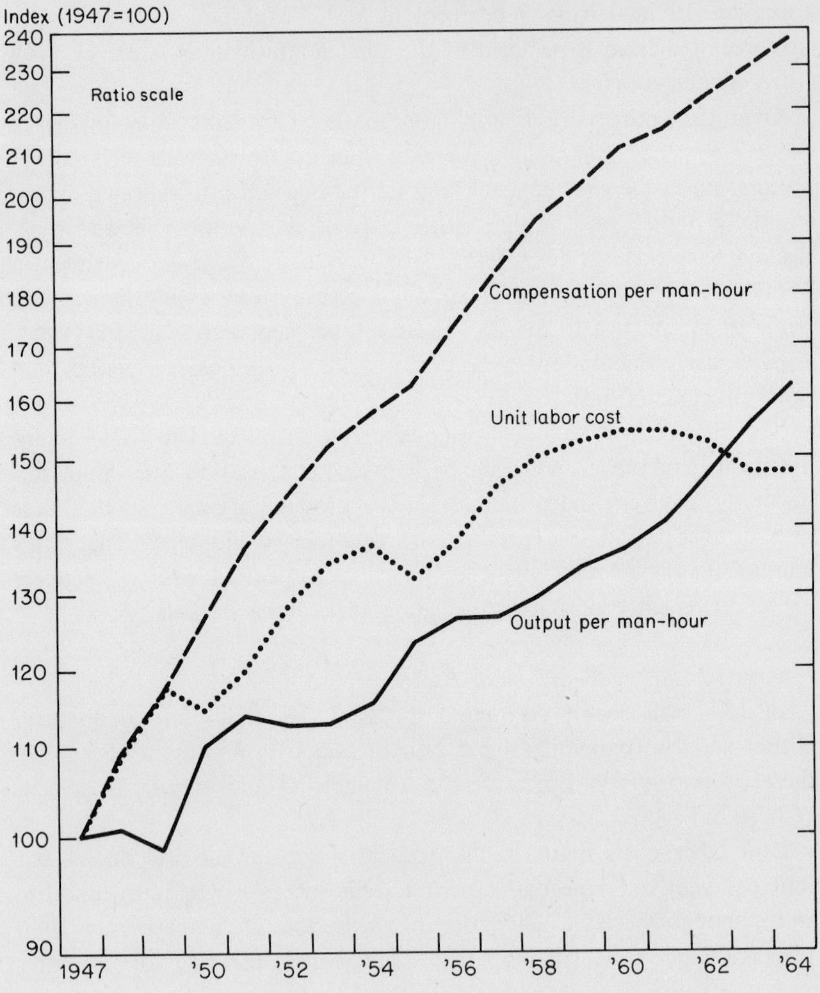

CHART 11

Indexes of Unit Labor Costs: Hourly Compensation and Output per Man-Hour for Employees in Finance, Insurance, and Real Estate, 1947–64
(1947 = 100)

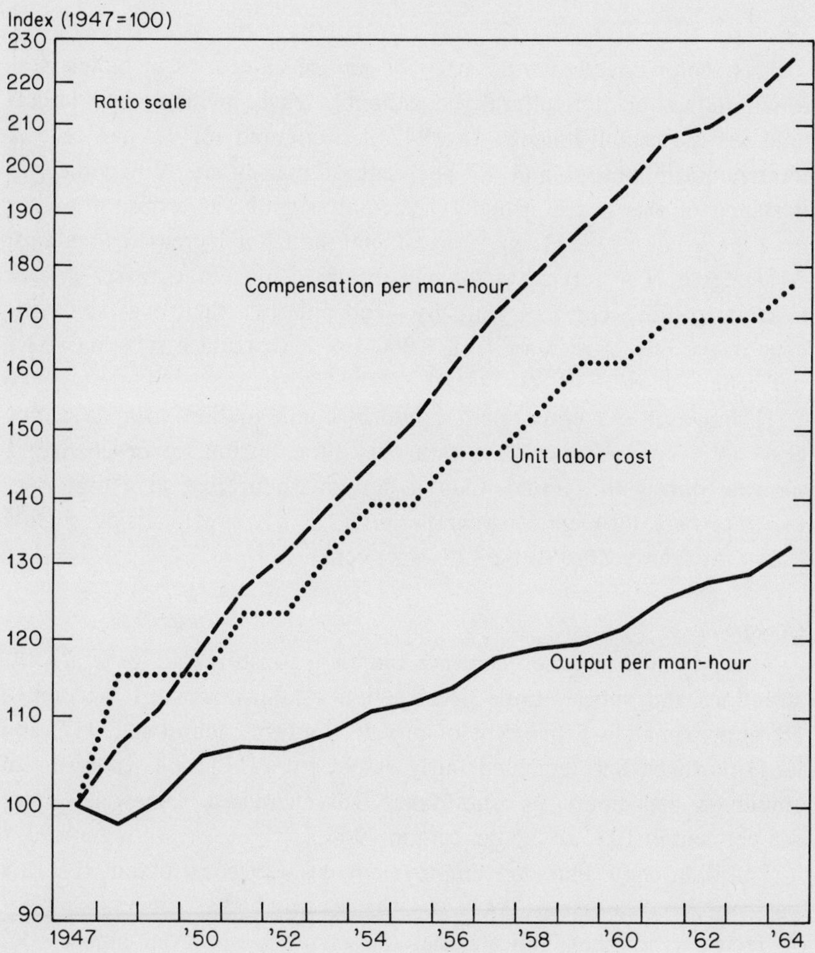

Although output per employee man-hour rose at a slightly higher rate from 1960–64 than before (2.0 per cent versus 1.6 per cent) the smaller increase in unit labor costs was primarily a reflection of the decline in the rate of increase in hourly compensation. From 1947–60, the annual gain was 5.3 per cent. It dropped to 3.4 per cent per year from 1960–64.

Services

This sector covers a wide array of service categories including personal, industrial, agricultural, educational, legal, medical, and household service establishments. In 1947 it accounted for 12 per cent of total nonfarm output and 17 per cent of man-hours. While the importance of the sector actually decreased slightly in terms of output by 1964 (11 per cent), in terms of man-hours it increased to almost 20 per cent. The service sector had the third highest increases in unit labor costs—3.7 per cent annually—and although there was some decline in the rate of increase from 1960–64, it was still a substantial 3.2 per cent (Chart 12).

Throughout the entire period hourly compensation rose at a rate close to 5 per cent per year with very little fluctuation or change in the rate during the period. Output per man-hour rose at a uniformly low rate over the eighteen-year period (1.2 per cent)—rising slightly less in the later years 1960–64 (1.1 per cent).

Construction

This sector comprises contract building construction, general construction, and special trade construction establishments. It accounted for approximately 5 per cent of private nonfarm output in 1947, and its importance has remained fairly stable from 1947–64. In terms of employee man-hours its importance has increased somewhat—from 4.5 per cent in 1947 to 5.6 per cent in 1964.

The data show that unit employment costs in construction rose 2.8 per cent per year from 1947–64—the second highest of any sector.[10] In recent years they indicate that the increase was even higher—5.2

[10] Employee compensation is somewhat less complete as a basis for measuring movements in labor costs per unit of output for this sector than for perhaps any other nonfarm sector. Self-employed account for 24 per cent of the number of persons engaged in activities in this sector in contrast to the average of 15 per cent for the nonfarm sector as a whole.

CHART 12

Indexes of Unit Labor Costs: Hourly Compensation and Output per Man-Hour for Employees in Services, 1947–64
(1947 = 100)

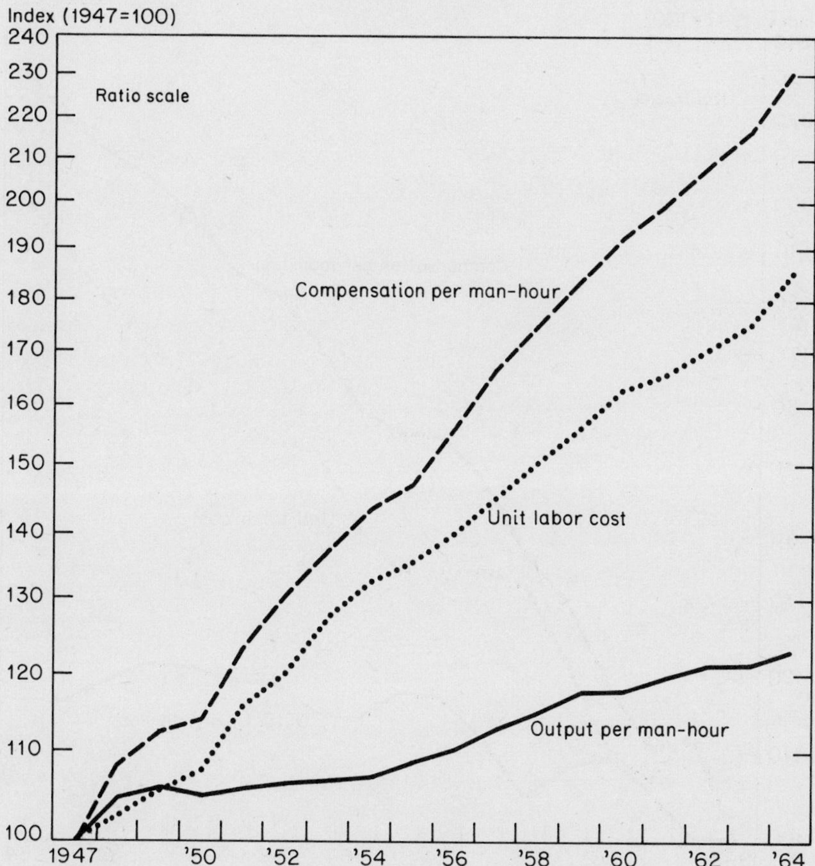

per cent per year from 1960–64. From 1947–60 the rate was 3.7 per cent, reflecting very sharp gains from 1950–52, then stability 1952–55, followed by a steep rise (Chart 13).

Hourly compensation averaged 4.9 per cent increases over the period with a slackening occurring from 1960–64 (4.0 per cent). But productivity according to the data rose very little—1 per cent per year from 1947–64—and declined by 1.1 per cent per year from 1960–64.

CHART 13

Indexes of Unit Labor Costs: Hourly Compensation and Output per Man-Hour for Employees in Construction, 1947–64

(1947 = 100)

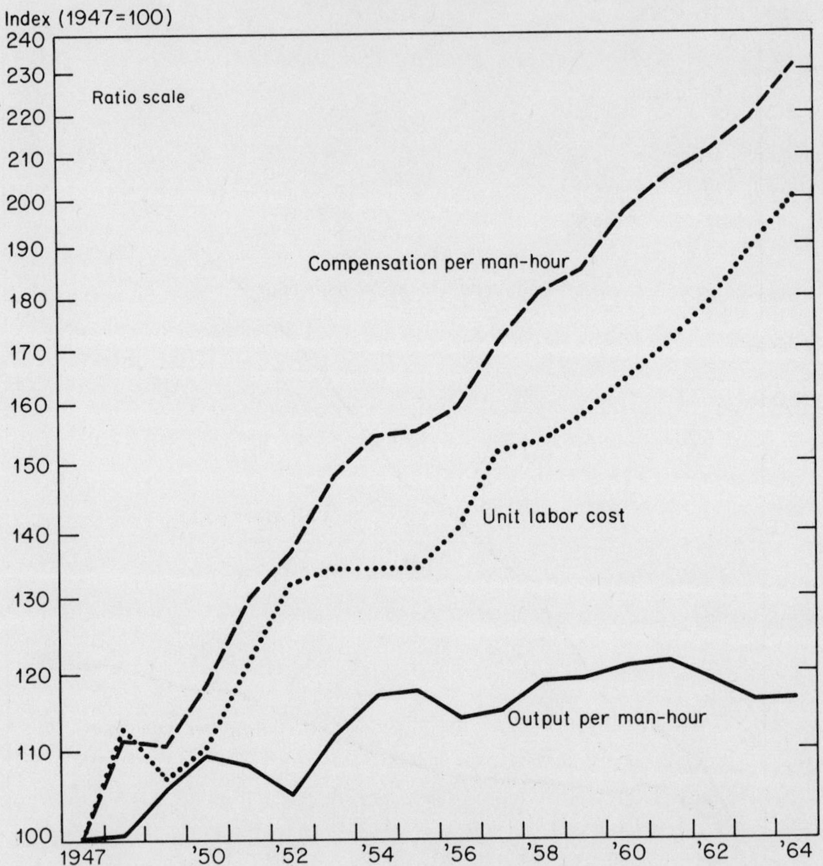

The output measure for this sector undoubtedly has a downward bias. Some of the components of the price index used to deflate the value data are based on costs which do not take adequate account of the decline in man-hours per unit of output.[11] Therefore, the produc-

[11] See Martin L. Marimont, "GNP by Major Industries," *Survey of Current Business,* October 1962, p. 10.

tivity and the unit labor-cost changes must be viewed critically. Other estimates, not necessarily consistent with the GNP framework of measures, would indicate that the increase in unit labor costs for this sector was substantially less than the figures derived from data on GNP originating in construction.[12]

Government Enterprises

As mentioned earlier, general government activities have been excluded from the examination of sector movements because of the nature of the output measure for these activities. However, one group of government activities is included in the "private" nonfarm economy—those whose major function involves the sale of a product or service. These activities—government enterprises—include, for example, the Post Office, Tennessee Valley Authority, publicly owned local utilities, and similar enterprises.

In 1947, government enterprises accounted for a little over 1 per cent of nonfarm output and almost 2 per cent of nonfarm man-hours. These proportions increased somewhat over the postwar period and by 1964 they were about 1.5 per cent and 2.5 per cent.

Unit labor costs of government enterprises rose substantially over the period—at a rate of 4.2 per cent per year. However, all of the increase occurred in the earlier part of the period, particularly from 1951 to 1956. Since 1960 they have declined about 0.2 per cent per year.

The break in the trend again reflects primarily the sharp increase in productivity in recent years. From 1947 to 1960 output per man-hour declined 0.4 per cent per year, reflecting a large gain from 1947–53 which was all but wiped out by a sharp and steady decline from 1953 through 1956. But since 1960 the rate has soared to 4.0 per cent per year. Hourly compensation also rose less in recent years, dropping from 4.6 per cent per year from 1947–60 to 3.7 per cent from 1960–64 (Chart 14).

[12] Estimates of construction output and output per man-hour for postwar years prepared by Dacy and others indicate at least a 3.0 per cent annual increase in output man-hours for this sector. See Douglas C. Dacy, "Productivity and Price Trends in Construction Since 1947," *Review of Economics and Statistics,* November 1965, pp. 406–411.

CHART 14

Indexes of Unit Labor Costs: Hourly Compensation and Output per Man-Hour for Employees in Government Enterprises, 1947–64 (1947 = 100)

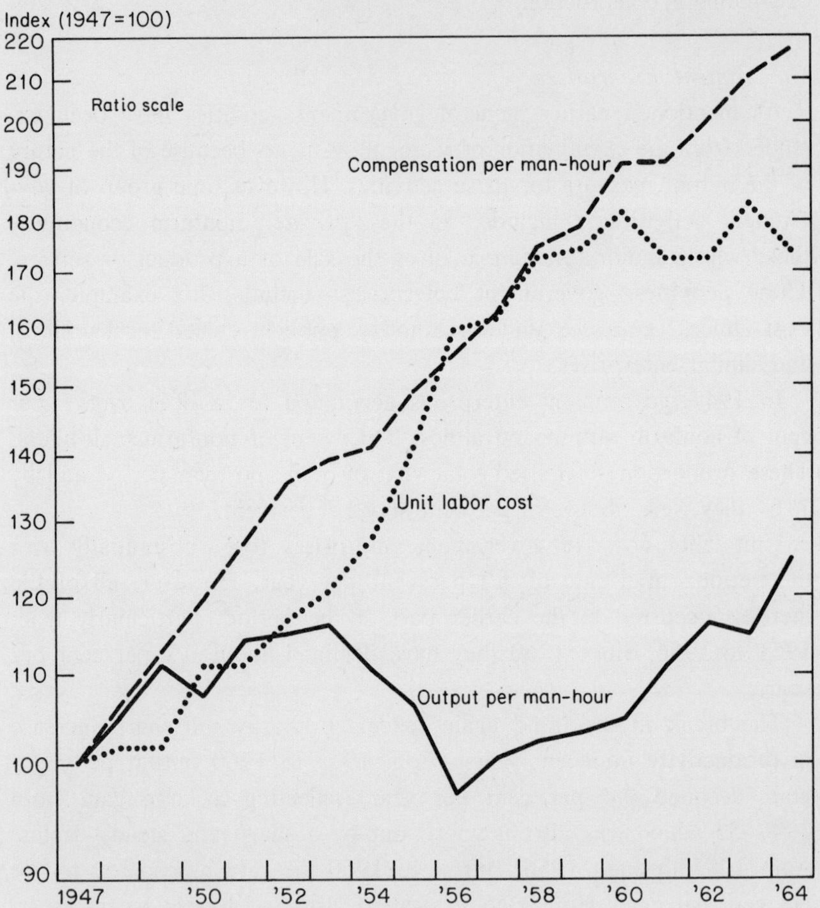

Common Intersector Elements

The above description of the trends for the individual sectors to some extent highlights the diversity of movement in unit labor costs, hourly compensation, and hourly output among the sectors. There are, however, some common elements which do emerge. First of all, with the exception of the services and construction sectors (where the data are perhaps less adequate), a distinct break in the trends in unit labor costs occurred around 1960 in each sector. This break was usually reflected by a substantial reduction in the rate of increase. (In one sector it reflected an actual decline.) Second, greater year-to-year fluctuations occurred in almost all sectors in the period from 1947–60 than from 1960–64.

Finally, in most sectors the relative decline in the rate of increase in unit labor costs was a reflection both of relative declines in the rates of hourly compensation and of relative increases in the average gain in output per man-hour. In general, however, the relative increase in the productivity rate exceeded the relative decline in the rise in hourly compensation.

Unit Labor Costs in the Total Private Economy

So far, the discussion of unit labor costs has related to the nonfarm economy. While this may be adequate for an understanding of the relationship between productivity and costs, there is still sufficient interest in the trends for the total private economy to warrant further computations and analysis in which both the farm and nonfarm sectors are included.

Inclusion of the farm sector in cost calculation forces us to deal with the question of proprietor income and wages. Employees constitute less than one-third of the work force in the farm sector so that estimates of "unit labor costs" based on employees only would be misleading, particularly for trend analyses since the proportion of employees to total work force has been increasing.

The importance of proprietors as a segment of the work force has long been recognized in the computation of productivity trends—they have been included in the denominator of the gross national product per man-hour ratio. A matching of these productivity figures with estimates of compensation per man-hour requires the inclusion of a comparable proprietor component in the denominator of the latter ratio as well. Proprietors could, of course, be excluded from both ratios but this would result in another, and possibly misleading, productivity figure. It may be elementary to note here that output per *employee* (proprietors excluded) could decrease merely because individual or partnership enterprises incorporated, and those who had been proprietors were, by legal definition, transformed into employees. Such transformation would have a similar effect on trends in unit costs.

If proprietors are included in the farm sector then, for comparability, they must be included in all other sectors. For most sectors, the proportion of proprietors in the work force is small and makes little or no difference in the productivity and cost trends.

There are no statistics of wage income of proprietors but several methods of determining or imputing a wage income share to proprietors have been developed. While they all have some logical basis, they are all also, unfortunately, open to criticism.[13] There appears to be no best or unique solution to the problem of estimating the wage income of proprietors. The method employed in this paper is to assume that compensation per man-hour of proprietors is the same as that of employees for each of the major sectors for which productivity and unit employment-cost estimates have been developed.[14]

Unit labor costs (for all persons) in the private economy rose 1.8 per cent a year in the postwar period 1947–64. The average gain was 0.3 per cent for the recent period 1960–64, compared with 2.1 per cent for the period 1947–60 (Tables 3 and 4).

These differential trend movements in unit costs were again the product of different trends in productivity and labor payments. Productivity rose faster in the latter period than in the earlier one (3.9 versus 3.2 per cent); compensation per man-hour rose more slowly (4.2 versus 5.3 per cent).

The trends for the private economy were substantially influenced by the large relative and absolute decline of proprietors, especially in the farm sector, during the period covered. This does not, of course, mean that the productivity of proprietors increased more and that of employees less, in the sense of physical output per worker. It is a con-

[13] For a discussion of this problem, see Stanley Lebergott, "Factor Shares in the Long Term, Some Theoretical and Statistical Aspects," in *The Behavior of Income Shares,* Studies in Income and Wealth 27, p. 80, Princeton for NBER, 1964.

[14] This method does lead to an implied negative nonlabor share (or return on investment) for a few sectors during isolated years. While not necessarily wrong it is not what might be reasonably expected. Using an alternative method of imputing proprietor wage income (e.g., using the trends in corporate labor-nonlabor shares to allocate noncorporate proprietor income) indicates that, for the total private economy, the trends in unit labor costs for all persons in the postwar period would not be substantially different from that obtained by the method used.

TABLE 3

Indexes of Unit Labor Costs, Hourly Compensation, and Output Per Man-Hour for All Persons in the Private Economy and Major Sectors, 1947–64

(1947 = 100)

Years	Private Economy[a]			Farm			Nonfarm			Mining		
	Unit Labor Costs[b]	Hourly Compensation	Output Per Man-Hour	Unit Labor Costs[b]	Hourly Compensation	Output Per Man-Hour	Unit Labor Costs[b]	Hourly Compensation	Output Per Man-Hour	Unit Labor Costs[b]	Hourly Compensation	Output Per Man-Hour
1948	104.7	109.1	104.4	89.2	103.5	116.9	105.9	109.1	103.1	109.4	114.3	104.8
1949	102.8	110.6	107.5	82.4	93.0	114.3	104.8	111.9	106.9	109.4	117.5	107.9
1950	101.5	118.2	116.3	77.0	100.0	129.9	104.0	118.3	113.9	106.3	127.9	118.9
1951	108.2	129.7	119.8	82.4	107.0	129.9	110.8	128.6	116.2	112.5	139.6	125.1
1952	112.6	137.3	122.0	79.7	114.0	141.6	115.7	135.5	117.0	115.6	146.1	127.6
1953	114.7	146.1	126.9	73.0	117.5	161.0	118.9	143.2	120.5	115.6	155.2	135.7
1954	115.5	150.3	130.0	70.3	119.3	168.8	119.7	147.4	123.2	109.4	156.5	142.9
1955	113.4	154.1	135.7	58.1	98.2	170.1	118.6	152.6	128.6	106.3	161.0	150.0
1956	120.5	163.9	136.1	58.1	101.8	177.9	126.4	161.6	127.8	112.5	173.4	152.5
1957	124.6	174.5	140.1	59.5	110.5	188.3	130.6	170.9	130.9	115.6	180.5	153.9
1958	125.9	181.8	144.1	58.1	121.1	207.8	132.4	177.3	134.0	115.6	183.8	159.3
1959	127.2	190.2	149.3	58.1	122.8	211.7	133.6	185.1	138.6	112.5	185.1	163.7
1960	130.0	197.6	151.5	50.0	112.3	223.4	137.1	192.5	140.2	112.5	191.6	172.0
1961	130.4	204.7	156.8	51.4	124.6	240.3	137.4	198.2	144.4	109.4	198.7	183.2
1962	130.1	213.7	164.3	52.7	131.6	246.8	136.7	206.4	151.0	106.3	205.8	191.7
1963	130.6	222.2	170.0	50.0	133.3	268.8	137.5	213.9	155.6	106.3	209.1	198.3
1964	132.1	233.5	176.2	50.0	135.1	268.8	139.0	224.0	161.0	106.3	215.6	203.3

(continued)

TABLE 3 (continued)

Years	Construction			Manufacturing			Transportation			Communications		
	Unit Labor Costs[b]	Hourly Compen-sation	Output Per Man-Hour	Unit Labor Costs[b]	Hourly Compen-sation	Output Per Man-Hour	Unit Labor Costs[b]	Hourly Compen-sation	Output Per Man-Hour	Unit Labor Costs[b]	Hourly Compen-sation	Output Per Man-Hour
1948	109.2	111.6	102.0	104.0	109.4	105.1	110.2	109.5	100.4	104.3	107.1	103.0
1949	102.6	111.0	107.8	106.0	114.4	108.7	120.4	117.5	97.9	104.3	115.7	110.4
1950	106.6	118.7	111.8	104.0	120.1	115.9	116.3	127.0	108.2	104.3	122.1	118.2
1951	110.5	129.7	117.6	112.0	132.4	119.2	122.4	137.2	112.5	102.1	129.3	126.3
1952	117.1	136.8	117.2	118.0	141.0	119.2	130.6	145.3	110.7	108.5	140.0	129.6
1953	118.4	147.7	124.5	122.0	148.9	122.8	136.7	152.6	111.1	108.5	147.1	135.4
1954	115.8	154.2	133.8	126.0	155.4	124.6	138.8	157.7	113.6	112.8	154.3	137.4
1955	111.8	154.8	139.2	122.0	161.2	132.2	132.7	162.8	121.8	110.6	160.0	146.1
1956	115.8	159.4	137.7	132.0	171.9	130.8	138.8	173.7	124.6	112.8	165.7	147.5
1957	123.7	171.0	137.7	138.0	182.0	133.3	146.9	184.7	124.6	110.6	175.0	157.2
1958	126.3	181.3	142.6	144.0	189.9	133.3	153.1	194.2	127.1	108.5	184.3	171.7
1959	127.6	185.2	144.6	142.0	197.8	140.9	153.1	202.2	131.4	106.4	196.4	186.5
1960	135.5	196.8	145.6	144.0	205.8	143.1	157.1	210.9	134.3	106.4	204.3	194.3
1961	140.8	205.2	145.6	146.0	212.2	146.7	155.1	216.1	138.2	104.3	215.7	209.1
1962	147.4	211.0	143.1	142.0	220.9	155.8	153.1	223.4	145.0	100.0	224.3	224.6
1963	155.3	218.7	141.2	142.0	228.8	162.0	151.0	229.9	153.2	97.9	232.9	239.7
1964	163.2	231.6	142.2	142.0	238.8	169.6	149.0	238.0	159.3	97.9	245.7	251.2

(continued)

TABLE 3 (continued)

Years	Public Utilities			Trade			Finance, Insurance, and Real Estate			Government Enterprises		
	Unit Labor Costs[b]	Hourly Compen-sation	Output Per Man-Hour	Unit Labor Costs[b]	Hourly Compen-sation	Output Per Man-Hour	Unit Labor Costs[b]	Hourly Compen-sation	Output Per Man-Hour	Unit Labor Costs[b]	Hourly Compen-sation	Output Per Man-Hour
1948	100.0	109.0	109.2	107.3	107.0	100.0	113.3	106.9	99.2	101.9	106.3	105.1
1949	97.3	115.2	117.0	107.3	107.8	101.0	113.3	110.8	102.3	101.9	112.6	110.6
1950	97.3	121.4	123.4	103.6	113.9	109.0	113.3	119.2	107.8	111.1	119.7	107.7
1951	94.6	131.7	138.4	112.7	121.7	108.1	120.0	126.2	108.1	111.1	126.8	114.5
1952	97.3	141.4	146.8	114.5	125.2	109.0	126.7	131.5	107.2	116.7	135.4	115.3
1953	97.3	150.3	154.2	118.2	132.2	111.9	133.3	138.5	107.7	120.4	139.4	116.2
1954	94.6	158.6	168.4	120.0	135.7	112.9	133.3	145.4	109.4	127.8	140.9	110.2
1955	91.9	165.5	178.1	116.4	140.9	120.0	140.0	150.8	112.1	140.7	148.8	106.4
1956	94.6	175.2	187.3	123.6	148.7	120.5	146.7	161.5	114.6	159.3	155.1	97.4
1957	94.6	184.1	195.9	127.3	157.4	123.3	146.7	170.8	118.6	161.1	162.2	100.4
1958	97.3	199.3	205.1	129.1	162.6	124.8	153.3	177.6	120.5	172.2	174.8	102.1
1959	94.6	210.3	221.6	129.1	169.6	131.4	160.0	187.7	122.1	174.1	178.7	103.0
1960	91.9	218.6	234.4	134.5	176.5	131.0	160.0	195.4	123.9	181.5	190.6	104.7
1961	94.6	230.3	246.3	134.5	181.7	135.2	166.7	206.9	127.7	172.2	190.6	110.6
1962	91.9	239.3	260.8	132.7	189.6	142.9	166.7	210.0	130.3	172.2	200.0	116.2
1963	91.9	249.0	269.7	132.7	198.3	148.6	166.7	216.2	131.9	183.3	210.2	114.9
1964	91.9	261.4	281.2	132.7	206.1	154.3	173.3	225.4	135.5	174.1	217.3	124.7

(continued)

TABLE 3 (concluded)

Years	Services		
	Unit Labor Costs[b]	Hourly Compensation	Output Per Man-Hour
1948	103.8	108.1	104.2
1949	105.8	111.6	105.4
1950	109.6	114.0	104.8
1951	115.4	123.3	106.0
1952	121.2	130.2	106.0
1953	126.9	137.2	106.6
1954	132.7	141.9	107.2
1955	132.7	146.5	109.6
1956	140.4	155.8	110.8
1957	144.2	165.1	113.3
1958	150.0	173.3	115.7
1959	151.9	182.6	118.7
1960	159.6	190.7	118.7
1961	163.5	197.7	119.9
1962	167.3	205.8	122.3
1963	173.1	214.0	122.9
1964	182.7	227.9	124.7

Source: Output and compensation data are from the U.S. Department of Commerce, Office of Business Economics. Man-hour data are from the U.S. Department of Labor, Bureau of Labor Statistics.

[a]Excludes general government.

[b]Compensation of all persons per unit of output.

TABLE 4

Average Annual Rates of Change[a] in Unit Labor Costs, Hourly Compensation, and Output per Man-Hour for All Persons in the Private Economy and Major Sectors, Selected Periods 1947–64

Sector	1947–64			1947–60			1960–64		
	Unit Labor Costs	Output Per Man-Hour	Hourly Compensation	Unit Labor Costs	Output Per Man-Hour	Hourly Compensation	Unit Labor Costs	Output Per Man-Hour	Hourly Compensation
Private economy[b]	1.8	3.2	5.0	2.1	3.2	5.3	0.3	3.9	4.2
Farm	–4.0	5.9	1.7	–4.6	6.1	1.3	–0.3	5.0	4.5
Nonfarm	2.1	2.6	4.7	2.5	2.6	5.1	0.3	3.6	3.9
Public utilities	–0.4	6.2	5.8	–0.5	6.7	6.2	–0.3	4.7	4.5
Communications	–0.2	5.5	5.3	0.5	5.0	5.5	–2.3	6.7	4.6
Mining	0.1	4.2	4.2	0.6	4.2	4.9	–1.4	4.2	2.9
Trade	1.7	2.5	4.3	2.1	2.2	4.4	–0.4	4.3	4.1
Transportation	2.3	2.7	5.1	3.1	2.4	5.7	–1.3	4.5	3.1
Manufacturing	2.4	2.7	5.2	3.1	2.6	5.7	–0.6	4.5	3.8
Finance, insurance, and real estate	3.1	1.8	5.0	3.5	1.7	5.3	1.6	2.1	3.4
Services	3.6	1.3	4.9	3.7	1.2	5.0	3.3	1.2	4.5
Construction	2.5	2.3	4.9	1.9	3.1	5.1	4.8	–0.8	4.0
Government enterprises	4.2	0.4	4.6	–5.3	–0.4	4.8	–0.2	4.0	3.7

Source: Output and compensation data are from the U.S. Department of Commerce, Office of Business Economics. Man-hour data are from the U.S. Department of Labor, Bureau of Labor Statistics.

[a]All rates computed from the least squares trend of the logarithms of the index numbers.

[b]Excluding general government.

sequence of the changing occupational and employment structure of the economy; in fact, some of the farm proprietors probably went into nonfarm employment.

The inclusion of proprietors in the nonfarm sector had very little impact on the productivity and unit labor-cost trends in that sector, as might be expected since proprietors are a relatively small part of the nonfarm labor force. However, the all-person–employee trends in con-

CHART 15

Indexes of Unit Labor Costs: Hourly Compensation and Output per Man-Hour for All Persons in the Total Private Economy, 1947–64 (1947 = 100)

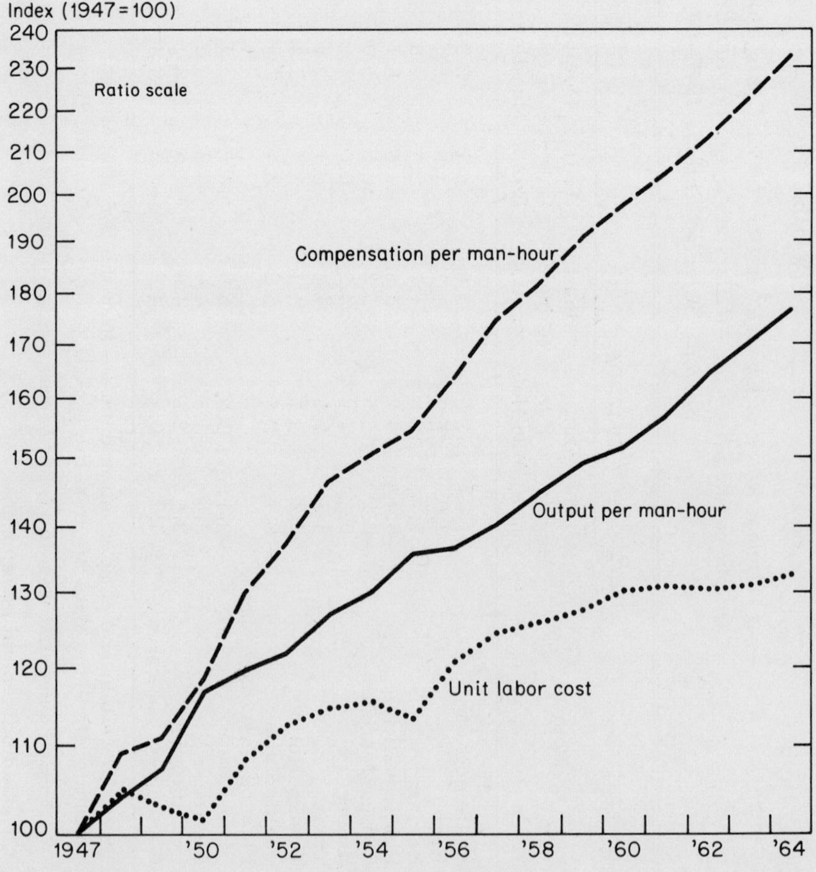

struction and trade were different; in both sectors proprietors have declined in relative importance.

THE FARM SECTOR

The importance of this sector has declined substantially during the postwar period, both in terms of man-hours and output. Man-hours dropped from 18 per cent of the total private economy in 1947 to 8 per cent in 1964. The relative share of output declined from 6 per cent in 1947 to 4 per cent in 1964.

Unit labor costs in the farm sector declined at the record rate of 4.0 per cent since 1947 (Chart 16). This decline by far exceeds the decline in any of the nonfarm sectors. The major part of the over-all decline occurred during the eight years before 1956. During this period, the annual rate of decline averaged 5.2 per cent. Since 1956, the decline amounted to 2.4 per cent per year with a slight decline of 0.3 per cent since 1960. On an annual basis there were four years with unit labor-cost increases, thirteen years with decreases, and six trend reversals.

The farm output per man-hour increased, on average, 5.9 per cent per year since 1947. During the first eleven years before 1958 the increase was somewhat higher (6.4 per cent). Since 1960 output per man-hour increases amounted to 5.0 per cent.

The movement in compensation shows a basically different pattern. The over-all increases average 1.7 per cent, with very low increases (1.0 per cent) until 1957 and a substantially higher rate of increase (4.5 per cent) since 1960. The farm sector shows two major reversals in the compensation trends. One major decline occurred in 1955 (7.7 per cent) and one in 1960 (8.6 per cent). This pattern contrasts sharply with the compensation movement in the nonfarm sectors, where compensation steadily moved upward from year-to-year for every single year.

ROLE OF SHIFTS AMONG SECTORS

The indexes of unit labor costs for the private economy and for the nonfarm economy were derived by dividing the total compensation of all component sectors by total output. These indexes would show changes, even if there were no change in the unit labor costs in each sector, if any of the sectors with higher (or lower) unit labor costs

CHART 16

Indexes of Unit Labor Costs: Hourly Compensation and Output per Man-Hour for All Persons in the Farm Sector, 1947–64

(1947 = 100)

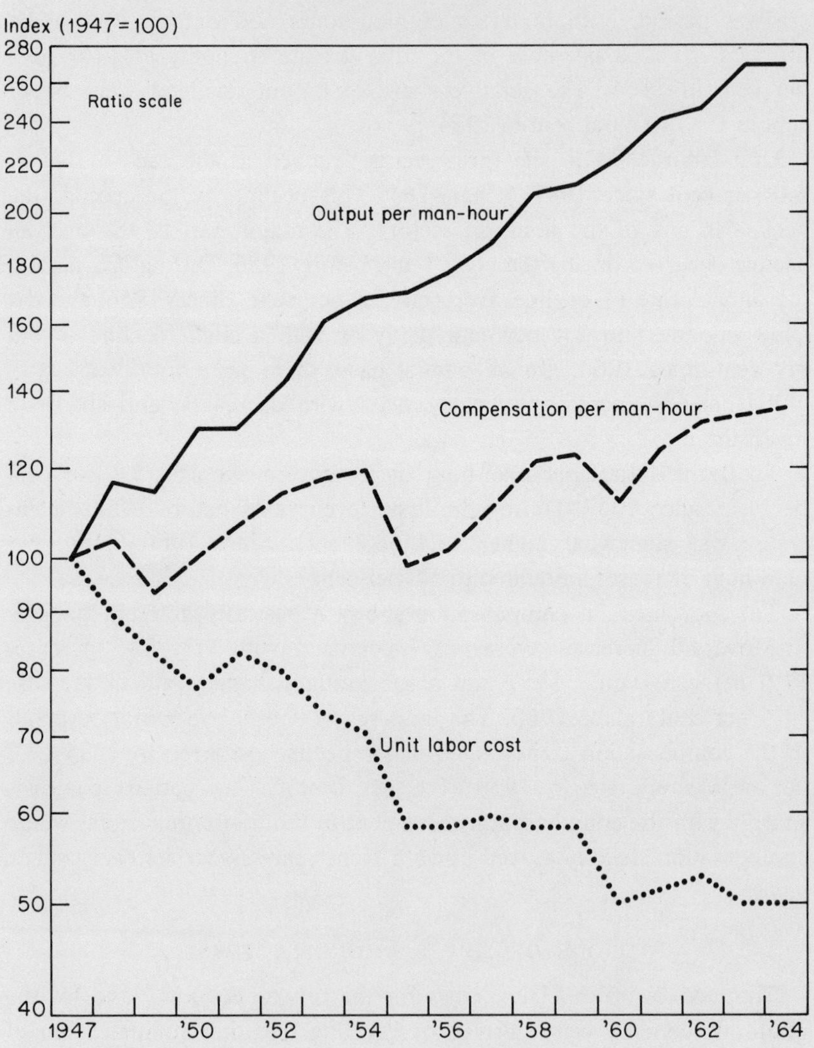

were to become more important. That is, the over-all changes in unit labor costs reflect both changes in the unit labor costs of component sectors and shifts in the relative importance of sectors with different levels of unit labor costs.

The relative importance of a sector can be measured either in terms of output or in terms of compensation—i.e., shifts can reflect either changes in output "mix" or changes in compensation "mix." The relevant measure depends on the analytical purpose of the unit labor-cost trend. One of the main purposes is to compare unit labor costs with price movements. Average price changes for the private economy are affected by sector changes in price and by shifts in the relative importance of sectors. In this case, the relative importance of the sectors can be measured in terms of output or value. The one dimension which is common to price and unit labor cost is output, so it seems appropriate to use the output proportions for measuring shift effects for both.

Similarly, with regard to output per man-hour, shifts in importance can be measured in terms of output or in terms of man-hours. Since the output per man-hour measure is examined in relation to the measure of compensation per unit of output, the mix in terms of output is relevant. In the case of hourly compensation, the relevant mix would appear to be in terms of compensation rather than man-hours.

In order to examine the movements of unit labor cost excluding the effect of shifts, the procedure employed was first to derive indexes of unit labor cost holding the output proportions of each sector constant; second, to derive indexes of shift by holding sector unit labor costs constant, allowing output proportions to change; and finally to allocate the interaction to each of the two elements.[15] A similar approach was followed with regard to output per man-hour and hourly compensation.

Table 5 shows for the entire postwar period and selected years the average annual rates of change in unit labor costs, hourly compen-

[15] The interaction amounted to less than 0.1 per cent per year and this was allocated equally to the two components. For a discussion of this problem of the transformation of the multiplicative relation into the additive one, see Irving H. Siegel, "Concepts and Measurement of Production and Productivity," Working Paper of National Conference on Productivity, 1952, p. 88; also H. Osborne and J. Epstein, "Corporate Profits Since World War II," *Survey of Current Business,* January 1956, p. 20.

TABLE 5

Average Annual Changes in Unit Labor Costs, Hourly Compensation, and Output Per Man-Hour in Private Economy and Nonfarm Sector

Item	Average Annual Percentage Change: Private Economy (All Persons)			Nonfarm Sector (Employees)		
	1947–64	1947–60	1960–64	1947–64	1947–60	1960–64
Unit Labor Costs						
Actual change	1.8	2.1	0.3	2.2	2.6	0.5
Change excluding sector output shifts[a]	2.0	2.3	0.4	2.4	2.8	0.5
Compensation per Man-Hour						
Actual change	5.0	5.3	4.2	4.8	5.2	3.8
Change excluding sector compensation shifts[a]	4.7	5.0	4.0	4.9	5.2	3.9
Output per Man-Hour						
Actual change	3.2	3.2	3.9	2.5	2.5	3.3
Change excluding sector output shifts[a]	2.9	2.9	3.6	2.3	2.2	3.2

[a]Excludes effects of shifts plus allocated interaction.

sation, and output per man-hour excluding the effects of these shifts. As can be seen the effect was small. The 1.8 per cent annual increase in unit labor costs for the private economy resulted in part from the 0.2 per cent decline in unit labor costs because of shifts among the sectors (including the allocated interaction). In other words, if no shifts had taken place unit labor costs in the private economy would have increased 2.0 per cent per year.

The results are primarily a reflection of the shifts within the nonfarm economy. The decline in the importance of the farm sector with its higher-than-average unit labor costs added less than 0.1 percentage points.

Within the nonfarm sector the effect was similar whether or not unit employment costs or unit labor costs of all persons are considered. Shifts among these sectors reduced the trend from 1947–64 by 0.2 percentage points.

Over the whole period shifts in sector importance had a similar effect on hourly compensation trends for the private economy. The over-all 5.0 per cent rate from 1947–64 reflected 0.3 per cent per year from shifts and 4.7 per cent per year from changes in component sectors. Since 1960 the annual rate reflected 0.2 percentage points from shifts.

Finally, with regard to output per man-hour, the effect of shifts in output proportions was also small. Over the whole period, the average annual gain in productivity for the private economy reflected plus 0.3 percentage points from shifts.

COMMENT

ALBERT REES, Princeton University

The Greenberg-Mark paper is, as we would all have expected, a very competent paper. The results seem generally reasonable (if by reasonable we mean consistent with earlier work), particularly in the ranking of industrial sectors by changes in unit labor cost.

The major methodological innovation is the inclusion in unit labor costs of the value of labor supplied by proprietors, partners, and their families. Conceptually, the case for this innovation is unassailable, and empirically it produces differences that are not negligible. While the procedures used to impute a value to proprietors' labor are admittedly somewhat arbitrary, the authors point out that the results do not appear to be sensitive to alternative imputation procedures.

The authors also emphasize that some of the results are improbable; for example, the apparent decline in output per man-hour in construction from 1960 to 1964. The most improbable results seem to arise from the lack of reliable output measures for construction and services. The case of construction is particularly noteworthy because it would not be difficult to improve present methods substantially. Suggestions for improving the index of construction prices were made by the Stigler Committee in 1960.[1] An improved construction price index would, of course, lead to improved real-output measures when the price index was used to deflate construction expenditures.

On the input side, an important data deficiency noted in the paper is the lack of establishment data on the hours and earnings of nonproduction workers. Again such data would not be difficult to collect, and their value, even on an occasional basis, would be great.

The authors, as befits good civil servants, have refrained from drawing any broad implications from their data. Not being similarly situated, I shall be a little bolder.

One of the most general findings of the paper is that the increase in unit labor costs was much slower in the period 1960–64 than in the period 1947–60, a difference that arises in part because the rise in compensation per man-hour was smaller in the later period. Of course, a slower increase in unit costs is in and of itself a good thing. However, it occurred in part because the unemployment rate in the period 1960–64 averaged 5.8 per cent. If this is the price of more nearly stable measured unit labor costs, the price is, in my judgment, too high.

It is also of interest to note that if the nonfarm sectors are ranked by the size of the rise in unit labor cost over the whole period 1947–64, we find in the last three places, widely separated from the rest, three heavily unionized sectors: mining, communication, and public utilities. Among the top three places, where measurement errors may be more important, we find two weakly unionized sectors, services and finance. These findings should surprise those who accept the simpler versions of the wage-push inflation hypothesis—those who argue that strong

[1] Price Statistics Review Committee, *The Price Statistics of the Federal Government,* New York, NBER, 1961, Appendix B, pp. 87–94.

unions cause wages to rise faster than labor productivity in their jurisdictions.

To avoid being misunderstood, I should add that these findings are not inconsistent with more subtle forms of the wage-push inflation hypothesis. It may be that in the absence of union pressures, unit labor costs in the industries with large productivity gains would have risen still less or fallen still more, and that these industries could then have made a larger contribution to stability of the general price level.

Industry Changes in Nonlabor Costs

JOHN W. KENDRICK
THE GEORGE WASHINGTON UNIVERSITY

Changes in the forces of both demand and supply interact to produce changes in industry structure. This paper deals with one aspect of changing industrial structure—industry changes in nonlabor costs. I first look at these changes as the product of relative industry changes in outputs and in unit nonlabor costs—largely accepting the former as given, despite the obvious interactions. I then look behind the industry changes in unit property costs to note the relative changes in capital productivity and in the gross price of capital and analyze the relationships of these two variables to each other and to selected additional variables.

Since changes in industry shares of property costs are related to changes in the property share of gross national income by industry, these changes are also examined. Changes in factor shares are "explained" statistically in terms of relative changes in factor prices and in factor inputs. The general patterns of these changes and the associated coefficients of substitution are set forth and an effort is made to explain them in terms of general economic forces.

Although the emphasis of the paper is on property costs, I will also briefly treat changes in indirect business taxes by industry.

Most of the basic industry series were provided by the Office of Business Economics: gross national product and income by major types of income; real gross product (1958 dollars); persons engaged in production; and average compensation per full-time equivalent employee.[1]

[1] The estimates of the Office of Business Economics, U.S. Department of Commerce, are published in the national income statistical supplement to the *Survey of Current Business,* November 1966. The gross income and product

NOTE: The author gratefully acknowledges the statistical assistance of Maximilian Goepp, Dorothy Juengst, and Yvonne Lethem.

Since the "profit-type income" category of OBE includes net proprietors' income, it was necessary to estimate the portion of this which is believed to represent compensation for the labor of proprietors in order to split gross national income into the labor and property shares. There are a number of alternative methods for doing this as noted by Greenberg and Mark; I chose the simplest method, which consists of imputing the average earnings per full-time equivalent employee in each industry to the numbers of proprietors in the industry. "Labor productivity" is estimated as the ratio of real product originating to numbers of persons engaged.

The Statistical Framework

The sector studied was limited to the private domestic business economy, for the simple reason that only in the industries comprising private business is there the full complement of nonlabor as well as labor income. In the government, household, and nonprofit institutions sectors a net property return is not even imputed in the Commerce Department accounts. Even if it were, an analysis of its share would reveal merely the assumptions of the estimators! In a few instances, the industry detail provided by OBE was combined for pragmatic reasons.[2]

Real capital stock estimates for twenty-eight of the fifty basic industries used in the study were kindly provided by Michael Gort and Rayford Boddy.[3] They have developed estimates of gross and net capital stock in current and constant prices, with a number of variants of the net stock estimates. I have chosen to work with the gross stock estimates, partly in order to simplify the analysis, and partly in order to avoid the problem of choosing among alternative depreciation patterns and the associated valuation adjustments on net profits. Thus, my capi-

---

estimates are published only for major industry groups and subgroups. The two-digit industry detail was furnished by OBE to the authors of papers for the December 1966 sessions of the Conference on Research in Income and Wealth for their analytical use.

[2] Chiefly, I combined those service industries which comprised private-nonprofit institutions as well as private businesses, prior to eliminating the income originating in the former.

[3] These estimates will be published by Michael Gort and Raford Boddy in a forthcoming article. Their capital stock estimates cover the period 1948–63, but the estimates for the years 1961–63 were received too late for use in this study; I extrapolated their estimates for 1948–60 by similar sources and methods, but my estimates for 1961–63 are subject to revision.

tal productivity estimates are the ratios of real gross product to real gross capital stock (the inverted ratios representing capital coefficients); and the "price" of capital is a gross price, computed as the ratio of gross property compensation and the real gross capital stock. This unorthodox variable thus reflects changes in the rate of depreciation, as well as in the net rate of return, and in the average prices of the underlying stock of capital goods.[4] Using gross "cash flow" has the advantage of avoiding a separation of depreciation and profits before taxes, but if time had permitted, I would also have treated depreciation and profits separately.

The analysis is confined to trends of industry shares of nonlabor costs between the two three-year periods 1948–50 and 1961–63. Each of these periods includes one recession year, but the earlier period probably represents a somewhat higher average rate of capacity utilization. Nevertheless, apart from a few exceptional industry situations, the periods chosen for comparison would appear to reveal basic trends in the several variables rather well. The framework developed here could be used for analyses of cyclical movements and movements from one cycle-average to another, as well as the trend over the period as a whole.

The limited time since receipt of the basic industry product estimates has forced me to make this paper more of a preliminary survey of the field than a thorough analysis. I hope that the paper will stimulate further work on factor costs by industry. Certainly the estimates now available from OBE on industry product make possible quantitative analyses which go beyond any previously attempted.

Indirect Business Taxes

Before turning our attention to gross property compensation, I believe it is worthwhile to take at least a passing look at indirect business taxes by industry. In 1948–50, these taxes accounted for 9.4 per cent of gross private domestic business product, increasing to 11.2 per cent in 1961–

[4] This is demonstrated in the following equation, in which K is the real gross stock of capital, P the average prices of the underlying capital goods (so that PK is the current-dollar value of the gross stock), r the gross rate of return on PK, and C the current-dollar gross property compensation:

$$\frac{C}{K} = \frac{rPK}{K} = rP$$

63. According to the Commerce estimates, there is a wide variation among industries in the proportions of gross product accounted for by indirect business taxes, as well as in the changes in these proportions. Concomitantly, there have been substantial differences among industries in the proportions they contribute to the government's total indirect business tax take, as implied in Table 1. Relative percentage changes in industry proportions are spelled out in Table 2, column 5. (All tabular matter is grouped at the end of this article.)

Before discussing the changes, it should be pointed out that about two-thirds of indirect business taxes are levied directly on commodities in the form of sales taxes, excises, and customs duties. About one-third are represented by property taxes, which differ according to the volume of taxable property commanded by an industry. OBE must have experienced some difficulties in allocating indirect taxes by industry, especially in the case of property taxes; and an appraisal of OBE methodology is needed. But the divergences in trends are so marked in many instances that the probable margins of error in the estimating procedures could hardly be a significant element in the results.

The changing proportions of total indirect business taxes contributed by an industry can be factored into relative changes in output and in unit tax payments (see Table 2, columns 5, 1, and 3). Sharply increasing relative tax payments (over 25 per cent in the period from 1948–50 to 1961–63) were a result *both* of relative increases in output and in unit taxes in a few industries: real estate, brokerage, and selected services. In more cases of sharp industry increases, the relative increase in unit taxes much more than offset the effect of declining relative output, i.e., in the cases of the petroleum industry; stone, clay, and glass; contract construction; insurance agents; repair services; and nonfarm agriculture. In almost as many cases, the sharp relative increase in tax take was due entirely to sharp relative increases in output, with unit taxes falling relatively for chemicals, transportation equipment (excluding motor vehicles), air transportation, radio-TV, and banking.

Marked declines of industry shares in total indirect business taxes were generally due to relative declines in both output and in unit taxes (in about ten industries). Relative declines in output much more than offset relative increases in unit taxes in the coal industry and in leather and leather products. Conversely, relative declines in unit taxes much more than offset relative increases in output in electrical machinery, instrument manufacture, and pipeline transportation.

The most important thing to notice is that there have been wide divergences among industries in the changes in indirect business taxes per unit of output over the period studied. These have obviously influenced relative prices, and thus relative changes in sales, output, and resource allocation. I do not attempt to trace the impacts—to do so would require data on gross industry prices and sales, as well as the industry product estimates and deflators, plus more time than was at my disposal. Yet it seems clear that the wide divergences noted must have distorted resource allocation considerably as compared with a competitive model in which prices reflect unit resource costs unaffected by indirect taxes.

The OBE has performed a service in allocating indirect business taxes on an industry basis: by spelling out the differential industry impact of changes in these taxes, it has made possible more rational action on the part of legislators. Possibly our legislators at the several levels have wished to raise indirect tax rates more than average in the petroleum industry, construction, and primary metals, to name a few, and to lower or raise them less than average on foods, apparel, electrical machinery, and pipelines. But they should know what they are doing, and in what degree, when they indirectly influence resource allocations. This objective would be further facilitated if the OBE estimates were provided in greater detail, possibly on a commodity-group as well as an industry basis, with the related gross sales and price information, and if the impact of indirect business taxes on prices were traced through to demand for goods and for the underlying factor services by industry.

Relative Changes in Gross Property Compensation

The industry shares of gross property compensation (GPC) have varied widely between 1948–50 and 1961–63, as shown in Table 1. The percentage changes in industry shares are indicated by the index numbers of relative GPC in Table 2, column 6. To take a few extreme examples from that table, gross property compensation in radio and TV broadcasting increased 3.6 times more than in the private domestic economy, while that of insurance carriers rose only 21.2 per cent as much (i.e., the industry percentage of GPC fell by over 78 per cent).

The relative industry changes in gross property compensation can be decomposed into relative changes in output and in GPC per unit of output (columns 1 and 4). Thus, in the case of radio-TV broadcasting, relative industry output rose by 80 per cent; the rest of the rise in the GPC percentage was due to a doubling of GPC per unit of output. With regard to insurance agents, relative output actually rose a bit—by 12 per cent; the decline in the industry share of total GPC was accounted for by an 81 per cent drop in GPC per unit of output.

There does not appear to be a significant correlation between relative industry changes in output and in unit GPC. In half the industries, both variables moved in the same direction, and in the other half of the industries, they moved in opposite directions. One might expect a significant negative correlation between relative industry changes in output and in unit *total* cost (the gross industry product price deflator): the correlation is negative, but not significant at the .05 level.[5] In any case, GPC on the average accounted for little more than one-third of total industry gross product in the private domestic business economy, and the relationship between relative changes in unit GPC and in total unit cost was not close between 1948–50 and 1961–63.[6]

In over half the industries—28—I was able to probe behind the relative changes in unit GPC. This variable may, of course, be viewed as the product of the gross capital coefficient and the gross "price of capital" (gross property compensation per unit of real gross capital stock). In the private domestic business economy, for example, the gross capital coefficient rose by 2 per cent over the period observed, while the gross price of capital rose by 19.3 per cent—accounting for the 21.7 per cent increase in unit property return. In looking at the component industries, however, I am concerned with the changes in these variables *relative* to the economy changes, as shown in the first two columns of Table 3. Thus, to take the first industry in the table, farming, a 13 per cent increase in the gross capital coefficient was more

[5] The coefficient of correlation is –.175. The estimating equation follows, with Y = relative unit total cost and X = relative output:

$$\log Y = 2.16219 - .0826 \log X$$

[6] The coefficient of correlation between these two variables was only 0.056. This implies a significant negative correlation between relative unit labor cost and output, which seems to have been the case, based on examination of a scatter diagram.

than offset by a 31 per cent decline in the gross price of capital—which "explains" the 22 per cent drop in unit property compensation shown in Table 2. The products of columns 1 and 2 in Table 3 should equal the link relatives shown in column 4 of Table 2 (unit gross property compensation), allowing for small discrepancies due to rounding.

When the two components of unit GPC are related to each other, a significant negative correlation emerges.[7] That is, a relative increase in the gross price of capital is associated with a relative drop in the real gross stock of capital per unit of output (capital coefficient), and the relative quantity change appears to be somewhat less than proportionate to the relative price change.

There may, of course, be a spurious element in this correlation (and subsequent ones) between variables containing a common component. Yet, from the theoretical viewpoint, one would expect this inverse relationship, especially if relative industry changes in the gross price of capital were closely related to those in the ratio of the gross price of capital to the gross compensation per employee (or per man-hour).

Since (as Greenberg and Mark point out) there was a rather narrow dispersion in rates of change in average labor compensation over the period, while at the same time there was a wide dispersion in rates of change in property return, relative industry changes in the latter were quite similar to changes in the ratios of the two factor prices. Thus, industry changes in the gross capital coefficients are also significantly related to industry changes in the ratio of the price of labor (measured as average annual compensation per full-time equivalent employee) to the gross price of capital.[8] A priori, one would expect a relatively more intensive use of capital if its relative price had fallen in relation to wage rates.

[7] The coefficient of correlation is −.796. The estimating equation follows, with X = the relative industry real gross stock of capital per unit of real gross product and Y = the relative gross price of industry capital (gross property compensation per unit of real gross capital stock):

$$\log Y = 4.5842 - 1.0286 \log X$$

[8] The coefficient of correlation is .621. The estimating equation follows, with X = the relative industry gross capital coefficient defined as in footnote 7, and Y = the relative ratio of the price of labor (average annual compensation per full-time equivalent employee) to the gross price of capital, as defined above (data presented in Table 3):

$$\log Y = .1343 + .9300 \log X$$

Since a thirteen-year period is being studied, I have been treating gross capital return per unit of real capital stock as a "price." Yet, it must be remembered that there is a residual, profit element in the "price," and that relative industry changes in the price of capital will be affected by the differential industry impact of dynamic change. This suggests that there is a reciprocal interaction in the relationship just discussed which may be more obvious if we speak of a *positive* relationship between relative industry changes in "capital productivity" and in the gross property return per unit of real capital. That is, in industries in which capital productivity is increasing fastest, one would expect a favorable impact on profit rates, as well as a continuing effort to economize on capital per unit of output.

Looking further at the output-capital ratio, it was interesting to discover a significant positive correlation between relative industry changes in capital productivity and in output.[9] This is also true of relative changes in labor productivity (measured as real product per person engaged) and in output.[10] The significantly positive correlations between relative industry changes in productivity of both factors and in output are behind the negative correlation between relative changes in total unit costs and in output.[11]

The positive correlation between relative industry changes in output and in capital productivity would have suggested a possible negative correlation between relative changes in output and in unit GPC, were it not for the fact I noted earlier: that is, the association between output and capital productivity is offset by the positive correlation between capital productivity and the gross price of capital, so that no significant correlation exists between output and unit GPC.

[9] The coefficient of correlation is .612. The estimating equation follows, with Y = relative industry capital productivity (real gross product per unit of real gross capital stock), and X = relative industry real gross product:

$$\log Y = 1.1039 + 0.4342 \log X$$

[10] The coefficient of correlation is 0.388, which is barely significant at the .05 level. The estimating equation follows, with Y = relative industry labor productivity (real gross product per person engaged in production) and X = relative real industry gross product:

$$\log Y = 1.5686 = .2126 \log X$$

[11] See John W. Kendrick, *Productivity Trends in the United States,* Princeton for NBER, 1961, Chapter 7.

The Property Share of Gross Factor Income

Changes in industry shares of gross factor income by type of compensation are related to changes in factor shares of gross income originating in each industry. For example, if an industry (such as manufactured food, as shown in Table 1) experiences a greater drop in its share of gross property compensation than in its share of gross factor income, this is associated with a fall in the property share of gross factor income. In the case of manufactured food, as shown in Table 4, the property share of gross income fell by 11 per cent between 1948–50 and 1961–63—somewhat more than the 3 per cent drop in the private domestic business economy as a whole.

In this section, I will examine the changes in factor shares of gross income over the chosen period. One approach to this analysis is demonstrated for all industries in Table 4. The percentage shares of property are shown for the two periods in the first two columns, and the link relatives indicating the proportionate changes in shares are shown in column 3. It will be noted that in the majority of industries, the property share declined, although in several industries there were marked increases, notably in communications.

Columns 4 and 5 "explain" the changes in property shares in terms of changes in unit property cost relative to unit total factor cost. If GPC per unit of output rises less than total cost per unit, then obviously the property share declines. Looking behind this relationship, one might inquire as to the conditions under which unit labor cost, and thus unit total cost, rises more than unit property cost.

One way of describing these conditions would be in terms of the relative movements of productivity and price for each of the factors. A decline in the property share would indicate that an increase in the price of labor exceeded the increase in labor productivity by a wider margin than the increase in the price of capital exceeded the increase in average capital productivity.

Another way of putting it is that if the relative decrease in the price of a factor is proportionately greater than the relative increase in its quantity of input, that factor's share will decline. This approach has been implemented for the twenty-eight industries for which capital data are available in Table 5. The "coefficient of substitution" in column 4 shows the ratio of rates of change in relative quantities to rates of change in relative prices. This concept is familiar as the "elasticity of substitution"; but since I am applying it to historical time series affected by dynamic changes, I merely term it a "coefficient."

Looking now at Table 5, it will be noted that in all industries and industry groups but one (transportation equipment manufacturing, except motor vehicles), the real gross capital stock (or "input") rose in relation to persons engaged (labor input). Conversely, the gross price of capital fell in relation to the price of labor (average compensation per employee, or per person engaged) in all but four of the industries. One of the four is transportation equipment excluding motor vehicles, which preserves an inverse relationship. In the other three industries (and in the communications group), the direct relationship is indicated by the minus (−) sign before the substitution ratio.

Examining the coefficients of substitution in column 4 of Table 5, one sees that in ten out of the thirty-five industries and groups the coefficients are greater than unity. This means that if relative capital input increased (which it did in all of these industries), the capital share increased, since the relative capital price declined less (or rose less, in the case of negative coefficients) than the proportionate increase in the relative volume of capital. In the one industry in which the relative capital input fell, the property share of income also rose, which is consistent with a coefficient of substitution below 1.

In twenty-five of the thirty-five industries and groups, and in the private domestic business economy as a whole, the coefficients of substitution were less than unity—and in all but transportation equipment excluding motor vehicles (in which relative capital input fell), the gross property share of income fell. In all but four of the industries, the coefficients were well above 0.5, indicating that generally the rate of change in the relative price of capital was well under twice the rate of change in the relative quantity of capital input. In the private domestic business economy as a whole, the coefficient was 0.89—considerably higher than the 0.58 which R. Sato and I computed for the U.S. economy over the period 1919–60,[12]—but still below unity.

In speculating about the prevailing pattern of relative factor prices, inputs, and shares, I believe the following general points may be made

[12] See J. W. Kendrick and R. Sato, "Factor Prices, Productivity, and Economic Growth," *American Economic Review,* December 1963, p. 981.

with considerable confidence.[13] The relative growth of capital in relation to the work force in the private economy as a whole reflects the saving and investment propensities of the community. As a result largely of research and development outlays, resulting in new products and cost-reducing inventions, investment demand schedules have shifted upwards enough to offset the tendency towards diminishing returns to capital. Rates of return on new investment have fluctuated, but have shown no sustained trend in either direction, while the real stock of capital grew by at least one per cent a year faster than the labor force, on the average, over the past half-century—and relatively even faster since World War II.

In analyzing the downward tendency in the relative price of capital, it must be remembered that this consists of two elements: prices of the underlying capital goods, and the gross rate of return on the stock of capital. As far as the average prices of reproducible capital goods are concerned, it is clear that these have risen significantly less than wage rates generally, since labor productivity has risen significantly in the capital-goods industries while factor prices in these industries change more or less proportionately to factor prices in the economy as a whole. As noted above, the rate of return on capital shows no sharp trend, and over the period in question this rate probably declined somewhat in most private industries—thus reenforcing the tendency for capital prices to rise less than the price of labor. But as has been pointed out elsewhere,[14] a general trend in the profit rate tends to be self-limiting through its effect on saving and investment.

If I am correct in positing no substantial longer-run trends in interest-plus-profit rates in conjunction with significant upward trends in productivity in the private economy including capital goods industries, then a relative decline in the ratio of capital to labor prices follows. Indeed, this would seem to be the chief mechanism whereby the relative growth of the capital stock is absorbed by the various industries. The fact that the over-all coefficient of substitution is less than unity reflects the basic fact that the rate of growth of productivity has exceeded the rate of growth of the capital stock per worker.[15] So the general tendency has been for property shares of factor income to drop, and thus for industry

[13] *Ibid.*, p. 975.
[14] *Ibid.*, p. 982.
[15] See Kendrick, *Productivity Trends,* Chapters 3 and 4.

shares of gross property cost to fall more, or rise less, than industry shares of gross national income.

It has been noted that a substantial majority of the thirty-five industries studied here tend to follow the private business economy pattern—a rise in the capital-labor ratio (one exception), a drop in the gross price of capital relative to average labor compensation (four exceptions), and a coefficient of substitution less than unity (ten exceptions). The variations among industries in the coefficients are due to: (a) differences in rates of growth of the capital-labor ratio due to differences and changes in the relative unit factor requirements of innovations in the various industries, and differential rates of shift in investment demand schedules; (b) differential changes in the price of capital, particularly the rate-of-return component, and/or in average labor compensation.

Of these variables, my judgment is that differential changes in the rate of return is probably the most important factor over shorter- or intermediate-term periods. It was certainly a key element in the communications industry, for example, reflecting changes in regulatory agency policies over the period studied.

Hopefully, the analysis here points the way to the further research needed to provide full economic explanations for the changing factor shares of income by industry, and for changing industry shares of factor compensation.[16]

[16] After completion of this paper, my attention was called to a recent econometric study of changing factor shares, "The Share of Corporate Profits in the Postwar Period," by Murray Brown (U.S. Department of Commerce, Staff Working Paper in Economics and Statistics No. 11, April 1965). This paper provides excellent parallel reading for the discussion in this volume.

TABLE 1
Industry Proportions of Gross Private Domestic Business Product By Major Type of Cost (Income), 1948–50, and 1961–63
(per cent)

	Total Gross Product		Total Gross Income		Gross Property Compensation	
	1948–50 (1)	1961–63 (2)	1948–50 (3)	1961–63 (4)	1948–50 (5)	1961–63 (6)
Private domestic business economy	100.0	100.0	100.0	100.0	100.0	100.0
Agriculture, forestry, and fisheries	9.0	4.7	9.6	5.0	15.5	9.2
Farms	8.7	4.5	9.2	4.7	15.4	9.1
Agricultural services, forestry, and fisheries	.32	.28	.36	.33	.07	.12
Mining	3.7	2.8	3.9	2.9	6.5	5.3
Metals	.38	.25	.39	.26	.62	.34
Coal	.97	.31	1.05	.34	.66	.24
Petroleum and natural gas	3.1	2.8	2.9	2.4	5.4	4.2
Nonmetallic mining	.26	.27	.27	.29	.33	.32
Contract construction	4.9	5.2	5.3	5.7	.78	1.07
Manufacturing	32.4	32.8	32.7	33.8	25.1	23.68
Nondurables	15.4	13.9	14.7	13.5	11.6	10.1
Food	4.4	3.6	3.7	3.3	3.1	2.6
Tobacco	.76	.68	.22	.28	.32	.50
Textile mills	2.0	1.01	2.1	1.1	1.5	.62
Apparel	1.5	1.2	1.7	1.3	.56	.44
Paper	1.1	1.3	1.2	1.4	1.4	1.3
Printing and publishing	1.6	1.6	1.7	1.8	.76	.82
Chemicals	2.0	2.5	2.2	2.8	3.0	3.5
Rubber and miscellaneous plastics	.61	.80	.59	.79	.31	.53
Leather	.51	.36	.55	.40	.21	.14

(continued)

TABLE 1 (continued)

	Total Gross Product		Total Gross Income		Gross Property Compensation	
	1948–50 (1)	1961–63 (2)	1948–50 (3)	1961–63 (4)	1948–50 (5)	1961–63 (6)
Durables	17.0	18.9	18.0	20.3	13.8	13.6
Lumber and wood	1.2	.78	1.3	.86	.95	.49
Furniture	.55	.49	.60	.55	.30	.25
Stone, clay, and glass	1.09	1.2	1.2	1.3	.98	1.1
Primary metals	2.8	2.6	3.0	2.9	2.6	2.2
Fabricated metals	2.0	2.0	2.2	2.2	1.5	1.2
Machinery, except electrical	2.8	3.0	3.0	3.3	2.1	2.2
Electrical machinery	1.9	2.7	2.0	2.9	1.3	1.5
Transportation equipment, except motor vehicles and ordnance	.94	2.2	1.01	2.4	.36	.91
Motor vehicles	2.5	2.6	2.4	2.5	2.9	3.0
Instruments	.46	.74	.48	.81	.20	.61
Miscellaneous manufacturing	.70	.56	.75	.60	.44	.28
Transportation	6.4	5.0	6.4	5.2	3.9	3.0
Railroads	3.4	1.7	3.4	1.8	2.2	1.1
Nonrailway transportation	3.0	3.3	3.0	3.4	1.7	1.9
Local and highway passenger	.74	.47	.74	.45	.33	.22
Motor freight and warehouses	1.3	1.7	1.3	1.8	.65	.78
Water	.48	.38	.50	.42	.24	.13
Air	.23	.49	.23	.50	.16	.35
Pipeline	.12	.10	.12	.11	.17	.19
Transportation services	.15	.16	.16	.18	.12	.16
Communications	1.7	2.5	1.6	2.4	1.2	3.4
Telephone and telegraph	1.6	2.3	1.4	2.2	1.1	3.1
Radio and TV	.13	.24	.14	.27	.08	.28

(continued)

TABLE 1 (concluded)

	Total Gross Product		Total Gross Income		Gross Property Compensation	
	1948–50 (1)	1961–63 (2)	1948–50 (3)	1961–63 (4)	1948–50 (5)	1961–63 (6)
Electric, gas, and sanitary services	2.0	2.9	2.0	2.9	1.1	3.1
Wholesale and retail trade	20.7	19.3	19.9	17.9	14.7	9.1
Wholesale	7.4	7.7	6.6	6.6	6.4	5.5
Retail	13.3	11.6	13.3	11.3	9.1	4.6
Finance, insurance, and real estate	11.8	15.9	11.1	14.8	23.1	31.2
Finance and insurance	2.8	3.8	2.8	3.9	1.8	1.6
Banking	1.2	1.7	1.3	1.9	1.9	2.7
Brokerage	.17	.35	.16	.35	–	.10
Insurance carriers	1.0	1.2	1.02	1.2	.49	.10
Insurance agents, etc.	.34	.50	.35	.53	.22	.37
Real estate	9.0	12.2	8.3	10.9	21.3	30.0
Services	7.3	8.8	7.6	9.5	6.3	8.2
Hotels and lodging places	.71	.65	.74	.68	.34	.37
Personal services	1.4	1.2	1.5	1.3	.57	.23
Miscellaneous business services	.72	1.5	.77	1.6	.36	.84
Repair services	.72	.84	.78	.92	.08	.20
Amusement, except motion pictures	.53	.60	.43	.53	.23	.27
Motion pictures	.54	.26	.45	.26	.34	.14
Other services (private business)	2.7	3.8	2.9	4.2	4:3	6.1

TABLE 2

Relative Changes in Real Product and Selected Unit and Total Costs[a]*, Private Domestic Business Economy by Industry, Based on Index Numbers, 1961–63*
(1948–50=100)

		Unit Costs (income)			Total Cost	
	Real Product (1)	Total (2)	Indirect Bus. Taxes (3)	Gross Property Compensation (4)	Indirect Bus. Taxes (5)	Gross Property Compensation (6)
Private domestic business economy (1948–50=100)	157.4	127.8	151.7	121.7	238.7	191.6
Private domestic business economy (1961–63 index Nos. = 100)						
Agriculture, forestry, and fisheries	75.3	70.0	102.2	78.7	77.2	59.2
Farms	75.1	68.0	100.9	78.2	75.8	58.7
Agricultural services, forestry, and fisheries	80.2	111.0	155.6	213.1	125.1	172.0
Mining	83.6	88.5	106.5	97.7	89.4	81.8
Metals	83.4	81.1	77.9	66.6	65.3	54.7
Coal	47.6	67.3	110.7	78.8	53.6	36.1
Petroleum and natural gas	95.0	97.8	151.7	81.8	144.2	77.6
Nonmetallic mining	116.8	88.5	61.9	83.2	74.9	97.2
Contract construction	91.7	115.5	149.6	149.9	137.0	137.5

(continued)

TABLE 2 (continued)

	Real Product	Unit Costs (income)			Total Cost	
		Total	Indirect Bus. Taxes	Gross Property Compensation	Indirect Bus. Taxes	Gross Property Compensation
Manufacturing	99.3	101.9	85.7	95.3	85.2	94.4
Nondurables	96.0	94.1	82.1	90.9	78.8	87.4
Food	85.0	98.2	69.8	96.1	59.4	81.9
Tobacco	94.4	94.9	69.0	168.9	65.2	156.5
Textile mills	75.9	67.6	67.6	53.7	51.4	40.7
Apparel	85.1	90.2	87.0	93.3	74.2	79.4
Paper	104.8	105.2	110.5	91.4	116.7	95.6
Printing and publishing	91.4	112.5	94.7	118.0	86.5	107.7
Chemicals	149.3	82.7	88.4	78.8	132.2	117.6
Rubber and misc. plastics	110.0	117.7	92.1	153.7	101.3	169.3
Leather	60.9	115.3	100.7	109.0	61.5	66.4
Durables	102.0	109.1	101.5	96.5	103.6	98.4
Lumber and wood	76.6	84.1	107.0	66.6	82.1	51.0
Furniture	81.3	110.6	112.0	105.3	91.3	85.6
Stone, clay, and glass	92.6	115.1	138.0	121.3	128.2	112.3
Primary metals	66.5	141.3	156.0	125.8	104.5	83.6
Fabricated metals	99.2	100.2	102.6	83.9	102.3	83.2
Machinery, except electrical	92.4	116.8	116.2	113.4	107.5	104.6
Electrical machinery	161.9	86.6	46.3	70.8	74.7	114.6
Transportation equipment, except motor vehicles and ordnance	194.7	117.9	69.4	129.0	134.8	251.1

(continued)

TABLE 2 (continued)

		Unit Costs (income)			Total Cost	
	Real Product	Total	Indirect Bus. Taxes	Gross Property Compensation	Indirect Bus. Taxes	Gross Property Compensation
Motor vehicles	104.6	101.3	114.8	96.4	120.4	100.8
Instruments	136.4	118.5	43.6	218.0	62.5	297.7
Miscellaneous manufacturing	87.0	90.0	78.2	74.5	68.0	64.8
Transportation	77.3	101.1	76.0	99.2	58.7	76.7
Railroads	60.8	82.2	53.4	84.8	32.6	51.5
Nonrailway transportation						
Local and highway	3.3	189.7	244.1	205.2	81.7	67.7
Motor freight and warehouse	135.8	96.9	79.8	87.2	107.6	118.6
Water	69.4	115.9	55.9	76.9	39.3	53.3
Air	274.7	75.7	51.5	80.9	140.5	222.2
Pipeline	126.2	64.7	34.0	89.0	43.0	112.2
Transportation services	58.0	188.9	185.8	229.9	108.1	133.3
Communications	147.2	97.6	58.6	190.2	86.0	280.0
Telephone and telegraph	144.7	96.8	59.2	190.4	85.5	275.4
Radio and TV	180.2	105.6	103.9	199.6	187.0	360.0
Electric, gas, and sanitary services	157.2	92.7	67.8	119.8	106.6	187.9
Wholesale and retail trade	99.2	93.8	109.8	62.4	108.8	62.2
Wholesale	111.8	92.9	96.4	77.1	107.7	86.1
Retail	91.7	94.8	120.0	55.2	110.1	50.7

(continued)

TABLE 2 (concluded)

		Unit Costs (income)			Total Cost	
	Real Product	Total	Indirect Bus. Taxes	Gross Property Compensation	Indirect Bus. Taxes	Gross Property Compensation
Finance, insurance, and real estate	117.0	115.7	116.0	115.7	135.7	135.2
Finance and insurance	97.0	140.6	127.2	96.5	123.2	93.3
Banking	81.9	170.6	152.1	175.7	125.0	143.8
Brokerage	128.0	174.7	105.3	209.2	134.4	
Insurance carriers	112.4	106.0	100.9	18.9	113.2	21.2
Insurance agents, etc.	100.1	147.9	133.6	166.1	133.4	166.3
Real estate	124.3	108.7	110.7	111.8	137.5	138.7
Services	99.0	122.6	74.3	131.6	73.6	130.5
Hotels and lodging places	88.2	103.9	110.4	123.8	97.6	109.2
Personal services	80.6	111.0	108.9	49.1	87.8	39.6
Miscellaneous business services	151.3	133.6	78.9	152.8	119.4	231.2
Repair services	199.2	116.9	156.5	244.1	155.6	242.2
Amusement, except motion pictures	98.5	115.5	77.9	118.6	76.8	118.6
Motion pictures	36.2	131.1	39.7	110.3	14.4	39.9
Other services (private business)	106.7	132.9	130.9	132.7	139.9	141.6

[a]The industry index numbers for 1961–63 in the table are obtained by dividing their values on a 1948–50 base by the index numbers for the total private domestic economy shown in the first line. Thus, we see for the several variables the industry movements between 1948–50 and 1961–63 *relative* to the movements for the private domestic economy.

TABLE 3

Relative Changes in the Capital Coefficient[a], Gross Price of Capital[b], and Associated Variables, Private Domestic Business Economy, by Selected Industries, 1961–63

(index numbers, 1948–50 = 100)

	Capital Coefficient[a] (1)	Gross Price of Capital[b] (2)	Output Per Worker (3)	Price of Labor[c] (4)	Ratio, Prices of Labor to Capital[d] (5)	Capital Per Worker[e] (6)
Farms	112.9	68.8	126.5	69.2	100.6	142.8
Mining	213.6	38.7	130.5	101.7	262.8	278.7
Petroleum	127.7	64.0	90.4	97.8	152.8	94.2
Contract construction	206.1	73.0	89.5	102.4	140.3	184.5
Manufacturing	103.8	91.5	97.2	102.9	112.5	100.9
Nondurables	103.5	87.7	101.3	97.4	111.1	104.8
Food	98.6	97.3	94.3	100.1	102.9	93.0
Tobacco	99.3	166.6	114.4	112.9	67.8	113.6
Textile mills	103.0	51.0	115.5	84.8	166.3	119.0
Apparel	96.0	96.6	89.2	81.5	84.4	85.6
Paper	123.0	73.4	87.4	102.4	139.5	107.5
Printing and publishing	104.1	113.2	80.7	91.7	81.0	84.0
Chemicals	81.0	96.9	121.3	107.5	110.9	98.3
Rubber	92.0	167.1	90.0	99.4	59.5	82.8
Leather	143.9	74.2	74.7	87.5	117.9	107.5
Durables	104.4	93.5	94.9	107.4	114.9	99.1
Furniture	96.1	110.6	81.8	91.3	82.5	78.6
Stone, clay, and glass	138.6	87.3	93.2	104.5	119.7	129.2
Primary metals	157.7	79.4	75.6	109.3	137.7	119.2
Fabricated metals	117.5	71.3	94.8	100.5	141.0	111.4
Machinery, except electrical	115.3	98.2	86.0	103.0	104.9	99.2
Electrical machinery	69.3	102.5	108.6	105.2	102.6	75.3
Transportation equipment, except motor vehicles	57.5	225.3	95.1	112.8	50.1	54.7
Motor vehicles	124.0	78.5	125.1	109.5	139.5	155.1

(continued)

TABLE 3 (concluded)

	Capital Coefficient[a] (1)	Gross Price of Capital[b] (2)	Output Per Worker (3)	Price of Labor[c] (4)	Ratio, Prices of Labor to Capital[d] (5)	Capital Per Worker[e] (6)
Transportation	89.1	111.4	99.4	104.6	93.9	88.6
Railroads	90.2	93.6	117.6	100.9	107.8	106.0
Water	113.0	67.3	88.2	111.8	166.1	99.7
Air	83.0	98.8	134.5	106.7	108.0	103.3
Communications	84.5	226.0	143.4	110.5	48.9	121.2
Telephone and telegraph	81.2	236.9	147.0	110.1	46.5	119.4
Radio and TV broadcast	100.1	197.7	73.7	99.0	50.1	73.8
Electric and gas, etc.	70.5	169.7	150.1	109.6	64.6	105.8
Wholesale and retail trade	121.3	51.5	94.4	94.8	184.1	114.5
Wholesale	125.7	60.9	101.4	99.3	163.1	127.5
Retail	121.2	45.2	88.7	92.1	203.8	107.5

[a] Real gross stock of capital per unit of output (real gross product).

[b] Gross capital compensation per unit of real gross capital stock.

[c] Average annual compensation per full-time equivalent employee.

[d] Column 3 divided by column 2.

[e] Real gross stock of capital per person engaged in production.

TABLE 4

The Changing Property Share of Gross Factor Income, Private Domestic Business Economy, by Industry
(percentages, and index numbers 1961–63 on a 1948–50 base)

	Property Shares of Gross Factor Income (per cent)		Link Relatives, 1961–63 (1948–50 = 100)		
	1948–50	1961–63	Property Share[a]	Unit Property Cost	Unit Total Cost
	(1)	(2)	(3)	(4)	(5)
Private domestic business economy	35.3	34.3	97.2	121.7	125.5
Agriculture, forestry, and fisheries	57.0	63.2	110.0	95.8	86.3
Farms	59.1	66.7	112.9	95.2	84.3
Agricultural services, forestries, and fisheries	7.44	12.63	192.3	259.4	134.9
Mining	58.1	62.5	107.7	119.1	110.6
Metals	55.90	43.81	79.4	81.0	102.0
Coal	22.16	24.44	109.9	95.9	83.7
Petroleum and natural gases	64.87	59.16	91.2	99.4	109.0
Nonmetallic mining	43.30	38.01	87.8	101.2	115.5
Contract construction	51.3	64.0	124.8	182.4	146.1
Manufacturing	27.1	24.0	88.9	116.0	130.5
Nondurables	21.1	19.5	92.4	110.6	119.9
Food	29.86	26.65	89.0	117.0	131.5
Tobacco	51.37	61.33	119.7	201.9	168.7
Textile mills	24.28	18.94	78.0	65.4	86.0
Apparel	11.82	11.64	98.5	113.5	115.5
Paper	38.53	31.96	83.0	112.2	133.9
Printing and publishing	16.00	15.94	99.9	143.6	143.8
Chemicals	47.73	43.46	91.1	95.9	105.3
Rubber and miscellaneous plastics	18.77	23.13	123.1	187.1	152.0
Leather	13.59	12.26	90.2	132.7	147.1

(continued)

TABLE 4 (continued)

	Property Shares of Gross Factor Income (per cent)		Link Relatives, 1961–63 (1948–50 = 100)		
	1948–50 (1)	1961–63 (2)	Property Share[a] (3)	Unit Property Cost (4)	Unit Total Cost (5)
Durables	27.0	22.9	84.7	117.5	138.7
Lumber and wood	25.18	19.40	77.0	81.0	105.2
Furniture	17.54	15.99	91.2	128.1	140.5
Stone, clay, and glass	29.25	29.64	101.3	147.6	145.7
Primary metals	30.04	25.62	85.3	153.1	179.4
Fabricated metals	23.98	19.15	79.8	102.1	127.9
Machinery, except electrical	24.27	22.31	91.9	138.0	150.1
Electrical machinery	22.63	17.16	75.8	86.2	113.7
Transportation equipment, except motor vehicles and ordnance	12.66	13.15	103.8	157.0	151.3
Motor vehicles	42.69	40.78	95.5	117.3	122.8
Instruments	15.15	25.73	169.8	265.3	156.2
Miscellaneous manufacturing	20.52	16.05	78.1	90.7	116.1
Transportation	21.1	19.5	92.4	120.7	130.6
Railroads	22.81	21.84	95.7	103.2	107.7
Nonrailroad transportation					
Local and highway passenger	15.64	16.84	107.7	249.7	231.9
Motor freight and warehouse	17.47	14.94	85.3	106.1	124.4
Water	17.13	10.56	61.6	93.5	151.7
Air	24.69	24.46	99.3	98.5	99.2
Pipeline	49.61	61.63	124.3	108.3	87.1
Transportation services	26.53	30.94	116.4	279.8	240.4
Communications	27.4	47.6	173.9	231.5	133.1
Telephone and telegraph	28.01	49.11	175.3	231.7	132.2
Radio and TV	19.64	35.36	180.1	242.9	134.9

(continued)

TABLE 4 (concluded)

	Property Shares of Gross Factor Income (per cent)		Link Relatives, 1961–63 (1948–50 = 100)		
	1948–50 (1)	1961–63 (2)	Property Share[a] (3)	Unit Property Cost (4)	Unit Total Cost (5)
Electric, gas, and sanitary services	52.3	63.0	120.8	145.8	120.7
Wholesale and retail trade	26.0	17.5	67.3	76.0	113.0
Wholesale	34.21	28.60	83.6	93.8	112.2
Retail	23.95	13.99	58.4	67.2	115.1
Finance, insurance, and real estate	73.5	72.4	98.6	140.8	142.8
Finance and insurance	22.2	14.6	65.8	117.4	178.4
Banking	49.33	48.50	98.3	213.8	217.5
Brokerage		10.28			211.4
Insurance carriers	16.82	2.90	17.3	23.0	133.1
Insurance agents, etc.	21.97	23.62	107.6	202.2	188.0
Real estate	90.8	92.9	102.5	136.1	132.8
Services	29.2	29.6	101.3	160.2	158.2
Hotels and lodging places	16.37	18.89	115.4	150.7	130.6
Personal services	13.90	5.89	42.4	59.8	141.1
Miscellaneous business services	16.68	17.91	107.5	185.9	172.9
Repair services	3.64	7.31	201.0	297.1	147.8
Amusements, except motion pictures	18.96	17.28	91.3	144.3	158.1
Motion pictures	26.72	17.78	66.5	134.2	201.8
Other services (private business)	52.28	50.56	96.7	161.5	167.0

[a]Columns 2 ÷ 1 equals columns 4 ÷ 5.

TABLE 5

Relative Capital Input, Relative Price of Capital, and Capital Share of Income Private Domestic Business Economy, by Selected Industries, 1961–63

(index numbers 1948–50=100)

	Relative Capital Input[a]	Relative Price of Capital[b]	Capital Share of Income[c] (1×2)	Coefficient of Substitution[d]
	(1)	(2)	(3)	(4)
Private domestic business economy	126.4	76.9	97.2	.89
Farms	127.1	88.7	112.7	1.99
Mining	146.4	73.5	107.6	1.24
Petroleum	117.0	77.9	91.1	.62
Contract construction	250.2	49.9	124.8	.21
Manufacturing	132.2	67.1	88.7	.70
Nondurables	134.6	68.7	92.5	.79
Food	123.6	72.2	89.2	.65
Tobacco	120.0	99.4	119.3	28.2
Textile mills	149.3	52.2	77.9	.61
Apparel	122.6	80.2	98.3	.92
Paper	129.5	64.1	83.0	.58
Printing and publishing	119.5	85.6	99.9	.99
Chemicals	119.4	76.3	91.1	.65
Rubber	117.3	104.9	123.0	-3.36
Leather	147.0	61.3	90.1	.78
Durables	130.1	65.2	84.8	.61
Furniture	112.9	80.9	91.3	.57
Stone, clay, and glass	150.8	67.2	101.3	1.04
Primary metals	143.4	59.5	85.3	.69
Fabricated metals	142.5	56.1	79.9	.61
Machinery, except electrical	131.7	69.8	91.9	.76
Electrical machinery	108.4	69.9	75.8	.22
Transportation equipment, except motor vehicles	82.7	125.5	103.8	.84
Motor vehicles	147.7	64.6	95.4	.89

(continued)

TABLE 5 (concluded)

	Relative Capital Input[a] (1)	Relative Price of Capital[b] (2)	Capital Share of Income[c] (1×2) (3)	Coefficient of Substitution[d] (4)
Transportation	122.9	75.2	92.4	.72
Railroads	138.6	69.1	95.8	.88
Water	136.1	45.2	61.5	.38
Air	142.2	69.7	99.1	1.00
Communications	147.2	118.2	174.0	-2.33
Telephone and telegraph	145.2	120.8	175.4	-2.00
Radio and TV broadcast	148.6	121.8	181.0	-2.02
Electric and gas, etc.	120.9	99.6	120.4	49.00
Wholesale and retail trade	143.3	47.1	67.5	.47
Wholesale	144.5	57.8	83.5	.67
Retail	139.1	42.0	58.4	.32

[a]Index numbers of ratio of real gross capital stock to average of the real stock and persons engaged, each weighted by its share in gross factor income, 1948–50.

[b]Index numbers of the ratio of gross property compensation per unit of real gross capital stock to an average of this variable compensation per full-time equivalent employee, weighted by gross income shares, 1948–50.

[c]Columns (1) × (2) should equal column 3 of Table 4, except for errors due to rounding.

[d]Rate of change in relative capital input (Column 1) divided by rate of change in relative capital price (Column 2).

COMMENT

DALE W. JORGENSON, University of California at Berkeley

INTRODUCTION

In this note I compare two alternative methods for measuring capital input: (1) the method developed by John W. Kendrick and employed in his paper, "Industry Changes in Nonlabor Costs"; (2) the method developed by Zvi Griliches and myself, which was published in "Sources of Measured Productivity Change: Capital Input." [1] Both of these methods are consistent with an accounting framework for national product and national wealth. The problem of choosing between the methods amounts to answering the questions, what is capital input? what is the price of capital? Definite answers to these questions may be obtained by appealing to the economic theory of capital. This theory suggests measures of capital input that may be employed in studies of total factor productivity or in estimating production functions. Data on capital and labor input comprise an explicit set of real-factor accounts corresponding to the real-product accounts. These accounts may be constructed with available data; the measurement of real input could be considerably refined through the introduction of new data.

THE KENDRICK APPROACH

The basis of the Kendrick approach is a definition of capital input as real gross capital stock. In an earlier paper Kendrick gives the following justification for this definition:

> . . . the prices of the underlying capital goods, as established in markets or imputed by owners, can be appropriately combined (with variable quantity weights) to provide a deflator to convert capital values into physical volumes of the various types of underlying capital goods at base-period prices. Or, the result can be achieved directly by weighting quantities by constant prices.
>
> As I view it, this is the most meaningful way to measure "real capital stock," since the weighted aggregate measures the physical complex of capital goods in terms of its estimated ability to contribute to production as of the base period.[2]

The "ability to contribute to production" is, of course, measured by the price of capital services, just as the ability of labor input to contribute to production is measured by the price of labor services. The price of capital services is not the same as the price of investment goods, the "deflator" of Kendrick's definition of real capital stock.

Kendrick takes the price of capital to be the ratio of gross property compensation to real gross capital stock and capital productivity to be the ratio of real gross product to real gross capital stock. While these

[1] *American Economic Review,* May 1966, pp. 50–61.

[2] John W. Kendrick, "Some Theoretical Aspects of Capital Measurement," *American Economic Review,* May 1961, p. 106.

definitions are consistent with his definition of capital input, they suffer from the same deficiencies. When the resulting estimates of the price of capital and capital input are employed to estimate the elasticity of substitution between labor and capital, a number of anomalies result. For example, the elasticity of substitution for the rubber industry is estimated to be −3.36 while the elasticities for communications, telephone and telegraph, and radio and TV broadcasting are −2.33, −2.00, and −2.02, respectively. None of these estimates can be interpreted as elasticities of substitution. These anomalous results may reflect the fact that the price of capital services, as defined by Kendrick, does not provide a conceptually adequate measure of the ability of capital goods to contribute to production.

AN ALTERNATIVE APPROACH

To provide a measure of capital input that reflects the productivity of capital goods, it is necessary to answer the questions, what is capital input? what is the price of capital? The answers to these questions are intimately related since it is necessary to aggregate over different kinds of capital to obtain the quantity and price of capital input. To perform this aggregation correctly, prices and quantities of capital input for each kind of capital are required. The values of the capital services must be added together to obtain total capital input in current prices. A deflator constructed as an index of capital service prices must be applied to the capital input in current prices to obtain an index of real capital input. Conceptually, this problem is identical to that of measuring real labor input. Denison [3] and Kendrick [4] have made important contributions to the measurement of real labor input. The problem to be posed is the construction of an analogous measure of real capital input. The two measures of real-factor input may then be combined into a set of real factor accounts, corresponding to the familiar real-product accounts.[5]

If capital services were bought and sold by distinct economic units in the same way as labor services, there would be no conceptual or

[3] E. Denison, *The Sources of Economic Growth in the United States and the Alternatives Before Us,* Supplementary Paper No. 13, New York, Committee for Economic Development, 1962.

[4] John W. Kendrick, *Productivity Trends in the United States,* Princeton for NBER, 1961.

[5] Factor accounts are usually given only in current prices; implicit in any study of total factor productivity is a set of factor accounts in constant prices.

empirical difference between the construction of a quantity index of total capital input and the construction of the corresponding index of total labor input. Beginning with data on the value of transactions in each type of capital service, this value could be separated into a price of capital service or rental and a quantity of capital service in, say, machine-hours. These data would correspond to the value of transactions in each type of labor service, which could be separated into a price of labor service or wage and a quantity of labor service in, say, man-hours. A quantity index of total capital input would be constructed from the quantities of each type of capital service, using the relative shares of the rental value of each capital service in the rental value of all capital services as weights.

The measurement of capital services is less straightforward than the measurement of labor services because the consumer of a capital service is usually also the supplier of the service; the whole transaction is recorded only in the internal accounts of individual economic units. The obstacles to extracting this information for purposes of social accounting are almost insuperable; the information must be obtained by a relatively lengthy chain of indirect inference. The data with which the calculation begins are the values of transactions in new investment goods, just as in Kendrick's construction of an index of real capital stock. These values must be separated into a price and quantity of investment goods. Second, the quantity of new investment goods reduced by the quantity of old investment goods replaced must be added to the accumulated stocks. The third step in this procedure is to calculate the quantity of capital services corresponding to each stock. In the measurement of capital it is conventional to assume that capital services are proportional to capital stock. Where independent data on the rates of utilization of capital are available, this assumption may be dispensed with.

Paralleling the calculation of quantities of capital services beginning with the quantities of new investment goods, the prices of capital services must be calculated beginning with the prices of new investment goods. Finally, a quantity index of total capital input must be constructed from the quantities of each type of capital service, using the relative shares of the implicit rental value of each capital service in the implicit rental value of all capital services as weights. The implicit rental value of each capital service is obtained by simply multiplying the quantity of that service by the corresponding price. At this stage the construction of a quantity index of total capital input is formally identical with the construction of a quantity index of total labor input or total output. The chief difference between the construction of price and quantity indexes of total capital input and any other aggregation problem is in the circuitous route by which the necessary data are obtained.

In effect, Kendrick assumes that the price of capital services is proportional to the price of the corresponding investment good for all types of stock—land, buildings, equipment, and inventories. This assumption is invalid so long as different depreciation rates and rates of capital gain or loss prevail for different classes of assets. As we shall see, the calculation of a conceptually correct index of capital input requires precisely the same data as those employed by Kendrick so that the assumption of proportionality between capital service prices and investment goods prices may be dispensed with.

The following notation is used to represent the capital accounts which provide the basis for measuring total capital input:

I_k—quantity of output of the kth investment good,
K_k—quantity of input of the kth capital service,
q_k—price of the kth investment good,
p_k—price of the kth capital service.

Under the assumption that the proportion of an investment replaced in a given interval of time declines exponentially, the cumulated stock of past investments in the kth capital good, net of replacements, satisfies the well-known relationship:

$$I_k = \dot{K}_k + \delta_k K_k, \tag{1}$$

where δ_k is the instantaneous rate of replacement of the kth investment good. Similarly, in the absence of direct taxation the price of the kth capital service satisfies the relationship:

$$p_k = q_k \left[r + \delta_k - \frac{\dot{q}_k}{q_k} \right], \tag{2}$$

where r is the rate of return on all capital, δ_k is the rate of replacement of the kth investment good, and $\dot{q}_k/q_k$ is the rate of capital gain on that good. Given these relationships between the price and quantity of investment goods and the price and quantity of the corresponding capital services, the only data beyond values of transactions in new investment goods required for the construction of price and quantity indexes of total capital input are rates of replacement for each distinct investment good and the rate of return on all capital. We turn now to the problem of measuring the rate of return.

First, to measure the values of output and input it is customary to exclude the value of capital gains from the value of input rather than to include the value of such gains in the value of output. This convention has the virtue that the value of output may be calculated directly from the values of transactions. Second, to measure total factor productivity, depreciation is frequently excluded from both input and output; this convention is adopted, for example, by Kendrick.[6] Exclusion of depreciation on capital introduces an entirely arbitrary distinction between labor input and capital input, since the corresponding exclusion of depreciation of the stock of labor services is not carried out.[7] To calculate the rate of return on all capital, I subtract from the value of output plus capital gains the value of labor input and of replacement. This results in the rate of return multiplied by the value of accumulated stocks. The rate of return is calculated by dividing this quantity by the value of the stock.[8] The implicit rental value of the kth capital good is:

$$p_k K_k = q_k \left[r + \delta_k - \frac{\dot{q}_k}{q_k} \right] K_k.$$

To calculate price and quantity indexes for total capital input, the prices and quantities of each type of capital service are aggregated, using the relative shares of the implicit rental value of each capital service in the implicit rental value of all capital services as weights.

I have outlined a method for computing the price of capital services in the absence of direct taxation of business income. In the presence of direct taxes we may distinguish between the price of capital services before and after taxes. The expression given above for the price of capital services is the price after taxes. The price of capital services before taxes is:

[6] Kendrick, *Productivity Trends.*

[7] This point is made by Evsey Domar, "On the Measurement of Technological Change," *Economic Journal,* December 1961, pp. 709–729.

[8] The procedure proposed by Domar, *ibid.,* p. 717, n. 3, fails to correct for capital gains. Implicitly, Domar is assuming either no capital gains or that all capital gains are included in the value of output, whether realized or not.

$$p_k = q_k\left[\frac{1-uv}{1-u}r + \frac{1-uw}{1-u}\delta_k - \frac{1-ux}{1-u}\frac{\dot{q}_k}{q_k}\right],$$

where u is the rate of direct taxation, v the proportion of return to capital allowable as a charge against income for tax purposes, w the proportion of replacement allowable for tax purposes, and x the proportion of capital gains included in income for tax purposes.

I estimate the variables describing the tax structure as follows: The rate of direct taxation is the ratio of profits tax liability to profits before taxes. The proportion of the return to capital allowable for tax purposes is the ratio of net interest to the total return to capital. Total return to capital is the after tax rate of return, r, multiplied by the current value of capital stock. The proportion of replacement allowable for tax purposes is the ratio of capital consumption allowances to the current value of replacement. The proportion of capital gains included in income is zero by the conventions of the U.S. national accounts. Given the value of direct taxes, the after tax rate of return is estimated by subtracting from the value of output plus capital gains the value of labor input, replacement, and direct taxes. This results in the total return to capital. The rate of return is calculated by dividing this quantity by the current value of the stock of capital. Given data on the rate of return and the variables describing the tax structure, the price of capital services before taxes is calculated for each investment good.[9] These prices of capital services may be used in calculating indexes of capital input, total input, and total factor productivity.

DOES IT MATTER?

We have presented two alternative approaches to the measurement of capital input. In both approaches the value of gross property compensation is taken as given. Both approaches employ data on investment in each type of capital good and deflators for each good together with data on gross property compensation to obtain a measure of capital input. Given data on taxation of income from capital, the measurement of capital service prices before taxes is feasible. The sum of the products of these service prices and the corresponding quantities of capital services must add up to gross property compensation. The economic theory of capital suggests a price for capital services that is a weighted

[9] Further details are given in Zvi Griliches and D. Jorgenson, "The Explanation of Productivity Change," *Review of Economic Studies,* July 1967, pp. 249–283; see especially the Statistical Appendix.

TABLE 1

Index of Total Factor Productivity, 1945–65
(1958 =1.000)

Year	Kendrick Measure of Capital Input and Analogous Measure of Labor Input (1)	Column 1 Adjusted for Utilization Rates (2)	Griliches–Jorgenson Measure of Capital Input (3)
1945	.913	.968	1.030
1950	.922	.963	.992
1955	1.016	1.023	1.032
1960	1.061	1.046	1.040
1965	1.209	1.172	1.157

sum of the cost of capital, the rate of replacement, and capital losses. This price will be proportional to the price of investment goods only if rates of replacement and capital gain or loss are the same for all capital goods. Kendrick's method for measuring capital input is based on the assumption that service prices and investment goods prices are proportional. The method which Griliches and I developed dispenses with this invalid assumption.

Now that I have compared the two alternative approaches to the measurement of capital input from the theoretical point of view, one may ask, does the difference between the two approaches matter empirically? To answer this question I offer some results from a recent study of growth in total factor productivity in the United States, beginning in 1945.[10] In the accompanying table three alternative indexes of total factor productivity are presented. The first index employs a Kendrick-type measure of capital input and the corresponding index of labor input. The second adjusts both labor and capital for rates of utilization; employment is converted to man-hours while numbers of machines are converted to machine-hours. Finally, the third index replaces capital goods prices by capital service prices in the measurement of capital input. This index employs measures of both capital input and labor input that conform to the principles outlined

[10] *Ibid.*

above. The growth in real product unexplained by growth in real input is reduced from 1.41 per cent per year in the first index to .96 per cent per year in the second index and, finally, to .58 per cent per year in the third index. I conclude that errors in the measurement of capital input are extremely important in the measurement of real input and, hence, in the measurement of real factor productivity. The correct measurement of capital input does matter empirically for real factor accounting, for studies of total factor productivity, and for studies of production functions. For all these reasons the conceptually correct method of measuring capital input, based on capital service prices rather than capital goods prices, is to be preferred.

Changing Factor Shares by Industry: Factor Prices and Factor Substitutions

ALVIN C. EGBERT
U.S. DEPARTMENT OF AGRICULTURE

According to Scitovsky, writing in 1964, "The theory of income distribution is in a highly unsatisfactory state" [19, p. 15].[1] No evidence of improvement in the theory since that time has been found. Moreover, this paper makes no claim to improve it. Here data are presented that indicate that factor shares have changed since the end of World War II. Relationships are derived which help to throw some light on the so-called mystery of changing or unchanging factor shares. These relationships are used to explain and measure some of the shifts that have taken place. Some suggestions for future investigation of factor shares grow out of this appraisal.

It is relevant to ask why there is such great concern with the distribution of factor shares. One reason is that the need to explain is at the heart of all scientific inquiry. Brown suggests another reason for investigating functional income distribution [3, p. 180].

> Stated simply, the question of relative shares is important because it represents the relative pay-off to various groups that is usually associated with their relative contribution to production. It is the end result of all their productive efforts; for once their productive efforts are established their relative remuneration is determined and only an extraneous force can alter the final distribution. In this sense a factor's relative income share is a variable of last resort. Hence, the question of shares is at the centre of controversy between certain pressure groups, and motivates the appeals to

[1] Numbers in square brackets refer to literature cited in the bibliography at the end of this paper.

NOTE: I wish to acknowledge the helpful comments and suggestions of my colleagues, R. F. Daly, Shlomo Reutlinger, William Mo, and John Layng, who contributed much to the development of this paper. They, of course, should not be held responsible for its defects.

political bodies to effectuate policies that alter the functional (and size) distribution of income. This in itself is sufficient justification for their examination.

The implication of this statement seems to be that all the economist needs to do is determine the factors' relative contribution, presumably on the basis of neoclassical theory, and then confront various groups with this evidence in settling disputes over distributive shares. But this is a gross oversimplification because marginal theory, as a basis for specifying income distribution, has numerous defects. First, in a dynamic economy the marginal conditions will never be satisfied. Second, if they were satisfied the economist could only grossly approximate them. Third, factor ownership is a function of past income distributions which may not have been desirable. Marginal theory may be a good frame of reference for thinking about economic systems and for specifying economic efficiency under certain conditions, but that is about all.

A more realistic reason for investigating income distribution is the relationship between income distribution and economic growth. Income could be distributed according to marginal-productivity criteria and yet the rate of growth may be lower than some feasible and desirable level. (A desirable growth rate as used here is one for which society would express a preference and for which it would also be willing to provide the necessary savings.)

Much empirical research attempting to explain changes in factor shares has been based on neoclassical theory and has dealt primarily with estimation of aggregate production functions. Early investigations assumed that the aggregate production function of an economy was characterized by an elasticity of substitution between factors of one and constant returns to scale. This approach was taken because of the apparent constancy of shares in aggregative data. More recent investigations have been directed toward fitting production functions in which elasticity of substitution is a parameter to be estimated [3, 11, 12, 17, 21]. If the estimated elasticity parameter is not unity, then changing factor shares would be expected over time.

There are at least three possible defects in the aggregate production function approach to changing factor shares. First, there is the well-known aggregation problem. Certainly aggregate production functions for a total economy do not represent homogeneous firms. Consequently, all that these functions can tell us is the average relationships between inputs and outputs for the total firms in the economy, averages for firms that range all the way from marginal to highly efficient. Thus, they can tell us very little about the basic forces affecting factor shares. Second, even if these aggregate production functions summarize relationships for a set of homogeneous firms, it is not likely, given the dynamic environment of industry, that factor use even approximates the marginal-productivity conditions. Empirical investigations by aggregate production functions support this contention. Furthermore, no studies have been noted demonstrating that entrepreneurs think in the terms of marginal economics as assumed under neoclassical theory. Third, aggregate production function investigations usually assume constant returns to scale. But according to the well-known Eurler theorem, the product is completely allocated by the marginal productivities if, and only if, constant returns to scale exist. If returns to scale are greater than unity, the firm owner or the corporation obtains a residual income. If returns to scale are less than one, the firm gets less than the so-called fair share. Consequently, changing factor shares under neoclassical theory are possible with changing returns to scale over time. But to our knowledge, this possible explanation of changing factor shares has not been investigated. For reasons stated above, however, analysis of this type is not recommended.

Other analyses of the factor shares, theoretical and empirical, have been macroeconomic in nature [8, 9, 13] or deviants from the neoclassical tradition [10]. By their own admission these studies, too, leave much of the relevant factor share theory to be uncovered.

In this paper none of these approaches is followed. However, an attempt is made to relate factor shares to a micro-analytical framework, which then is related to national income accounts.

Factor Shares and the Firm

Consider first a firm's profit or loss equation (1).

$$O_{it}P_{it} \equiv W_{it}L_{it} + G_{it}g_{it} + K_{it} + T_{it}O_{it} + \pi_{it} \tag{1}$$

where O_{it} = output of firm i at time t

P_{it} = price of O_{it} per unit

W_{it} = average wage rate paid by firm

L_{it} = total labor input in hours

G_{it} = total goods and services used to produce current output

g_{it} = average price of goods and services purchased

K_{it} = depreciation of plant and equipment and other fixed costs
T_{it} = indirect business tax per unit of output
π_{it} = residual income or profit before taxes

After some manipulation we have,

$$\frac{\pi_{it}}{O_{it}P_{it}} \equiv 1 - \frac{L_{it}W_{it}}{O_{it}P_{it}} - \frac{G_{it}g_{it}}{O_{it}P_{it}} - \frac{K_{it}}{O_{it}P_{it}} - \frac{T_{it}O_{it}}{O_{it}P_{it}} \tag{2}$$

This is the old standby profit-sales ratio which is used as a test of efficiency by many firms and also is a standard analysis ratio used in accounting circles.

Multiplying through by

$$\frac{O_{it}P_{it}}{O_{it}P_{it} - G_{it}g_{it}}$$

we have

$$\frac{\pi_{it}}{O_{it}P_{it} - G_{it}g_{it}} \equiv 1 - \frac{L_{it}W_{it}}{O_{it}P_{it} - G_{it}g_{it}} - \frac{K_{it}}{O_{it}P_{it} - G_{it}g_{it}} - \frac{T_{it}O_{it}}{O_{it}P_{it} - G_{it}g_{it}} \tag{3}$$

The denominator of each of the terms in Equation 3 is, of course, the gross product of the firm as used in national income accounts. Equations 2 and 3 can be converted into the labor and nonlabor share of total value of product (sales) or gross product by appropriate manipulations.

We see from Equations 2 and 3 that any action taken to increase the profit-sales ratio will also increase the profit-GNP ratio. How a firm might go about increasing the profit–sales ratio would depend on its market environment, i.e., monopoly, monopsony, pure competition.[2]

Firms in competitive markets, we usually assume, must take factor and product prices as given. The alternatives open to them for increasing the profit-sales ratio will only involve labor-output, variable capital-output and fixed capital-output ratios. The firm would, presumably, want to make all of these ratios as small as possible for each

[2] It is not assumed that the firm maximizes the ratio, but only that it will take any action which appears to increase the ratio. The knowledge and information required for maximization are too great. If maximization is assumed, we should revert to neoclassical theory.

level of output. However, on considering alternative production techniques and technologies, this will not always be possible. Consequently, a firm presumably would consider alternative techniques as to their net impact on the profit-sales ratio.

Firms having some degree of monopoly power may choose to influence product or factor prices or both. This could be achieved either through advertising or bargaining. It seems reasonable that some firms can, and do, increase their profit-sales ratio by raising product prices and driving down the prices of purchased inputs. However, it may not be possible for a firm to reduce wages, even in a contracting economy. But in an economy of generally rising prices it may be able to hold wages constant or below the growth rate of general prices.

If it can be assumed that fixed and variable nonlabor costs are always proportional to value of output, then the profit-sales ratio is increased by reducing the labor share, as shown in Equation 2. This can be accomplished by one or all of four alternatives—decreasing labor inputs, decreasing wages, increasing output, and increasing product prices under the constraints mentioned above. Wages and prices, as already noted, can be modified independently of the production levels. Labor inputs can be reduced in some cases by changing production techniques, which may or may not require increased capital inputs. Similarly, output can be increased by changing production techniques without necessarily increasing inputs. Many such changes can be effected only over time as equipment wears out or becomes obsolete and employees can be trained or employees with the necessary skills hired. The specific strategy a firm might follow, given the profit-sales ratio as a decision guide, is not at all certain and may vary from firm to firm depending on the technologies available and on the products produced.

The profit-sales ratio is just one of a number of alternatives that may have some role in firm decision making. Another is the profit-capital ratio. However, the profit-sales ratio is cited as being the most prevalent [7, p. 1]. The above derivation is used as a means for developing a hypothesis about changing factor shares. No attempt is made to prove its general applicability.

Before proceeding to the analysis of factor shares, I relate this framework to national income accounts since all analysis is in terms of these accounts.

Factor Shares in Gross National Product Accounts

First, let us assume that the proper aggregations over firms have been performed. Then, omitting time subscripts,

O_j = the physical output of industry j
P_j = average price per unit of output of industry j
W_j = the average wage rate per hour of labor in industry j
L_j = labor input in man-hours in industry j
$\bar{G}_j$ = value of goods and services used in industry j to produce output O_j[3]
$\bar{K}_j$ = depreciation of plant and equipment and other fixed costs
T_j = indirect business taxes
π_j = residual income, or profit before taxes, in industry j

For simplification let us assume that there are just two industries, $j = 1, 2$, and that each product can be used as either a producer or consumer good. We can now form two identity equations

$$(4) \qquad O_1P_1 \equiv W_1L_1 + \bar{G}_1 + \bar{K}_1 + T_1 + \pi_1$$

$$(5) \qquad O_2P_2 \equiv W_2L_2 + \bar{G}_2 + \bar{K}_2 + T_2 + \pi_2$$

Further we define

$$(6) \qquad \bar{G}_1 \equiv C_2O_2P_2$$

$$(7) \qquad \bar{G}_2 \equiv C_1O_1P_1$$

Then substituting Equations 6 and 7 in 4 and 5 we have

$$(8) \qquad (O_1P_1 - C_2O_2P_2) \equiv W_1L_1 + K_1 + T_1 + \pi_1$$

$$(9) \qquad (O_2P_2 - C_1O_1P_1) \equiv W_2L_2 + K_2 + T_2 + \pi_2$$

The left side of Equations 8 and 9 represents industry GNP. Then aggregating Equations 4 and 5,

$$(10) \quad (1 - C_1)\,O_1P_1 + (1 - C_2)\,O_2P_2 \equiv W_1L_1 + W_2L_2 + \bar{K}_1 + \bar{K}_2 + T_1 + T_2 + \pi_1 + \pi_2$$

The left side of Equation 10 represents the value of final goods and services produced in the economy or total GNP. Dividing each right side of Equations 8, 9 and 10 by the left results in,

[3] $\bar{G}_j$ is used here to represent value, cf. pp. 187–188.

$$1 \equiv \frac{W_1L_1}{(O_1P_1 - C_2O_2P_2)} + \frac{\bar{K}_1 + T_1 + \pi_1}{(O_1P_1 - C_2O_2P_2)} \tag{11}$$

$$1 \equiv \frac{W_2L_2}{(O_2P_2 - C_1O_1P_1)} + \frac{\bar{K}_2 + T_2 + \pi_2}{(O_2P_2 - C_1O_1P_1)} \tag{12}$$

$$1 \equiv \frac{W_1L_1 + W_2L_2}{(1 - C_1)O_1P_1 + (1 - C_2)O_2P_2} + \frac{\bar{K}_1 + \bar{K}_2 + T_1 + T_2 + \pi_1 + \pi_2}{(1 - C_1)O_1P_1 + (1 - C_2)O_2P_2} \tag{13}$$

The first term of Equations 11, 12, and 13 is, of course, the labor share of value added or GNP. The second term on the right is the nonlabor share or capital, rent, and profit share. (The term profit is used here to mean a return greater than total costs.) Equations 11 and 12 show that even though labor, wages, output, and prices change at the same rates, the labor share can increase or decrease if the ratio between nonlabor variable inputs and value of output changes over time. (Such a change has occurred in agriculture, but it has been more than offset by increases in the agricultural wage bill. The hired labor force in agriculture has declined very rapidly in the post-World War II period, but wages have increased relatively more.) Equation 13 indicates that if C_1 and C_2—the proportion of intermediate goods used up in the production process—increase or decrease, the labor share can change over time even though growth in the wage bill and value of output remain the same.

The customary procedure of considering only the labor share and nonlabor share is used in the analysis which follows. Because (1) changes in one of these shares imply offsetting changes in the other and (2) because of lack of data on capital inputs, only changes in the labor share are analyzed.

Labor Share of Gross National Product by Industry Since World War II

Total employee compensation as a percentage of gross national product (labor share) has increased moderately since World War II. It trended upward from about 55 per cent in 1947 to 58 per cent in 1957, but has changed little since then. The labor share by industry, however, does not exhibit this general uptrend. In a number of industries the labor share has declined. But in a statistical sense, not all of these trends have been significant (Table 1). The downtrend in the labor share has been significant in coal mining, instruments, local and suburban passenger transportation, pipeline transportation and transportation services, telephone and telegraph, radio and television, auto repair and several miscellaneous groups.[4] On the other hand, the labor share has trended significantly upward in food, tobacco, fabricated metal, electrical machinery and miscellaneous manufacturing. But, the most significant uptrend in the labor share runs through the service group.

This simple trend analysis, summarized in Table 1, points up several things related to changing labor and other factor shares: (a) changes in labor's share of GNP have ranged from large declines to large increases, (b) these changes have not been consistent within industry groups, i.e., mining, construction, etc., and (c) the technological nature of the industry—as related to automation—appears to have had some influence on changing labor shares, cf., e.g., telephone and telegraph and services.

We now turn to some probings into explanation of trends in labor shares. First, let us consider the problem somewhat superficially. The labor share is given by the following identity:

$$LS_{jt} \equiv \frac{L_{jt}W_{jt}}{\bar{O}_{jt}P_{jt}} \tag{14}$$

where LS_{jt} = labor share in industry j at time t
L_{jt} = total labor input in hours
W_{jt} = average labor compensation per hour
$\bar{O}_{jt}$ = output[5]
P_{jt} = price per unit of output t[5]

Of course, changes in the labor share are affected by changes in each of the four variables in Equation 14, changing individually or col-

[4] The statistical significance of these trends is, of course, a function of the average change, the b value, and the consistency of the change, R^2. The labor share may have declined dramatically as indicated by the b value, but the decline is erratic, e.g., coal mining.

[5] Because of the nature of the data, output is gross output less intermediate goods used. See Equations 11 and 12. Price is the implicit price deflator which is a weighted average of product and intermediate goods prices. Available data indicate that product and intermediate goods prices are highly correlated for some industries.

TABLE 1

Average Annual Trend in Employee Compensation as Percentage of Gross National Product

Industry	Average Annual Trend[a]	T value	R^2
Agriculture, forestry, and fisheries	.095	1.78	.17
Farms	.007	.23	.00
Agricultural services, forestry and fisheries	.077	2.02	.21
Total mining	-.453	-7.05	.77
Metal	.721	2.61	.31
Coal	-.608	-3.15	.40
Crude petroleum and natural gas	.062	1.62	.15
Nonmetallic	.377	2.88	.36
Contract construction	.505	7.78	.80
Total manufacturing	.216	3.35	.43
Total nondurable goods	.130	2.24	.25
Food	.332	4.83	.61
Tobacco	.115	4.05	.52
Textile	.276	1.44	.12
Apparel	.121	1.46	.12
Paper	.558	4.66	.59
Printing	.107	1.98	.21
Chemicals	.240	2.15	.24
Petroleum refining	-.315	-1.13	.08
Rubber	-.075	-.57	.02
Leather	.199	1.12	.08
Total durable goods	.229	2.45	.29
Lumber	.116	1.19	.09
Furniture	.217	2.90	.36
Stone, clay, and glass	-.082	-.72	.03
Primary metals	.311	2.15	.24
Fabricated metals	.350	3.26	.42
Machinery, except electric	.183	1.92	.20
Electrical machinery	.549	5.05	.63
Transportation equipment, except motor vehicles	-.004	-.03	.00
Motor vehicles	-.169	-.75	.04
Instruments	-.595	-6.70	.75
Miscellaneous manufacturing	.332	4.20	.54

(continued)

TABLE 1 (continued)

Industry	Average Annual Trend[a]	*T* value	R^2
Total transportation	.136	2.18	.24
Railroads	.243	2.58	.31
Local and suburban passenger	-.462	-10.33	.88
Motor freight	.510	11.90	.90
Water	.484	1.82	.18
Air	.325	1.91	.20
Pipeline	-.646	-3.83	.49
Services	-.307	-3.84	.50
Total communication	-.998	-12.75	.92
Telephone and telegraph	-1.023	-12.44	.91
Radio and television	-1.112	-10.55	.88
Electric, gas, and sanitary	-.617	-13.93	.93
Total trade	.351	8.90	.84
Wholesale	.141	2.36	.27
Retail	.494	11.58	.90
Total finance, insurance, and real estate	.036	1.96	.20
Banking	.083	1.11	.08
Security brokers	-.403	-1.36	.11
Insurance carriers	.906	3.71	.48
Insurance agents	.182	1.61	.15
Real estate	.123	12.07	.91
Total services	.111	6.25	.72
Hotels	.144	2.95	.37
Personal	-.113	-2.86	.35
Miscellaneous business	.284	4.19	.54
Auto repair	-.747	-6.65	.75
Miscellaneous repairs	.555	4.39	.56
Motion pictures	1.174	5.00	.63
Commencements	.177	4.51	.58
Medical	.548	7.92	.81
Legal	.292	6.86	.76
Educational	.208	4.22	.54
Nonprofit membership organizations	-.163	-9.02	.84
Miscellaneous professional	.407	3.99	.51

(continued)

TABLE 1 (concluded)

Industry	Average Annual Trend[a]	T value	R^2
Total government	-.015	-.44	.01
Federal	.148	1.93	.20
Federal enterprises	1.911	1.19	.09
State and local	.034	2.50	.29
State and local enterprises	-.234	-3.44	.44
Rest of the world	-.054	-7.13	.77

[a]Least squares regression coefficient (b) from equation $Y = a + bT$. The regression log $Y = a + bT$ gave similar results, therefore it is not shown. To reduce the influence of the World War II, only 1948 through 1964 data were used.

lectively. In most instances, all variables change but not in the same direction or at the same rates. It is obvious from Equation 14 that the labor share depends on the relative rates of growth in each of the four factors. Increases in the labor input and the wages have a positive effect on the labor share, *ceteris paribus*. In contrast, increases in output and product prices reduce the labor share, *ceteris paribus*.

Because of a lack of comparable data, relative changes in these factors could only be analyzed for thirty-one industries. The annual growth rates for labor, wages, output and prices for these industries are presented in Table 2.

Growth rates of factors which directly affect the labor share differ significantly among industries, as shown in Table 2. Annual growth in labor use ranges from -4.5 per cent in local and suburban transportation to 3 per cent in motor freight and warehousing.[6] Other industries such as crude petroleum and natural gas, leather and leather products, primary metals and telephone and telegraph show small rates of change in labor use over the 1947–64 period.

Growth and changes in wage rates, as is to be expected, exhibit less variation than labor use, growth is positive throughout, and the

[6] Growth as used here is $r \times 100$ where r is from the formula $A_{t+n} = A_{t+o}(1 + r)^n$.

TABLE 2

Average Annual Growth Rates of Factors Affecting Labor's Share of Gross National Product, Selected Industries, 1948 to 1964[a]

(per cent)

Industry	Labor	Average Compensation Per Hour	Output	Price
Total mining	-2.1	4.1	2.1	0.9
Metal	-1.4	5.8	2.1	0.1
Crude petroleum and natural gas	0.6	4.2	3.0	1.7
Mining and quarrying of nonmetallic minerals, except fuels	1.6	5.2	4.7	1.3
Contract construction	2.0	4.8	2.8	3.2
Total nondurable goods	0.4	4.6	3.3	1.4
Food and kindred products	-0.4	5.3	2.5	1.5
Tobacco manufactures	-1.2	0.7	0.3	1.5
Textile mill products	-2.2	3.0	1.7	1.3
Apparel and other finished products made from fabrics and similar material	0.9	2.5	2.5	0.3
Paper and allied products	1.8	5.1	4.1	2.1
Printing, publishing, and allied industries	1.6	4.5	0.6	2.7
Chemicals and allied products	2.2	5.5	6.8	0.4
Petroleum refining and related industries	-1.1	5.7	3.5	1.6
Rubber and miscellaneous plastic products	2.6	6.9	4.6	2.9
Leather and leather products	-0.7	3.8	0.0	3.0
Total durable goods	1.5	5.3	3.9	2.4
Lumber and wood products, except furniture	-1.9	4.4	1.8	0.6
Furniture and fixtures	1.0	4.2	2.2	2.6
Stone, clay, and glass products	0.9	4.6	3.2	2.6
Primary metal industries	-0.1	5.7	0.8	4.4
Fabricated metal products[a]	1.3	4.6	3.6	1.9

(continued)

TABLE 2 (concluded)

Industry	Labor	Average Compensation Per Hour	Output	Price
	%	%	%	%
Machinery, except electrical	1.6	4.9	3.3	3.0
Electrical machinery, equip. and supplies	3.7	4.8	7.5	0.5
Transportation equipment, except motor vehicles	2.0	9.8	8.8	3.0
Motor vehicles	0.0	6.5	4.6	1.7
Instruments[a]	2.8	5.8	6.3	3.0
Miscellaneous manufacturing industries	-0.3	4.5	2.5	1.1
Railroads	-4.4	4.9	0.0	0.2
Local and surburban transit and interurban passenger transportation	-4.5	6.0	-4.7	6.9
Motor freight and warehousing	3.0	5.5	5.9	1.6
Telephone and telegraph	0.6	5.2	6.8	1.5
Electric, gas, and sanitary	1.0	5.4	7.1	1.2
Wholesale trade	1.6	4.6	4.5	1.2
Retail trade	1.1	4.4	3.0	1.4

[a]See appendix table for definitions.

variance over all industries is 1.5. The lowest rate of increase took place in the apparel industry—2.5 per cent—and the highest in transportation equipment, except motor vehicles—9.8 per cent. However, the extreme rate of increase in the latter is probably explained by the lag in growth of the aircraft industry following World War II and its subsequent resurgence during the Korean conflict. The explanation could also lie in data problems. Transportation equipment aside, wage rates rose most in tobacco manufactures—7.0 per cent.

Differences in output growth by industries were considerable in the post-World War II period, ranging from −4.7 per cent for local and suburban transportation to 8.8 per cent for transportation equipment, except motor vehicles. As noted above, growth in wage rates in the latter industry, this growth rate may be distorted by the period of measurement and unrepresentative of secular growth. Other industries showing growth rates in GNP of over 6 per cent are chemicals, electrical machinery, instruments, telephone and telegraph, and electric, gas, and sanitary. The variance of the growth rates for all industries listed is 6.5.

Price changes, as measured by the GNP price deflator, showed a little more variation than wage rates—the variance of this set being 1.8. Prices increased only 0.2 per cent per year for railroads, but 6.9 per cent for local and suburban transit. Primary metals and contract construction were two other industries for which prices rose rapidly—4.4 per cent and 3.2 per cent, respectively.

Note that industries in which the labor share has declined are either high growth industries—instruments, telephone and telegraph, radio and television, electric, gas, and sanitary, and pipelines—or declining industries—coal mining, local transportation, and transportation services. This fact seems to imply that with high rates of growth an industry may be able to extract an increasing share of the income pie, at least for an intermediate period of time. On the other hand, a decreasing labor share in a declining industry may indicate a lack of mobility in the labor force. However, this is not a possible explanation for the decreasing share in local transportation. Because the labor input and output in this industry declined at about the same rate, the declining labor share resulted from the fact that net prices increased faster than wages, as shown in Table 2.

As just noted, to explain net changes in the labor share, changes in each of the four factors impinging on the labor share must be considered simultaneously. The net impacts of labor use, wages, output, and prices on the labor share can be specified with a little mathematical manipulation. First, Equation 14 is written in logarithmic form:

$$\log LS_t = \log L_t + \log W_t - \log O_t - \log P_t \tag{15}$$

and

$$\log LS_{t+1} = \log L_{t+1} + \log W_{t+1} - \log O_{t+1} - \log P_{t+1} \tag{16}$$

Taking the difference of Equations 15 and 16 we have,

$$\Delta \log LS = \Delta \log L + \Delta \log W - \Delta \log O - \Delta \log P \tag{17}$$

and dividing through by Δ log *LS*, the relative influence of each factor on the change in the labor share can be obtained.

$$(18)\qquad 1 = \frac{\Delta \log L}{\Delta \log LS} + \frac{\Delta \log W}{\Delta \log LS} - \frac{\Delta \log O}{\Delta \log LS} - \frac{\Delta \log P}{\Delta \log LS}$$

Equation 18 can be used to distribute the percentage change in the labor share by multiplying each term of Equation 14 by the percentage change in the labor share. Let

$$\frac{\Delta LS\ 100}{LS} = y$$

then

$$(19)\qquad y = y\frac{\Delta \log L}{\Delta \log LS} + y\frac{\Delta \log W}{\Delta \log LS} - y\frac{\Delta \log O}{\Delta \log LS} - y\frac{\Delta \log P}{\Delta \log LS}$$

Each term of Equation 19 can be interpreted as the contribution of each variable to specified changes in the labor share when the net change in the labor share is allocated approximately on the basis of the relative elasticities.[7]

While the labor share has been changing industry by industry in the post-World War II period, these changes have been by no means smooth or always in the same direction, as shown in Table 3. (Averages for 1948–50, 1955–57, and 1962–64 were used to make comparisons of changes in the labor share over the postwar period and between industries. Three-year averages were used to even out short-term fluctuations, and 1947 was omitted because World War II apparently was still significantly affecting the labor share.)

The apparent declining labor share in all mining is something of a hybrid. Although not shown in Table 3, part of the indicated decline is

[7] As pointed out by the discussant, Dr. Liu, given

$$\log LS = \log W + \log L - \log O - \log P$$

the time derivative is

$$\frac{1}{LS}\frac{dLS}{dt} = \frac{1}{W}\frac{dW}{dt} - \frac{1}{L}\frac{dL}{dt} - \frac{1}{O}\frac{dO}{dt} - \frac{1}{P}\frac{dP}{dt}$$

But this differential equation is approximate and only satisfactory for small changes, and it is equivalent to the analysis of rates of change discussed in the previous section. For the large changes in the labor share that are dealt with in this section, this method leaves a significant part of the change in the labor share unexplained or unallocated.

TABLE 3

Net Influence of Factors Affecting Labor's Share of Gross National Product, Selected Industries, 1948 to 1964 and Selected Subperiods

(per cent)

Industry	Period[a]	Labor	Wage	Output	Price	Change in Labor Share
Total mining	1	-7.4	33.6	-24.1	-12.7	-10.6
	2	-21.3	19.9	-4.6	0.4	-5.6
	3	-27.4	51.6	-27.7	-12.0	-15.6
Metal	1	7.2	58.8	-26.0	-29.3	10.7
	2	-29.1	24.2	-4.4	27.7	18.4
	3	-22.9	89.8	-33.0	-2.8	31.1
Crude petroleum and natural gas	1	24.9	34.0	-35.2	-19.4	4.3
	2	-15.0	24.7	-6.6	-4.2	-1.1
	3	9.3	59.2	-41.8	-23.6	3.1
Mining and quarrying of nonmetallic minerals, except fuels	1	16.8	46.6	-48.1	-10.8	4.5
	2	6.8	25.2	-17.8	-7.7	6.4
	3	24.1	73.3	-67.4	-18.8	11.2
Contract construction	1	34.1	47.4	-46.6	-23.0	11.9
	2	2.1	30.4	-3.6	-26.3	2.7
	3	29.5	70.5	-41.0	-46.6	12.4
Total nondurable goods	1	3.9	36.9	-25.0	-12.1	3.7
	2	0.8	27.2	-22.2	-7.3	-1.5
	3	4.6	63.8	-47.0	-19.3	2.1
Food and kindred products	1	-0.2	42.5	-22.2	-9.8	10.3
	2	-6.1	32.6	-12.9	-13.2	0.4
	3	6.5	76.2	-35.6	-23.4	10.7
Tobacco manufactures	1	-7.2	52.6	-11.8	-20.1	13.5
	2	-10.2	40.1	-29.2	-2.0	-1.3
	3	-18.0	94.5	-42.7	-21.9	11.9
Textile mill products	1	-20.4	20.6	-7.3	19.3	12.3
	2	-11.4	20.3	-17.0	0.0	-8.1
	3	-31.2	40.7	-24.6	18.3	3.2

(continued)

TABLE 3 (continued)

Industry	Period[a]	Labor	Wage	Output	Price	Change in Labor Share
Apparel and other finished products made from fabrics and similar materials	1	3.2	19.5	-15.5	-6.5	0.6
	2	8.8	16.9	-19.6	2.7	8.8
	3	12.2	37.4	-36.0	-4.1	9.5
Paper and allied products	1	18.0	36.0	-32.6	-22.9	-1.5
	2	7.0	35.0	-24.0	-5.4	12.6
	3	26.0	72.9	-58.3	-29.6	10.9
Printing, publishing, and allied industries	1	14.1	38.1	-26.2	-17.1	8.9
	2	8.5	23.7	-15.3	-21.4	-4.5
	3	22.2	61.1	-40.9	-38.3	4.1
Chemicals and allied products	1	22.3	45.3	-54.3	-7.9	5.4
	2	7.5	29.0	-37.2	2.0	1.3
	3	30.4	76.5	-94.4	-5.8	6.8
Petroleum refining and related products	1	6.6	44.7	-28.9	-14.4	8.0
	2	-19.9	31.4	-19.0	-7.5	-14.9
	3	14.5	74.1	-46.5	-21.1	-8.1
Rubber and miscellaneous plastic products	1	22.4	33.4	-26.2	-36.0	-6.3
	2	11.6	25.2	-35.6	-3.5	-2.2
	3	33.5	57.5	-60.4	-39.0	-8.4
Leather and leather products	1	-3.3	26.6	3.7	-26.1	0.9
	2	-6.0	24.8	-3.0	-13.9	1.9
	3	-9.7	52.9	0.6	-40.9	2.9
Total durable goods	1	21.8	43.4	-36.3	-25.5	3.4
	2	-0.4	30.1	-19.1	-9.8	0.8
	3	21.4	73.3	-55.3	-35.2	4.2
Lumber and wood products, except furniture	1	-12.9	41.8	-8.4	-14.4	6.1
	2	-13.9	19.5	-16.3	5.2	-5.4
	3	-26.8	60.6	-24.8	-8.7	0.3

(continued)

TABLE 3 (continued)

Industry	Period[a]	Labor	Wage	Output	Price	Change in Labor Share
Furniture and fixtures	1	7.6	37.0	-23.7	-19.8	1.2
	2	6.4	22.8	-7.9	-17.1	4.2
	3	13.9	59.5	-31.3	-36.7	5.4
Stone, clay, and glass products	1	11.1	34.7	-26.6	-27.9	-8.6
	2	1.2	26.6	-15.9	-9.3	2.7
	3	12.4	60.9	-42.3	-37.2	-6.1
Primary metal industries	1	10.9	46.4	-21.6	-40.4	-4.7
	2	-12.7	31.3	12.1	-20.0	10.8
	3	-0.8	79.1	-11.0	-61.8	5.5
Fabricated metal products[b]	1	18.0	39.4	-32.4	-19.2	5.8
	2	0.1	24.6	-18.4	-8.2	-1.9
	3	17.8	63.8	-50.6	-27.2	3.8
Machinery, except electrical	1	21.8	36.2	-29.6	-27.3	1.1
	2	-0.2	31.8	-17.1	-15.3	-0.8
	3	23.7	71.8	-49.7	-45.4	0.4
Electrical machinery, equipment and supplies	1	33.5	35.6	-57.1	-7.8	4.2
	2	18.5	32.8	-47.5	0.3	4.1
	3	52.6	69.2	-105.8	-7.5	8.4
Transportation equipment, except motor vehicles	1	43.6	84.2	-99.3	-29.3	-0.8
	2	-16.0	45.7	-17.8	-12.4	-0.5
	3	27.4	129.8	-116.8	-41.6	-1.3
Motor vehicles	1	8.3	52.0	-34.5	-21.5	4.3
	2	-9.2	35.4	-29.8	-3.0	-6.5
	3	-1.2	86.4	63.7	-23.9	-2.4
Instruments[c]	1	29.6	48.2	-55.8	-24.2	-2.2
	2	8.2	28.6	-27.8	-16.4	-7.4
	3	36.4	74.2	-80.7	-39.2	-9.4
Miscellaneous manufacturing industries	1	-2.7	42.3	-22.3	-8.4	8.9
	2	-2.1	22.2	-14.0	7.3	-1.2
	3	-4.8	64.6	-36.4	-15.7	7.7

(continued)

TABLE 3 (concluded)

Industry	Period[a]	Labor	Wage	Output	Price	Change in Labor Share
Railroads	1	-22.9	36.9	-2.4	-10.6	1.0
	2	-39.5	31.5	2.4	9.0	3.4
	3	-64.4	71.5	-0.2	-2.4	4.5
Local and surburban transit and interurban passenger transportation	1	-33.4	39.6	43.6	-52.3	-2.5
	2	-30.7	41.2	23.4	-40.5	-6.6
	3	-62.2	78.5	64.7	-89.9	-8.9
Motor freight and warehousing	1	26.6	46.6	-52.0	-15.5	5.6
	2	15.2	28.4	-32.7	-7.0	3.9
	3	42.6	76.5	-86.5	-23.0	9.7
Telephone and telegraph	1	13.6	34.9	-43.0	-14.0	-8.5
	2	-5.0	31.4	-40.3	-5.9	-19.8
	3	7.4	61.5	-77.3	-18.2	-26.6
Electric, gas, and sanitary	1	10.8	36.1	-52.6	-9.3	-15.0
	2	2.3	33.4	-36.8	-6.3	-7.4
	3	12.5	65.6	-84.8	-14.8	-21.4
Wholesale trade	1	12.9	35.3	-31.1	-13.3	3.8
	2	9.3	29.6	-32.2	-4.3	2.4
	3	22.2	64.9	-63.3	-17.6	6.2
Retail trade	1	10.7	32.6	-24.8	-7.4	11.2
	2	5.8	28.9	-18.5	-12.7	3.4
	3	17.2	64.3	-45.2	-21.1	15.1

[a] 1 = 1949-50 to 1955-57 period; 2 = 1955-57 to 1962-64 period; 3 = 1948-50 to 1962-64 period.

[b] Fabricated metal products, excluding ordnance machinery and transportation equipment.

[c] Instruments include professional, scientific, and controlling instruments; photographic and optical goods, watches and clocks.

due to an actual decline in the labor share in coal mining. But part of the measured decline is due to the rapid growth in crude petroleum and natural gas, which [1] now accounts for 71 per cent of total output of the mining sector compared with 65 per cent in 1947 and [2] the relatively small labor share in this industry. The reason for this elaboration is to point out that analysis of aggregates may lead to the wrong conclusions.

In some industries—crude petroleum and natural gas, tobacco manufactures, textiles, printing, fabricated metals, machinery, except electrical, and miscellaneous manufactures—the labor share declined in the last half of the period, even though for the entire period the general trend was up. On the other hand, in paper and allied products and primary metals, the labor share trended downward in the last half of the period even though the over-all trend was up. These examples point out only that the labor share is not stable, and that the trend may change direction within relatively short periods of time and probably reflects the effect of short-term shifts in market forces.

It is not possible at this stage to glean any general conclusions from these data. But several areas loom large as possible explanations for the changes in the labor share among industries. These are differential rates of growth in: (a) the demand for products, (b) the supply and demand for labor of various skills, and (c) technological developments.

Changes in factor share are the product of a very dynamic economy in which demand for many products has been increasing rapidly. An industry facing a rapidly expanding demand for its products may elect to increase output at constant prices or increase both output and prices. For example, output in telephone and telegraph, electric, gas and sanitary, instruments, transportation equipment, electrical machinery, and chemicals grew very rapidly, as shown in Table 2. Prices grew at an above average rate in transportation equipment and instruments, but at a below average rate for the telephone and telegraph, electric, gas and sanitary industries, and at a much below average rate for chemicals. But each of these rates of growth reflects a different degree of control over markets and prices. Decisions with respect to output, advertising, and prices, however, cannot be made without considering their impacts on labor, wage rates, and prices of raw materials and inputs. Increases in output may have various effects on wages, depending on the labor market faced by a particular industry.

In an economy of generally rising wages, an industry may need to increase wages even though it is unable to raise the prices of its products. Moreover, wages may be forced up by strong labor unions. But in planning over time, a firm or industry has the alternative of substituting technology and capital for labor—with or without changes in output. Moreover, an industry may be able to increase output without increasing its demand for labor or even its demand for capital. Data in previous tables point out that many determinative factors such as prices, wages, output, labor, and technology have changed across industries, though at differential rates, and result in various patterns of changing factor shares.

For example, in the telephone and telegraph and electric, gas and sanitary sectors, where the labor share has decreased in the post-World War II period, output has increased very rapidly and the labor-input has risen very slowly, but wage increases have remained near average. In spite of very rapid increases in output, prices were increased as fast as for some other industries which experienced slower growth in output, as shown in Table 2. Moreover, the net-output–labor ratio for these utilities increased much more rapidly than for all other industries analyzed, except transportation equipment, and the net-output–capital ratio declined slowly in spite of large applications of capital, as shown in Table 4.

Relative rates of change in the output-capital and capital-labor ratios are indicators of changes in productivity and technological advance. Available crude measures of productivity increases—as defined by Professor Kendrick [11]—have been greatest in the telephone and telegraph and electric, gas, and sanitary sectors. The replacement of the telephone operator by automatic switching systems has been one of the important factors increasing productivity in the telephone sector.

Summary and Conclusions

Quite a bit of kicking in the bushes has been done in hope that a white rabbit would jump out. If one has appeared it has been a gray one. The mystery of changing factor shares has not been solved, and it is not certain that much light has been shed on it.

A final decision must await considerable probing in depth—probing for the purpose of testing alternative hypotheses which may explain

TABLE 4

Average Annual Percentage Change in Output-Capital, Output-Labor, and Capital-Labor Ratios, 1948–50 to 1962–64

(per cent)

Industries	Output-Capital[a]	Output-Labor	Capital-Labor
Total mining	-2.89	4.35	7.35
Metal	-5.25	3.55	9.70
Crude petroleum and natural gas	-2.20	2.26	4.65
Mining and quarrying of nonmetallic minerals, except fuels	-3.10	2.96	6.23
Contract construction	-2.94	0.74	3.85
Total nondurable goods	-3.14	3.04	6.34
Food and kindred products	-2.15	2.98	5.05
Tobacco manufactures	-5.26	4.20	9.82
Textile mill products	-0.65	4.02	4.68
Apparel and other finished products made from fabrics and similar material	0.25	1.68	1.34
Paper and allied products	-4.35	2.25	6.97
Printing, publishing, and allied industries	-3.85	1.32	5.35
Chemicals and allied products	-2.88	4.55	7.57
Petroleum refining and related industries	-1.74	4.66	6.55
Rubber and miscellaneous plastic products	-4.34	2.04	6.65
Leather and leather products	-2.08	0.64	3.10
Total durable goods	-3.70	2.50	6.44
Lumber and wood products, except furniture	-1.29	3.78	5.00
Furniture and fixtures	-1.55	1.21	2.60
Stone, clay, and glass products	-5.68	2.25	8.81
Primary metal industries	-7.16	1.40	8.61
Fabricated metal products[b]	-3.09	2.35	5.56
Machinery, except electrical	-4.18	1.71	6.02
Electrical machinery, equipment, and supplies	-1.50	3.65	5.38
Transportation equipment, except motor vehicles	-3.36	5.97	9.69
Motor vehicles	-3.34	4.91	8.52
Instruments[b]	-8.50	3.39	13.02
Miscellaneous manufacturing industries	3.06	2.85	0.09

(continued)

TABLE 4 (concluded)

Industries	Output-Capital[a]	Output-Labor	Capital-Labor
Railroads	-4.06	4.55	8.89
Local and surburban transit and interurban passenger transportation	-4.44	-0.25	4.71
Motor freight and warehousing	0.09	3.01	2.95
Telephone and telegraph	-1.19	5.93	7.24
Electric, gas, and sanitary	-1.20	5.97	7.26
Wholesale trade	0.33	2.92	2.60
Retail trade	0.10	1.88	1.81

[a]Capital is the GNP capital consumption allowance deflated by the wholesale price index for producers' finished goods. For definitions of output and labor see appendix tables.

[b]See appendix tables for definitions.

changing factor shares industry by industry and for the economy as a whole. What we have observed in this chapter may be only an aggregative mirage—changing rates of internal growth. However, this is unlikely for the fairly homogeneous communications sector.

Analysis of the functional distribution of income must be built on a dynamic model. The long-run equilibrium concept is a never-never land that is only a beginning point—a point of departure—especially in growing capitalist economies. Such economies are in a continuous state of adjustment where the long-run equilibrium is always at least one step ahead. And so involved is the adjustment process that even if there were no "random shocks" impinging on the system, it might take a lifetime to reach the steady state.

The whole area of the changing quality of inputs, which is a facet of the technological development process, needs to be explored in depth. Both labor and capital inputs need to be measured in this dimension.

Ideally, we would like to specify and measure the relevant behavioral or supply and demand relations for each industry at a satisfactory level of disaggregation. In the first part of this paper, it was suggested that the profit-sales ratio might be a relevant model for initiating a study of

TABLE 5

Labor Use, Wages, Output and Prices, by Selected Industries, 1947 to 1964

Year	Labor[a]	Wage[b]	Output[c]	Price[d]	Labor[a]	Wage[b]	Output[c]	Price[d]
	Total Mining				*Metal Mining*			
1947	2,026	1.53	10,183	0.666	224	1.38	975	0.769
1948	2,037	1.77	10,733	0.863	230	1.53	1,006	0.957
1949	1,756	1.82	9,569	0.846	208	1.64	904	0.772
1950	1,775	1.97	10,677	0.860	212	1.75	1,042	0.978
1951	1,855	2.16	11,739	0.865	228	1.99	1,120	1.012
1952	1,803	2.28	11,652	0.865	227	2.22	1,034	0.911
1953	1,747	2.40	12,049	0.876	239	2.36	1,150	0.958
1954	1,588	2.39	11,656	0.929	211	2.42	941	1.146
1955	1,676	2.45	12,842	0.956	223	2.59	1,194	1.247
1956	1,744	2.69	13,570	0.986	238	2.76	1,258	1.296
1957	1,727	2.78	13,556	0.994	236	2.90	1,328	1.034
1958	1,519	2.83	12,359	1.000	187	2.98	1,096	1.000
1959	1,542	2.85	12,848	0.952	175	3.12	1,025	0.914
1960	1,496	2.94	13,141	0.970	204	3.18	1,286	0.988
1961	1,415	3.04	13,265	0.969	188	3.36	1,288	1.000
1962	1,382	3.18	13,579	0.956	178	3.47	1,295	0.893
1963	1,374	3.20	13,951	0.979	173	3.52	1,291	0.912
1964	1,379	3.33	14,378	0.989	183	3.49	1,350	0.967
	Crude Petroleum and Natural Gas				*Mining and Quarrying of Non-metallic Minerals, Except Fuels*			
1947	556	1.47	5,831	0.549	228	1.15	588	0.794
1948	606	1.66	6,428	0.778	229	1.27	639	0.883
1949	572	1.79	6,087	0.802	213	1.41	618	0.947
1950	581	1.85	6,667	0.785	217	1.56	706	0.953
1951	636	1.98	7,530	0.781	238	1.67	771	1.002
1952	678	2.12	7,777	0.808	242	1.80	806	0.988
1953	691	2.21	8,144	0.823	245	1.92	827	1.002
1954	695	2.30	8,144	0.902	239	2.02	911	0.989
1955	734	2.35	8,699	0.929	250	2.12	991	1.034
1956	753	2.52	9,135	0.942	266	2.25	1,071	1.044
1957	750	2.65	9,126	0.978	260	2.36	1,068	1.020
1958	717	2.64	8,537	1.000	259	2.40	1,051	1.000
1959	730	2.71	8,998	0.957	278	2.41	1,154	0.965
1960	675	2.87	8,981	0.973	280	2.44	1,197	1.012
1961	659	3.01	9,169	0.975	274	2.55	1,193	0.960
1962	651	3.10	9,382	0.970	272	2.68	1,196	1.062
1963	633	3.23	9,596	0.999	272	2.77	1,222	1.129
1964	641	3.28	9,818	1.004	283	2.81	1,294	1.135

(continued)

TABLE 5 (continued)

Year	Labor[a]	Wage[b]	Output[c]	Price[d]	Labor[a]	Wage[b]	Output[c]	Price[d]
	Total Contract Construction				*Total Nondurable Goods*			
1947	3,937	1.54	12,880	0.686	14,965	1.34	39,956	0.833
1948	4,297	1.72	14,097	0.791	14,942	1.46	41,845	0.875
1949	4,244	1.72	14,675	0.762	14,065	1.53	40,612	0.860
1950	4,537	1.85	16,191	0.782	14,754	1.59	44,903	0.847
1951	5,157	2.02	18,245	0.821	15,002	1.73	47,507	0.911
1952	5,328	2.12	18,336	0.883	15,037	1.82	47,322	0.931
1953	5,167	2.28	18,916	0.880	15,316	1.91	49,456	0.935
1954	5,053	2.39	19,321	0.866	14,571	2.01	48,192	0.945
1955	5,406	2.40	20,770	0.866	15,229	2.06	52,902	0.951
1956	5,848	2.48	21,842	0.917	15,257	2.19	54,602	0.974
1957	5,624	2.65	21,130	0.988	14,919	2.32	54,914	0.979
1958	5,314	2.80	20,683	1.000	14,357	2.41	54,039	1.000
1959	5,695	2.84	22,049	1.012	15,076	2.49	58,989	1.016
1960	5,506	3.05	21,736	1.044	14,953	2.60	59,930	1.033
1961	5,403	3.18	21,402	1.093	14,828	2.69	60,697	1.038
1962	5,583	3.28	21,693	1.146	15,183	2.77	64,664	1.034
1963	5,747	3.37	21,850	1.204	15,197	2.86	66,729	1.043
1964	5,912	3.57	22,522	1.263	15,372	2.99	71,060	1.045
	Food and Kindred Products				*Tobacco Manufactures*			
1947	4,041	1.24	11,391	0.828	239	0.87	2,011	0.812
1948	3,971	1.35	11,880	0.859	227	0.95	2,144	0.814
1949	3,874	1.41	11,380	0.897	211	1.08	2,273	0.807
1950	3,900	1.48	12,360	0.858	204	1.18	2,184	0.841
1951	3,991	1.60	12,567	0.886	208	1.33	2,418	0.833
1952	3,982	1.69	13,017	0.935	211	1.40	2,522	0.901
1953	3,968	1.80	13,946	0.912	205	1.53	2,341	1.001
1954	3,905	1.89	13,478	0.948	202	1.61	2,200	1.028
1955	3,938	1.97	14,174	0.972	206	1.64	2,336	0.998
1956	3,956	2.08	14,739	0.952	201	1.80	2,467	0.981
1957	3,830	2.22	15,126	0.944	194	1.93	2,570	0.994
1958	3,761	2.31	14,996	1.000	192	2.00	2,738	1.000
1959	3,815	2.42	15,098	1.056	192	2.11	2,906	0.994
1960	3,798	2.54	15,464	1.057	187	2.35	3,027	0.999
1961	3,776	2.62	15,256	1.102	184	2.38	3,174	0.987
1962	3,757	2.73	15,794	1.099	182	2.55	3,293	0.983
1963	3,708	2.83	16,656	1.077	176	2.69	3,346	1.019
1964	3,568	3.09	17,598	1.092	184	2.75	3,266	1.031

(continued)

TABLE 5 (continued)

Year	Labor[a]	Wage[b]	Output[c]	Price[d]	Labor[a]	Wage[b]	Output[c]	Price[d]
	Textile Mill Products				*Apparel and Other Finished Products Made From Fabrics and Similar Materials*			
1947	2,675	1.16	3,733	1.260	2,160	1.30	3,687	0.968
1948	2,715	1.31	4,100	1.281	2,215	1.38	3,896	0.944
1949	2,321	1.37	3,790	1.109	2,159	1.36	3,847	0.916
1950	2,586	1.40	3,965	1.159	2,250	1.41	4,203	0.861
1951	2,497	1.51	4,082	1.284	2,235	1.48	4,501	0.891
1952	2,365	1.55	4,078	1.143	2,296	1.50	4,488	0.920
1953	2,348	1.57	3,987	1.129	2,343	1.56	4,603	0.928
1954	2,076	1.60	3,793	1.032	2,173	1.62	4,300	0.948
1955	2,190	1.61	4,222	1.044	2,301	1.62	4,613	0.938
1956	2,130	1.69	4,284	1.051	2,290	1.73	4,701	0.982
1957	1,985	1.76	4,190	1.027	2,246	1.79	4,629	0.983
1958	1,844	1.80	4,122	1.000	2,139	1.83	4,559	1.000
1959	1,987	1.87	4,542	1.035	2,314	1.86	4,894	0.997
1960	1,899	1.95	4,400	1.076	2,270	1.94	5,101	1.000
1961	1,854	1.98	4,396	1.025	2,236	1.99	5,068	1.032
1962	1,905	2.05	4,808	1.031	2,379	2.04	5,432	1.046
1963	1,876	2.10	4,971	1.010	2,411	2.08	5,516	1.061
1964	1,818	2.31	5,379	1.036	2,655	2.01	5,891	1.072
	Paper and Allied Products				*Printing, Publishing, and Allied Industries*			
1947	1,042	1.35	3,631	0.689	1,507	1.56	4,627	0.699
1948	1,053	1.49	3,342	0.787	1,516	1.72	4,743	0.740
1949	987	1.56	3,329	0.738	1,493	1.84	4,797	0.769
1950	1,092	1.63	4,328	0.705	1,513	1.93	4,986	0.779
1951	1,146	1.79	4,626	0.831	1,553	2.04	5,091	0.814
1952	1,121	1.91	4,100	0.874	1,578	2.15	5,110	0.865
1953	1,186	2.00	4,551	0.837	1,628	2.26	5,409	0.886
1954	1,168	2.10	4,572	0.858	1,629	2.37	5,688	0.875
1955	1,233	2.17	5,103	0.867	1,688	2.45	6,049	0.900
1956	1,264	2.31	5,296	0.945	1,744	2.55	6,280	0.925
1957	1,255	2.42	4,877	0.995	1,746	2.69	6,364	0.969
1958	1,299	2.38	4,820	1.000	1,724	2.79	6,128	1.000
1959	1,307	2.61	5,480	0.986	1,774	2.91	6,594	1.016
1960	1,316	2.72	5,392	1.026	1,820	3.02	6,764	1.053
1961	1,329	2.84	5,737	1.000	1,822	3.11	6,765	1.070
1962	1,358	2.96	6,121	1.001	1,845	3.20	7,041	1.092
1963	1,377	3.05	6,285	0.985	1,854	3.29	7,069	1.130
1964	1,275	3.46	6,749	0.969	1,940	3.36	7,687	1.127

(continued)

TABLE 5 (continued)

Year	Labor[a]	Wage[b]	Output[c]	Price[d]	Labor[a]	Wage[b]	Output[c]	Price[d]
	Chemicals and Allied Products				*Petroleum Refining and Related Industries*			
1947	1,390	1.56	4,072	0.905	467	2.07	2,070	0.909
1948	1,403	1.68	4,823	0.913	481	2.27	2,261	1.087
1949	1,308	1.82	4,985	0.920	463	2.45	2,269	0.852
1950	1,371	1.92	6,023	0.902	462	2.51	2,595	0.872
1951	1,518	2.11	6,503	1.006	491	2.84	2,624	1.066
1952	1,553	2.24	6,563	0.985	494	3.09	2,658	1.021
1953	1,638	2.37	7,018	0.983	511	3.18	2,824	1.113
1954	1,597	2.52	7,252	0.994	504	3.37	2,746	1.074
1955	1,652	2.60	8,530	0.992	504	3.49	3,100	1.027
1956	1,702	2.80	8,981	0.977	502	3.70	3,179	1.157
1957	1,723	3.00	9,395	0.987	493	4.04	3,144	1.047
1958	1,681	3.12	9,218	1.000	476	4.13	3,124	1.000
1959	1,742	3.25	10,917	0.987	462	4.38	3,310	1.130
1960	1,779	3.37	10,975	0.981	453	4.42	3,498	1.220
1961	1,783	3.50	11,534	0.968	434	4.75	3,530	1.186
1962	1,836	3.60	12,446	0.961	422	4.81	3,826	1.102
1963	1,867	3.72	13,189	0.964	412	5.08	3,835	1.214
1964	1,791	4.11	14,139	0.969	375	5.60	3,912	1.189
	Rubber and Miscellaneous Plastics Products				*Leather and Leather Products*			
1947	670	1.52	2,584	0.574	827	1.19	1,668	0.696
1948	636	1.58	2,403	0.600	797	1.28	1,735	0.743
1949	565	1.67	2,185	0.610	740	1.32	1,576	0.735
1950	663	1.71	2,552	0.622	772	1.36	1,545	0.748
1951	708	1.89	3,210	0.677	729	1.47	1,647	0.838
1952	718	2.01	3,181	0.706	767	1.51	1,535	0.910
1953	758	2.11	3,159	0.748	763	1.57	1,582	0.885
1954	680	2.21	2,773	0.745	716	1.62	1,491	0.932
1955	790	2.26	3,183	0.792	760	1.65	1,555	0.921
1956	776	2.43	3,105	0.906	748	1.75	1,572	0.976
1957	785	2.57	3,067	0.959	725	1.84	1,553	0.998
1958	702	2.75	2,878	1.000	686	1.89	1,456	1.000
1959	800	2.79	3,609	0.914	735	1.94	1,651	0.971
1960	786	2.88	3,768	0.889	697	2.01	1,553	1.072
1961	788	2.91	3,747	0.913	697	2.04	1,484	1.061
1962	871	3.01	4,275	0.912	705	2.10	1,614	1.076
1963	886	3.10	4,341	0.933	684	2.16	1,558	1.141
1964	889	3.34	4,806	0.908	708	2.21	1,655	1.129

(continued)

TABLE 5 (continued)

Year	Labor[a]	Wage[b]	Output[c]	Price[d]	Labor[a]	Wage[b]	Output[c]	Price[d]
	Total Durable Goods				*Lumber and Wood Products, Except Furniture*			
1947	17,659	1.43	53,481	0.628	1,771	1.00	3,285	0.807
1948	17,491	1.57	55,675	0.684	1,701	1.15	3,224	0.925
1949	15,344	1.66	51,083	0.726	1,511	1.15	2,979	0.860
1950	17,298	1.73	61,203	0.747	1,660	1.24	3,239	0.992
1951	19,614	1.92	69,676	0.794	1,717	1.38	3,301	1.097
1952	20,175	2.06	71,896	0.818	1,632	1.46	3,206	1.064
1953	21,660	2.17	79,381	0.829	1,571	1.51	3,108	1.075
1954	19,036	2.29	71,252	0.852	1,439	1.56	3,018	1.060
1955	20,490	2.37	80,797	0.873	1,519	1.66	3,486	1.077
1956	20,966	2.53	79,545	0.925	1,475	1.75	3,475	1.093
1957	20,654	2.68	79,779	0.973	1,305	1.80	3,281	1.026
1958	18,137	2.85	69,634	1.000	1,234	1.86	3,306	1.000
1959	19,837	2.93	79,916	1.016	1,360	1.92	3,619	1.067
1960	19,724	3.07	80,922	1.019	1,271	2.01	3,546	1.036
1961	19,007	3.15	79,733	1.018	1,194	2.04	3,479	0.994
1962	20,162	3.27	90,449	1.016	1,220	2.12	3,788	0.984
1963	20,551	3.38	96,093	1.012	1,223	2.22	4,004	1.007
1964	21,125	3.52	102,548	1.021	1,285	2.30	4,312	1.039
	Furniture and Fixtures				*Stone, Clay, and Glass Products*			
1947	725	1.24	1,425	0.711	1,145	1.31	3,405	0.607
1948	738	1.34	1,657	0.747	1,162	1.46	3,638	0.657
1949	659	1.44	1,575	0.774	1,061	1.54	3,388	0.703
1950	791	1.47	1,901	0.768	1,169	1.61	4,057	0.726
1951	763	1.61	1,807	0.887	1,264	1.77	4,356	0.769
1952	769	1.71	1,950	0.859	1,205	1.85	4,113	0.781
1953	787	1.77	1,946	0.867	1,233	1.98	4,425	0.815
1954	711	1.87	1,872	0.874	1,164	2.08	4,323	0.851
1955	783	1.92	2,171	0.872	1,267	2.15	4,973	0.887
1956	795	2.01	2,186	0.925	1,294	2.28	4,897	0.933
1957	777	2.12	2,091	0.972	1,251	2.42	4,755	0.971
1958	737	2.17	1,911	1.000	1,170	2.57	4,661	1.000
1959	815	2.19	2,178	1.002	1,294	2.64	5,242	1.023
1960	797	2.28	2,147	1.030	1,275	2.77	5,128	1.029
1961	764	2.33	2,066	1.060	1,232	2.83	5,043	1.029
1962	815	2.38	2,218	1.079	1,260	2.94	5,358	1.023
1963	827	2.46	2,284	1.089	1,292	3.02	5,736	1.015
1964	863	2.56	2,462	1.105	1,305	3.20	6,051	1.022

(continued)

TABLE 5 (continued)

Year	Labor[a]	Wage[b]	Output[c]	Price[d]	Labor[a]	Wage[b]	Output[c]	Price[d]
	Primary Metal Industry				*Fabricated Metal Products*[e]			
1947	2,654	1.57	11,796	0.481	2,103	1.49	5,913	0.698
1948	2,697	1.69	11,711	0.536	2,072	1.65	6,026	0.769
1949	2,264	1.80	10,168	0.589	2,025	1.57	5,403	0.782
1950	2,652	1.90	12,430	0.618	2,119	1.80	6,558	0.814
1951	2,951	2.11	14,866	0.662	2,343	1.93	6,908	0.920
1952	2,720	2.30	13,171	0.679	2,308	2.08	7,088	0.889
1953	2,949	2.41	15,235	0.712	2,514	2.18	7,875	0.883
1954	2,460	2.54	11,899	0.774	2,270	2.30	7,601	0.878
1955	2,840	2.66	14,572	0.809	2,434	2.37	8,089	0.912
1956	2,890	2.86	14,308	0.880	2,499	2.47	8,208	0.954
1957	2,791	3.11	13,984	0.951	2,483	2.63	8,409	0.986
1958	2,297	3.28	10,912	1.000	2,234	2.75	7,804	1.000
1959	2,491	3.40	12,181	1.015	2,387	2.86	8,725	0.989
1960	2,497	3.57	12,001	1.049	2,391	2.95	8,741	0.996
1961	2,353	3.64	11,275	1.033	2,284	3.02	8,752	1.005
1962	2,437	3.78	12,043	1.058	2,410	3.09	9,464	1.014
1963	2,498	3.82	12,598	1.056	2,481	3.16	9,856	1.022
1964	2,623	3.99	13,578	1.074	2,529	3.36	10,400	1.059
	Machinery, Except Electrical				*Electrical Machinery, Equipment, and Supplies*			
1947	2,967	1.51	9,509	0.613	2,169	1.47	5,235	0.796
1948	2,946	1.69	10,126	0.660	2,066	1.62	5,079	0.871
1949	2,434	1.79	8,782	0.702	1,770	1.69	4,895	0.847
1950	2,636	1.84	9,572	0.727	2,118	1.69	6,157	0.855
1951	3,295	2.02	12,272	0.791	2,386	1.87	7,062	0.894
1952	3,393	2.19	13,323	0.803	2,539	2.00	8,299	0.875
1953	3,427	2.32	13,212	0.817	2,829	2.10	9,096	0.889
1954	3,000	2.42	11,926	0.834	2,464	2.21	8,123	0.900
1955	3,164	2.46	12,194	0.854	2,626	2.28	8,779	0.885
1956	3,457	2.60	13,470	0.919	2,807	2.40	9,501	0.913
1957	3,389	2.75	12,802	0.983	2,802	2.55	9,767	0.978
1958	2,820	2.92	10,921	1.000	2,572	2.75	9,348	1.000
1959	3,134	3.02	12,687	1.020	2,941	2.86	11,085	1.009
1960	3,153	3.12	12,722	1.030	3,036	3.00	11,660	0.989
1961	3,024	3.22	12,636	1.038	3,080	3.08	12,262	0.982
1962	3,238	3.32	14,135	1.048	3,311	3.18	14,034	0.947
1963	3,328	3.43	14,585	1.057	3,262	3.29	14,790	0.922
1964	3,423	3.70	16,422	1.075	3,284	3.38	15,678	0.898

(continued)

TABLE 5 (continued)

Year	Labor[a]	Wage[b]	Output[c]	Price[d]	Labor[a]	Wage[b]	Output[c]	Price[d]
	Transportation Equipment, Except Motor Vehicles				*Motor Vehicles*			
1947	2,632	0.68	2,655	0.629	1,589	1.52	6,024	0.658
1948	2,602	0.73	3,215	0.671	1,591	1.67	6,595	0.698
1949	2,492	0.75	3,151	0.696	1,551	1.78	6,988	0.807
1950	2,723	0.70	3,324	0.710	1,787	1.96	9,889	0.759
1951	3,246	1.04	4,890	0.803	1,751	2.25	9,427	0.756
1952	3,702	1.39	7,598	0.798	1,674	2.41	8,296	0.904
1953	4,260	1.46	9,139	0.800	2,003	2.50	10,419	0.875
1954	3,731	1.56	8,763	0.811	1,652	2.67	9,071	0.872
1955	4,079	1.45	8,448	0.830	2,020	2.75	13,058	0.900
1956	3,988	1.71	8,495	0.917	1,698	3.06	9,781	0.937
1957	4,050	1.89	9,322	0.976	1,636	3.24	10,254	0.969
1958	3,343	2.23	8,791	1.000	1,252	3.62	7,092	1.000
1959	3,517	2.25	8,749	1.018	1,480	3.52	9,980	1.026
1960	3,358	2.31	8,525	1.030	1,544	3.66	11,000	0.998
1961	3,070	2.60	8,868	1.035	1,319	3.90	9,827	0.993
1962	3,369	2.63	10,136	1.040	1,536	4.15	13,440	0.976
1963	3,523	2.64	10,658	1.043	1,650	4.34	15,388	0.964
1964	3,412	2.77	10,664	1.077	1,684	4.59	16,246	0.953
	Instruments[f]				*Misc. Manufacturing Industries*			
1947	561	1.37	1,363	0.663	887	1.25	1,729	0.879
1948	548	1.52	1,466	0.691	891	1.36	1,927	0.873
1949	493	1.63	1,429	0.713	793	1.43	1,738	0.890
1950	537	1.77	1,675	0.727	849	1.49	1,974	0.899
1951	646	1.88	2,015	0.795	855	1.59	2,067	0.908
1952	682	2.07	2,300	0.796	833	1.69	2,115	0.905
1953	728	2.19	2,476	0.822	886	1.78	2,195	0.926
1954	668	2.36	2,468	0.834	804	1.90	2,105	0.939
1955	687	2.45	2,610	0.846	830	1.95	2,328	0.926
1956	720	2.63	2,759	0.902	838	2.06	2,350	0.967
1957	719	2.83	2,646	0.969	799	2.18	2,310	0.989
1958	670	2.97	2,604	1.000	766	2.25	2,284	1.000
1959	733	3.04	2,980	1.025	804	2.30	2,504	0.987
1960	744	3.14	3,017	1.045	797	2.41	2,448	1.003
1961	735	3.24	3,016	1.067	777	2.48	2,500	1.031
1962	763	3.34	3,251	1.084	804	2.54	2,602	1.027
1963	774	3.48	3,540	1.078	798	2.64	2,621	1.034
1964	779	3.64	3,916	1.061	817	2.76	2,773	1.033

(continued)

TABLE 5 (continued)

Year	Labor[a]	Wage[b]	Output[c]	Price[d]	Labor[a]	Wage[b]	Output[c]	Price[d]
	Total Railroads				*Local and Suburban Transit and Interurban Passenger Transportation*			
1947	3,757	1.45	10,684	0.687	441	2.89	3,962	0.446
1948	3,644	1.60	10,451	0.793	391	3.19	3,782	0.470
1949	3,106	1.73	8,718	0.862	375	3.28	3,193	0.541
1950	2,951	1.89	9,482	0.873	349	3.47	2,943	0.586
1951	3,089	2.07	10,590	0.868	335	3.80	2,830	0.650
1952	2,956	2.18	10,137	0.935	322	4.08	2,767	0.694
1953	2,907	2.22	9,917	0.950	312	4.26	2,658	0.717
1954	2,578	2.29	8,946	0.922	306	4.19	2,371	0.769
1955	2,626	2.32	9,870	0.906	284	4.51	2,222	0.839
1956	2,580	2.54	10,040	0.935	266	4.88	2,123	0.892
1957	2,431	2.72	9,468	0.984	249	5.41	2,071	0.959
1958	2,070	2.95	8,430	1.000	236	5.59	1,982	1.000
1959	2,015	3.08	8,871	0.947	232	5.83	1,915	1.069
1960	1,919	3.20	8,748	0.929	227	6.15	1,863	1.123
1961	1,797	3.23	8,674	0.909	220	6.46	1,750	1.238
1962	1,763	3.33	9,155	0.889	201	7.10	1,708	1.295
1963	1,722	3.39	9,575	0.857	195	7.48	1,704	1.336
1964	1,710	3.48	9,969	0.842	186	8.02	1,627	1.459
	Motor Freight Transportation And Warehousing				*Total Telephone and Telegraph*			
1947	1,312	1.11	3,120	0.784	1,276	1.41	3,759	0.763
1948	1,359	1.23	3,403	0.832	1,433	1.47	4,375	0.797
1949	1,271	1.37	3,462	0.847	1,388	1.59	4,604	0.824
1950	1,294	1.59	4,335	0.810	1,356	1.70	4,810	0.873
1951	1,420	1.67	4,586	0.836	1,415	1.77	5,248	0.892
1952	1,454	1.82	4,718	0.908	1,449	1.93	5,611	0.921
1953	1,521	1.97	5,176	0.927	1,507	1.99	6,065	0.952
1954	1,502	2.03	5,180	0.942	1,503	2.06	6,151	0.954
1955	1,643	2.11	5,890	0.937	1,548	2.20	6,703	0.950
1956	1,717	2.21	6,217	0.965	1,618	2.29	7,202	0.961
1957	1,719	2.35	6,449	0.992	1,648	2.37	7,706	0.976
1958	1,687	2.43	6,411	1.000	1,547	2.52	7,993	1.000
1959	1,853	2.54	7,047	1.015	1,527	2.69	8,621	1.017
1960	1,847	2.68	7,222	1.020	1,538	2.80	9,109	1.026
1961	1,828	2.76	7,459	1.018	1,502	3.00	9,687	1.029
1962	1,909	2.85	7,974	1.035	1,508	3.12	10,483	1.027
1963	1,973	2.93	8,485	1.031	1,498	3.20	11,222	1.027
1964	2,004	3.10	9,043	1.034	1,548	3.42	12,162	1.027

(continued)

TABLE 5 (concluded)

Year	Labor[a]	Wage[b]	Output[c]	Price[d]	Labor[a]	Wage[b]	Output[c]	Price[d]
	Electric, Gas, and Sanitary				*Wholesale Trade*			
1947	1,005	1.59	4,354	0.867	5,046	1.61	19,591	0.793
1948	1,115	1.61	5,013	0.851	5,306	1.70	20,322	0.853
1949	1,131	1.77	5,510	0.880	5,276	1.68	20,162	0.825
1950	1,163	1.81	5,930	0.890	5,329	1.78	21,957	0.855
1951	1,184	1.94	6,806	0.891	5,529	1.93	23,023	0.926
1952	1,190	2.10	7,284	0.910	5,687	1.98	23,526	0.915
1953	1,217	2.22	7,796	0.926	5,757	2.07	24,021	0.912
1954	1,229	2.36	8,565	0.937	5,768	2.13	24,244	0.915
1955	1,263	2.38	9,095	0.958	5,918	2.22	27,156	0.926
1956	1,281	2.58	9,740	0.967	6,074	2.40	28,497	0.964
1957	1,287	2.72	10,279	0.975	6,063	2.54	28,990	0.993
1958	1,297	2.85	10,710	1.000	5,954	2.66	29,408	1.000
1959	1,305	3.06	11,582	1.010	6,220	2.74	32,218	1.007
1960	1,311	3.20	12,355	1.029	6,326	2.86	33,147	1.007
1961	1,306	3.37	12,919	1.036	6,303	2.96	34,629	1.004
1962	1,301	3.46	13,639	1.038	6,452	3.05	36,824	1.001
1963	1,307	3.60	14,163	1.034	6,585	3.15	38,497	1.002
1964	1,315	3.80	14,878	1.025	6,715	3.30	40,911	1.003
		Retail Trade						
1947	14,060	1.02	33,101	0.842				
1948	14,426	1.09	33,929	0.915				
1949	14,451	1.12	35,066	0.894				
1950	14,678	1.18	38,421	0.846				
1951	15,177	1.23	38,334	0.915				
1952	15,410	1.28	39,414	0.939				
1953	15,563	1.35	40,847	0.926				
1954	15,475	1.39	41,222	0.938				
1955	15,938	1.44	44,480	0.923				
1956	16,213	1.51	45,333	0.947				
1957	16,083	1.60	46,107	0.977				
1958	15,902	1.64	45,713	1.000				
1959	16,466	1.71	48,570	1.020				
1960	16,793	1.79	49,157	1.035				
1961	16,531	1.84	48,910	1.067				
1962	16,774	1.92	52,127	1.071				
1963	17,071	2.00	54,068	1.077				
1964	17,237	2.13	57,321	1.083				

Notes to Table 5

[a]Labor, million man-hours. Estimated from employment – all employees – and average hours worked, production workers. (Source: *Employment and Earnings Statistics for the United States, 1909–64,* Bulletin 1312–2, U. S. Department of Labor, December 1964.)

[b]Wage, average compensation per hour, dollars. Estimated by dividing total employees compensation by estimated total man-hours worked. (Source: Office of Business Economics, Department of Commerce.)

[c]Gross national product, million dollars. (Source: Office of Business Economics, Department of Commerce.)

[d]Price. Implicit industry price deflator, index 1958=100. (Source: Office of Business Economics, Department of Commerce.)

[e]Fabricated metal products, excluding ordnance machinery and transportation equipment.

[f]Instruments include professional, scientific and controlling instruments; photographic and optical goods, watches and clocks.

factor shares. It was pointed out that under certain conditions attainment of larger profit-sales ratios would lead to smaller labor shares. It was noted, too, that important factors affecting the profit-sales ratio and the labor share, such as wages and prices, are outside the influence of many firms but may be controlled to some extent by others. Such things would need to be taken into account in formal behavioral relations.

It is obvious that in order to specify rigorously the relevant behavioral relations within and between industries—and both are needed—reliable data on all factor inputs and their prices, and outputs and their prices are needed but are not presently available. Even if these data were available, the statistical problem involved might defy solution. With the behavioral relations at hand, changing factor shares could be readily explained, at least to the satisfaction of most economists.

Bibliography

1. Bell, Frederick, "The Theory of Relative Shares: Comment," *Quarterly Journal of Economics,* November 1965, pp. 671–676.
2. Bronferrner, M., "A Note on Relative Shares and the Elasticity of Substitution," *Journal of Political Economy,* June 1960, pp. 284–287.

3. Brown, M., *On The Theory and Measurement of Technological Change,* New York, 1966.
4. Denison, E. F., "Distribution of National Income," *Survey of Current Business,* June 1952, pp. 16–24.
5. Heady, E. O., "Changes in Income Distribution in Agriculture with Special Reference to Technological Progress," *Journal of Farm Economics,* August 1944, pp. 435–438.
6. Heady, E. O. and Dillon, J. L., *Agricultural Production Functions,* Ames, Iowa, 1961, Chapter 1.
7. Hultgren, T., *Cost, Prices and Profits: Their Cyclical Relations,* New York, NBER, 1965.
8. Kaldor, N., "Alternative Theories of Distribution," *The Review of Economic Studies,* 1955–56, pp. 83–100.
9. ——— "A Model of Economic Growth," *The Economic Journal,* pp. 591–625.
10. Kalechi, M., "The Determinants of Distribution of National Income," *Econometrica,* April 1938, pp. 97–113.
11. Kendrick, J. W., *Productivity Trends in the United States,* Princeton for NBER, 1961.
12. Kendrick, J. W. and Sato, R., "Factor Prices, Productivity and Economic Growth," Mimeograph, undated.
13. Kravis, I. B., "Relative Income Shares in Fact and Theory," *American Economic Review,* December 1959.
14. Marimont, M. L., "GNP by Major Industries—Comparative Pattern of Postwar Growth," *Survey of Current Business,* October 1962, pp. 6–19.
15. Mendershausen, H., "On the Significance of Professor Douglas' Production Function," *Econometrica,* April 1938, pp. 143–153.
16. National Bureau of Economic Research, Studies in Income and Wealth 25, Princeton, 1961.
17. ———, Studies in Income and Wealth 5, Part I, New York, 1943.
18. Sen, A. K., "Neoclassical and Neo-Keynesian Theories of Distribution," *The Economic Record,* March 1963, pp. 53–64.
19. Scitovsky, T., "A Survey of Some Theories of Income Distribution," in *The Behavior of Income Shares,* Princeton for NBER, 1964.
20. Solow, R. M., "A Skeptical Note on the Constancy of Relative Shares," *American Economic Review,* September 1958, pp. 618–631.
21. ———, "Capital, Labor and Income in Manufacturing," in *The Behavior of Income Shares,* Princeton for NBER, 1964.

COMMENT

TA-CHUNG LIU, Cornell and Brandeis Universities

An analysis of income shares is important in evaluating the efficiency, the equity, and the growth prospects of an economy. Egbert is not satisfied with the customary approach to the problem through the use of aggregate production functions in a neoclassical model. The well-known complications due to aggregation in estimating production functions, the unlikely fulfillment of the familiar marginal conditions at any moment of time in a dynamic world of change, and the assumption of constant returns to scale involved in much of the literature are valid objections which Egbert has raised. The author has, instead, attempted to analyze factor shares in a micro-analytical framework which is then related to national income accounts in Equations 1–14. His approach is an interesting exercise in rearranging the identity that profits are equal to sales minus various categories of costs.

The empirical work in this paper, however, is carried out on the basis of the following relationship through time for a given industry: [1]

$$\frac{1}{LS}\frac{d(LS)}{dt} = \frac{1}{L}\frac{dL}{dt} + \frac{1}{W}\frac{dW}{dt} - \frac{1}{O}\frac{dO}{dt} - \frac{1}{P}\frac{dP}{dt}$$

This relationship holds approximately for a finite span of time and where *LS, L, W, O, P* and *t* denote labor share, labor input, wage rate, output, price of output, and time, respectively.

The main empirical result is presented in Table 3. It decomposes the rate of change of labor share into the four components corresponding to the four terms on the right side of the equation given above. It tells clearly, for instance, that the *decline* of the labor share in the net output of the telephone and telegraph industry and the gas, electric, and sanitary industry from 1948–50 to 1962–64 reflected largely the greater rates of increase in the quantities and prices of outputs (both having negative influence on the labor share) than those of labor inputs and the wage rates. The reverse happened in the case of contract construction, motor freight, and warehousing, and wholesale and retail

[1] This is derived directly from Equation 16.

NOTE: These comments are based on the original version of the paper as presented at the Conference.

trade; the labor share increased because labor inputs and wage rates increased at faster rates than the quantities and prices of output.

The usefulness of the approach formulated in this paper is quite similar to that of the quantity equation of money. The author's approach decomposes the changes in the labor share into the four elements mentioned above, whereas the latter identifies the change in the price level as the algebraic sum of the changes in M, V and T. Similar to the quantity equation of money, the equation given above is an identity and does not provide us with a theory explaining the change in labor share.

As a summary or a classification of the component elements of the change in labor share, the equation presented above suffers a disadvantage in that the four components are not the results of the working of mutually exclusive underlying forces. The basic parameters determining the labor shares are, among others, the elasticity of demand for output, the elasticity of substitution between labor and nonlabor factors, the elasticity of supply of labor, the speed of adjustment toward equilibrium and the extent of the deviation from equilibrium in the labor market, and the rate of technological advance. The elasticity of demand for output acts directly on both O and P. The elasticity of supply of labor and the elasticity of substitution have a direct bearing on both L and W. The rate of technological advance affects directly both O and L. Perhaps only the speed of adjustment toward equilibrium in the labor market is, in the first instance, related to one term alone (L). This compares rather unfavorably with the quantity equation of money because there are perhaps a large number of factors which have a direct effect on P through one component only (M, V or T).

For an explanation of the change in factor shares, a theoretical model must be constructed to include the basic parameters, some of which have been mentioned above. The complications of aggregation cannot be avoided in any approach to the problem, including the one formulated by Egbert. Some of the other difficulties mentioned by Egbert (e.g., deviations from equilibrium and nonconstant returns to scale) can be, and have been, to some extent, overcome in the literature. Nevertheless, the approach formulated by Egbert and the empirical results obtained are a useful contribution. The information given by Egbert on the four components of the change in labor share for the different industries is quite valuable in formulating realistic industry models. Algebraic solutions for the growth rates of *LS, L, W, O* and *P* can be obtained from the theoretical model constructed for a given industry in terms of the basic parameters. The empirical results concerning the various growth rates given in this paper can then be used to infer the magnitudes of the basic parameters. Complicated problems of identification would be involved in such an attempt, but the Egbert framework would be helpful in resolving these difficulties. Egbert has initiated an approach which may yield interesting analytical results.

Part III

The Basic Industry Product Estimates

Comparison of Federal Reserve and OBE Measures of Real Manufacturing Output, 1947–64

JACK J. GOTTSEGEN
RICHARD C. ZIEMER
OFFICE OF BUSINESS ECONOMICS
U.S. DEPARTMENT OF COMMERCE

Annual estimates of gross product originating in manufacturing industries and the subgroups, durable and nondurable goods industries, for the postwar period were first published in the October 1962 issue of the *Survey of Current Business*. These OBE measures have been compared with those of the Federal Reserve Board (FRB) and differences in growth rates and in year-to-year changes noted.

Although the two series differ conceptually and statistically the broad pattern of manufacturing output reflected by both the OBE and FRB series has been similar for the postwar period. As discussed in

NOTE: The following abbreviations are used in this article:

OBE = Office of Business Economics
FRB = Federal Reserve Board
GPO = Gross product originating; an industry's contribution to GNP
Real Product = Gross product originating in constant (1958) prices.

Similar comparisons for the mining industries and for the utilities industries, the remaining components of the FRB's "Index of Industrial Production," are not made for the following reasons. The OBE indexes for mining are based on the indexes for the separate mining activities as computed by the Federal Reserve Board. The utility industry, as defined by the SIC, determines the industry composition for purposes of compiling GNP data. The latter (Major Group 49) includes only privately owned companies engaged in the generation, transmission, and/or distribution of electricity or gas or steam and also those operating water and irrigation systems, and sanitary systems engaged in collecting and disposing of garbage, sewage, and other wastes. In contrast, the output of utilities as measured by the FRB indexes relates to the production and distribution of only electricity and gas by both privately owned and publicly owned utilities as well as by power plants which are auxiliary units or departments of manufacturing and mining establishments.

more detail below, both series exhibit a sharp rate of increase from 1948–53, a slower rate of gain until 1960, and rapid gains since 1960 (Chart 1). However, manufacturing output has increased more rapidly from 1948–64, when measured by the FRB series. Higher growth rates reflected by the latter measures, compared with the indexes of real product, also prevail during the 1953–60 period. The FRB and OBE series for the durable (Chart 2) and nondurable (Chart 3) manufacturing industries also show similar movements.

A detailed examination of the relationship between the manufacturing components of the FRB index and the OBE gross-product-originating measures has been postponed until the latter could be revised to reflect the statistical and definitional revisions which were incorporated into the national accounts in August 1965. The revised GPO series also incorporate information from more recent and comprehensive sources including the 1958 input–output study, as well as improvements in estimating methods, and reflect changes in industry classifications as provided by the 1957 edition of the *Standard Industrial Classification (SIC) Manual.* It is recognized that some of the observations indicated below may not apply when the FRB revisions are completed, but explanations of the fundamental relationships, particularly at a detailed manufacturing industry level, are possible.[1]

Conceptual Differences and Measurement Problems

While the annual production indexes prepared by both OBE and FRB and those developed from the Census data are designed to measure changes in real output for manufacturing industries, they differ with respect to concepts and methods of measurement.

GPO AND FRB MEASURES

Gross product originating in an industry is a measure of an industry's contributions to the nation's total output of goods and services as

[1] The revised FRB series are planned for release in 1968. They will be adjusted to the Census-Federal Reserve Benchmark Indexes of Manufacturing for 1958 and 1963. (The authors are indebted to Mr. C. Gehman and Mrs. C. J. Motheral, Federal Reserve Board, for their cooperation and assistance in providing information on procedures and making available unpublished FRB data including some of the tabulations prepared for *Industrial Production Measurement in the United States: Concepts, Uses and Compilation Practices,* Board of Governors of the Federal Reserve System, February 1964.)

defined in the national income and product accounts. An industry's gross product or value added may be measured as the amount by which the total value of its output exceeds the cost of purchased intermediate products (materials and business services) used in production. The gross product is also equal to the sum of the industry's factor payments (employee compensation, profits, net interest, etc.) and of its nonfactor costs of production (indirect business taxes, depreciation, etc.). OBE uses the latter procedure to measure an industry's output (value added) in current dollars. The constant-dollar total is calculated by deflating the current-dollar total by an implicit deflator derived by the "double deflation" procedure.[2] The constant-dollar series represents an industry's value added for the given year's composite of output minus purchases, valued in base-year prices.

The FRB indexes for a two-digit SIC industry are also designed to be measures of its value added in constant prices. In these indexes, however, the Census value-added concept is used and this value added, as discussed below,[3] differs from the GPO concept principally by including the value of purchased services. The Census value added for a base year is extrapolated by quantity series representative of an industry's total output.

Changes in total output may differ from changes in value added (also called net output or gross product). Such differences will arise when, for any number of reasons, the material requirements per unit of output vary over time. Such variations may occur, for example, because: (a) improved production techniques result in savings of materials or in substituting less expensive materials; (b) changes in the degree of integration of production processes or in the kinds of products produced result in a shift to the use of more (or less) highly fabricated materials; and (c) the proportion of products within an industry with higher value added per unit of output increases (or decreases) relative to those with lower unit value added.

In principle, the OBE data on real product should reflect the "true" movements in net output. In practice, however, the OBE series may not, because of imperfections, for example, in the data for price changes or the lack of this information. The price index problems arise primarily because of limitations in sample coverage, the markets

[2] See Appendix A for description.
[3] See Census value added and GPO, p. 230.

in which prices are measured, the differences between quoted and transaction prices, and their adequacy to account for quality changes (the quality issue is mentioned again in the paragraph below which refers to the quantity series on output used in the FRB calculations). Even when individual price indexes are available, there may be difficulties because adequate information is unavailable on weights needed to calculate composite indexes for deflating outputs and inputs. (See Appendix A.) Furthermore, the current-dollar measures of value of production, cost of materials, purchased services, and gross product originating in a manufacturing industry have statistical limitations.

The FRB series, in principle, also represent changes in net output if the ratio of value added per unit of output remains constant at the detailed level selected by the FRB for estimating output. If stability at this level, which is generally a SIC three-digit level, does not occur, the movements of value added and total output are not parallel. Similarly, the relationship for a major (two-digit SIC) industry is dependent upon the value-added–output ratios for the component series. (The FRB indexes will, however, reflect changes in the value added for a major industry if output shifts occur only among the component industries at the measured level with different value-added–output ratios.)

Like the OBE measures, the FRB measures are affected by inadequacies of data sources. Series on the quantity of output may not be representative or adequate in coverage.[4] The available quantity series may also not be sufficiently detailed and thus not reflect properly changes in the composite of output or in the quality of goods produced. Where the deflation method is used by FRB, the shortcomings of the price data, which are a consideration in the constant-dollar OBE data, must be considered as well. For those industries where labor inputs (or, in a few cases, material inputs) are used to estimate output, there may also be a question of reliability.

The FRB indexes for manufacturing industries are calculated by using about 200 series. These 200 series include, for a number of industries, a man-hour or employment series adjusted for estimated productivity as measures of physical volume of output. About 9 per

[4] The issue frequently is whether the production movements of a given product follow more closely that of another product or whether the price movements of the products are more closely related.

cent of manufacturing activity through 1957 and 55 per cent since 1958 is represented by such labor-input series. The remainder are represented primarily by physical units of output. The productivity estimates used with man-hour or employment figures are derived from a wide variety of data including productivity patterns based on the FRB physical product series.[5]

The constant-(1958) dollar GPO for a given two-digit industry is calculated by deflating the current-dollar totals by an implicit deflator derived by a "double deflation" procedure. In this procedure, the output of each four-digit manufacturing industry (about 425 industries) is derived from Census Bureau data on the value of shipments and of inventory change; these are deflated separately, and then aggregated to about sixty subgroups represented in the manufacturing segment of OBE's 1958 input–output study. The Census cost-of-materials data for each of these groups are also deflated separately, and subtracted from deflated output to yield "Census" value-added figures in constant prices. The current- and constant-dollar totals for output, materials input and value added of the sixty groups are then aggregated to the SIC two-digit level. At this level the current-dollar totals for value added are divided by the corresponding constant-dollar totals to yield the value added or GPO implicit deflator. In this deflation process, more than 1200 price indexes, about 70 per cent of which are specially tabulated by the U.S. Bureau of Labor Statistics, are used by OBE. Limitations of these price indexes have been indicated above.

The GPO implicit deflator has the quality that small differences in the level of output or input prices yield larger differences in the GPO deflator since the latter is derived as a residual—that is, the output price index has a positive weight but the input price index has a negative weight.[6] In addition, the GPO price index does not explicitly include representation of prices for purchased business services. Some preliminary tests, however, indicate that even for industries where such purchases are large, an approximation of an all-inclusive GPO deflator differs little from the ones actually used by OBE.[7]

[5] See Appendix A for the proportion of each SIC two-digit industry's output that is based on measures of labor input. These measures are also discussed in *Industrial Production Measurement in the United States: Concepts, Uses and Compilation Practices,* Board of Governors of the Federal Reserve System, February 1964, p. 13.

[6] See *GNP by Major Industry,* Methods and Concepts, p. 3.

[7] See Appendix A.

CENSUS VALUE ADDED AND GPO

The OBE gross product totals exclude all intermediate purchases by the industry and include the excise taxes for which the industry has legal responsibility. Census value added excludes excise taxes paid by the industry and is net only of purchased goods including fuels and electricity consumed in the production processes but not purchased services other than contract work done on reported output.

In addition, the Census value-added total does not include an adjustment for inventory valuation (IVA), which is included in the GPO figures. Census value added is currently derived by subtracting the cost of materials consumed, energy used, and the cost of resales from the value of output. The latter is determined by the value of shipments (including receipts for resales and other activities) adjusted for change in inventories of finished goods and work in process valued at beginning of the year and end-of-the-year prices.[8]

According to the basic concepts of national income accounting, the value of current production is only truly reflected when the change in inventories is valued at average prices during the period. Reported corporate profits and income of unincorporated enterprises is adjusted for inventory profit or loss. The adjustment to reported book value of inventories results in having the change in the physical volume of inventories valued at average prices during the current year instead of in book values.[9] When an industry's ratio of changes in inventory valuations to value added is relatively large, which occurs when prices fluctuate greatly, the inventory valuation adjustments can affect significantly the current-dollar totals of GPO.

Furthermore, gross-product-originating data and Census value-added figures for a specified industry differ for other reasons. The Census data exclude intermediate purchases of materials and services used by administrative and auxiliary establishments associated with the manufacturing establishments; classification differences arise from independent decisions made by the Census Bureau and by the Internal Revenue Service, and State Unemployment Insurance Agencies, which are the principal sources of data for GPO; total compensation used by OBE differs from the Census sources; value added is derived by the Census

[8] Census value of production as computed by OBE differs slightly.

[9] For further explanation and procedures which vary with the method of inventory valuations (FIFO or LIFO), see *National Income,* 1954 edition, supplement to the *Survey of Current Business,* pp. 44–45 and 135–138.

Bureau from reported values of shipments, inventories and cost of materials, supplies, and energy consumed, while OBE derives this total by adding the factor and nonfactor charges, which involves estimating from companies' total profits and capital consumption allowances for all establishments classified in an industry; since 1954, the procedure for calculating Census value added has been changed and there is undercoverage in the 1947 and 1949–64 Census data as well as sampling errors for some years.

Statistical Framework for Analysis

Disparities between the OBE and FRB measures of manufacturing output stem from differences in weighting patterns, in the data and methods used to measure output for the component manufacturing series, and in the definitions of output. The OBE series is a measure of the manufacturing industries' contributions to total GNP. A current-dollar series, representing at market prices the increase in value resulting from the industry's activity, is deflated so that this total (real product) may be expressed in base-year prices. The FRB indexes are based on detailed quantity (pounds or number produced) or proxy (man-hours or materials consumed) measures of the total output, which are aggregated to industry and group levels by using as weights Census value added for a base period.

The statistical framework for analyzing the relationship between the OBE and FRB indexes is shown in Table 1. The 1964 FRB indexes as published, but on a 1958 rather than 1957–59 base, are shown in column 1. These indexes reweighted by 1958 GPO and by 1958 Census value of production appear respectively in columns 2 and 3. The next four columns contain indexes based on a constant-dollar (1958) series for Census measures showing total output, material inputs, net output, and net output including the appropriate federal excise taxes for which the manufacturer has legal responsibility. The GPO indexes appear in column 8. These statistics provide the necessary information so that among other comparisons, the following become evident:

1. The difference between the published FRB and OBE indexes, when disparities due to base periods are removed (column 1 minus column 8 or column 9).

TABLE 1

Selected Indexes of Manufacturing Activity, 1964

Industry	Indexes (1958 = 100): FRB			Deflated Census Data				OBE	Point Differences in Indexes[a]					
	As Pub. (1)	Re-weighted GPO (2)	Re-weighted VP (3)	VP (4)	Cost of Materials (5)	VA (6)	VA Plus Excise (7)	Gross Product (8)	Total (FRB Minus OBE) (9)	FRB (Net Minus Gross Wtd.) (10)	Total Output (Quantity Minus Deflated) (11)	Total Minus Net Output (12)	Excise Tax (13)	Net Output (Census Minus OBE) (14)
All manufacturing industries	142.8	143.1	141.3	136.6	134.0	140.0	139.5	140.4	2.4	1.5	4.7	-3.4	.5	-.9
Nondurable goods industries	137.0	135.8	133.4	130.9	128.2	135.0	133.5	132.0	5.0	3.6	2.5	-4.1	1.5	1.5
Food and kindred products	121.7	121.8	121.4	121.3	123.1	116.9	117.3	117.1	4.6	.3	.1	4.4	-.4	.2
Tobacco manufacturers	120.4	118.8	114.5	116.3	116.3	116.3	115.0	119.0	1.4	5.9	-1.8	.0	1.3	-4.0
Textile mill products	130.3	130.2	130.1	138.7	142.7	132.6	132.6	130.1	.2	.2	-8.6	6.1	.0	2.5
Apparel and other fabricated textile products	140.7	140.6	141.6	126.7	128.3	124.7	124.7	128.1	12.6	-.9	14.9	2.0	.0	-3.4
Paper and allied products	137.2	137.2	137.8	135.4	131.9	139.9	139.9	140.0	-2.8	-.6	2.4	-4.5	.0	-.1
Printing, publishing, and allied industries	127.2	127.2	127.5	126.3	128.0	125.4	125.4	125.7	1.5	-.3	1.2	.9	.0	-.3
Chemicals and allied products	166.6	165.9	165.5	155.3	149.0	160.8	160.8	152.0	14.6	1.1	10.2	-5.5	.0	8.8
Petroleum refining and related industries	124.2	125.5	123.1	126.4	116.6	174.7	152.5	144.3	-20.1	1.1	-3.3	-48.3	22.2	8.2
Rubber and miscellaneous plastic products	169.5	170.9	172.3	159.8	154.3	165.4	162.8	163.4	6.1	-2.8	12.5	-5.6	2.6	-.6
Leather and leather products	106.9	107.0	106.7	104.3	102.7	105.9	105.9	112.8	-5.9	.2	2.4	-1.6	.0	-6.9
Durable goods industries	147.8	148.8	149.4	142.4	140.8	144.1	144.9	146.9	.9	-1.6	7.0	-1.7	-.8	-2.0
Lumber and wood products, except furniture	117.8	119.2	119.0	126.1	123.1	130.1	130.1	128.9	-11.1	-1.2	-7.1	-4.0	.0	1.2
Furniture and fixtures	154.7	155.0	155.7	128.6	134.1	123.1	123.1	128.7	26.0	-1.0	27.1	5.5	.0	-5.6
Stone, clay, and glass products	135.2	135.6	136.2	132.1	132.2	132.1	132.1	131.2	4.0	-1.0	4.1	.0	.0	.9
Primary metal industries	147.5	148.2	147.8	140.2	144.9	133.7	133.7	130.2	17.3	-.3	7.6	6.5	.0	3.5
Fabricated metal products	142.8	142.5	140.5	126.5	126.2	126.8	126.8	135.2	7.6	2.3	14.0	-.3	.0	-8.4
Machinery, except electrical	161.7	162.0	161.3	145.4	145.6	145.2	145.2	153.3	8.4	.4	15.9	.2	.0	-8.1
Electrical machinery	156.2	154.6	153.8	166.7	150.6	179.9	179.1	167.1	-10.9	2.4	-12.9	-13.2	.8	12.0
Transportation equipment and ordnance, except motor vehicles	124.4	124.6	125.7	108.6	101.7	115.2	115.2	123.8	.6	-1.3	17.1	-6.6	.0	-8.6
Motor vehicles and motor vehicle equipment	181.1	182.1	181.7	179.4	173.3	192.6	192.6	213.0	-31.9	-.6	2.3	-13.2	.0	-20.4
Instruments	148.1	147.8	147.5	159.5	149.5	165.5	165.5	139.1	9.0	.6	-12.0	-6.0	.0	26.4
Miscellaneous manufacturing industries	141.9	141.9	141.9	134.3	133.4	135.1	135.1	119.3	22.6	.0	7.6	-.8	.0	15.8

Note: VP = value of production; VA = value added. For other abbreviations see note at beginning of Appendix C.

[a]Col. 9 = col. 1 minus 8; col. 10 = col. 1 minus 3; col. 11 = col. 3 minus 4; col. 12 = col. 4 minus col. 6; col. 13 = col. 6 minus col. 7; col. 14 = col. 7 minus col. 8.

2. The difference when the underlying FRB output series are combined with Census gross rather than with net value weights (column 1 minus column 3 or column 10).

3. The difference between total real output when measured by quantity (column 3) and by deflation (column 4), which appears in column 11.

4. The difference between deflated total (column 4) and net output (column 6) which is shown in column 12.

5. The difference in real net output resulting from the exclusion or inclusion of excise taxes in the calculation of this measure. Column 13 is derived by subtracting column 7 from column 6.

6. The difference (column 14) between Census value added with tax (column 7) and OBE net value-added series (column 8).

While in principle the differences between the measures compared are conceptual, a portion of the disparities may actually be due to data inconsistencies. For example, comparisons between columns 3 and 4 imply that the same outputs are reflected by both the FRB quantity series and data derived from Census shipments and changes in inventories of finished goods and goods in process. For some industries, such as foods, the coverage of the FRB and Census total-output series differs markedly and for years prior to 1958 Census data were adjusted to reflect SIC changes. Limitations of the various series are described in Appendix C, which also contains a more detailed description of the indexes shown in columns 1 through 8 of Table 1 and of similar tables shown in this article. The procedures, weights, and data sources used to construct the FRB and OBE indexes are briefly discussed in Appendix A. The GPO current-dollar totals and their components as well as the GPO constant-(1958) dollar totals by industry (1947–64) are shown in Appendix B. Lastly, the implicit price deflators for total output, cost of materials, value added, and GPO, by industry are listed in Appendix D.

Conclusions

The OBE and FRB indexes may be compared from many viewpoints. Although the magnitudes of the difference and an industry's contribution to the spread between the two indexes may vary when trends, year-to-year changes, or other stated periods are compared, the underlying causes for disparities between the two series may be illustrated by a comparison of the 1964 OBE and FRB indexes—the most recent year for which the data are available.

If both the FRB and OBE indexes had the same (GPO) weights, then the 2.4 points excess of the 1964 FRB index over the OBE figure for total manufacturing would have been increased to 2.7 points. This small change arises from a relatively larger decrease in the reweighted FRB indexes for nondurables, which is offset by an increase in the FRB reweighted indexes for durables. Weighting patterns account for 1.2 points of the 5.0 points spread between the OBE and published FRB series for the nondurables. For the durable goods industries, weighting differences increase the FRB and OBE gap from 0.9 to 1.9 points. Weighting the 1964 FRB relatives by 1958 Census value of production also results in reducing the point spread for nondurables and increasing the gaps for durables.

The influence of the weights stems principally from the inclusion of excise taxes in the GPO weights and their exclusion from the Census value-added weights used by FRB. For total manufacturing, weights reduced the point spreads because the tax incidence is associated with industries whose 1964 output increased less rapidly since 1958 than the average. This applies particularly to the nondurables, where the influence of these taxes almost halved the spread due to other weighting differences.

The FRB indexes reweighted by 1958 Census value of production exceeds the deflated Census value of production series by 4.7 points for total manufacturing. The spread however is 2.5 points for the nondurables and 7.0 points for the durables. The point difference due to measuring total output by quantity or man-hour series rather than by deflation is 4 points or more for four of ten nondurable industries accounting for 18.4 per cent of the 1964 all manufacturing total (based on deflated Census value of production). For durables, the corresponding figures are ten of the eleven industries, which account for 46.6 per cent of the 1964 manufacturing total. The point differences at the aggregate levels—total durable and nondurable manufacturing industries—are reduced because of offsetting movements. The FRB total-output weighted indexes are higher than the deflated Census value of production figures by 4 points or more for ten industries (54.1 per cent of total manufacturing) and lower by 4 points or more for four industries (14.7 per cent of the 1964 manufacturing total).

TABLE 2

Frequency Distribution of 1964 Point Differences Resulting from Measuring Total Output by Quantity Versus Deflation

Class Interval	Number of Industries	Percentage of Total Manufacturing (1957–59 = 100)	
		Quantities	Man-Hours
Less than -12.1	1	2.1	5.3
-8.1 to -12.0	2	2.8	2.5
-4.1 to - 8.0	1	1.6	0.4
-0.1 to - 4.0	2	3.2	0.0
0 to 3.9	5	16.8	11.2
4.0 to 7.9	3	9.1	4.2
8.0 to 11.9	1	3.7	5.0
12.0 and more	6	5.7	26.4
Total	21	45.0	55.0

About 55 per cent of the 1964 FRB index is based on a man-hour or employment series adjusted for estimated changes in productivity and the remainder by a physical quantity series (Table 2). For durables, where the larger gap between the two measures of total output occurs, about 70 per cent of the output is measured by man-hour series in contrast to about 37 per cent for the nondurables.[10] However, the largest positive difference in the 1964 FRB reweighted index and deflated Census value of production occurred for the furniture and fixtures industry where FRB measures the entire output by a man-hour series and the largest negative difference occurred in electrical machinery where 77.8 per cent, based on 1957–59 proportions, are based on man-hours adjusted for productivity. As shown in Table 2, those industries which FRB measures primarily on quantity data generally show less disparity with deflated Census value of production in 1964 than those whose total output is measured by a man-hour series.

As previously indicated, the difference between the published FRB and OBE indexes is 2.7 points if only movements between the two indexes are considered. The 2.7 points difference when distributed by

[10] See Appendix A for weights and types of series used by FRB.

categories which show changes between the Census measures of total (VP) and net (VA) output is as follows:

As indicated in Table 3, the following may be concluded:

(1) Of the 2.7 points discrepancy due to movements between the FRB and OBE series for total manufacturing, 3.9 points are contributed by industries whose 1964 Census total-output index (1958 = 100) exceeded net output. Based on 1957–59 proportions, these industries accounted for 44.4 per cent of total manufacturing.

(2) Offsetting the increase for the above series by 1.4 points are the contributions from twelve industries which fall into the category of larger 1958–64 increases in value added than in value of production.

TABLE 3

Frequency Distribution of 1964 Point Differences Between FRB and OBE Indexes, Classified by Movements of Census Measures of Total and Net Output

		Percentage of Total Manufacturing (1957–59 = 100)		
	Number of Industries	Quantities	Man-Hours	Point Contributions
VP = VA	2	2.0	2.4	0.2
OBE higher than FRB	0	0.0	0.0	0.0
FRB higher than OBE	2	2.0	2.4	0.2
VA higher than VP	12	20.5	30.7	-1.4
OBE higher than FRB	6	14.3	8.1	-3.7
FRB higher than OBE	6	6.2	22.6	2.3
VA smaller than VP	7	22.5	21.9	3.9
OBE higher than FRB	0	0.0	0.0	0.0
FRB higher than OBE	7	22.5	21.9	3.9
Totals	21	45.0	55.0	2.7

Note: VP = Value of production; VA = Value added. For other abbreviations see note at the beginning of Appendix C.

For six industries, which account for about 22 per cent of total manufacturing, the OBE indexes are higher; for six industries, contributing about 29 per cent, the FRB indexes are higher.

(3) The remaining two industries fall into the category where, since 1958, the 1964 indexes of gross and net output are identical. These industries, accounting for 4.4 per cent of total manufacturing, contribute only 0.2 points to the 2.7 point spread between the published FRB and OBE indexes.

(4) The FRB use of a man-hour series rather than a quantity series to measure output predominates only in one category, namely where net output has increased faster than total output. Differences in 1964 levels again appear to arise almost as much from quantity measures (pounds of plastics, number of tires, tons of steel) as from the use of a man-hour series, when compared with the deflation procedure.

This should not suggest, however, that deflated Census value added or GPO are necessarily correct, despite the fact that movements of these two indexes for total manufacturing are almost identical. There are of course, the limitations noted below with respect to deflated outputs. In addition, the deflation of the inputs depends not only on the validity of the price indexes but also on the weights used to aggregate them.

Table 4 below summarizes differences between the FRB and OBE indexes for 1964 (1958 = 100) for total manufacturing, durable, and nondurable goods industries and also isolates the differences by SIC two-digit industries. Summary figures indicating the point spread arising from weights and movements are shown separately. Because the industry weights in the FRB and OBE series differ, the sums of the industry point contributions do not equal the respective durable and nondurable point contributions. The weight differences between the two series also explain why the point contributions for the durables and nondurables do not add to the total for all manufacturing industries.

For the nondurable goods industries, the 1964 gap principally arises from the food, apparel, chemicals, and petroleum industries. For the food and petroleum industries, the FRB indexes approximate the indexes of Census deflated value of production and the OBE indexes reflect the Census deflated value-added levels. For the chemicals industry the FRB index, which is 14.6 points higher than the OBE index, is closer to the Census value-added index and the OBE series

TABLE 4

FRB and OBE Indexes, Point Spreads and Contributions to Total Manufacturing Spread for 1964

(1958 = 100)

	Point Spreads			Point Contributions		
		Due to			Due to	
	Total	Movements	Weights	Total[a]	Movements	Weights
Total manufacturing[a]	2.4	2.7	-.3	2.4	2.7	-.3
Durables and nondurables sum[b]	n.a.	n.a.	n.a.	2.6	2.7	-.1
Two-digit sum[c]	n.a.	n.a.	n.a.	2.7	2.7	0
Nondurable goods[a]	5.0	3.8	1.2	2.2	1.7	.5
Two-digit sum[c]	n.a.	n.a.	n.a.	1.8	1.7	.1
Food and kindred products	4.6	4.7	-.1	.6	.6	(*)
Tobacco manufactures	1.4	-.2	1.6	(*)	(*)	(*)
Textile mill products	.2	.1	.1	(*)	(*)	(*)
Apparel and other fabricated textile products	12.6	12.5	.1	.5	.5	(*)
Paper and allied products	-2.8	-2.8	0	-.1	-.1	0
Printing, publishing, and allied industries	1.5	1.5	0	.1	.1	0
Chemicals and allied products	14.6	13.9	.7	1.1	1.0	.1
Petroleum refining and related industries	-20.1	-18.8	-1.3	-.5	-.5	(*)
Rubber and miscellaneous plastic products	6.1	7.5	-1.4	.2	.2	(*)
Leather and leather products	-5.9	-5.8	-.1	-.1	-.1	(*)

(continued)

TABLE 4 (concluded)

	Point Spreads			Point Contributions		
		Due to			Due to	
	Total	Movements	Weights	Total[a]	Movements	Weights
Durable goods[a]	.9	1.9	-1.0	.4	1.0	-.6
Two-digit sum[c]	n.a.	n.a.	n.a.	.9	1.0	-.1
Lumber and wood products, except furniture	-11.1	-9.7	-1.4	-.3	-.3	(*)
Furniture and fixtures	26.0	26.3	-.3	.4	.4	(*)
Stone, clay, and glass products	4.0	4.4	-.4	.2	.2	(*)
Primary metal industries	17.3	18.0	-.7	1.5	1.6	-.1
Fabricated metal products	7.6	7.3	.3	.5	.5	(*)
Machinery, except electrical	8.4	8.7	-.3	.7	.7	(*)
Electrical machinery	-10.9	-12.5	1.6	-.8	-.9	.1
Transportation equipment and ordnance, except motor vehicles	.6	.8	.2	(*)	(*)	(*)
Motor vehicles and motor vehicle equipment	-31.9	-30.9	-1.0	-1.9	-1.8	-.1
Instruments	9.0	8.7	.3	.2	.2	(*)
Miscellaneous manufacturing industries	22.6	22.6	0	.4	.4	0

Note: The following symbols are used in this table: * = less than .05. n.a. = not applicable. For other abbreviations see note at the beginning of Appendix C.

[a]FRB series with FRB weights throughout; GPO series with GPO weights throughout.

[b]FRB durable and nondurable series with FRB two-digit weights and GPO weights for durable and nondurable goods; GPO series with GPO weights throughout.

[c]FRB series with two-digit GPO weights and FRB weights within two-digits; GPO series with GPO weights throughout.

is closer to the Census measure of total output (the gap between these two Census measures is 5.5 points). For the apparel industry, whose relative importance is about one-half that of the chemicals industry, the published 1964 FRB index exceeds both Census measures as well as the OBE index. For both the chemicals and the apparel industry, the OBE and Census value-added series differ markedly and move in opposite directions.

If signs are ignored, the movement differences for durables are approximately 7 points and not 1 point. About one-half of the absolute difference of 7 points in movements within the durable group is accounted by the indexes for primary metals (1.6 points) and for motor vehicles and equipment (1.8 point). For both of these industries, the 1964 published FRB indexes approximate the movement of total Census deflated output; and the OBE indexes, net output. About 26 per cent of the difference occurs in four industries (SIC 32, 34, 35, 39) where total and net output are approximately the same, but the FRB series is consistently higher than the OBE indexes. For the stone, clay, and glass products industry (SIC 32) the OBE index approximates the Census value-added figure. The gaps between the OBE and Census value-added series for the remaining three industries approximate the same magnitude as between the OBE and FRB series. About 16 per cent of the difference for durables occurs in the lumber and electrical machinery industries where Census net exceeds total output and the OBE series are higher than the FRB indexes. The 1964 OBE and Census value-added indexes reflect about the same change from 1958 for the lumber industry, but the electrical machinery figure for Census value added is considerably higher than for the OBE series. Lastly, about 9 per cent of the gap is accounted for by two industries where the FRB exceeds OBE. For the furniture industry Census deflated net output is less than total output, and for instruments the converse is true.

Comparison Between the OBE and Published FRB Series

The broad pattern of manufacturing output as reflected by the two measures has been similar during the postwar period (Chart 1). As summarized in the table below (Table 5), both series exhibit a sharp rate of increase from 1948 to 1953, a slower rate of gain until 1960, and a large percentage gain since 1960.

CHART 1

All Manufacturing Industries: OBE and FRB Indexes of Real Output, 1947–64

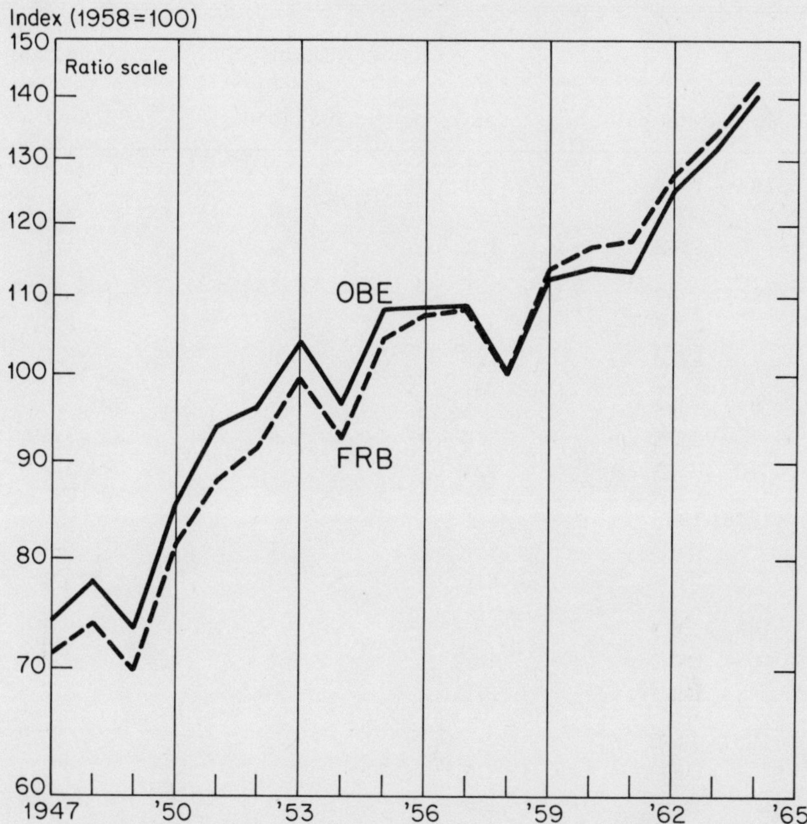

Despite these similarities, a larger growth rate is reflected by the FRB than by the OBE series. For 1948–64, the average annual growth for manufacturing is 3.8 per cent according to GPO, and 4.2 per cent based on the FRB index. Approximately the same differences in trends between the two series are indicated for the ten-year period, 1948–57, and for the eight-year period since 1957. Comparing the peak-to-peak years of successive business cycles, the growth rates as measured by OBE indexes are less than those indicated by the FRB for all periods, except for the incomplete cycle period 1960–64.

The indexes for the durable and nondurable goods industries also show similar patterns but with some recent exceptions. During 1948–64,

TABLE 5

Average Annual Percentage Change for Manufacturing Output for Selected Periods, OBE and FRB Indexes

Year and Series	Total	Durable Goods Industries	Nondurable Goods Industries
1948–1964			
OBE	3.8	4.0	3.5
FRB	4.2	4.4	4.1
1948–1957			
OBE	3.8	4.2	3.2
FRB	4.3	5.0	3.7
1957–1964			
OBE	3.7	3.6	3.8
FRB	4.0	3.6	4.6
1948–1953			
OBE	6.0	7.7	3.7
FRB	6.1	8.3	3.8
1953–1957			
OBE	1.1	0.1	2.7
FRB	2.1	1.0	3.7
1957–1960			
OBE	1.5	0.6	2.9
FRB	2.6	1.4	4.2
1960–1964			
OBE	5.4	6.0	4.5
FRB	5.2	5.3	4.9

Note: Figures show the average annual compounded rate of change between the initial and terminal years of each period.

CHART 2

Durable Goods Industries: OBE and FRB Indexes of Real Output, 1947–64

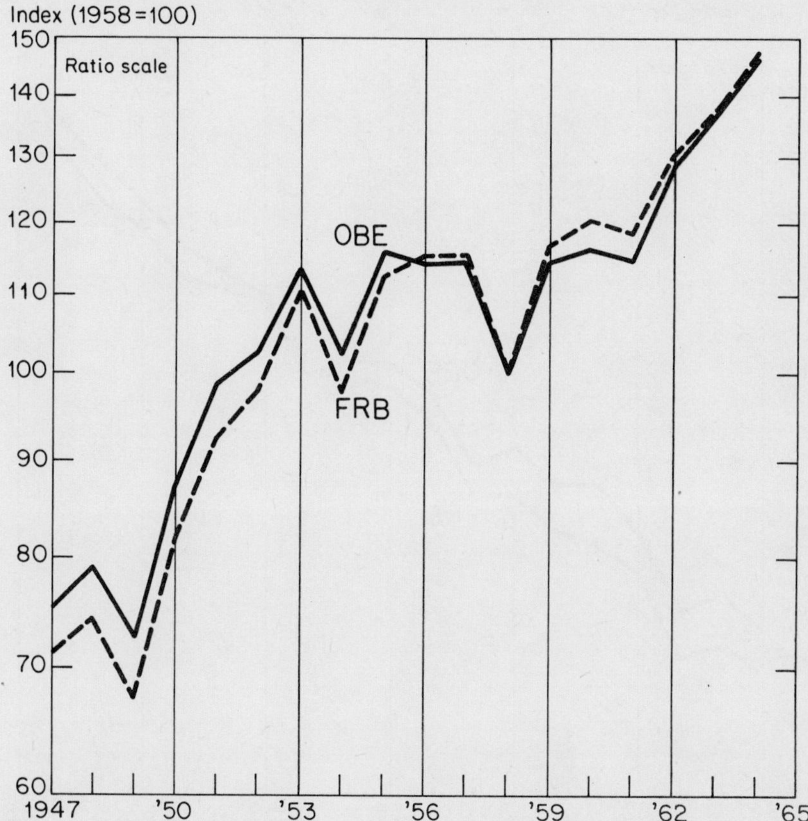

the average annual change for durable goods is 4.4 per cent according to the FRB indexes and 4.0 per cent for the OBE series. The rates for both durable goods series, however, are the same for the period since 1957 because of the sharper acceleration in the GPO series since 1960 (Chart 2). The 1960–64 rate for the OBE series is 6.0 per cent compared with 5.3 per cent for the FRB index.

For the nondurable goods industries, the OBE indexes always indicate a smaller growth than do the FRB series throughout 1948–64 and its subperiods (Chart 3). A partial explanation is the inclusion of excise

CHART 3

Nondurable Goods Industries: OBE and FRB Indexes of Real Output, 1947–64

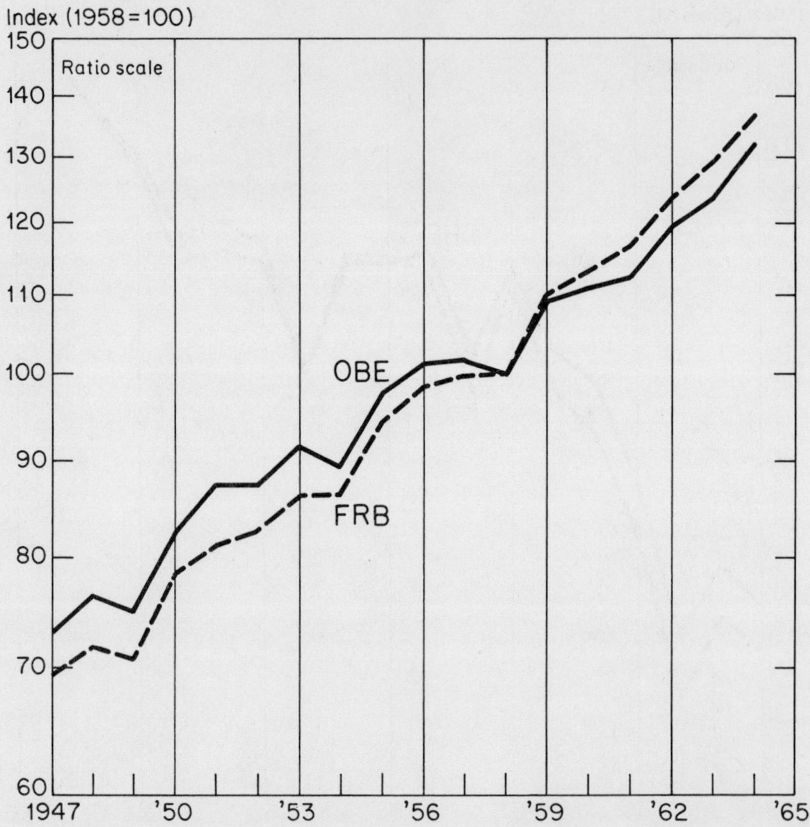

taxes in the OBE series, which gives added weight to the slower moving components of the nondurable group. (See discussion below.)

The difference in growth rates between the FRB and OBE indexes for durables is smaller than for the nondurables goods industries because the trend differences for industries within the former group are largely offsetting, but are not for the nondurables. Significantly higher growth rates occur in the FRB measures for the primary metals, and transportation equipment and ordnance, except motor vehicles industries, which in both the FRB and OBE series account for about 29 per cent of the total for the durable goods industries (Table 6). However, these

TABLE 6

Average Annual Percentage Change by Manufacturing Industries for Selected Periods, OBE and FRB Indexes

	1948–64		1948–57		1957–64	
	OBE	FRB	OBE	FRB	OBE	FRB
Total manufacturing	3.8	4.2	3.8	4.3	3.7	4.0
Nondurable goods	3.5	4.1	3.2	3.7	3.8	4.6
Food and kindred products	2.5	2.6	2.7	2.2	2.1	3.2
Tobacco manufactures	2.7	2.3	2.0	1.4	3.4	3.6
Textile mill products	1.7	1.9	0.2	0.7	3.6	3.5
Apparel and other fabricated textile products	2.6	3.5	2.0	2.5	3.4	4.8
Paper and allied products	4.5	4.7	4.3	4.6	4.7	4.8
Printing, publishing, and allied industries	3.1	3.3	3.4	3.4	2.8	3.2
Chemicals and allied products	6.9	8.2	7.7	8.6	5.9	7.8
Petroleum refining and related industries	4.4	3.7	3.7	4.2	5.3	3.0
Rubber and miscellaneous plastic products	4.3	6.5	2.8	6.1	6.3	7.0
Leather and leather products	-0.3	0.9	-1.3	1.3	0.9	0.5
Durable goods	4.0	4.4	4.2	5.0	3.6	3.6
Lumber and wood products, except furniture	1.8	1.3	0.2	0.5	3.8	2.3
Furniture and fixtures	2.5	4.6	2.6	3.6	2.3	5.8
Stone, clay, and glass products	3.3	3.6	3.0	3.6	3.7	3.6
Primary metal industries	1.2	2.0	2.0	1.9	0.2	2.0
Fabricated metal products	3.6	3.4	3.8	3.1	3.3	3.9
Machinery, except electrical	3.2	3.7	2.6	3.4	3.9	4.2
Electrical machinery	6.9	6.3	6.8	7.4	6.9	4.8
Transportation equipment and ordnance, except motor vehicles	7.9	10.3	12.5	17.3	2.2	1.9
Motor vehicles and motor vehicle equipment	5.3	4.4	5.0	4.1	5.7	4.8
Instruments	5.8	5.8	6.8	6.6	4.6	4.8
Miscellaneous manufacturing industries	2.2	2.9	2.0	1.7	2.4	4.4

Note: Figures show average annual compounded rate of change between the initial and terminal years of each period.

TABLE 7

Frequency Distribution of Number of Manufacturing Industries by Size of Average Annual Rate of Change, 1948–64

	Number of Industries	
Percentage Change	OBE Series	FRB Series
Negative	1	0
0–0.9	0	1
1–1.9	3	2
2–2.9	5	4
3–3.9	4	6
4–4.9	3	3
5–5.9	2	1
6 or higher	3	4

are offset by higher growth rates in the OBE series for the electrical machinery, motor vehicles and equipment, and lumber industries which, in aggregate, account for about 27 per cent of the group total for both the FRB and OBE series. For the nondurable goods industries the 1948–64 growth rates as measured by the FRB indexes are higher for almost all of the industries within this group.

A frequency distribution of the number of manufacturing industries by size of the 1948–64 annual average rates of change is shown in Table 7. The OBE series contains one industry with a negative rate of change and the FRB has none. The industry is leather and leather products, which has a rate of −0.3 per cent in the OBE series and 0.9 per cent in the FRB series. The OBE real product indexes show that only three industries have a growth rate of 6 per cent or more. The same three industries and also the rubber and miscellaneous plastic products industry are included in the same class interval for the FRB series.

YEAR-TO-YEAR CHANGES

For ten of the seventeen years, the differences in the year-to-year change in indexes between the OBE and published FRB series for total manufacturing is less than 1 point, and differences of 1.5 or more

TABLE 8

Frequency Distribution of Number of Years: Point Differences in Year-to-Year Changes Between the FRB and OBE Indexes, 1947-64

Point Differences	All Manufacturing Industries	Durable Goods Industries	Nondurable Goods Industries
Under 0.5	5	5	4
0.5–0.9	5	1	5
1.0–1.4	3	1	2
1.5–1.9	1	5	4
2.0–2.4	2	3	2
Over 2.5	1	2	0
Total	17	17	17

between the indexes occur only for four periods—1950–51, 1951–52, 1955–56, 1961–62. Larger differences appear among the durables than the nondurables. The number of years for which the indexes differ by 1.5 points or more is ten for durable and six for the nondurables.

The 1951 OBE index for total manufacturing is 10.2 per cent higher and the FRB index 8.1 per cent higher than the respective 1950 figures. For the durable goods industries the percentage changes are 13.7 per cent for OBE and 12.7 per cent for the FRB series. However, for the nondurable goods industries the 1951 OBE index is 5.6 per cent higher and the FRB index 3.3 per cent higher than the respective 1950 figures. The larger FRB-OBE gap for the nondurable industries stems largely from diverse movements between total and net output and between the Census value-added and OBE series. Such differences in the annual changes are particularly significant in the tobacco, textiles, chemicals, rubber, and leather and leather products industries, which are also characterized by relatively large changes in the inventory valuation adjustment.

The FRB indexes show higher annual percentage changes in 1952 compared with 1951 for both durable and nondurable goods industries. In the durable goods industries, this difference largely disappears if GPO weights are substituted for the FRB weights in the FRB series. In the nondurable goods industries weighting is less important, and the differences stem primarily from the diverse annual movements occurring in the apparel, paper, chemicals, and rubber industries.

The difference in the FRB-OBE percentage change from 1955 to 1956 for total manufacturing is largely due to the diverse movements for the durable goods industries. The FRB index for this group increased 2.1 per cent and the OBE index declined 1.6 per cent. This difference is caused primarily by the larger decline in the indexes for the motor vehicle and equipment industry (SIC 371) as measured by the OBE indexes than by the FRB indexes. The relatively large differences in the year-to-year movements in the indexes for total manufacturing from 1961 to 1962 again stem from the relative size of the changes in the OBE and FRB indexes for Industry 371.

Differences due to weighting for year-to-year changes are more significant in the earlier than the more recent years of the period reviewed. Generally, from 1947 through 1952 reweighting the FRB series by GPO weights brings the annual changes for this series closer to those reflected by the OBE series (Tables 9–11). With some exceptions, this is not true for the years since 1957.

While a portion of the dissimilarities in year-to-year movements between the FRB and OBE indexes arises from the diverse movements between gross and net output, these differences are relatively small for total durable and nondurable manufacturing industries. In addition, only a small amount of the differences for these groups is explained by the disparities in year-to-year changes between the current-dollar series for Census value added and gross product originating. Differences due to these factors for individual industries, however, are large; and are discussed below for selected industries.

DIFFERENCES DUE TO WEIGHTS

The effect of weighting differences on the growth rates for the 1948–64 period and for the two major subperiods is summarized below. The comparisons include a measure of the differences which result when the FRB indexes are weighted by 1958 GPO weights as well as when these indexes are recalculated with *total*-output rather than net-output weights.

Only a small portion of the FRB-OBE differences in the 1948–64 annual growth rates for total manufacturing is due to value-added

TABLE 9

Selected Measures of Manufacturing Activity, All Manufacturing Industries, 1947–64

	Indexes (1958 = 100)								Point Differences In Indexes[a]					
	FRB			Deflated Census Data				OBE						
		Reweighted												
Year	As Pub. (1)	GPO (2)	VP (3)	VP (4)	Cost Mat. (5)	VA (6)	VA Plus Excise (7)	Gross Product (8)	Total (FRB Minus OBE) (9)	FRB (Net Minus Gross Wtd.) (10)	Total Output (Quantity Minus Defltd.) (11)	Total Minus Net Output (12)	Excise Tax (13)	Net Output (Census Minus OBE) (14)
1947	71.2	73.1	73.7	75.7	75.6	75.8	76.2	74.2	-3.0	-2.5	-2.0	-.1	-.4	2.0
1948	73.9	75.5	76.1					77.8	-3.9	-2.2				
1949	69.8	71.0	72.2	73.4	76.7	69.3	70.2	73.5	-3.7	-2.4	-1.2	4.1	-.9	-3.3
1950	81.3	82.8	83.3	83.9	83.8	84.0	84.6	85.3	-4.0	-2.0	-.6	-.1	-.6	-.7
1951	87.9	89.8	89.5	90.7	89.4	92.2	92.4	93.9	-6.0	-1.6	-1.2	-1.5	-.2	-1.5
1952	91.4	92.2	91.7	94.1	94.0	94.2	94.1	96.0	-4.6	-.3	-2.4	-.1	.1	-1.9
1953	99.5	101.0	99.8	103.7	104.0	103.3	103.1	104.0	-4.5	-.3	-3.9	.4	.2	-.9
1954	92.6	93.3	93.1	94.9	95.5	94.2	94.1	96.6	-4.0	-.5	-1.8	.7	.1	-2.5
1955	104.4	105.9	105.6	107.0	107.6	106.2	106.1	108.0	-3.6	-1.2	-1.4	.8	.1	-1.9
1956	107.5	108.3	107.6	108.3	107.9	108.8	108.5	108.4	-.9	-.1	-.7	-.5	.3	.1
1957	108.2	108.7	107.9	107.8	107.6	108.2	107.9	108.8	-.6	.3	.1	-.4	.3	-.9
1958	100.0	100.0	100.0	100.0	100.0	100.0	100.0	100.0	.0	.0	.0	.0	.0	.0
1959	113.7	114.1	113.4	111.3	110.4	112.6	112.4	112.4	1.3	.3	2.1	-1.3	.2	.0
1960	116.8	117.3	116.6	113.3	113.0	113.7	113.7	113.9	2.9	.2	3.3	-.4	.0	-.2
1961	117.6	117.6	117.1	113.2	113.2	113.2	113.2	113.5	4.1	.5	3.9	.0	.0	-.3
1962	127.4	127.5	126.4	122.5	121.4	123.9	123.6	125.0	2.4	1.0	3.9	-1.4	.3	-1.4
1963	134.0	134.2	133.0	128.8	126.5	131.7	131.5	131.3	2.7	1.0	4.2	-2.9	.2	.2
1964	142.8	143.1	141.3	136.6	134.0	140.0	139.5	140.4	2.4	1.5	4.7	-3.4	.5	-.9

Note: VP = value of production; VA = value added. For other abbreviations see note at the beginning of Appendix C.

[a]Col. 9 = col. 1 – col. 8; col. 10 = col. 1 – col. 3; col. 11 = col. 3 – col. 4; col. 12 = col. 4 – col. 6; col. 13 = col. 6 – col. 7; col. 14 = col. 7 – col. 8.

TABLE 10

Selected Measures of Manufacturing Activity, Nondurable Goods Industries, 1947–64

	Indexes (1958 = 100)								Point Differences In Indexes[a]					
	FRB			Deflated Census Data				OBE Gross Product	Total (FRB Minus OBE)	FRB (Net Minus Gross Wtd.)	Total Output (Quantity Minus Defltd.)	Total Minus Net Output	Excise Tax	Net Output (Census Minus OBE)
	As Pub.	Reweighted GPO	Reweighted VP	VP	Cost Mat.	VA	VA Plus Excise							
Year	(1)	(2)	(3)	(4)	(5)	(6)	(7)	(8)	(9)	(10)	(11)	(12)	(13)	(14)
1947	69.4	72.0	73.0	73.2	72.9	73.7	74.6	73.0	-3.6	-3.6	-.2	-.5	-.9	1.6
1948	71.8	73.7	74.3					76.4	-4.6	-2.5				
1949	70.6	72.3	73.2	74.1	75.8	71.6	72.6	74.8	-4.2	-2.6	-.9	2.5	-1.0	-2.2
1950	78.5	80.0	80.1	80.1	78.4	82.8	83.4	82.8	-4.3	-1.6	.0	-2.7	-.6	.6
1951	81.1	82.6	83.0	83.1	81.8	85.1	85.5	87.4	-6.3	-1.9	-.1	-2.0	-.4	-1.9
1952	82.6	83.7	84.9	85.0	85.8	83.8	84.6	87.4	-4.8	-2.3	-.1	1.2	-.8	-2.8
1953	86.4	87.0	87.8	89.0	88.2	90.2	90.5	91.5	-5.1	-1.4	-1.2	-1.2	-.3	-1.0
1954	86.4	86.7	87.8	88.3	88.5	88.1	88.3	89.3	-2.9	-1.4	-.5	.2	-.2	-1.0
1955	94.6	94.7	95.6	96.1	95.9	96.5	96.4	97.8	-3.2	-1.0	-.5	-.4	.1	-1.4
1956	98.6	98.6	99.4	100.3	99.7	101.0	100.8	101.1	-2.5	-.8	-.9	-.7	.2	-.3
1957	99.9	99.7	99.9	100.6	99.3	102.6	102.1	101.7	-1.8	.0	-.7	-2.0	.5	.4
1958	100.0	100.0	100.0	100.0	100.0	100.0	100.0	100.0	.0	.0	.0	.0	.0	.0
1959	110.0	109.9	109.4	108.3	107.5	109.7	109.1	109.2	.8	.6	1.1	-1.4	.6	-.1
1960	113.1	112.8	112.0	110.2	109.5	111.4	110.9	110.9	2.2	1.1	1.8	-1.2	.5	.0
1961	116.6	116.3	115.4	112.6	112.5	112.7	112.4	112.3	4.3	1.2	2.8	-.1	.3	.1
1962	123.8	123.0	121.5	118.5	117.6	120.0	119.2	119.6	4.2	2.3	3.0	-1.5	.8	-.4
1963	129.4	128.5	126.7	123.6	121.8	126.4	125.4	123.7	5.7	2.7	3.1	-2.8	1.0	1.7
1964	137.0	135.8	133.4	130.9	128.2	135.0	133.5	132.0	5.0	3.6	2.5	-4.1	1.5	1.5

Note: VP = value of production; VA = value added. For other abbreviations see note at the beginning of Appendix C.

[a]Col. 9 = col. 1 – col. 8; col. 10 = col. 1 – col. 3; col. 11 = col. 3 – col. 4; col. 12 = col. 4 – col. 6; col. 13 = col. 6 – col. 7; col. 14 = col. 7 – col. 8.

TABLE 11

Selected Measures of Manufacturing Activity, Durable Goods Industries, 1947–64

	Indexes (1958 = 100)								Point Differences In Indexes[a]					
	FRB			Deflated Census Data				OBE Gross Product						
		Reweighted												
Year	As Pub. (1)	GPO (2)	VP (3)	VP (4)	Cost Mat. (5)	VA (6)	VA Plus Excise (7)	(8)	Total (FRB Minus OBE) (9)	FRB (Net Minus Gross Wtd.) (10)	Total Output (Quantity Minus Defltd.) (11)	Total Minus Net Output (12)	Excise Tax (13)	Net Output (Census Minus OBE) (14)
1947	71.2	73.9	74.5	78.2	78.9	77.5	77.5	75.2	-4.0	-3.3	-3.7	.7	.0	2.3
1948	74.2	76.9	77.8					78.9	-4.7	-3.6				
1949	67.4	70.0	71.3	72.7	77.7	67.5	68.0	72.5	-5.1	-3.9	-1.4	5.2	-.5	-4.5
1950	82.1	84.9	86.6	87.7	90.3	85.0	85.6	87.3	-5.2	-4.5	-1.1	2.7	-.6	-1.7
1951	92.5	95.4	96.1	98.3	98.5	98.0	98.4	99.0	-6.5	-3.6	-2.2	.3	-.4	-.6
1952	98.0	98.7	98.5	103.3	103.9	102.6	102.5	102.6	-4.6	-.5	-4.8	.7	.1	-.1
1953	110.6	111.8	112.1	118.5	123.0	113.9	114.1	113.7	-3.1	-1.5	-6.4	4.6	-.2	.4
1954	97.9	98.3	98.5	101.6	103.9	99.1	99.3	102.2	-4.3	-.6	-3.1	2.5	-.2	-2.9
1955	112.8	114.5	115.7	117.9	121.7	113.9	114.7	115.9	-3.1	-2.9	-2.2	4.0	-.8	-1.2
1956	115.2	115.7	115.9	116.3	117.6	115.1	115.2	114.1	1.1	-.7	-.4	1.2	-.1	1.1
1957	115.2	115.7	116.1	115.1	117.4	112.7	113.0	114.3	.9	-.9	1.0	2.4	-.3	-1.3
1958	100.0	100.0	100.0	100.0	100.0	100.0	100.0	100.0	.0	.0	.0	.0	.0	.0
1959	116.9	117.4	117.5	114.4	113.9	115.0	115.2	114.8	2.1	-.6	3.1	-.6	-.2	.4
1960	120.2	120.7	121.2	116.4	117.2	115.7	116.1	116.3	3.9	-1.0	4.8	.7	-.4	-.2
1961	118.5	118.7	118.8	113.8	113.9	113.7	113.9	114.5	4.0	-.3	5.0	.1	-.2	-.6
1962	130.6	130.9	131.4	126.5	126.0	127.1	127.6	129.2	1.4	-.8	4.9	-.6	-.5	-1.6
1963	137.9	138.7	139.3	134.0	132.1	136.1	136.8	137.3	.6	-1.4	5.3	-2.1	-.7	-.5
1964	147.8	148.8	149.4	142.4	140.8	144.1	144.9	146.9	.9	-1.6	7.0	-1.7	-.8	-2.0

Note: VP = value of production; VA = value added. For other abbreviations see note at the beginning of Appendix C.

[a]Col. 9 = col. 1 – col. 8; col. 10 = col. 1 – col. 3; col. 11 = col. 3 – col. 4; col. 12 = col. 4 – col. 6; col. 13 = col. 6 – col. 7; col. 14 = col. 7 – col. 8.

TABLE 12

Point Differences in Trends Between Published and Reweighted FRB and OBE Indexes

Year and Series	Total	Durable Goods Industries	Nondurable Goods Industries
1948–64			
Pub. FRB minus OBE	0.4	0.4	0.6
FRB rewtd. GPO minus OBE	0.3	0.2	0.4
FRB rewtd. VP minus OBE	0.1	0.2	0.2
Pub. minus FRB rewtd. GPO	0.1	0.2	0.2
Pub. minus FRB rewtd. VP	0.3	0.2	0.4
1948–57			
Pub. FRB minus OBE	0.5	0.8	0.5
FRB rewtd. GPO minus OBE	0.3	0.4	0.2
FRB rewtd. VP minus OBE	0.2	0.3	0.1
Pub. minus FRB rewtd. GPO	0.2	0.4	0.3
Pub. minus FRB rewtd. VP	0.3	0.5	0.4
1957–64			
Pub. FRB minus OBE	0.3	0.0	0.8
FRB rewtd. GPO minus OBE	0.3	0.1	0.7
FRB rewtd. VP minus OBE	0.2	0.1	0.4
Pub. minus FRB rewtd. GPO	0.0	-0.1	0.1
Pub. minus FRB rewtd. VP	0.1	-0.1	0.4

Note: VP = value of production. For other abbreviations see note at the beginning of Appendix C.

weights.[11] However, when the FRB indexes are reweighted by the 1958 Census value of production the spread in the growth rates for 1948–64 and for the two subperiods is sizeably reduced. For 1948–64, the difference in growth rates between the OBE series and the FRB indexes

[11] However, if 1947 is used as the initial year, the trend differences between the OBE and the FRB series reweighted by 1958 GPO weights are halved for the period, as a whole, and the gap between the 1947–57 growth rates for the two series is substantially reduced.

reweighted by value of production is only 0.1 point rather than 0.4 points because of the closer relationship in trends for the nondurable goods industries.

In contrast with the impact on the total indexes, differences due to weighting in the 1948–64 trends are more important for the durables than for the nondurable goods industries. For this period when the FRB indexes are reweighted by the 1958 GPO, the differences for the durables are halved; for the nondurables, these are reduced by one-third. On the other hand, the influence of total-output weights is more pronounced on the spreads for the nondurables.

DIFFERENCES IN REAL TOTAL OUTPUT AS MEASURED BY QUANTITY OR BY DEFLATION

As previously indicated and described in detail in Appendix A, the measures that the FRB uses to estimate output are based on a count of quantities produced, or proxies of such counts. In recent years the principal proxy has been man-hours adjusted for changes in productivity. In the OBE series the derivation of total output is by deflation.

To measure differences between the two methods, the detailed FRB indexes used for manufacturing were weighted by appropriate 1958 Census production data and recalculated for 1947–64. Trends for 1947–64 (there are no 1948 Census data) based on these reweighted FRB series and corresponding Census measures appear in Table 13 below.

For 1947–64, the trends for the reweighted FRB series are higher than for the deflated Census value of production data for total manufacturing and for the subgroups. The point differences in the 1947–64 trends between the reweighted FRB and Census value of total production indexes for total manufacturing is 0.4 points. Differences in output for the durables are 0.6, and 0.2 points for the nondurables.

The 1947–64 trends for fourteen of the twenty-one manufacturing industries also show that the reweighted FRB series grows faster than the deflated Census VP series. Of the remaining seven industries, the deflated Census series grows faster for five, and the trends are identical for two industries.

For 1957–64, the growth of the FRB series is substantially larger (2.0 points or more) in apparel, furniture, and transportation equipment and ordnance, except motor vehicles; and substantially smaller for elec-

TABLE 13

Trends in Total Output for Manufacturing: FRB Indexes Weighted by 1958 Census Value of Production and Indexes of Deflated Census Value of Total Production, 1947–64, 1947–57, 1957–64

SIC Number	Industry	1947–64 FRB Wtd.	1947–64 Deflated Census	1947–57 FRB Wtd.	1947–57 Deflated Census	1957–64 FRB Wtd.	1957–64 Deflated Census
Manufacturing		3.9	3.5	3.9	3.6	3.9	3.4
	Nondurable goods	3.6	3.5	3.2	3.2	4.2	3.8
20	Food and kindred products	2.4	2.6	1.9	2.4	3.1	3.0
21	Tobacco manufactures	2.1	1.4	1.7	0.3	2.6	2.9
22	Textile mill products	2.1	3.2	1.2	2.2	3.5	4.5
23	Apparel and other fabricated textile products	3.6	2.9	2.7	3.1	4.9	2.7
26	Paper and allied products	4.5	4.0	4.3	3.8	4.9	4.2
27	Printing, publishing, and allied industries	3.6	3.1	3.8	3.0	3.2	3.3
28	Chemicals and allied products	7.9	6.7	8.1	7.0	7.6	6.3
29	Petroleum refining and related industries	3.8	4.1	4.5	4.8	2.8	3.1
30	Rubber and miscellaneous plastic products	5.6	4.4	4.4	2.9	7.3	6.6
31	Leather and leather products	0.5	-0.1	0.5	-0.2	0.4	0.1

(continued)

TABLE 13 (concluded)

SIC Number	Industry	1947–64 FRB Wtd.	1947–64 Deflated Census	1947–57 FRB Wtd.	1947–57 Deflated Census	1957–64 FRB Wtd.	1957–64 Deflated Census
	Durable goods	4.2	3.6	4.5	3.9	3.7	3.1
24	Lumber and wood products, except furniture	1.6	1.9	1.0	1.0	2.5	3.3
25	Furniture and fixtures	4.6	3.2	3.6	3.3	5.9	3.0
32	Stone, clay, and glass products	4.3	4.3	4.6	4.8	3.8	3.6
33	Primary metal industries	2.3	1.8	2.4	1.8	2.1	1.7
34	Fabricated metal products	3.4	2.8	3.1	3.1	3.8	2.3
35	Machinery, except electrical	3.6	2.7	3.2	2.3	4.3	3.4
36	Electrical machinery	5.9	5.9	6.9	4.9	4.6	6.5
37+19-371	Transport. equip. and ord., except motor veh.	9.2	7.1	14.7	12.9	1.9	-0.7
371	Motor vehicles and equipment	4.7	4.3	4.7	4.5	4.8	4.0
38	Instruments	5.6	5.5	6.1	4.8	4.8	6.5
39	Miscellaneous manufacturing industries	3.1	3.2	2.2	2.2	4.4	4.7

trical machinery. For all of these industries, except apparel, the FRB measures the quantity of output entirely or principally by the proxy, man-hours adjusted for productivity. For the eight industries where the 1957–64 trend differences are small (0.5 points or less) three are measured only by quantity measures and one only by man-hours. Of the remaining four industries, about 75 per cent of the output for the leather and rubber industries; 57 per cent for foods; and about 30 per cent of the output for the printing and publishing, and stone, clay, and glass products industries are measured by quantity measures.

OBE, FRB, and Census Measures of Net Output

In the discussion above, the FRB indexes reweighted by 1958 Census production data and corresponding deflated Census totals were compared to determine differences in total output when measured by quantity or by deflation. In this section the OBE and published FRB indexes are compared with Census measures of net output. When the OBE series are compared with Census value added, the latter have been adjusted to include federal excise taxes. Thus these two series are comparable.

The relationship between the OBE and Census data reflects differences or similarities in the underlying measures of net output in current dollars. The FRB-Census differences reflect the patterns of change in the underlying real-total-output measures as discussed above.

Differences in growth rates between Census value of production (VP) and value added (VA) for total manufacturing, durables, and nondurables are relatively small for 1947–64 and 1947–57. For the 1957–64 period the trend differences are relatively large for the durable goods industries, and this difference is also reflected in the figures for total manufacturing (Table 14).

From 1947 to 1957 both the OBE and FRB measures of output show larger increases than the Census value-added series. However, the gap between the FRB and Census is substantially larger for total manufacturing and for the durable goods industries than the OBE-Census growth rate differences. Since 1957, the OBE and Census value-added series have shown about the same rate of gain. On the other hand, the FRB growth rate for nondurables is considerably larger than the Census value-added rate.

TABLE 14

Comparison of Trends in Real Product as Measured by FRB, OBE, and Census Measures for Selected Periods
(point differences between compounded annual average rates of change)

Year and Series	Total	Durable Goods Industries	Nondurable Goods Industries
1947-64			
Pub. FRB minus OBE	0.4	0.4	0.6
Census VP minus VA	-0.2	-0.1	-0.1
OBE minus Census VA, plus tax	0.2	0.3	0.0
Pub. FRB minus Census VA	0.5	0.7	0.5
1947–57			
Pub. FRB minus OBE	0.4	0.6	0.3
Census VP minus VA	-0.0	0.1	-0.2
OBE minus Census VA, plus tax	0.4	0.5	0.2
Pub. FRB minus Census VA	0.7	1.1	0.3
1957–64			
Pub. FRB minus OBE	0.3	0.0	0.8
Census VP minus VA	-0.3	-0.5	-0.2
OBE minus Census VA, plus tax	0.0	0.0	-0.1
Pub. FRB minus Census VA	0.3	0.0	0.6

Note: VP = value of production; VA = value added. For other abbreviations see beginning of Appendix C.

COMPARISONS BY TWO-DIGIT INDUSTRIES, 1957–64

While the 1957–64 OBE and Census VA growth rates for total manufacturing and the durable goods industries are identical, this relationship does not hold for any two-digit industry. On the other hand, the 1957–64 trends based on the FRB and on the Census value-added indexes are identical for three industries.

As shown in Table 15, point differences in the 1957–64 trends for thirteen of the twenty-one industries are smaller when the OBE and

Census value-added series are compared than for the FRB and Census value-added series. The largest disparity occurs for the petroleum refining industry, which has a 3.0 per cent growth rate for 1957–64 according to the FRB indexes and a 7.7 per cent rate based on Census deflated value added. The largest gap between the OBE and Census value-added measures occurs for the instrument industry, which has a 2.5 point higher growth rate according to the Census measure. More rapid growth is shown for only eight industries (SIC 22, 24, 29, 31, 32, 36, 371, and (37 + 19 − 371)) by the OBE measures, when compared with the FRB series. For five of these industries, the 1957–64 average annual rate of change for the Census value-added series is higher than for the corresponding Census value-of-production series; for one industry, Census net and gross output trends are identical; and for two industries, Census total output is higher than value added.

Comparison by Industry

In this section, the principal reasons for differences in the OBE and FRB measures of output for two-digit (SIC) manufacturing industries are summarized. While data for all two-digit SIC industries are shown (see Appendix C), only selected industries are discussed below.[12] These industries illustrate more specifically the principal conditions causing variations between the FRB and OBE series in trends or year-to-year movements.

Disparities in the FRB and OBE trends for some industries and for some periods are related primarily to different movements in total and net output as reflected by the Census measures. Changes in the ratio of value added per unit of output have occurred because the composition of the products produced by an industry over time has changed and the FRB series selected to measure the industry output did not reflect this change. This is illustrated by the varying proportions of metal to wooden furniture produced by the household furniture industry (SIC 251), which is described below. Significant changes in product composition even within product groupings (radios, TV's, freezers, communications equipment, etc.) for the electrical machinery

[12] Discussions for all two-digit SIC manufacturing industries are available upon request to the Office of Business Economics, U.S. Department of Commerce, Washington, D.C. 20035.

TABLE 15

Comparison of Trends in Real Product as Measured by FRB, OBE, and Census Measures, by Industries, 1957–64
(point differences between compounded annual average rates of change)

SIC Number		Pub. FRB Minus OBE	Census VP Minus Census VA	OBE Minus Census VA Plus Tax	Pub. FRB Minus Census VA
	Total manufacturing	0.3	-0.3	0.0	0.3
	Nondurable goods	0.8	-0.2	-0.1	0.6
20	Food and kindred products	1.1	1.5	0.4	1.7
21	Tobacco manufactures	0.2	-0.8	0.2	-0.1
22	Textile mill products	-0.1	0.6	-0.3	-0.4
23	Apparel and other fabricated textile products	1.4	-0.0	0.7	2.1
26	Paper and allied products	0.1	-0.6	-0.1	0.0
27	Printing, publishing, and allied industries	0.4	0.4	-0.1	0.3
28	Chemicals and allied products	1.9	-0.7	-1.1	0.8
29	Petroleum refining and related industries	-2.3	-4.6	-0.7	-4.7
30	Rubber and miscellaneous plastic products	0.7	0.0	-0.1	0.4
31	Leather and leather products	-0.4	-0.4	0.4	0.0

(continued)

TABLE 15 (concluded)

SIC Number		Pub. FRB Minus OBE	Census VP Minus Census VA	OBE Minus Census VA Plus Tax	Pub. FRB Minus Census VA
	Durable goods	0.0	-0.5	0.0	0.0
24	Lumber and wood prod., except furniture	-1.5	0.0	0.5	-1.0
25	Furniture and fixtures	3.5	0.8	0.1	3.6
32	Stone, clay, and glass products	-0.1	0.1	0.2	0.1
33	Primary metal industries	1.8	0.8	-0.7	1.1
34	Fabricated metal products	0.6	0.0	1.0	1.6
35	Machinery, except electrical	0.3	0.0	0.5	0.8
36	Electrical machinery	-2.1	-1.3	-0.8	-3.0
37-371+19	Transportation equipment and ordnance, except motor vehicles	-0.3	-1.6	1.3	1.0
371	Motor vehicles and motor vehicle equipment	-0.9	-1.5	0.3	-0.7
38	Instruments	0.2	-0.6	-2.5	-2.3
39	Miscellaneous manufacturing industries	2.0	0.3	-2.0	0.0

Note: VA = value added; VP = Value of production. For other abbreviations see note at the beginning of Appendix C.

industry (SIC 36) have also occurred, which apparently are not fully reflected by the FRB methodology. Changes in technology have also caused shifts in the unit cost of materials. For example, the value added per unit of output for the blast furnace and steel mills industry (SIC 331) has declined because the ores shipped from the mines in more recent years are of a higher grade than those previously shipped. Refinery gases, which are a source of petrochemicals, represent an increasing contribution to the output for the petroleum refinery industry (SIC 291), but have no explicit representation in the FRB indexes. Value added per unit of output in the dairy industry (SIC 202), which has been reduced by a shift from home to store and institutional deliveries, is not reflected by the total quantities of milk produced. Representation of tobacco stemming and drying, which accounts for a varying unit value added for the tobacco industry (SIC 21), by measures of the quantities of chewing and smoking tobacco produced contributed to differences between the OBE and FRB measures for this industry.

Differences in the measure of net output also reflect differences in total output which arise because FRB has measured output based on counts of quantities produced or proxies (principally man-hours) of such counts and the OBE has derived such output by deflation. For example, the 1947–64 average annual rates for the FRB indexes reweighted by 1958 value of production grow faster than the deflated Census value of production series for fourteen of the twenty-one manufacturing industries (See Table 13). Large differences (1.0 point or more) occur in the furniture, chemicals, rubber and plastics, fabricated metal products, and transportation equipment and ordnance, except motor vehicles, industries. Since 1957, almost 100 per cent of the total output for all of these industries, except chemicals, and rubber and plastics, was determined by a man-hour series adjusted for changes in productivity. Differences in output also arise for specified time periods in the apparel and shoe industries when output determined by number of garments cut or shoes produced is compared with deflated value of production.

The use of different data sources to determine output trends also contributes to varying movements. As shown below, the 1958–64 FRB movements for meat products (SIC 201) and dairy products (SIC 202) differ markedly from those of deflated value of production partially because the FRB measures are based on agricultural data whose coverage includes establishments not classified as manufacturing plants.

Differences in trends between the OBE and FRB series also are caused by the inclusion of taxes in the OBE series and their omission from the FRB measures. For example, the higher OBE growth rate compared with the FRB rate for tobacco manufactures (SIC 21) is partially due to this factor. Reweighting the FRB index by 1958 GPO weights also results in a greater similarity in the 1947–64 trends for rubber and plastics products (SIC 30) and transportation equipment and ordnance, except motor vehicles (SIC 37 + 19 – 371) industries.

Differences between the published FRB and OBE series in the year-to-year movements is also frequently related to varying movements for total and net output. This is particularly true for the years immediately after World War II and during the Korean conflict. In addition, for some industries, the discrepancies between the OBE and FRB series for years prior to 1952 arise because the weights used for the OBE series reflect 1958 price relationships for the 1947–64 period, while the currently published FRB indexes are combined with weights that embody 1957 price relationships for post-1952 data and 1947 price relationships for the years 1947–52. This relationship partially accounts for the pre-1957 variations in movements for the paper and allied products industry and transportation equipment and ordnance, except motor vehicles industries. Reweighting the FRB indexes reduces differences between year-to-year changes for the FRB and OBE series for some years for the same industries.

The direction or amplitude of change for the OBE series for some industries differs from the FRB or Census measures because the current-dollar totals for only the former series are adjusted for inventory valuation. These differences appear during years when large price movements occur, such as during 1949–51. For example, the year-to-year changes between the OBE and Census measures of value added would be similar for the apparel industry, particularly for 1949–53 and 1960–61, if the comparisons were based on GPO figures before adjustment for inventory valuation. The movements between Census value added and OBE indexes would also be more similar for the tobacco, furniture, rubber and leather industries, if the OBE series were adjusted to make them comparable in concept with the other measures.

Differences in classification of industries or activities also account for annual variations. For example, during the Korean conflict substantial amounts of war goods were produced as secondary products in the machinery, fabricated metal, transportation equipment, and instruments industries. The Federal Reserve in its 1959 revision added "representation for these products to the private ordnance plant series rather than to the appropriate two-digit groups with the result that the former series is overstated and the latter industries understated in the year 1951, 1952, and possibly 1953." [13]

The sources from which the Census Bureau and the OBE derive their data also contribute to differences among the several measures. Such variations in coverage and classification of establishments are noticeable in the lumber and apparel industries particularly for the pre-1954 period when the Census data were subject to high sampling errors, and the OBE data include estimates of establishment profits based on the 1958 Census-IRS link project. Significant differences in OBE and Census payroll figures have also occurred since 1958 for instruments, fabricated metal products, leather, and lumber industries. Variations in the movements between the Census value added and OBE indexes have also caused differences between the FRB and OBE series.

Each of the industries which are discussed below have been selected because they contain examples of the major causes of differences between the OBE and FRB series. The discussion of the printing industry (SIC 27) is included for contrast since it illustrates how the OBE and FRB movements for some industries are similar despite differences in methodology and data sources.

FOOD AND KINDRED PRODUCTS (SIC 20)

The OBE and published FRB series show approximately the same 1948–64 annual rates of growth for the food, beverage, and kindred products industries.[14] The figures are 2.5 per cent and 2.6 per cent respectively. The annual average rates of change for both series, however, differ substantially for the periods prior to and subsequent to 1957 and are principally explained by varying movements between net and total output. For 1948–57, the average annual rate for the

[13] Letter of May 18, 1966, from Clayton Gehman.

[14] The relative importance of this industry expressed as a percentage of the respective manufacturing total is as follows:

	1947	*1958*	*1964*
OBE	12.4	12.1	10.1
FRB (as pub.)	13.4	11.9	10.1

OBE series is 2.7 per cent, and for the FRB series, 2.2 per cent.[15] Since 1957, the rates are 2.1 and 3.2 per cent respectively for the OBE and the FRB series (Appendix C). Reweighting the FRB series by either 1958 GPO or by 1958 Census value of production affects the 1948–57 growth rates. The trend for the FRB indexes is 0.2 points lower when weighted by GPO weights, and 0.2 points higher, when weighted by gross weights, than the rates for the published series. The 1957–64 trends for the reweighted and published FRB series are approximately the same.

The deflated 1947–57 Census data for the food and kindred products [16] industry show a slightly declining ratio of quantity of materials and energy consumed to the amount of goods produced, but a more rapidly rising ratio since 1957. Thus, the Census measures of net output increased less rapidly since 1957 compared with 1947–57, and the converse applies to the annual rates of change for total output.[17] The OBE indexes of real product reflect the Census net-output pattern, and the trend of the FRB indexes follows that of the Census value-of-production series, which shows 1957–64 as a period of more rapid increase compared with 1947–57.

The FRB-OBE differences in year-to-year changes for some years are also due to diverse movements between total and net output. For example, larger changes in quantity of value added than in total output occurred between 1949–50, 1952–53, 1956–57, and even in the direction of the change as for 1957–58 or 1960–61 (see Appendix Table C-2). Differences in weighting also result in disparities in the year-to-year movements, particularly for 1947–52, between the OBE and FRB indexes.

Another cause for trend and year-to-year disparities between the OBE and FRB series is the derivation of output by deflation versus quantity measures. Many of the twenty-three series used by FRB to

[15] If the terminal year of 1957 is not used, then the percentage changes from 1948 to 1956 or to 1958 for both indexes are approximately the same.

[16] Adjusted for SIC changes. The adjustments in the Census and OBE data and in the *Annual Survey of Manufacturers* data for the fluid milk industry, the fats and oils industries, and other SIC changes are relatively large in the early years of this subperiod.

[17] The 1957–64 higher growth rates for value of production compared with value added are largely due to higher than average increases in output by industries characterized by low unit value added such as SIC 201—meat products or SIC 2092—soybean oil mills.

measure output for this industry are quantity series based on information compiled by the U.S. Department of Agriculture. These product data are not necessarily representative of the Census shipment data because the food producing establishments may not be classified as a manufacturing unit.[18] Variations resulting from the sources as well as from the measures employed may be illustrated by the 1958–63 percentage changes for selected food industries as indicated by the FRB series, the Census bench mark, and deflated value of shipments as shown below.

	FRB Indexes	*Census Bench-mark Indexes*	*Deflated Census Shipments*
201 Meat products [a]	22.3	15.5	24.1
202 Dairy products [a]	9.8	14.4	1.7
203 Canned and frozen foods [b]	36.8	d	28.8
205 Bakery products [b]	16.0	6.4	3.5
206 Sugar [a]	13.0	18.6	16.4
207 Candy and related products [c]	18.4	20.7	9.1

[a] FRB indexes based on quantity data compiled by U.S. Dept. of Agriculture.
[b] FRB indexes based on man-hours adjusted for productivity changes.
[c] FRB indexes based on quantity data compiled by Census Bureau.
[d] Not shown because comparable quantity data were not obtained for a significant portion of these products. (*1963 Census of Manufactures,* Vol. 2, 20C [preliminary version].)

The percentage changes from 1958 shown in the FRB series for bakery products (SIC 205) and for canned and frozen foods (SIC 203), which are based on man-hours, are higher than for the Census bench-mark series or deflated shipments. When the FRB indexes are based on U.S. Department of Agriculture data they are higher than the Census bench-mark figures for meat products (SIC 201) and lower for dairy products (SIC 202) and sugar (SIC 206). When the FRB is based on Census data, such as for SIC 207, the percentage changes for this series and the Census bench-mark series are approximately the same.

In addition to differences in coverage, represented by varying series, outputs derived from a quantity series and by deflation may differ because of differences in product mix. This is illustrated by the figures for the dairy products industry (SIC 202). More than 60 per cent of

[18] For meat products see *1958 Census of Manufactures,* p. 20A-2; for dairy products, p. 20B-3; for grain mill products, p. 20C-1.

the shipment values for industry 202 arise from the fluid milk industry (2026), and its principal product class, packaged milk and related products (20262). The 1963 product class figure in current dollars is 4.8 per cent higher than the 1958 total, but 7.6 per cent less when expressed in 1958 dollars. The Census production indexes, principally based on quantity of products shipped, show that 1963 output is 8.1 per cent higher than for 1958, and that unit values declined by 2.8 per cent. In contrast, the BLS price composite for this product class shows an increase of 13.4 per cent since 1958. The price decline in average unit prices resulting from measuring changes in output by quantities for relatively broad categories does not reflect shifts in quantities between home and retail store deliveries, nor in shifts from quarts to half-gallon packages, or for all other "quality" changes. Some of these changes are measured by specification prices.

Variations in the amplitude of change between the Census value added plus excise taxes and the OBE series are caused by differences in the current-dollar totals for the respective series. In part, these disparities are generally explained by the IVA adjustments to the GPO totals. For example, the 1955 figure for IVA raised the GPO total for that year, while the 1956 and 1957 figures were lowered by IVA (Appendix B). The change from 1955 to 1956 in the real product index is 4.2 per cent, but would be 6.7 per cent if there were no IVA adjustment. These figures compare with the 8.0 per cent increase for deflated Census value added plus excise tax. For the other periods indicated, the differences between the OBE and Census value added plus excise taxes series would also have been reduced.

FURNITURE AND FIXTURES (SIC 25)

The 1948–64 average annual rate of increase of this major group [19] when measured by the FRB index is almost twice (4.6 per cent) the figure based on the OBE series (2.5 per cent). The rates also differ markedly for the subperiods 1948–57 and 1957–64. For the former period, the trends are 2.6 and 3.6 per cent respectively for the OBE

[19] The relative importance of this industry, expressed as a percentage of the respective manufacturing total, is as follows:

	1947	*1958*	*1964*
OBE	1.6	1.5	1.4
FRB (As pub.)	1.8	1.8	1.9

and the FRB series. In the post-1957 period, the compound annual rate of change for the OBE series is 2.3 per cent and 5.8 per cent for the FRB series. The reweighted FRB indexes (1958 GPO or Census value of production weights) do not differ significantly in trends or in year-to-year changes from the published FRB series. The spread between the 1964 published or reweighted FRB indexes and the OBE index is 26 or more points (Appendix Table C-7).

The movements of the OBE series generally parallel those of Census value added (VA). The annual rates of change in the Census VA series since 1947 are smaller (2.6 per cent) than in the Census production series (3.2 per cent). The 1947–64 trend toward less value added per unit of output stems from the relative changes in the product mix. These shifts occur between the household furniture industry (SIC 251) and the rest of the industries included in this major group as well as from changes within the household furniture industry. The varying average annual rates of change in the Census and FRB measures by industry sectors [20] are indicated below:

	Household Furniture (SIC 251)		*Other Furniture and Fixtures (SIC 252-9)*	
Census Measures	1947–57	1957–64	1947–57	1957–64
VP	3.7	2.8	2.4	3.6
CM	4.0	3.6	3.0	4.8
VA	3.3	1.9	2.0	2.7
FRB Indexes	3.4	7.0	4.1	3.3

In addition, within the household furniture group (SIC 251) there has also been a significant shift of product mix. For example, metal household furniture shipments (2514), which have a relatively lower value added per unit of output than "other furniture," increased relatively more than other household furniture from 1947 to 1957 but have been decreasing since then.[21] Conceptually, the trend for FRB indexes for

[20] The FRB measures output for this industry by two series; one for SIC 251, and the other for SIC 252-9.

[21] The ratios of constant-dollar shipment values of metal household furniture (SIC 2514) to the total for household furniture (SIC 251) for selected years are as follows:

1947	10.2	1957	15.7
1950	13.4	1958	15.0
1954	14.6	1963	13.5
		1964	13.6

SIC 251 and SIC 252-9 should show the same growth rates as Census value of production (VP) for each of these sectors.

Differences between the FRB and OBE series are due not only to the lower growth rate for net compared with total output but also to disparities in measures of total output. Prior to 1958, the FRB determined output by deflated value data, and since then by man-hours. While the 1947–57 rates of increase for the published and reweighted FRB and deflated Census value of production series are thus approximately the same (3.6 per cent and 3.3 per cent, respectively), the 1957–64 growth rate of 5.8 per cent for the published FRB index is almost twice the figure of 3.0 per cent for the deflated Census value-of-production series.

Differences in movement between Census value added and GPO are primarily explained by the IVA. When the IVA is excluded from the calculations of the indexes for GPO, the year-to-year movements of the two series are similar.

PRINTING, PUBLISHING, AND ALLIED INDUSTRIES (SIC 27)

The trends and annual movements when measured by either the FRB or OBE series are almost identical for this industry.[22] For 1948–64, the OBE series shows a compounded annual rate of increase of 3.1 per cent while the rate for the FRB series is 3.3 per cent. The difference between the two series is accounted for by the post-1957 trends of 3.2 per cent for the FRB indexes and 2.8 per cent for the OBE series, since identical 1948–57 growth rates of 3.4 per cent are reflected by both series. The FRB indexes when reweighted by either the 1958 GPO or value of production do not differ significantly in level or movement from the published FRB figures.

The implicit deflator for GPO is derived by double deflation from the Census data on production and cost of materials, supplies, fuels, and electricity. Since the Wholesale Price Index includes no representation for printing, publishing, and allied industries, special price series were constructed. These were used to deflate Census product groupings of subscriptions and sales of newspapers and periodicals, advertising

[22] The relative importance of this industry, expressed as a percentage of the respective manufacturing total, is as follows:

	1947	*1958*	*1964*
OBE	5.0	5.0	4.3
FRB (As pub.)	5.5	5.5	4.9

receipts by medium, sales for books published by subject as well as for job printing and allied activities. On the other hand, the FRB uses four series to measure activity in this major group. Based on 1957–59 industry proportions, 68 per cent was based on deflated value of shipments prior to 1958, and 68 per cent based on man-hours adjusted for productivity since 1958. Nevertheless, the trends and year-to-year changes between the FRB series reweighted by 1958 Census value-of-production and the deflated Census value-of-production series are very similar, except for the years prior to 1952 (Appendix Table C-9).

The similarities in trends and year-to-year movements between the OBE and FRB series also stem from the fact that the differences between total and net output are not large. Furthermore, the differences in movements between Census value added and OBE are not large.

PRIMARY METAL INDUSTRIES (SIC 33)

For 1948–57, the OBE and FRB indexes show an almost identical growth rate of 2 per cent. If the terminal year is extended to 1964, the compounded annual rate of increase for this industry[23] is 0.2 per cent for the OBE series compared with 2.0 per cent for the FRB. Reweighting the FRB indexes by 1958 GPO or Census value of production results in a higher growth rate (2.2 per cent) for 1948–57, but no change for 1957–64. Disparities between the FRB and OBE series largely arise from differences when output is derived from quantity measures or by deflation and by the differing movements between total and net output.

In measuring output for the primary metal industries the FRB employs twenty-three quantity series (see Appendix A). These represent production and may include, as in the case of ferrous castings, the quantities shipped to other plants of the same company as well as the amounts produced by departments (e.g., foundries) of plants classified in industries other than SIC 33. Because the ferrous and nonferrous industries are composed of nonintegrated, partially integrated, and fully integrated plants, Census shipment data include varying amounts of duplication. The large differences in Appendix Table C-15, column 11, for 1950–53 may partially reflect comparisons of measures relating

[23] The relative importance of this industry expressed as a percentage of the respective manufacturing total is as follows:

	1947	*1958*	*1964*
OBE	12.8	8.8	8.2
FRB (As pub.)	11.6	8.0	8.3

to production and to shipments. These differences are also magnified during these years by the independent adjustments to the Census data by FRB and OBE to reflect Census reporting procedures and the 1953 FRB link.

The Census measures for Major Group 33 show a higher growth rate for total compared with net output for 1947–64 as well as for the eleven years ending in 1957 and for the eight-year period since 1957. The 1957–64 trends for the subgroups iron and steel and the non-ferrous industries, compared with those for the major industry group, are as follows:

	Value of Production	*Cost of Materials*	*Value Added*
Industry 33 total	1.7	2.4	0.9
Iron and steel [a]	0.9	1.4	0.4
Nonferrous metals	3.7	4.4	2.4

[a] According to the output measures for the steel industry (SIC 331) computed by BLS, the compounded rate of change from 1957 to 1964 is 0.7 per cent. *Indexes of Output per Man-hour,* Steel Industry, 1947–65, U.S. Department of Labor, BLS report 306, p. 9, June 1966.

The trends in the industry averages principally stem from the movements in the iron and steel subgroup, which accounts for about two-thirds of the industry total. Illustrative of the declining value added per unit of output for the blast furnaces and steel mills industry has been the shipment of higher grade ores from the mines.[24] Thus more work is done at the latter establishment and less processing is required by the iron- and steel-making industry.

The effect of diverse trends for total and net output is further magnified by the FRB procedure in assigning the value-added weights for Industries 3312 and 3399. Value added for each series used in determining output for this industry is estimated by subtracting the estimated value of its major inputs from the estimated value of output.[25] Any errors in such procedures such as in computing the selling prices for pig iron (about 99 per cent of which is captive production) and in costs of its raw materials may overstate its importance relative to the more highly fabricated products of the industry.

Differences in levels between the OBE real product and deflated

[24] *Minerals Year Book,* Washington, D.C., 1962, pp. 668–669.

[25] This procedure was used by the Census Bureau in preparing the 1954 benchmark indexes. For details, see *1954 Census of Manufactures,* Vol. 4, Indexes of Production, p. 32.

Census value-added series for some years are relatively large. These differences are the result of disparities between the movements of the current-dollar series. For example, the 1963 gap between the two indexes is 6 points (Appendix Table C-15, column 14). The IVA adjustment and the difference between the OBE and Census payroll totals accounted for 3 of these 6 points. Other differences may be accounted for by the relatively large percentage of intracompany shipments and their evaluations. When these are between establishments in the same industry group, the Census value-added figure is unaffected, but when the industry classification of the establishment receiving these goods differs or the reporting of the values is inconsistent, then differences may arise. Also contributing to differences in movement between the Census value-added and the OBE figure is the fact that OBE figures are partially dependent upon the establishment allocation of company total for profit and capital consumption allowances.

FABRICATED METAL PRODUCTS (SIC 34)

The 1948–64 compounded average annual rates of change for this industry[26] as measured by the OBE and FRB indexes are 3.4 and 3.6 per cent respectively. However, the subperiod trends differ. For 1948–57, the growth rate for the OBE series is 3.8 per cent and 3.1 per cent for the FRB series, while the converse occurs for 1957–64 when the trend for the FRB series is 3.9 per cent and for the OBE series, 3.3 per cent. The reweighted FRB series compared with the published FRB data show no significant differences in trends or in year-to-year movements. The Census measures of value of production and value added show lower annual average rates of change and the year-to-year movements differ when compared with the FRB and OBE series.

Disparities between the FRB and OBE indexes stem principally from differences in the measurement of total output. The average annual rates of change for the FRB indexes, reweighted by value of production and the deflated Census measure of total output are identical for 1947–57, when the former series is also dependent upon "deflated values." However, for 1957–64 the gap between these two series is 1.5 per cent. In this period, almost 90 percent of output of this

[26] The relative importance of this industry, expressed as a percentage of the respective manufacturing total, is as follows:

	1947	*1958*	*1964*
OBE	6.4	6.3	6.1
FRB (As pub.)	7.1	6.2	6.2

industry is measured by the FRB by a man-hour series. (See Appendix Table C-16.)

Industry classification differences may also contribute to the difference between the two output series. The FRB includes representation for the lighting fixture industry (SIC 3642) in this major group but excludes information for the valves and pipe fittings industry (SIC 3494) and the fabricated pipe and fittings industry (SIC 3498) which are assigned to Major Group 35. In addition during the Korean conflict the FRB assigned war material made by the establishments classified in this industry to private ordnance plants.

While the trends for the Census measures of total and net output are approximately the same, this situation is a result of the relationship prevailing for the terminal years only. The variations in movements between total and net output generally explain the variations during 1948–64 in the amplitudes and direction of year-to-year changes. In 1951–54, the FRB-OBE gap is partially explained by the different movements for the Census measures of gross and net output. During these years there were also large disparities in the current-dollar totals for Census value added and GPO.

Since 1957, the growth rates for the Census value-added series is considerably less than that for the OBE indexes. The difference in current-dollar totals for these series appears to be primarily due to industry classification as indicated below (percentage changes in current dollars, 1958–64).

	Census Value Added	*Gross Product Originating*
Total	32.2	41.1
Payroll	26.7	35.1
Other	5.5	6.0

MOTOR VEHICLES AND EQUIPMENT (SIC 371)

Throughout the 1948–64 period, the OBE indexes for this industry [27] show higher levels of activity when compared with the FRB measures.

[27] The relative importance of this industry, expressed as a percentage of the respective manufacturing total, is as follows:

	1947	*1958*	*1964*
OBE	6.6	5.7	8.7
FRB (As pub.)	6.3	5.4	6.8

The 1948–64 average annual rate of change for the OBE series is 5.3 per cent; and 4.4 per cent for the FRB index. The growth rates for 1948–57 are 5.0 and 4.1 per cent respectively for the OBE and FRB series; and the corresponding figures for 1957–64 are 5.7 and 4.8 per cent. The magnitude of these differences remains whether the FRB indexes are reweighted by 1958 GPO or Census value of production.

In measuring the output of the motor vehicle industry, the FRB uses nine series. Since 1958 about 47 per cent, based on 1957–59 proportions, of the industry output are based on man-hours adjusted for estimated changes in productivity. The quantity indexes for passenger cars include adjustments to reflect quality changes but, "there is no allowance in the index for the marked gains in performance of late model trucks compared with those produced in the period immediately after the Second World War." [28] The adjustments for quality changes are based on production by (a) make and model, (b) certain items of equipment, and (3) body styles.[29] Since the late 1950's, the quality adjustment has been based on less detailed methods than employed for the preceding years.

Adjustments for quality changes in the OBE series are largely dependent upon the BLS wholesale prices and their specifications. The difficulties encountered in this area are well known. In addition, prices for original equipment may move differently from that for the replacement market. This error, if any, is cancelable to the extent that the original equipment represents an intraindustry shipment. The double deflation procedure also measures changes in value added when "trading up or down" [30] by consumers occurs.

Between 1952 and 1955, there are large differences between the FRB indexes, reweighted by 1958 value of shipments, and the Census deflated value-of-production series (Appendix Table C-20, column 11). A part of this difference stems from the reclassification by FRB of war goods produced as secondary products in this industry to the private ordnance

[28] "The Revised Index of Industrial Production," reply by Clayton Gehman, *American Economic Review,* June 1963, p. 520.

[29] For more detailed description, see *1954 Census of Manufactures,* Vol. IV, pp. 33–34.

[30] The term "trading up" refers to the shift in consumer demand from low price cars or standard models to more expensive makes, body styles, or with additional equipment. An example of "trading down" is the shift from standard-sized cars to economy compacts.

series.[31] The Census data represent total activities for all establishments classified in this industry.

Despite differences between outputs calculated from quantity measures and those derived by deflation, average annual rates of change in the FRB series are more closely approximated by those for Census value of production than by Census value added. The OBE trend, however, is more closely approximated by the Census value-added series. Differences between the growth rates for the FRB and Census value of production series are larger for the post-1957 period than for the earlier subperiod, while the converse is true when the OBE and Census value-added trends are compared.

The point differences between total and net output vary greatly (Appendix Table C-20, column 12). A varying value-added ratio rather than a constant ratio is realistic for this industry, since value added per unit of output increases as output rises. As indicated below, when total motor vehicle sales increase sizeably over the previous year's sales, larger increases occur in value added (Census and OBE) than in the Census value-of-production series. On the other hand, a sizeable decline in output is not necessarily accompanied by a larger decrease in value added than in value of production. This is partly due to replacement parts sales, which apparently decline less than sales of other products of the industry,[32] and partly to the curtailment of direct expenses.

Levels and amplitudes of the annual movements for the OBE and

	Increases						*Decreases*				
	Number of Vehicles	Census VP	Census VA	FRB	OBE		Number of Vehicles	Census VP	Census VA	FRB	OBE
1949–50	28.0	29.9	42.7	28.6	41.5	1950–51	18.1	11.3	4.3	8.3	4.7
1952–53	32.2	31.2	23.5	26.9	25.6	1953–54	9.9	13.6	15.3	9.8	12.9
1954–55	38.9	41.0	51.4	43.0	43.9	1955–56	24.5	22.0	21.7	19.8	25.1
1958–59	31.0	27.5	33.8	31.1	40.7	1957–58	28.9	26.8	24.8	23.4	30.8
1961–62	22.4	26.3	26.7	19.9	36.7	1960–61	15.1	13.5	11.1	9.9	10.6

[31] See pp. 262–263.

[32] In 1958 the Census Bureau established a product class (37176): parts and accessories for passenger cars, trucks, and busses, shipped to other than motor vehicles manufacturers. For 1960–61, the constant-dollar percentage decline was 3.5 per cent for this product class and 14.0 per cent for the remainder of Industry 3717.

Census value-added series differ from 1949 through 1955 because of disparities in the two current-dollar series (Appendix Table C-20, column 14). The current-dollar figures of gross product originating during this period exceed Census value added, while for other years the usual relationship between these figures prevails. Significant differences in OBE and Census payroll figures also occur since 1958, as indicated by percentage changes in current dollars shown below.

	Census Value Added and GPO	
	Census Value Added	Gross Product Originating
Total	97.4	118.3
Payroll	70.0	59.6
Other	117.0	185.3

In summary, the OBE indexes display higher growth rates than the FRB series for 1948–64. The gap between the trends for these two series is identical for 1948–57 and for 1957–64. The largest disparities occur in 1950–55 and since 1962. The 1950–55 disparities are principally explained by differences in measuring output and by the current-dollar movements of GPO, which in contrast to the FRB series reflect total activity for the establishments classified in the industry. The disparities since 1962 are largely due to the variation in movement between total and net output. The OBE measures of value added are more volatile than the FRB measures because the former reflect the volatility of profits due to scale of operation as well as shifts in margins as consumers "trade up," or "trade down" in make, model, or added equipment. In addition, when the data for new cars appearing in the final product accounts are compared with the GPO indexes, there is some evidence that increases since 1961 in GPO for Industry 371 have been offset by declines in the value added for industries whose principal activity relates to transporting or marketing new vehicles.

Appendix A: Description of FRB and OBE Indexes of Manufacturing Output

1. FEDERAL RESERVE BOARD'S INDEXES

Based on the value-added weights in the 1957–59 base period, slightly less than 90 per cent of the FRB index of industrial production is accounted for by manufacturing activity; the remainder represents the output for mining and electric and gas utilities. While the measures include production at Government owned and operated installations,[1] the indexes for manufacturing predominantly relate to activities of the privately operated sectors.

The FRB published indexes show changes in physical output by industry as well as for market categories, including a division between final products and materials and a subdivision of final products between output of consumer goods and output of equipment (including ordnance) for business and government use.

The current indexes of the FRB reflect major revisions described in detail in *Industrial Production, 1959 Revisions,* and those made in October 1962 when the comparison and weight bases were shifted from 1957 to 1957–59.[2] These revisions established new market groupings, expanded coverage and representation, refined procedures for estimating changes in industries represented by man-hour series, and revised the seasonal-adjustment factors. In addition, the 1959 revisions incorporated the 1947–54 production indexes derived from the comprehensive Census of Manufactures data for 1947 and 1954,[3] and also adjusted the 1955–57 production indexes using information compiled in the *Annual Surveys of Manufactures.* Moreover, the industry grouping was made to conform to the 1957 edition of *Standard Industrial Classification* (*SIC*) *Manual.* In the 1962 revision, the annual levels for eight series in the apparel, food, and chemical groups were adjusted to take account of the information appearing in the preliminary *1958 Census of Manufactures* and the 1959 and 1960 *Annual Survey of Manufactures.*

The total and other aggregate indexes are derived from weighted averages of relatives. Various measures are used to represent changes

[1] These include arsenals (0.12 per cent) and Navy shipyards (0.35 per cent).

[2] For further details, see Board of Governors of the Federal Reserve System, *Industrial Production: 1959 Revision,* Washington, D.C., 1960; *Industrial Production: 1957–59 Base,* Washington, D.C., 1962; and *Industrial Production Measurements in the United States* (reply to an inquiry from the Economic Commission for Europe), Washington, D.C., February 1964.

[3] *1954 Census of Manufactures,* Vol. IV, Indexes of Production, G.P.O., Washington, D.C., 1958. "In the 1954 bench-mark 82 percent of the total value added for manufacturing was represented by indexes derived from product data. Of these indexes, products represented by both quantity and value data made up about 75 percent and products represented only by deflated value data about 25 percent. Another 3½ percent was represented by indexes based on materials consumption and the remaining 14½ percent consisted of industry values indexes deflated by selected price or unit value indexes." (Industrial Production Measurement in the U.S., p. 36.)

in the quantity of output. These changes are expressed as relatives with 1957–59 = 100; each series of relatives is multiplied by a base-year-weight factor; and the product summed. The weight used for manufacturing components is the average of the 1957–59 Census of Manufactures value added expressed in 1957 prices. For each series the 1957–59 value-added figure in 1957 prices was obtained by dividing 1957 value added by the ratio of production in 1957 to production in 1957–59. Census value-added data are available either at an industry (four-, three-, or two-digit SIC) level, and for many product groupings (plants specializing in shipments of specified product classes) for some series. Value-added weights are based on the assumption that value added is proportional to the value of the product within the group.[4]

Since the indexes prior to 1953 were not recalculated, but linked in the 1959 revision, the weighting pattern for these indexes is based on weights derived from the 1947 Census value-added data. Because of the subsequent revision from the 1957 base to the 1957–59 base, the linked indexes on the 1957 base were converted to the 1957–59 base period by a multiplying factor for each aggregate index.

The indexes of output for the annual series discussed in this paper are based on a variety of measures—number of physical units produced, deflated values, man-hours, or materials consumed. The 200 series used for manufacturing measures and the proportions of 1957–59 value added for manufacturing accounted for by these series are shown in Table A-1.

2. INDEXES OF REAL PRODUCT FOR MANUFACTURING INDUSTRIES

Indexes of GPO for major manufacturing industries (two-digit SIC industries) are derived by deflation. The current-dollar figures for a two-digit industry, compiled from the national income accounts of the gross national product, represent the unique contribution (value added), in market prices by the specified industry to the nation's economy. To secure a measure in "real terms," the current-dollar total is deflated by a gross product price index calculated by the double deflation method.[5]

[4] For blast furnaces and rolling mills (SIC 331) and a few other industries, other estimating procedures are used.

[5] The limitations of the value added implicit deflator are discussed in the OBE unpublished document, "GNP by Major Industry; Concepts and Methods," and also by Paul A. David, "The Deflation of Value Added," *The Review of Economics and Statistics,* May 1962, pp. 148 ff.

TABLE A-1

Percentage of the 1957–59 Industry Proportion

SIC No.	Prior to 1958: Annual Quantity Produced	Prior to 1958: Deflated Value	Prior to 1958: Man-Hours Adjusted for Productivity[a]	Prior to 1958: Imputed or Extrapolated	Prior to 1958: Quantity of Materials Consumed	1958–64: Monthly Quantity Produced	1958–64: Deflated Value	1958–64: Man-Hours Adjusted for Productivity[a]	1958–64: Imputed or Extrapolated	1958–64: Quantity of Materials Consumed
All mfg.	43.0	43.2	8.6	2.2	3.0	33.7	--	55.0	6.1	5.2
20	76.7	20.5	--	2.8	--	39.3	--	43.0	17.7	--
21	100.0	--	--	--	--	100.0	--	--	--	--
22	38.3	36.6	--	18.6	6.5	35.9	--	16.9	19.3	27.9
23	67.1	9.8	20.3	2.8	--	59.1	--	38.7	2.2	--
26	93.9	--	--	6.1	--	61.5	--	--	38.5	--
27	--	67.7	--	--	32.3	--	--	67.7	--	32.3
28	30.5	52.9	15.4	1.2	--	33.7	--	57.4	0.3	8.6
29	94.9	--	--	5.1	--	90.9	--	--	9.1	--
30	38.7	61.3	--	--	--	33.7	--	26.1	--	40.2
31	75.7	24.3	--	--	--	75.7	--	24.3	--	--
24	68.2	--	14.5	17.3	--	51.9	--	20.8	17.3	--
25	--	100.0	--	--	--	--	--	100.0	--	--
32	50.5	36.4	0.7	6.7	5.7	29.1	--	70.2	0.7	--
33	93.8	--	--	1.4	4.8	91.4	--	--	3.9	4.7
34	5.8	77.7	9.1	--	7.4	3.0	--	89.6	--	7.4
35	5.8	94.2	--	--	--	7.0	--	93.0	--	--
36	25.9	74.1	--	--	--	28.1	--	71.9	--	--
371	85.3	14.7	--	--	--	47.0	--	38.3	14.7	--
37+19–371	4.0	40.0	56.0	--	--	2.0	--	98.0	--	--
38	--	92.4	7.6	--	--	--	--	100.0	--	--
39	--	42.4	57.6	--	--	--	--	100.0	--	--

Source: *Industrial Production Measurement in the U.S.*, p. 36 ff.

[a]Representation in the monthly and annual series also include employment adjusted for changes in productivity. These series, however, account for about one-half of 1 per cent.

Indexes for durable and nondurable goods industries and for total manufacturing are calculated by summing the constant-dollar totals for selected industries.

As described in detail in "GNP by Major Industries; Concepts and Methods," [6] current-dollar figures are compiled by summing the appropriate factor payments and nonfactor costs for an industry (two-digit SIC).[7] Since the corporate profits and capital consumption allowance (CCA) components of gross product are compiled on a company rather than on an establishment basis, adjustments are made in these totals to reflect the establishment composition of the manufacturing industries, as defined by the *Standard Industrial Classification Manual.* For all industries, except the petroleum refining industry (SIC 29), these adjustments are based on the company-establishment pattern weighted to reflect industry variations in profits or CCA per employee. The employment data appear in the U.S. Bureau of the Census publication, *Enterprise Statistics: 1958 Part 3, Link of Census Establishment and IRS Corporation Data.* For the petroleum refining industry, profits represent a residual after determining the amount due to mining activities (based on depletion allowances) and for wholesale and retail trade (based on industry averages). Depreciation charges for the petroleum refining industry are allocated on the basis of information for "assets by departments" as compiled in the Chase Manhattan Bank's studies for integrated oil companies.

The current-dollar measures of an industry's gross product, derived as the sum of its factor payments and nonfactor costs, are not directly convertible to constant dollars because the components (employee compensation, profits, interest, etc.) cannot be expressed in quantity and unit prices suitable for this purpose. To calculate constant-dollar figures, the gross product originating is deflated by implicit deflators derived by deflating output and purchases separately (double deflation). This method involves the derivation of measures of output and input by specified manufacturing industry groups separately expressed in current dollars and also in base-year dollars and the value added obtained by

[6] A methodology is available upon request to the Office of Business Economics.

[7] The only exception is for Major Group 37, transportation equipment, which is combined with Major Group 19, ordnance. The subtotals: (a) motor vehicles (SIC 371) and transportation equipment, except motor vehicles (SIC 37-371 and 19), are considered as industry groups, rather than the combination of the major SIC industries.

subtraction. The implicit price deflator is calculated by dividing the current-dollar figure by the constant-dollar figure for value added.

The data sources showing current dollars for total output (shipments figures adjusted for changes in inventories of finished goods and goods in process) and inputs for specified industries are the *Census of Manufactures* and *The Annual Survey of Manufactures*. To reflect the industry classifications appearing in the 1957 edition of the SIC manual, shipments and cost of materials, supplies, etc. for years prior to 1958 were adjusted when necessary on basis of the "bridge" data appearing in the *1958 Census of Manufactures, Vol. I, Summary,* Appendix C, Part 2. The price information is obtained primarily from *The Wholesale Price Indexes,* U.S. Bureau of Labor Statistics.

In order that the constant-dollar aggregate for value added may consist of the current year's quantity valued at prices prevailing in the base year, an industry's current value of shipments, inventory, and cost of materials and other items consumed in the manufacturing process should be deflated by a price index representing the given year's composite of products. For nearly all industries, the output composite for each year may be reliably approximated by the Census annual shipment values of each product class wherever made. However, the output for a small number of industries consists of a significant amount of products classified in other industries. In these cases, the annual data on total product class shipments are inadequate. For such industries, output price indexes with current-year weights are estimated from information contained in the *1947, 1954, and 1958 Censuses of Manufactures,* which provide information on the product composition of each industry's total value of shipments. Weights were calculated for the three Census years using these detailed product-mix data. Linear interpolations yielded the weighting pattern for the intercensal years.

Current-year weighted price indexes, as described above, are thus used to derive a constant-dollar series at a four-digit SIC industry level. These are then summed to the 1958 input–output sectors (industry) and again aggregated to the SIC two-digit manufacturing levels.[8]

Inventory data for the input–output industries are adjusted to provide one set of inventory figures which reflect average prices during the given

[8] Because of differences stemming from definitional changes affecting the compiled industry statistics prior to, and subsequent to, 1958, two sets of data were compiled: (a) 1947 through 1958 and (b) 1958 to date. Whenever a continuous series from 1947 was needed, 1958 served as a link for the two series.

year and a second set which reflect 1958 prices. The deflators used for this adjustment are adapted from the price indexes used in the calculation of the "inventory valuation adjustment" [9] included in the national accounts.

A basic problem in deflating Census data on cost of materials, supplies, components, fuel, and electricity for manufacturing industries is that information on the annual composition of their intermediate purchases is incomplete. The 1947 input–output study conducted by BLS, and the 1958 study, conducted by OBE, provide estimates of the relative dollar values of the items purchased by an industry. Composite price indexes were constructed using the data appearing in these studies as weights; these two sets of deflators (1947-weighted and 1958-weighted) were then interpolated to provide an approximation of a current-year-weighted-input-price index. The weights for 1958 and subsequent years are based on the 1958 study.

Value added at the two-digit industry level was computed in given year prices and in 1958 prices by subtracting cost of materials from value of production (shipments plus inventory changes) valued at the respective price levels. These two-digit industry totals were adjusted to include excise taxes. From the current- and constant-dollar totals of value added, as adjusted, implicit price deflators (1958 = 100) were computed. These deflators then are used to calculate the constant-dollar (1958) gross product originating in the specified industry.

The preceding discussion relates to the calculation of real gross product for all years except 1948 and for all manufacturing industries, except petroleum refining (SIC 29). With respect to 1948, no full-scale Census surveys of manufacturing industries were conducted for that year. Consequently, implicit price deflators for that year are obtained by using 1948 price indexes weighted by the 1947 shipments and purchases.

The data for Industry 29, are dominated by the figures for Industry 2911, petroleum refining. The ratio of cost of materials to value of shipments for the latter industry is among the highest, and for many years the highest, of all manufacturing industries. (The ratio varies from 80 to 84 per cent from 1950 to the present). Since value added is a residual, small differences in the price levels of output and input and small inconsistencies in the measures of output and input may yield larger differences in the price movements for value added. This was the experience

[9] See above.

when the double deflation method was used for SIC 29. In addition, the number of series and/or items priced and the weights used to derive geographic and national price composites do not coincide with the regional activities represented by the annual values of shipments and costs of crude petroleum and intra-industry purchases, as compiled by the Bureau of the Census. Furthermore, the BLS annual prices are arithmetic averages of monthly prices while shipments of the major products of this industry are generally seasonal.

Unusually complete physical measures of output and input for petroleum refineries for the required number of years are compiled by the U.S. Bureau of Mines. The data also reflect the technical changes which result in varied proportions of product outputs derived principally from a single material input. Therefore, these statistics are used to calculate indexes of physical volume comparable to the Census product classes. By extrapolating the 1958 product class shipment values by the appropriate indexes, a constant-dollar series is calculated. For the input crude petroleum oil a realized price based on the U.S. Bureau of Mines data is substituted for the BLS price series. For all other industries [10] in Major Group 29, the standard procedures as described above are followed.

For each two-digit industry, the implicit deflator based on Census value added is used to derive a constant-dollar series for the corresponding total of gross product originating. For Industry 29, petroleum and related products and Industry 21, tobacco manufactures, the deflator derived from the Census data is used only for the sum of all components, except excise taxes. The total for these taxes is deflated separately, based on changes in the latter tax rates. For other industries, excise taxes are not separately deflated since they represent a relatively small proportion of the gross product originating in that industry.

Data for Census cost of materials are only a partial measure of intermediate purchases, since purchased business services such as advertising fees, legal services, rents, telephone and postal bills, and royalties are not included in these totals. When the relative proportion of these business expenses to total costs is large and the price behavior of purchased services differs markedly from value added, the calculated implicit deflator may be affected.

To secure an estimate of what the implicit deflator might be if data on purchases of services were available annually, information was

[10] Data for Industry 2992, lubricating oils and greases, are included with the figures for Industry 2911.

utilized from the 1958 and preliminary 1961 input–output tables. Based on the calculations for three industries, for which purchased services are known to be relatively high, the following results for 1961 were derived:

		Implicit Deflator for GPO, 1958 = 100	
SIC	Industry	As Used	Adjusted for Services
20	Food and kindred products	110.2	110.7
21	Tobacco manufactures[11]	98.7	96.8
371	Motor vehicles and equipment	99.5	98.3

While these results are inconclusive, it is believed that for most of the manufacturing industries, for which purchased services are relatively small, the implicit deflator based on Census value added represents the price movement of GPO.

3. THE WEIGHT BASE

As indicated above, the weight base for the Federal Reserve Board's index for manufacturing is the 1957–59 Census value-added figures in 1957 prices. The base for gross product originating is 1958, a year of relatively low output, and is based on gross national product, which differs in concept from Census value added. In production indexes, different weight periods will result in changes only if relative proportions are widely different. If this occurs, then the use of different weights may result in changes in the general levels and also affect the timing and amplitude of the fluctuations in the indexes.[12] A comparison of the 1958 weight proportions for the two indexes appears below (Table A-2). The differences in proportions shown partly stem from the conceptual differences between Census value added and gross national product. The larger relative weights for the food and kindred products, tobacco, and petroleum refining industries are principally accounted for by the inclusion of excise taxes in the GPO totals and their exclusion from the Census value-added figures. These payments are not offset by purchased services which are relatively high in these industries. Other differences in proportions are partly accounted for by classification differences.

[11] For this industry, the implicit deflator for GPO is based on a composite for Census value added and for excise taxes. The implicit deflator for Census value added, excluding taxes, is 96.4 (1958=100).

[12] *1954 Census of Manufactures,* Vol. IV, Indexes of Production, pp. 20–26.

TABLE A-2

Assigned 1958 Weights for Indexes of Manufacturing: Office of Business Economics and Federal Reserve Board

Industry	OBE	FRB	OBE	FRB
Manufacturing	100.00	100.00	--	--
Nondurable goods	43.70	46.13	100.00	100.00
Food and kindred products	12.13	12.64	27.76	27.41
Tobacco manufactures	2.21	1.02	5.06	2.21
Textile mill products	3.33	3.39	7.62	7.35
Apparel and other fabricated textile products	3.69	4.24	8.44	9.19
Paper and allied products	3.90	4.13	8.92	8.95
Printing, publishing, and allied industries	4.95	5.71	11.33	12.38
Chemicals and allied products	7.45	9.02	17.05	19.55
Petroleum refining and related industries	2.53	2.38	5.79	5.16
Rubber and misc. plastic products	2.33	2.27	5.33	4.92
Leather and leather products	1.18	1.33	2.70	2.88
Durable goods	56.30	53.87	100.00	100.00
Lumber and wood products, except furniture	2.67	2.06	4.74	3.82
Furniture and fixtures	1.55	1.77	2.75	3.29
Stone, clay, and glass products	3.77	3.46	6.70	6.42
Primary metal industries	8.82	7.54	15.67	14.00
Fabricated metal products	6.31	6.20	11.21	11.51
Machinery, except electrical	8.83	9.19	15.68	17.05
Electrical machinery	7.56	7.11	13.43	13.20
Transportation equipment and ordnance, except motor vehicles	7.11	8.01[a]	12.63	14.87[a]
Motor vehicles and motor vehicle equipment	5.73	4.82	10.18	8.95
Instruments	2.11	1.95	3.75	3.62
Miscellaneous manufacturing industries	1.85	1.76	3.29	3.27

[a]Includes government owned and government operated establishments.

For example, the FRB includes representation for the lighting fixture industry (SIC 3642) in Major Group 34 but excludes information for the valves and pipe fitting industry (SIC 3494) and the fabricated pipe and fittings industry (SIC 3498), which are assigned to Major Group 35. In addition, the company profits and capital consumption allowances are adjusted by OBE to an establishment industry basis.[13]

The amount of the adjustment for profits and capital consumption allowances, other than for the petroleum refining industry, when related to the company industry totals, is less than 5 per cent for eight of the twenty listed manufacturing industries. For only five industries is the adjustment more than 15 per cent. These adjustments when expressed as a percentage of total GPO are considerably less. For example, the percentage adjustment in 1958 company profit totals to represent activity for establishments classified in the industry only are as follows in Table A-3:

TABLE A-3

Percentage Adjustment	Industries Number	Industries SIC Number
Less than 0.5 per cent	7	21, 23, 27, 24, 25, 32, 34
0.5–0.9	5	20, 28, 30, 31, 35
1.0–1.4	3	33, 36 (37 + 19 - 371)
1.5–1.9	0	
2.0–2.4	1	26
2.5–2.9	3	22,38,39
Over 3 per cent	2	29, 371

Appendix B: Gross Product Originating, by Industry, 1947–64

EXPLANATION OF ABBREVIATIONS USED IN TABLES

These tables show Gross Product Originating in 1958 dollars, in current dollars, and the current dollar totals for components.

[13] See above for adjustment procedures.

CO(1958) $ = Gross product originating in 1958 dollars. For derivation, see Appendix A; for deflators, see Appendix D.

CU $, Total = Gross product originating in current dollars. The sum of factor and nonfactor charges, which appears in the columns on the right.

Employee Compensation = Employee compensation, which consists of wages, salaries, and supplements.

Interest = Net interest component of national income.

CCA = Capital consumption allowances, which consist of depreciation and accidental damage to fixed business property. These figures represent establishment totals (see Appendix A).

IBT = Indirect business tax and nontax liability and business transfer payments. Includes federal excise taxes for which the industry has legal responsibility.

Profit Type Income:

Total = Sum of profits and IVA.

Profits = Sum of corporate profits on an establishment basis and income of unincorporated enterprises.

IVA = Inventory valuation adjustment. See *National Income,* 1954 edition, supplement to the *Survey of Current Business,* pp. 44–45 and 135–138.

Appendix C: Selected Measures of Manufacturing Activity by Industry Groups and by Industry, 1947–64

The statistical framework for analyzing the relationship between the OBE and FRB indexes involves comparisons with reweighted FRB series and Census measures of total and net output. The text discussions and tables below include data for selected measures of total and net output. Point differences between these selected measures of manufacturing activity are also shown. In addition, the trends of the various measures for 1948–64 and for the subperiods ending and beginning with 1957 were computed and are shown below. A brief description and derivation of the series appearing in these tables appears below:

FRB As Pub. (column 1) = The published indexes of the Federal Reserve Board for the given industry or groups rebased to 1958 = 100. The weights for these indexes are discussed in Appendix A. The series shown is derived by dividing the given year FRB index by the 1958 FRB index.

FRB Reweighted (columns 2 and 3) = The FRB (output) relatives rebased to 1958 = 100 from 1957–59 = 100 and reweighted by (1) 1958 gross product originating (column 2) and (2) 1958 Census Value of Production (column 3).

Value of Production—VP (column 4) = Deflated Census value of shipments plus deflated change in inventories of finished goods and work in

TABLE B-1

Gross Product Originating, by Industry, 1947–64

(million dollars)

	Gross Product Originating		Current-Dollar Components						
							Profit-Type Income		
Year	CO(1958) $	CU $ Total	Employee Compensation	Interest	C C A	I B T	Total	Profits	I V A
			All Manufacturing Industries						
1947	91,788	66,869	45,271	-27	2,418	6,079	13,128	16,971	-3,843
1948	96,264	74,696	49,367	-14	2,855	6,245	16,243	17,631	-1,388
1949	90,907	72,012	46,983	-14	3,242	6,449	15,352	14,245	1,107
1950	105,517	83,752	53,528	-135	3,492	7,082	19,785	23,001	-3,216
1951	116,172	98,602	63,572	-92	4,044	7,510	23,568	24,173	-605
1952	118,710	102,868	68,726	9	4,698	8,591	20,844	20,198	646
1953	128,599	112,048	76,229	11	5,567	9,235	21,006	21,652	-646
1954	119,450	106,248	72,743	51	6,372	8,687	18,395	18,723	-328
1955	133,561	120,846	79,884	-47	7,171	9,694	24,144	25,460	-1,316
1956	134,050	126,761	86,321	9	7,741	10,148	22,542	24,188	-1,646
1957	134,556	131,386	90,089	129	8,551	10,714	21,903	22,774	-871
1958	123,673	123,673	86,242	296	9,103	10,580	17,452	17,658	-206
1959	138,950	141,128	95,776	120	9,426	11,494	24,312	24,678	-366
1960	140,904	144,368	99,424	99	9,831	12,428	22,586	22,254	332
1961	140,423	144,172	99,718	199	10,405	12,531	21,319	21,451	-132
1962	154,605	158,759	108,158	320	12,189	13,477	24,615	24,467	148
1963	162,439	167,035	112,888	328	12,765	14,294	26,760	27,264	-504
1964	173,613	179,808	120,460	338	13,742	15,135	30,133	30,466	-333

(continued)

TABLE B-1 (continued)

	Gross Product Originating		Current-Dollar Components						
							Profit-Type Income		
Year	CO(1958) $	CU $ Total	Employee Compensation	Interest	C C A	I B T	Total	Profits	I V A
			Nondurable Goods Industries						
1947	39,446	33,283	20,036	-2	1,154	4,756	7,339	9,011	-1,672
1948	41,292	36,614	21,826	23	1,373	4,712	8,680	8,395	285
1949	40,415	34,926	21,514	42	1,595	4,811	6,964	6,256	708
1950	44,732	38,033	23,514	13	1,699	5,157	7,650	9,524	-1,874
1951	47,217	43,279	25,970	30	1,899	5,378	10,002	9,870	132
1952	47,250	44,057	27,258	33	2,102	6,147	8,517	7,749	768
1953	49,455	46,241	29,159	23	2,338	6,250	8,471	8,313	158
1954	48,281	45,541	29,265	66	2,721	6,064	7,425	7,445	-20
1955	52,872	50,310	31,266	45	3,073	6,381	9,545	9,504	41
1956	54,620	53,182	33,367	43	3,341	7,019	9,412	9,647	-235
1957	54,944	53,761	34,649	92	3,677	7,265	8,078	8,387	-309
1958	54,039	54,039	34,665	148	4,074	7,526	7,626	7,511	115
1959	59,010	59,933	37,553	73	4,280	7,925	10,102	10,120	-18
1960	59,939	61,908	38,945	21	4,334	8,592	10,016	9,866	150
1961	60,697	63,004	39,897	119	4,652	8,847	9,489	9,602	-113
1962	64,650	66,863	42,136	189	5,453	9,197	9,888	9,805	83
1963	66,823	69,604	43,507	224	5,800	9,611	10,462	10,692	-230
1964	71,323	74,408	46,003	260	6,237	10,141	11,767	11,680	87

(continued)

TABLE B-1 (continued)

	Gross Product Originating		Current-Dollar Components						
							Profit-Type Income		
Year	CO(1958) $	CU $ Total	Employee Compensation	Interest	C C A	I B T	Total	Profits	I V A
			Durable Goods Industries						
1947	52,342	33,586	25,235	-25	1,264	1,323	5,789	7,960	-2,171
1948	54,972	38,082	27,541	-37	1,482	1,533	7,563	9,236	-1,673
1949	50,492	37,086	25,469	-56	1,647	1,638	8,388	7,989	399
1950	60,785	45,719	30,014	-148	1,793	1,925	12,135	13,477	-1,342
1951	68,955	55,323	37,602	-122	2,145	2,132	13,566	14,303	-737
1952	71,460	58,811	41,468	-24	2,596	2,444	12,327	12,449	-122
1953	79,144	65,807	47,070	-12	3,229	2,985	12,535	13,339	-804
1954	71,169	60,707	43,478	-15	3,651	2,623	10,970	11,278	-308
1955	80,689	70,536	48,618	-92	4,098	3,313	14,599	15,956	-1,357
1956	79,430	73,579	52,954	-34	4,400	3,129	13,130	14,541	-1,411
1957	79,612	77,625	55,440	37	4,874	3,449	13,825	14,387	-562
1958	69,634	69,634	51,577	148	5,029	3,054	9,826	10,147	-321
1959	79,940	81,195	58,223	47	5,146	3,569	14,210	14,558	-348
1960	80,965	82,460	60,479	78	5,497	3,836	12,570	12,388	182
1961	79,726	81,168	59,821	80	5,753	3,684	11,830	11,849	-19
1962	89,955	91,896	66,022	131	6,736	4,280	14,727	14,662	65
1963	95,616	97,431	69,381	104	6,965	4,683	16,298	16,572	-274
1964	102,290	105,400	74,457	78	7,505	4,994	18,366	18,786	-420

(continued)

TABLE B-1 (continued)

	Gross Product Originating		Current-Dollar Components				Profit-Type Income		
Year	CO(1958) $	CU $ Total	Employee Compensation	Interest	C C A	I B T	Total	Profits	I V A
			Food and Kindred Products, SIC 20						
1947	11,391	9,432	5,014	16	352	2,454	1,596	2,193	-597
1948	11,880	10,205	5,342	26	433	2,285	2,119	1,857	262
1949	11,380	10,208	5,445	32	497	2,346	1,888	1,825	63
1950	12,360	10,605	5,779	33	522	2,542	1,729	2,030	-301
1951	12,552	11,134	6,386	50	579	2,567	1,552	1,771	-219
1952	13,017	12,171	6,728	45	604	2,835	1,959	1,795	164
1953	13,977	12,719	7,141	28	616	2,908	2,026	1,978	48
1954	13,478	12,777	7,396	34	664	2,797	1,886	1,944	-58
1955	14,174	13,777	7,747	34	741	2,892	2,363	2,160	203
1956	14,771	14,032	8,246	35	761	3,087	1,903	2,046	-143
1957	15,158	14,279	8,521	46	808	2,953	1,951	1,991	-40
1958	14,996	14,996	8,701	46	989	3,030	2,230	2,239	-9
1959	15,098	15,944	9,215	37	1,045	3,129	2,518	2,434	84
1960	15,464	16,345	9,662	34	1,081	3,178	2,390	2,451	-61
1961	15,256	16,812	9,901	47	1,134	3,287	2,443	2,445	-2
1962	15,794	17,358	10,248	66	1,298	3,389	2,357	2,397	-40
1963	16,615	18,077	10,484	66	1,323	3,502	2,702	2,876	-174
1964	17,553	19,361	11,000	67	1,401	3,911	2,982	2,806	176

(continued)

TABLE B-1 (continued)

	Gross Product Originating		Current-Dollar Components						
							Profit-Type Income		
Year	CO(1958) $	CU $ Total	Employee Compensation	Interest	C C A	I B T	Total	Profits	I V A
			Tobacco Manufactures, SIC 21						
1947	2,011	1,633	207	15	9	1,268	134	189	-55
1948	2,144	1,746	215	19	11	1,317	184	241	-57
1949	2,273	1,834	229	20	13	1,326	246	262	-16
1950	2,184	1,836	241	20	14	1,354	207	291	-84
1951	2,418	2,013	278	21	15	1,452	247	299	-52
1952	2,522	2,272	295	22	14	1,672	269	289	-20
1953	2,341	2,343	314	25	17	1,624	363	346	17
1954	2,200	2,262	326	24	19	1,552	341	332	9
1955	2,336	2,331	339	23	21	1,604	344	395	-51
1956	2,467	2,419	362	24	24	1,645	364	415	-51
1957	2,570	2,554	374	28	27	1,713	412	448	-36
1958	2,738	2,738	385	22	31	1,829	471	526	-55
1959	2,906	2,889	405	19	36	1,872	557	574	-17
1960	3,027	3,025	439	22	40	1,968	556	597	-41
1961	3,174	3,132	438	18	42	2,035	599	650	-51
1962	3,293	3,236	463	22	52	2,048	651	641	10
1963	3,346	3,410	476	17	59	2,135	723	675	48
1964	3,259	3,348	504	18	59	2,087	680	650	30

(continued)

TABLE B-1 (continued)

	Gross Product Originating		Current-Dollar Components						
							Profit-Type Income		
Year	CO(1958) $	CU $ Total	Employee Compensation	Interest	C C A	I B T	Total	Profits	I V A
			Textile Mill Products, SIC 22						
1947	3,730	4,703	3,114	-6	131	59	1,405	1,559	-154
1948	4,098	5,253	3,556	-5	157	67	1,478	1,540	-62
1949	3,776	4,203	3,172	-5	173	62	801	639	162
1950	3,965	4,595	3,630	-1	192	70	704	1,196	-492
1951	4,079	5,241	3,771	14	208	76	1,172	922	250
1952	4,078	4,661	3,655	10	216	69	711	460	251
1953	3,987	4,501	3,690	7	229	71	504	470	34
1954	3,793	3,914	3,322	11	240	68	273	258	15
1955	4,226	4,408	3,531	11	267	73	526	501	25
1956	4,284	4,502	3,602	22	281	74	523	511	12
1957	4,190	4,303	3,497	28	299	73	406	406	0
1958	4,122	4,122	3,318	23	289	69	423	346	77
1959	4,542	4,701	3,722	15	282	74	608	645	-37
1960	4,396	4,734	3,708	19	290	77	640	563	77
1961	4,396	4,506	3,663	23	320	74	426	480	-54
1962	4,808	4,957	3,906	37	339	83	592	593	-1
1963	4,967	5,012	3,950	39	349	90	584	604	-20
1964	5,361	5,511	4,210	38	367	95	801	752	49

(continued)

TABLE B-1 (continued)

	Gross Product Originating		Current-Dollar Components						
							Profit-Type Income		
Year	CO(1958) $	CU $ Total	Employee Compensation	Interest	C C A	I B T	Total	Profits	I V A
			Apparel and Related Products, SIC 23						
1947	3,676	3,569	2,806	-7	46	38	686	797	-111
1948	3,888	3,678	3,051	-4	55	41	535	530	5
1949	3,839	3,524	2,944	-5	64	42	479	377	102
1950	4,184	3,619	3,172	1	66	44	336	559	-223
1951	4,480	4,010	3,313	8	71	44	574	474	100
1952	4,483	4,129	3,453	-3	73	45	561	481	80
1953	4,603	4,272	3,666	-1	77	48	482	441	41
1954	4,300	4,076	3,530	-2	79	49	420	410	10
1955	4,613	4,327	3,740	3	87	53	444	453	-9
1956	4,701	4,616	3,970	1	89	56	500	489	11
1957	4,629	4,550	4,026	1	82	55	386	381	5
1958	4,559	4,559	3,918	-2	95	59	489	447	42
1959	4,894	4,879	4,300	5	95	63	416	479	-63
1960	5,101	5,101	4,414	4	92	64	527	497	30
1961	5,068	5,230	4,451	8	107	70	594	587	7
1962	5,432	5,682	4,864	16	121	76	605	613	-8
1963	5,526	5,874	5,030	24	123	81	616	629	-13
1964	5,840	6,295	5,337	29	134	87	708	731	-23

(continued)

TABLE B-1 (continued)

	Gross Product Originating		Current-Dollar Components				Profit-Type Income		
Year	CO(1958) $	CU $ Total	Employee Compensation	Interest	C C A	I B T	Total	Profits	I V A
			Lumber and Wood Products, Except Furniture, SIC 24						
1947	3,285	2,651	1,778	4	103	35	731	910	-179
1948	3,224	2,982	1,957	7	144	45	829	857	-28
1949	2,979	2,562	1,732	8	174	48	600	550	50
1950	3,239	3,213	2,066	6	188	52	901	1,071	-170
1951	3,301	3,621	2,377	7	229	58	950	925	25
1952	3,206	3,411	2,378	9	242	61	721	719	2
1953	3,106	3,339	2,369	9	247	60	654	633	21
1954	3,018	3,199	2,247	8	250	65	629	651	-22
1955	3,487	3,755	2,515	9	292	69	870	912	-42
1956	3,475	3,798	2,588	14	304	77	815	776	39
1957	3,272	3,367	2,350	23	330	77	587	544	43
1958	3,306	3,306	2,297	20	295	82	612	646	-34
1959	3,619	3,861	2,616	20	322	81	822	862	-40
1960	3,550	3,674	2,555	32	339	88	660	574	86
1961	3,479	3,458	2,438	38	331	89	562	548	14
1962	3,784	3,727	2,591	50	347	95	644	657	-13
1963	3,965	4,009	2,723	53	353	102	778	816	-38
1964	4,263	4,425	2,970	64	397	109	885	896	-11

(continued)

TABLE B-1 (continued)

Year	Gross Product Originating		Current-Dollar Components						
			Employee Compensation	Interest	C C A	I B T	Profit-Type Income		
	CO(1958) $	CU $ Total					Total	Profits	I V A
Furniture and Fixtures, SIC 25									
1947	1,425	1,013	901	1	45	27	39	236	-197
1948	1,657	1,238	991	1	37	20	189	221	-32
1949	1,569	1,219	949	-1	43	22	206	179	27
1950	1,901	1,458	1,163	0	46	25	224	303	-79
1951	1,807	1,603	1,229	1	54	28	291	282	9
1952	1,950	1,675	1,312	0	57	29	277	268	9
1953	1,946	1,687	1,394	0	58	29	206	229	-23
1954	1,872	1,636	1,329	0	63	30	214	209	5
1955	2,171	1,893	1,503	2	71	34	283	325	-42
1956	2,186	2,022	1,597	2	71	36	316	340	-24
1957	2,091	2,032	1,643	0	70	38	281	277	4
1958	1,911	1,911	1,597	1	78	37	198	214	-16
1959	2,180	2,182	1,787	0	87	41	267	278	-11
1960	2,147	2,211	1,817	3	91	41	259	254	5
1961	2,066	2,190	1,782	5	92	44	267	257	10
1962	2,218	2,393	1,943	7	99	50	294	296	-2
1963	2,282	2,487	2,030	5	91	52	309	331	-22
1964	2,460	2,716	2,204	6	83	55	368	380	-12

(continued)

TABLE B-1 (continued)

Year	Gross Product Originating		Current-Dollar Components						
							Profit-Type Income		
	CO(1958) $	CU $ Total	Employee Compensation	Interest	C C A	I B T	Total	Profits	I V A
Paper and Allied Products, SIC 26									
1947	3,631	2,502	1,408	-5	114	40	945	1,086	-141
1948	3,342	2,630	1,573	-4	140	46	875	905	-30
1949	3,329	2,457	1,544	-4	162	49	706	637	69
1950	4,328	3,051	1,785	-9	177	54	1,044	1,145	-101
1951	4,626	3,844	2,053	-14	206	69	1,530	1,571	-41
1952	4,114	3,583	2,138	-12	233	75	1,149	1,118	31
1953	4,528	3,808	2,369	-14	266	81	1,106	1,114	-8
1954	4,567	3,923	2,451	-7	314	80	1,085	1,081	4
1955	5,109	4,424	2,679	-3	386	88	1,274	1,327	-53
1956	5,280	5,005	2,913	1	423	99	1,569	1,575	-6
1957	4,882	4,853	3,032	12	480	110	1,219	1,244	-25
1958	4,820	4,820	3,094	26	531	112	1,057	1,060	-3
1959	5,480	5,403	3,415	17	546	114	1,311	1,319	-8
1960	5,397	5,532	3,573	20	568	121	1,250	1,199	51
1961	5,737	5,737	3,769	37	622	128	1,181	1,167	14
1962	6,121	6,127	4,020	35	750	140	1,182	1,155	27
1963	6,584	6,171	4,197	40	755	148	1,031	1,071	-40
1964	6,746	6,598	4,414	38	832	157	1,157	1,175	-18

(continued)

TABLE B-1 (continued)

	Gross Product Originating		Current-Dollar Components						
							Profit-Type Income		
Year	CO(1958) $	CU $ Total	Employee Compensation	Interest	C C A	I B T	Total	Profits	I V A
			Printing and Publishing, SIC 27						
1947	4,613	3,234	2,344	-7	82	54	761	825	-64
1948	4,724	3,510	2,605	-6	103	62	746	795	-49
1949	4,803	3,689	2,750	-3	123	69	750	744	6
1950	4,992	3,884	2,925	-5	135	72	757	792	-35
1951	5,078	4,144	3,164	-5	151	76	758	821	-63
1952	5,092	4,420	3,386	-8	161	79	802	837	-35
1953	5,402	4,792	3,679	-9	175	89	858	862	-4
1954	5,688	4,977	3,865	-8	184	85	851	851	0
1955	6,042	5,444	4,131	-12	217	92	1,016	1,037	-21
1956	6,280	5,809	4,447	-14	235	99	1,042	1,070	-28
1957	6,364	6,167	4,700	-20	265	105	1,117	1,147	-30
1958	6,128	6,128	4,819	-20	295	110	924	925	-1
1959	6,594	6,700	5,159	-17	311	115	1,132	1,148	-16
1960	6,764	7,122	5,487	-27	340	125	1,197	1,201	-4
1961	6,765	7,239	5,668	-25	355	130	1,111	1,109	2
1962	7,041	7,689	5,900	-10	430	141	1,228	1,233	-5
1963	7,018	7,923	6,138	2	460	153	1,170	1,170	0
1964	7,701	8,671	6,550	3	505	161	1,452	1,449	3

(continued)

TABLE B-1 (continued)

	Gross Product Originating		Current-Dollar Components				Profit-Type Income		
Year	CO(1958) $	CU $ Total	Employee Compensation	Interest	C C A	I B T	Total	Profits	I V A
			Chemicals and Allied Products, SIC 28						
1947	4,072	3,685	2,174	-17	216	62	1,250	1,617	-367
1948	4,817	4,403	2,364	-13	279	70	1,703	1,523	180
1949	4,985	4,586	2,377	-16	331	80	1,814	1,574	240
1950	6,023	5,433	2,632	-27	374	86	2,368	2,657	-289
1951	6,503	6,542	3,200	-32	435	103	2,836	2,843	-7
1952	6,570	6,465	3,476	-5	548	126	2,320	2,205	115
1953	7,018	6,899	3,880	-3	672	133	2,217	2,233	-16
1954	7,252	7,208	4,017	8	801	131	2,251	2,272	-21
1955	8,530	8,462	4,300	5	931	145	3,081	2,983	98
1956	8,981	8,774	4,773	-4	987	166	2,852	2,903	-51
1957	9,395	9,273	5,161	8	1,058	178	2,868	2,953	-85
1958	9,218	9,218	5,238	34	1,144	191	2,611	2,547	64
1959	10,928	10,775	5,660	13	1,252	201	3,649	3,564	85
1960	10,975	10,766	5,992	-16	1,244	220	3,326	3,297	29
1961	11,534	11,165	6,233	17	1,366	229	3,320	3,324	-4
1962	12,446	11,961	6,600	22	1,660	251	3,428	3,365	63
1963	13,088	12,604	6,939	30	1,768	293	3,574	3,674	-100
1964	14,009	13,491	7,367	34	1,854	311	3,925	4,042	-117

(continued)

TABLE B-1 (continued)

	Gross Product Originating		Current-Dollar Components				Profit-Type Income		
Year	CO(1958) $	CU $ Total	Employee Compensation	Interest	C C A	I B T	Total	Profits	I V A
			Petroleum and Related Industries, SIC 29						
1947	2,070	1,881	965	9	124	575	208	314	-106
1948	2,261	2,458	1,095	6	107	630	620	652	-32
1949	2,269	1,934	1,134	19	148	650	-17	-44	27
1950	2,595	2,264	1,163	1	135	707	258	265	-7
1951	2,624	2,798	1,395	-11	128	770	516	532	-16
1952	2,658	2,713	1,529	-16	135	1,023	42	30	12
1953	2,824	3,144	1,626	-18	156	1,065	315	349	-34
1954	2,746	2,948	1,700	-2	276	1,091	-117	-145	28
1955	3,100	3,184	1,759	-25	252	1,192	6	15	-9
1956	3,179	3,678	1,858	-34	351	1,508	-5	21	-26
1957	3,144	3,291	1,991	-24	443	1,742	-861	-733	-128
1958	3,124	3,124	1,968	-1	451	1,787	-1,081	-1,137	56
1959	3,310	3,740	2,020	-30	462	1,977	-689	-726	37
1960	3,498	4,268	2,003	-57	413	2,458	-549	-499	-50
1961	3,530	4,187	2,059	-29	419	2,473	-735	-747	12
1962	3,826	4,217	2,033	-26	469	2,572	-831	-831	0
1963	4,068	4,700	2,068	-37	603	2,699	-633	-649	16
1964	4,508	4,925	2,081	-17	717	2,790	-646	-656	10

(continued)

TABLE B-1 (continued)

	Gross Product Originating		Current-Dollar Components				Profit-Type Income		
Year	CO(1958) $	CU $ Total	Employee Compensation	Interest	C C A	I B T	Total	Profits	I V A
			Rubber and Misc. Plastic Products, SIC 30						
1947	2,584	1,483	1,018	2	60	191	212	174	38
1948	2,403	1,442	1,008	5	65	178	186	190	-4
1949	2,185	1,333	941	5	58	170	159	126	33
1950	2,556	1,590	1,133	-1	60	212	186	410	-224
1951	3,210	2,173	1,339	-3	80	203	554	514	40
1952	3,181	2,246	1,441	0	90	205	510	379	131
1953	3,193	2,363	1,599	5	103	213	443	385	58
1954	2,766	2,066	1,500	6	118	193	249	295	-46
1955	3,187	2,521	1,785	7	142	223	364	459	-95
1956	3,105	2,813	1,887	9	157	265	495	454	41
1957	3,067	2,941	2,015	10	180	316	420	392	28
1958	2,878	2,878	1,930	15	213	319	401	418	-17
1959	3,609	3,299	2,233	9	213	360	484	509	-25
1960	3,764	3,350	2,268	14	224	358	486	408	78
1961	3,751	3,421	2,296	17	249	398	461	450	11
1962	4,275	3,899	2,623	20	297	473	486	476	10
1963	4,322	4,028	2,736	28	309	484	471	463	8
1964	4,703	4,360	2,969	32	321	511	527	522	5

(continued)

TABLE B-1 (continued)

Year	Gross Product Originating		Current-Dollar Components						
							Profit-Type Income		
	CO(1958) $	CU $ Total	Employee Compensation	Interest	C C A	I B T	Total	Profits	I V A
			Leather and Leather Products, SIC 31						
1947	1,668	1,161	986	-2	20	15	142	257	-115
1948	1,735	1,289	1,017	-1	23	16	234	162	72
1949	1,576	1,158	978	-1	26	17	138	116	22
1950	1,545	1,156	1,054	1	24	16	61	179	-118
1951	1,647	1,380	1,071	2	26	18	263	123	140
1952	1,535	1,397	1,157	0	28	18	194	155	39
1953	1,582	1,400	1,195	3	27	18	157	135	22
1954	1,491	1,390	1,158	2	26	18	186	147	39
1955	1,555	1,432	1,255	2	29	19	127	174	-47
1956	1,572	1,534	1,309	3	33	20	169	163	6
1957	1,545	1,550	1,332	3	35	20	160	158	2
1958	1,456	1,456	1,294	5	36	20	101	140	-39
1959	1,649	1,603	1,424	5	38	20	116	174	-58
1960	1,553	1,665	1,399	8	42	23	193	152	41
1961	1,486	1,575	1,419	6	38	23	89	137	-48
1962	1,614	1,737	1,479	7	37	24	190	163	27
1963	1,589	1,805	1,489	15	51	26	224	179	45
1964	1,643	1,848	1,571	18	47	31	181	209	-28

(continued)

TABLE B-1 (continued)

	Gross Product Originating		Current-Dollar Components						
							Profit-Type Income		
Year	CO(1958) $	CU $ Total	Employee Compensation	Interest	C C A	I B T	Total	Profits	I V A
			Stone, Clay, and Glass Products, SIC 32						
1947	3,405	2,067	1,495	-2	84	32	458	519	-61
1948	3,636	2,389	1,699	-2	105	36	551	609	-58
1949	3,388	2,382	1,629	-3	121	40	595	597	-2
1950	4,058	2,946	1,880	-6	136	42	894	927	-33
1951	4,356	3,350	2,237	-7	159	50	911	936	-25
1952	4,114	3,213	2,225	-6	186	55	753	763	-10
1953	4,423	3,605	2,439	-9	230	70	875	920	-45
1954	4,323	3,679	2,419	-9	250	65	954	973	-19
1955	4,973	4,411	2,727	-14	288	77	1,333	1,368	-35
1956	4,897	4,569	2,953	-13	305	80	1,244	1,288	-44
1957	4,755	4,617	3,030	-5	383	86	1,123	1,161	-38
1958	4,661	4,661	3,010	-1	478	99	1,075	1,105	-30
1959	5,242	5,363	3,416	-8	484	102	1,369	1,382	-13
1960	5,128	5,277	3,531	7	538	106	1,095	1,095	0
1961	5,043	5,189	3,485	8	549	111	1,036	1,036	0
1962	5,358	5,481	3,707	8	633	123	1,010	1,012	-2
1963	5,739	5,825	3,904	11	653	132	1,125	1,123	2
1964	6,114	6,236	4,191	14	690	144	1,197	1,207	-10

(continued)

TABLE B-1 (continued)

Year	Gross Product Originating		Current-Dollar Components						
							Profit-Type Income		
	CO(1958) $	CU $ Total	Employee Compensation	Interest	C C A	I B T	Total	Profits	I V A
			Primary Metal Industries, SIC 33						
1947	11,796	5,674	4,173	-1	325	111	1,066	1,453	-387
1948	11,711	6,277	4,548	1	352	111	1,265	1,539	-274
1949	10,168	5,989	4,080	6	384	122	1,397	1,284	113
1950	12,430	7,682	5,041	-14	422	131	2,102	2,315	-213
1951	14,866	9,841	6,225	-16	514	152	2,966	3,025	-59
1952	13,171	8,943	6,265	24	711	176	1,767	1,776	-9
1953	15,233	10,846	7,106	63	1,057	221	2,399	2,457	-58
1954	11,899	9,210	6,243	41	1,229	193	1,504	1,565	-61
1955	14,572	11,789	7,558	1	1,313	216	2,701	2,939	-238
1956	14,308	12,591	8,262	11	1,347	227	2,744	2,826	-82
1957	13,984	13,299	8,675	20	1,400	247	2,957	2,818	139
1958	10,912	10,912	7,542	90	1,290	244	1,746	1,782	-36
1959	12,181	12,364	8,469	59	1,212	246	2,378	2,420	-42
1960	12,001	12,589	8,905	58	1,328	269	2,029	1,970	59
1961	11,286	11,647	8,562	34	1,384	278	1,389	1,407	-18
1962	12,055	12,742	9,216	59	1,723	307	1,437	1,357	80
1963	12,722	13,371	9,492	51	1,778	323	1,727	1,782	-55
1964	14,208	15,132	10,476	47	1,942	344	2,323	2,480	-157

(continued)

TABLE B-1 (continued)

	Gross Product Originating		Current-Dollar Components				Profit-Type Income		
Year	CO(1958) $	CU $ Total	Employee Compensation	Interest	C C A	I B T	Total	Profits	I V A
			Fabricated Metal Products, SIC 34						
1947	5,913	4,127	3,135	-9	150	68	783	1,097	-314
1948	6,026	4,634	3,418	-6	164	82	976	1,196	-220
1949	5,403	4,225	3,176	-8	179	86	792	785	7
1950	6,566	5,338	3,804	-11	192	94	1,259	1,387	-128
1951	6,908	6,355	4,524	-11	234	108	1,500	1,590	-90
1952	7,088	6,301	4,798	-5	264	116	1,128	1,202	-74
1953	7,875	6,954	5,472	-3	296	132	1,057	1,203	-146
1954	7,601	6,674	5,214	-4	318	132	1,014	1,054	-40
1955	8,089	7,377	5,768	-4	361	139	1,113	1,279	-166
1956	8,208	7,830	6,174	7	362	151	1,136	1,325	-189
1957	8,409	8,291	6,526	7	397	168	1,193	1,312	-119
1958	7,804	7,804	6,146	13	437	171	1,037	1,084	-47
1959	8,726	8,630	6,830	12	453	174	1,161	1,176	-15
1960	8,750	8,706	7,063	22	501	189	931	921	10
1961	8,751	8,795	6,891	18	523	197	1,166	1,157	9
1962	9,464	9,596	7,455	28	648	215	1,250	1,234	16
1963	9,745	10,008	7,814	31	667	230	1,266	1,301	-35
1964	10,550	11,004	8,503	48	706	245	1,502	1,519	-17

(continued)

TABLE B-1 (continued)

	Gross Product Originating		Current-Dollar Components						
							Profit-Type Income		
Year	CO(1958) $	CU $ Total	Employee Compensation	Interest	C C A	I B T	Total	Profits	I V A
			Machinery, Except Electrical, SIC 35						
1947	9,509	5,829	4,476	-1	214	124	1,016	1,440	-424
1948	10,126	6,683	4,973	-14	258	147	1,319	1,740	-421
1949	8,782	6,165	4,345	-11	291	151	1,389	1,361	28
1950	9,572	6,959	4,847	-26	319	162	1,657	1,910	-253
1951	12,256	9,707	6,658	-23	376	201	2,495	2,731	-236
1952	13,323	10,698	7,428	-6	441	230	2,605	2,630	-25
1953	13,212	10,794	7,939	-7	493	260	2,109	2,320	-211
1954	11,926	9,946	7,250	-10	566	253	1,887	1,930	-43
1955	12,194	10,414	7,768	-13	649	275	1,735	2,026	-291
1956	13,470	12,379	9,005	-5	711	313	2,355	2,708	-353
1957	12,802	12,584	9,322	-6	780	335	2,153	2,386	-233
1958	10,921	10,921	8,246	10	796	324	1,545	1,590	-45
1959	12,687	12,941	9,475	0	910	337	2,219	2,334	-115
1960	12,722	13,104	9,832	11	945	371	1,945	1,965	-20
1961	12,624	13,116	9,728	7	1,008	376	1,997	2,021	-24
1962	14,121	14,813	10,763	5	1,159	394	2,492	2,515	-23
1963	14,696	15,475	11,383	13	1,122	415	2,542	2,598	-56
1964	16,739	17,927	12,684	26	1,313	443	3,461	3,544	-83

(continued)

TABLE B-1 (continued)

	Gross Product Originating		Current-Dollar Components						
							Profit-Type Income		
Year	CO(1958) $	CU $ Total	Employee Compensation	Interest	C C A	I B T	Total	Profits	I V A
			Electrical Machinery, SIC 36						
1947	5,235	4,167	3,189	-5	83	303	597	842	-245
1948	5,389	4,424	3,342	-3	114	332	639	826	-187
1949	4,895	4,146	2,998	-5	120	280	753	656	97
1950	6,157	5,264	3,580	-20	136	375	1,193	1,361	-168
1951	7,062	6,313	4,450	-12	157	454	1,264	1,365	-101
1952	8,299	7,262	5,072	0	187	480	1,523	1,523	0
1953	9,096	8,086	5,931	-7	226	552	1,384	1,479	-95
1954	8,123	7,311	5,444	1	258	399	1,209	1,240	-31
1955	8,779	7,769	5,996	0	304	440	1,029	1,192	-163
1956	9,501	8,674	6,725	11	342	448	1,148	1,240	-92
1957	9,767	9,552	7,153	22	380	464	1,533	1,518	15
1958	9,348	9,348	7,063	15	431	456	1,383	1,391	-8
1959	11,085	11,185	8,415	-3	425	517	1,831	1,877	-46
1960	11,660	11,532	9,097	-2	460	518	1,459	1,418	41
1961	12,274	12,041	9,498	11	522	539	1,471	1,461	10
1962	14,034	13,290	10,521	21	591	590	1,567	1,538	29
1963	14,770	13,633	10,717	20	664	634	1,598	1,614	-16
1964	15,622	14,091	11,083	-10	718	667	1,633	1,702	-69

(continued)

TABLE B-1 (continued)

	Gross Product Originating		Current-Dollar Components						
							Profit-Type Income		
Year	CO(1958) $	CU $ Total	Employee Compensation	Interest	C C A	I B T	Total	Profits	I V A
			Motor Vehicles and Equipment, SIC 371						
1947	6,024	3,964	2,413	6	132	465	948	1,080	-132
1948	6,595	4,603	2,660	-21	154	579	1,231	1,491	-260
1949	6,988	5,639	2,763	-35	167	718	2,026	1,997	29
1950	9,889	7,506	3,507	-64	190	849	3,024	3,178	-154
1951	9,427	7,127	3,933	-61	200	874	2,181	2,282	-101
1952	8,296	7,500	4,027	-55	234	1,074	2,220	2,252	-32
1953	10,419	9,117	5,007	-71	309	1,406	2,466	2,517	-51
1954	9,071	7,910	4,411	-50	374	1,259	1,916	1,948	-32
1955	13,058	11,752	5,549	-70	433	1,823	4,017	4,186	-169
1956	9,781	9,165	5,203	-73	519	1,523	1,993	2,173	-180
1957	10,254	9,936	5,296	-67	633	1,736	2,338	2,431	-93
1958	7,092	7,092	4,535	-46	640	1,338	625	659	-34
1959	9,980	10,239	5,210	-87	623	1,748	2,745	2,726	19
1960	11,011	10,978	5,657	-125	621	1,921	2,904	2,907	-3
1961	9,807	9,758	5,137	-93	615	1,690	2,409	2,401	8
1962	12,923	13,117	6,369	-108	740	2,119	3,997	3,995	2
1963	14,912	14,972	7,095	-148	768	2,368	4,889	4,919	-30
1964	15,103	15,481	7,706	-150	798	2,533	4,594	4,609	-15

(continued)

TABLE B-1 (continued)

	Gross Product Originating		Current-Dollar Components				Profit-Type Income		
Year	CO(1958) $	CU $ Total	Employee Compensation	Interest	C C A	I B T	Total	Profits	I V A
			Transportation Equipment and Ordnance, Except Motor Vehicles, SIC 37+19–371						
1947	2,655	1,670	1,797	-19	55	49	-212	-74	-138
1948	3,215	2,157	1,906	-4	62	61	132	260	-128
1949	3,151	2,193	1,860	-8	71	61	209	207	2
1950	3,324	2,360	1,913	-14	68	71	322	393	-71
1951	4,890	3,927	3,391	-2	98	81	359	444	-85
1952	7,598	6,063	5,145	8	137	98	675	684	-9
1953	9,139	7,311	6,240	5	168	118	780	948	-168
1954	8,763	7,107	5,813	0	187	113	994	1,031	-37
1955	8,428	7,012	5,935	-7	204	119	761	960	-199
1956	8,495	7,790	6,827	0	220	133	610	1,043	-433
1957	9,322	9,098	7,671	25	261	153	988	1,190	-202
1958	8,791	8,791	7,440	24	317	158	852	902	-50
1959	8,756	8,905	7,926	37	351	164	427	504	-77
1960	8,534	8,781	7,768	52	392	170	399	375	24
1961	8,877	9,179	7,994	40	404	191	550	554	-4
1962	10,145	10,541	8,866	47	445	209	974	973	1
1963	10,666	11,167	9,445	40	483	230	969	1,005	-36
1964	10,885	11,636	9,614	2	544	242	1,234	1,279	-45

(continued)

TABLE B-1 (continued)

	Gross Product Originating		Current-Dollar Components						
							Profit-Type Income		
Year	CO(1958) $	CU $ Total	Employee Compensation	Interest	C C A	I B T	Total	Profits	I V A
			Instruments and Related Products, SIC 38						
1947	1,366	904	766	-2	19	50	71	104	-33
1948	1,466	1,013	835	-1	21	60	98	121	-23
1949	1,429	1,019	806	-2	23	53	139	115	24
1950	1,675	1,218	950	-2	27	60	183	189	-6
1951	2,015	1,602	1,217	-3	47	63	278	299	-21
1952	2,300	1,831	1,413	0	56	53	309	306	3
1953	2,500	2,035	1,595	1	60	61	318	336	-18
1954	2,468	2,058	1,576	0	66	42	374	383	-9
1955	2,610	2,208	1,682	-1	79	49	399	408	-9
1956	2,759	2,489	1,892	2	107	59	429	443	-14
1957	2,646	2,564	2,035	6	116	61	346	389	-43
1958	2,604	2,604	1,990	10	134	63	407	423	-16
1959	2,980	3,054	2,226	9	143	72	604	611	-7
1960	3,017	3,153	2,336	8	160	73	576	589	-13
1961	3,019	3,218	2,382	6	209	77	544	563	-19
1962	3,251	3,524	2,550	8	232	81	653	662	-9
1963	3,531	3,813	2,677	13	256	91	776	760	16
1964	3,622	3,941	2,785	18	192	100	846	839	7

(continued)

TABLE B-1 (concluded)

	Gross Product Originating		Current-Dollar Components						
							Profit-Type Income		
Year	CO(1958) $	CU $ Total	Employee Compensation	Interest	C C A	I B T	Total	Profits	I V A
			Miscellaneous Manufacturing Industries, SIC 39						
1947	1,729	1,520	1,112	3	54	59	292	353	-61
1948	1,927	1,682	1,212	5	71	60	334	376	-42
1949	1,740	1,547	1,131	3	74	57	282	258	24
1950	1,974	1,775	1,263	3	69	64	376	443	-67
1951	2,067	1,877	1,361	5	77	63	371	424	-53
1952	2,115	1,914	1,405	7	81	72	349	326	23
1953	2,195	2,033	1,578	7	85	76	287	297	-10
1954	2,105	1,977	1,532	8	90	72	275	294	-19
1955	2,328	2,156	1,617	5	104	72	358	361	-3
1956	2,350	2,272	1,728	10	112	82	340	379	-39
1957	2,310	2,285	1,739	12	124	84	326	361	-35
1958	2,284	2,284	1,711	12	133	82	346	351	-5
1959	2,504	2,471	1,853	8	136	87	387	388	-1
1960	2,445	2,455	1,918	12	122	90	313	320	-7
1961	2,500	2,577	1,924	6	116	92	439	444	-5
1962	2,602	2,672	2,041	6	119	97	409	423	-14
1963	2,588	2,671	2,101	15	130	106	319	323	-4
1964	2,724	2,811	2,241	13	122	112	323	331	-8

Note: See the beginning of this appendix for the explanation of the abbreviations used in these tables.

process. Value is generally fob plant and excludes excise taxes. For more detailed explanation, see *1958 Census of Manufactures.*

Cost of Materials (column 5) = Deflated cost of materials, supplies, components, semifinished goods, fuels and electricity actually consumed or put into production during the year and cost of products purchased for resale. Cost includes direct charges actually paid or payable for items consumed after discounts and including freight and other direct charges. For more detailed explanation, see *1958 Census of Manufactures.*

Value Added—VA (column 6) = Deflated value of production (above) less deflated cost of materials, etc. (above). Equivalent to adjusted Census value added by manufactures.

VA plus Excise (column 7) = Deflated value added (above) plus deflated federal excise taxes for which the given industry is legally liable.

OBE Gross Product (column 8) = Deflated current-dollar total of gross product originating in the specified industry. For derivation, see Appendix A.

Total (FRB – OBE) (column 9) = Published FRB index (column 1) minus published OBE index (column 8). Differences between the two series may arise from weights and measures of output.

FRB (Net Minus Gross Wtd.) (column 10) = Published FRB index weighted by 1957–59 Census value added (column 1) minus FRB series weighted by 1958 Census value of production (column 3). Since the identical FRB output relatives are used in the calculations of both indexes, discrepancies between the two series arise because of weighting differences. Such disparities are the result of relative differences in the individual industry's contribution to the major group when computed on a net- or gross-output basis.

Total Output (Quantity Minus Deflated) (column 11) = FRB series weighted by 1958 Census value of production (column 3) minus Census series of deflated value of production (column 4). This series generally reflects the difference in total output derived by a quantity extrapolation technique vis-à-vis a deflation procedure. However, differences between the series may arise from data limitations. For example, the two series may differ because of coverage (see discussion for Major Group 34), adjustments due to SIC changes particularly in years when the FRB indexes are linked (Major Group 26) and in changes since 1958 in FRB procedures to derive annual measures (Major Group 25).

Total Minus Net Output (column 12) = Deflated Census value of production (column 4) minus deflated Census value added (column 6). This series measures differences between the movement of gross and net output as derived from deflated Census data. Movement differences between total and net output reflect the industry changes in unit costs relative to unit output because of shifts in product mix, substitutions of materials, technological changes, and other circumstances influencing the amount of work done in an industry.

Excise Tax (column 13) = Deflated Census value added (column 6) minus deflated Census value added plus excise tax (column 7). This difference illustrates the effect of the addition of manufacturer's excise taxes to the value of net output. Since Census value added excluding excise taxes is used to weight the published FRB series and the OBE series includes this nonfactor payment, the difference between the two series quite often is related to these taxes, cf. SIC 20, 21, 29, 30, 36 and 371.

Net Output (Census – OBE) (column 14) = Census value added plus excise taxes (column 7) minus published OBE (column 8). Disparities between these two measures are based on differences in the movements of the current-dollar series and partially reflect changes occasiond by the conceptual differences between the two measures including inventory valuation adjustment (IVA) in the GPO series. The use of independent data sources may also be a cause of differences and reflect differencs in classification by the several government agencies.

In addition to measures of trend, shown below, averages of the absolute value of the percentage changes over the entire period for each of the series shown in columns 1 through 8 were computed. The standard deviation of these percentage changes was also calculated. The results indicated that generally the averages and the distribution about these averages for each of the series were approximately of the same magnitude by industry. The variation in any one series was not significantly greater than the variation in the others.

GROWTH RATES

The average annual growth rates of the various series by industry for selected periods are shown below. These measures show the average annual compounded rate of change between the initial and terminal years of each period. The computations are based on the "Growth Rate Conversion Tables" appearing in Bureau of the Census, *Long Term Economic Growth 1860–1965,* ES-4-No. 1, October 1966, p. 115.

Appendix D: Implicit Price Deflators by Industry Groups and by Industry, 1947–64

EXPLANATION OF ABBREVIATIONS USED IN TABLES

These tables contain implicit price deflators (current-dollar series divided by constant-dollar series) for the series indicated below. A description of how these price deflators are derived appears in Appendix A.

Value of Production (VP) = Census value of shipments plus change in inventory of finished goods and work in process.

TABLE C-1

Average Annual Rates of Growth by Industry for Selected Periods

Periods	FRB As Pub.	FRB Reweighted GPO	FRB Reweighted VP	Deflated Census Data VP	Deflated Census Data Cost of Materials	Deflated Census Data VA	Deflated Census Data VA Plus Excise	OBE Gross Product
				All Manufacturing Industries				
1947–64	4.2	4.0	3.9	3.5	3.4	3.7	3.6	3.8
1948–64	4.2	4.1	3.9					3.8
1947–57	4.3	4.0	3.9	3.6	3.6	3.6	3.5	3.9
1948–57	4.3	4.1	4.0					3.8
1957–64	4.0	4.0	3.9	3.4	3.2	3.7	3.7	3.7
				Nondurable Goods Industries				
1947–64	4.1	3.8	3.6	3.5	3.4	3.6	3.5	3.5
1948–64	4.1	3.9	3.7					3.5
1947–57	3.7	3.3	3.2	3.2	3.1	3.4	3.2	3.4
1948–57	3.7	3.4	3.3					3.2
1957–64	4.6	4.5	4.2	3.8	3.7	4.0	3.9	3.8
				Durable Goods Industries				
1947–64	4.4	4.2	4.2	3.6	3.5	3.7	3.7	4.0
1948–64	4.4	4.2	4.2					4.0
1947–57	4.9	4.6	4.5	3.9	4.1	3.8	3.8	4.3
1948–57	5.0	4.6	4.5					4.2
1957–64	3.6	3.7	3.7	3.1	2.6	3.6	3.6	3.6
				Food and Kindred Products, SIC 20				
1947–64	2.4	2.3	2.4	2.6	2.7	2.4	2.2	2.6
1948–64	2.6	2.6	2.7					2.5
1947–57	1.9	1.6	1.9	2.4	2.1	3.0	2.5	2.9
1948–57	2.2	2.0	2.4					2.7
1957–64	3.2	3.2	3.1	3.0	3.7	1.5	1.7	2.1
				Tobacco Manufactures, SIC 21				
1947–64	2.3	2.6	2.1	1.4	0.6	3.1	2.5	2.9
1948–64	2.3	2.5	1.9					2.7
1947–57	1.5	2.1	1.7	0.3	–0.7	2.6	2.0	2.5
1948–57	1.4	1.8	1.4					2.0
1957–64	3.6	3.4	2.6	2.9	2.5	3.7	3.2	3.4

(continued)

TABLE C-1 (continued)

Periods	FRB As Pub.	FRB Reweighted GPO	FRB Reweighted VP	Deflated Census Data VP	Deflated Census Data Cost of Materials	Deflated Census Data VA	Deflated Census Data VA Plus Excise	OBE Gross Product
Textile Mill Products, SIC 22								
1947–64	2.2	2.2	2.1	3.2	3.5	2.7	2.7	2.2
1948–64	1.9	1.9	1.8					1.7
1947–57	1.3	1.2	1.2	2.2	2.5	1.9	1.9	1.2
1948–57	0.7	0.6	0.6					0.2
1957–64	3.5	3.5	3.5	4.5	4.9	3.9	3.9	3.6
Apparel and Related Products, SIC 23								
1947–64	3.5	3.5	3.6	2.9	3.1	2.7	2.7	2.8
1948–64	3.5	3.4	3.5					2.6
1947–57	2.7	2.6	2.7	3.1	3.3	2.8	2.8	2.3
1948–57	2.5	2.4	2.5					2.0
1957–64	4.8	4.7	4.9	2.7	2.7	2.7	2.7	3.4
Lumber and Wood Products Except Furniture, SIC 24								
1947–64	1.4	1.6	1.6	1.9	2.9	0.9	0.9	1.5
1948–64	1.3	1.5	1.5					1.8
1947–57	0.8	1.0	1.0	1.0	2.7	-0.7	-0.7	0.0
1948–57	0.5	0.7	0.7					0.2
1957–64	2.3	2.6	2.5	3.3	3.2	3.3	3.3	3.8
Furniture and Fixtures, SIC 25								
1947–64	4.5	4.5	4.6	3.2	3.8	2.6	2.6	3.3
1948–64	4.6	4.6	4.6					2.5
1947–57	3.6	3.6	3.6	3.3	3.7	2.9	2.9	3.9
1948–57	3.6	3.6	3.6					2.6
1957–64	5.8	5.9	5.9	3.0	3.9	2.2	2.2	2.3
Paper and Allied Products, SIC 26								
1947–64	4.6	4.4	4.5	4.0	4.3	3.7	3.7	3.7
1948–64	4.7	4.5	4.6					4.5
1947–57	4.4	4.2	4.3	3.8	4.6	2.9	2.9	3.0
1948–57	4.6	4.4	4.5					4.3
1957–64	4.8	4.8	4.9	4.2	3.7	4.8	4.8	4.7

(continued)

TABLE C-1 (continued)

Periods	FRB As Pub.	FRB Reweighted GPO	FRB Reweighted VP	Deflated Census Data VP	Deflated Census Data Cost of Materials	Deflated Census Data VA	Deflated Census Data VA Plus Excise	OBE Gross Product
			Printing and Publishing, SIC 27					
1947–64	3.4	3.5	3.6	3.1	3.8	2.8	2.8	3.1
1948–64	3.3	3.4	3.4					3.1
1947–57	3.6	3.8	3.8	3.0	3.4	2.7	2.7	3.3
1948–57	3.4	3.5	3.5					3.4
1957–64	3.2	3.2	3.2	3.3	4.2	2.9	2.9	2.8
			Chemicals and Allied Products, SIC 28					
1947–64	8.2	8.1	7.9	6.7	5.7	7.7	7.7	7.5
1948–64	8.2	8.1	8.0					6.9
1947–57	8.6	8.4	8.1	7.0	5.9	8.1	8.1	8.7
1948–57	8.6	8.5	8.2					7.7
1957–64	7.8	7.7	7.6	6.3	5.4	7.0	7.0	5.9
			Petroleum and Related Industries, SIC 29					
1947–64	3.9	3.8	3.8	4.1	3.8	5.1	4.8	4.7
1948–64	3.7	3.7	3.5					4.4
1947–57	4.6	4.3	4.5	4.8	5.1	3.4	4.0	4.3
1948–57	4.2	4.1	4.1					3.7
1957–64	3.0	3.1	2.8	3.1	2.0	7.7	6.0	5.3
			Rubber and Miscellaneous Plastic Products, SIC 30					
1947–64	6.2	5.4	5.6	4.4	5.0	3.9	3.7	3.6
1948–64	6.5	6.0	6.1					4.3
1947–57	5.6	4.2	4.4	2.9	4.0	2.0	1.8	1.7
1948–57	6.1	5.1	5.3					2.8
1957–64	7.0	7.1	7.3	6.6	6.6	6.6	6.4	6.3
			Leather and Leather Products, SIC 31					
1947–64	0.6	0.6	0.5	−0.1	0.7	−0.7	−0.7	−0.1
1948–64	0.9	0.9	0.8					−0.3
1947–57	0.7	0.7	0.5	−0.2	1.4	−1.6	−1.6	−0.8
1948–57	1.3	1.3	1.1					−1.3
1957–64	0.5	0.5	0.4	0.1	−0.4	0.5	0.5	0.9

(continued)

TABLE C-1 (continued)

Periods	FRB As Pub.	FRB Reweighted GPO	FRB Reweighted VP	Deflated Census Data VP	Deflated Census Data Cost of Materials	Deflated Census Data VA	Deflated Census Data VA Plus Excise	OBE Gross Product
				Stone, Clay, and Glass Products, SIC 32				
1947–64	3.8	4.0	4.3	4.3	5.3	3.7	3.7	3.5
1948–64	3.6	3.8	4.0					3.3
1947–57	3.9	4.3	4.6	4.8	6.4	3.8	3.8	3.4
1948–57	3.6	3.9	4.1					3.0
1957–64	3.6	3.7	3.8	3.6	3.8	3.5	3.5	3.7
				Primary Metal Industries, SIC 33				
1947–64	2.1	2.2	2.3	1.8	2.3	1.1	1.1	1.1
1948–64	2.0	2.1	2.2					1.2
1947–57	2.1	2.4	2.4	1.8	2.2	1.2	1.2	1.7
1948–57	1.9	2.2	2.2					2.0
1957–64	2.0	2.0	2.1	1.7	2.4	0.9	0.9	0.2
				Fabricated Metal Products, SIC 34				
1947–64	3.3	3.4	3.4	2.8	2.7	2.8	2.8	3.5
1948–64	3.4	3.5	3.5					3.6
1947–57	3.0	3.0	3.1	3.1	3.0	3.2	3.2	3.6
1948–57	3.1	3.2	3.2					3.8
1957–64	3.9	3.9	3.8	2.3	2.3	2.3	2.3	3.3
				Machinery, Except Electrical, SIC 35				
1947–64	3.5	3.7	3.6	2.7	2.8	2.7	2.7	3.4
1948–64	3.7	3.9	3.8					3.2
1947–57	3.1	3.3	3.2	2.3	2.3	2.2	2.2	3.0
1948–57	3.4	3.6	3.4					2.6
1957–64	4.2	4.3	4.3	3.4	3.4	3.4	3.4	3.9
				Electrical Machinery, SIC 36				
1947–64	6.1	6.0	5.9	5.6	4.2	6.7	6.7	6.6
1948–64	6.3	6.1	6.0					6.9
1947–57	7.1	7.0	6.9	4.9	3.7	6.0	6.0	6.4
1948–57	7.4	7.3	7.1					6.8
1957–64	4.8	4.7	4.6	6.5	4.8	7.8	7.7	6.9

(continued)

TABLE C-1 (concluded)

Periods	FRB As Pub.	FRB Reweighted GPO	FRB Reweighted VP	Deflated Census Data VP	Deflated Census Data Cost of Materials	Deflated Census Data VA	Deflated Census Data VA Plus Excise	OBE Gross Product
Trans. Equip. and Ord. Except Mot. Vehicles, SIC 37 + 19 - 371								
1947–64	10.3	9.8	9.2	7.1	6.7	7.4	7.4	8.7
1948–64	10.3	10.1	9.3					7.9
1947–57	16.6	15.7	14.7	12.9	13.6	12.3	12.3	13.4
1948–57	17.3	16.9	15.5					12.5
1957–64	1.9	1.6	1.9	-0.7	-2.4	0.9	0.9	2.2
Motor Vehicles and Equipment, SIC 371								
1947–64	4.6	4.7	4.7	4.3	3.9	5.1	5.1	5.6
1948–64	4.4	4.5	4.5					5.3
1947–57	4.5	4.7	4.7	4.5	4.4	4.9	4.9	5.5
1948–57	4.1	4.3	4.2					5.0
1957–64	4.8	4.7	4.8	4.0	3.2	5.5	5.4	5.7
Instruments and Related Products, SIC 38								
1947–64	5.6	5.6	5.6	5.5	4.9	5.8	5.8	5.9
1948–64	5.8	5.8	5.7					5.8
1947–57	6.2	6.2	6.1	4.8	4.5	4.9	4.9	6.8
1948–57	6.6	6.6	6.5					6.8
1957–64	4.8	4.8	4.8	6.5	5.4	7.1	7.1	4.6
Miscellaneous Manufacturing Industrial, SIC 39								
1947–64	3.1	3.1	3.1	3.2	3.0	3.4	3.4	2.7
1948–64	2.9	2.9	2.9					2.2
1947–57	2.2	2.2	2.2	2.2	1.6	2.6	2.6	2.9
1948–57	1.7	1.7	1.7					2.0
1957–64	4.4	4.4	4.4	4.7	5.2	4.4	4.4	2.4

Note: VA = Value added; VP = Value of production. For other abbreviations see note at the beginning of Appendix C.

TABLE C-2

Selected Measures of Manufacturing Activity 1947–1964: Food and Kindred Products, SIC 20

	Indexes (1958 = 100)								Point Differences In Indexes[a]					
	FRB			Deflated Census Data				OBE Gross Product	Total (FRB Minus OBE)	FRB (Net Minus Gross Wtd.)	Total Output (Quantity Minus Defltd.)	Total Minus Net Output	Excise Tax	Net Output (Census Minus OBE)
	As Pub.	Reweighted GPO	Reweighted VP	VP	Cost Mat.	VA	VA Plus Excise							
Year	(1)	(2)	(3)	(4)	(5)	(6)	(7)	(8)	(9)	(10)	(11)	(12)	(13)	(14)
1947	81.0	83.2	81.5	78.0	77.8	78.6	81.2	76.0	5.0	-.5	3.5	-.6	-2.6	5.2
1948	80.2	81.4	79.2					79.2	1.0	1.0				
1949	81.1	81.8	80.6	78.5	80.4	73.9	76.2	75.9	5.2	.5	2.1	4.6	-2.3	.3
1950	84.0	85.7	83.2	80.3	79.4	82.4	84.7	82.4	1.6	.8	2.9	-2.1	-2.3	2.3
1951	85.6	87.2	85.5	82.4	80.9	85.9	87.5	83.7	1.9	.1	3.1	-3.5	-1.6	3.8
1952	87.4	87.4	88.1	85.3	84.8	86.6	87.9	86.8	.6	-.7	2.8	-1.3	-1.3	1.1
1953	88.7	89.2	89.1	87.6	85.6	92.3	93.1	93.2	-4.5	-.4	1.5	-4.7	-.8	-.1
1954	90.7	90.6	91.2	87.3	86.9	88.2	89.0	89.9	.8	-.5	3.9	-.9	-.8	-.9
1955	94.2	94.3	95.4	92.9	93.0	92.6	93.3	94.5	-.3	-1.2	2.5	.3	-.7	-1.2
1956	97.8	98.2	98.9	97.7	96.6	100.3	100.8	98.5	-.7	-1.1	1.2	-2.6	-.5	2.3
1957	97.7	97.6	98.1	98.5	95.6	105.4	104.4	101.1	-3.4	-.4	-.4	-6.9	1.0	3.3
1958	100.0	100.0	100.0	100.0	100.0	100.0	100.0	100.0	.0	.0	.0	.0	.0	.0
1959	104.5	104.7	105.1	104.2	106.4	99.2	99.7	100.7	3.8	-.6	.9	5.0	-.5	-1.0
1960	107.4	107.5	107.8	107.4	108.5	104.7	104.7	103.1	4.3	-.4	.4	2.7	.0	1.6
1961	111.0	111.1	111.4	109.4	112.4	102.2	103.0	101.7	9.3	-.4	2.0	7.2	-.8	1.3
1962	114.3	114.1	114.1	112.7	115.3	106.6	107.2	105.3	9.0	.2	1.4	6.1	-.6	1.9
1963	117.7	117.4	117.5	115.8	117.4	111.9	112.1	110.8	6.9	.2	1.7	3.9	-.2	1.3
1964	121.7	121.8	121.4	121.3	123.1	116.9	117.3	117.1	4.6	.3	.1	4.4	-.4	.2

Note: VP = value of production; VA = value added. For other abbreviations see note at the beginning of Appendix C.

[a]Col. 9 = col. 1 – col. 8; col. 10 = col. 1 – col. 3; col. 11 = col. 3 – col. 4; col. 12 = col. 4 – col. 6; col. 13 = col. 6 – col. 7; col. 14 = col. 7 – col. 8.

TABLE C-3

Selected Measures of Manufacturing Activity, 1947–64: Tobacco Manufactures, SIC 21

	Indexes (1958 = 100)								Point Differences In Indexes[a]					
	FRB			Deflated Census Data				OBE Gross Product						
		Reweighted												
Year	As Pub. (1)	GPO (2)	VP (3)	VP (4)	Cost Mat. (5)	VA (6)	VA Plus Excise (7)	(8)	Total (FRB Minus OBE) (9)	FRB (Net Minus Gross Wtd.) (10)	Total Output (Quantity Minus Defltd.) (11)	Total Minus Net Output (12)	Excise Tax (13)	Net Output (Census Minus OBE) (14)
1947	81.4	76.3	81.0	92.0	105.5	69.7	75.3	73.4	8.0	.4	-11.0	22.3	-5.6	1.9
1948	83.4	80.0	84.2					78.3	5.1	-.8				
1949	82.8	79.7	83.6	98.9	109.1	82.2	82.7	83.0	-.2	-.8	-15.3	16.7	-.5	.3
1950	83.8	81.2	84.9	99.0	113.3	75.4	80.8	79.8	4.0	-1.1	-14.1	23.6	-5.4	1.0
1951	88.8	86.9	90.5	99.5	106.2	88.4	88.6	88.3	.5	-1.7	-9.0	11.1	-.2	.3
1952	91.8	90.8	94.2	101.0	109.7	86.7	89.5	92.1	-.3	-2.4	-6.8	14.3	-2.8	-2.6
1953	89.8	88.9	92.3	95.7	111.8	69.2	80.4	85.5	4.3	-2.5	-3.4	26.5	-11.2	-5.1
1954	86.0	85.0	88.2	88.9	104.0	64.1	75.9	80.4	5.6	-2.2	-.7	24.8	-11.8	-4.5
1955	88.0	87.3	90.1	92.5	101.8	77.2	83.2	85.3	2.7	-2.1	-2.4	15.3	-6.0	-2.1
1956	90.3	90.0	92.3	93.6	96.6	88.5	89.4	90.1	.2	-2.0	-1.3	5.1	-.9	-.7
1957	94.1	93.9	95.6	95.1	98.1	90.0	92.1	93.9	.2	-1.5	.5	5.1	-2.1	-1.8
1958	100.0	100.0	100.0	100.0	100.0	100.0	100.0	100.0	.0	.0	.0	.0	.0	.0
1959	105.0	104.9	103.0	103.0	101.0	106.4	104.1	106.1	-1.1	2.0	.0	-3.4	2.3	-2.0
1960	107.1	107.9	104.3	110.8	111.5	109.6	108.5	110.6	-3.5	2.8	-6.5	1.2	1.1	-2.1
1961	110.5	112.2	106.9	112.7	110.6	116.3	113.5	115.9	-5.4	3.6	-5.8	-3.6	2.8	-2.4
1962	111.7	113.5	107.0	113.3	108.8	121.2	116.0	120.3	-8.6	4.7	-6.3	-7.9	5.2	-4.3
1963	114.9	117.1	109.1	113.4	113.6	113.1	115.1	122.2	-7.3	5.8	-4.3	.3	-2.0	-7.1
1964	120.4	118.8	114.5	116.3	116.3	116.3	115.0	119.0	1.4	5.9	-1.8	.0	1.3	-4.0

Note: VA = value added; VP = value of production. For other abbreviations see note at the beginning of Appendix C.

[a]Col. 9 = col. 1 – col. 8; col. 10 = col. 1 – col. 3; col. 11 = col. 3 – col. 4; col. 12 = col. 4 – col. 6; col. 13 = col. 6 – col. 7; col. 14 = col. 7 – col. 8.

TABLE C-4

Selected Measures of Manufacturing Activity, 1947–64: Textile Mill Products, SIC 22

	Indexes (1958 = 100)								Point Differences In Indexes[a]					
	FRB			Deflated Census Data				OBE Gross Product						
		Reweighted												
Year	As Pub. (1)	GPO (2)	VP (3)	VP (4)	Cost Mat. (5)	VA (6)	VA Plus Excise (7)	(8)	Total (FRB Minus OBE) (9)	FRB (Net Minus Gross Wtd.) (10)	Total Output (Quantity Minus Defltd.) (11)	Total Minus Net Output (12)	Excise Tax (13)	Net Output (Census Minus OBE) (14)
1947	90.1	90.5	91.0	81.7	80.0	84.1	84.1	90.5	-.4	-.9	9.3	-2.4	.0	-6.4
1948	96.3	96.9	97.2					99.4	-3.1	-.9				
1949	89.1	89.4	89.5	82.1	80.5	84.6	84.6	91.6	-2.5	-.4	7.4	-2.5	.0	-7.0
1950	101.4	101.7	101.8	94.9	91.6	99.6	99.6	96.2	5.2	-.4	6.9	-4.7	.0	3.4
1951	100.3	100.1	100.2	93.6	95.8	90.2	90.2	99.0	1.3	.1	6.6	3.4	.0	-8.8
1952	99.5	99.4	99.3	94.0	97.7	88.5	88.5	98.9	.6	.2	5.3	5.5	.0	-10.4
1953	101.5	101.5	101.4	99.5	102.2	95.5	95.5	96.7	4.8	.1	1.9	4.0	.0	-1.2
1954	94.9	95.0	94.9	91.6	92.1	90.9	90.9	92.0	2.9	.0	3.3	.7	.0	-1.1
1955	104.9	104.9	105.0	103.6	105.7	100.6	100.6	102.5	2.4	-.1	1.4	3.0	.0	-1.9
1956	106.5	106.7	106.9	104.7	105.6	103.4	103.4	103.9	2.6	-.4	2.2	1.3	.0	-.5
1957	102.3	102.4	102.5	101.9	102.2	101.5	101.5	101.6	.7	-.2	.6	.4	.0	-.1
1958	100.0	100.0	100.0	100.0	100.0	100.0	100.0	100.0	.0	.0	.0	.0	.0	.0
1959	115.8	115.9	116.1	111.8	112.2	111.2	111.2	110.2	5.6	-.3	4.3	.6	.0	1.0
1960	111.3	111.4	111.5	109.8	110.9	108.2	108.2	106.6	4.7	-.2	1.7	1.6	.0	1.6
1961	113.6	113.5	113.4	114.2	115.8	111.8	111.8	106.6	7.0	.2	-.8	2.4	.0	5.2
1962	122.3	122.2	122.3	123.5	125.5	120.4	120.4	116.6	5.7	.0	-1.2	3.1	.0	3.8
1963	124.0	123.9	124.0	127.9	131.0	123.1	123.1	120.5	3.5	.0	-3.9	4.8	.0	2.6
1964	130.3	130.2	130.1	138.7	142.7	132.6	132.6	130.1	.2	.2	-8.6	6.1	.0	2.5

Note: VA = value added; VP = value of production. For other abbreviations see note at the beginning of Appendix C.

[a]Col. 9 = col. 1 – col. 8; col. 10 = col. 1 – col. 3; col. 11 = col. 3 – col. 4; col. 12 = col. 4 – col. 6; col. 13 = col. 6 – col. 7; col. 14 = col. 7 – col. 8.

TABLE C-5

Selected Measures of Manufacturing Activity, 1947–64: Apparel and Related Products, SIC 23

	Indexes (1958 = 100)								Point Differences In Indexes[a]					
	FRB			Deflated Census Data				OBE Gross Product	Total (FRB Minus OBE)	FRB (Net Minus Gross Wtd.)	Total Output (Quantity Minus Defltd.)	Total Minus Net Output	Excise Tax	Net Output (Census Minus OBE)
	As Pub.	Reweighted GPO	Reweighted VP	VP	Cost Mat.	VA	VA Plus Excise							
Year	(1)	(2)	(3)	(4)	(5)	(6)	(7)	(8)	(9)	(10)	(11)	(12)	(13)	(14)
1947	77.8	78.7	77.9	77.7	76.8	78.7	78.7	80.6	-2.8	-.1	.2	-1.0	.0	-1.9
1948	81.1	82.3	81.6					85.3	-4.2	-.5				
1949	80.4	80.9	80.2	83.4	86.8	79.1	79.1	84.2	-3.8	.2	-3.2	4.3	.0	-5.1
1950	86.5	87.7	87.2	83.3	81.8	85.2	85.2	91.8	-5.3	-.7	3.9	-1.9	.0	-6.6
1951	84.9	83.9	83.6	82.6	75.4	91.5	91.5	98.3	-13.4	1.3	1.0	-8.9	.0	-6.8
1952	89.3	89.3	89.1	88.2	86.7	90.0	90.0	98.3	-9.0	.2	.9	-1.8	.0	-8.3
1953	90.9	91.1	91.0	93.4	87.6	100.6	100.6	101.0	-10.1	-.1	-2.4	-7.2	.0	-.4
1954	87.8	88.1	87.8	91.6	90.7	92.8	92.8	94.3	-6.5	.0	-3.8	-1.2	.0	-1.5
1955	96.4	97.0	96.9	99.6	99.2	100.2	100.2	101.2	-4.8	-.5	-2.7	-.6	.0	-1.0
1956	100.3	100.9	100.7	103.2	105.0	101.0	101.0	103.1	-2.8	-.4	-2.5	2.2	.0	-2.1
1957	101.4	101.7	101.6	105.0	106.3	103.6	103.6	101.5	-.1	-.2	-3.4	1.4	.0	2.1
1958	100.0	100.0	100.0	100.0	100.0	100.0	100.0	100.0	.0	.0	.0	.0	.0	.0
1959	113.5	113.9	113.9	106.8	106.1	107.8	107.8	107.3	6.2	-.4	7.1	-1.0	.0	.5
1960	117.4	117.6	117.8	108.6	107.3	110.3	110.3	111.9	5.5	-.4	9.2	-1.7	.0	-1.6
1961	117.6	117.6	117.9	109.3	110.6	107.6	107.6	111.2	6.4	-.3	8.6	1.7	.0	-3.6
1962	124.8	124.9	125.4	115.6	118.4	112.0	112.0	119.1	5.7	-.6	9.8	3.6	.0	-7.1
1963	131.8	131.9	132.6	121.8	122.6	120.9	120.9	121.2	10.6	-.8	10.8	.9	.0	-.3
1964	140.7	140.6	141.6	126.7	128.3	124.7	124.7	128.1	12.6	-.9	14.9	2.0	.0	-3.4

Note: VA = value added; VP = value of production. For other abbreviations see note at the beginning of Appendix C.

[a]Col. 9 = col. 1 – col. 8; col. 10 = col. 1 – col. 3; col. 11 = col. 3 – col. 4; col. 12 = col. 4 – col. 6; col. 13 = col. 6 – col. 7; col. 14 = col. 7 – col. 8.

TABLE C-6

Selected Measures of Manufacturing Activity, 1947–64: Lumber and Wood Products, Except Furniture, SIC 24

	Indexes (1958 = 100)								Point Differences In Indexes[a]					
	FRB			Deflated Census Data				OBE Gross Product						
		Reweighted												
Year	As Pub. (1)	GPO (2)	VP (3)	VP (4)	Cost Mat. (5)	VA (6)	VA Plus Excise (7)	(8)	Total (FRB Minus OBE) (9)	FRB (Net Minus Gross Wtd.) (10)	Total Output (Quantity Minus Defltd.) (11)	Total Minus Net Output (12)	Excise Tax (13)	Net Output (Census Minus OBE) (14)
1947	92.3	90.3	90.3	91.1	75.7	111.3	111.3	99.4	-7.1	2.0	-.8	-20.2	.0	11.9
1948	96.0	94.1	94.1					97.5	-1.5	1.9				
1949	84.7	83.0	83.1	80.9	73.4	90.7	90.7	90.1	-5.4	1.6	2.2	-9.8	.0	.6
1950	102.9	101.5	101.7	97.7	87.8	110.6	110.6	98.0	4.9	1.2	4.0	-12.9	.0	12.6
1951	102.7	101.3	101.4	97.6	88.9	108.9	108.9	99.8	2.9	1.3	3.8	-11.3	.0	9.1
1952	101.4	100.3	100.4	97.7	90.8	106.7	106.7	97.0	4.4	1.0	2.7	-9.0	.0	9.7
1953	107.1	105.0	105.1	98.9	93.5	105.9	105.9	94.0	13.1	2.0	6.2	-7.0	.0	11.9
1954	104.2	102.9	103.1	94.2	92.0	97.0	97.0	91.3	12.9	1.1	8.9	-2.8	.0	5.7
1955	114.5	114.2	114.3	107.4	104.8	110.8	110.8	105.5	9.0	.2	6.9	-3.4	.0	5.3
1956	110.3	109.2	109.1	108.4	104.7	113.2	113.2	105.1	5.2	1.2	.7	-4.8	.0	8.1
1957	100.3	99.9	99.9	100.7	98.6	103.4	103.4	99.0	1.3	.4	-.8	-2.7	.0	4.4
1958	100.0	100.0	100.0	100.0	100.0	100.0	100.0	100.0	.0	.0	.0	.0	.0	.0
1959	113.5	114.3	114.2	109.3	108.6	110.3	110.3	109.5	4.0	-.7	4.9	-1.0	.0	.8
1960	106.8	106.4	106.1	107.0	107.8	105.8	105.8	107.4	-.6	.7	-.9	1.2	.0	-1.6
1961	106.0	106.9	106.6	106.5	106.9	106.0	106.0	105.2	.8	-.6	.1	.5	.0	.8
1962	111.0	111.9	111.6	112.4	111.4	113.7	113.7	114.5	-3.5	-.6	-.8	-1.3	.0	-.8
1963	113.9	115.1	114.8	118.8	116.3	122.2	122.2	119.9	-6.0	-.9	-4.0	-3.4	.0	2.3
1964	117.8	119.2	119.0	126.1	123.1	130.1	130.1	128.9	-11.1	-1.2	-7.1	-4.0	.0	1.2

Note: VA = value added; VP = value of production. For other abbreviations see note at the beginning of Appendix C.

[a]Col. 9 = col. 1 – col. 8; col. 10 = col. 1 – col. 3; col. 11 = col. 3 – col. 4; col. 12 = col. 4 – col. 6; col. 13 = col. 6 – col. 7; col. 14 = col. 7 – col. 8.

TABLE C-7

Selected Measures of Manufacturing Activity, 1947–64: Furniture and Fixtures, SIC 25

	Indexes (1958 = 100)								Point Differences In Indexes[a]					
	FRB			Deflated Census Data				OBE Gross Product	Total (FRB Minus OBE)	FRB (Net Minus Gross Wtd.)	Total Output (Quantity Minus Defltd.)	Total Minus Net Output	Excise Tax	Net Output (Census Minus OBE)
	As Pub.	Reweighted GPO	Reweighted VP	VP	Cost Mat.	VA	VA Plus Excise							
Year	(1)	(2)	(3)	(4)	(5)	(6)	(7)	(8)	(9)	(10)	(11)	(12)	(13)	(14)
1947	72.9	73.0	72.9	75.7	71.2	79.9	79.9	74.6	-1.7	.0	-2.8	-4.2	.0	5.3
1948	75.6	75.8	75.7					86.7	-11.1	-.1				
1949	69.9	70.0	69.9	71.4	68.2	74.4	74.4	82.1	-12.2	.0	-1.5	-3.0	.0	-7.7
1950	85.3	85.2	85.4	87.2	82.0	92.0	92.0	99.5	-14.2	-.1	-1.8	-4.8	.0	-7.5
1951	80.6	80.7	80.4	84.1	80.7	87.3	87.3	94.6	-14.0	.2	-3.7	-3.2	.0	-7.3
1952	82.8	82.8	82.8	87.3	82.6	91.7	91.7	102.0	-19.2	.0	-4.5	-4.4	.0	-10.3
1953	86.6	86.7	86.4	94.6	91.1	97.8	97.8	101.8	-15.2	.2	-8.2	-3.2	.0	-4.0
1954	90.3	90.3	90.2	91.7	88.4	94.7	94.7	98.0	-7.7	.1	-1.5	-3.0	.0	-3.3
1955	102.6	102.6	102.5	104.6	100.8	108.2	108.2	113.6	-11.0	.1	-2.1	-3.6	.0	-5.4
1956	105.9	105.9	105.5	107.5	103.7	111.1	111.1	114.4	-8.5	.4	-2.0	-3.6	.0	-3.3
1957	104.1	104.1	103.9	104.3	102.5	106.0	106.0	109.4	-5.3	.2	-.4	-1.7	.0	-3.4
1958	100.0	100.0	100.0	100.0	100.0	100.0	100.0	100.0	.0	.0	.0	.0	.0	.0
1959	119.5	119.6	119.8	110.8	110.5	111.0	111.0	114.1	5.4	-.3	9.0	-.2	.0	-3.1
1960	124.6	124.6	124.5	108.0	108.5	107.6	107.6	112.3	12.3	.1	16.5	.4	.0	-4.7
1961	124.4	124.5	124.5	105.3	108.5	102.2	102.2	108.1	16.3	-.1	19.2	3.1	.0	-5.9
1962	136.7	136.9	137.1	114.3	117.5	111.3	111.3	116.1	20.6	-.4	22.8	3.0	.0	-4.8
1963	143.6	143.8	144.1	119.8	121.1	118.5	118.5	119.4	24.2	-.5	24.3	1.3	.0	-.9
1964	154.7	155.0	155.7	128.6	134.1	123.1	123.1	128.7	26.0	-1.0	27.1	5.5	.0	-5.6

Note: VP = value of production; VA = value added. For other abbreviations see note at the beginning of Appendix C.

[a]Col. 9 = col. 1 – col. 8; col. 10 = col. 1 – col. 3; col. 11 = col. 3 – col. 4; col. 12 = vol. 4 – col. 6; col. 13 = col. 6 – col. 7; col. 14 = col. 7 – col. 8.

TABLE C-8

Selected Measures of Manufacturing Activity, 1947–64: Paper and Allied Products, SIC 26

	Indexes (1958 = 100)								Point Differences In Indexes[a]					
	FRB			Deflated Census Data				OBE Gross Product						
	As Pub.	Reweighted GPO	Reweighted VP	VP	Cost Mat.	VA	VA Plus Excise		Total (FRB Minus OBE)	FRB (Net Minus Gross Wtd.)	Total Output (Quantity Minus Defltd.)	Total Minus Net Output	Excise Tax	Net Output (Census Minus OBE)
Year	(1)	(2)	(3)	(4)	(5)	(6)	(7)	(8)	(9)	(10)	(11)	(12)	(13)	(14)
1947	64.2	65.7	64.9	69.8	64.9	75.8	75.8	75.3	-11.1	-.7	-4.9	-6.0	.0	.5
1948	65.9	67.4	66.7					69.3	-3.4	-.8				
1949	63.1	64.3	64.0	65.7	65.9	65.5	65.5	69.1	-6.0	-.9	-1.7	.2	.0	-3.6
1950	75.9	77.1	76.7	80.1	75.9	85.4	85.4	89.8	-13.9	-.8	-3.4	-5.3	.0	-4.4
1951	80.5	81.3	80.7	83.8	78.8	89.8	89.8	96.0	-15.5	-.2	-3.1	-6.0	.0	-6.2
1952	76.6	76.9	76.5	80.0	81.5	78.2	78.2	85.4	-8.8	.1	-3.5	1.8	.0	-7.2
1953	83.4	83.5	83.1	90.6	88.1	93.8	93.8	93.9	-10.5	.3	-7.5	-3.2	.0	-.1
1954	84.4	84.4	84.0	91.6	89.7	94.0	94.0	94.8	-10.4	.4	-7.6	-2.4	.0	-.8
1955	95.2	95.3	95.0	100.1	97.6	103.2	103.2	106.0	-10.8	.2	-5.1	-3.1	.0	-2.8
1956	99.7	99.8	99.5	102.2	101.3	103.4	103.4	109.5	-9.8	.2	-2.7	-1.2	.0	-6.1
1957	99.0	99.0	98.9	101.6	102.2	100.8	100.8	101.3	-2.3	.1	-2.7	.8	.0	-.5
1958	100.0	100.0	100.0	100.0	100.0	100.0	100.0	100.0	.0	.0	.0	.0	.0	.0
1959	109.8	109.9	110.0	110.8	107.5	115.0	115.0	113.7	-3.9	-.2	-.8	-4.2	.0	1.3
1960	110.8	110.8	110.9	110.9	109.7	112.4	112.4	112.0	-1.2	-.1	.0	-1.5	.0	.4
1961	117.0	117.0	117.2	115.9	115.3	116.6	116.6	119.0	-2.0	-.2	1.3	-.7	.0	-2.4
1962	123.1	123.1	123.5	122.6	121.5	124.0	124.0	127.0	-3.9	-.4	.9	-1.4	.0	-3.0
1963	128.7	128.8	129.2	129.5	126.5	133.2	133.2	130.4	-1.7	-.5	-.3	-3.7	.0	2.8
1964	137.2	137.2	137.8	135.4	131.9	139.9	139.9	140.0	-2.8	-.6	2.4	-4.5	.0	-.1

Note: VA = value added; VP = value of production. For other abbreviations see note at the beginning of Appendix C.

[a]Col. 9 = col. 1 – col. 8; col. 10 = col. 1 – col. 3; col. 11 = col. 3 – col. 4; col. 12 = col. 4 – col. 6; col. 13 = col. 6 – col. 7; col. 14 = col. 7 – col. 8.

TABLE C-9

Selected Measures of Manufacturing Activity, 1947–64: Printing and Publishing, SIC 27

	Indexes (1958 = 100)								Point Differences In Indexes[a]					
	FRB			Deflated Census Data				OBE Gross Product	Total (FRB Minus OBE)	FRB (Net Minus Gross Wtd.)	Total Output (Quantity Minus Defltd.)	Total Minus Net Output	Excise Tax	Net Output (Census Minus OBE)
	As Pub.	Reweighted												
Year	As Pub. (1)	GPO (2)	VP (3)	VP (4)	Cost Mat. (5)	VA (6)	VA Plus Excise (7)	(8)	(9)	(10)	(11)	(12)	(13)	(14)
1947	71.9	70.4	70.4	74.8	68.3	78.6	78.6	75.3	-3.4	1.5	-4.4	-3.8	.0	3.3
1948	75.6	74.9	74.7					77.1	-1.5	.9				
1949	77.6	75.4	75.0	75.9	72.4	77.9	77.9	78.4	-.8	2.6	-.9	-2.0	.0	-.5
1950	81.2	79.8	79.4	78.6	73.9	81.2	81.2	81.5	-.3	1.8	.8	-2.6	.0	-.3
1951	82.8	81.8	81.5	82.5	78.1	85.0	85.0	82.9	-.1	1.3	-1.0	-2.5	.0	2.1
1952	82.6	82.1	81.8	81.2	76.5	83.8	83.8	83.1	-.5	.8	.6	-2.6	.0	.7
1953	86.4	86.3	86.1	84.4	81.1	86.3	86.3	88.2	-1.8	.3	1.7	-1.9	.0	-1.9
1954	89.9	89.9	89.7	90.9	87.4	92.8	92.8	92.8	-2.9	.2	-1.2	-1.9	.0	.0
1955	95.5	95.4	95.1	95.1	92.0	96.8	96.8	98.6	-3.1	.4	.0	-1.7	.0	-1.8
1956	100.4	100.4	100.2	100.5	95.4	103.4	103.4	102.5	-2.1	.2	-.3	-2.9	.0	.9
1957	102.2	102.0	102.0	100.4	95.8	103.0	103.0	103.9	-1.7	.2	1.6	-2.6	.0	-.9
1958	100.0	100.0	100.0	100.0	100.0	100.0	100.0	100.0	.0	.0	.0	.0	.0	.0
1959	107.5	107.5	107.6	108.1	108.2	108.1	108.1	107.6	-.1	-.1	-.5	.0	.0	.5
1960	113.5	113.5	113.7	111.9	112.8	111.4	111.4	110.4	3.1	-.2	1.8	.5	.0	1.0
1961	115.1	115.1	115.4	113.6	116.4	112.0	112.0	110.4	4.7	-.3	1.8	1.6	.0	1.6
1962	118.3	118.3	118.6	117.0	120.0	115.3	115.3	114.9	3.4	-.3	1.6	1.7	.0	.4
1963	120.1	120.0	120.4	118.2	120.4	116.9	116.9	114.5	5.6	-.3	2.2	1.3	.0	2.4
1964	127.2	127.2	127.5	126.3	128.0	125.4	125.4	125.7	1.5	-.3	1.2	.9	.0	-.3

Note: VP = value of production; VA = value added. For other abbreviations see note at the beginning of Appendix C.

[a]Col. 9 = col. 1 – col. 8; col. 10 = col. 1 – col. 3; col. 11 = col. 3 – col. 4; col. 12 = col. 4 – col. 6; col. 13 = col. 6 – col. 7; col. 14 = col. 7 – col. 8.

TABLE C-10

Selected Measures of Manufacturing Activity, 1947–64: Chemicals and Allied Products, SIC 28

	Indexes (1958 = 100)								Point Differences In Indexes[a]					
	FRB			Deflated Census Data				OBE Gross Product	Total (FRB Minus OBE)	FRB (Net Minus Gross Wtd.)	Total Output (Quantity Minus Defltd.)	Total Minus Net Output	Excise Tax	Net Output (Census Minus OBE)
	As Pub.	Reweighted GPO	Reweighted VP	VP	Cost Mat.	VA	VA Plus Excise							
Year	(1)	(2)	(3)	(4)	(5)	(6)	(7)	(8)	(9)	(10)	(11)	(12)	(13)	(14)
1947	43.3	44.0	45.2	51.5	58.2	45.9	45.9	44.2	-.9	-1.9	-6.3	5.6	.0	1.7
1948	46.9	47.5	48.6					52.3	-5.4	-1.7				
1949	46.2	46.7	47.6	55.1	61.8	49.5	49.5	54.1	-7.9	-1.4	-7.5	5.6	.0	-4.6
1950	57.8	58.3	59.2	67.2	70.8	64.3	64.3	65.3	-7.5	-1.4	-8.0	2.9	.0	-1.0
1951	65.6	65.7	66.5	72.3	79.4	66.4	66.4	70.5	-4.9	-.9	-5.8	5.9	.0	-4.1
1952	68.5	69.0	69.8	75.1	80.9	70.2	70.2	71.3	-2.8	-1.3	-5.3	4.9	.0	-1.1
1953	74.1	74.5	75.5	79.5	84.8	75.0	75.0	76.1	-2.0	-1.4	-4.0	4.5	.0	-1.1
1954	73.9	74.3	75.1	79.9	84.3	76.2	76.2	78.7	-4.8	-1.2	-4.8	3.7	.0	-2.5
1955	86.3	86.6	87.7	92.4	96.0	89.5	89.5	92.5	-6.2	-1.4	-4.7	2.9	.0	-3.0
1956	93.0	93.1	93.8	99.3	102.1	97.0	97.0	97.4	-4.4	-.8	-5.5	2.3	.0	-.4
1957	98.5	98.6	98.9	101.4	103.3	99.9	99.9	101.9	-3.4	-.4	-2.5	1.5	.0	-2.0
1958	100.0	100.0	100.0	100.0	100.0	100.0	100.0	100.0	.0	.0	.0	.0	.0	.0
1959	114.6	114.5	114.9	116.3	113.8	118.4	118.4	118.6	-4.0	-.3	-1.4	-2.1	.0	-.2
1960	121.7	121.4	121.7	116.9	114.6	119.0	119.0	119.1	2.6	.0	4.8	-2.1	.0	-.1
1961	128.8	128.3	128.5	120.5	116.6	123.9	123.9	125.1	3.7	.3	8.0	-3.4	.0	-1.2
1962	142.1	141.5	141.3	132.9	128.3	136.9	136.9	135.0	7.1	.8	8.4	-4.0	.0	1.9
1963	155.1	154.5	154.2	143.6	138.2	148.4	148.4	142.0	13.1	.9	10.6	-4.8	.0	6.4
1964	166.6	165.9	165.5	155.3	149.0	160.8	160.8	152.0	14.6	1.1	10.2	-5.5	.0	8.8

Note: VA = value added; VP = value of production. For other abbreviations see note at the beginning of Appendix C.

[a]Col. 9 = col. 1 – col. 8; col. 10 = col. 1 – col. 3; col. 11 = col. 3 – col. 4; col. 12 = col. 4 – col. 6; col. 13 = col. 6 – col. 7; col. 14 = col. 7 – col. 8.

TABLE C-11

Selected Measures of Manufacturing Activity, 1947–64: Petroleum and Related Industries, SIC 29

	Indexes (1958 = 100)								Point Differences In Indexes[a]					
	FRB			Deflated Census Data				OBE Gross Product						
	As Pub.	Reweighted							Total (FRB Minus OBE)	FRB (Net Minus Gross Wtd.)	Total Output (Quantity Minus Defltd.)	Total Minus Net Output	Excise Tax	Net Output (Census Minus OBE)
Year	(1)	GPO (2)	VP (3)	VP (4)	Cost Mat. (5)	VA (6)	VA Plus Excise (7)	(8)	(9)	(10)	(11)	(12)	(13)	(14)
1947	64.6	66.4	65.6	64.0	61.8	74.8	68.5	66.3	-1.7	-1.0	1.6	-10.8	6.3	2.2
1948	69.9	70.6	71.0					72.4	-2.5	-1.1				
1949	67.8	69.7	68.5	67.4	64.9	79.5	74.4	72.6	-4.8	-.7	1.1	-12.1	5.1	1.8
1950	74.6	76.7	75.8	74.2	69.9	95.3	86.3	83.1	-8.5	-1.2	1.6	-21.1	9.0	3.2
1951	83.5	84.6	85.2	84.3	82.5	93.1	86.4	84.0	-.5	-1.7	.9	-8.8	6.7	2.4
1952	85.5	86.2	86.8	86.4	86.1	87.7	85.7	85.1	.4	-1.3	.4	-1.3	2.0	.6
1953	90.6	90.7	90.9	89.9	88.6	96.0	91.8	90.4	.2	-.3	1.0	-6.1	4.2	1.4
1954	89.8	89.7	89.9	90.3	91.0	87.1	87.7	87.9	1.9	-.1	-.4	3.2	-.6	-.2
1955	96.5	96.4	96.5	97.5	96.4	102.8	100.1	99.2	-2.7	.0	-1.0	-5.3	2.7	.9
1956	101.3	100.8	101.5	102.9	102.7	104.1	102.4	101.8	-.5	-.2	-1.4	-1.2	1.7	.6
1957	101.2	101.2	101.6	101.8	101.3	104.1	101.5	100.6	.6	-.4	-.2	-2.3	2.6	.9
1958	100.0	100.0	100.0	100.0	100.0	100.0	100.0	100.0	.0	.0	.0	.0	.0	.0
1959	106.7	106.8	106.2	105.9	105.9	105.8	104.8	106.0	.7	.5	.3	.1	1.0	-1.2
1960	109.3	110.1	109.0	108.0	107.0	112.9	110.0	112.0	-2.7	.3	1.0	-4.9	2.9	-2.0
1961	111.6	111.9	111.1	108.7	107.0	117.2	112.9	113.0	-1.4	.5	2.4	-8.5	4.3	-.1
1962	115.9	116.5	115.3	112.3	108.9	129.0	121.5	122.5	-6.6	.6	3.0	-16.7	7.5	-1.0
1963	120.2	120.9	119.6	119.3	113.8	146.8	134.7	130.2	-10.0	.6	.3	-27.5	12.1	4.5
1964	124.2	125.5	123.1	126.4	116.6	174.7	152.5	144.3	-20.1	1.1	-3.3	-48.3	22.2	8.2

Note: VA = value added; VP = value of production. For other abbreviations see note at the beginning of Appendix C.

[a]Col. 9 = col. 1 – col. 8; col. 10 = col. 1 – col. 3; col. 11 = col. 3 – col. 4; col. 12 = col. 4 – col. 6; col. 13 = col. 6 – col. 7; col. 14 = col. 7 – col. 8.

TABLE C-12

Selected Measures of Manufacturing Activity, 1947–64: Rubber and Misc. Plastic Products, SIC 30

	Indexes (1958 = 100)								Point Differences In Indexes[a]					
	FRB			Deflated Census Data				OBE Gross Product	Total (FRB Minus OBE)	FRB (Net Minus Gross Wtd.)	Total Output (Quantity Minus Defltd.)	Total Minus Net Output	Excise Tax	Net Output (Census Minus OBE)
	As Pub.	Reweighted GPO	Reweighted VP	VP	Cost Mat.	VA	VA Plus Excise							
Year	(1)	(2)	(3)	(4)	(5)	(6)	(7)	(8)	(9)	(10)	(11)	(12)	(13)	(14)
1947	61.0	69.8	68.6	76.9	66.8	86.7	87.9	89.8	-28.8	-7.6	-8.3	-9.8	-1.2	-1.9
1948	61.8	67.4	66.4					83.5	-21.7	-4.6				
1949	58.4	62.1	61.3	69.2	61.8	76.3	77.3	75.9	-17.5	-2.9	-7.9	-7.1	-1.0	1.4
1950	75.6	76.2	75.3	85.1	66.0	103.6	104.4	88.8	-13.2	.3	-9.8	-18.5	-.8	15.6
1951	77.2	79.3	78.3	89.7	71.3	107.5	107.3	111.5	-34.3	-1.1	-11.4	-17.8	.2	-4.2
1952	79.3	80.7	79.8	90.6	79.2	101.5	101.6	110.5	-31.2	-.5	-10.8	-10.9	-.1	-8.9
1953	85.0	86.1	85.2	97.6	86.6	108.2	108.1	110.9	-25.9	-.2	-12.4	-10.6	.1	-2.8
1954	83.4	84.0	83.4	92.2	80.4	103.6	103.1	96.1	-12.7	.0	-8.8	-11.4	.5	7.0
1955	103.4	104.1	103.4	104.4	92.3	116.2	116.0	110.7	-7.3	.0	-1.0	-11.8	.2	5.3
1956	100.9	101.2	100.9	101.9	96.4	107.1	107.1	107.9	-7.0	.0	-1.0	-5.2	.0	-.8
1957	105.3	105.6	105.4	102.1	98.7	105.4	105.2	106.6	-1.3	-.1	3.3	-3.3	.2	-1.4
1958	100.0	100.0	100.0	100.0	100.0	100.0	100.0	100.0	.0	.0	.0	.0	.0	.0
1959	120.1	120.6	120.8	121.6	114.8	128.4	127.4	125.4	-5.3	-.7	-.8	-6.8	1.0	2.0
1960	120.4	121.4	121.8	122.6	115.9	129.3	128.1	130.8	-10.4	-1.4	-.8	-6.7	1.2	-2.7
1961	121.4	122.3	123.0	126.3	119.1	133.7	132.1	130.3	-8.9	-1.6	-3.3	-7.4	1.6	1.8
1962	141.6	142.5	143.4	140.7	134.2	147.4	145.4	148.5	-6.9	-1.8	2.7	-6.7	2.0	-3.1
1963	151.8	152.6	153.7	148.7	142.4	155.1	152.8	150.2	1.6	-1.9	5.0	-6.4	2.3	2.6
1964	169.5	170.9	172.3	159.8	154.3	165.4	162.8	163.4	6.1	-2.8	12.5	-5.6	2.6	-.6

Note: VA = value added; VP = value of production. For other abbreviations see note at the beginning of Appendix C.

[a]Col. 9 = col. 1 – col. 8; col. 10 = col. 1 – col. 3; col. 11 = col. 3 – col. 4; col. 12 = col. 4 – col. 6; col. 13 = col. 6 – col. 7; col. 14 = col. 7 – col. 8.

TABLE C-13

Selected Measures of Manufacturing Activity, 1947–64: Leather and Leather Products, SIC 31

	Indexes (1958 = 100)								Point Differences In Indexes[a]					
	FRB			Deflated Census Data				OBE Gross Product	Total (FRB Minus OBE)	FRB (Net Minus Gross Wtd.)	Total Output (Quantity Minus Defltd.)	Total Minus Net Output	Excise Tax	Net Output (Census Minus OBE)
	As Pub.	Reweighted GPO	Reweighted VP	VP	Cost Mat.	VA	VA Plus Excise							
Year	(1)	(2)	(3)	(4)	(5)	(6)	(7)	(8)	(9)	(10)	(11)	(12)	(13)	(14)
1947	96.7	96.6	98.5	105.3	91.3	120.0	120.0	114.6	-17.9	-1.8	-6.8	-14.7	.0	5.4
1948	92.1	92.0	93.6					119.2	-27.1	-1.5				
1949	87.6	87.5	88.7	96.6	91.9	101.6	101.6	108.2	-20.6	-1.1	-7.9	-5.0	.0	-6.6
1950	94.8	94.6	95.7	96.4	86.9	106.3	106.3	106.1	-11.3	-.9	-.7	-9.9	.0	.2
1951	88.9	88.8	89.5	91.4	84.5	98.7	98.7	113.1	-24.2	-.6	-1.9	-7.3	.0	-14.4
1952	94.6	94.5	95.0	97.9	100.5	95.3	95.3	105.4	-10.8	-.4	-2.9	2.6	.0	-10.1
1953	94.9	94.7	95.5	102.1	97.4	107.0	107.0	108.7	-13.8	-.6	-6.6	-4.9	.0	-1.7
1954	94.0	93.8	94.3	97.3	98.0	96.7	96.7	102.4	-8.4	-.3	-3.0	.6	.0	-5.7
1955	102.1	102.1	102.4	104.3	104.1	104.6	104.6	106.8	-4.7	-.3	-1.9	-.3	.0	-2.2
1956	104.0	103.9	104.1	104.8	105.0	104.6	104.6	108.0	-4.0	-.1	-.7	.2	.0	-3.4
1957	103.3	103.4	103.5	103.7	105.3	102.0	102.0	106.1	-2.8	-.2	-.2	1.7	.0	-4.1
1958	100.0	100.0	100.0	100.0	100.0	100.0	100.0	100.0	.0	.0	.0	.0	.0	.0
1959	109.1	109.2	108.9	103.5	89.3	118.5	118.5	113.3	-4.2	.2	5.4	-15.0	.0	5.2
1960	103.8	103.8	103.6	100.2	99.0	101.5	101.5	106.7	-2.9	.2	3.4	-1.3	.0	-5.2
1961	104.3	104.3	104.3	98.6	94.8	102.5	102.5	102.1	2.2	.0	5.7	-3.9	.0	.4
1962	106.6	106.7	106.4	99.9	96.2	103.8	103.8	110.9	-4.3	.2	6.5	-3.9	.0	-7.1
1963	104.0	104.0	103.9	99.0	100.9	97.0	97.0	109.1	-5.1	.1	4.9	2.0	.0	-12.1
1964	106.9	107.0	106.7	104.3	102.7	105.9	105.9	112.8	-5.9	.2	2.4	-1.6	.0	-6.9

Note: VA = value added; VP = value of production. For other abbreviations see note at the beginning of Appendix C.

[a]Col. 9 = col. 1 – col. 8; col. 10 = col. 1 – col. 3; col. 11 = col. 3 – col. 4; col. 12 = col. 4 – col. 6; col. 13 = col. 6 – col. 7; col. 14 = col. 7 – col. 8.

TABLE C-14

Selected Measures of Manufacturing Activity, 1947–64: Stone, Clay, and Glass Products, SIC 32

	Indexes (1958 = 100)								Point Differences In Indexes[a]					
	FRB			Deflated Census Data				OBE Gross Product	Total (FRB Minus OBE)	FRB (Net Minus Gross Wtd.)	Total Output (Quantity Minus Defltd.)	Total Minus Net Output	Excise Tax	Net Output (Census Minus OBE)
	As Pub.	Reweighted GPO	Reweighted VP	VP	Cost Mat.	VA	VA Plus Excise							
Year	(1)	(2)	(3)	(4)	(5)	(6)	(7)	(8)	(9)	(10)	(11)	(12)	(13)	(14)
1947	71.9	69.2	67.0	64.6	54.9	71.4	71.4	73.1	-1.2	4.9	2.4	-6.8	.0	-1.7
1948	76.5	74.4	72.7					78.0	-1.5	3.8				
1949	71.4	69.5	68.0	65.5	63.0	67.2	67.2	72.7	-1.3	3.4	2.5	-1.7	.0	-5.5
1950	86.4	84.2	83.1	80.3	73.0	85.5	85.5	87.1	-.7	3.3	2.8	-5.2	.0	-1.6
1951	95.4	93.6	92.5	88.6	83.4	92.4	92.4	93.5	1.9	2.9	3.9	-3.8	.0	-1.1
1952	91.2	90.2	89.7	87.3	83.4	90.0	90.0	88.3	2.9	1.5	2.4	-2.7	.0	1.7
1953	93.5	92.6	91.6	90.0	85.9	92.9	92.9	94.9	-1.4	1.9	1.6	-2.9	.0	-2.0
1954	89.9	89.2	88.3	88.8	86.3	90.6	90.6	92.7	-2.8	1.6	-.5	-1.8	.0	-2.1
1955	102.6	102.0	101.3	101.9	99.2	103.8	103.8	106.7	-4.1	1.3	-.6	-1.9	.0	-2.9
1956	107.4	107.0	106.6	105.4	102.3	107.6	107.6	105.1	2.3	.8	1.2	-2.2	.0	2.5
1957	105.6	105.1	104.7	103.1	102.0	104.0	104.0	102.0	3.6	.9	1.6	-.9	.0	2.0
1958	100.0	100.0	100.0	100.0	100.0	100.0	100.0	100.0	.0	.0	.0	.0	.0	.0
1959	116.3	116.7	117.2	115.2	116.1	114.5	114.5	112.5	3.8	-.9	2.0	.7	.0	2.0
1960	115.7	115.9	116.3	113.0	114.1	112.1	112.1	110.0	5.7	-.6	3.3	.9	.0	2.1
1961	114.2	114.5	115.0	112.1	113.7	110.8	110.8	108.2	6.0	-.8	2.9	1.3	.0	2.6
1962	119.2	119.4	119.8	117.0	118.0	116.3	116.3	115.0	4.2	-.6	2.8	.7	.0	1.3
1963	126.1	126.5	127.1	125.9	125.8	126.0	126.0	123.1	3.0	-1.0	1.2	-.1	.0	2.9
1964	135.2	135.6	136.2	132.1	132.2	132.1	132.1	131.2	4.0	-1.0	4.1	.0	.0	.9

Note: VA = value added; VP = value of production. For other abbreviations see note at the beginning of Appendix C.

[a]Col. 9 = col. 1 – col. 8; col. 10 = col. 1 – col. 3; col. 11 = col. 3 – col. 4; col. 12 = col. 4 – col. 6; col. 13 = col. 6 – col. 7; col. 14 = col. 7 – col. 8.

TABLE C-15

Selected Measures of Manufacturing Activity, 1947–64: Primary Metal Industries, SIC 33

	Indexes (1958 = 100)								Point Differences In Indexes[a]					
	FRB			Deflated Census Data				OBE Gross Product						
		Reweighted												
Year	As Pub. (1)	GPO (2)	VP (3)	VP (4)	Cost Mat. (5)	VA (6)	VA Plus Excise (7)	(8)	Total (FRB Minus OBE) (9)	FRB (Net Minus Gross Wtd.) (10)	Total Output (Quantity Minus Defltd.) (11)	Total Minus Net Output (12)	Excise Tax (13)	Net Output (Census Minus OBE) (14)
1947	103.7	101.6	100.7	104.0	98.7	111.2	111.2	108.1	-4.4	3.0	-3.3	-7.2	.0	3.1
1948	107.8	105.9	104.7					107.3	.5	3.1				
1949	90.7	89.9	89.0	91.4	91.2	91.6	91.6	93.2	-2.5	1.7	-2.4	-.2	.0	-1.6
1950	114.2	112.5	111.5	103.9	94.1	117.2	117.2	113.9	.3	2.7	7.6	-13.3	.0	3.3
1951	124.2	123.8	121.6	128.0	120.0	138.9	138.9	136.2	-12.0	2.6	-6.4	-10.9	.0	2.7
1952	113.5	113.1	111.6	119.2	114.5	125.4	125.4	120.7	-7.2	1.9	-7.6	-6.2	.0	4.7
1953	128.6	129.7	127.8	140.6	135.8	147.1	147.1	139.6	-11.0	.8	-12.8	-6.5	.0	7.5
1954	104.3	104.6	103.8	103.9	99.3	110.0	110.0	109.0	-4.7	.5	-.1	-6.1	.0	1.0
1955	135.3	135.7	133.9	131.3	126.6	137.7	137.7	133.5	1.8	1.4	2.6	-6.4	.0	4.2
1956	133.0	133.3	132.1	133.3	129.9	137.8	137.8	131.1	1.9	.9	-1.2	-4.5	.0	6.7
1957	128.2	128.9	127.8	124.2	123.1	125.7	125.7	128.2	.0	.4	3.6	-1.5	.0	-2.5
1958	100.0	100.0	100.0	100.0	100.0	100.0	100.0	100.0	.0	.0	.0	.0	.0	.0
1959	114.7	114.6	113.7	114.8	112.9	117.5	117.5	111.6	3.1	1.0	-1.1	-2.7	.0	5.9
1960	115.8	115.8	115.3	115.2	117.7	111.8	111.8	110.0	5.8	.5	.1	3.4	.0	1.8
1961	113.0	113.2	113.6	113.0	116.2	108.6	108.6	103.4	9.6	-.6	.6	4.4	.0	5.2
1962	119.5	119.7	119.9	120.7	125.0	114.9	114.9	110.5	9.0	-.4	-.8	5.8	.0	4.4
1963	129.5	130.0	129.9	126.3	129.3	122.1	122.1	116.6	12.9	-.4	3.6	4.2	.0	5.5
1964	147.5	148.2	147.8	140.2	144.9	133.7	133.7	130.2	17.3	-.3	7.6	6.5	.0	3.5

Note: VP = value of production; VA = value added. For other abbreviations see note at the beginning of Appendix C.

[a]Col. 9 = col. 1 – col. 8; col. 10 = col. 1 – col. 3; col. 11 = col. 3 – col. 4; col. 12 = col. 4 – col. 6; col. 13 = col. 6 – col. 7; col. 14 = col. 7 – col. 8.

TABLE C-16

Selected Measures of Manufacturing Activity, 1947–64: Fabricated Metal Products, SIC 34

	Indexes (1958 = 100)								Point Differences In Indexes[a]					
	FRB			Deflated Census Data				OBE Gross Product						
	As Pub.	Reweighted GPO	Reweighted VP	VP	Cost Mat.	VA	VA Plus Excise		Total (FRB Minus OBE)	FRB (Net Minus Gross Wtd.)	Total Output (Quantity Minus Defltd.)	Total Minus Net Output	Excise Tax	Net Output (Census Minus OBE)
Year	(1)	(2)	(3)	(4)	(5)	(6)	(7)	(8)	(9)	(10)	(11)	(12)	(13)	(14)
1947	81.7	81.1	79.9	79.3	79.9	78.7	78.7	75.8	5.9	1.8	.6	.6	.0	2.9
1948	83.1	82.5	81.5					77.2	5.9	1.6				
1949	75.1	74.5	74.0	69.9	71.9	67.9	67.9	69.2	5.9	1.1	4.1	2.0	.0	-1.3
1950	91.9	91.4	90.5	87.9	90.4	85.5	85.5	84.1	7.8	1.4	2.6	2.4	.0	1.4
1951	98.2	97.8	96.4	95.0	98.5	91.6	91.6	88.5	9.7	1.8	1.4	3.4	.0	3.1
1952	95.8	95.6	94.5	92.0	92.8	91.1	91.1	90.8	5.0	1.3	2.5	.9	.0	.3
1953	108.0	108.1	106.5	104.3	105.5	103.2	103.2	100.9	7.1	1.5	2.2	1.1	.0	2.3
1954	97.1	97.4	96.6	94.4	93.3	95.5	95.5	97.4	-.3	.5	2.2	-1.1	.0	-1.9
1955	105.8	106.3	105.3	104.7	105.5	103.9	103.9	103.7	2.1	.5	.6	.8	.0	.2
1956	106.4	106.6	106.0	107.6	107.9	107.2	107.2	105.2	1.2	.4	-1.6	.4	.0	2.0
1957	109.3	109.1	108.5	107.9	107.7	108.1	108.1	107.8	1.5	.8	.6	-.2	.0	.3
1958	100.0	100.0	100.0	100.0	100.0	100.0	100.0	100.0	.0	.0	.0	.0	.0	.0
1959	113.6	113.4	112.5	110.0	108.1	111.9	111.9	111.8	1.8	1.1	2.5	-1.9	.0	.1
1960	115.8	115.5	114.6	108.7	107.1	110.4	110.4	112.1	3.7	1.2	5.9	-1.7	.0	-1.7
1961	114.6	114.3	113.4	108.0	107.3	108.8	108.8	112.1	2.5	1.2	5.4	-.8	.0	-3.3
1962	126.0	125.6	124.1	115.5	114.5	116.5	116.5	121.3	4.7	1.9	8.6	-1.0	.0	-4.8
1963	132.8	132.5	130.7	118.5	116.6	120.5	120.5	124.9	7.9	2.1	12.2	-2.0	.0	-4.4
1964	142.8	142.5	140.5	126.5	126.2	126.8	126.8	135.2	7.6	2.3	14.0	-.3	.0	-8.4

Note: VA = value added; VP = value of production. For other abbreviations see note at the beginning of Appendix C.

[a]Col. 9 = col. 1 – col. 8; col. 10 = col. 1 – col. 3; col. 11 = col. 3 – col. 4; col. 12 = col. 4 – col. 6; col. 13 = col. 6 – col. 7; col. 14 = col. 7 – col. 8.

TABLE C-17

Selected Measures of Manufacturing Activity, 1947–64: Machinery, Except Electrical, SIC 35

	Indexes (1958 = 100)								Point Differences In Indexes[a]					
	FRB			Deflated Census Data				OBE Gross Product						
	As Pub.	Reweighted GPO	Reweighted VP	VP	Cost Mat.	VA	VA Plus Excise		Total (FRB Minus OBE)	FRB (Net Minus Gross Wtd.)	Total Output (Quantity Minus Defltd.)	Total Minus Net Output	Excise Tax	Net Output (Census Minus OBE)
Year	(1)	(2)	(3)	(4)	(5)	(6)	(7)	(8)	(9)	(10)	(11)	(12)	(13)	(14)
1947	89.4	87.3	87.7	91.9	91.2	92.4	92.4	87.1	2.3	1.7	-4.2	-.5	.0	5.3
1948	89.9	87.9	89.0					92.7	-2.8	.9				
1949	76.7	75.2	76.5	76.5	78.9	74.7	74.7	80.4	-3.7	.2	.0	1.8	.0	-5.7
1950	86.0	84.3	85.1	86.7	87.3	86.2	86.2	87.6	-1.6	.9	-1.6	.5	.0	-1.4
1951	109.3	107.4	107.7	109.9	108.9	110.7	110.7	112.2	-2.9	1.6	-2.2	-.8	.0	-1.5
1952	118.7	116.5	116.1	116.7	116.7	116.8	116.8	122.0	-3.3	2.6	-.6	-.1	.0	-5.2
1953	122.4	120.8	120.0	117.8	119.2	116.7	116.7	121.0	1.4	2.4	2.2	1.1	.0	-4.3
1954	104.4	103.5	103.1	101.3	98.9	103.1	103.1	109.2	-4.8	1.3	1.8	-1.8	.0	-6.1
1955	112.2	110.7	110.5	111.1	110.5	111.5	111.5	111.7	.5	1.7	-.6	-.4	.0	-.2
1956	125.1	123.6	123.0	120.9	120.2	121.4	121.4	123.3	1.8	2.1	2.1	-.5	.0	-1.9
1957	121.0	120.9	120.3	114.9	114.9	114.9	114.9	117.2	3.8	.7	5.4	.0	.0	-2.3
1958	100.0	100.0	100.0	100.0	100.0	100.0	100.0	100.0	.0	.0	.0	.0	.0	.0
1959	120.3	119.7	119.4	114.8	114.4	115.1	115.1	116.2	4.1	.9	4.6	-.3	.0	-1.1
1960	123.8	123.5	122.9	113.1	112.8	113.2	113.2	116.5	7.3	.9	9.8	-.1	.0	-3.3
1961	121.2	121.2	120.5	111.5	111.2	111.7	111.7	115.6	5.6	.7	9.0	-.2	.0	-3.9
1962	136.2	136.5	135.6	123.8	122.5	124.8	124.8	129.3	6.9	.6	11.8	-1.0	.0	-4.5
1963	144.4	144.7	143.9	131.6	129.7	133.1	133.1	134.6	9.8	.5	12.3	-1.5	.0	-1.5
1964	161.7	162.0	161.3	145.4	145.6	145.2	145.2	153.3	8.4	.4	15.9	.2	.0	-8.1

Note: VA = value added; VP = value of production. For other abbreviations see note at the beginning of Appendix C.

[a]Col. 9 = col. 1 – col. 8; col. 10 = col. 1 – col. 3; col. 11 = col. 3 – col. 4; col. 12 = col. 4 – col. 6; col. 13 = col. 6 – col. 7; col. 14 = col. 7 – col. 8.

TABLE C-18

Selected Measures of Manufacturing Activity, 1947–64: Electrical Machinery, SIC 36

	Indexes (1958 = 100)								Point Differences In Indexes[a]					
	FRB			Deflated Census Data				OBE Gross Product						
	As Pub.	Reweighted GPO	Reweighted VP	VP	Cost Mat.	VA	VA Plus Excise		Total (FRB Minus OBE)	FRB (Net Minus Gross Wtd.)	Total Output (Quantity Minus Defltd.)	Total Minus Net Output	Excise Tax	Net Output (Census Minus OBE)
Year	(1)	(2)	(3)	(4)	(5)	(6)	(7)	(8)	(9)	(10)	(11)	(12)	(13)	(14)
1947	56.8	57.1	57.6	66.3	75.3	59.3	59.3	56.0	.8	-.8	-8.7	7.0	.0	3.3
1948	58.9	59.6	60.5					57.6	1.3	-1.6				
1949	55.2	55.3	56.2	60.0	68.2	53.5	53.3	52.4	2.8	-1.0	-3.8	6.5	.2	.9
1950	75.7	71.4	73.5	78.8	89.0	70.8	70.6	65.9	9.8	2.2	-5.3	8.0	.2	4.7
1951	76.1	75.9	77.1	86.4	92.2	81.9	82.1	75.5	.6	-1.0	-9.3	4.5	-.2	6.6
1952	87.0	89.2	89.8	96.7	101.1	93.3	93.1	88.8	-1.8	-2.8	-6.9	3.4	.2	4.3
1953	101.0	101.3	102.1	109.4	119.5	101.6	101.6	97.3	3.7	-1.1	-7.3	7.8	.0	4.3
1954	91.7	91.3	91.8	94.8	102.9	88.4	88.2	86.9	4.8	-.1	-3.0	6.4	.2	1.3
1955	104.1	104.5	105.3	105.6	111.4	101.1	101.3	93.9	10.2	-1.2	-.3	4.5	-.2	7.4
1956	114.8	115.2	115.4	111.0	114.3	108.4	108.3	101.6	13.2	-.6	4.4	2.6	.1	6.7
1957	112.3	112.3	112.3	107.4	108.5	106.5	106.4	104.5	7.8	.0	4.9	.9	.1	1.9
1958	100.0	100.0	100.0	100.0	100.0	100.0	100.0	100.0	.0	.0	.0	.0	.0	.0
1959	120.9	120.9	120.8	118.8	118.4	119.2	119.1	118.6	2.3	.1	2.0	-.4	.1	.5
1960	126.2	125.2	124.5	125.7	122.8	128.0	127.5	124.7	1.5	1.7	-1.2	-2.3	.5	2.8
1961	128.6	126.8	126.0	131.9	128.0	135.2	134.6	131.3	-2.7	2.6	-5.9	-3.3	.6	3.3
1962	142.8	141.2	140.2	151.9	143.7	158.7	157.8	150.1	-7.3	2.6	-11.7	-6.8	.9	7.7
1963	147.0	145.4	144.5	157.9	146.3	167.5	166.8	158.0	-11.0	2.5	-13.4	-9.6	.7	8.8
1964	156.2	154.6	153.8	166.7	150.6	179.9	179.1	167.1	-10.9	2.4	-12.9	-13.2	.8	12.0

Note: VA = value added; VP = value of production. For other abbreviations see note at the beginning of Appendix C.

[a]Col. 9 = col. 1 – col. 8; col. 10 = col. 1 – col. 3; col. 11 = col. 3 – col. 4; col. 12 = col. 4 – col. 6; col. 13 = col. 6 – col. 7; col. 14 = col. 7 – col. 8.

TABLE C-19

Selected Measures of Manufacturing Activity, 1947–64: Transportation Equipment and Ordnance, Except Motor Vehicles, SIC 37+19–371

	Indexes (1958 = 100)								Point Differences In Indexes[a]					
	FRB			Deflated Census Data				OBE						
	As	Reweighted												
Year	As Pub. (1)	GPO (2)	VP (3)	VP (4)	Cost Mat. (5)	VA (6)	VA Plus Excise (7)	Gross Product (8)	Total (FRB Minus OBE) (9)	FRB (Net Minus Gross Wtd.) (10)	Total Output (Quantity Minus Defltd.) (11)	Total Minus Net Output (12)	Excise Tax (13)	Net Output (Census Minus OBE) (14)
1947	23.5	25.3	28.1	33.8	33.7	34.0	34.0	30.2	-6.7	-4.6	-5.7	-.2	.0	3.8
1948	26.0	26.7	30.1					36.6	-10.6	-4.1				
1949	25.2	27.0	30.1	34.5	37.3	32.0	32.0	35.8	-10.6	-4.9	-4.4	2.5	.0	-3.8
1950	26.7	27.9	30.2	37.5	38.4	36.7	36.7	37.8	-11.1	-3.5	-7.3	.8	.0	1.1
1951	53.9	60.8	63.6	60.1	58.8	61.3	61.3	55.6	-1.7	-9.7	3.5	-1.2	.0	5.7
1952	81.2	87.2	88.8	101.8	107.8	96.3	96.3	86.4	-5.2	-7.6	-13.0	5.5	.0	9.9
1953	101.9	110.0	111.4	126.0	139.4	113.9	113.9	104.0	-2.1	-9.5	-14.6	12.1	.0	9.9
1954	88.3	91.8	91.9	109.9	116.5	104.0	104.0	99.7	-11.4	-3.6	-18.0	5.9	.0	4.3
1955	90.0	93.2	93.9	101.4	105.5	97.6	97.6	95.9	-5.9	-3.9	-7.5	3.8	.0	1.7
1956	98.7	99.7	100.9	102.9	105.5	100.6	100.6	96.6	2.1	-2.2	-2.0	2.3	.0	4.0
1957	109.2	109.1	110.3	114.1	120.4	108.4	108.4	106.0	3.2	-1.1	-3.8	5.7	.0	2.4
1958	100.0	100.0	100.0	100.0	100.0	100.0	100.0	100.0	.0	.0	.0	.0	.0	.0
1959	106.5	107.7	108.1	102.8	104.9	100.7	100.7	99.6	6.9	-1.6	5.3	2.1	.0	1.1
1960	102.2	104.2	104.8	97.6	98.4	96.9	96.9	97.1	5.1	-2.6	7.2	.7	.0	-.2
1961	105.2	108.2	108.0	96.4	99.0	94.0	94.0	101.0	4.2	-2.8	11.6	2.4	.0	-7.0
1962	114.7	118.0	118.3	103.0	101.0	104.8	104.8	115.4	-.7	-3.6	15.3	-1.8	.0	-10.6
1963	120.5	123.8	124.2	108.1	100.7	115.0	115.0	121.3	-.8	-3.7	16.1	-6.9	.0	-6.3
1964	124.4	124.6	125.7	108.6	101.7	115.2	115.2	123.8	.6	-1.3	17.1	-6.6	.0	-8.6

Note: VA = value added; VP = value of production. For other abbreviations see note at the beginning of Appendix C.

[a]Col. 9 = col. 1 – col. 8; col. 10 = col. 1 – col. 3; col. 11 = col. 3 – col. 4; col. 12 = col. 4 – col. 6; col. 13 = col. 6 – col. 7; col. 14 = col. 7 – col. 8.

TABLE C-20

Selected Measures of Manufacturing Activity, 1947–64: Motor Vehicles and Equipment, SIC 371

Year	Indexes (1958 = 100): FRB: As Pub. (1)	FRB: Reweighted: GPO (2)	FRB: Reweighted: VP (3)	Deflated Census Data: VP (4)	Deflated Census Data: Cost Mat. (5)	Deflated Census Data: VA (6)	Deflated Census Data: VA Plus Excise (7)	OBE Gross Product (8)	Point Differences In Indexes[a]: Total (FRB Minus OBE) (9)	FRB (Net Minus Gross Wtd.) (10)	Total Output (Quantity Minus Defltd.) (11)	Total Minus Net Output (12)	Excise Tax (13)	Net Output (Census Minus OBE) (14)
1947	83.8	83.0	83.2	87.7	90.3	82.2	82.4	84.9	-1.1	.6	-4.5	5.5	-.2	-2.5
1948	91.0	90.2	90.5					93.0	-2.0	.5				
1949	93.2	95.0	94.6	97.4	106.2	78.5	83.0	98.5	-5.3	-1.4	-2.8	18.9	-4.5	-15.5
1950	119.9	122.8	122.1	126.5	131.2	116.5	118.4	139.4	-19.5	-2.2	-4.4	10.0	-1.9	-21.0
1951	109.9	111.8	111.3	112.2	112.4	111.7	113.3	132.9	-23.0	-1.4	-.9	.5	-1.6	-19.6
1952	94.2	95.4	95.1	105.0	106.3	102.1	101.9	117.0	-22.8	-.9	-9.9	2.9	.2	-15.1
1953	119.5	122.5	121.8	137.8	143.7	124.9	125.8	146.9	-27.4	-2.3	-16.0	12.9	-.9	-21.1
1954	107.8	109.0	108.6	119.1	125.7	104.9	106.5	127.9	-20.1	-.8	-10.5	14.2	-1.6	-21.4
1955	154.2	156.7	155.7	167.9	171.3	160.5	161.2	184.1	-29.9	-1.5	-12.2	7.4	-.7	-22.9
1956	123.6	125.0	124.6	131.0	133.2	126.2	126.3	137.9	-14.3	-1.0	-6.4	4.8	-.1	-11.6
1957	130.6	131.8	131.3	136.6	138.6	132.3	133.0	144.6	-14.0	-.7	-5.3	4.3	-.7	-11.6
1958	100.0	100.0	100.0	100.0	100.0	100.0	100.0	100.0	.0	.0	.0	.0	.0	.0
1959	131.1	132.1	131.8	127.5	124.3	134.4	133.8	140.7	-9.6	-.7	4.3	-6.9	.6	-6.9
1960	149.9	152.1	151.3	144.5	141.2	151.7	150.8	155.3	-5.4	-1.4	6.8	-7.2	.9	-4.5
1961	135.0	134.2	134.4	125.0	120.2	135.3	134.1	138.3	-3.3	.6	9.4	-10.3	1.2	-4.2
1962	161.8	162.3	162.0	157.9	151.7	171.2	169.9	182.2	-20.4	-.2	4.1	-13.3	1.3	-12.3
1963	176.2	177.7	177.2	174.3	168.2	187.2	186.5	210.3	-34.1	-1.0	2.9	-12.9	.7	-23.8
1964	181.1	182.1	181.7	179.4	173.3	192.6	192.6	213.0	-31.9	-.6	2.3	-13.2	.0	-20.4

Note: VP = value of production; VA = value added. For other abbreviations see note at the beginning of Appendix C.

[a]Col. 9 = col. 1 – col. 8; col. 10 = col. 1 – col. 3; col. 11 = col. 3 – col. 4; col. 12 = col. 4 – col. 6; col. 13 = col. 6 – col. 7; col. 14 = col. 7 – col. 8.

TABLE C-21

Selected Measures of Manufacturing Activity, 1947–64: Instruments and Related Products, SIC 38

	Indexes (1958 = 100)								Point Differences In Indexes[a]					
	FRB			Deflated Census Data				OBE Gross Product						
	As Pub.	Reweighted GPO	Reweighted VP	VP	Cost Mat.	VA	VA Plus Excise		Total (FRB Minus OBE)	FRB (Net Minus Gross Wtd.)	Total Output (Quantity Minus Defltd.)	Total Minus Net Output	Excise Tax	Net Output (Census Minus OBE)
Year	(1)	(2)	(3)	(4)	(5)	(6)	(7)	(8)	(9)	(10)	(11)	(12)	(13)	(14)
1947	58.3	58.2	58.7	64.3	66.4	63.2	63.2	52.5	5.8	-.4	-5.6	1.1	.0	10.7
1948	59.9	59.8	60.3					56.3	3.6	-.4				
1949	53.4	53.3	53.7	57.5	57.8	57.3	57.3	54.9	-1.5	-.3	-3.8	.2	.0	2.4
1950	62.2	62.2	62.6	70.9	69.0	72.0	72.0	64.3	-2.1	-.4	-8.3	-1.1	.0	7.7
1951	71.3	71.2	71.7	81.1	80.5	81.4	81.4	77.4	-6.1	-.4	-9.4	-.3	.0	4.0
1952	84.8	84.7	85.4	92.0	95.7	89.9	89.9	88.3	-3.5	-.6	-6.6	2.1	.0	1.6
1953	92.6	92.4	93.2	97.0	96.7	97.2	97.2	96.0	-3.4	-.6	-3.8	-.2	.0	1.2
1954	90.0	90.1	90.4	88.6	88.8	88.4	88.4	94.8	-4.8	-.4	1.8	.2	.0	-6.4
1955	96.3	96.5	96.4	96.8	92.0	99.6	99.6	100.2	-3.9	-.1	-.4	-2.8	.0	-.6
1956	103.6	103.5	103.4	102.0	97.7	104.5	104.5	106.0	-2.4	.2	1.4	-2.5	.0	-1.5
1957	106.4	106.4	106.3	102.5	103.3	102.1	102.1	101.6	4.8	.1	3.8	.4	.0	.5
1958	100.0	100.0	100.0	100.0	100.0	100.0	100.0	100.0	.0	.0	.0	.0	.0	.0
1959	119.3	119.1	119.0	117.7	112.9	120.6	120.6	114.4	4.9	.3	1.3	-2.9	.0	6.2
1960	126.5	126.4	126.0	124.3	120.3	126.6	126.6	115.9	10.6	.5	1.7	-2.3	.0	10.7
1961	125.7	125.8	125.4	126.6	126.6	126.6	126.6	115.9	9.8	.3	-1.2	.0	.0	10.7
1962	133.6	133.4	133.1	135.5	133.3	136.9	136.9	124.8	8.8	.5	-2.4	-1.4	.0	12.1
1963	141.4	141.5	141.3	152.1	144.7	156.6	156.6	135.6	5.8	.1	-10.8	-4.5	.0	21.0
1964	148.1	147.8	147.5	159.5	149.5	165.5	165.5	139.1	9.0	.6	-12.0	-6.0	.0	26.4

Note: VA = value added; VP = value of production. For other abbreviations see note at the beginning of Appendix C.

[a]Col. 9 = col. 1 – col. 8; col. 10 = col. 1 – col. 3; col. 11 = col. 3 – col. 4; col. 12 = col. 4 – col. 6; col. 13 = col. 6 – col. 7; col. 14 = col. 7 – col. 8.

TABLE C-22

Selected Measures of Manufacturing Activity, 1947–64: Miscellaneous Manufacturing Industries, SIC 39

	Indexes (1958 = 100)								Point Differences In Indexes[a]					
	FRB			Deflated Census Data				OBE Gross Product						
	As Pub.	Reweighted GPO	Reweighted VP	VP	Cost Mat.	VA	VA Plus Excise		Total (FRB Minus OBE)	FRB (Net Minus Gross Wtd.)	Total Output (Quantity Minus Defltd.)	Total Minus Net Output	Excise Tax	Net Output (Census Minus OBE)
Year	(1)	(2)	(3)	(4)	(5)	(6)	(7)	(8)	(9)	(10)	(11)	(12)	(13)	(14)
1947	84.5	84.5	84.5	78.4	80.2	77.0	77.0	75.7	8.8	.0	6.1	1.4	.0	1.3
1948	90.2	90.2	90.2					84.4	5.8	.0				
1949	83.6	83.6	83.6	77.9	82.6	74.0	74.0	76.2	7.4	.0	5.7	3.9	.0	-2.2
1950	94.1	94.1	94.1	88.2	93.6	83.8	83.8	86.4	7.7	.0	5.9	4.4	.0	-2.6
1951	91.2	91.2	91.2	83.1	81.7	84.3	84.3	90.5	.7	.0	8.1	-1.2	.0	-6.2
1952	93.8	93.8	93.8	83.9	83.4	84.4	84.4	92.6	1.2	.0	9.9	-.5	.0	-8.2
1953	105.7	105.7	105.7	95.2	93.0	97.0	97.0	96.1	9.6	.0	10.5	-1.8	.0	.9
1954	95.7	95.7	95.7	87.2	86.9	87.4	87.4	92.2	3.5	.0	8.5	-.2	.0	-4.8
1955	107.1	107.1	107.1	96.1	93.4	98.3	98.3	101.9	5.2	.0	11.0	-2.2	.0	-3.6
1956	110.4	110.4	110.4	100.0	98.0	101.7	101.7	102.9	7.5	.0	10.4	-1.7	.0	-1.2
1957	105.0	105.0	105.0	97.2	93.8	100.0	100.0	101.1	3.9	.0	7.8	-2.8	.0	-1.1
1958	100.0	100.0	100.0	100.0	100.0	100.0	100.0	100.0	.0	.0	.0	.0	.0	.0
1959	114.0	114.0	114.0	109.1	108.8	109.5	109.5	109.6	4.4	.0	4.9	-.4	.0	-.1
1960	118.3	118.3	118.3	112.4	112.8	112.1	112.1	107.0	11.3	.0	5.9	.3	.0	5.1
1961	120.0	120.0	120.0	116.0	120.3	112.3	112.3	109.5	10.5	.0	4.0	3.7	.0	2.8
1962	130.0	130.0	130.0	122.8	123.6	122.1	122.1	113.9	16.1	.0	7.2	.7	.0	8.2
1963	133.0	133.0	133.0	127.6	126.4	128.7	128.7	113.3	19.7	.0	5.4	-1.1	.0	15.4
1964	141.9	141.9	141.9	134.3	133.4	135.1	135.1	119.3	22.6	.0	7.6	-.8	.0	15.8

Note: VA = value added; VP = value of production. For other abbreviations see note at the beginning of Appendix C.

[a]Col. 9 = col. 1 – col. 8; col. 10 = col. 1 – col. 3; col. 11 = col. 3 – col. 4; col. 12 = col. 4 – col. 6; col. 13 = col. 6 – col. 7; col. 14 = col. 7 – col. 8.

TABLE D-1

Implicit Price Deflators, 1947–64

(1958 = 100)

Year	VP	Cost of Materials	VA	VA Plus Excise	GPO	VP	Cost of Materials	VA	VA Plus Excise	GPO	VP	Cost of Materials	VA	VA Plus Excise	GPO
	All Manufacturing Industries					*Nondurable Goods Industries*					*Durable Goods Industries*				
1947	76.3	79.2	72.7	72.9	72.9	88.8	92.3	83.4	83.0	84.4	64.7	64.8	64.5	64.4	64.2
1948	81.8	86.8	75.9	75.8	77.6	92.5	99.3	83.0	82.6	88.7	71.2	72.5	69.8	69.5	69.3
1949	81.1	82.4	79.3	79.0	79.2	88.7	90.6	85.7	85.0	86.4	73.4	72.9	73.9	73.5	73.4
1950	82.9	85.8	79.3	79.0	79.4	90.3	94.8	83.8	83.3	85.0	76.2	76.6	75.7	75.3	75.2
1951	90.5	95.0	85.0	84.5	84.9	100.3	106.7	90.9	89.9	91.7	82.1	83.4	80.8	80.5	80.2
1952	89.5	92.1	86.2	86.4	86.7	97.4	100.6	92.5	92.3	93.2	82.9	83.8	82.0	82.1	82.3
1953	89.2	91.4	86.5	86.7	87.1	95.5	97.7	92.2	92.0	93.5	84.5	86.0	82.9	83.0	83.1
1954	90.7	92.3	88.6	88.7	88.9	96.0	97.6	93.5	93.1	94.3	86.1	86.9	85.2	85.2	85.3
1955	91.9	93.2	90.3	90.3	90.5	95.2	95.5	94.8	94.3	95.2	89.2	91.0	87.3	87.3	87.4
1956	95.8	96.9	94.4	94.4	94.6	96.7	96.4	97.0	96.8	97.4	95.0	97.3	92.5	92.5	92.6
1957	98.7	99.5	97.8	97.8	97.6	98.9	99.5	98.1	98.2	97.8	98.6	99.6	97.5	97.5	97.5
1958	100.0	100.0	100.0	100.0	100.0	100.0	100.0	100.0	100.0	100.0	100.0	100.0	100.0	100.0	100.0
1959	100.6	100.1	101.4	101.4	101.6	99.4	98.2	101.3	101.4	101.6	101.9	102.2	101.5	101.5	101.6
1960	100.9	99.9	102.2	102.4	102.5	99.8	97.9	102.6	103.1	103.3	102.0	102.2	101.8	101.8	101.8
1961	100.6	99.1	102.6	102.9	102.7	99.7	97.3	103.6	104.1	103.8	101.5	101.2	101.9	101.8	101.8
1962	100.6	99.1	102.6	102.8	102.7	99.8	97.6	103.2	103.7	103.4	101.4	100.7	102.2	102.1	102.2
1963	100.3	98.6	102.5	102.7	102.8	99.4	96.9	103.3	103.8	104.2	101.2	100.5	102.0	101.9	101.9
1964	100.7	98.9	103.0	103.2	103.6	99.1	96.4	103.1	103.6	104.3	102.3	101.6	103.0	102.9	103.0

(continued)

TABLE D-1 (continued)

Year	VP	Cost of Materials	VA	VA Plus Excise (GPO)	VP	Cost of Materials	VA	VA Plus Excise	GPO	VP	Cost of Materials	VA	VA Plus Excise (GPO)
	Food and Kindred Products, SIC 20				*Tobacco Manufactures, SIC 21*					*Textile Mill Products, SIC 22*			
1947	93.2	98.0	82.0	82.8	74.2	77.8	65.3	78.5	81.2	110.5	99.4	126.1	126.1
1948	99.3	105.2	85.7	85.9	76.0	79.4	67.3	79.6	81.4	116.5	107.3	128.2	128.2
1949	91.5	92.0	90.2	89.7	77.8	82.7	67.3	78.7	80.7	105.4	101.1	111.3	111.3
1950	92.8	96.0	85.6	85.8	81.2	83.4	75.9	82.8	84.1	112.9	110.6	115.9	115.9
1951	103.0	109.4	88.7	88.7	83.5	90.9	68.8	80.6	83.3	127.6	127.1	128.5	128.5
1952	101.6	105.6	92.3	93.5	83.8	89.9	71.0	87.7	90.1	112.1	110.8	114.3	114.3
1953	96.2	99.3	89.6	91.0	92.3	89.2	100.3	100.1	100.1	108.4	105.5	112.9	112.9
1954	98.3	100.2	93.9	94.8	96.2	91.3	109.3	103.4	102.8	103.7	104.1	103.2	103.2
1955	94.2	93.1	96.7	97.2	93.6	91.0	99.3	99.7	99.8	103.9	103.6	104.3	104.3
1956	93.4	93.0	94.3	95.0	94.2	94.1	94.3	97.5	98.1	103.6	102.6	105.1	105.1
1957	95.8	97.0	93.4	94.2	97.3	96.8	98.2	99.2	99.4	103.1	103.4	102.7	102.7
1958	100.0	100.0	100.0	100.0	100.0	100.0	100.0	100.0	100.0	100.0	100.0	100.0	100.0
1959	97.7	94.3	106.5	105.6	101.6	103.6	98.3	99.3	99.4	101.8	100.7	103.5	103.5
1960	97.7	94.1	106.5	105.7	101.2	102.1	99.7	99.9	99.9	102.6	99.3	107.7	107.7
1961	99.2	94.4	111.8	110.2	103.0	106.9	96.5	98.4	98.7	99.5	97.5	102.5	102.5
1962	99.7	95.2	111.4	109.9	103.4	108.5	95.5	97.9	98.3	100.4	98.6	103.1	103.1
1963	99.2	94.9	110.1	108.8	103.0	101.8	105.2	102.2	101.9	99.6	98.9	100.9	100.9
1964	99.2	94.1	111.8	110.3	103.4	101.1	107.4	103.3	102.7	99.9	98.1	102.8	102.8

(continued)

TABLE D-1 (continued)

Year	VP	Cost of Materials	VA	VA Plus Excise (GPO)	VP	Cost of Materials	VA	VA Plus Excise (GPO)	VP	Cost of Materials	VA	VA Plus Excise (GPO)
	Apparel and Related Products, SIC 23				*Lumber and Wood Products, Except Furniture, SIC 24*				*Furniture and Fixtures, SIC 25*			
1947	103.4	108.6	97.1	97.1	79.6	78.5	80.7	80.7	74.0	77.5	71.1	71.1
1948	105.1	114.6	94.6	94.6	91.2	89.7	92.5	92.5	79.0	84.4	74.7	74.7
1949	98.8	103.9	91.8	91.8	85.0	84.0	86.0	86.0	79.2	81.1	77.7	77.7
1950	99.2	110.0	86.5	86.5	97.0	94.9	99.2	99.2	81.7	87.8	76.7	76.7
1951	106.0	122.4	89.5	89.5	106.2	103.0	109.7	109.7	92.0	95.8	88.7	88.7
1952	101.0	108.4	92.1	92.1	103.5	100.9	106.4	106.4	88.9	92.5	85.9	85.9
1953	99.5	105.9	92.8	92.8	103.7	100.4	107.5	107.5	89.9	93.5	86.7	86.7
1954	99.2	102.8	94.8	94.8	102.1	99.0	106.0	106.0	90.1	93.1	87.4	87.4
1955	99.1	103.4	93.8	93.8	105.5	103.8	107.7	107.7	91.3	96.0	87.2	87.2
1956	100.7	102.7	98.2	98.2	107.4	105.8	109.3	109.3	95.6	99.1	92.5	92.5
1957	100.5	102.2	98.3	98.3	102.1	101.5	102.9	102.9	98.5	99.9	97.2	97.2
1958	100.0	100.0	100.0	100.0	100.0	100.0	100.0	100.0	100.0	100.0	100.0	100.0
1959	100.9	101.8	99.7	99.7	106.5	106.4	106.7	106.7	101.0	101.9	100.1	100.1
1960	102.0	103.6	100.0	100.0	102.8	102.3	103.5	103.5	102.1	101.1	103.0	103.0
1961	101.7	100.5	103.2	103.2	98.6	98.0	99.4	99.4	102.6	99.4	106.0	106.0
1962	102.4	100.7	104.6	104.6	99.0	99.4	98.5	98.5	103.7	99.7	107.9	107.9
1963	102.9	100.2	106.3	106.3	101.2	101.3	101.0	101.1	104.6	100.2	109.0	109.0
1964	103.9	100.9	107.8	107.8	103.0	102.4	103.8	103.8	105.1	100.3	110.4	110.4

(continued)

TABLE D-1 (continued)

Year	VP	Cost of Materials	VA	VA Plus Excise (GPO)	VP	Cost of Materials	VA	VA Plus Excise (GPO)	VP	Cost of Materials	VA	VA Plus Excise (GPO)
	Paper and Allied Products, SIC 26				*Printing and Publishing, SIC 27*				*Chemicals and Allied Products, SIC 28*			
1947	73.2	77.2	68.9	68.9	69.8	69.2	70.1	70.1	90.4	90.3	90.5	90.5
1948	77.2	75.9	78.7	78.7	74.9	76.3	74.3	74.3	93.2	95.0	91.4	91.4
1949	74.5	75.1	73.8	73.8	77.2	78.0	76.8	76.8	89.0	86.1	92.0	92.0
1950	76.3	81.5	70.5	70.5	78.3	79.1	77.8	77.8	89.0	87.6	90.2	90.2
1951	90.4	97.1	83.1	83.1	83.4	86.8	81.6	81.6	100.1	99.7	100.6	100.6
1952	88.8	90.1	87.1	87.1	88.0	90.4	86.8	86.8	96.7	95.0	98.4	98.4
1953	87.8	91.0	84.1	84.1	89.6	91.2	88.7	88.7	96.9	95.5	98.3	98.3
1954	88.5	90.7	85.9	85.9	88.7	90.9	87.5	87.5	97.7	95.9	99.4	99.4
1955	90.6	94.0	86.6	86.6	91.1	93.1	90.1	90.1	97.8	96.2	99.2	99.2
1956	97.0	98.9	94.8	94.8	94.2	97.5	92.5	92.5	98.1	98.5	97.7	97.7
1957	99.4	99.3	99.4	99.4	98.2	100.8	96.9	96.9	99.5	100.5	98.7	98.7
1958	100.0	100.0	100.0	100.0	100.0	100.0	100.0	100.0	100.0	100.0	100.0	100.0
1959	100.2	101.5	98.6	98.6	101.2	100.6	101.6	101.6	98.8	98.9	98.6	98.6
1960	101.5	100.7	102.5	102.5	104.1	102.0	105.3	105.3	99.0	100.0	98.1	98.1
1961	98.6	97.4	100.0	100.0	105.1	101.9	107.0	107.0	97.8	99.1	96.8	96.8
1962	99.1	98.3	100.1	100.1	106.8	102.7	109.2	109.2	96.2	96.4	96.1	96.1
1963	98.3	98.3	98.2	98.2	109.4	103.5	112.9	112.9	95.6	94.8	96.3	96.3
1964	98.5	99.1	97.8	97.8	109.6	104.7	112.6	112.6	95.4	94.2	96.3	96.3

(continued)

TABLE D-1 (continued)

Year	VP	Cost of Materials	VA	VA Plus Excise	GPO	VP	Cost of Materials	VA	VA Plus Excise (GPO)	VP	Cost of Materials	VA	VA Plus Excise (GPO)
	Petroleum and Related Industries, SIC 29					*Rubber and Misc. Plastic Products, SIC 30*				*Leather and Leather Products, SIC 31*			
1947	74.6	71.6	86.5	75.5	90.9	69.6	86.9	56.8	57.4	92.8	122.2	69.6	69.6
1948	71.2	89.3	45.3	47.1	108.7	72.3	89.0	59.7	60.0	95.2	120.2	74.3	74.3
1949	82.3	84.3	74.2	66.9	85.2	71.2	84.4	60.9	61.0	91.3	110.3	73.5	73.5
1950	79.9	83.8	65.9	62.0	87.2	78.0	104.0	62.1	62.2	96.8	122.6	74.8	74.8
1951	89.3	87.4	97.5	83.1	106.6	91.4	128.0	68.1	67.7	111.4	142.5	83.8	83.8
1952	89.6	87.2	101.2	88.9	102.1	88.0	110.4	71.2	70.6	96.2	101.0	91.0	91.0
1953	91.5	90.5	96.2	86.2	111.3	86.2	100.8	74.9	74.0	96.3	104.6	88.5	88.5
1954	92.9	91.4	100.7	87.6	107.4	86.5	101.0	75.6	74.7	94.1	94.9	93.2	93.2
1955	93.8	92.0	101.9	89.1	102.7	92.9	109.3	80.4	79.1	93.8	95.3	92.1	92.1
1956	98.3	93.8	120.1	106.3	115.7	97.3	104.2	91.4	90.6	98.8	100.0	97.6	97.6
1957	105.0	102.0	119.1	111.9	104.7	98.6	102.1	95.5	95.9	99.3	98.3	100.3	100.3
1958	100.0	100.0	100.0	100.0	100.0	100.0	100.0	100.0	100.0	100.0	100.0	100.0	100.0
1959	99.3	97.5	108.5	108.3	113.0	96.8	103.4	90.8	91.4	109.8	125.6	97.2	97.2
1960	99.5	97.4	109.6	117.9	122.0	95.2	103.0	88.2	89.0	108.9	110.5	107.2	107.2
1961	100.1	97.5	112.0	119.3	118.6	93.2	96.9	89.8	91.2	109.3	112.7	106.0	106.0
1962	98.8	97.9	102.7	113.0	110.2	92.1	95.6	88.9	91.2	110.9	114.3	107.6	107.6
1963	97.4	97.5	96.9	108.6	115.5	92.5	94.1	91.1	93.2	109.2	105.3	113.6	113.6
1964	93.4	96.6	82.8	97.7	109.3	91.9	93.3	90.7	92.7	109.3	106.2	112.5	112.5

(continued)

TABLE D-1 (continued)

Year	VP	Cost of Materials	VA	VA Plus Excise (GPO)	VP	Cost of Materials	VA	VA Plus Excise (GPO)	VP	Cost of Materials	VA	VA Plus Excise (GPO)
	Stone, Clay, and Glass Products, SIC 32				*Primary Metal Industries, SIC 33*				*Fabricated Metal Products, SIC 34*			
1947	63.7	69.3	60.7	60.7	56.6	63.8	48.1	48.1	64.1	58.3	69.8	69.8
1948	69.4	76.2	65.7	65.7	64.6	74.3	53.6	53.6	71.3	65.5	76.9	76.9
1949	73.1	77.5	70.3	70.3	66.3	71.7	58.9	58.9	73.2	68.3	78.2	78.2
1950	75.3	79.7	72.6	72.6	70.1	77.7	61.8	61.8	75.8	70.4	81.3	81.3
1951	80.1	85.1	76.9	76.9	76.1	84.6	66.2	66.2	84.5	77.3	92.0	92.0
1952	81.3	86.1	78.1	78.1	77.7	85.6	67.9	67.9	83.4	77.9	88.9	88.9
1953	84.3	88.5	81.5	81.5	81.2	89.2	71.2	71.2	84.8	81.3	88.3	88.3
1954	86.9	89.6	85.1	85.1	84.3	90.0	77.4	77.4	85.3	82.8	87.8	87.8
1955	89.7	91.0	88.7	88.7	90.0	97.4	80.9	80.9	89.0	86.7	91.2	91.2
1956	94.1	95.2	93.3	93.3	98.0	105.9	88.0	88.0	94.5	93.7	95.4	95.4
1957	97.8	98.7	97.1	97.1	99.9	103.5	95.1	95.1	98.5	98.5	98.6	98.6
1958	100.0	100.0	100.0	100.0	100.0	100.0	100.0	100.0	100.0	100.0	100.0	100.0
1959	101.4	100.2	102.3	102.3	102.6	103.5	101.5	101.5	100.5	102.0	98.9	98.9
1960	102.0	100.9	102.9	102.9	103.9	103.2	104.9	104.9	101.1	102.6	99.5	99.5
1961	101.8	100.3	102.9	102.9	102.5	102.1	103.2	103.2	101.2	101.8	100.5	100.5
1962	101.6	100.7	102.3	102.3	102.0	99.6	105.7	105.7	101.5	101.6	101.4	101.4
1963	101.0	100.4	101.5	101.5	101.5	99.0	105.1	105.1	102.1	101.4	102.7	102.7
1964	101.2	100.2	102.0	102.0	103.5	101.5	106.5	106.5	103.3	102.4	104.3	104.3

(continued)

TABLE D-1 (continued)

Year	VP	Cost of Materials	VA	VA Plus Excise (GPO)	VP	Cost of Materials	VA	VA Plus Excise (GPO)	VP	Cost of Materials	VA	VA Plus Excise (GPO)
	Machinery, Except Electrical, SIC 35				*Electrical Machinery, SIC 36*				*Motor Vehicles and Equipment, SIC 371*			
1947	61.0	60.5	61.3	61.3	73.5	68.9	78.0	79.6	65.4	63.3	70.3	65.8
1948	66.3	66.8	66.0	66.0	77.2	74.2	80.1	82.1	71.7	70.1	75.5	69.8
1949	69.6	68.9	70.2	70.2	77.6	72.3	83.0	84.7	77.5	73.8	88.4	80.7
1950	72.1	71.3	72.7	72.7	80.2	76.6	83.7	85.5	76.9	75.2	81.2	75.9
1951	78.9	78.5	79.2	79.2	86.7	85.3	87.9	89.4	80.6	81.0	79.9	75.6
1952	79.5	78.4	80.3	80.3	85.6	84.9	86.2	87.5	86.0	83.3	92.1	90.4
1953	81.4	81.0	81.7	81.7	87.0	86.4	87.5	88.9	85.6	84.4	88.6	87.5
1954	83.0	82.5	83.4	83.4	88.2	86.8	89.4	90.0	85.9	85.1	88.0	87.2
1955	85.5	85.7	85.4	85.4	88.5	88.9	88.2	88.5	88.9	88.1	90.8	90.0
1956	92.1	92.5	91.9	91.9	93.3	96.0	91.1	91.3	93.5	93.3	94.1	93.7
1957	98.1	98.0	98.3	98.3	98.4	99.2	97.8	97.8	97.4	97.6	96.9	96.9
1958	100.0	100.0	100.0	100.0	100.0	100.0	100.0	100.0	100.0	100.0	100.0	100.0
1959	101.9	101.8	102.0	102.0	101.3	101.7	100.9	100.9	102.1	101.8	102.7	102.6
1960	102.8	102.7	103.0	103.0	100.2	102.0	98.9	98.9	100.7	101.2	99.6	99.7
1961	103.1	102.1	103.9	103.9	99.1	100.2	98.2	98.1	100.4	100.9	99.3	99.5
1962	103.7	102.2	104.9	104.9	96.9	99.8	94.7	94.7	101.0	100.6	101.8	101.5
1963	104.1	102.6	105.3	105.3	95.4	99.7	92.3	92.3	100.2	100.0	100.7	100.4
1964	105.6	103.7	107.1	107.1	94.2	100.0	90.2	90.2	101.4	100.5	103.1	102.5

(continued)

TABLE D-1 (concluded)

Year	VP	Cost of Materials	VA	VA Plus Excise (GPO)	VP	Cost of Materials	VA	VA Plus Excise (GPO)	VP	Cost of Materials	VA	VA Plus Excise (GPO)
	Trans. Eq. and Ord., Except Mot. Vehicles, SIC 37+19-371				*Instruments and Related Products, SIC 38*				*Miscellaneous Manufacturing Ind., SIC 39*			
1947	61.6	60.1	62.9	62.9	69.3	74.4	66.2	66.2	84.6	80.8	87.9	87.9
1948	66.7	66.2	67.1	67.1	73.2	80.0	69.1	69.1	86.9	86.4	87.3	87.3
1949	69.3	69.1	69.6	69.6	74.2	79.4	71.3	71.3	86.2	83.2	88.9	88.9
1950	71.3	71.7	71.0	71.0	75.5	80.6	72.7	72.7	88.1	86.2	89.9	89.9
1951	79.9	79.5	80.3	80.3	82.5	87.8	79.5	79.5	94.1	98.3	90.8	90.8
1952	80.2	80.5	79.8	79.8	82.3	86.7	79.6	79.6	92.3	94.5	90.5	90.5
1953	81.6	83.2	80.0	80.0	84.4	89.6	81.4	81.4	93.5	94.7	92.6	92.6
1954	83.0	84.9	81.1	81.1	85.4	88.7	83.4	83.4	94.3	94.8	93.9	93.9
1955	86.0	88.8	83.2	83.2	87.0	91.5	84.6	84.6	94.7	97.4	92.6	92.6
1956	93.0	94.4	91.7	91.7	92.3	96.1	90.2	90.2	98.0	99.5	96.7	96.7
1957	98.1	98.6	97.6	97.6	97.6	98.8	96.9	96.9	99.4	100.0	98.9	98.9
1958	100.0	100.0	100.0	100.0	100.0	100.0	100.0	100.0	100.0	100.0	100.0	100.0
1959	101.4	101.1	101.7	101.7	102.4	102.3	102.5	102.5	100.1	101.8	98.7	98.7
1960	102.5	102.1	102.9	102.9	104.0	103.2	104.5	104.5	101.0	101.8	100.4	100.4
1961	102.7	102.0	103.4	103.4	105.2	102.8	106.6	106.6	101.5	99.7	103.1	103.1
1962	103.0	101.9	103.9	103.9	106.6	103.5	108.4	108.4	101.7	100.6	102.7	102.7
1963	103.1	101.3	104.7	104.7	106.2	103.1	108.0	108.0	102.0	100.6	103.2	103.2
1964	104.9	102.5	106.9	106.9	106.9	103.5	108.8	108.8	102.5	101.8	103.2	103.2

Note: VA = value added; VP = value of production. For other abbreviations see note at the beginning of Appendix D.

Cost of Materials = Census cost of materials, supplies, components, semifinished goods, fuel and electricity, actually consumed or put into production during the year and cost of goods purchased for resale.

Value Added (VA) = Value of production (above) less cost of materials (above).

VA + Excise = Value added (above) plus federal excise taxes for which the given industry is legally liable.

Gross Product Originating (GPO) = Gross product originating in a given industry. The deflators for the two-digit industries are the same as those for VA plus Excise except for SIC industries 21 and 29 where different procedures are used. For all manufacturing, durable, and nondurable goods industries, the GPO and VA plus Excise deflators are not the same because of differences in the two-digit industry deflators and weights.

COMMENT

CLAYTON GEHMAN AND CORNELIA MOTHERAL, Federal Reserve Board

The Gottsegen-Ziemer paper and its appendixes provide new data on deflated gross product series in manufacturing which can be used to compare two-digit industry groups with annual averages of the presently published Federal Reserve monthly production indexes. Until these new data can be examined in detail and analyzed in relation to the results of the Census-Federal Reserve bench mark indexes for 1947–54, 1954–58, and 1958–63, it is not possible to judge whether the gross product data provide more accurate indicators of growth in this sector of the economy. However, it is possible—before completing the general revision of the Federal Reserve monthly index now underway—to agree that the manufacturing total index may be slightly overstated in 1959 and 1960 and that changes in series and weights are likely to result in various revisions in the total and the parts for more recent years. Detailed analysis would involve study of differences in deflators for the 425 four-digit industries and the several thousand product classes directly represented in the Census-Federal Reserve bench-mark indexes.

Comparisons of the corrected two-digit results of the two systems of measurement can be made only for the 1947–54 period since the published Federal Reserve indexes are not yet adjusted to subsequent bench-mark levels. Here the record shows practically identical results for total manufacturing—increases of 30.1 and 30.2 per cent. But if the same weight periods are used, the presently revised gross product series rises more than the Federal Reserve manufacturing production index, as noted below. The previously published gross product series available for the comparison made in the February 1964 U.S. reply to the ECE rose 25.0 per cent from 1947 to 1954. That increase was just about the same as the increase in the Federal Reserve manufacturing production index adjusted to the Census-Federal Reserve bench mark, when allowances were made for differences in scope and when weights in the gross product series were used.

The Federal Reserve indexes have not yet been adjusted to the 1954–58 bench mark, but the bench-mark results for manufacturing and mining have been distributed to the contributors to this discussion. They show an output increase of 8.5 per cent for manufacturing based on the 1958 weight year used for the gross product series for manufacturing (which rises only 3.5 per cent), while the published Federal Reserve manufacturing index rises 8.0 per cent. Much of the difference between the bench-mark and the gross product series in this period is between the gross product current-dollar data and current-dollar Census value added, which implies (aside from statistical differences, which may actually be at issue here) a substantial increase in business services per unit of product; it would be of interest to try to develop a direct measure of business services for this period as a check.

The 1958–63 bench-mark compilations, still in a preliminary stage, suggest that while there are many differences at the two-digit and more detailed levels from the presently published Federal Reserve indexes, the totals for manufacturing are about as close in 1963 as in 1958.

In 1964, the year after the last bench-mark period, the Federal Reserve manufacturing index rises 6.6 per cent which is quite close to the increase of 6.8 per cent shown by the gross product series. Preliminary Census Annual Survey shipments for 1965, after adjustment for inventory and price changes at the total level only, show an increase of 8.2 per cent from 1964 to 1965. Allowing for the tendency of both the Federal Reserve and OBE net measures to rise more than such a gross value series in recent years, this suggests that the 8.9 per cent rise shown by the Federal Reserve series for 1965 will be borne out by more detailed calculations. The finding that annual averages of the monthly production index are still close to comprehensive annual Census data twelve years after the last bench-mark adjustment should not be overlooked in appraising the adequacy of the Federal Reserve monthly production index results.

We see little basis for the indication in the Gottsegen-Ziemer paper and the Moss commentary of any persistent divergence in the two sets of numbers and the emphasis that "an essential difference" is the larger growth rate of the presently published Federal Reserve series than of the revised gross product series. Over the seventeen-year interval of changes shown, a major portion of the divergence for the total comes within several annual periods which might be largely isolated by a more detailed comparison of gross product data with the bench-mark results. The Federal Reserve index is higher at the end of the seventeen-year interval and the differences are even greater at the extremes reached in 1951 and 1961, but the evidence of persistent differences is not clear from the presently available data. We do hold the view that a net industry measure would probably rise more in certain periods than the presently published Federal Reserve index (see the comparisons for total industrial production presented in a paper on "Estimating Aggregate Output" in the 1964 *Proceedings* of the American Statistical Association).

The accompanying table shows that for the bench-mark interval from 1947 to 1954, the gross product series rises 2 per cent more than the Federal Reserve series, as reweighted by the OBE. Although the widest margin was 3 per cent in 1951, it was still plus 0.5 in 1955. After downward shifts in the 1954–58 bench-mark period and from 1958 to 1960, the gross product series again rises more than the Federal Reserve series to 1964.

Gross Product Series Relative to the Manufacturing Production Index, 1947 = 100

Year	Index	Year	Index
1947	100.0	1956	98.6
1948	101.3	1957	98.7
1949	102.1	1958	98.5
1950	101.3	1959	96.9
1951	103.0	1960	95.6
1952	102.6	1961	95.1
1953	101.4	1962	96.9
1954	102.0	1963	96.5
1955	100.5	1964	96.6

NOTE: Calculated from reweighted Federal Reserve indexes shown in the paper in this volume, "Comparison of Federal Reserve and OBE Measures of Real Manufacturing Output, 1947–64."

As the Gottsegen-Ziemer paper and Moss's comments indicate, differences in results shown stem not only from changes in input–output relationships but also from differences in the measurement of gross output. We expect that a more detailed examination of the gross product and bench-mark industry gross output deflators could lead to more similarity of results between the two approaches.

The Gottsegen-Ziemer paper apparently finds little evidence of an over-all bias in the man-hour portion of the index in the unbenchmarked interval since 1954. Moss uses the two-digit furniture group, which accounts for 1.8 per cent of total manufacturing, as an illustration of the hazards of projecting adjusted man-hour data. His comparison was only for the change from 1958 to 1964 and it was not noted that the increase for the presently published furniture index from 1954 to 1958 was about the same as the Census-Federal Reserve bench mark (that was 11 per cent, while the gross product series increased only 2 per cent) and that the published annual changes since 1959–60 are close to deflated Census value results. The Federal Reserve published furniture group is doubtless too high for the 1959–60 period. The gross product series for furniture shows an irregular downtrend over this period. By 1962 it is only 2 per cent higher than seven years earlier and thus implies little change in labor productivity for most of the period, which seems unlikely. Moss correctly notes the problems of measuring price changes for these products but another basic question is whether an adequate monthly sample of the value of factory sales or shipments of furniture can be maintained—various attempts to do so in the past have not been successful.

As was stated in our paper, it is planned to exclude estimated purchases of business services from the value-added weights in the forthcoming revision of the Federal Reserve monthly index and to use 1958 price relationships for recent periods. We do not think it would be appropriate to take the other three steps which would be necessary to make the weights of the two series completely comparable: (1) using 1958 price relationships for earlier periods; (2) adding excise taxes to weights which are intended to approximate factor costs; and (3) shifting from the Census weighting universe to the gross product weighting universe.

We have reservations about series whose year-to-year movements are affected by various company-establishment and inventory valuation adjustments. Admittedly the annual movements of Census value of output data may also be affected by inventory valuation and sampling and coverage problems; in these cases we prefer to rely as much as possible on appropriate quantity indicators for annual indexes which are used to adjust the levels of the monthly indexes.

Assuming that there were no differences in weights or in deflation of gross output, the question has been raised whether it would be desirable to adjust the Federal Reserve monthly series to reflect changes in input–output relationships that have apparently occurred in some industries such as primary metals, autos, petroleum refining, and (to go outside manufacturing) electric utilities. Some adjustments might be accomplished by increased use of value added weights below the industry level. If an increase in output per unit of input in the auto industry is due to more fabrication of components within the industry, such an increase could be imputed to the original equipment auto parts series. Changes due to more efficient use of materials (as in electric utilities) or to use of more highly processed materials (as in primary metals) could be allowed for by adjusting an industry group total index rather than the component product series, so that the components could still be aggregated with gross weights for analyzing commodity flows in the over-all economy, as outlined in our paper.

We would like to underscore, however, the comments made in the Gottsegen-Ziemer paper on the sensitivity to error of double deflation measures and to note that they did not accept the resulting calculations for the petroleum refining industry, although in that industry input and price data can be more exactly determined than in other larger and more heterogeneous industry groups. For a further example, in the course of our bench-mark work two experimental double deflations were made of the auto industry for 1954–58, one using wholesale price index components and another using unit values derived from quantity indexes. The difference between the input deflators was negligible; the difference between the output deflators was 4 per cent, or 1 per cent per year, and the resulting difference between the residual net output indexes was 14 per cent, nearly 3.5 per cent per year.

We chose in our paper to develop the analytical value of using the monthly production measures as links to final demand and prices and to raise some questions concerning the data currently available for analyzing output and inventory changes in the goods sector of the economy. The

OBE elected to contribute additional statistical comparisons and points of possible reconciliation of the two sets of series for the manufacturing sector. Without the new, more detailed gross product data which became available at this Conference, it was not possible for us to go much beyond the analysis for manufacturing which we presented two years ago in the reply to the ECE. That analysis compared the Federal Reserve indexes with the then published gross product series of the BLS as well as the OBE; also, the net versus gross comparisons were presented in an ASA paper cited above.

More direct comparisons are now possible within the Census framework; we plan to be working further on such comparisons, particularly with regard to gross output deflators. We hope that the efforts of others at OBE and Census will include consideration of such matters as comparison of Census current-dollar values with gross product data and direct measurement of at least the current-dollar value of business services.

Cornelia Motheral

The following comments represent scattered further observations on the Gottsegen-Ziemer paper.

Mr. Gottsegen has indicated that some differences between the OBE measures, on the one hand, and OBE's deflated Census value-added measures and the Federal Reserve measures, on the other, stem from the inventory valuation adjustment to the former, particularly in year-to-year movements for 1950–51. With Census data it is only necessary to adjust for changes in valuation of finished and in-process inventories and sometimes not even those, since in many industries where changes in such inventories are important, value of production or value of work done rather than value of shipments is reported to the Census. The industries in which the differences stemming from IVA occur, according to Gottsegen, are tobacco, textiles, furniture, chemicals, rubber, and leather. Many of the Federal Reserve monthly series in these groups, and more of the annual series, are based on quantity of production data, so that no adjustment for inventory change is necessary, with or without IVA. Some of the monthly and somewhat more of the annual data use shipments as a proxy for production; these will be in error by the amount of real inventory change, not by the amount of IVA. I have inspected two of the series where man-hours—a production proxy not needing inventory adjustment of any kind—are used monthly, and the annual indexes are based on deflated value of shipments. It does not seem likely that adjustment for inventory change, with or without IVA, would change the direction of the plastics products component of the rubber and plastics products index for the 1950–51 period. The other rubber series are based on quantities of production or rubber consumption. I conclude that the IVA is more likely to be at fault than the production indexes in this area. Another area where deflated value of shipments is used annually is furniture. Here I inspected the 1953–54 difference, where the Federal Reserve series goes up while the OBE series goes down. Adjustment for inventory change, with or without IVA, would have little effect on the movement of the Federal Reserve series; however, the Federal Reserve household furniture series is based on wherever-made product shipments—industry shipments decline from 1953 to 1954, and should have been used.

Doing the IVA in three- and four-digit detail is often more work than it's worth. We have done it in the 1947–54 and 1954–58 bench marks, and of course it is necessary and makes a difference in certain years such as 1947 and 1950. For 1954 and 1958 it was hardly worth the effort. We are now setting up a system in which our annual indexes will be based on deflated Census data to a greater extent, and the possibility that we will have to apply an IVA for some years and some industries will have to be borne in mind.

In our attempt to monitor current index levels, it would be a help if BLS published monthly wholesale price indexes classified to correspond to the industry groupings used in the Census Bureau's monthly manufacturers' shipments survey. Such indexes would be useful for deflating shipments and finished and in-process inventories.

Gottsegen ascribes the differences between the OBE and Federal Reserve series for Group 30, rubber and plastics products, to the Federal Reserve use of unrepresentative quantity or man-hour indicators. But the greatest trend divergence for this industry occurs in the 1947–57 period when the Federal Reserve series are adjusted to bench-mark and annual levels; in the period for 1957 to date when we are dependent on tire quantity series and man-hours with estimated productivity adjustments, the trends are not dissimilar. I think that the difference in the earlier period is caused partly by our use of 1947 weights through 1952, not only in combining the series but also internally in the detailed bench-mark indexes to which the series are adjusted; and partly by our bench-mark and annual measures for plastics products, which represent a Census value deflated with a deflator derived from Tariff Commission quantity and value data for plastics materials. We realize that it is often not appropriate to deflate a product value with a materials deflator, but we believe that the Tariff data provided better coverage of this field than available wholesale price index components, and think that in this area we were probably more nearly correct than the OBE measure.

The differences that arise from weighting are associated more with choice of weight year than with choice of weight concept. The basic question involved is whether it is really appropriate to measure the output of the late 1940's and early 1950's with the price relationships of 1958.

We are surprised at many of the differences shown because as Spencer indicated, the Federal Reserve manufacturing index is very close to the 1954–58 bench mark and a preliminary 1958–63 bench mark; it is also very close in 1962 and 1964, relative to 1963, to Annual Survey data deflated in some detail with BLS wholesale price indexes, and in 1965 to deflated totals from the very recently available 1965 Annual Survey.

We recognize that legitimate and plausible differences can arise because of changes in materials input per unit of output, as in primary metals. In primary metals these changes arise from use of more highly processed ores, yet this increase is not reflected in the OBE mining measures since they use the Federal Reserve mining series based on usable ore, which are considerably understated as measures of mining gross product.

We are also surprised, however, to see that the two "gross" measures for primary metals—Federal Reserve indexes gross weighted versus deflated Census gross output—show such differences for the 1958–64 period. Primary metals has usually been our best index, requiring little bench-mark revision. If both of the two gross measures are correct—that is, if we are measuring the quantities correctly and the deflators applied to the Census data measure the prices correctly—they seem to me to imply a decline in quality of primary metals. Or, if we assume that such difficult aspects of quality as strength and durability are equally badly measured by the production and price indexes, then the difference between the two measures suggest that in this period there was a movement toward the cheaper grades within the types of metal and metal product measured by the Federal Reserve indexes for primary metals. The only other possibility I can think of is some peculiarity in the detailed product weights, which in the steel industry are open to question.

On the other hand, as Spencer has suggested from study of Census unit value and BLS price indications at the five-digit product class level, there may be an upward bias in the BLS price indexes for these products. Of course, to the extent that these products become inputs to other manufacturing industries, the errors will cancel at the total manufacturing level, although the gross product series for primary metals would be understated, and those for metal fabricating would be overstated.

VIVIAN E. SPENCER, Bureau of the Census

The first comment on this extremely valuable paper, which maintains the high quality of work to be expected from these authors, must be on its excellence.

The second comment must be on the really striking similarity, considering the differences in methods and concepts used in their construction, of the FRB and OBE series as presented in the paper. In the deflated Census value-added series plotted on the charts attached to this paper, the latter series usually fall between the OBE and FRB series—but closer to the OBE figures. In one sense, the differences between these series furnish a measure of their reliability. Where the differences are significant, one would like to analyze them as indicators of the effect of differences in the basic concepts and methods. Some such discussion is included in the paper. However, time has not permitted me to expand upon them.

One desirable study would be comparing the behavior of the 1954–58 and 1958–63 relationships with that of the new Census bench-mark indexes based on data for the approximately 7,000 commodities on which information is collected in the Census of Manufactures. These indexes use value-added weights at the five-digit commodity level and are also available with employment, man-hour, current-capital-input, and value of shipment weights, and at the four-digit level with energy-input weights. Such a study could not as yet be made: Although the wherever-made commodity indexes for most areas were published in the final 1963 publications of the censuses of Manufactures and Mineral Industries, and the 1954–58 industry indexes have had limited distribution, nevertheless, work on the 1958–63 industry indexes is not yet entirely complete.

In the course of the index work, one bit of analysis which we did may have some bearing on the relations between series in this paper. In the total series and many of the two-digit group comparisons, it is notable that the FRB series rises throughout most of the period more rapidly than the OBE series. The 1947–54 Census bench-mark index was found to be five points higher than the FRB. It appears that the final Census bench marks for 1954–58 and 1958–63 will also be slightly higher than the FRB, but in each case only by one or two points.

The OBE series depends entirely for deflation on the especially constructed BLS price indexes. The FRB depends to a much lesser extent on BLS price series. Although the final Census indexes incorporate many BLS price series for areas where inadequate or no quantity data are available, they do so to a still lesser extent. In our working analysis of the relation between BLS indexes and the raw Census four-digit implied unit value indexes constructed with maximium use of Census quantity and value data, scatter diagrams were constructed comparing the two-price measures. A tendency was noted for the BLS indexes to show higher increases in price than the Census series. This seemed particularly clear in both periods for areas like Major Groups 28—chemicals and 33—primary metals where this pattern of more rapid increase of FRB than OBE is notable. If the BLS price indexes do tend to overstate price increases, this might be a significant factor in the lower rate of increase in the OBE series than in the FRB series, and again would contribute to the FRB index falling somewhat below the Census bench marks.

The divergence of the FRB and OBE series for Group 29 in 1964 and certain other years, and the even greater divergence when they are compared with the deflated value-added series, point to the need for a further restudy of the special methods used for construction of these series and of alternative methods possible. There are, of course, significant problems in arriving at good petroleum refining measures.

MILTON MOSS, Bureau of the Budget

It is probably fair to say that the figures in the national accounts which are used most intensively here and abroad are those in *constant* prices. The past decade has witnessed a considerable advance in the measurement and publication of estimates in constant prices in the United States, partly reflecting the strong interest in the analysis of economic growth.

Such advances include the following: (1) United States gross national product by major type of purchaser which, formerly available only annually, was put on a quarterly basis early in the decade; (2) GNP by major type of product for durable and nondurable goods, services, and structures, with a breakdown for goods as between final sales and change in business inventories on a quarterly basis; (3) industrial production indexes, published more promptly and in greater detail than before and developed along market categories to provide comparisons with final sales and between materials and finished products; (4) real gross product originating by industry on an annual basis, building on earlier estimates by Alterman and Jacobs, and which opens the door to analysis of productivity change in industry detail within a consistent accounting framework; (5) coincident with the preceding, the regrouping and reweighting of prices along industry lines to provide the framework for developing industry or so-called sector price indexes; (6) integration of the input–output table with the income and product accounts, making possible a consistent accounting of changes in the industrial distribution of final demand.

Partly in consequence of this work, we are faced with an embarassment of riches exposing various differences in the existing bodies of information.

The period ahead, with its continued pressure to increase the timeliness and detail of data in constant prices, will necessarily involve decisions about the extent to which differences between measures such as the Index of Industrial Production and GNP by industry can be adequately resolved.

NOTE: I should like to take this occasion to acknowledge my association with Gary G. Schlarbaum, who worked with me as a summer intern at the Budget Bureau in 1966 and who made intensive study of problems involved in reconciling the Index of Industrial Production with real gross product by industry.

What have the papers in this section contributed to our understanding of differences and what have they contributed to resolving them?

It is clear from both Gottsegen-Ziemer and Gehman-Motheral papers that there are significant differences between the movements of the Index of Industrial Production and of the gross product figures—over the long term, from year to year, and for quarterly changes—whether industry or commodity comparisons are made. In a broad sense, of course, the two measures show similar results and the error margins implied by the differences in movement would not trouble many other countries where the data base is far poorer than ours.

But, for the uses to which the data are put, the fact that the FRB measure for manufactures rises 4.2 per cent per year and OBE's corresponding measure rises 3.8 per cent over the whole postwar period, and the fact that for durable manufactures one rose (FRB) and the other fell (OBE) from 1955–56 pose serious questions for analysis of growth and fluctuations.

The Gottsegen-Ziemer paper, which I have been asked to discuss, should be highly commended for making available a wealth of material for indicating some of the possible factors making for differences between the two measures. Much work will need to be done, however, to resolve the difficulties, and I hope this conference will provide the push necessary to get this work done.

I would like to illustrate (Table 1) what the difficulties are and what we might conclude about the directions ahead. My remarks will be similar in many respects to those of Jack Gottsegen, but my emphasis will be different and I would like to suggest some remedies. The figures in the table are adapted from appendix material mostly supplied with the Gottsegen-Ziemer paper and which shows indexes for manufacturing for the year 1964 with the year 1958 = 100.

Analyzing the difference between the Federal Reserve and OBE measures based only on the span of two years, which I have done in the table, has severe limitations, particularly since the size and nature of the differences between the indexes will depend on the particular pair of years chosen. Moreover, the fact that 1958 was a recession year and 1964 a prosperous one tends to exaggerate differences for a number of groups—although at the total level the difference between the two series is very small. Also, at this level of aggregation, the operation of the various influences cannot be separated. For example,

TABLE 1

Indexes of Manufacturing Activity: 1964

(in constant prices, 1958 = 100)

	Federal Reserve		Census – OBE			OBE	
Manufacturing Industry	Value-Added Weights (1)	Gross Weights (2)	Gross Output (3)	Input (4)	Value Added (5)	Value-Added Plus Excise (6)	Product Originating (7)
Total	142.8	141.8	136.6	134.0	140.1	139.6	140.4
Nondurables	137.0	134.2	130.9	128.2	135.1	133.6	132.0
Durables	147.8	149.9	142.4	140.8	144.1	144.9	146.9
Food	121.7	121.6	121.3	123.1	116.9	117.3	117.1
Tobacco	120.4	115.2	116.3	116.3	116.3	115.0	119.0
Textiles	130.3	130.1	138.7	142.7	132.6	132.6	130.1
Apparel	140.7	143.1	129.4	128.3	130.8	130.8	128.1
Lumber	117.8	120.5	126.1	123.1	130.1	130.1	128.9
Furniture	154.7	155.6	128.6	134.1	123.1	123.1	128.7
Paper	137.2	138.9	135.4	131.9	139.9	139.9	140.0
Printing	127.2	127.7	124.2	128.0	121.9	121.9	125.7
Chemicals	166.6	167.3	155.3	149.0	160.8	160.8	152.0
Petroleum	124.2	122.9	126.4	116.6	174.7	152.5	144.3
Rubber	169.5	174.0	159.8	154.3	165.4	162.8	163.4
Leather	106.9	106.9	104.3	102.7	105.9	105.9	108.9
Stone, clay, and glass	135.2	136.3	132.1	132.2	132.1	132.1	131.2
Primary metals	147.5	148.7	140.2	144.9	133.7	133.7	130.2
Fabricated metals	142.8	140.7	126.5	126.2	126.8	126.8	135.2
Nonelectrical machinery	161.7	159.3	145.4	145.6	145.2	145.2	153.3
Electrical machinery	156.2	155.9	166.7	150.6	179.9	179.1	167.3
Motor vehicles	181.1	186.1	179.4	173.3	192.6	192.6	213.0
Transportation equipment, ordnance, except motor vehicles	122.2	125.5	108.6	101.7	115.2	115.2	123.8
Instruments	148.1	153.4	159.5	149.5	165.5	165.5	139.6
Miscellaneous manufacturing	141.9	142.8	134.3	133.4	135.1	135.1	119.3

Source: Data are based on figures from paper by J. J. Gottsegen and R. C. Ziemer, except for column 2 which is based on unpublished Federal Reserve Board data.

differences between aggregate input and output indexes could result from differences in output movements of individual industries with different ratios of input to output, even though input–output relations in individual industries might not have changed—the familiar product mix problem. Still another problem—a perennial one—is that 1964 is not a bench-mark year and we are dealing with preliminary figures in both systems. Whatever the difficulties, however, the table does provide a convenient framework for illustrating the main factors accounting for differences between the measures

At the risk of being too obvious, let me quickly describe the figures in each column. The first column of figures represents the Federal Reserve indexes as published, but on a 1958 rather than 1957–59 base. These indexes are based on series that are gross of material inputs but combined with value-added weights. The second column represents the same series combined with gross value weights. Aside from some generally minor problems of aggregation, columns 1 and 2 differ merely because of differences between value-added and gross value weights. The underlying series are identical.

Column 3 represents deflated gross value of output of individual industries combined with gross value weights using Census data. At the individual industry level these indexes should be identical in theory with indexes in columns 1 and 2, except in those few cases where FRB has developed value-added weights for individual products. They differ from column 1 at aggregate levels because of the use of gross value weights, but they should be identical with those in column 2 at the levels of aggregation shown. That they do in fact differ and that they ought to conform will be emphasized at later points in my discussion.

Columns 4 and 5 are also based on Census data giving indexes of constant-dollar input and value added. These figures, including column 3, are based on values from the Census of Manufactures and the Annual Survey of Manufactures deflated by OBE with BLS wholesale price series. While the data do not necessarily represent bench marks, they provide, by and large, a consistent set of information for analyzing changes in the movement of material inputs and outputs in constant prices as measured by OBE and hence provide one basis for inferring whether differences between the FRB and OBE measures reflect differences between gross output and *value added*.

The last two columns, shown here as OBE data, represent in column 6 indexes of value added in constant prices but inclusive of excise taxes, and the last column, gross product originating in constant prices. These two columns show different results only because they use different current-dollar figures for measuring value added. The deflators are the same. The first and last columns provide us with the comparison between the two measures under consideration in this session. The columns in between help interpret those differences.

For total manufacturing, we note that in the change from 1958 to 1964 the FRB index rises 42.8 per cent (col. 1) and OBE 40.4 per cent (col. 7)—a rather similar increase. It is instructive to try to interpret even this small difference, using the indexes in the other columns to seek clues. Is the difference shown a result of the fact that the FRB index is gross, i.e., does not allow for differences between gross output of products and input of materials while the OBE measure is net in this respect? The table suggests otherwise. Comparison of columns 3 and 4 shows that gross output rose relative to input, and therefore value added has risen relative to gross output.

If the Federal Reserve index were regarded as simply a gross output index, on that account it should have risen less than OBE but in fact it has risen more. So whatever differences exist between the two measures at the total level it has apparently not arisen as a result of differences between input and output. However, when we look at some of the underlying two-digit groups shown in the table, a fuller appreciation of the role played by the various factors is more clearly revealed.

In the food group, for example, the lower OBE index (117.1) compared with the Federal Reserve (121.7) appears to result from a difference between value added and gross output as indicated in columns 4 and 5. The deflated Census data indicate that input has increased faster than output and consequently value added has increased less than gross output. This would seem to explain, at least statistically, why product originating showed an increase of only 17 per cent while the Federal Reserve showed an increase of 22 per cent, or closer to the gross output figure in column 3. To determine whether this is the underlying reason *in fact,* however, would require more detail. That is, additional detail would be needed to determine, for example, whether the difference arose because the FRB index included in its food index the increase in packaging materials; or in other words, was or was not duplicating some of the output of the paper industry.

It is instructive to compare columns 2 and 3. Since the figures in the two columns are broadly similar as to weights, and assuming they deal with the same value data, the differences result from the fact that quantity-type data are used in one case (FRB) and BLS price data for deflation are used in the other. *Conceptually* the figures in these two columns should be identical, as I indicated earlier; that is, with ideal quantity and price data the use of quantity indexes with base-period price weights should provide the same results as indexes based on deflation of value data with detailed price indexes with current-year quantity weights. In fact, the results are quite different. Differences are sizeable in some groups and go in different directions. At bench-mark intervals when both measures rely heavily on identical Census value data such differences ought to be fully explained. Is it because detailed quantity data are inferior or superior to price data or is it because FRB and Census are in fact "deflating" different value aggregates because of classification or other reasons?

The indexes in columns 6 and 7 use identical deflators but different current-dollar data. Here, too, differences in a number of groups are quite sizeable and in my conclusion later I wish to emphasize the need to reconcile these figures.

I should like now to illustrate two problems which are thorns of criticism in the series under review. I refer to the problem of reliance on man-hours in the FRB measure and the difficulty with double deflation in the OBE measure.

First, the man-hour problem. I can illustrate this with the index shown in the table for the furniture industry. Note that this index at 154.7 (col. 1) compares with an OBE measure of 128.7.

Monthly changes in the FRB index for the furniture industry are equal to percentage changes in man-hours for this industry multiplied by assumed changes in output per man-hour. These monthly changes are interpolated between and extrapolated beyond bench marks, at which time levels of output and of output per man-hour are calculated using Census production and BLS employment. Generally value data deflated by wholesale price indexes rather than quantity-type data are used to estimate output for this industry because a sample of price data for major items is more readily available than is a detailed listing for the great heterogeneity of physical quantities of furniture.

Assuming that selected price data are broadly representative of price changes for all furniture items and that they allow for quality change (heroic assumptions of course), the deflated value data constitute a basic approach to measurement of physical volume for this type of industry. But the published index has not been adjusted regularly to Census bench marks or Annual Survey of Manufactures data for some time. It may well be that a detailed study of this industry will expose weaknesses in the price data for deflating the Census value data, in which case price data should be improved. But I see no better alternative for such an industry.

The problem then for resolving difficulties of the type exemplified by the furniture industry is for the FRB to have more frequent bench marks using the Census Annual Survey of Manufactures. A sizeable fraction of the total Index of Industrial Production (approximately half) requires the bench-mark study of adjusted man-hour series. While these series are monitored by FRB in the aggregate by comparisons with product-type indexes and other data such as electric power and freight transport, their detailed adjustment at approximately annual intervals is highly desirable.

I know how difficult it is to carry out bench-mark studies frequently —it is one of the most thankless and exacting jobs. But it must be done and whatever can be done to make this task less slavish, more expeditious, and even more interesting, if possible, should be done.

To illustrate the problem with double deflation in the OBE measure, attention is now directed to the indexes in the table for petroleum refining. The table shows, for example, that gross output of petroleum rose 26.4 per cent (col. 3) and input rose 16.6 per cent (col. 4). Value added, as a consequence, rose 75 per cent (col. 5). This enormous difference between value added and gross output raises serious questions. The level of input is large relative to output in this industry and small errors in both can be magnified in the value-added residual, as is well known. But as a matter of fact, have refined products, for example, increased relative to inputs or is this a result of the oddities of double deflation? I ask this question because this happens to be an industry with especially good physical volume information on outputs, as Gottsegen and Ziemer recognize. But we also know a great deal about inputs of crude oil, electric power, additives, fuel, etc., which they do not recognize as well.

Gottsegen and Ziemer have apparently done a good deal of work on this industry, which at first I had not fully appreciated. But the irony of this example consists in this simple fact—despite an unusually rich amount of information of both inputs and outputs, double deflation procedures have been found seriously wanting. I suspect that refined products have not risen relative to crude oil, fuels, electric power, additives, etc., by the differences suggested in columns 3, 4, and 5. The index finally accepted by OBE (144.3 in column 7) is still considerably higher than the gross output measure, 126.4 in column 3 and than the FRB measure, 124.2 in column 1.

What Do We Do?

The following recommendations spell out in slightly more detail what has been already said on eliminating unnecessary differences between the FRB and OBE figures.

1. The figures in column 2 and column 3 should be made as identical as possible at bench-mark intervals. The figures in these two columns theoretically are deflating the same value base in the individual industries. As mentioned earlier, they differ only because quantity-type information with base-year price weights are used in the Federal Reserve, and BLS price data with quantity weights are used by OBE.

2. The basic data from which columns 6 and 7 are derived should be made as identical as possible. Differences arise because the current-dollar data on value added come from different sources, one from Census, and the other from IRS and other sources. The Census data include business services, while the OBE data require difficult problems of allocation of company-based data to an establishment order. In order that the figures in columns 6 and 7 be made as identical as possible, two things need to be done; one involves a strengthening of the Enterprise Statistics Program at Census to improve our links between company and establishment data and classifications, the other is that Census value-added data should be made less duplicative to exclude purchased business services.

3. The detail in GPO by industry should be made available for analysis. Not only should two-digit and lower orders of aggregation be made available on net output but the data for analyzing the significance of the net output measures, namely, relations between gross output and input, should also be made available. In other words, at

least at bench-mark intervals, the figures on gross output, input, and net output, in current dollars, constant dollars, and implied deflators should be made available—if not for publication, for special analysis. These data were made available to this conference and I hope this practice will continue.

4. The price indexes need to be strengthened, both in those areas where these indexes are apparently less accurate than quantity-type information, but more importantly in those areas where they are presently woefully incomplete. The latter include particularly the area of producers durable equipment. Where the price data are clearly more accurate than quantity-type information they should be used in the FRB index. At bench-mark intervals these judgments can be made.

5. A problem remains if we put all emphasis on net output measures. For one thing, information for commodities tends to disappear in the framework of GNP originating so long as indexes are shown only for net output. It is true that on a bench-mark basis we can show indexes of dollar values for outputs, inputs, and net outputs. Such detail would be extremely useful as indicated above. But quarterly or monthly data on this detailed basis is not likely to be developed for a long, long time.

The detailed commodity flows that can be shown monthly for materials and finished products in the Index of Industrial Production, from producing through distributing channels, should be encouraged.

As pointed out in the Gehman-Motheral paper, these detailed commodity flows can help in understanding the bases for inventory and price change and can provide the basis for a more detailed understanding of short-run fluctuations.

One possibility is to have value-added type measures at bench-mark intervals supplemented by gross output series for monthly movements and for special groupings. The value-added type measures of FRB and OBE should be reconciled and the gross output type measures in FRB should be reconciled with those which OBE calculates as an early step in its procedures. If this is done at bench-mark intervals (annual as much as possible), differences could be resolved, say at two-digit levels, and a major element of confusion would thereby be eliminated.

6. At more frequent intervals (monthly and quarterly), I recommend that we look to the wider use of the Monthly Industry Survey of Shipments, Inventories, and Orders for use in those series in which the Board relies heavily on man-hours for current changes. While

man-hour data provide very useful indicators in many industries where the production process is long, the need for current measures of productivity change requires that these man-hour measures be supplemented as much as possible by production-type data on a monthly basis. This will require further strengthening of the Monthly Industry Survey, including a strengthening of its sample, the more frequent bench-mark extrapolation of these monthly data to annual survey levels (last bench mark was for 1962), and a closer tie with employment information so that analysis of output in relation to employment on a current basis may be strengthened.

7. More detailed input–output studies (which will require continual improvement in data on material and service inputs) will help in reconciling many problems of data and analysis of intermediate and final output.

Conclusion

All, or nearly all, the people needed to bring a little more peaceful coexistence between IP and GPO are in attendance at this conference. It seems to me that there is an opportunity ahead for these people to develop an imaginative solution to the problems posed by the differences between the Index of Industrial Production and GNP. The different approaches in the two measures challenge us to reap the benefits of both without necessarily attempting an ironclad solution that would end up with only one type of measure. The advantages of a detailed industry analysis of productivity changes within a consistent accounting framework are clear, and we should direct the statistics program to strengthen this work to make it more detailed and more timely. The advantages of a commodity-flow type of analysis for both short-run and long-term analysis, but particularly for the short-run, should be made more widely understood. The flexibility that the Index of Industrial Production provides for this type of commodity-flow analysis suggests that this work should be encouraged.

While we of course look for a lessening of unnecessary tensions in this area of disparate statistics—I would like to end my discussion with a request for a constructive variety in our approach to the study of output and demand developments.

"In My Father's house are many mansions."

FRANK R. GARFIELD

In my view the Gottsegen-Ziemer paper marks the beginning of a new phase in the discussion of measuring manufacturing production in the United States. This developing discussion may well have a significant bearing on production measurement problems in other areas and on policy problems relating to productivity, unit labor costs, growth, and the like. These policy problems are of great practical importance and measurement issues affecting them call for the most careful study.

The two-digit data made available with this paper and the analysis by two-digit groups, which is begun here and to be extended in later papers, will provide students in this area with important basic material essential for appraising certain alternative methods of measurement and considering what methods may be appropriate in different types of situations. For example, this new material will offer an opportunity for study at the two-digit level of differences between indexes of deflated value of product, deflated value of input and deflated value-added, as derived here from Census data in current-value terms through deflation by regrouped Bureau of Labor Statistics price data.

The new material will also make possible, for years of comprehensive censuses, comparisons between the results of this double deflation work and of the work embodied in the Census-Federal Reserve bench-mark indexes. Such comparisons could be made now for 1947–54 and 1954–58, and comparison for 1958–63 will be possible in the near future when the Census-Federal Reserve indexes become available.

In the Gottsegen-Ziemer analysis emphasis is on other comparisons and especially on those relating to recent years. For recent years, as the authors point out, the comparisons between the GPO measures of the Office of Business Economics and the Federal Reserve Board measures must be regarded as preliminary because some of the two-digit indexes in the Federal Reserve index will probably be revised appreciably when the new bench marks become available, even though, as reported in the Gehman-Motheral paper, the total for manufacturing is not expected to be altered much. The present showing is one of significant similarities but also of significant differences.

In commenting on measurement problems, Gottsegen and Ziemer note a number of issues associated with representation of real value added (or gross product originating) by physical output series and by such proxies as adjusted man-hours. They also note various different problems associated with measurement of gross product originating by the double deflation approach in which price deflators obtained by deflating Census value of output and of input are used to transform current-dollar gross product originating into real terms. The authors take the view that this approach can be accepted for all two-digit groups in manufacturing, with the single exception of petroleum refining. There, a constant-dollar output series derived from physical volume measures is substituted for deflated dollar figures. This substitution is probably desirable and I think it likely that for some other groups also constant-dollar series might better be derived by means other than deflating dollar figures; and beyond questions concerning particular series lie broader questions concerning the best general (or selective) approach.

As the authors suggest, production measurement problems are many. Comment on a single issue must, therefore, leave much unsaid. But I think the nature of the double deflation approach particularly needs to be explored further, especially with respect to one aspect noted by the authors. They say: "The GPO implicit deflator has the quality that small differences in the level of output or input prices yield larger differences in the GPO deflator since the latter is derived as a residual—that is, the output price index has a positive weight but the input price index has a negative weight." And again, in discussing the petroleum refining problem they say: "Since value added is a residual, small differences in price levels of output and input and small inconsistencies in the measures of output and input may yield large differences in the price movements for value added. This was the experience when the double deflation method was used for SIC 29."

In citing this reason as one of several for making a substitution here, but not elsewhere, the authors point out that the ratio of cost of materials to value of shipments in that industry is unusually high, ranging from 80 to 84 per cent in the 1950–58 period. Another way of stating the situation for 1958 in petroleum refining is to say that value added (the residual to be approximated) was 16 per cent of value of output and a little less than 9 per cent of value of output plus value of input, the values deflated to arrive at a price deflator for value added. Considering the proportions shown for petroleum refining and the problems involved in matching prices in price series and prices in value series, it hardly seems surprising that the results shown for this industry were found to be unsatisfactory. When errors occur in deflating inputs or outputs they may, of course, be offsetting—or they may not. In this connection, it may be noted that equal percentage errors in input and output measures will not exactly offset each other.

In 1958, the 16 per cent for petroleum refining was the extreme low for the two-digit industry ratios of value added to value of output. But in the food industry, value added was only 29 per cent of value of product—and 17 per cent of the sum of value of product and value of input. The behavior of the food processing series shown in their chart and the behavior of corresponding real output and input series shown in the tables raise questions: Did real GPO (or value added) actually show little net change from 1957 to 1960 or 1961? Little change for real value added implies a decline in real value added in relation to real value of output in that period of 9 per cent or more. This sharp decline was preceded and followed by increases in the ratio of real value added to real value of output. Independent evidence seems to me essential to corroborate this finding before it can be accepted. The 9 per cent decline in the ratio, from 31.4 to 28.6 per cent, reflected the difference between a 9 per cent rise in real output and a 13 per cent rise in real input (comparing 1957 and 1960). Is this perhaps a case where rather small errors in price measurement and matching could have accounted for much or all of the temporary levelling off in real value added? Would either input or output perhaps have provided a better representation of real value added?

At the other extreme from petroleum refining and food processing in 1958 were printing and publishing and instruments and allied products, with value added to value of product ratios of 63 and 62 per cent. But even for printing and publishing the deflation process is applied to a total of 100 (for output) plus 37 (for input) or 137 altogether in obtaining a residual for 63 (i.e., 100 minus 37). Thus, at best, with respect to this aspect of the problem, the risks of important effects from small errors seem to me considerable over the whole range of industries.

The analysis in the Gottsegen-Ziemer paper is largely in terms of changes over long periods; while year-to-year percentage changes shown in the tables provide a ready reference for those interested, the discussion of year-to-year changes by industry, for the most part, will come later.

I expect this to be a very significant part of the whole analytical project.

The problems of current monthly or even quarterly figures are rather different from those of annual figures—in many respects they are more difficult—and the answers as to the most appropriate approaches may not be the same as those arrived at for annual figures. But it is of great importance that the issues relating to annual figures be discussed further in quite some detail to improve our understanding both of what has been happening from year to year and of what can be learned by various approaches to annual production measurement.

Measures of Industrial Production and Final Demand

CLAYTON GEHMAN
CORNELIA MOTHERAL
FEDERAL RESERVE BOARD

Since the early 1920's, economists at the Federal Reserve have been developing monthly measures of activity and prices in the commodity sector of the economy with a view to analyzing the more crucial influences in the over-all economic situation. The compilation of such industry-type information has facilitated comparisons among economic time series similarly organized to study interrelationships of demand and supply for different types of commodities and utilization of labor and capital.

Market groupings of these industry data have been developed for major categories of consumer goods, equipment, and materials, as well as for many subdivisions of these categories to provide links between final demand, commodity prices, and industrial activity. Such market groupings of Bureau of Labor Statistics wholesale price indexes were compiled in 1937–41 for analysis of economy-wide price fluctuations. During World War II a market grouping of industrial production indexes was developed for studying cyclical and growth trends in consumption and investment.

At that time, the extent of the diversion of industrial resources for war purposes proved to be of critical importance in appraising developments in the private economy and in anticipating postwar economic changes. For example, direct comparisons of physical quantity series on consumer goods output showed more reduction during the war and thus the likelihood of more expansion in general economic activity in the immediate postwar period than was indicated by the aggregate expenditure data.[1] The strength shown after the war in the private

[1] A possible expansion of 60 per cent in consumer goods output above the 1935–39 average was noted in the leading article on "Wartime Production and

economy more than offset the widely expected deflationary effects of the cutback in federal war expenditures. With the unfolding of events in the postwar period and as more adequate data became available, work on market groupings of the production index continued and regular monthly publication was undertaken in 1959. A related development was the Census Bureau's publication beginning in 1963 of market groupings for the monthly series on value of manufacturers' shipments, inventories, and orders.

Two chapters in *Industrial Production—1959 Revision* provide a description of the composition of the market groupings, their relationships to other series, and possible uses of such groupings in cyclical analysis, with various qualifications. These analyses have been carried forward in special articles and in the U.S. reply to the Economic Commission for Europe inquiry on industrial production measurement.[2] The present paper brings some of the earlier comparisons up to date and discusses various improvements which will be provided by new features of a comprehensive revision of the production indexes. This revision is now underway and should be published in a year or so.

This paper also recommends future development of additional monthly measures of production and distribution in the commodity-producing and construction sectors of the economy. Such measures, with weights to represent gross flows, would provide monthly measures of input and output in constant dollars for these sectors; when combined with value-added weights they comprise a monthly measure of real gross product originating in those sectors.

I. Measurement Considerations

In a number of respects, the production measures differ in concept, in measurement techniques, and in scope and classification from the

Incomes," *Federal Reserve Bulletin,* September 1944. An exact comparison of this change became available in a recalculation of the Census-Federal Reserve bench-mark production index from 1939 to 1947, which showed an increase of 58 per cent for consumer goods, as described in Board of Governors of the Federal Reserve System, *Industrial Production Measurement in the United States,* February 1964, p. 5. Since 1939 was 6 per cent above the 1935–39 average the actual rise was about 65 per cent. See also Frank R. Garfield, "Measuring and Forecasting Consumption," *Journal of the American Statistical Association,* September 1946, pp. 322–333.

[2] Board of Governors of the Federal Reserve System, *Industrial Production Measurement in the United States,* February 1964.

Department of Commerce constant-dollar final-expenditure series in the national product accounts and the revised specially calculated annual real gross product originating by major industries presented at this conference. In some periods and some areas of measurement these differences lead to differences in indicated changes in apparently similar categories. We are mainly concerned in this paper with describing some of the analytical purposes for which the monthly production measures may be used and the inferences that may be drawn from their relationships to each other and to the final-expenditure series.

CONCEPT

In concept, the Commerce Department's gross product measures are net, whereas the Board's value-added-weighted production measures use gross series. The quarterly final-expenditure series are net since they measure output at only one stage, the last. The same approach is used for certain purposes in production index analysis when gross weighted end products of industry are used to compile an unduplicated output measure. In both cases, inputs from outside the measured sector are netted out—imports in the case of GNP, and imported, farm, and service inputs in the case of the net industry measure.[3]

The annual industry real gross product series are net by virtue of using the double deflation technique wherever input and output data are available. A complete system of measures of constant-dollar input, output, and net output for all sectors of the economy, or even just for the business or commodity sectors, would be of great usefulness. It should be pointed out that relatively small errors in the input or output measures for a given industry or sector may cause larger errors in the value-added residual and impair the usefulness of the industry detail; input measurement is particularly subject to error since reported detail is incomplete even in the industrial censuses. But if input and output measures are so constructed as to provide a consistent accounting for the flow of goods and services from one sector to another, the errors in measurement of intermediate output cancel out and the total will be the same as that derived by the final-expenditure approach. And the study of behavior of the flows and their interrelationships is of interest in itself, and is a main subject of this paper.

[3] See Clayton Gehman, "Alternative Measures of Economic Activity," *Annual Proceedings of the Business and Economics Statistics Section,* 1964 Annual Proceedings of the American Statistical Association.

The annual industry gross product data do not account consistently for these flows of goods and services, partly because the input and output series are not separately published for the sectors where double deflation was used and partly because data—and the fact that the compilations are based on the current-dollar series for employee compensation, interest, capital consumption, indirect taxes, and profits—did not permit consistent application of the double deflation technique. Manufacturing, utilities, and agriculture are double deflated but mining and trade are not. Changes in materials input–output relationships may be insignificant in mining and trade; the point is, however, that it is important for the consistency of a set of net output measures with each other, and with the measure of final unduplicated output, that (for example) iron ore as output of domestic mines be deflated by the same deflator (except for changes in transportation and distribution charges) as domestic ore used in the domestic iron and steel industry.

The production indexes provide accounting for real gross flows, and can be combined into measures of real value added, under the assumption that at the level of weighting there are no (or there are offsetting) changes in output per unit of material input. For short periods this can be accepted with little question. Even for a longer period such as the years since 1947, evidence has not been presented that there has been significant change in material and business service input per unit of output for the U.S. industrial sector as a whole. Of course, there have been changes in individual industries or industry groups (another reason why if double deflation is to be applied it is best to apply it consistently throughout the industrial sector), and some tests suggest the likelihood that the exclusion of these inputs would result in a net output index showing somewhat more growth than the value-added-weighted index since the mid-1950's (Gehman, "Alternative Measures," cited in footnote 3 above). In any event, for current analysis of monthly fluctuations in real terms, such value-added-weighted series are the only information available.

The expenditure and industry-originating series are both on a market-price basis: excise taxes are included in the manufacturing gross product data and retail excise and sales taxes are in the trade margin. The industrial production indexes are on a factor-cost basis, which is considered more appropriate for measurement of industry utilization of capital and labor. (In practice they include some indirect taxes, mainly property taxes.) The exclusion of manufacturing excise taxes has little effect on over-all manufacturing indexes, but the retail taxes may cause some difficulty in attempts to link consumer demands measured in market prices with trade and industrial activity measurements.

Finally, the production indexes use 1947 weights for the 1947–52 period and, therefore, show somewhat more growth than the 1958-weighted expenditure series.

SCOPE AND CLASSIFICATION

The industrial production system differs in several respects from the expenditure series in scope and classification. Some of the differences could be resolved by adoption of common standards, others are less tractable. Although these differences have been described in detail in the *1959 Revision* publication, it may be useful to summarize some of their main features here.

The expenditure series measure goods output at the point of sale, including all value added by trade and transportation. The production indexes exclude value added by trade and transportation, except in a few cases where the industry boundary includes distribution, as in utilities and dairy products. The production indexes can be supplemented by monthly measures of distribution activity to add up to series for total commodity output and distribution. For some experiments with this concept see Gehman, "Alternative Measures."

In the expenditure series, consumer purchases of electricity and gas are classified as services and oil and gas well drilling is included in structures, while the production groupings include these as consumer goods and business equipment, respectively. The expenditure series for nondurable goods includes consumption of unmanufactured farm products not in the industrial production series. Motor vehicle parts used in repairs are classified in the services sector of the expenditure series, whereas the production index includes all replacement parts.

The expenditure series cover exports net of imports, whereas the production index includes exports of domestic industrial products and when gross-value-weighted includes imported materials (raw or processed) that are consumed in further processing. To complete the measurement of commodity flows, a high priority should be placed on developing monthly measures of quantity and price as well as the value of merchandise exports and imports for (1) manufactured consumer goods, business equipment, defense equipment, and industrial materials;

(2) the latter preferably subdivided between construction materials, materials for processing, and miscellaneous finished materials; and (3) fresh foods and foodstuffs and other raw materials for processing. Such measures should also contribute new insights into changes in the merchandise trade balance and hence analysis of balance of payments problems.

Finally, the production grouping classification is, with the major exception of aircraft, by type of product rather than by type of purchaser. Thus, consumer goods include purchases of autos and other consumer products by business and government, business equipment includes government purchases, etc. This type of classification has advantages for some types of analysis. Electric power generating equipment adds to the nation's capacity to produce whether it is purchased by a utility company or a Federal power project. The purchase of autos by rental fleets reflects consumer as well as business demands. (Indeed, the shifting importance of auto rental raises the question of whether the fixed percentage split of auto sales between consumer and business use in the expenditure series is appropriate.)

MEASUREMENT AND INFERENCE

The final expenditure series is based on the value of final transactions, with output at earlier stages inferred from changes in deflated inventories of final products and materials. Inventory values are collected and published by holder—manufacturers and distributors—and are also combined by major type of products sold—durable and nondurable. From the point of view of the study of relationships of industrial production to final demand they can be more usefully divided into two broad stages of processing. On the one hand, all stocks of materials to be used for further industrial processing can be grouped, whether they are held by their purchasers or by their producers as "finished goods." The second grouping would combine the stocks of all end products of industry, whether held by manufacturers or distributors, including stocks of construction materials held by wholesalers and retailers.

The production index approach measures output directly at several stages of industrial activity. Changes in materials inventories may be inferred from comparison of the materials and end-product indexes; changes in inventories of end products from comparison of end-product output and final sales. Owing to the various considerations noted in the *1959 Revision,* such inferences must be made with considerable qualifications and a continuing check of other data. Even so, it is believed that these inferences have some advantages for current analysis because the production data are available from two to six weeks earlier than the book value inventory figures and are subject to little current revision, while the inventory change data have been subject to larger revisions and to special difficulties in allowing for changes in valuations.

II. New Market Measures of Production

There is presented below in Charts 1-a and 1-b an over-all monthly picture, going back to 1953, of the market groupings of the industrial production index and these results supply the main framework for the discussion in this paper. The weights used to compile the series from 1953 forward that are shown in these and subsequent charts are all new and relate to the year 1958. The main difference between the new

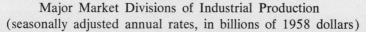

CHART 1-a

Major Market Divisions of Industrial Production

(seasonally adjusted annual rates, in billions of 1958 dollars)

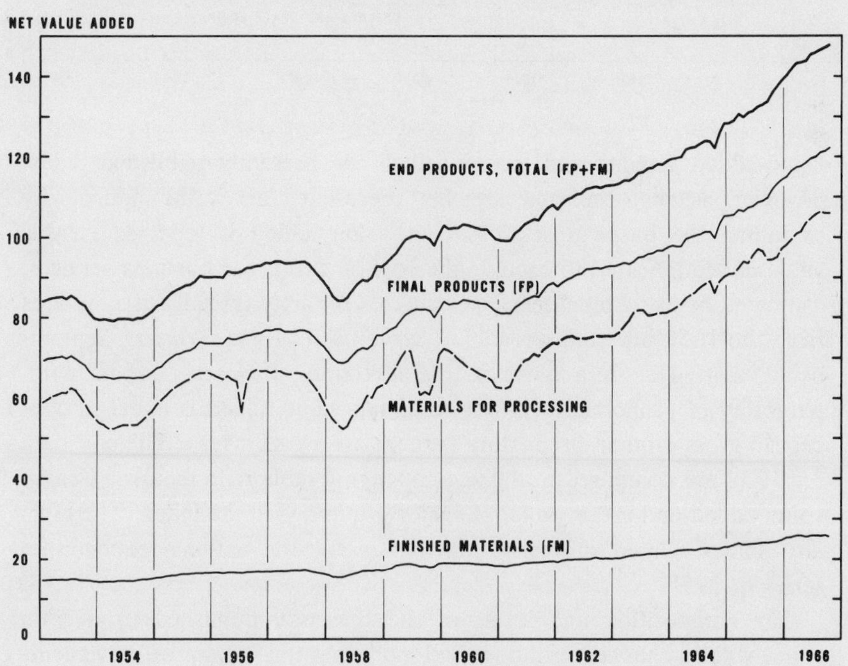

CHART 1-b

Major End-Product Groups of Industrial Production
(seasonally adjusted annual rates, in billions of 1958 dollars)

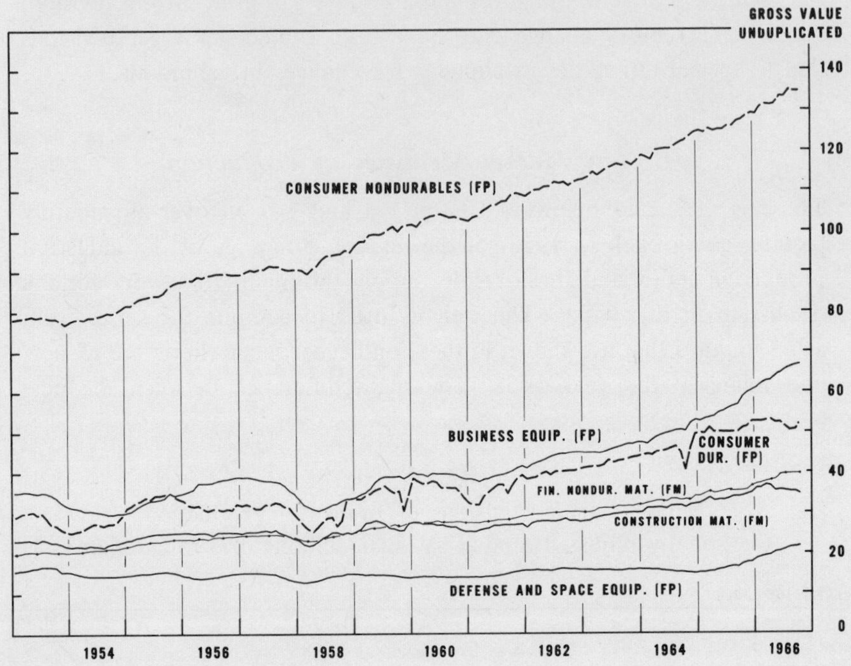

value-added weights and those used in the presently published index, however, is that the new weights represent "net value added" by excluding the business services. Net value added is reported Census value added adjusted to exclude the cost of purchased business services, estimated by using relationships calculated for sixty-three industry groups from the 1958 interindustry table (*Survey of Current Business,* September 1965). This is a move in the direction of closer national comparability of economic measures since net value added is equal in concept to gross product originating (except for excise taxes). The new data for 1958 are compared in the accompanying table with data for Census value added and gross value for major groupings in the index. The table also shows related summary information for the national expenditure series in 1958.

The composition and levels of the presently published production series will be changed in the revised index but the pattern of movements shown for the broad groupings will probably not be appreciably different from those indicated in these charts. Preliminary checks indicate that the total index and its major divisions will be revised little in 1958 and 1963 relative to 1954 as a result of the detailed Census-Federal Reserve bench-mark production index calculations now nearing completion, and the over-all results for 1964 and 1965 appear to be close to Census Annual Survey data. These indications do not include the effect of substituting the net value-added weights. The exclusion mainly of advertising outlays from these weights decreases the relative importance of consumer goods in the index, as the data indicate in the table, and increases the influence of equipment and materials output.

The two lower lines in Chart 1-a show new supplementary divisions for materials in the total index. The largest of these represents output of all mined and manufactured materials and components used for further processing or assembly in the industrial sector. It also includes utility output of gas and electricity for industrial-type users. The division for "finished materials" represents output of those materials produced largely for use outside the industrial sector of the economy. It includes all construction materials and various nondurable materials, such as feeds, fertilizer, and gas and electricity for commercial-type users.

This division for finished materials is combined with the present grouping for final products to provide a new total for end products.[4] This combination accounts for three-fifths of total industrial production in the 1958 period. Currently, end-product output is shown in Chart 1-a to be at an annual rate of $148 billion (1958 dollars) in "net value added."

In gross value terms—the terms in which the components of end products are shown in Chart 1-b—end-product output is at an annual rate of 350 billion dollars in 1958 prices. The latter chart presents separately six major groups of end products in the total index: two of these, construction materials and finished nondurable materials, are a subdivision of the finished materials grouping shown in Chart 1-a, while the remaining four groups are subdivisions of the presently published final-product total. The consumer goods groupings used in the chart are based on the durability of products—automotive and home goods are durable, and apparel and staples are nondurable—partly in order to

[4] For an earlier discussion of these subjects and comparisons with alternative weight systems see pages 14–17, Chart 2 following page 38, and page 49 of *Industrial Production Measurement in the United States.*

TABLE 1

Value of Output in 1958
(billion dollars)

	Department of Commerce[a]	Federal Reserve Production Index Data		
		Net Value Added	Census Value Added	Gross Value
GNP total	444.5			
Goods, total	229.4			
Farm	21.3	21.3		37.6[b]
Industrial (private)[c]	142.6			
Industrial production		144.7	164.7	351.7[b]
End products		86.6	99.8	214.8
Final products		65.1	75.3	167.1
Consumer goods		41.4	49.2	121.2
Automotive products		3.3	4.0	13.3
Home goods and apparel		13.7	15.7	29.8
Consumer staples		24.3	29.5	78.1
Equipment		23.7	26.1	45.9
Business equipment		16.0	17.7	32.1
Defense and space equipment		7.7	8.4	13.8
Finished materials		21.6	24.5	47.8
Construction materials		11.1	12.2	23.8
Finished nondurable materials		10.5	12.3	24.0
Materials for processing		58.0	64.9	136.8[b]

[a]*Survey of Current Business*, September 1963.

[b]Includes duplication.

[c]Sum of gross product originating in manufacturing, mining, and public utilities (GNP goods total excludes such utilities' sales to residential users, which are classified as consumer services). Differs from production index values by inclusion of excise taxes and utilities other than electricity and gas, by exclusion of logging, fluid milk, and government-owned manufacturing and utility plants, and because of differences in data sources and methods of estimation.

show how the relative levels and monthly fluctuations of consumer durable goods compare with the business and defense equipment groups and with construction materials.

All six major end-product groups are shown in constant-dollar industrial gross value terms (excluding excise and sales taxes and distribution margins) but are without duplication since only one stage of output is included; they do include, of course, the value of farm products, imported materials, business services, etc. incorporated in those products. Gross values of this type have been compiled for each series in the revised index. The use of gross values as weights to combine series into constant-dollar aggregates provides more useful measures of commodity flows and comparisons with other gross-basis series such as merchandise exports and retail sales.

Before considering the relationship of these more detailed market groupings to the most comparable expenditure series, the behavior of the two major divisions for end products and for materials for processing which were shown in net value-added dollar amounts in Chart 1-a will be reviewed. These series have some characteristics of a monthly input–output measure as is illustrated in Chart 2 which shows their relative movements using indexes on a 1957–59 base plotted on ratio scale chart paper.

MATERIALS AND END PRODUCT RELATIONS

It is a well-established fact that output of industrial materials fluctuates more than output of final products because of changes in business inventories and other influences. It is partly because of this greater instability—which is a cause of instability in incomes, as well as in production—that the direct representation of the series for materials contributes to the analytical value of the monthly production index and its market groupings. Also, under modern technology, the output facilities for steel, cement, chemicals, and other major materials have a much greater capital ratio than those for the production of final goods and services. Consequently, an appreciation of the greater volatility of materials output contributes to a better understanding of changes in fixed investment. A related point which helps account for the temporary over-building of plant capacity is the fact that in periods of expansion 8 per cent or so of materials output has gone into inventory accumulation. The extent of apparent over-building has subsequently been exaggerated by sharply reduced rates of materials output associated with inventory liquidation.

CHART 2

Industrial Production by Two Broad Stages
(seasonally adjusted, 1957–59 = 100)

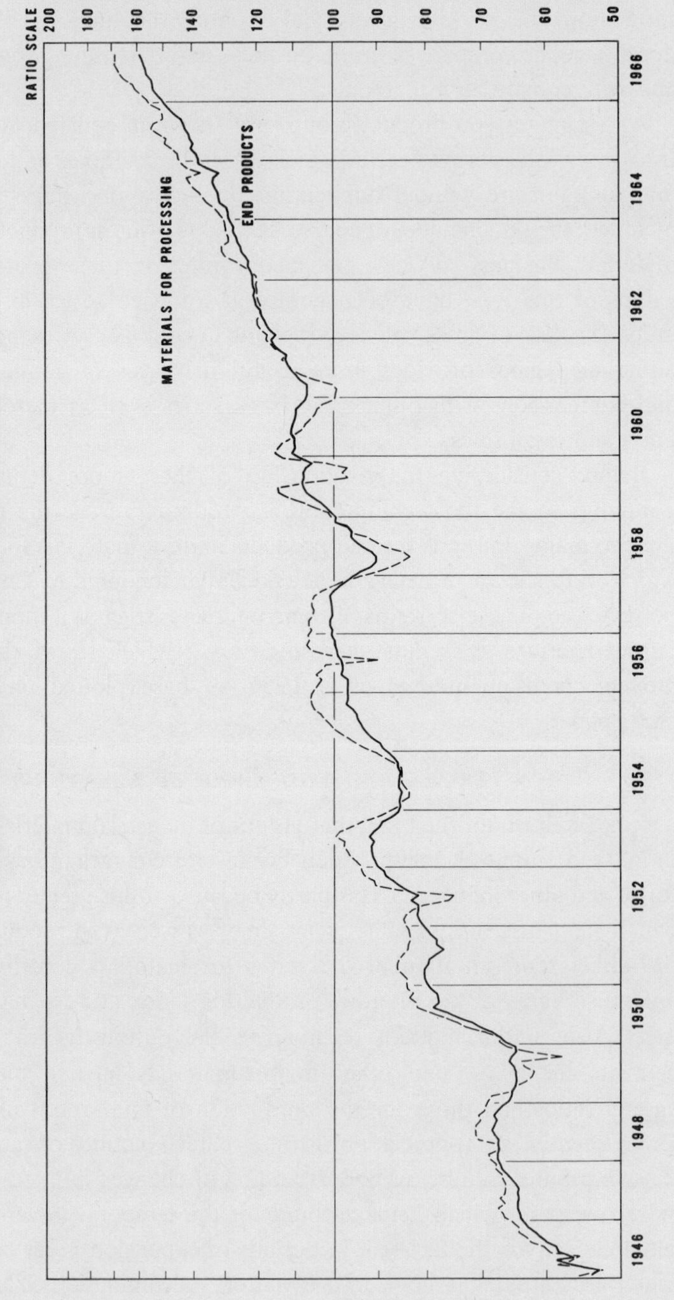

During the post-World War II period there have been three general declines in materials output of about 14 per cent and one shorter but sharper 22 per cent readjustment (apart from the steel strike decreases in 1959, 1956, 1952, and late 1949). These followed varying intervals of major economic expansions which crested in 1948, 1953, 1957, and 1960 with markedly larger rises in output of materials than in final products. The expansions were influenced by inventory, price, and growth expectations which for various reasons were not fully supported by trends in output and sales of final products.

It is beyond the scope of this paper to analyze each of those situations, but a few comments on the earliest and the latest of those periods may indicate some of the advantages of studying changes in the production indexes in relation to other data. Thus, Chart 2 (and a later Chart 10) shows that a major feature of the immediate postwar period was the sharp recovery and expansion in output of materials and final products which contributed to an end of the immediate postwar inflationary trend and the first major postwar economic readjustment beginning in the autumn of 1948.

In the latest period of 1960, too, output of materials, as well as total industrial production, reached relatively advanced levels. The inventory imbalances accompanying the extended steel strike of 1959, in addition to other influences, contributed to the shallow economic downturn in 1960. As may be noted in Charts 1-a and 2, about 9 billion dollars of the drop was in materials output which declined about 14 per cent. There was a sizable decline in output of consumer durable goods, but business equipment fell off only a few per cent (Chart 1-b). In view of these changes in relationship to the relatively sustained levels of final sales of goods and construction (Chart 10), it became apparent by the spring of 1961 that a rapid recovery in production was likely by midyear. Within another year, output of consumer goods and total end products was up to 118 per cent of the 1957–59 average, back on or above the longer-run growth trend of 4 or 5 per cent per year which these production series indicated had been resumed by 1959.

In each of these and other periods of accelerated increases in output of industrial materials it has not been possible to judge in advance the extent of the subsequent production adjustments that might be involved. This is because of various coverage and data problems and structural shifts which occur over time—as, for example, changes in the volume of inventories needed per unit of output or final sale, or in the balance of foreign trade in industrial materials. Another coverage consideration is that while output of some of the more stable final products such as manufactured foods and tobacco products consumes an important volume of manufactured materials—chemicals and paper, for example—some of their major materials are purchased from agricultural sources. Regularly published monthly series measuring the real flow of domestic agricultural products into manufacturing, as well as the previously recommended foreign trade series, would be useful in this context.

Since the differences between the two monthly series in Chart 2 reflect structural changes as well as coverage and weighting influences, in addition to straight data problems, the differential movements need to be interpreted with some caution. For example, it is apparent from the movement of these series and other data that requirements of domestic industrial materials per unit of domestic output of industrial end products fell off after 1956–57. Only relatively large changes that are sustained for some time are likely to suggest important cyclical imbalances in output relationships and provide an advance indicator of changes in the real volume of inventories of materials.

The differences between the two output series may be compared with changes in total materials inventories, wherever held. For this purpose, Department of Commerce data on the current-dollar book value of business inventories have been regrouped, and the results for two new series are shown as total values and monthly changes in Chart 3. The materials series includes all manufacturers' stocks of "materials and supplies" and "work in process" and also the stocks of "finished goods" held by manufacturers of materials such as primary metals and textiles. The finished goods series includes "finished goods" holdings of manufacturers of final products and total distributors' stocks (as revised in the November *Survey of Current Business*). The finished goods series in combination with the materials data, and after various adjustments for coverage and inventory valuation, provide the main basis for compiling the regularly published expenditure series for quarterly nonfarm inventory change shown in the bottom panel.

Differences between the processing materials and end-product output series were calculated monthly, after first making their difference in the base period equal to the change in the special materials inventory grouping in that period. The difference series (published in a chart in "Industrial Production in 1966," *Federal Reserve Bulletin,* January 1967) shows fluctuations generally similar in direction and amount to the series

CHART 3

Nonfarm Inventory Levels and Changes by Stage
(seasonally adjusted, billions of current dollars)

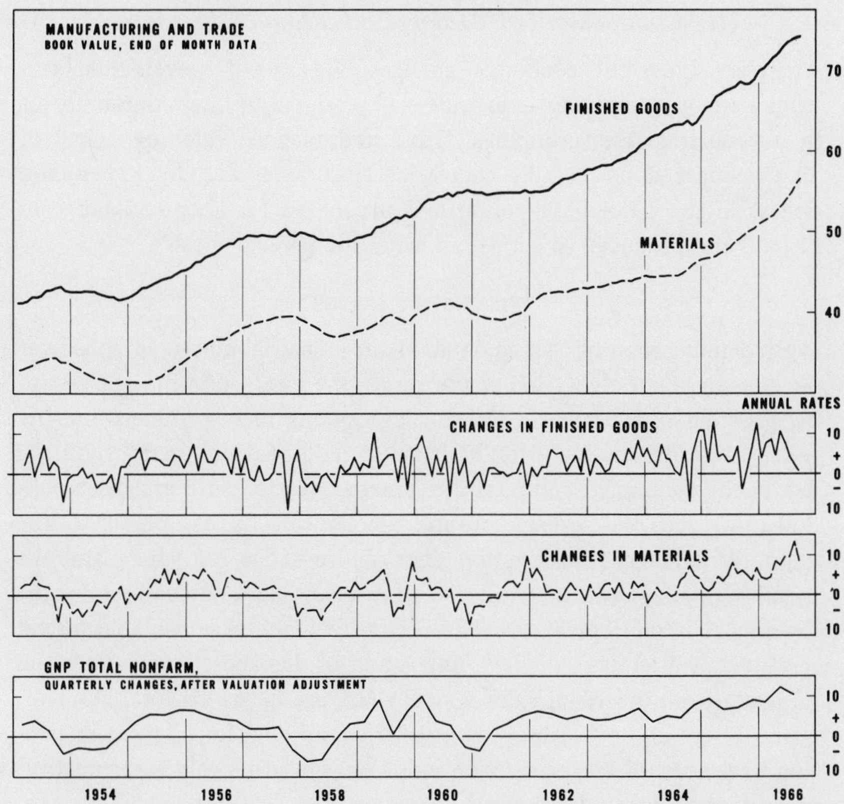

presented in the third panel on Chart 3, but with much less month-to-month variation than the book value series. Since the difference series is apparently less subject to random influences and free of the valuation problems in the book value series, it can provide a useful addition to current information on inventory change.

Over the past eighteen months and in some other periods, the behavior of these and other production data in relation to other information has provided a useful indicator of impending inventory changes supplementary to the usual projections of the nonfarm inventory expenditure series. The results of business surveys of manufacturers' expectations of inventory change, which have figured heavily in the projections of little change or less accumulation in the expenditure series, have proved to be quite wide of the mark.

III. Comparison of Major End Product Measures

Analysis of current economic changes and growth developments is facilitated by combining industrial end products by their durability or by particular market groupings. Gross unduplicated value of output of all consumer goods at the industrial level amounted to 121 billion dollars in the 1958 base period and accounted for about 55 per cent of total end products, as shown above in the preceding table.

CONSUMER GOODS

By defining monthly the fluctuations in industrial output of consumer goods with about eighty individual series, the production market grouping provides a picture of leads and lags among these products and between these products and other parts of industrial production and the rest of the economy. The total consumer goods measure and its breakdown for durable and nondurable goods can be compared to the quarterly personal consumption expenditure series for goods and the monthly retail trade data, with due allowances and qualifications for the differences in concept and scope. The individual series available permit more detailed analysis of the composition of demand changes than can be made from the retail sales series which are based on total store reports. They can be weighted with value-added data for analysis in relation to the rest of the production index or with gross values for analysis in relation to demand measures.

At various times during the postwar period comparisons between output and final sales of consumer goods have provided clues as to changes in relationships at different stages of activity and as to changes in stocks of finished goods held by manufacturers and distributors. On many occasions, however, the differences displayed have been within the limits of the statistical discrepancies involved and subject to relatively large revisions of the final-sales data (and of inventory data for comparison) a year or two or even a decade or two later. The accuracy of inferences regarding final-product inventories might be improved if the margin of error in the advance monthly retail trade series could be reduced.

In addition to the analytical use of the separation for durable and nondurable consumer goods, the available alternative production group-

CHART 4

Fluctuations in Consumer Goods Output, Exclusive of Automotive Products

(seasonally adjusted, 1957–59 = 100)

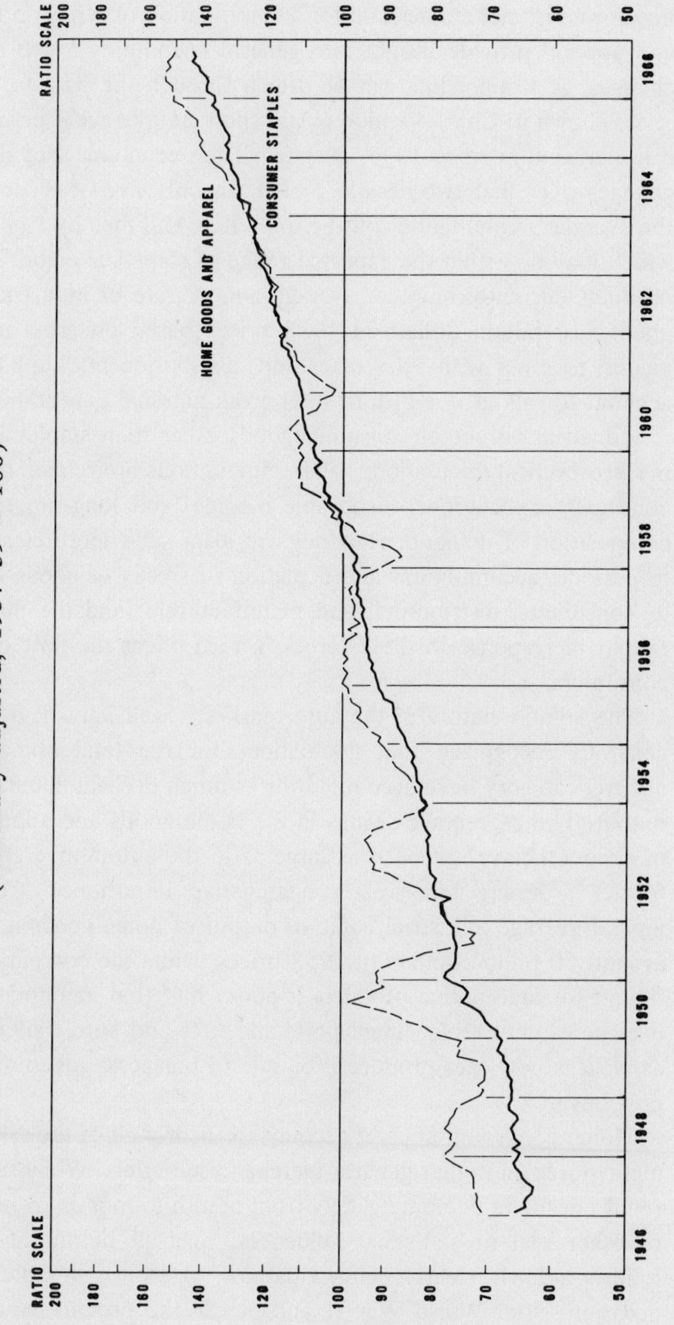

ings for consumer staples and for a combination of series on home goods and apparel provide insight into general economic growth and cyclical changes. A straight line can be drawn through the data for the staples series shown in Chart 4 which would show an average 4 per cent growth rate per annum since 1947, despite all the economic and demographic changes over that two-decade period. In only five of those years were the average annual figures off the trend line, and then by 1 per cent or so, which may be within the expected range of statistical error. These staple products currently have an average annual rate of industrial output of about 110 billion dollars in 1958 prices based on gross unduplicated values; together with sales taxes and distribution markups these values account for about one-fifth of total gross national expenditures.

Industrial output of consumer goods other than staples is subject to marked cyclical fluctuations. These fluctuations are related to changes in consumer expectations, disposable income, and long-run trends in the composition of demand. But they are also—and more closely—related to periodic accumulation and depletion of stocks of goods in the hands of consumers, distributors, and manufacturers; and the fluctuations of output in response to these forces in turn affect the flow of income to consumers.

The volatile nature of the auto market is well known; it is much less generally recognized that fluctuations for the total home goods and apparel category have accounted for as much cyclical fluctuation as auto output. The percentage swings in the home goods and apparel grouping of products have not been as large as in the automotive group, but the former grouping has greater aggregative importance. Currently, the annual average industrial value of output of home goods and apparel is around 50 billion dollars in 1958 prices, while the comparable value of output for automotive products is about half that amount, even though it includes auto replacement parts and tires and auto trailers and boats, as well as new cars produced for sale to business, government, and export buyers.

Home goods and apparel account for nearly all of the sales of department stores and other general merchandise outlets. While their available retail sales data fluctuate widely from month to month, owing to weather or other real or statistical influences, over-all output of these goods follows a fairly clearly defined pattern, as shown in Chart 4. On five occasions after World War II and before the present expansion began in 1961, output of these goods reached advanced levels relative to their longer-run growth trend for periods varying from a year to two prior to a general downward readjustment in the private economy—although in the Korean War period of 1951 the downturn was offset by a massive expansion in federal military activities and outlays.

Historically, it has been possible to compile fairly adequate data from department store-type outlets on monthly changes in their stocks of goods. Since sales of these types of outlets, as well as stocks, have been relatively sensitive to general economic changes, they have been of strategic value in analysis—both along with, and in addition to, changes in the auto market where the count of dealers' new-car stocks (in transit and at outlets at ten-day intervals) is of unparalleled accuracy and importance in the field of inventory data. Moreover, there are available relatively adequate physical quantity monthly data on factory and wholesalers' stocks of major home goods. From these data certain broad relationships of monthly changes in output, stocks, and retail deliveries can be fairly firmly established. In summary, too, this information can be related to the over-all changes in the monthly book value inventory figures for finished goods shown in Chart 3, which as specially grouped for this purpose are largely consumer goods. Some of the divergent movements shown between stocks of these goods and of materials are of considerable importance in appraising current trends. Early in the autumn of 1966 the over-all rate of business inventory accumulation slowed down not because of any basic shift in trends but as a temporary result of a sharp readjustment in auto output and stocks. This was reversed shortly and inventory accumulation of other goods and especially materials continued at a rapid pace in the fourth quarter as their output was at or above earlier advanced levels while final sales in constant dollars had slowed.

It is evident from study of Charts 1-b and 5 that over-all cyclical changes in output of consumer goods have contributed about as much or more to economic fluctuations as have business equipment and construction materials. This does not mean, of course, that consumer goods changes have been of equal significance in initiating expansions and contractions in general business activity, since many other economic and political events have also been involved.

Even allowing for a considerable range of uncertainty in the data, the monthly behavior of the total consumer goods production grouping shown in Chart 5 provides little evidence as to the primacy of income changes—although in 1964 the effects of anticipation and enactment of

CHART 5

Changes in Consumer Goods Output and Incomes Compared
(seasonally adjusted annual rates, in billions of 1958 dollars)

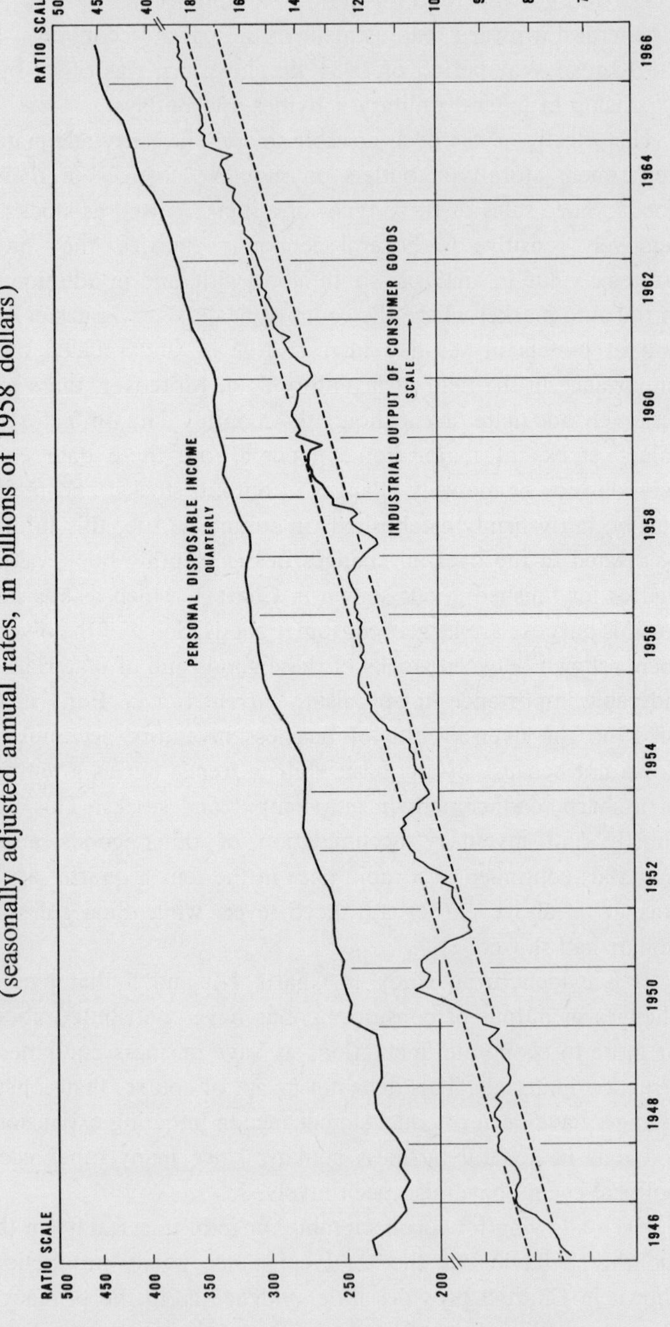

income tax reductions were clearly evident. On the contrary, it seems that in many instances output changes are independent of, or precede, changes in personal income. The comparison in Chart 5 is made with the latest revised quarterly series for personal disposable income in constant dollars (admittedly something of an artifact) against the monthly total industrial output measure for consumer goods which combines the two series shown in Chart 4 for staples and home goods and apparel with the production series for automotive products.

The fact that personal consumption expenditures are intermediate to income and output is of importance in influencing business inventory changes in consumer goods but it is doubtful if their fluctuations can account for all the pattern of differences in Chart 5. The periodic postwar fluctuations of consumer goods output are shown to have been within a range of about 8 per cent of their average growth trend of around 4 per cent per annum. During the 1957–58 period there was a limited interruption when consumer goods output fell below the trend through the 1949, 1951, 1954, and 1960 low points.

With the outbreak of the Korean War in 1950 there were sharp increases in demand for consumer durables; production indexes revealed an expansion in output of these goods of one-half and a subsequent sharp cutback which reflected mainly an accumulation of excessive inventories. Analysis of these developments by stage of activity indicated less upward pressures on prices after the spring of 1951 than might have been anticipated from observing over-all changes in income and expenditure data.

CONSTRUCTION MEASURES

Construction materials is another major industrial end-product grouping for which direct production measures are useful for analytical purposes. As shown above, this grouping had a net value of 11.1 billion dollars in 1958 while its gross weighted value was more than twice as much. In the current revision of the total index, the construction materials category will be more exactly defined by excluding, for example, the glass and paint used for manufacturing purposes. There will still be some overlap of uses in the materials measured. For the purposes of the present comparison of the grouping shown in Charts 1-b and 6, the presently published monthly production index grouping for construction materials has been rebased and multiplied by revised estimates of

CHART 6

Construction Series by Stages Compared
(seasonally adjusted annual rates, in billions of 1958 dollars)

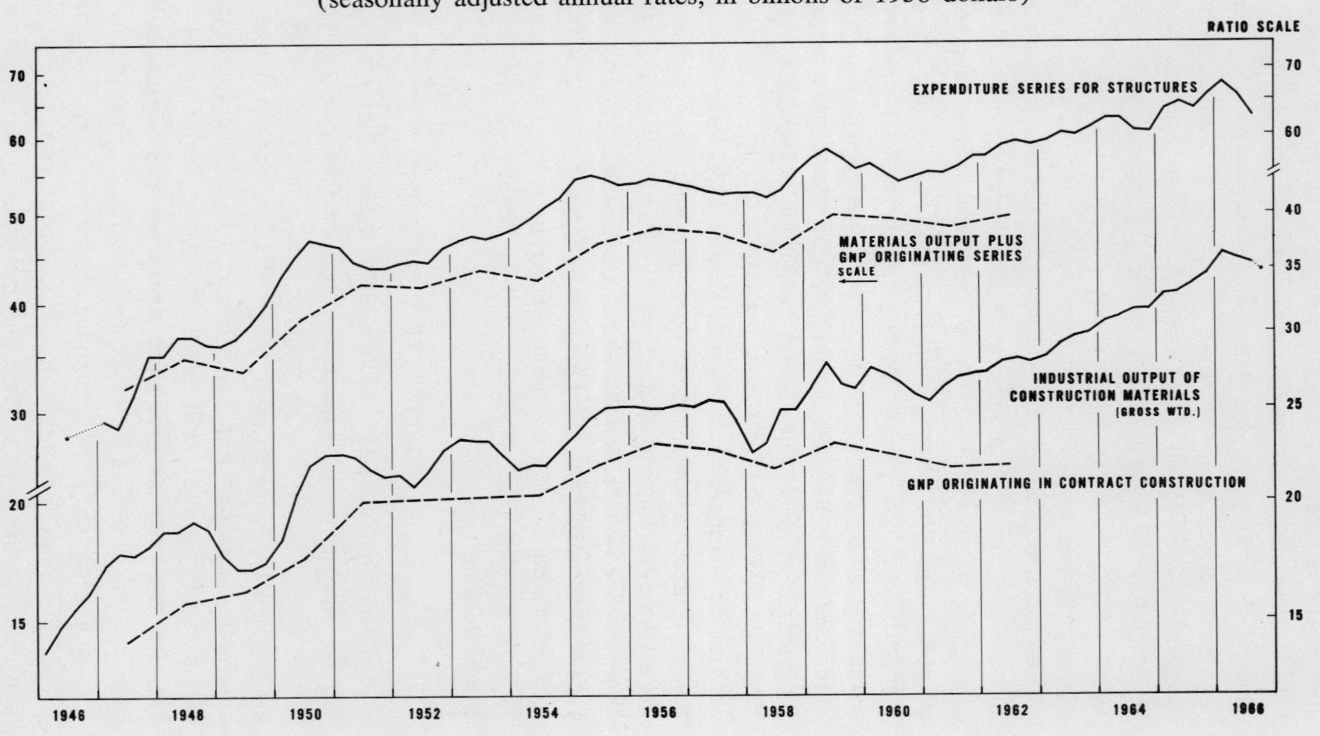

the unduplicated gross value of construction materials output in 1958. The quarterly average results are shown as the third series from the top of Chart 6.

These construction materials are largely incorporated in new structures, additions, and alterations as represented by the constant-dollar expenditure series which is also shown quarterly as the top line on the chart in 1958 prices. The bottom line is an annual series for gross product originating in the contract construction industry, which accounts for a considerable part of the value added to construction materials in building. This series was compiled by the Office of Business Economics and published in the October 1962 and September 1963 *Surveys of Current Business*. This annual gross-product-originating series is combined with annual averages of construction materials output to provide the results shown by the dash line second from the top.

The quarterly and annual differences in movements and levels among these series present some challenging problems for future study in this area. In addition to statistical discrepancies, the difference between the two top lines (ranging from a minus 2 per cent in 1947 to a plus 20 per cent in 1954 and 1962) is in transportation and distribution of materials to the construction site, in force account construction (not included in the gross product originating), and in oil and gas well drilling which is included in the structures but not in the construction materials component of the production index. On the other hand, both the gross product and the construction materials are affected by maintenance and repair activities which are not represented in the expenditure series for new structures.

It is questionable, however, that these differences in scope alone account for the differences among the series; some stem from inventory building and liquidation at industrial and trade establishments, others from federal government purchases for defense-related use and also from the fact that the monthly representation in the expenditure series is based partly on projections rather than directly observed data. A monthly construction activity index based on construction materials output (with some lag), employment or man-hours worked in the contract construction industry adjusted for productivity changes, and rough allowances for distribution and force account construction might throw some light on views based on the presently available construction series concerning the course of construction activity and its response to financial and other influences in periods of economic contraction and expansion. Of special interest in recent years has been the showing that industrial output of construction materials has risen at least 15 per cent more than the expenditure series (and a difference also is shown by the composite output index for construction materials compiled by the Department of Commerce).

EQUIPMENT MEASURES

The production index grouping for equipment is based on the same family of industry statistics that are available for use in comparing other information on commodity output and flows in the industrial sector and that can be systematically related to detailed and comprehensive data at Annual Survey and complete Census intervals. Monthly changes in these establishment-type data can be readily compared to changes in labor, power, and other resource use and compared to changes in industrial capacity and labor-cost trends. The monthly compilation of the indexes permits current comparisons and early judgments of rates of change and turning points. The monthly movements, and especially their quarterly averages, are subject to little revision before and after seasonal adjustment, partly because they are based on a number of individual industry series. These individual series also facilitate more detailed analysis of short-run changes.

The business equipment component of the production index is not designed to provide an exact separation from federal defense products or from other government purchases. In the revised production index this grouping will be improved by a clearer separation from defense-type goods, as well as by the calculation of new subtotals for three types of industrial equipment—manufacturing, electric power, and construction and mining. Separate series will be developed for electronic communications equipment, scientific instruments, and military ships built in private yards, which will all be included in the revised defense and space equipment category. Military aircraft and missile production is included in the presently compiled defense grouping of end products shown on a gross weight basis in Chart 1-b.

A detailed 1954–58 Census-Federal Reserve bench-mark production index for business equipment has been calculated which uses these improved groupings, and it suggests relatively little difference in 1958 compared to 1954. Very preliminary 1963 calculations suggest no significant revision in that year relative to 1958.

The presently published business equipment grouping expressed in 1958 constant dollars is shown in Chart 7 with quarterly average annual rates based on the revised 1958 unduplicated gross value weights. For purposes of this comparison, the production series is also shown, excluding oil and gas well drilling. The third line shows the published expenditure series for private purchases of producers' durable equipment (PDE), while the fourth line shows the same series exclusive of the fixed proportion of new-auto sales estimated as purchased for business use.

The separation provided by PDE for domestic, private purchases of these goods is an important feature for some but not all purposes of economic analysis. Various financial as well as real volume influences

CHART 7

Output Trends in Equipment

(seasonally adjusted annual rates, in billions of 1958 dollars)

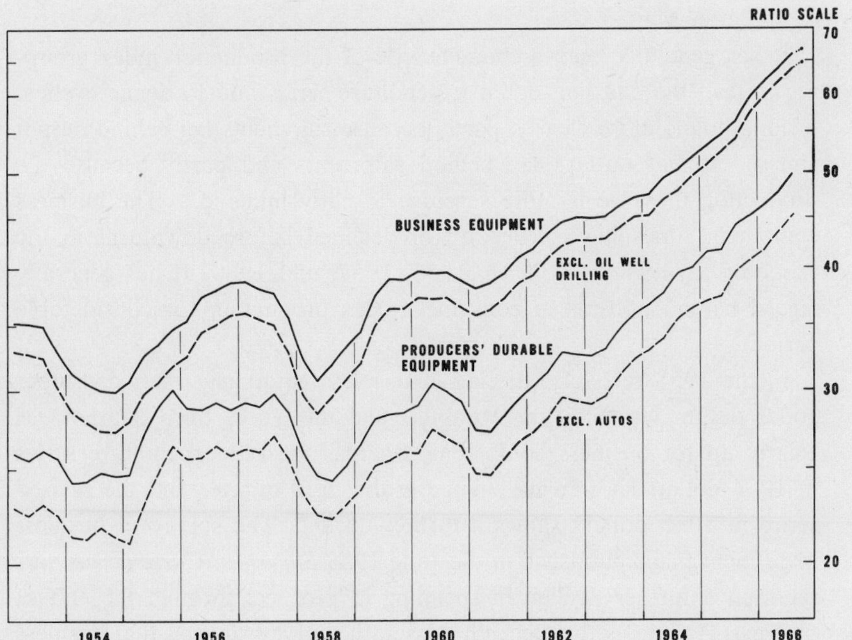

affect capital equipment developments; usually, however, it is difficult to establish systematic relationships based on profits and other financial flows and expectations thereof which apply from one time period to another.

The business equipment measures are roughly comparable in scope with the Census Bureau monthly industry survey data in current dollars for manufacturers' new and unfilled orders, inventories, and shipments of these types of goods. Analysis of changes in these series suggests that new orders tend to precede production changes by four months or so, while changes in inventory holdings of equipment establishments lag about six months after changes in production.

Since business equipment is in the long run an intermediate product, used largely to produce and distribute other industrial commodities, the relationship between measures for business equipment and total industrial production is of interest. Over the entire post-World War II period the index of the ratio of business equipment to total industrial production has fallen to 95 or 90 during cyclical low periods and risen to 105 or 110 during cyclical expansions—until 1966 when it rose above a level of 115 after May.

It has generally been a characteristic of the production index grouping to lead the constant-dollar expenditure series and to define cyclical turning points more clearly, partly because shipments lag behind output and investment outlays lag behind shipments and partly because the production measure is more sensitive to early influences. The business equipment series has levelled off or declined before downturns in the economy as a whole in 1948, 1953, 1957, and 1960. It has generally lagged behind upturns in consumer goods production for considerable periods.

In the 1958 recovery, the lag in business equipment after consumer goods output was only three months and the whole third quarter was clearly up for business equipment, whereas the old expenditure series in 1954 dollars showed no change in the third quarter and the revised series in 1958 dollars shows a further decline. The survey of business investment plans published in the June 1958 *Survey of Current Business* reported a further decline in spending in prospect through the end of the year. As late as the December issue the survey showed that business investment outlays were scheduled in early 1959 to approximate the

1958 average rate. In the period preceding the downturn neither the June nor December 1957 survey provided an advance indication, while activity in the machinery industries began to fall off in the early part of that year. A similar delayed sequence of anticipated and reported events occurred in the 1960–61 readjustment.

The business investment survey results on spending are of a different order than on expectations; and the regularly published results, together with the business equipment index and other data, led to the view that capital goods output was on a continued downtrend during 1954 and expanded only after a boom in autos and housing late in 1954 and in early 1955. The investment expenditure series, which is not charted here, reached its low point in the first quarter of 1955 and subsequently rose steadily to a peak in the third quarter of 1957, reflecting in part rising prices and costs.

In the revised PDE figures, the low point was moved from the fourth quarter of 1954 to the first quarter of the year, before the low for the economy as a whole was reached. A peak was reached in the fourth quarter of 1955 which was not exceeded until 1960, and then by only a slight amount in a single quarter. (Comparison of the bottom line in Chart 7 shows that the expenditure series before the addition of the auto sales data behaves somewhat more like the production series.)

Differences in cyclical patterns shown by the production and the expenditure series reflect partly changes in work in process at establishments manufacturing equipment. Comparison of the monthly finished goods and work-in-process series for the machinery industry suggests that inventory buildups of this type probably contributed to differences of several per cent in the continued business equipment buildup in 1955–57 while the expenditure figures showed little change.

Quarterly movements of current-dollar PDE are derived largely by subtracting estimates of the value of plant construction from figures on total company dollar outlays for new plant and equipment. The construction estimates are from quite unrelated sources. Residual values for PDE are then deflated by price series whose movements and levels may not be wholly appropriate for the deflation process. Other things being similar, the probabilities are greater that more adequate measurement indications may be obtained if they are made as close as possible to the point where the economic activity occurs.

Apparently, a major reason for the upward revision in 1965 of about one-fifth in the PDE series is that it was adjusted directly to Census Annual Survey data up through 1962 for equipment shipments by industrial establishments, adjusted to exclude sales to government agencies and sales for export and with price and other allowances.[5] The production equipment series is largely based in the first instance on monthly reports of man-hours at such establishments adjusted for broad productivity trends, and quantity output data for a few major products such as motor trucks. For equipment production, labor input is generally the most important component of its real value, and use of monthly man-hours has the additional advantage of directly representing work done on items with long production times.

It is sometimes suggested that differences in the concept of capital measured are a cause of differences between the production and expenditure series. Such differences would be reflected in the deflators implicit in the two series but for the intervals measured by the Census-Federal Reserve bench-mark indexes, 1947–54 and 1954–58, there are no significant differences in the deflators for the two series; both of them rely extensively on the equipment series in the BLS wholesale price index.

IV. Comparison of Durable and Nondurable Groupings

Some of the major differences arising from the allocation of goods by type of purchaser in the expenditure series are submerged at the level of totals for durable and nondurable goods. However, changes in the expenditure categories so designated cannot be appropriately compared with production series for durable and nondurable manufacturing partly because the latter groups do not include the mining and farm values represented in final sales of durable and nondurable goods, and because the classification of "durable" goods by combining total two-digit SIC groups embodies some "nondurable" materials and vice versa—for example, glass and metal containers for food products. The comparisons that follow will instead use special durable and nondurable groupings composed of final products of each type combined, with net value-added weights, with new materials groupings. These new materials groupings

[5] Revisions in other components of the goods category of the expenditure series were less as the postwar increase in the total was revised upwards by 6 per cent in August 1965.

approximate those which will be used in the revised production index, organized according to the durability of the products in which they are used.

DURABLE GOODS OUTPUT

While some differences in the behavior of the business equipment and PDE series may be expected because of differences in the scope of the measurements, these are largely submerged in a comparison of total durable goods output series. For this purpose of comparison the expenditure series for constant-dollar final sales of durable goods after adjustment for durable goods inventory change is shown in Chart 8. The industrial output series most comparable is a specially compiled total of durable final products, including consumer durables and business and defense equipment, combined with industrial output of durable materials for processing—all with net value-added weights. Construction materials are excluded from the comparison, except to the extent that the materials series includes some metals that may be used in the manufacture of construction materials and to the extent that the inventory change series includes changes in manufacturers' and distributors' inventories of construction materials. The materials-for-processing series is shown separately at the bottom of the chart. It is generally more volatile than the series for final-product output.

The decline in materials output relative to final products between the mid-1950's and the early 1960's is most noticeable in this durable materials series, which rose only 7 per cent from 1956 to 1962 while final products rose 18 per cent. One of the major elements in this difference was a sharp increase in steel imports while steel exports showed little net change.

The average margin of about one-fourth between the total-production series and the expenditure series reflects mainly the trade and transportation markup for consumer durable goods, but it would also be affected by the level of exports of durable goods relative to imports and, of course, by errors and miscellaneous statistical differences.

In the period since 1953, the production and expenditure series show considerable similarity for most short-run movements but there are differences in some crucial periods. For example, industrial output declines gradually in the first three quarters of 1957 from a fourth quarter 1956 peak, while the expenditure series peaks in the third quarter of 1957.

CHART 8

Durable Goods Output by Broad Stages

(seasonally adjusted annual rates, in billions of 1958 dollars)

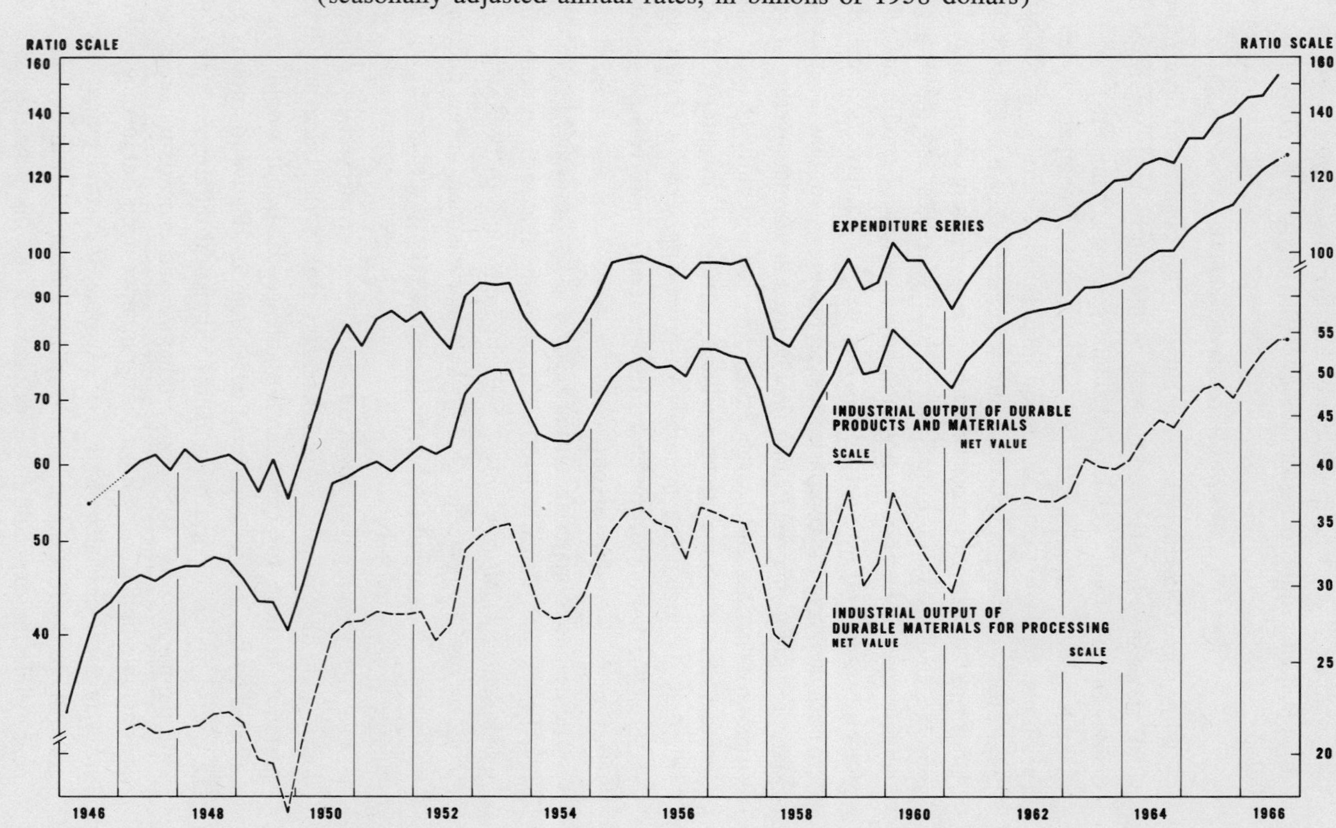

The industrial output series declines further in the third quarter of 1960, whereas the expenditure series shows no change. In both of these cases, the movements reflect differences between the amount and direction of inventory change indicated by the constant-dollar business inventory series and the amount and direction of inventory change indicated by comparison of materials output, final-product output, and final sales.

In the period before 1953, the expenditure series show quarterly reversals so large and frequent, and so different from the movements of the output series, as to raise some questions about the usefulness for analysis of this expenditure series. Part of the problem may lie in the allocation of expenditure series data between durable and nondurable goods, since the nondurable expenditure series to be presented in the next chart often shows offsetting movements.

Differences in seasonal allowance are also involved in some cases but here, too, differences at lower levels are submerged as the relatively high third-quarter figures shown in Chart 7 for PDE in the years 1953–57 are less apparent in Chart 8. In this connection it may be noted that the production indexes are built up from a relatively large number of seasonally adjusted groupings of monthly series.

Both the various similarities and differences involved here suggest that a continuing analysis of detailed monthly measures of production and other data on final sales of durable goods would increase our understanding of cyclical processes and the development of cyclical imbalances. One consideration of major interest is the relative current contribution of changes in government expenditures on resource use. This is a major gap of general interest in economic analysis not directly supplied by the production index measurements. As shown in Chart 1-b, only output of the most specialized federal defense and space equipment can be identified monthly. This equipment has a present valuation of about 20 billion dollars in 1958 prices and is subject to relatively larger changes and longer lead times than the remainder of government outlays. A large part of these other government outlays, of course, is reflected in demands for construction and consumer outlays. Even in the national expenditure accounts, however, it is often a long and uncertain path to trace government appropriations and outlays to their current impact on resources.

NONDURABLE GOODS OUTPUT

While the more volatile durable goods sector requires special consideration, the larger category for nondurable goods has shown changes which are also of concern in judging over-all rates of growth in the economy and the possibility of important fluctuations in inventories and other cyclical influences.

Chart 9 shows the expenditure series for output of nondurable goods in constant 1958 dollars. Below it is shown a broadly comparable production series for nondurable goods at the industrial establishment level exhibiting relatively marked differences from the expenditure series in many quarters. The production measure is the sum, with net value-added weights, of nondurable consumer goods (apparel and staples), nondurable materials, and farm output. The farm output series is based on quarterly averages of a monthly Federal Reserve measure of output of livestock and products and other farm data, adjusted to the annual farm GNP series.

Apart from the differences noted earlier, a substantial portion of the margin between the output and expenditure series represents distribution, including the large volume of services contained in the expenditure series representation for eating and drinking places. As with durable goods, the quarter-to-quarter differences between changes in materials and final products and between changes in final-product production and sales reflect inventory fluctuations, but there are puzzling differences between the reported inventory figures and the inferred movements. From 1947 to 1956, there were a number of quarterly intervals when it would be difficult to relate the inferred output changes for the expenditure series to the production measures—an especially striking difference developed between the two series from the fourth quarter of 1950 to the fourth quarter of 1951. A relatively recent dramatic difference, which figured in the interpretation of the economic situation during last year, occurred in the fourth quarter of 1965, when nondurable goods inventories (revalued and deflated) showed the largest increase since 1952 in spite of an increase in final sales greater than the increase in final-product output.

While the two total series for durable goods show about the same over-all trend from 1953 to date, the expenditure series for nondurables rises about one-tenth less than the production series. Detailed analysis

CHART 9

Nondurable Goods Output by Broad Stages

(seasonally adjusted annual rates, in billions of 1958 dollars)

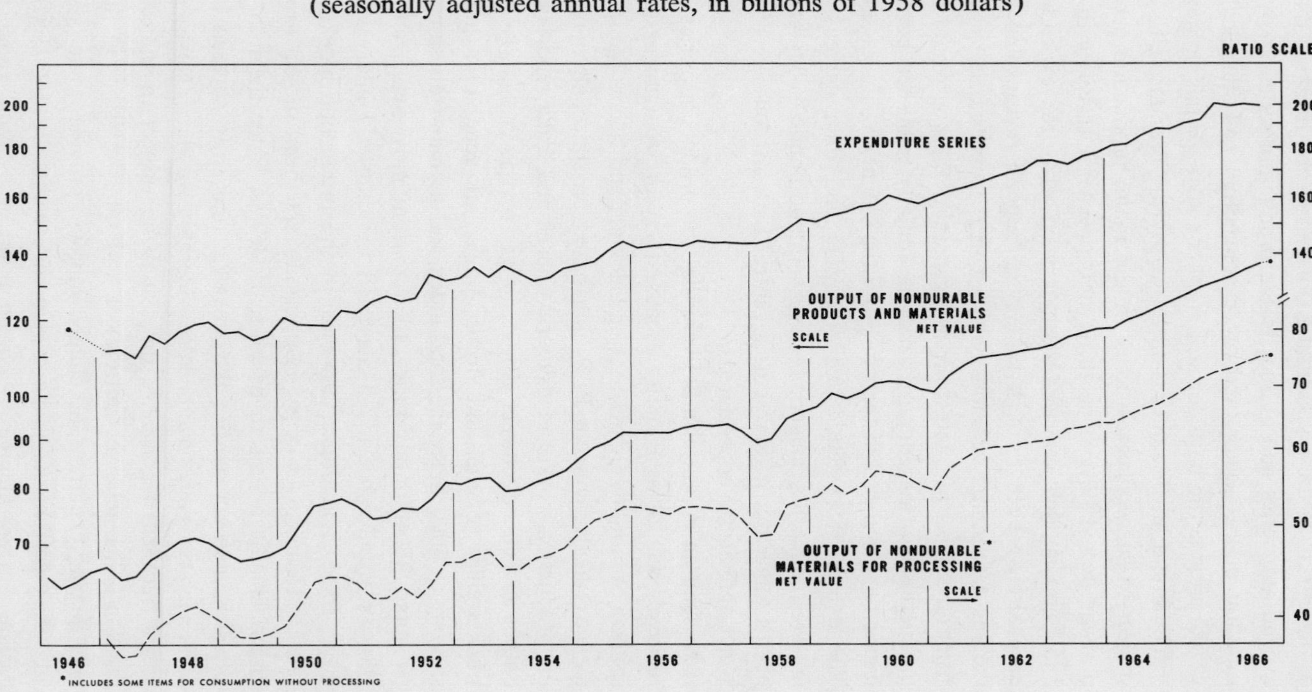

of the effects of the representation of eating and drinking places in the expenditure series and utilities in the production series, the rate of distribution in this sector, and other conceptual and statistical problems would provide the basis for still another paper for this volume.

These and all the other data shown by the present charts have been subject to successive revisions. In the main, production series for the postwar period have gone through two general revisions in 1953 and 1959 and another one is now underway, while the expenditure series have already been through three such general revisions in addition to the regular annual revisions which carry changes back several years. Another subject of interest for this general discussion would be how the production and expenditure series as initially published portrayed economic developments at the time, and the extent of subsequent revisions. The nature of currently available data and their current impact on analysts and policy makers, both private and public, is beyond the scope of this paper but it represents a central part of economic history which is not sufficiently appreciated.

In such an appraisal it is likely that the production series would fare relatively well. This is partly because there are four major independent sources of monthly figures used to calculate and review the index's overall movements—current BLS data based on state employment reports for production worker man-hours, Census and trade reports on product output and manufacturers' shipments and inventory data, rail and motor truck freight volume, and electric power self-generation and industrial sales by utilities. Since the total index and its major divisions are based on about 200 monthly series, their current movements, after seasonal allowance and especially if averaged for quarterly intervals, are fairly firmly fixed. The slopes, however, of the production indexes and their rates of change over longer-run periods have been subject to some large historical adjustments to bench-mark levels. Since the introduction of adjusted man-hour series for areas not currently covered by product data, such revisions have been considerably smaller. Year-to-year movements between bench-mark dates may be subject to somewhat larger revisions. The relatively infrequent and small revisions in the monthly and quarterly pattern of changes shown provide some assurance in analyzing current economic developments and drawing conclusions regarding current changes in consumption and capital goods trends and their relationships to each other, and even in indicated changes in inventories, which have been subject to the largest percentage revisions.

V. In Conclusion

These comparisons of output by stage and by particular markets underscore the value of using commodity flow measures to help illuminate developments in the general economy. One of the most strategic aspects of these studies is the appraisal of the growth of capital goods demands and needs relative to the over-all economy together with the cumulative effects of changes in stocks of goods held by businesses and consumers. The latter are especially difficult to appraise.

A continuing broad summary of major changes in production relations and shifts in business holdings of goods can be provided by examining the kinds of comparison illustrated in the final Chart 10. The main lines of divergence involved here in real terms generally reflect changes in output and business inventories of consumer products and of industrial materials—the latter especially as they may be influenced by fluctuations in equipment production.

Owing to the qualifications already referred to in this paper, not all of the divergences or the similarities in movements shown in Chart 10 should be interpreted as providing measures of output imbalances, or balances, or changes, or lack of changes, in business inventories. It is necessary to allow for inventory shifts in the comparison base period used, which in the most recent period shown for 1960–61 included a rise in business stocks of both materials and final products. Also, part of the larger recent rise in the production series reflects the more rapid growth of the equipment series and its relatively lesser importance in the expenditure measure for final sales of goods; this was also the case in the Korean War period.

Such comparisons do provide, however, a useful framework within which to examine questions of changing output and inventory relations and also to review the matter of statistical consistency which is one of the considerations of this volume. Large sustained changes in industrial production, which now accounts for nearly all of total commodity output and changes in domestic new supplies of goods, relative to the sum of final sales of goods and construction can be expected to be reflected in business inventories. More immediately, large current shifts in the rates

CHART 10

Industrial Production and Final Sales Compared
(seasonally adjusted, four comparison base periods)

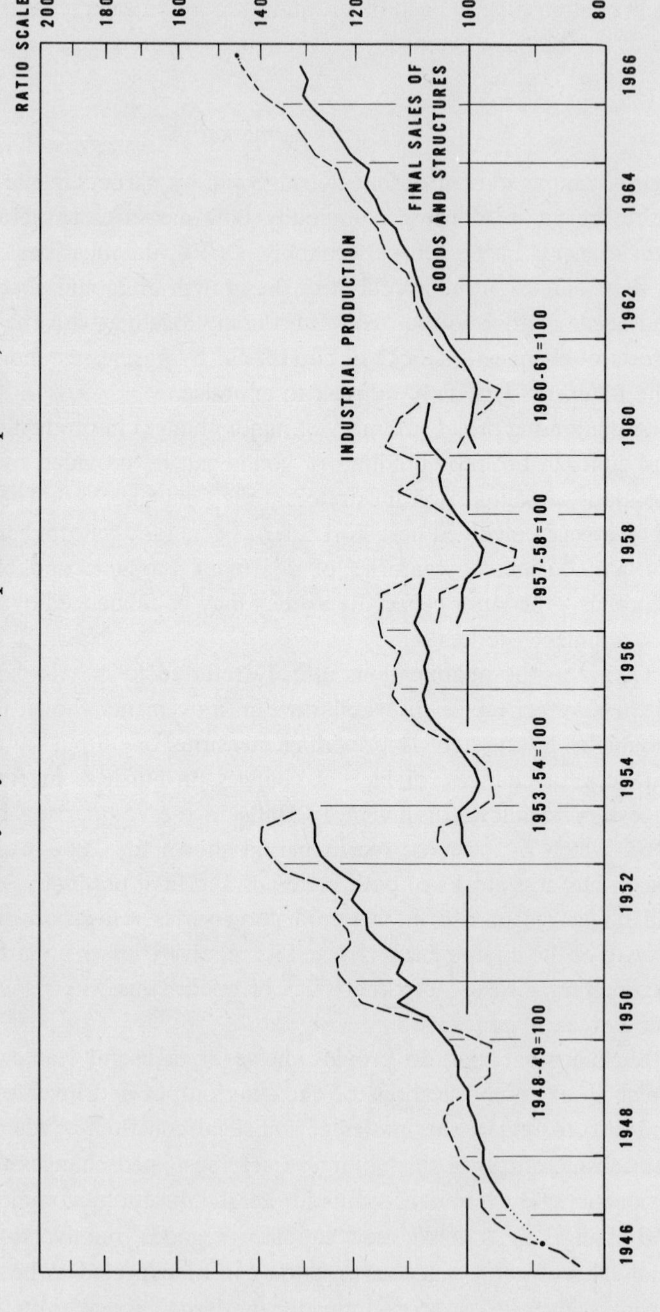

of inventory accumulation or liquidation cannot be expected without marked changes in industrial production or in the real volume of retail purchases. These factors must be taken into consideration in analysis of price developments and the formulation of economic policy.

The production accounts provide only a part of the framework of economic analysis and a whole variety of other economic influences, including institutional and political forces, must be continuously studied to accomplish even the modest objective of describing adequately economic developments, let alone attempting to explain them. It would be a step ahead in both description and explanation, however, if monthly constant-dollar measures were developed for regular publication of farm output, commodity transportation, wholesale and retail distribution, and foreign merchandise trade to complete the system of measures here proposed for the goods and construction sectors of the economy.

COMMENT

MICHAEL D. GODFREY, Princeton University

I frequently find myself critical of economic research on the ground that too little attention is paid to the nature and sources of the data involved in the research. The value of the research ultimately depends on these data. Clearly, however, the Gehman-Motheral paper cannot be criticized on that ground. Instead, I would venture to raise a few questions concerning the economic theory which forms the framework for the results reported here and comment on the potential value of the indicated measures of production in the context of aspects of this theory.

It would seem desirable to justify data operations on the basis of the consistency of these operations with a particular theoretical framework. The choice of theoretical framework is itself partially determined by policy objectives or other considerations. We might consider briefly two extreme objectives in order to indicate the impact that these choices have on the forms of data which we require. First, I will consider the kinds of data required in policy planning for long-term economic growth. Second, I will consider data needs for short-term stabilization policy. Though it is clear that these two categories are interdependent, I will, in general, ignore that interesting fact for purposes of simplicity and brevity of exposition.

If our objective is to determine the long-run growth behavior of the economy we could consider the following simple procedure. We have available a number of time series which we wish to aggregate into one series representing the long-run variation indicated by the original series. Though the actual procedure for doing this will be complicated by considerations of price and structural variations in the economy, we will generally want to perform an aggregation which will smooth out erratic or high frequency variations in the resultant series. We would be willing to pay for this smoothness by accepting relatively slow response to rapid (and usually transient) changes in the original series.

On the other hand, the objective of producing a series which would best represent the variation in the economy for the purposes of stabilization policy will lead to quite a different aggregation procedure. In this case we would require that the aggregate series respond as quickly as possible to any significant variation in the underlying series. Whether the series accurately reflects the trend or long-term variation in the original series would be of relatively minor importance.

Procedures for achieving each of these two objectives are statistically straightforward for linear combinations of the data. The consideration of objectives such as these would both be feasible technically and would bring the development of indexes, such as the measure of industrial production proposed here, into closer contact with the economic uses to which these indexes are put.

Finally, I would like to emphasize that this comment is intended as an encouragement to extend and develop the thorough and obviously valuable work which this paper clearly describes. If more economists demonstrated the concern for, and understanding of, data sources represented here we would all be better off.

COMMENT ON THE GOTTSEGEN-ZIEMER AND GEHMAN-MOTHERAL PAPERS

STANLEY J. SIGEL

The two papers in the present session make substantial contributions to an understanding of the statistical, conceptual, and analytic relationships between the income and product accounts and the index of industrial production. The detailed and searching work and the knowledge revealed in these papers and in the subsequent discussion, as well as in other papers delivered in earlier sessions of this meeting, indicate that the creation of an explicit, detailed, and systematic reconciliation and comparison between these two systems of data (covering both their major aggregates and their various components and alternative concepts and regroupings) should now be possible. Such a task would not necessarily be a simple or an easy one nor one to be undertaken without expert knowledge. But, given the amount of information now available as a basis for such a comparison in the OBE's work on input–output and real product and in the recent work on the index at the Federal Reserve, it is somewhat disappointing that one or more papers presenting such a systematic comparison were not given at this meeting of the Conference.

Although both of the papers in this session contained elements relevant to such a comprehensive comparison, neither of them was specifically directed toward this task; my disappointment is caused thus not by the papers that were presented but by the absence of those which were not and by the circumstance that all of the relevant information for a comprehensive comparison was probably not available soon enough or distributed widely enough to have permitted the preparation of such a comparison.

I gather that I am not the only one who feels the need for these missing background papers. Thus the discussion following the presentation of the two papers indicates that both papers might, in some respects, have been strengthened or made clearer if a satisfactory reconciliation had been available to the authors and to the profession generally. For example, in the discussion it was pointed out that some of the statistical differences between real-product and index measures noted in the Gottsegen-Ziemer paper may have been attributable to industry boundary and classification differences; discussion of the Gehman-Motheral paper revealed that there is some uncertainty and misunderstanding even among the knowledgeable economists at this Conference as to the exact scope of series in the production index system, particularly in relation to series in the income and product system.

The need for an effective comparison between the two sets of data is an obvious one and this is certainly not the first time that someone has mentioned it. And there have, of course, been more than one attempt at statistical comparison of various aspects of the series. But until a satisfactory comparison—that is, one that is sufficiently systematic and comprehensive—is provided, it is worthwhile repeating the suggestion. But anyone who does repeat the suggestion ought also to give at least some rough indications of the form and contents of a comparison that he would consider to be satisfactory.

A comprehensive comparison of the kind I am urging here would contain several elements. It should include comparisons of the aggregate measures and of the individual components and special regroupings of the two systems in terms of detailed examinations of boundaries, weighting, and use and interpretation of data. While there will be many instances where these three major elements of difference will overlap or be inextricably linked, it would be extremely helpful, to me at least, if the comparison could distinguish as sharply as possible among these sources of difference.

With respect to comparison of boundaries, what is probably needed is the construction of a schematic master framework that would be in sufficient detail to encompass the differences between the two systems—in total and in parts—with respect to industry classification and coverage, commodity classification and coverage, final product classification and coverage, identification of value added, the stages of the production and distribution process to which the various measures refer, gross and net characteristics, and, perhaps, choice of unit (i.e., establishment, enterprise, etc.). For purposes of the delineation of boundary differences, the framework on which the respective boundary lines would be drawn could be schematic, that is, it would not be necessary at this stage of the comparison to indicate magnitudes for every cell and for every difference. Indeed, as has been pointed out in the discussion this afternoon, there are no estimates available at the present time for some of the differences; this need not, and should not, be taken as a barrier to making a comprehensive and systematic comparison of boundaries and coverage.

Such a schematic framework for the comparison of boundaries and coverage would probably have a general format not unlike an input–output transactions table. In details, however, it would differ from the present input–output table by whatever additions, deletions, regroupings, and other adjustments might be called for in order to focus on the specific comparisons needed. In particular, the framework might have to have special features to accommodate both industry and commodity boundary comparisons.

The drawing of boundary lines on such a framework would by no means provide all of the important comparisons that have to be made between the two data systems. A separate area of comparison would focus on differences in weighting, on the implications of weighting for the interpretation of what it is the measures are a measure of, and thus for comparisons between particular measures. This analysis of weighting would be done at whatever level of detail is necessary to get to actual operational comparisons. It should cover, of course, not only explicit weighting of production measures but also the implicit weighting produced by the use of particular price indices as deflators.

A third area of comparison would deal with data questions—choice of data, interpretation and evaluation of data, revision and bench-mark practices, the use of direct or indirect measures and other statistical procedures. The data and statistical comparisons should, like the boundary and weighting comparisons, be made at whatever level of detail is operational, that is, at the level where the specific decisions on data and statistical procedures are made.

The distinction between data differences and boundary and weighting differences will in many cases be a fuzzy one. For example, the difference between a gross output series and a net output series may be considered a matter of boundaries and definition, or it may be considered to be a statistical difference with the two series having the same definition but using different data series as proxies for what is being measured. Similarly, the industry classification of particular establishments may differ between two series, even though they use identical industry definitions and intend identical industry boundaries, because of different interpretations of the exact contents of available data or because the raw data available to the two sets of measures contain inconsistent treatments. This would result in differing industry coverage in the two measures, but it obviously can be considered to be either a boundary problem or a data problem. There is, however, no need to agonize over such marginal problems in the classification of differences as long as the paper makes quite explicit what is being compared.

After the boundary, weighting, and statistical comparisons and differences have been systematically sorted out and identified at both a detailed level and at appropriate summary levels, the results can be used—either in the same project or in subsequent analyses—to make the kinds of comparisons and judgments that can be made at present only in less satisfactory and more impressionistic ways. These comparisons might include such things as the comparison of the movements of different series over time, the explanation of any differences between specific series, and the exploration of the implications of these differences for our understanding of what is happening in the economy; the allocation of differences in level and movement as between conceptual and statistical reasons; the better understanding of the conceptual characteristics and differences of various series and thus of their appropriate analytic applications; the confrontation of "accidental" statistical differences (that is, those not basically related to differences in analytic purpose, concept, or fundamental statistical procedure) with a view, hopefully, of reaching agreement on the adoption of the better statistical choices and procedures; the construction of a special purpose index or set of indices to serve as a monthly estimator of real GNP and its major components, etc. Without the firm basis of a comprehensive and systematic comparison, these things can be done only crudely, if at all; the detailed comparison and reconciliation of boundary and definition and concept is thus not an alternative but a prerequisite to working statistical comparisons that themselves must form the background of substantive analysis.

It should be clear that the kind of comparison I am urging would not be an easy task, despite all the information that exists. There are many reasons to believe that it probably can be accomplished most effectively, or maybe only, by those who have the most intimate working knowledge of the details and operations of the two measures. Since it is a tedious task and since those in the best position to do it usually have many other pressing tasks to perform, the risk is great that this particular task may be neglected or given very low priority and that we will have to make-do with cruder comparisons. Undoubtedly work on many of the elements needed for the comparison is already underway. Such work should be continued and strengthened, but it is hoped that serious attention and adequate resources can also be devoted to the kind of systematic and comprehensive approach suggested here.

REPLY

CORNELIA MOTHERAL

In response to the question as to whether we had tried to relate production indexes to production functions: Part of our new annual index program is an attempt to relate production to man-hours and to electric power use, using the latter as a proxy for capital input. In response to Godfrey's question whether electric power was not a better proxy for labor input: That is true in industries where electricity is used only to turn on the lights; but many industries such as primary metals, chemicals, and paper use electric power in conjunction with heavy capital equipment.

In response to questions on problems in market classification: We did have a little more detail than your input–output industries. There are still difficulties, of course, and there were some cats and dogs that were so difficult to classify that we just called them general business supplies. It seemed to us that one of the principal problems was that exports of materials are part of final demand, and it is for this reason that we recommend compilation of special measures for this export category. The other big problem is government purchases, which are not distinguished from consumer and business equipment except in the case of defense and space equipment.

Problems in the Estimation of Industry Output in Current and Constant Dollars in Canada

GORDON J. GARSTON
DAVID A. WORTON
DOMINION BUREAU OF STATISTICS, CANADA

I. Introduction

In May 1963, the Dominion Bureau of Statistics (DBS) published a basic reference paper which embodied the results of a number of years of research and development relating to industry of origin real output measurement.[1] This publication made available production indexes for the entire array of Canadian domestic industries on an annual basis going back to 1935, and on a quarterly basis from the beginning of 1946. It encompassed and supplemented the latest Index of Industrial Production Reference Paper, which had been published in 1959 [2] and which contained both monthly and annual production indexes starting in 1935.[3] The Index of Industrial Production components contained in this latter publication and subsequent supplements were used in the comprehensive industry of origin real domestic product system without further adjustment. Thus the real domestic product industry of origin estimates represented both an extension of the official Index of Industrial Pro-

[1] DBS Occasional Paper, 61-505, *Indexes of Real Domestic Product by Industry of Origin, 1935–61,* Ottawa, 1963.

[2] DBS Occasional Paper, 61-502, *Revised Index of Industrial Production, 1935–1957,* Ottawa, 1959.

[3] A monthly Index of Industrial Production, dating back to January 1919, has been published in Canada since January 1926. For pre-1935 data see DBS publication 61-005, *Monthly Index of Industrial Production,* Annual Supplement, May 1963, Ottawa.

NOTE: The opinions expressed in this paper are the responsibility of the authors alone and do not necessarily represent the official position of the Dominion Bureau of Statistics.

duction and, at the same time, a new dimension of the Canadian system of national accounts. The basic need for such a study can best be demonstrated by a brief review of the historical background of industry of origin production measures in Canada.

The Index of Industrial Production has always been considered a timely and comprehensive coincident measure of economic production; but in the early 1950's it became increasingly clear that a broader setting for the Index was needed that could take account of the growing importance of the service-producing industries in Canada as well as short-term fluctuations of output in such volatile goods-producing industries as agriculture and construction. At the same time, the increasing interest in problems of economic growth and the need for a means of checking the validity of the quarterly estimates of deflated GNE being developed at the time lent a strong stimulus to the refinement of concepts and the improvement of national income and product measures. In particular, concern with the industrial distribution of longer-term production gains underlined the need for industry of origin data in both current dollar and real or constant dollar terms. Prior to the development of official measures of industry real product and for longer-term studies predating them, this need had to be met by private estimates, of which Kuznets' work in the United States is the most notable example.

In Canada, official estimates of current dollar national income by industry first became available in 1951 for the years back to 1926.[4] Although providing detail for eleven industry divisions within the business sector, they suffered from three principal defects from the standpoint of analysis. In the first place, being calculated at the net level, they reflected the errors implicit in the estimation of capital consumption by means of current accounting allowances for depreciation, etc. Secondly, it was not possible to adjust these estimates for price change at the industry level, although this could be done at the aggregate level by shifting to the concept of constant dollar expenditure on gross national product at market prices. Finally, the difficulty of allocating the profits of multiestablishment[5] companies or enterprises between industry divisions inevitably resulted in a distortion of the pattern of income distri-

[4] DBS *National Accounts, Income and Expenditure, 1926–50,* Ottawa, 1951.

[5] An establishment is defined as the smallest unit which is a separate operating entity capable of reporting all elements of basic industrial statistics, p. 8, DBS Catalogue No. 12-501, *Standard Industrial Classification,* Ottawa, 1960.

bution, particularly for the resource industries, manufacturing and trade, between which vertical integration is quite widespread.

In 1958, as part of the historical revision of the national accounts,[6] the Dominion Bureau of Statistics replaced the (net) national income concept in the published industrial distribution by that of gross domestic product at factor cost. This change was primarily an acknowledgement of the practical difficulties of deriving an industrial distribution of national income. However, the problem of finding appropriate deflators for the several kinds of domestic income flows remained and, while the inclusion of capital cost allowances resulted in more meaningful aggregates, the problem of the proper identification of particular factor shares and nonfactor costs by industry still remained.

The income side of the national accounts has continued to consist of a mixture of company and establishment data. Establishment data are used for labor income series while company data are used for such other factor shares and nonfactor costs as profits and capital consumption allowances. The need for a closer integration of financial flow data into the national accounts is a predisposing factor towards a completely company-oriented data framework. This point is presently under active consideration and thus the next historical revision to the national accounts, now being planned, could result in tables derived from company records only. This would involve reassembling establishment-based labor data to form company aggregates, and there would subsequently be no industry aggregates of establishment-based current dollar data in the Canadian national accounts.

Such an eventuality would underline even more emphatically the need for a parallel system of economic statistics, in both current and constant dollar terms, relating to the supply side of domestic production and based on establishment data. The use of the establishment as the basic building block would permit the integration of the system at the aggregate level with national accounts concepts and data and, at the same time, provide the maximum of industrial detail permitted by the Standard Industrial Classification system. The primary purposes of this paper are to describe the progress already achieved in the development of industry

[6] DBS Catalogue No. 13-502, *National Accounts, Income and Expenditure, 1926–56,* Ottawa, 1958. It should be noted that unless otherwise stated the term "national accounts" is used throughout this paper to mean the income and expenditure accounts.

of origin domestic product measures within this framework, to indicate the remaining major conceptual and statistical problems which stand in the way of fully consistent and integrated industry of origin data, and to present some statistical results and analytical uses.

Until the release of the industry of origin real output reference paper, the detailed expenditure aggregates were the only tools for a comprehensive real product analysis. The refinement of detail afforded by the new estimates thus permits a major analytical breakthrough. The simultaneous availability of current dollar value added by factor shares and nonfactor costs, although for the time being a less immediately attainable objective because of the conceptual and data difficulties involved, would reinforce the constant dollar data and extend their range of uses considerably. Cyclical behavior and growth studies of output and intermediate input at various levels of aggregation, the analysis of production shifts, productivity change, etc., could be supplemented by price and factor cost analysis. Furthermore, the use of establishment data would open up the possibility of eventually preparing such studies on a regional basis.[7]

While the conceptual and data requirements for current-dollar estimates of gross domestic product by industry of origin are mostly discussed in this paper in terms of gross output and intermediate input flows, the authors are of the opinion that the ability to separate the resultant value added into its factor and nonfactor cost shares is a prerequisite for exploiting the full potential of industry of origin measurements.

II. The Conceptual Framework for Industry of Origin Estimates

THE BASIC CONCEPT USED

From the beginning of work in Canada on the estimation of production by industry of origin, the goal has been to derive measures which sum to a complete and unduplicated aggregate. Working within the framework of an integrated statistical system, with the national accounts at its center, the requirements of industry disaggregation dictated a domestic

[7] A number of regional allocation problems, such as the treatment of the armed forces and shipping, would have to be solved by convention. Once these were solved, cost considerations would probably confine such comprehensive studies to individual provinces or groups of provinces.

product concept of economic production. In an open economy such as Canada's, the use of a national product concept presents very difficult conceptual and data problems at the individual industry level. This is true of both current and constant dollar data and is a well-known area of difficulty which it does not appear useful to explore further here.

The concept of economic production has been discussed by many writers, for example, Richard Stone, who in one of his earlier papers referred to "bringing into being goods and services (or perhaps more strictly the utilities associated with these) on which members of the community or the community as a whole through its agents sets a valuation." [8]

A definition given in the national accounts publication amplifies this statement somewhat and makes explicit a number of corollary points such as the fact that the creation or loss of economic value can occur in relation to products already in existence:

> While to many people the idea of production is restricted to the activities of a manufacturing plant, a mine, or a farm, to the economist any process that creates value or adds value to already existing goods is production. Thus, while the transformation of raw materials into finished goods is obviously production, the transportation of these goods from the factory to the market where they can be sold is also production. The distribution of these goods through wholesale and retail trade channels to the user adds value since goods which were inaccessible to the user now become available. Production may also occur which has little, if any, connection with goods. The services provided by a physician or lawyer and the entertainment of an actor all create value and are therefore production.
>
> The use of value as a criterion permits comparison of the relative amounts produced by different types of production and provides a measuring rod by means of which heterogeneous goods and services can be added together and expressed as a value total. It also follows that each item entering into the value of production total is capable of being expressed in terms of a quantity component and a price component.[9]

Here the idea of creating value or adding value to existing goods is of paramount importance. Purely physical units of output, whether they be tons of steel produced, the number of automobiles assembled, loaves of bread sold or haircuts given, are all imperfect proxies for the quantity

[8] *The Role of Measurement in Economics,* Cambridge, 1951, pp. 38–39.

[9] DBS Catalogue No. 13-502, p. 105, par. 25–26. In the latter paragraph the authors have taken the liberty of replacing the words "physical volume" with the word "quantity" and for this they take full responsibility.

of output being produced—even though, on practical grounds, these units may have to be used for measurement purposes. Product mix, for instance, implies much more than mere differing physical characteristics within a collection of goods. Also included, and often of much more importance, are mixes in sales conditions such as sales in bulk or by individual item, export sales as opposed to domestic sales, delivered products or products sold separately of transportation, products sold with and without warranties and servicing, etc., all of which can, and generally do, result in identical physical units attracting varying market values.

A further point should be made. The "creation of value" concept restricts the boundary of economic production to the production process itself. No further implication or imputation should be read into the creation of value. For example, a consumer's own time is outside the production process so that, when he switches from home-delivery laundry service to the use of a "coinwash," a portion of economic production has moved outside the scope of measurement. It would be a long step into welfare economics to consider consumer time or participation as an input into economic production.

What then is the most appropriate statistical expression of this concept? The costs encountered in creating economic product values provide an obvious starting point. From this point of view, a net domestic product (or domestic income) concept is by far the best of a number of possible choices. This concept of economic production expresses the market value boundary of the factors of production. Factor costs accumulate in the individual production processes and when summed across industry yield an unduplicated measure of aggregate economic production. In Canada, for practical reasons noted in the next section, capital consumption allowances have been included in the industry measures, thus modifying the concept in its pure form to one of gross domestic product at factor cost. Such a measure, although exaggerated due to the duplication inherent in capital consumption allowances, fully reflects technological change. (The constant dollar form, with which this paper is most concerned, measures current year output in terms of a base-period valuation but current year technology.) The desired gross domestic product at factor cost measure can be derived in current dollar terms either by deducting intermediate goods and services inputs from shipments (adjusted for finished goods and goods-in-process inventory changes) or from accrued operating revenue, or by summing accrued factor incomes earned and nonfactor costs incurred in the production process. The former approach makes operationally possible the calculation of gross domestic product in constant dollars by the double deflation method.

Two other aspects of the basic concept of economic production need to be considered in an industry of origin context. One of these is the question of *when* economic production occurs and the other that of *where* it takes place, i.e., in what industry. The production process is of course a function of the factors of labor, capital, and entrepreneurship working in combination over a period of time which can vary considerably in length, according to the nature of the product. The valuation of the resultant product, however, is determined at a point in time, i.e., when the market transaction takes place.

The cost of intermediate goods and services, and all labor costs (or returns) have to be paid for as they are acquired at prevailing market rates. The returns to entrepreneurship and capital, on the other hand, are determined residually when the product or service is finally sold. An excess of revenue over related costs results in profit but, if the entrepreneur has not gauged the market properly, he may have to pay a penalty in the form of a loss. Such a loss reflects negative factor income (and thus a reduction in net worth), the effect being to offset the production which was contributed by other factors at an earlier stage of the production process.

When measuring production on an annual basis, the actual duration of the production process is of minor importance since the full production cycle is, in most instances, completed within the span of one year. The areas of production which overlap annual periods can be usually ignored, except in cases such as construction where progress payments are made. When the period of measurement is shortened however, as in the case of monthly or quarterly industry measures of economic production, differences of timing between the accrual of factor and intermediate costs and the recognition of the resultant value created attain major significance. Failure to measure sales and inventory change (finished goods and goods-in-process) separately leads to timing errors in an output measure, and the use of indicators based only on quantities produced during a particular period must always be deficient from an economic production point of view.

The basic point is well illustrated in agriculture, where the costs incurred by a farmer in ploughing and seeding have little or no marketable value until the crop is harvested and sold. It is true, of course, that the factor and other inputs used such as hired labor, seed, gasoline, etc., all have economic value as reflected in their purchase price, but whether their combination as reflected in the potential crop will have value or not cannot be determined until the crop is sold. The only value added at the time of marketing is the return to the farmer for assuming risk in combining these inputs, since the value of the inputs themselves would have been previously accounted for and determined by other industries or imports. If, just prior to marketing, the crop is destroyed by accident or act of God then, at that time, all accumulated costs must be written off. In this latter case the factor costs accrued earlier in other industries producing the materials and services used as well as accrued labor and other costs incurred by the farmer are nullified by a negative entry in farm net income. In this case, the production of earlier time periods was destroyed in a later time period. Such additions to economic production in one time period and deductions from economic production in a later time period are completely consistent with the concept of economic production described earlier.

The other question of *where* economic production actually originates raises a number of very basic problems requiring more extensive treatment than is possible within the scope of this paper. It may be noted, however, that it makes a substantial difference to industry of origin measures for factor income and capital consumption allowances to be accrued to "using" industries rather than "owning" industries in cases where the use and ownership of assets are not synonymous. It can be argued that it is desirable that the "owning" industry concept be followed for industry of origin economic production measurement purposes, although the "using" industry concept would clearly be very useful for many purposes. The choice of concept here directly affects the industrial origin of such important items as capital consumption allowances, net rents, and interest. In the case of capital consumption allowances, for example, it is not normally possible for a using industry to report these allowances unless it is also the owning industry. What is needed to clarify these issues is a reexamination of basic concepts relating to the industrial origin and definition of factor income. It seems to us that gross interest on loaned capital and rent payments on rented assets should be considered nonfactor incomes if industry of origin output measures are to be as useful and meaningful throughout the industrial structure as they might be. This point is further elaborated in the section dealing with "Some Major Conceptual Problems."

FACTOR COST VS. MARKET PRICE VALUATION

As noted earlier, the Canadian industry of origin approach to an aggregate measure of economic production utilizes the gross domestic product at factor cost concept. This is in accordance with the United Nations Statistical Office's preliminary recommendations for the revision of the System of National Accounts (SNA), although market price is considered by that office to be the most basic measure.[10] A net domestic product at factor cost[11] approach is also suggested as part of the production system. Wherever industry of origin estimates are required for purposes of industrial structure analysis, or are to be related to other macroeconomic aggregates such as labor and capital inputs, the factor cost approach is favored. As will be elaborated later, we believe that the factor cost approach facilitates the preparation of a broad range of naturally consistent output and input measures classified by industry of origin. Such a range of measures should be capable of reconciliation with the national accounts at the aggregate level, but the component detail should be free of the distorting effects of unevenly applied indirect taxes and excluded subsidies. As noted earlier, the authors believe that the net domestic product at factor cost concept provides the best conceptual approach to industry analyses.

Demand analysis requires that market prices be used because it is these which determine the quantities of consumption and in turn affect the quantities of factors demanded. However, market prices are largely irrelevant to the broad class of problems relating to the contribution of the different factors, changes of efficiency in their use, etc.

Again, the difficulty of deciding whether indirect taxes originate with purchasing industries or selling industries obscures the meaning of the market price concept of gross domestic product by industry of origin, so that there are both practical and conceptual grounds for favoring the use of a factor cost concept when dealing with the supply side of economic production.

[10] See United Nations Statistical Commission Report, E/CN.3/345, p. 77, and Annex II, The Standard Tables, June 1966.

[11] Also recommended by the UN Statistical Office. See United Nations Statistical Commission Report, E/CN.3/345, p. 78.

In reconciling expenditure and production measures at the aggregate level, it is conceptually clearer, and more accurate statistically, to remove indirect taxes in constant dollars from the constant dollar GNE detailed components than to add indirect taxes to, and subtract subsidies from, the various products of each industry. An analysis of expenditure in terms of industrial source is in no way facilitated by industry measures at market prices if these measures have in them an unknown amount of distortion introduced by arbitrary decisions relating to the industrial origin of certain indirect taxes. An analysis of the industrial source of final products based on factor cost is free of this distortion and serves the purpose as well if not better.

The census and annual survey sales or shipments data, on which the DBS industry of origin real output estimates are based, have traditionally excluded indirect taxes levied on the final products of each industry but have included subsidy receipts as, for instance, in agriculture, gold mines, railways, and feed mills. At the same time, where intermediate input data such as materials, fuel, and electricity have been collected, the valuation boundary has always included all indirect taxes levied, and excluded all subsidies paid. Where census value added has been calculated from these data, it has contained some indirect taxes levied on the industry's assets, both tangible and intangible. An estimate of the magnitude of these residual indirect taxes was made for the year 1949 using 1949 input–output table worksheets, and their relationship with total indirect taxes is shown in the following table:

It may be seen from Table 1 that indirect taxes normally included in census value-added data comprised, in 1949, about 32 per cent of total indirect taxes and about 4 per cent of GDP at factor cost. Indirect taxes originating in manufacturing accounted for 53 per cent of the all-industry total, but only 79 million dollars, or 8 per cent of the manufacturing total of 991 million dollars, could be identified with census value added. In terms of GDP at factor cost originating in manufacturing this amounted to only 2 per cent.

Property taxes represent the major indirect tax component of census value added and in Table 2 the industrial distribution of these taxes is shown. It is interesting to note that the bulk (58 per cent) of property taxes originates with the real estate "industry" which includes the rent imputations on housing and government buildings.

These two tables and the following comments help to appraise possible

TABLE 1

Indirect Taxes Included in Census Value-Added Data Compared With Total Indirect Taxes in 1949

Type of Indirect Tax	All Industries		Manufacturing	
	$ Million	%	$ Million	%
Miscellaneous federal tax	16.0	0.8	0.4	–
Corporation tax[a]	21.0	1.1	6.8	0.7
Public domain tax	39.9	2.1	–	–
License fees and permits	37.0	2.0	4.2	0.4
Motor vehicle license fees and permits	36.0	1.9	5.0	0.5
Miscellaneous provincial and municipal taxes	76.0	4.0	10.5	1.1
Subtotal	225.9	12.0	26.9	2.7
Real and personal property tax	374.0	19.8	52.4	5.3
Indirect taxes included in Census value added	599.9	31.8	79.3	8.0
Total indirect taxes, (all types)	1,885.0	100.0	991.0	100.0
Gross domestic product at factor cost, 1949	14,885.0[b]		4,191.5	
Gross domestic product at market prices, 1949	16,693.0[bc]			

[a]Tax on paid up capital and place of business.

[b]Source: *National Accounts, Income and Expenditure, 1926–1956,* Table 4, p. 35.

[c]Consists of gross domestic product at factor cost (14,885.0), plus total indirect taxes (1,885.0), and less subsidies (77.0).

TABLE 2

Incidence of Real and Personal Property Tax, by Industry, 1949

Industry	$ Million	%
Agriculture	29.0	7.7
Mining	1.6	0.4
Manufacturing (including repair establishments)	52.4	14.0
Construction	3.9	1.0
Transportation	9.6	2.6
Storage	0.4	0.1
Communication	3.4	0.9
Electric power and gas utilities	3.5	0.9
Wholesale trade	2.1	0.6
Retail trade	24.0	6.4
Finance, insurance, real estate	239.1	63.8
(Real estate)	(217.8)	(58.1)
Community, recreation, business and personal service	6.0	1.6
Total	374.0	100.0

distortion in the industry of origin annual measures due to residual indirect taxes. In the over-all real gross domestic product framework the census value added concept has been successfully measured in industries accounting for 30 per cent (within manufacturing 12 per cent) of aggregate GDP at factor cost. Labor input measures are used for about 15 per cent and single item industry projectors for another 5 per cent of coverage. Thus about 50 per cent of GDP originating is, for the most part, free of the distorting influence of indirect taxes and can be said to be on a factor cost basis of valuation. With improvements now under way in price index and intermediate input surveys we believe that about 60 per cent of GDP can be covered by measures based on value added within three to four years' time.

The presently remaining 50 per cent of coverage is mainly represented by the gross output concept, measured for the most part by deflated sales or shipments (adjusted for inventory change where necessary). This level of valuation includes all indirect taxes paid on intermediate input, plus all indirect taxes levied on the industry's assets or privileges, but it excludes sales and excise taxes levied at the sales or shipments boundary as well as subsidies paid on intermediate inputs used. Individual industry projectors of the gross output type are thus free of distortion due to indirect taxes or subsidies only to the extent that all these taxes and subsidies were proportional to gross output unit values in the base year, or that the industry's output consisted of only one product, or the product distribution remains constant.

It is unnecessary to know all the indirect taxes paid by each industry to obtain factor cost values unless one starts with a gross value that includes all indirect taxes levied on that industry. Canada's measures would, of course, be improved if that portion of indirect taxes levied on assets or privileges were collected on a regular survey basis and could be properly deflated and removed from each industry's projector. We believe that this could be done without introducing significant error into the net measures. The base for such taxes is relatively stable and it would be possible to deflate property taxes by moving them on real capital stocks or by the use of specially constructed price indexes relating to property taxes. Of course, if a gross output projector must be used, or even an intermediate input projector, it is clear that such a projector will be questionable on more serious grounds than those of its indirect tax content. But, in the double deflation approach, it is unnecessary to know the indirect tax content of intermediate input.

In Canada, the problems of assigning indirect taxes to (and excluding subsidies from) particular products within an industry are virtually impossible to overcome without knowledge of the use to which a product is to be put. Depending on its end use, a product may be relatively free of indirect taxes (materials or products used in further processing, and essential consumer goods such as bread, for example), or it may attract additional indirect taxes (cigarettes and liquor, and building materials sold as such to persons, for example). Even in normally taxable end uses, sales may be made without a tax being levied, as for example when the federal government purchases the product. Records of the use of the individual products of an industry are not generally available from producers nor easily estimated. Thus, even if it were desirable to build an industry of origin market value system, it would not seem to be feasible in Canada.

DOMESTIC VS. NATIONAL PRODUCT

As noted earlier, the industry of origin studies have been confined to a gross domestic product at factor cost concept. Thus the economic production measured is that produced by industries located within the geographical boundaries of Canada.[12] The term "domestic" differs from the term "national" as used for national accounting purposes by excluding production in foreign countries accruing to Canadian owners residing in Canada, and including all production taking place within the boundaries of Canada, regardless of the ownership of the means of production. The domestic concept flows naturally out of the basic industrial data while the national concept requires that a number of adjustments be made. To adjust the domestic measure of production (GDP) to a national measure (GNP), it is necessary to deduct not only interest and dividends and certain labor income but also depreciation and unremitted profits where applicable, which accrue to nonresident owners of capital located within the geographical boundaries of Canada and to add these same items accruing to Canadian owners of foreign assets. Such additions and deductions can only be estimated satisfactorily on an aggregate basis. Corresponding industry adjustments are frustrated by both practical and conceptual difficulties.

Table 3 shows the adjustments needed to reconcile GNP at market prices with GDP at factor cost in 1949.[13] Table 4 illustrates a reconciliation in constant dollar terms between the industry of origin GDP results and the deflated expenditure on GDP. The basic approach used in this reconciliation is that of deflating the current dollar indirect tax content of final expenditure category market values using input–output relationships.[14] The approach followed in previous studies,[15] in which

[12] There are a number of exceptions to this general rule. In the case of shipping and airlines, the services of Canadian-flag carriers are covered regardless of where the service occurred. On the other hand, the service of foreign-registered ships and aircraft are excluded even though the service performed occurred in Canadian waters or in Canadian skies. Another exception is the case of the armed forces and diplomatic services. Canadian forces and diplomatic personnel stationed abroad are included in domestic product while the personnel of foreign countries stationed in Canada are excluded.

[13] Both tables 3 and 4 are adapted from *Indexes of Real Domestic Product by Industry of Origin, 1935–61,* Appendix D, "Problems in the Reconciliation of Real Gross Domestic Product at Factor Cost with Constant Dollar Expenditure on Gross National Product at Market Prices."

[14] The technique used is described in Appendix D, *Ibid.,* pp. 135–144. As noted earlier in this paper certain indirect taxes such as property taxes should be de-

TABLE 3

Relation Between Gross National Product at Market Prices and Gross Domestic Product at Factor Cost, Canada, 1949
(million dollars)

	1949
Gross national product at market prices	16,343
Minus:	
Residual error of estimate	-43
Indirect taxes less subsidies	1,808
Income received from nonresidents	83
Plus:	
Income paid to nonresidents	390
Equals:	
Gross domestic product at factor cost	14,885

the industry of origin studies were placed on a GDP at market price basis, has been discarded due to the fact that the allocation of indirect taxes to industries and to industry product detail is both too arbitrary and too difficult.

NET VS. GROSS DOMESTIC PRODUCT

Although it would be desirable for conceptual and other reasons to develop industry measures that are net of capital consumption allowances, it has not yet been possible to do so because of the practical difficulties encountered in isolating these allowances. Current dollar capital cost allowance data are available from taxation records, but these are usually calculated with a view to minimizing taxable income and do not necessarily reflect cost expiration even in the conventional account-

---

flated by moving them on such series as real capital stocks rather than the gross or net output of industries.

[15] One such study was discussed in an earlier paper to this Conference: V. R. Berlinguette and F. H. Leacy, *The Estimation of Real Domestic Product by Final Expenditure Categories and by Industry of Origin in Canada.* See *Output, Input, and Productivity Measurement,* Studies in Income and Wealth 25, Princeton for NBER, 1961, pp. 214–216.

TABLE 4

Gross Domestic Product at Factor Cost in Constant (1949) Dollars, 1953 and 1954
(million dollars)

Industry approach	1953	1954	Expenditure approach	1953	1954
1. Index of gross domestic product at factor cost, 1949 = 100	(127.4)	(124.7)	1. Expenditure on gross national product at market prices	20,794	20,186
			2. Minus: Residual error of estimate[a]	-117	-11
			3. Interest and dividend receipts from nonresidents	-151	-135
			4. Plus: Interest and dividend payments to nonresidents	360	381
			5. Expenditure on gross domestic product at market prices	21,120	20,421
			6. Minus: Constant–dollar indirect taxes less subsidies	2,130	-2,119
2. Gross domestic product at factor cost (before statistical difference)[b]	18,963	18,562	7. Expenditure on gross domestic product at factor cost (before statistical difference)	18,990	18,302
3. Statistical difference[c]	13	-130	8. Statistical difference[c]	-14	130
4. Gross domestic product at factor cost	18,976	18,432	9. Expenditure on gross domestic product at factor cost	18,976	18,432

[a]As per Table 5, *National Accounts, Income and Expenditure, 1926–1956*. This is the current value national accounts residual error of estimate, expressed in constant (1949) dollars.

[b]These estimates have been obtained by converting the indexes of gross domestic product at factor cost to constant dollars, using $14,885 millions as the estimate of gross domestic product at factor cost for the year 1949.

[c]This is the statistical difference between the two estimates of gross domestic product at factor cost, in constant dollars, and should not be confused with item 2 of the expenditure approach.

ing sense. Further, capital consumption allowances are so far generally available on a company basis only and not on the more desirable establishment basis. These source records are far from adequate in providing data corresponding to the required economic concept of capital consumption allowances for industry of origin studies. It is hoped that the research program underway in DBS on the preparation of estimates of constant dollar capital formation, capital stock, and capital consumption allowances by industry using the "perpetual inventory" method will eventually permit the needed refinement of the real GDP industry measures.[16]

It should be noted that, when this refinement is achieved, real net domestic product at factor cost can be isolated. In our view this is the conceptually desirable level of valuation for supply-side analysis. Of course, factor cost and market price valuation (of the factors of production) are identical at this stage.

COMMERCIAL VS. NONCOMMERCIAL PRODUCTION

In the Canadian industry of origin estimates, a rough split has been made between industries that operate for gain and those that do not. In general, those production units that are classified in the national accounts to the business sector are included in the commercial group of industries, while those classified to the personal and government sectors are included in the noncommerical group. Commercial industries both sell their products and purchase their intermediate inputs in the market; thus the basic data are generally available from which current- and constant-dollar net output can be determined.

Noncommercial industries do not operate primarily for the purpose of making a gain. Examples are charitable organizations, public schools, and hospitals. Some noncommercial establishments do charge the user for their services, but this charge usually falls short of covering expenses and may not be related to the specific service rendered in each case. Establishments classified to the public administration and defense industries do not operate for gain and are included with the noncommercial group of industries.

[16] The results of this program to date are shown in DBS Occasional Papers 13-522, *Fixed Capital Flows and Stock, Manufacturing, Canada, 1926–60* (*Methodology*) and 13-523, *Fixed Capital Flows and Stock, Manufacturing, Canada, 1926–60* (*Statistical Supplement*), Ottawa, 1967.

Institutions in the personal sector and in the government sector (such as municipal schools) have no transactions which uniquely define the cost to the user of the individual service being produced. They do, of course, have records of labor costs, some purchased goods and services, and some capital consumption allowances which permit the derivation of current dollar aggregates for national accounting purposes and industry of origin estimation. But any attempt to measure output in constant dollar terms founders on the lack of meaningful product detail. A decision could possibly be made as to what the products are, but the problem of deriving an appropriate weighting pattern would still remain. Attempts to do so in terms of relative base-period costs could not be considered satisfactory because there is no way of knowing how well these would parallel the judgment on the use of primary and other inputs which only the market place can render. Thus, since output is not evaluated, it cannot be properly measured, and a cost convention has to be used which necessarily has a limited meaning.

In Canada, the industry of origin real output measures for noncommercial industries follow the concepts laid down for the current-dollar national accounts series. In the latter, the contribution to gross domestic product of public administration and defense and most other noncommercial industries is measured by salaries, wages, and supplementary labor income. In a few cases such as public hospitals, labor costs are supplemented by depreciation charges. In the deflated final expenditure categories approach, these primary costs are supplemented by the deflated value of all purchased materials and services. In the industry of origin approach, the latter are not included since to do so would cause duplication, such inputs being measured as the products of other industries.

The procedure of measuring the real output of public administration and defense and other noncommercial industries by deflated labor costs leaves much to be desired but seems preferable to presently available alternatives. However, the importance of developing useful output and efficiency measures for these industries is becoming increasingly recognized by governments and others. In turn, this is leading to improved data on program-costing and eventually might well permit some breakthrough in output measurement for these industries.

IMPUTATIONS AND OTHER PROBLEMS RELATING TO PRODUCTION BOUNDARIES

The industry of origin GDP estimates are designed to cover all the industries specified in the Canadian Standard Industrial Classification Manual.[17] In addition, they encompass extensions made for purposes of the Canadian System of National Accounts.[18] These extensions take the form of imputations of a market value to a good or service that does not pass through normal market channels but which does have a reasonable market counterpart, as for example farm income in kind.

A major imputation is made in respect of owner-occupied houses, on the assumption that home owners are in fact business units, renting houses to themselves. This convention serves to make production accruing from the use of residential real estate invariant to ownership, and thus differs from the treatment of other consumer durables such as cars. The present Canadian industry of origin real output measures follow the conventions of the national accounts and include imputed rents in a special real estate (rents) industry, although it might be considered desirable to eliminate this imputation for purposes of industry of origin output and productivity studies because of the difficulty of isolating labor income or input into this "rents industry."

SOME MAJOR CONCEPTUAL PROBLEMS

Public Administration and Defense

There is probably no single industry that has given rise to more theoretical discussion among national accountants than public administration and defense. This results from the fact that its products are not sold on the market. Admittedly less than perfect conventions have been set up to evaluate the goods and services provided by the public administration and defense industries in Western countries. National accounting practice treats production in these industries in the same way as it treats households, the outputs of the various goods and services provided being valued at cost, i.e., in terms of salaries and wages paid and/or the cost of the goods and services purchased, and the economic process covered is deemed to have ended at this point.

[17] *Standard Industrial Classification Manual,* Ottawa, 1948, and as revised in DBS Occasional Paper No. 12-501, 1960.

[18] For the importance of these imputations see *National Accounts Income and Expenditure, 1926–56,* Table 49 and accompanying text.

Thus, this approach to the valuation of the goods and services provided by the public administration and defense industries tacitly assumes that they are provided collectively. No residual rent is created by government activities.

This approach has been challenged in recent years. It is suggested that national income or national product can, on the one hand, be taken to reflect an evaluation of existing output, for the purpose of making comparisons of welfare among communities and through time. On the other hand, it can be taken to measure the value of potential output that might be produced with existing inputs of resources.[19] From both points of view, the present treatment of government is unsatisfactory. Kuznets, for instance, has argued that, in order to measure "welfare," items of expenditure that are not in themselves final consumption or investment should be excluded.[20] Thus, on this line of reasoning, "environmental outputs," which make private production possible, constitute duplication since they are already reflected in the value of final output for the business sector. Only the value of those publicly provided goods which have counterparts in the business sector should be counted as government production.

Apart from the difficulty of drawing the dividing line between such intermediate and final public goods and services, the inconsistency of adding the value of public goods at cost to private goods at market prices remains. Clearly a welfare connotation requires that national product be valued at market price and, as Forte and Buchanan have demonstrated, current procedures of measurement can only result in a mixture of welfare and opportunity cost valuation of the total national income or output.

Those who consider the public administration and defense industry as a producer of goods and services find the present method of measuring government output inadequate. It is argued that national income statistics can be reduced to one basic measurable total of the end product of business and government which would then be invariant to institutional changes. The advocates of this concept propose an imputation for the value of services of government assets. An imputation for gov-

[19] For a summary of this view see F. Forte and J. M. Buchanan, "The Evaluation of Public Services," *Journal of Political Economy,* April 1961, p. 107.

[20] See "On the Valuation of Social Income—Reflections on Professor Hicks' Article," *Economica,* February–May 1948.

ernment-used property, analogous to private property such as rentals (both gross and net) and with due regard for expenses incurred, depreciation, etc., has been made in Canada. However, for such government assets as roads and canals, it is impossible to assess a realistic market value based on returns. Colm proposes, for instance, that the imputation should include the application of some fixed rate of return to estimated capital values.[21] The approach Colm proposed would require a comprehensive survey of public capital assets, their valuation and depreciation. On the question of intermediate or final use of government goods and services, Colm has proposed that they should all be considered as final products.

The serious shortcoming of a cost approach to the measurement of goods and services produced by the public administration and defense industries is that only in a very few instances can asset use be evaluated. As noted earlier, any consistent evaluation would require some fixed rate of return to capital assets. The difficulties of deriving such rates, as well as those involved in the valuation of the capital assets, would be substantial.

The difficulties which present themselves from a national accounts standpoint are even more formidable in the industry of origin context, where the possibility of deriving a useful measure of output for the public administration and defense industries seems more remote. To provide useful comparisons of performance with resource cost, for instance, activity measures are necessary for individual products and services. This in turn depends on the availability of detailed cost accounting data.

Such data would permit valid estimates of primary input costs pertaining to both labor and capital, at least for major activities in the public administration portion, and these could be used to reflect productivity change in the utilization of these factors. Such cost accounting data are not available although progress in government program-costing is encouraging.

The present Canadian industry of origin approach uses a factor (labor input) valuation for services produced by the public administration and defense industries. When the volume of output is measured by means

[21] G. Colm, "A Re-examination of Controversial Issues," in *Problems in the International Comparison of Economic Accounts,* Studies in Income and Wealth 20, Princeton for NBER, 1957.

of a labor-input series, real output in the public administration and defense industries is almost certainly understated, since no allowance is made for the increased productivity of labor input. Advocates of a complete-cost approach are also unable to make allowance in the capital-cost series for productivity change, thus giving rise to a deficient measure. Current dollar measures can be constructed on a reasonably sound basis using the complete-cost approach, but real output and productivity measures require meaningful product detail with price and quantity data. In their absence, any adjustments for productivity must be arbitrary in nature.

A possible interim approach might be along the lines indicated by George Jaszi when he stated that, "It may be possible to focus not on the services provided by the government to the public, but on the services government employees render to the government, and perhaps derive a measurement of productivity that is tied to technical efficiency with which various detailed operations are performed and does not concern itself with the more ultimate purposes of these activities." [22]

The Service Industries

Although economics deals with the allocation of scarce resources in the production of both goods and services, the latter sector was neglected until comparatively recent times. This is understandable in view of the tendency for theoretical emphasis at any time or place to reflect the influence of the dominating sector in economic development. For example, the physiocrats tried to establish the criteria of productiveness in terms of agriculture, the mercantilists looked to foreign trade, while Adam Smith and the classical economists who followed him saw the production of material commodities in general as the key to economic prosperity—an outlook that has persisted almost to the present day.

Another more recent fact that has tended to inhibit the development of service industry measures is the difficulty encountered in defining their role and their products. Goods, being tangible, are usually easier to understand and measure than services and, on this account, have

[22] G. Jaszi, "The Measurement of Aggregate Economic Growth, A Review of Key Conceptual and Statistical Issues as Suggested by United States Experience," *Review of Economics and Statistics,* November 1961, p. 328.

tended to overshadow services in both theoretical and statistical development.

What has been accomplished to date in the measurement of service industry output certainly cannot be described as ideal, although it may be sufficient to gauge the requirements of an adequate system. Output measures are available for the majority of the goods-producing industries and, although they may suffer from biases, data gaps, and other deficiencies, they have generally been prepared in an atmosphere of understanding. This is far from being the case with the service industries. Before a really adequate data base can be developed for the service industries, it is necessary to understand clearly what should be measured and how it can be measured.

Considerable attention has been given to the problem of classifying economic activities into goods- or service-producing industries, a common criterion being whether or not the activity in question involves a physical transformation of materials. This has inevitably resulted in a number of borderline cases, among which public utilities come readily to mind. It seems to us that classification as such is a secondary issue which can quite satisfactorily be resolved by arbitrary treatment appropriate to particular situations. Inasmuch as the criteria involved have been carried over to the problem of measurement, however, they have had a misleading effect in creating confusion between superficial and fundamental characteristics of the production process. In the constant dollar approach particularly, the measurement of output has been so closely identified with a transformation process that the failure of the service industries to meet this criterion may have resulted in a somewhat negative attitude towards the problem. For example, a shirt being sewn or packaged is clearly seen as some form of production, but a packaged shirt that has been transported, sold, insured, etc., always looks the same even though it in fact represents a different aggregate of factor incomes.

There can, of course, be no doubt that when the creation of market value is synonymous with an act of physical transformation, supported by value data for both output and input which can be factored into quantity and price components, the measurement of constant dollar value added is greatly simplified. However, the lack of such data in certain durable goods industries is just as serious an obstacle to measurement as it is in the great majority of service industries, despite the fact that physical transformation is clearly evident in the one case and not in the other. The primary problem is thus one of recognizing the identity of measurement requirements throughout the whole industry of origin approach. Grave difficulties of application may exist in particular cases, but the availability of a common and consistent framework within which to view them should permit a more positive approach to what had hitherto been regarded as an intractable group of industries.

Notwithstanding these difficulties, it has been possible to prepare real output measures on a basis roughly equivalent in quality to those in the goods-producing industries for about one-third of the service-producing industries, concentrated for the most part in trade and transportation. Another third have serious data problems but these could be overcome without great difficulty by initiating statistical surveys designed to fill gaps and clarify ambiguities. The remaining commercial service industries, such as insurance, financial intermediaries, and business services, pose a much greater challenge from a conceptual point of view. If the problems in these areas can be solved, the way would be clear for meaningful statistical measures covering at least the commercial part of the services-producing industry sector.

Financial Intermediaries

The Canadian national accounts' income and expenditure system, in its presentation, has been largely concerned with aggregative relationships such as those between sectors (personal, business, etc.) of the economy and between income and expenditure flows at the total level. The current-dollar distribution of value added by industry of origin has been of subsidiary interest. A more detailed scrutiny by industry of origin brings to light certain problems which, in our opinion, do not show up in the more aggregative setting. One such problem concerns the origination by industry of certain factor incomes, particularly those arising out of gross interest and rents. On an aggregate basis, the allocation of factor incomes to individual industries is not required and it is sufficient merely to ensure that these be picked up somewhere in the aggregation. In an industry approach no such facile handling is possible, for here the critical question is one of exactly where in the industrial structure economic production does in fact originate.

The present practice in the Canadian national accounts, as well as in industry of origin data, is to treat interest paid as representative of factor income originating in the industry paying the interest. Thus interest receipts from other industries, which are included in the reported profits of the owning industry, must be deducted from these profits. In effect, interest received is treated as a transfer payment. In the case of financial intermediaries, which in total contribute about 3.5 per cent of gross domestic product, a banking imputation is made, the assumption being that certain services performed by the banking system are not reflected in the market transactions of the system. For example, commercial banks in Canada traditionally pay a lower rate of interest to their depositors than would prevail if services performed for the depositors were charged for at a rate designed to cover the costs of the services so performed.

We feel that the treatment of interest in the national accounts should be thoroughly reexamined from the point of view of considering interest receipts and payments as receipts from, and payments for, the sale of services, in conformity with normal business accounting practices.[23] The present treatment in the national accounts, discounting the banking imputation, results in negative factor income in certain financial industries and what the authors believe is a general distortion in the distribution of factor incomes as between financial and nonfinancial industries. It is believed too, that the banking imputation is not a proper solution for that industry. The distorted current dollar distributions in turn carry over into the measures of real output and productivity.

As noted earlier, industry output and income measurement must be related to the creation of market value. The suggestions which follow are an attempt to apply this concept to the measurement of current and constant dollar output in the banking industry, which is perhaps the most obvious example of the problems inherent in the present treatment of financial intermediaries. Market value in this industry arises out of its function in providing certain facilitating services incidental to the production and distribution activities of nonbanking industries, persons, etc. As with fixed capital assets, a

[23] While there is fairly general agreement in the DBS regarding the need for a reexamination of the problems posed by financial intermediaries for industry of origin measures, it should be made clear that our particular proposals represent a minority opinion.

business establishment may choose between ownership or rental of liquid capital, and thus the hiring of money may be thought of as analogous to the hiring of machines or the rental of property. Banks themselves treat interest receipts as revenue and interest payments as costs so that, from the production viewpoint, current dollar value added can be identified in a manner quite consistent with the procedures followed in goods-producing industries. A corollary of this treatment, of course, is that interest received and paid be similarly identified as revenue and intermediate input in other nonfinancial industries.[24]

Once the current dollar industry of origin measures are derived in the suggested manner, the preparation of constant dollar measures may be considerably facilitated. However, the task of obtaining a good breakdown of value into price and quantity components for the financial intermediaries will not be a very easy one. In deflating bank revenue, for example, several alternative methods of deriving constant dollar gross interest have been examined by writers such as Speagle and Kohn. One approach is simply to deflate with a price index of interest rates, while another requires additional deflation using a related price index such as the implicit price index of GNE, the Consumer Price Index or a price index representative of goods and services actually purchased with borrowed money. As Speagle and Kohn have pointed out, deflation with a price index of interest rates alone merely results in a series in which interest rates of the base year are held constant. To quote an analogy in the area of retail trade, this approach would be similar to deflating margins with an index of changes in gross margins which would in fact be no deflation at all since all it accomplishes is a revaluation with constant margins. On the other hand, a deflation of gross interest receipts with a price index of goods or services purchased by the borrower paying the interest equates the service provided with the quantity of goods or services purchased, rather than with the quantity of service actually rendered by the banking industry. Clearly, further research resources should be assigned to problems such as this if mean-

[24] For background discussion relating to the various conceptual issues and views, see National Bureau of Economic Research, Studies in Income and Wealth 10, pp. 28–84; and R. E. Speagle and L. Silverman, "The Banking Income Dilemma," *Review of Economics and Statistics,* May 1953.

For a discussion and analysis of various approaches to problems of deflation, see R. E. Speagle and E. Kohn, "Employment and Output in Banking, 1919–55," *Review of Economics and Statistics,* February 1958.

ingful growth, productivity, and price analyses are to be undertaken for these industries and if these, in turn, are to be integrated within the system of economic production statistics.

It is our contention that each individual establishment should be viewed as an integral operating unit with operating revenue and related intermediate operating expenses, permitting the calculation of domestic product or value added along conventional lines. It is, of course, recognized that a departure such as this from the traditional national accounting systems would ease some problems relating to financial intermediaries, the relationship of financial intermediaries to nonfinancial industries and sectors, and national-domestic concept differences, but would also add some problems in respect to deflation of the output and input of all industries, which would now include interest flows. Other added problems would include the necessity to reformulate basic related theory and concepts and to trace effects on the various flows and components within the entire system of national accounts. For instance, there would be a problem in the personal sector, where there will be gross interest receipts, which under the proposed system might be treated as receipts from the sale of services.

In raising these issues, we hope to stimulate discussion and research which may lead to a solution to the problems we believe are created by the existing treatment of interest.

In DBS, it has recently been proposed that rent receipts and payments be treated as operating income and expenses respectively in establishment surveys and the industry of origin measures. In making this proposal it is recognized that rental income arises in two general areas, namely (a) rental of immovables, such as land and buildings, and (b) rental of capital equipment. Under the proposal, whenever an asset, be it real property or equipment, is leased and where this leasing activity is separable from the other activities of an establishment so that a separate leasing establishment can be identified, rental income derived from such leases should be classified under that establishment and the establishment classified either under the real estate industry, where rent is derived from immovables, or under the appropriate industry where rent is derived from leasing capital equipment. When such rental and/or leasing activity is not classifiable as a separate establishment, then such rental income should be included with the operating income of the leasing establishment. This approach to the treatment of gross rents classifies net rent and associated capital consumption allowances under the owning or supplying industry rather than under the using industry. We recognize that there may be equally valid arguments for allocating rents to the using industry rather than the owning industry as, for example, in the construction of input–output tables.

III. The Data Base and Basic Methodology for Canadian Industry of Origin Output Measurement

THE DATA BASE FOR HISTORICAL MEASURES

On an historical basis, industry production measures have been dependent on a very broad range of decennial, occasional, annual, and subannual surveys of companies, establishments or locations, and activities. Using these and other source data the industrial distribution of gross domestic product in the Canadian national accounts has been, and still is, a mixture of company and establishment (including location) statistics. Another published current value series has presented census value added data (gross output less materials, fuel, and electricity) for the commodity-producing industries by province and territory [25] but does not provide similar data for the service-producing industries nor data for intermediate service inputs in the commodity-producing industries. Measures of real output such as the Index of Industrial Production and the real domestic product by industry of origin estimates were developed in annual and subannual form, using this mixture of survey data in such a way as to best approximate the desired concept.[26] Thus, the basic data inventory used so far for industry of origin studies, while quite extensive, cannot be described as ideal for most industries, and it has, of course, been much worse from the subannual than the annual point of view.

DATA BASE IMPROVEMENTS

In recognition of this general need for more comprehensive and consistent industrial data, the Dominion Bureau of Statistics has

[25] DBS Catalogue No. 61-202, *Survey of Production* (annual), Ottawa.

[26] Detailed descriptions of data used for both the subannual and annual industry measures may be found in Appendices B and C of *Indexes of Real Domestic Product by Industry of Origin, 1935–61* and in Appendix B of *Revised Index of Industrial Production, 1935–57.*

undertaken a number of programs aimed at improving the industrial data base. One of the main developments has been the introduction (in 1960) of a revised industrial classification of establishments, accompanied by a more practicable interpretation of the establishment itself. Work is also in progress on studies of the relationship between company and establishment classifications and reporting units, the accelerated development of industry selling-price indexes and matching value data, a review of commodity classifications, and the further integration of such systems as the national accounts, interindustry and financial flow tables, industry of origin real domestic product measures, industry prices and productivity measures.

The Basic Reporting Unit and Industry Coverage

In order to achieve a complete coverage of economic production using the establishment as the basic reporting unit, the definition of the establishment requires careful interpretation. Prior to 1960, in most industry surveys the "establishment" consisted of a reporting unit corresponding to "process" or "location" (store, plant, warehouse, mine, smelter, etc.) and was generally confined in scope to the main activity only of any multi-activity reporting unit. This resulted in many inconsistencies, and control over reporting procedures in different surveys could not possibly be tight enough to prevent gaps, duplication, and differences in coverage of establishments. With the introduction of the revised SIC the establishment was defined as "the smallest unit which is a separate operating entity capable of reporting all elements of basic industrial statistics." With this new definition, introduced in 1961, data on all operations of the establishment are covered as opposed to the previous emphasis on main activity only.[27] Furthermore, the products of these activities are, with some exceptions noted later, to be valued at whatever boundary—plant, gate, establishment sales outlet, delivery point, etc.—they leave the establishment. Of course this establishment concept results in some increased heterogeneity in the industry data, but it is felt that the advantages of improved accuracy and consistency far outweigh the disadvantages.

In order to illustrate this change in reporting procedures, it may

[27] Intermediate service inputs are not yet covered by annual censuses of industry although these have been collected in the Decennial Census of Merchandising and Services for 1961 and in a special survey of other industries designed to meet the needs of the 1961 input–output table.

be useful to consider the example of a manufacturing establishment which encompasses a factory or fabricating unit, a factory sales office, a warehousing unit removed from the factory, and several retail and wholesale sales branches located away from the factory. According to the new concept and the definitions related to it, this assortment of activities constitutes an establishment within which it is not possible to isolate value added relating to the various activities. The concept recognizes that, for each product item produced or sold, only one firm value—the actual transaction price—exists on the establishment's books and that only intermediate inputs from outside the establishment can be routinely valued at their actual purchase prices. In such a situation, it is thought better to accept the establishment as it actually operates rather than attempt to break it down into artificially separate activities. To attempt such a breakdown would be to force the establishment to file various reports covering the different activities, with arbitrary valuations as the products of the establishment flow from one stage to another. Subsequent to the complete implementation of this establishment-reporting-unit concept it might be possible, with the assistance of supplementary questions on annual survey questionnaires, to sum across establishments for main activities such as shipments of goods of own manufacture and own-account construction on a gross basis, although the problems of isolating value added for such activities within the establishment will remain unsolved because many inputs cannot be identified with specific activities.

This establishment approach to industry of origin measurement thus attempts to rectify the shortcomings of the pure activity system which existed heretofore, while at the same time avoiding the pitfalls inherent in the use of a company system with its broader, more heterogeneous, and changeable industrial structure. Of course, the establishment approach cannot solve all the problems. Establishments that have vertically integrated operations cutting across primary, secondary, and even tertiary industries (as, for example, mining, smelting, and refining; or crude oil production, refining, and distribution) must be split, if this can reasonably be achieved, in order to prevent too much heterogeneity in the industry measures. Errors introduced by such splits can be minimized, however, by means of careful analysis of input–output relations.

Most DBS data collecting divisions have already converted their industry surveys to the new establishment base and others are in process of doing so. Exceptions to this conversion are those surveys expressly intended to cover company data, such as corporation profits, financial assets and liabilities, and location data such as small area sales and employment. Progress in developing establishment surveys based on the new interpretation of the establishment has been good, but somewhat uneven throughout the industrial structure. If this were fully implemented in all industries, the new interpretation would afford a consistent statistical base for industrial analysis.

In the meantime, the process of implementation has itself given rise to some difficult statistical problems and inconsistencies in the industry of origin measures.

The implementation of the new concepts has progressed faster and further in the area of manufacturing than in any other industry division, although, so far at least, intermediate service inputs are not collected in the annual censuses. There are also a number of other problems. For example, some users require manufacturing (activity) census value-added data to be isolated within the total establishment activity framework. This is frequently difficult to accomplish in any consistent and meaningful way since it involves the separation of fabricating costs from selling costs, warehousing costs, etc., as well as the artificial valuation of products at different levels of processing and handling. Some of the outstanding data problems arise because of a lack of provision for the reporting of service outputs such as gross rents received, as well as certain transportation costs included in the transaction price of products sold and also purchased services.

In the manufacturing censuses of Canada and other countries, outward transportation charges paid to common or contract carriers are treated differently from transportation costs provided by the establishment itself. Products delivered by a producing establishment's own transportation facilities are reported inclusive of delivery costs, while payments made to common or contract carriers are excluded from the revenue or gross output data and are not collected as service inputs. This results in a confusion of value and price boundaries and an unknown amount of error is introduced into the net output of the producing establishments. The product of an establishment that is shipped via common or contract carrier, and for which the charges are met by the producing establishment, would show up on the purchasing establishment's books at the delivered cost. In current-dollar terms, the common or contract carrier transportation charges met by the producing establishment and the related revenue that it receives from the purchasing establishment may or may not cancel, depending on company policy, competition, etc. When these flows are expressed in constant dollar terms there will almost certainly be some non-cancelling effects or error. Such problems and inconsistencies as these are being systematically studied in DBS, and it is hoped that they can be substantially reduced over the next several years.

In the areas of merchandising and some selected personal, business, and recreation service surveys, substantial progress has been made in building an establishment-type set of total-activity data which, although by no means perfect, are reasonably consistent with the gross domestic product concept. For most of these areas, intermediate service input data for establishments have been collected with a fair degree of success in the latest decennial census and will continue to be collected on a triennial rotating basis. Subannual sales data will probably remain on a location basis for the foreseeable future, thus requiring periodic adjustment to the more comprehensive establishment surveys. There still remain, however, numerous data gaps in the service industries.

Some major industry divisions or sectors are still completely or mainly on an activity basis. The most important of these are construction and agriculture. Construction is, of course, a most difficult industry to survey, as evidenced by the fact that most countries do not have proper censuses of their construction industries.[28] In Canada some of these survey problems may result from attempting to measure the construction industry as a whole rather than breaking it down into a substantial number of relatively homogeneous subindustries as in other major industry divisions. The identification of establishments for this industry and a clear distinction between activity or commodity surveys and industry surveys might also help to overcome some of the present problems. Total activity or commodity statistics can be derived by summing the gross output data relating to construction as a primary and secondary activity from the entire spectrum of establishment-based

[28] See the United Nations Statistical Commission report E/CN.3/306, *Summary of the Comments Received from Various Countries Regarding the Study "Construction Statistics,"* January 1965.

industry surveys. We do not see any reason for treating construction differently in this regard than manufacturing and distribution.

What must be accepted here, as indeed for all other industries, if studies of structure, value added, growth, productivity, etc., are to be developed, is the principle of using reporting units of the establishment type. Activity-based statistics that incorporate "own-account" construction by nonconstruction reporting units can never yield these measures because it is generally impossible to match properly related output and input elements. Clearly too, the traditional approach to census value added, which is an unsatisfactory concept in any case in the context of establishment-based total activity measurement, is even less satisfactory in the case of the construction industry because of the wide prevalence of subcontracting.

As noted earlier, collection difficulties are admittedly severe for the construction industry, but it is believed that these could be mitigated by following the approach suggested. It is our belief too that the use of physical measures to project real output in these industries should be avoided because of the difficulty of assessing quality change in construction industry products. A far better approach to quantity measurement is through value deflation using specially constructed price indexes, which can be tailored to major components such as heating and air conditioning, landscaping, electrical, plumbing, steel, or masonry subcontracting.

Agriculture is also an industry which presents difficult statistical problems for industry of origin measures. Again, agricultural statistics need to be developed on an establishment and subindustry basis in order to permit their proper analysis and integration within the domestic industry structure. Historically, the collection of agricultural statistics has been oriented toward individual commodities to meet the specific requirements of governments and market analysts. These commodity data, although valuable from the latter point of view, have been inadequate for purposes of meeting all the technical requirements for the study of agriculture as an industry or group of industries. We recognize the difficulties inherent in obtaining establishment-based data for agriculture in a manner consistent with other industries such as manufacturing or retail trade but we believe such an approach would eliminate most of the present problems and inconsistencies in the industry of origin measures. Commodity statistics are undoubtedly required in addition to establishment statistics, but both objectives could be achieved simultaneously by giving primary emphasis to the establishment and summing commodity data across these establishments.

Establishment–Company Problems

For purposes of interindustry flow tables, as well as for industry of origin current and constant dollar measures, it is necessary to estimate establishment-type data for some components of gross domestic product from available company records. With the probability that the industrial distribution of income and gross domestic product in the official Canadian national accounts will become entirely company-based, there is, as was noted in the introduction, a pressing need to develop a parallel system of establishment-based current dollar statistics, and to be able to reconcile the two systems.

In the process of preparing both an input–output table and a new set of base-year industry weights for the real domestic product indexes for the year 1961, considerable attention has been given to methods of estimating establishment operating surplus (inclusive of capital consumption allowances) from multiestablishment company returns. With the adoption of a total-activity establishment concept for industry censuses and the gradual extension of these censuses to such industry areas as construction, merchandising, and services, such a task should become easier in the future. Of course insofar as establishment gross output and intermediate-input boundaries are arbitrarily drawn by the company to which they belong, the allocation of company operating surplus to its establishments will run into trouble. However, these difficulties with the establishment as a reporting unit will become better understood through a systematic company–establishment reconciliation and, in time, can be reduced.

One of the major problems encountered in the breakdown of multiestablishment company data has been the lack of complete coverage of the affected component establishments in DBS industry surveys outside those areas covered by full censuses. Other problems encountered, particularly in the early stages of this work, included some confusion in establishment valuation boundaries between industries such as manufacturing and merchandising and, occasionally, actual duplication of establishments. Such problems are gradually being eliminated, however, through such administrative devices as a central list of establishments and integrated company-establishment files. A considerable amount of attention is now being given to the preparation of matched company-establishment records which in turn should permit the eventual derivation of integrated and matched value-volume-price data for gross domestic product by industry of origin on an annual basis. The attainment of this goal may take a number of years, but there is general agreement that it should be pursued as rapidly as resources permit.

VALUE DEFLATION BY SPECIFIED PRICE INDEXES

Probably the most significant area of recent statistical advance in Canada relevant to industry of origin real output measures is the development of industry selling-price indexes and the matching of value and price boundaries for establishments.[29] Progress in these areas will have significant and direct effects on the quality of the industry real-output measures. Because of its importance, it is worthwhile discussing the background and current development of industry value deflation in Canada.

As may be seen from a study of the appropriate appendixes of the two basic industry real output reference documents previously referred to, annual, quarterly, and monthly real output measures have been developed in large part through the extensive use of value data deflation, either by price indexes based on specific prices or by indexes of average unit value. About 20 per cent of both the annual and subannual aggregates of real domestic product by industry of origin, as published in these basic historical documents and kept up to date in current monthly Index of Industrial Production releases,[30] is dependent on deflation methods using price indexes derived from price surveys of specified commodities. For the historical computation of these annual and subannual measures, price indexes were drawn from a wide variety of sources, including most DBS price index records. It should be noted that these published industry real output measures do not reflect any use of the new industry selling-price indexes. These indexes are being used quite extensively, however, in annual manufacturing industry bench mark updating now underway for the 1959–1961 and

[29] See DBS Occasional Paper No. 62-515, *Industry Selling Price Indexes, 1956–59,* Ottawa, 1961, for the initial stage of this development.

[30] DBS Catalogue No. 61-005, *Index of Industrial Production,* Ottawa, monthly.

post-1961 periods. The initial results of this work will not be available, however, until sometime in 1968.

At the annual level, the physical units, i.e., the average unit value deflation approach, have been principally used in the goods-producing industries other than construction, as well as in many transportation, storage, and communication industries where, depending on the extent and quality of the underlying data, net or gross output indexes have been constructed. Annual indexes for construction have followed the methods used in the calculation of constant dollar GNE, i.e., the value of new investment construction has been deflated by a "cost" price index composed of the prices of main materials used and average wage rates. This approach is, of course, deficient due to its inability to properly reflect productivity changes and gross profit margins. In the general area of retail and wholesale trade and some personal services, real output measures have generally been developed by the value deflation approach using base-weighted price indexes of specified products or services. In the noncommercial industries, as well as in certain components of the finance, insurance, and real estate industry, where labor input is the conventionally accepted measure of output, the deflation of payrolls by average wage and salary indexes has been used. This is tantamount to weighting labor time with base-period compensation rates and is thus analogous to average unit value deflation.

Data difficulties generally preclude the use of net output measures in monthly and quarterly indexes. In the industries where these measures were used at the annual level, the logical subannual substitute might appear to be gross output, calculated by the average unit value deflation approach or the value deflation by specified price index approach, as the case may be. Similarly, it might be expected that indexes based on gross output at the annual level would be calculated in the same way for subannual purposes with, as far as possible, the same distribution between the two alternative measurement approaches. This is generally so with the notable exception of manufacturing, where gaps in the framework of subannual commodity data and the scarcity of appropriate deflators for available shipments data necessitate substantial reliance on man-hour indicators adjusted for estimated productivity change. As with the annual indexes, subannual indexes for most service industries other than trade, personal, and recreation services, and transportation, storage, and communication are largely based on unadjusted labor input, with most being again derived by wage and salary deflation using some form of average wage deflator.

As can be seen from the foregoing remarks, the specified price index approach has so far played a secondary role in the DBS real output measurement program. The main thrust of effort has been through average unit value deflation, with the alternative approach representing a supporting position. It is being increasingly realized, however, that future refinements of the real output system depend importantly on a much more positive use of value deflation by specified price indexes which, in turn, implies the need for an expanded system of price statistics, classified in the same way as, and conceptually consistent with, the underlying value data.

As Stone has pointed out, the relative change between two periods in the aggregate value of a set of commodity transactions can be factored into a change of relative quantity times a change of relative price, and this identity can be expressed either as the product of a base-weighted quantity index and a current-weighted price index or of a current-weighted quantity index and a base-weighted price index.[31] The recognition of these two areas of index number construction as conceptually complementary and operationally parallel is thus the first step in the development of a truly integrated system of value-price-volume statistics by industry of origin.

However, within such a comprehensive approach there are certain independent and sometimes conflicting requirements of the component index number systems which need to be considered. For instance, because the concept of real domestic product requires that the quantity index number be a measure of net output or value added, primary interest focuses on the final net value result at the industry level. On the other hand, precisely specified commodity detail for both outputs and inputs is an essential feature of price indexes required for double-deflation-derived value added in constant dollars by industry of origin and, furthermore, this detail should be available on a monthly basis. Again, the requirements of comparability through time point to the need for base-weighted formulas in the construction of both price and quantity index numbers. When considered against the background of currently available data as well as the technical difficulties that would

[31] Richard Stone, *Quantity and Price Indexes in National Accounts,* Paris, 1956.

be involved with current weighting, for instance, constraints of this kind indicate quite clearly that the scope for readily deriving all requisite index numbers by the decomposition of a single set of value data falls short of theoretical possibilities. Clearly, very few of the requirements of industry price indexes could be satisfied in this manner.

At the present time, the most fruitful approach to this problem seems to lie in giving high priority within a coordinated conceptual framework to the further extension and strengthening of the existing program of industry price statistics for manufacturing and to the simultaneous refinement of corresponding monthly and annual value data. In manufacturing, available monthly value data relate to shipments reported by establishments on an aggregate basis, so that one requirement of the system of monthly price indexes is that it should permit the regrouping of component commodity relatives on an establishment basis with proper regard for seasonal patterns in shipments. For the deflation of annual census data for shipments and materials used, the main problems are those of developing sufficient commodity detail so as to minimize the difficulty of working with base-weighted aggregates of individual commodity relatives and of ensuring uniform price and valuation boundaries. The latter point is a particularly crucial one in the light of the more realistic reporting procedures now in force in the annual Census of Manufactures. The deflation of finished goods and work in process inventories, generally valued at cost, in order to permit the proper adjustment of shipments data to a production basis, is also an extremely important problem, particularly at the monthly level, and one on which very little progress has yet been made.

In this general connection, a brief review of progress to date at DBS in the development of wholesale price indexes by industry may be appropriate. The indexes so far published cover the selling prices f.o.b. plant of approximately 100 manufacturing industries at the three-digit level or below, as defined in the 1948 Standard Industrial Classification. They are available from 1956 to date on a monthly basis with a 1956 reference base and a 1953-weight base. In terms of coverage, they account for about 70 per cent of gross domestic product originating in manufacturing in 1953, or more than 20 per cent of GDP for the economy as a whole. Notable omissions from this coverage at the present time include the entire printing, publishing, and allied industries major group, a number of transportation equipment industries such as shipbuilding, railway rolling stock, and aircraft and parts, as well as some elements of clothing and iron and steel products. The problems of heterogeneity and discontinuity of commodity detail, and those associated with the definition of output itself, which have been encountered in the construction of selling-price indexes for these industries are, of course, precisely those which have made it impossible to calculate quantity indexes by the physical units approach.

The commodities and commodity groupings used for weighting purposes within each industry were selected from the respective Census of Manufactures establishment returns in the order of their importance so as to account for 75 per cent of base-year shipments. Underlying these broad classifications is an extensive system of price collection, embracing more than 3,300 individual price quotations from some 1,700 respondents. While the basic weighting diagram for each industry remains fixed for the duration of the indexes, individual indicators are reviewed regularly with respondents and changed if necessary to ensure their continuing representativeness. In contrast with the more demanding requirements of coverage associated with the selection of quantity indicators, economy of effort of this kind is a powerful argument in favor of the value-deflation approach to real output measurement, particularly when most or all of the work has to be done in any case for basic price measurement purposes.[32]

A major obstacle in the past to the realization of the full potential of this approach has been the lack of a corresponding set of intermediate-input price indexes by industry. In recent years, however, substantial progress has been made in the construction of input price indexes in manufacturing, where more than eighty such indexes have already been calculated on an experimental basis, covering industries accounting for about 45 per cent of GDP originating in manufacturing in 1953. One of the principal problems in this area is that of discontinuity in the collection of price quotations, since buyers covered by the sample do not necessarily make purchases in every monthly period for which data are required. This has been partially solved by adapting for use on the input side some of the available output prices, although the supplementary information on transportation charges, taxes, etc., needed to convert these prices to a laid-down basis at the point of delivery are frequently difficult to obtain.

[32] See Richard Stone, *Quantity and Price Indexes,* p. 99.

There are also certain conceptual inconsistencies between the published industry selling-price indexes and the value data of the Census of Manufactures. For instance, in recognition of other important uses, the price quotations on which the indexes are based refer to new orders rather than to shipments. Apart from the particular effects in those industries where there is a characteristic lag between the receipt of an order and its shipment, there may also be a general effect which varies in a cyclical fashion according to the degree of pressure on productive resources. Furthermore, the annual industry selling-price indexes are unweighted arithmetic averages of monthly data, so that their use for the deflation of annual value totals would distort the resultant output measure in a situation where there were seasonal patterns in sales and the related transactions prices. It is also the case that Census of Manufactures returns are frequently based on the fiscal year of the reporting entities, whereas the annual price indexes are on a calendar year basis. Problems of this type are, however, generally amenable to testing for their incidence and importance and can generally be dealt with by adjustments and recompilations of the basic pricing data.

The change in value reporting procedures in the Census of Manufactures which was implemented in 1961, and which was the second stage in the adoption of the 1960 Standard Industrial Classification, has further complicated the measurement of real output by the deflation approach. For instance, respondents were formerly instructed to value their shipments "f.o.b. plant," i.e., at a level corresponding to a boundary of the establishment defined in terms of manufacturing activity only. To the extent that an establishment was engaged in nonmanufacturing operations, it was assumed that these would be measured in other surveys such as those pertaining to wholesale trade, construction, etc. As noted earlier, this attempted fragmentation of the various activities within an establishment frequently found no parallel in the accounting records of respondents who were often forced to value shipments at the point of sale rather than at the desired manufacturing level. This resulted in inconsistencies within the statistics of individual industries, as well as in duplication between industry divisions. The new concept requires that each establishment be coded to only one industry, that its survey return should cover all its activities and that its shipments be valued "f.o.b. establishment."

Thus a problem of consistency arises between the current dollar shipments data of the Census of Manufactures and the corresponding industry selling-price indexes. For a given industry, the former now reflects a particular "marketing mix" which can change from year to year as a result of organizational changes within component establishments, and thus cannot be related to price indexes based on a uniform "f.o.b. plant" valuation covering manufacturing activity only. The forthcoming revisions to the industry selling-price indexes for manufacturing, in which a 1961 weight and reference basis will be adopted, are, however, also designed to reflect the new establishment concept by adjusting pricing boundaries to the corresponding valuation practices and by being extended to cover nonmanufacturing output. The revised indexes may be initially released for a somewhat smaller number of industries than was the case with the previous indexes, but it is intended to extend their coverage as rapidly as resources permit.

Without minimizing the difficulties involved, the calculation of quantity measures in manufacturing by value deflation thus seems to offer encouraging scope. It does in fact constitute the most realistic hope of a solution in such areas as the monthly Index of Industrial Production where excessive reliance on adjusted man-hour indicators has blunted the cyclical sensitivity of the index and where the gaps cannot realistically be filled by the extension or elaboration of commodity surveys. An alternative approach to increase cyclical sensitivity used by the Federal Reserve Board for the U.S. Index of Industrial Production, estimates short-term movements in output per unit of labor input for man-hour represented industries on the basis of implicit output/man-hour relationships in commodity represented industries. This approach has not yet been tried in Canada largely because of the basic differences in the nature of many of the industries represented by commodity surveys and those represented by man-hours. At the annual level, the deflation problems created by nonmanufacturing production and the possibility of changing levels of valuation in the reporting of manufacturing shipments quite obviously militate against the feasibility of the physical units approach.

This discussion of the problems involved in the derivation of quantity index numbers by the specified price index deflation approach has been entirely conducted within the context of manufacturing, where the annual census data provide perhaps the most detailed and historically complete statistical series within the DBS and were thus an obvious starting point for the development of industrial price indexes. In the immediate future, further development of the system is likely to be largely concentrated in the remaining industrial divisions covered by the annual Census of Industry, namely mining, forestry, and fishing, where the experience derived in manufacturing is expected to be directly relevant. Substantial progress has in fact already been made in mining. In the remaining goods-producing industries, agriculture and construction are likely to prove more difficult since the basic value data are assembled on a commodity rather than an establishment basis. Retail and wholesale trade, and the transportation, storage, and communication divisions offer the brightest prospect in the nongoods sector for the early development of industry price indexes. These areas already have substantial price coverage due to the relevance of their sales boundaries for consumer and general wholesale price indexes. However, there is need for further commodity and service coverage, for input price indexes, for indirect tax and other adjustments to bring the price relatives into line with reported sales value boundaries, and, of course, different weight structures. Refinements and extensions of industry price coverage in these and other service industry areas, while extremely important and urgent within the total industry real output framework, are not as amenable to early solution as those in the manufacturing, mining, forestry, and fishing industry divisions.

QUALITY CHANGES

The assessment of the effects of changes in the quality of the individual goods and services underlying quantity measures of economic production has always constituted an extremely difficult conceptual and practical problem. While it has been treated extensively in the theoretical literature, there has been but little effect on official statistics of prices and real output because of the lack of operational feasibility of most proposed solutions. It is not the intention here to attempt a comprehensive discussion of this complex topic but merely to bring to the fore those aspects of it which the authors feel explicit attention should be given in a real output measurement context and to comment on how they can be handled within the general approaches previously discussed.

In the first place, it should be stressed that we are concerned with a producer's view of quality change over time rather than a consumer's view of the same change. For example technologial advance is continually giving rise to changes in design, substitution of more efficient materials and component parts, closer engineering tolerances and better methods of quality control, etc., which can frequently increase the utility of the products to the consumer quite out of proportion to the costs involved. It is on the latter aspect rather than the former that attention should be focussed. The quantity measure of economic production should seek to identify the additional factor costs or returns which have contributed to the quality improvement and to distribute them properly by industry. The consumer does have a role in this process, and it is more than an indirect one, since his acceptance of the product in the market place determines the size of these factor returns. But the consumer's surplus or economic rent which emerges from the interaction of his own utility field with the market price is something which falls outside the scope of the statistical measure of production. It thus seems to us that the identification and quantification of quality change as we have defined it does not require any radically different approach. As demonstrated below, it should emerge naturally from a careful application of some of the techniques discussed previously.

The term "quality change," even in the restricted sense that is being considered here, actually embraces a number of logically separate phenomena, some of which are more amenable to treatment than others. For instance, changes over time in the proportional composition of the set of distinguishable product varieties contained in a prescribed total or aggregate—the product mix, in other words—can be thought of as group or structural quality change. If, for instance, a broadly defined product category such as "tractors" does in fact conceal a gradual shift from large to small units, a quantity index derived by weighting the total number of units by a base-year average unit value would have a progressive upward bias. This kind of quality change is not difficult to deal with in principle by either average unit value or specified price index deflation, since what is needed in each case is more detailed information on value and quantity and price quotations.

New varieties not previously represented in the aggregate can be handled in a manner similar to new products, i.e., by introducing them into the calculations with artificial weights and by providing for regular updating of weighting systems under both the average unit value and specified price index deflation approaches.

A further kind of quality change which cannot be handled nearly as well occurs in connection with model changes in products such as automobiles and farm machinery. From the standpoint of the unit value deflation approach, it would be formally correct to regard each change as a new variety. This, however, would result in considerable discontinuity of product detail, with excessive reliance on artificial weights, and perhaps a less satisfactory result than if no adjustment had been attempted at all.

When such a situation results in an increase in the price quotation for a particular product, conventional methodology in the construction of price indexes permits either of two extreme positions or some intermediate compromise. At one extreme, price quotations of the consecutive varieties may be regarded as directly comparable so that the difference between the two is embodied into the index as pure price change. Alternatively, the contiguous price quotations may be treated as directly proportional to the qualities of the varieties concerned so that the price index registers no change. When a higher current value of output in the later period is deflated by a price index determined according to the second of these alternatives, the resultant volume measure is higher than that which would be derived from the use of a price index based on the first assumption.

The industry selling-price indexes previously referred to take an intermediate position between these two extremes. The convention most extensively used seeks to measure quality change between two varieties by a comparison of the direct current-period quantities of both labor and material inputs of the new model with that of the old under the same price and technological conditions.[33] The implied assumption about the parallel movement of other costs (including profits) in this comparison may introduce some unknown element of bias and should also be taken into account. This, of course, is very difficult to do on an operational basis.

Thus, to the extent that industry selling-price indexes embody this kind of adjustment, their use as deflators of value data at appropriate levels of detail will yield quantity measures which also reflect quality change. In spite of the obvious limitations, this approach is clearly preferable to average unit value deflation which completely evades the

[33] The mechanics of this convention are explained in *Industry Selling Price Indexes, 1956–59,* DBS Catalog No. 62-515, Ottawa, 1961.

problem. From the standpoint of GDP by industry of origin, however, the impact of quality change must be assessed in terms of value added, not gross output. If, for instance, the increase in quality was known to have originated partly in a purchased component, it would be clear that the index of real gross output derived by deflation would overstate the volume increase, thus, in effect, allocating some of the quality change to the wrong industry or duplicating it. Correct allocation would require the use of a corresponding set of quality-adjusted purchase-price indexes, for the purpose of deflating material inputs and constructing a net measure, so that the appropriate part of the quality change could be netted out of the purchasing industry's output.

IV. Uses and Limitations of the Current- and Constant-Dollar Industry Data

GENERAL

The quarterly indexes of real domestic product by industry of origin and their monthly Index of Industrial Production component enjoy an extremely wide circulation among a variety of users including federal and provincial government departments and other official or semiofficial organizations, foreign governments and international organizations, Canadian and foreign business corporations, labor unions, private research and planning groups, universities, the financial press, and others. A common denominator in this broad range of interests is the value of the indexes as major indicators of economic activity. By complementing the changing expenditure patterns revealed by the quarterly national accounts with a detailed picture of the supply side, the indexes make possible improvements in the efficacy of short-term analysis, forecasting, and policy making. At the same time, the availability of a long series of annual data in considerable industry detail has opened up a wide range of medium- and long-term uses at both the macro- and microeconomic levels. No more than a few representative examples of such uses can be elaborated in any detail. Some uses of the measures by DBS itself are described immediately below. This is followed by a brief account of the way in which some other federal government departments have used them, and finally by a discussion of some potential uses which so far have not been extensively explored in Canada.

TABLE 5

Annual Rates of Industry Growth,[a] *1946–65*

Industry	Percentage
Electric power and gas utilities	9.6
Mining	9.1
Construction	5.1
Finance, insurance, and real estate	5.0
Manufacturing	4.8
Transportation, storage, and communication	4.6
Real domestic product	4.4
Trade	4.1
Public administration and defense	4.0
Community, recreation, business and personal service	3.6
Fishing and trapping	1.8
Forestry	1.7
Agriculture	1.5

[a]Calculated by fitting a least squares of logarithms trend line to the annual data for each industry.

Internal Consistency Checks

As previously mentioned, the development of real domestic product estimates by industry of origin was initiated as a check on the validity of the quarterly estimates of deflated GNE. The background of this testing is well documented,[34] but it may be briefly noted here that, even without adjustment for the statistical and conceptual differences involved, the two estimates generally move in the same direction and at approximately the same rate of change. In addition to this check at the aggregate level, individual production indexes are also used in statistical consistency checks for particular components of the GNE estimates.

Analyses of Growth, Change, and Cyclical Behavior

A major analytical use of the industry of origin real output measures in the related DBS publications has been the study of the growth of

[34] *Indexes of Real Domestic Product by Industry of Origin, 1935–61,* Part I (Introduction) and Appendix D.

the Canadian economy, in terms of both long-term trends and cyclical production movements. The most commonly used technique in this context has simply been to examine the relative expansion patterns of the various industries in order to ascertain the sources of past and future growth. Table 5 shows the average annual rates of growth ranked in order of size for the major industry groupings and for total real domestic product for the 1946–65 period.

The examination of a finer industrial breakdown, as in Table 6, which shows the growth rates in major manufacturing industries, indicates that industries producing radically new products and using new processes,

TABLE 6

Annual Rates of Growth[a] in Manufacturing Industries, 1946–65

Industry	Percentage
Miscellaneous manufacturing	9.1
Products of petroleum and coal	8.6
Chemicals and allied products	7.6
Electrical apparatus and supplies	7.0
Nonmetallic mineral products	6.9
Tobacco and tobacco products	6.1
Printing and publishing	5.3
Manufacturing	4.8
Iron and steel products	4.8
Rubber products	4.2
Textile products	4.2
Paper products	4.1
Transportation equipment	4.1
Foods and beverages	3.9
Nonferrous metal products	3.8
Wood products	3.4
Clothing	3.0
Leather products	1.6

[a]Calculated by fitting a least squares of logarithms trend line to the annual data for each industry.

TABLE 7

Percentage Distribution of Real Domestic Product by Industry of Origin for Major Industry Groupings, Selected Years

Industry Grouping	1949	1956	1965
Real domestic product	100.0	100.0	100.0
Agriculture	10.7	10.2	7.6
Forestry	2.1	2.0	1.6
Fishing and trapping	0.5	0.4	0.3
Mining	3.2	4.7	5.6
Manufacturing	27.3	27.6	29.7
Construction	6.4	7.1	6.4
Electric power and gas utilities	1.6	2.2	3.5
Other goods-producing industries, n.e.c.	1.1	1.1	0.8
Transportation, storage, and communication	8.4	8.3	8.9
Trade	14.6	14.0	13.6
Finance, insurance, and real estate	9.1	8.6	9.1
Public administration and defense	4.7	5.0	4.2
Community, recreation, business and personal service	10.2	8.7	8.6

such as petroleum products, chemicals, and electrical apparatus, expanded far more rapidly than traditional industries such as leather products and clothing, the latter of which grew at roughly the same rate as the Canadian population.

Such differences in the relative rates of expansion of individual industries result in certain structural changes in the economy which are reflected in the constant dollar industry of origin measures. The direct effect of the differential growth rates is shown by changes in the relative contribution of each industry to total real domestic product. Table 7 shows the distribution of real domestic product by major industry groupings for the years 1949, 1956, and 1965. A decline in the relative importance of agriculture and an increase in the contribution of manufacturing, mining, and electric power and gas utilities are immediately apparent. Analysis of structural changes is most appropriately performed with the aid of current dollar industry of origin data, as these reflect changes in relative prices—an important determinant of any industrial structure. Such data, however, are at present available on the preferred establishment basis only for weight-base years.

In addition to their uses in analyzing the long-term growth of the economy, the industry of origin measures are also used for studying short-term production movements and cyclical changes in production. For this purpose, the seasonally adjusted quarterly and monthly data are particularly suitable. However, even annual data can be used for analyzing certain shorter-term trends in the past record or to identify emerging trends in the current period. For example, in Table 8 the post-

TABLE 8

Percentage Rates of Growth[a] by Industry, Selected Time Periods

Industry Grouping	1946–50	1950–56	1956–60	1960–65
Real domestic product	4.4	5.8	2.1	5.4
Agriculture	-0.7	4.9	-2.5	3.2
Forestry	3.6	3.2	-0.3	2.5
Fishing and trapping	5.7	0.4	-1.7	3.0
Mining	10.1	12.2	6.0	5.8
Manufacturing	5.8	6.0	1.6	7.4
Nondurables	4.4	5.3	3.4	6.2
Durables	7.5	6.8	-0.3	8.8
Construction	11.8	7.6	-0.4	5.3
Electric power and gas utilities	9.3	10.4	9.9	8.5
Transportation, storage, and communication	3.4	6.3	2.4	6.5
Trade	4.6	5.1	2.1	4.8
Retail	5.1	4.8	1.7	4.0
Wholesale	3.5	5.8	2.8	6.1
Finance, insurance, and real estate	6.7	5.0	4.6	4.6
Public administration and defense	-3.8	6.9	2.9	1.4
Community, recreation, business and personal service	3.7	3.5	3.8	3.9

[a]Terminal years, using the compound interest formula.

war period has been divided into four shorter periods of four to six years each, the last three of which roughly measure expansion from peak to peak in total real output. In 1946, production was at a relatively low level. It is interesting to note that, except for the steady-growth industries, expansion during the late 1950's was generally much slower than during any of the other periods, with the output of some industries actually showing a decline over that period. During the 1960's, there has been a marked acceleration in growth for most industry groups, with the notable exceptions of mining and electric power and gas utilities whose rates of increase have been gradually decelerating since the early 1950's, and are now closer to those for the rest of the economy.

Detailed industry of origin data are also useful for analyzing period-to-period changes in total real domestic product, as can be seen from Table 9 below, which shows year-to-year percentage changes for the years 1959–65 and the percentage contributions of the various industry groups to the total change in each case. A similar analysis of quarter-to-quarter changes in seasonally adjusted data for a more detailed industry breakdown has been found very useful in interpreting particular movements in total output or the output of a particular industry group, assessing the effect of irregular factors affecting one industry, on higher aggregates, and in reconciling production with related data. Even in the annual data listed below for illustrative purposes, some of these points emerge clearly, particularly the marked differences in the contributions of the various industries to the small increase in 1960, the year most affected by the 1960–61 cyclical downturn. The strong irregular effect of agriculture on total production also emerges quite clearly.

As mentioned above, the monthly and quarterly seasonally adjusted real domestic product indexes are used for all types of short-term analysis and forecasting and business cycle analysis. The availability of current seasonally adjusted data for industries outside the area of the Index of Industrial Production greatly enhances the usefulness of the estimates. The indexes have been used for all the standard types of business cycle analysis, including the calculation of diffusion indexes, specific cycle turning points, contributions of individual industries to the change in aggregate production over various phases of the cycle, comparisons in the movements of various industries and aggregates over

TABLE 9

An Analysis of Year-To-Year Changes in Total Real Domestic Product and Industry Contribution to that Change
(percentages)

Industry or Group	1959	1960	1961	1962	1963	1964	1965
Year-to-Year Change in Real Domestic Product	5.5	1.7	2.0	6.5	5.6	6.2	6.9
Percentage Contributions to the Above Change (total real domestic product = 100)							
Agriculture	0.1	11.4	-39.8	8.2	13.8	7.6	7.6
Forestry	3.8	9.0	-7.2	1.7	1.9	1.7	0.2
Fishing and trapping	-0.8	-0.4	2.0	0.4	-0.3	0.3	-0.1
Mining	12.4	0.3	7.4	5.6	4.4	5.7	4.5
Manufacturing	35.7	23.7	47.8	28.1	35.0	29.3	36.5
Construction	-5.9	-18.7	10.7	6.2	1.7	6.1	9.7
Electric power and gas utilities	6.4	15.3	9.1	3.2	4.9	3.4	5.1
Other goods, n.e.c.	1.1	-1.5	0.5	0.9	0.9	0.9	0.2
Transportation, storage, communication	13.9	10.6	21.2	8.5	10.8	8.8	9.5
Trade	15.6	1.4	7.2	13.8	9.3	13.5	14.8
Finance, insurance, and real estate	8.0	20.8	16.9	9.5	10.6	9.4	6.0
Public administration and defense	2.1	4.9	8.9	5.0	0.1	4.5	0.3
Community, recreation, business and personal service	7.6	23.3	15.2	9.1	6.9	8.8	5.8

the same phases of the various cycles, and so forth. Tables 10 and 11 show some of these comparisons for the last three cycles in aggregate production in Canada using quarterly data.

Productivity Uses

Another important use of the real domestic product by industry of origin measures is in the official productivity measures published by DBS. In the initial stages of this program, priority was given to the development of aggregate measures, and this resulted in the publication, early in 1965,[35] of annual indexes of output per person employed [36] and per man-hour in the commerical nonagricultural economy and its manufacturing and nonmanufacturing sectors for the period 1947–63.

The noncommercial sector was excluded from the coverage of these measures for the same reason that the corresponding U.S. measures are restricted to the private economy. Canadian practice goes further, however, in excluding not only public administration and defense but also other noncommercial services, such as education, nonprofit institutions, and hospitals, where real output is conventionally measured by deflated primary inputs. In view of the conceptual difficulties involved in the development of true GDP measures for this sector, the present situation seems likely to persist for a long time.

However, the exclusion of agriculture from the first published measures was not meant to be more than temporary. In this case, the available output measures were not essentially at fault. Although they are based primarily on commodity rather than establishment statistics, their conceptual basis is considered to be generally adequate for broad trend or growth analysis. The problem was rather that the well-known difficulties of measuring labor inputs in agriculture, particularly those of man-hours, caused some doubts as to the validity of separate productivity series for this industry as well as the effect which their inclusion would have on the broader aggregate. Since that time, it has become much more apparent that, in spite of the somewhat tentative nature of the productivity measures for agriculture itself, the usefulness of the aggregate measures would be considerably enhanced by their inclusion,

[35] DBS Catalogue No. 14-501, *Indexes of Output per Person Employed and per Man-Hour in Canada, Commercial Nonagricultural Industries, 1947–63,* Ottawa, 1965.

[36] The term "persons employed" covers all persons engaged in the creation of output.

TABLE 10

Trough to Peak Changes in Major Industry Groupings Over Recent Cycles in Production and Their Contributions to Aggregate Change.

	IIQ'54–IVQ'56		IVQ'57–IQ'60		IQ'61–IVQ'65[a]	
	Effect on Real Domestic Product[b]	Percentage Change	Effect on Real Domestic Product[b]	Percentage Change	Effect on Real Domestic Product[b]	Percentage Change
Real domestic product	24.9	24.9	10.6	10.6	35.2	35.2
Agriculture	3.8	44.0	1.0	11.4	2.6	35.3
Forestry	0.4	17.9	0.5	33.7	0.4	22.0
Fishing and trapping	--	3.9	--	-7.4	-0.1	-12.9
Mining	2.0	48.6	0.9	16.2	2.1	39.2
Manufacturing	6.8	24.4	3.5	12.8	13.4	49.3
Nondurable	2.9	19.4	2.1	14.6	5.8	37.9
Durable	3.9	30.1	1.3	10.9	7.6	64.2
Construction	2.2	34.0	-0.3	-3.9	2.4	38.5
Electric power and gas utilities	0.7	33.9	0.7	28.9	1.7	55.5
Other goods industries, n.e.c.	0.2	21.2	--	1.5	0.1	15.2

(continued)

TABLE 10 (concluded)

	IIQ'54–IVQ'56		IVQ'57–IQ'60		IQ'61–IVQ'65[a]	
	Effect on Real Domestic Product[b]	Percentage Change	Effect on Real Domestic Product[b]	Percentage Change	Effect on Real Domestic Product[b]	Percentage Change
Transportation, storage, and communication	2.7	34.6	0.8	9.7	3.3	37.9
Transportation	2.2	40.1	0.6	9.0	2.6	40.4
Trade	3.4	24.5	1.4	9.7	4.4	31.4
Wholesale	1.5	31.9	0.8	16.8	2.2	45.2
Retail	2.0	20.8	0.6	6.1	2.2	24.3
Finance, insurance, and real estate	1.1	12.0	0.9	9.6	2.3	23.8
Public administration and defense	0.4	7.0	0.3	5.1	0.3	5.1
Community, recreation, business and personal service	1.0	10.6	1.0	11.1	2.1	22.2

[a]Production was still expanding at the end of 1965.

[b]The percentage contributions of the individual industry groups to the aggregate change may not add to the percentage change in total real domestic product due to rounding.

TABLE 11

Peak to Peak Percentage Changes in Major Industry Groupings Over Recent Cycles in Production

Industry or Grouping	IIIQ'53–IVQ'56	IVQ'56–IQ'60	IQ'60–IVQ'65[a]
Real domestic product	18.7	7.3	32.7
Agriculture	-1.0	-8.1	14.4
Forestry	19.0	1.3	8.9
Fishing and trapping	1.8	-18.4	42.7
Mining	55.5	24.7	31.9
Manufacturing	20.1	6.1	45.3
Nondurable	19.3	12.9	38.7
Durable	21.1	-1.2	53.3
Construction	27.8	-0.9	30.7
Electric power and gas utilities	44.4	38.1	61.1
Transportation, storage, and communication	26.4	7.9	41.1
Transportation	25.7	4.7	42.9
Trade	20.7	6.9	29.5
Wholesale	20.8	11.0	35.1
Retail	20.6	4.7	26.3
Finance, insurance, and real estate	16.9	15.5	28.2
Public administration and defense	10.4	9.1	10.0
Community, recreation, business and personal service	12.0	12.2	25.0

[a]Production was still expanding at the end of 1965.

so as to provide coverage of the entire commerical economy. The difficulties of measuring labor inputs in agriculture are not likely to be quickly resolved, but they are hardly any more serious than those originating in other primary industries already covered. Accordingly, in the subsequent updating of the measures, indexes of output per person employed and per man-hour have been released for the commercial economy as a whole, with separate detail for agriculture, manufacturing, and the residual nonmanufacturing sector. This enlarged coverage now accounts for almost 90 per cent of total base-year real domestic product.

The analytical potential of the aggregate productivity measures cannot, of course, be fully realized until complete detail by industry division is available. Among other advantages this would permit the distinction within the over-all measures between changes in levels of productivity in the component industries and shifts in the relative importance of industries having different levels of productivity. Such detail cannot at present be provided because of the lack of consistency and comparability between the methods and data sources used in the estimation of real output and employment for particular industries, where the criteria are more exacting than at higher levels of aggregation.

In construction, for example, published real output measures reflect value added in construction *activity* which cannot be meaningfully related to the reported employment figures of the construction *industry*. The ability to collect the two kinds of data within the common framework of a census of the construction industry at appropriate levels of industry detail would go a very long way towards solving this problem. Again, separate measures for industries such as finance, insurance and real estate, and business services, in which output is most commonly measured by labor inputs, would be misleading since they would almost certainly underestimate productivity gains.

Shift analysis has thus been confined so far to various combinations of shifts between agriculture, manufacturing, and the residual nonmanufacturing sector of the commercial economy. However, there are still levels of aggregation where problems arising from the quality, consistency, and comparability of the output and input measures for component industries are not too serious. Work is presently in progress to show, for the 1966 updating, separate figures for the goods- and service-producing sectors of the commercial economy and to measure the effect on over-all productivity change of shifts in their relative importance. In this connection, it may be noted that postwar Canadian experience in the growth of output, input, and productivity in the service industries will be the subject of a paper by one of the present authors at the 1967 Conference on Research in Income and Wealth.

Since a unique feature of the Canadian measures of real domestic product by industry of origin is their quarterly periodicity, there can be little doubt that their analytical usefulness would be considerably enhanced by relating them to the corresponding labor input measures in order to bring to light the variations in the rate of productivity change which occur over the course of the business cycle as the level of utilization of available capital resources changes. Many users do in fact make such calculations unofficially, generally by means of Labour Force Survey employment data, the annual changes in which, at the aggregate level, are very close to those of the composite series developed for the official productivity measures. In recognition of the growing demand for an official series of quarterly productivity measures, exploratory work is proceeding at DBS towards the development of quarterly labor input series consistent with those used for the annual measures.

Progress has also been made in the measurement and analysis of productivity change at the individual industry level. The present program covers some twenty manufacturing industries which were chosen as a cross-section of representative import-competing, export, and purely domestic industries. So far, studies covering the period 1947–61 have been completed for synthetic textile mills, breweries, and pulp and paper mills,[37] and others for iron and steel mills, sugar refineries, and hosiery mills are well advanced.

The conceptual basis of the industry productivity measures is essentially the same as that of the aggregate measures, with the principal measure of output being constant dollar census value added, as calculated by the double deflation approach from detailed annual data on shipments, inventories, and materials and supplies used. However, we see no reason at this time for forcing productivity measures at this level of detail into a rigid conceptual framework and we feel that all useful and practicable relationships between various output and input measures of a given industry should be explored. A familiar example is the BLS practice of weighting quantities of products with their unit man-hour requirements and relating these to current man-hours to derive a measure of changes in the total man-hours required to produce the base-year composite of goods.

A pressing concern at the moment is the need to fill out the framework of detail within manufacturing somewhat faster than this program of individual industry studies seems likely to permit. Present plans call for the publication of crude productivity measures at the major group level, using the appropriate monthly Index of Industrial Production components and the corresponding employment and man-hours

[37] DBS Catalogue No. 14-502, *Productivity Trends in Industry, Report No. 1: Synthetic Textile Mills, Breweries, Pulp and Paper Mills, 1947–61,* Ottawa, 1966.

data (which relate to wage earners only) of the monthly Employment Survey. While such measures would lack the precision of the more detailed studies, their greater timeliness and breadth of coverage would more than compensate for this defect, and the implementation of the project can proceed as soon as the Index of Industrial Production is converted to the new Standard Industrial Classification and a 1961 weight base.

Finally, it may be mentioned that the DBS recognizes the desirability of extending its program of individual industry productivity studies beyond manufacturing. Because of the heavy demands on resources which such studies impose, however, it is unlikely that more than a token commitment can be made in the immediate future. The choice of a particular industry or industries has yet to be made, but it is likely to be influenced by the availability of similar official U.S. studies.

OTHER USES OF THE CONSTANT-DOLLAR MEASURES

Perhaps one of the most important applications of the real domestic product by industry of origin estimates is their use in the economic review for the previous calendar year which usually accompanies the Minister of Finance's budget speech.[38] This review, which provides the background for determining broad budgetary objectives, has traditionally been based on current statistics of the components of national income and expenditure, employment and earnings, price and cost trends, as well as the balance of payments and the capital markets. Since the industry of origin estimates became available, however, they have been used in the review for progressively more sophisticated purposes—from a simple analysis of changes in the industrial distribution of real output to an analysis of the relationship between business investment and output by industry of origin and, most recently, as part of a longer-term review of the relationships between output and employment by major sectors, to estimate unit labor costs by industry and trends in the value, volume, and price components of current dollar value added by industry.

In 1963, the Economic Council of Canada was established by federal act of Parliament and directed to study and advise upon the medium-

[38] See, for example, "Budget Papers presented by the Honourable Mitchell Sharp, M.P., Minister of Finance, for the information of Parliament in connection with the Budget of 1966–67," *House of Commons Debates,* March 29, 1966, Ottawa.

and long-term development of the Canadian economy in relation to the attainment of the goals of full employment, a high rate of economic growth, reasonable stability of prices, a viable balance of payments, and an equitable distribution of rising income. The first annual review of the Council, released in January 1965,[39] was devoted to an appraisal of the prospects and problems of the Canadian economy over the five-year period to 1970 in order to provide a basis for the development of public policies and private decisions favorable to, or consistent with, the achievement of these goals. The Council's estimates of potential output to 1970 for the total economy were a composite of direct projections and estimates derived as the product of potential man-hours and potential man-hour productivity.[40] These were in turn based on historical data for the commercial nonagricultural economy, agriculture, and public administration and community services for the period 1946 to 1963. Thus, while the results were not intended to provide more than broad guidelines for potential growth over the period in question, the availability of this industrial detail made it possible to take into account important differences in output, labor input, and productivity trends in the components of the total.

In a related study prepared for the purpose of projecting the levels of investment consistent with a high rate of growth of output to 1970 considerably more detailed components of real output by industry of origin were used.[41] Historical capital-output ratios were prepared for a broad range of industry groups, which accounted for more than three-quarters of the 1963 real output of the commercial nonagricultural economy and over 80 per cent of business nonresidential investment. Projections of 1963 real output by industry division to 1970 consistent with the growth of total real output were then combined with projections of the corresponding capital output ratios to provide annual estimates of capital-stock levels. Constant dollar gross investment for each year to 1970 was then calculated as the sum of discard replacements and gross capital stock changes.

The Council's second annual review provided an appraisal of the

[39] Economic Council of Canada, First Annual Review, *Economic Goals for Canada to 1970,* Ottawa, December 1964.

[40] See B. J. Drabble, *Potential Output, 1946 to 1963,* Staff Study No. 2, Economic Council of Canada, Ottawa, December 1964.

[41] Derek A. White, *Business Investment to 1970,* Staff Study No. 5, Economic Council of Canada, Ottawa, December 1964.

recent performance of the economy in relation to the goals listed above, with particular emphasis on manufacturing which had not been singled out for special attention in the first reveiw.[42] The results of a number of studies of significant factors bearing on the achievement of the goals were also presented. These included some of the basic determinants of productivity, the forces contributing to sustained and stable growth, and the question of regionally balanced economic growth. These studies drew extensively on the real output by industry of origin estimates and have also focussed attention on the need for certain obvious refinements and extensions, for instance, the improvement of the cyclical sensitivity of the Index of Industrial Production and the provision of regional detail.

Following a reference from the Government of Canada, the Council is currently studying the factors affecting price determination and the interrelation between movements in prices and costs, and levels of productivity and incomes. This study, the results of which were published in the Council's third annual review late in 1966, has drawn extensively on detailed industrial data of real output. As part of its longer-term research program, the Council will extend its estimate of potential output to 1975, and it is expected that the program of revisions and refinements to the real output measures which is currently going forward will provide a sounder statistical basis for this exercise than was possible in the earlier case.

In addition, the industry of origin real output estimates have been extensively used in a variety of short-term forecasting exercises by the Departments of Trade and Commerce, and Labour. Studies of this kind are prepared for internal use only, but their methodology is based on simple arithmetic relationships between output, labor input, and productivity, on the basis of which either labor demand or potential output is estimated, using assumptions about the short-term behavior of productivity and the other related variable, in as much industrial detail as possible.

PRICE-COST ANALYSIS BY INDUSTRY

In the introduction, we affirmed our conviction that a set of establishment-based current dollar estimates of the income and cost components

[42] Economic Council of Canada, Second Annual Review, *Towards Sustained and Balanced Economic Growth,* Ottawa, December 1965.

of gross domestic product by industry of origin is an indispensable accompaniment of the constant dollar production-based estimates. To a significant extent, this view reflects the importance which we attach to the analysis of price change in value added by industry and the underlying cost-profit structures developed by Schultze [43] and exemplified by Marimont in his 1962 article presenting the new set of GNP by industry of origin accounts developed by the Office of Business Economics. Efforts along these lines in Canada have so far been fragmentary, both in regard to the number of industries and the kinds of factor income or nonfactor cost covered. Typically, they have been concerned with labor costs and corporate profits per unit of output by major industrial groupings such as manufacturing.[44] The limited and tentative nature of these studies reflects an awareness by their authors of the underlying data limitations but, even so, the available figures may be carrying more weight than they can properly bear. In the present climate of acute and increasing concern about the relationship of prices, costs, and incomes to sustained economic growth,[45] it would be extremely valuable to be able to identify problem areas by industry and by type of factor or nonfactor share; although an understanding of the underlying causes undoubtedly goes beyond this kind of statistical evidence into the areas of structure and institutional arrangements. It nevertheless seems a useful and timely exercise to review the available current dollar (income) and constant dollar (product) measures to indicate the major lines of development needed before truly comprehensive analysis in this field can be undertaken.

An industrial distribution of current dollar gross domestic product at factor cost and certain of its components is published annually as a supplement to the basic national accounts' income and expenditure tables.[46] The distribution is, for the greater part, at the industry division level of the 1948 Standard Industrial Classification and differs in minor detail from that of the real domestic product by industry of origin

[43] Charles L. Schultze, *Prices, Costs and Output: 1945–57,* New York, 1960.

[44] See, for example, Economic Council of Canada, *Second Annual Review,* Table 2-4, page 18 and Chart 2-5, page 19, also "Budget Papers," *House of Commons Debates,* March 29, 1966, Charts 15 and 16. As noted on page 73, the latter also contains (Table 23) a series of annual average growth rates of the value, volume and price components of GDP by industry.

[45] See page 474, above.

[46] *National Accounts, Income and Expenditure, 1926–56* and *National Accounts Income and Expenditure* (Annual), Tables 21, 22, 23 and 24.

estimates.[47] However, the availability of a detailed set of base-year weights for the latter makes it possible to recompile them to conformity with the national accounts' distribution.

Data on wages, salaries, and supplementary labor income by industry are published, as well as investment income, accrued net income of farm operators from farm production and net income of nonfarm unincorporated business. (It should be noted that the industrial distribution of corporation profits as published is not completely on a domestic basis, so that the figures cannot be subtracted from those of investment income to derive rent, interest, and miscellaneous investment income.)[48] The incomplete details of this distribution at the present time thus constitute the first obstacle to a comprehensive price-cost analysis of gross product by industry of origin.

However, the most serious difficulty arises out of the fact that all components of the national accounts' distribution by industry of origin of current dollar gross domestic product at factor cost, except for wages, salaries and supplementary labor income, net income of unincorporated businesses, and the inventory valuation adjustment, are compiled on a company basis of classification, following the Department of National Revenue's taxation statistics from which they largely derive. To the extent that manufacturing enterprises are integrated backward into resource industries and forward into wholesaling, retailing, finance, or other service industries, an industrial distribution of gross domestic product so importantly influenced by company statistics will show a larger proportion of productive resources engaged in manufacturing than if profits, capital consumption allowances, etc., were based on establishment statistics.

The distribution of 1949 gross domestic product by industry of origin which provides the weighting system for the real output measures was based largely on a recompilation of the national accounts' distribution along establishment (or, in some cases, activity) lines for the purposes

[47] In the industrial distribution of real domestic product by industry of origin estimates (also based primarily on the 1948 SIC), repair service is excluded from manufacturing; contract drilling (excluding drilling for oil and gas) and prospecting are excluded from mining, quarrying and oil wells; and water and sanitary services from public utility operations. These industries are then brought together in a separate division "other goods producing industries, n.e.s."

[48] *National Accounts, Income and Expenditure, 1926–56,* Tables 27 and 50, par. 194.

of the 1949 input-output table.[49] Thus, in addition to major regroupings of data relating to corporation profits, capital consumption allowances, etc., due to the reporting unit and classification differences just noted, the distribution reflected a different treatment of construction, in which the own-account new construction of other industries was also included so as to provide a measure of all construction activity regardless of where it originated. The greater part of this adjustment was effected in the wages, salaries, and supplementary labor income component, where the national accounts' figure of 523 million dollars for 1949 was increased by deductions from public administration and defense, public utilities, communication, transportation, and manufacturing amounting to 150 million dollars.

These examples, while not an exhaustive list, are sufficient to demonstrate the hazards of attempting to derive significant price-cost relationships from currently available data, even in the limited area of unit labor costs where the requisite figures are ostensibly prepared on a mutually consistent basis. Progress towards the solution of these difficulties will no doubt emerge as the developments such as those noted at various points in this paper are carried forward.

Statistical Integration

For some years the prevailing view in DBS has been that it would be unnecessarily restrictive to insist that all the basic systems of economic statistics utilize identical building blocks at their most detailed levels. Such an insistence would achieve a semblance of integration at the expense of the primary purposes the separate systems are designed to serve. Either explicitly or by implication, systems such as the inter-industry flow studies, domestic product by industry of origin measures, industry prices and productivity-price-cost relationships are most conveniently based on establishment data, while the income and expenditure accounts and the financial flow systems relate more naturally to company data. These systems should be capable of being integrated and reconciled at various levels of aggregation.

[49] See DBS Catalogue No. 13-513, *Supplement to the Inter-Industry Flow of Goods and Services, Canada, 1949,* Ottawa, 1960.

COMMENT

MICHAEL GORT, State University of New York at Buffalo

I am told that there are two classes of people in the world: those who classify people into two classes and those who don't. Apparently I belong to the first category, for I had always thought there were two classes of social accountants: the "thick-skinned" and the "thin-skinned" accountants. Those who are "thick-skinned" devote themselves to generating the best estimates of observable phenomena that their resources and tools permit without being unduly concerned about asymmetry in definitions and methods of measurement. Those who are "thin-skinned" find such conceptual inelegance intolerable and devote themselves to resolving the inconsistencies. Messrs. Garston and Worton, it seems, belong to both categories—which, I suppose, destroys my classification system. They are, however, considerably more successful in their capacity as "thick-skinned" than as "thin-skinned" social accountants.

The authors and their colleagues at the Dominion Bureau of Statistics have developed an extremely valuable body of data on industry real product, and have achieved this objective despite very serious deficiencies in the basic data available to them. In general, the methods they have used permit industry comparisons of Canadian output and of input–output relations with those developed by the Office of Business Economics for the United States. The methods they have used differ in a number of respects from those used by the Office of Business Economics, mainly because the same classes of data have not been available to them. For example, the authors would have preferred to rely more heavily on measures of real output based on value data deflated by price indexes for individual industries instead of on quantity indexes with base-year price weights. Conceptually the two approaches should yield the same results though, of course, there may be serious measurement discrepancies. As additional price data become available and as further improvements in industry estimates particularly of investment flows and of capital are carried out both in the United States and in Canada, a number of interesting comparisons should become possible. For example, we might learn if the consistently higher capital-output ratios that have been observed for Canadian as compared with American industries represent real differences or only a statistical illusion.

A few words are, perhaps, appropriate on questions of measurement as distinct from the logical structure of the accounts. It seems to me that the authors place undue emphasis on the errors that arise from industry estimates that pertain to establishments but that are derived from company data. As the development of company statistics [1] in recent years in the United States has shown, the discrepancy between company- and establishment-based data is not large for most sectors—mining and some other extractive industries are an exception—at least at the level of industry detail used in the current Canadian measures of output. Relatively simple methods of adjustment should reduce the error to tolerable dimensions. Thus I am somewhat puzzled by the fact that the authors consider this a serious obstacle to the measurement of capital consumption for an establishment-based industry classification. Surely this source of error is negligible by comparison with the information gaps to which capital consumption estimates are subject quite apart from errors in industry classification. Parenthetically, the authors' implicit endorsement of the perpetual inventory method of estimating capital consumption is, I think, premature. All of us who have indulged in the sport of measuring capital stocks and capital consumption by perpetual inventory techniques will, I think, agree that the method is simply a rule of thumb which is used for want of better information. From the standpoint of logical consistency it is far better than the customary accounting values of depreciation. Its superiority over the latter, or over other potential estimating techniques, as an empirical measure of the underlying phenomenon is, however, yet to be proven. It would be unfortunate if what is now done for convenience became a convention.

The authors' discussion of the conceptual problems in the measurement of real product covers most of the standard questions discussed in the literature. They deviate from the conventional view on two issues—namely on the definition of output for the financial and real estate sectors and on the way in which price indexes should be used to adjust for quality change in measuring real product. On both matters their position, I believe, is untenable. In addition, they express a strong preference on

[1] U.S. Bureau of the Census, *Enterprise Statistics: 1958,* Part I, 1963.

conceptual grounds for a factor-cost rather than a market-value measure of industry output. I am inclined to think that, for most analytical uses, the choice among these alternatives depends on data quality and thus I favor the market-value approach.

Messrs. Garston and Worton are uncomfortable about the fact that revenues minus purchases from other industries are considered output for most sectors but not so for financial intermediaries and real estate firms. They propose, therefore, that interest and rents be deemed factor returns to the owners of assets rather than to the industries in which the physical assets are used. One would hardly wish one's measure of the output of an industry to be affected by the choice of financing methods, and debt financing is simply an alternative to equity financing. Consequently, to carry the authors' suggestion to its logical conclusion, the same classification should be applied at least to dividends on common stock as to interest, if not also to retained earnings. Moreover if the interest or dividends paid to the holders of financial assets represent factor returns, they can hardly cease to be factor returns if paid to households rather than to business firms. The effect, therefore, of the authors' proposal, if carried out consistently, would be to attribute a large fraction of output to households while subtracting from the estimate of industry output most of the returns to capital. I doubt that the authors would wish to go this far, but any alternative interpretation of their proposal leads to far more arbitrariness than they seek to avoid by their suggestion. However, a user need not be unduly disturbed about how interest payments and rents are classified as long as the statistician shows enough detail in his breakdown to permit someone with different convictions or tastes to reclassify these items. In all the debates over definitions in the social accounts, this may well be the most important point to remember.

In their discussion of factor-cost versus market-value measures of industry output, the authors show much concern about the current statistical inconsistencies in the allocation of indirect taxes by industry and how these affect market-value estimates. They are also troubled by the conceptual issue of whether indirect taxes should be ascribed to buyers or to sellers. Thus they express a preference for factor-cost estimates. Whatever arbitrariness exists in the allocation of indirect taxes, it affects more the measure of the level of industry output than the measure of change in output over time. As long as we consistently use actual market values to measure all inputs as well as sales, double deflation in conjunction with correct price indexes should deflate out changes in tax rates that are shifted to product prices, thus leaving the measure of output unaffected. To be sure, accurate price indexes, especially for purchased materials, are difficult to construct without a detailed breakdown of the composition of all inputs. However, estimates of indirect taxes paid through the purchase of intermediate products cannot be made at all without detailed and currently applicable data on input–output relations.

For some purposes, such as intercountry comparisons of production relations, the level of output is important. However, for most analytical uses of data on industry output, it is the movement in the series over time rather than its level that is crucial. The absence of suitable indexes for directly deflating factor returns, or alternatively, for deflating indirect taxes (which must then be subtracted from the deflated market value of output) seems to render the factor-cost estimate less reliable for measuring the movements in output. Once again, however, even if the factor-cost measure were adopted, users could be given their choice of measures through the simple expedient of showing the amount that has been subtracted from market values for indirect taxes—assuming, of course, that factor incomes are not deflated directly.

I now come to the most difficult problem of all—the allowance for quality change in the measure of output. There are a number of approaches to this problem. One can, for example, deflate output by price indexes that ignore quality change in output, as most price indexes currently in use tend to do. Changes in inputs and in output will then measure changes in the quantities of units, and estimates of productivity change will reflect only those technical advances that permit a larger physical quantity of output to be produced from the same quantity of inputs, with both unadjusted for quality change. Alternatively, one can try to adjust all outputs and inputs for quality change, as measured by the valuations of buyers, and thereby allocate to each industry changes in productivity that arise both from increases in the quantity and the quality of output from a given (quality-adjusted) constant-dollar value of inputs. Still a third alternative is to deflate output by quality-adjusted price indexes and then impute to the factors of production all measured changes in the quantity or quality of output.[2] In this way, the value of inputs would be derived from the value of output, with technical advance allocated among the factors of production in accordance with independent information on various capital and labor augmenting variables such as education, research and development expenditures, etc.

Messrs. Garston and Worton take none of these approaches. Instead they prefer to measure quality change only when such quality change is associated with an increase in the quantity of inputs used. Thus, for example, if an automobile tire lasts twice as long but its production entails no increase in the quantity of labor or capital or materials, the authors would make no allowance for such quality change in their measure of output. It is only if the amount of rubber used in the tire, or some other input, increased that the quantity change would be reflected in measured output. This is a step in the direction of decomposing all outputs and inputs into their constituent particles, and the particles into their energy equivalents. Then by the law of the conservation of energy, outputs will always equal inputs. Since all definitions are arbitrary, the authors commit no logical error if they choose to define real output in terms of real inputs. But on the same principle, they should also exclude from their measure of output all increases in the quantity produced if unaccompanied by commensurate increases in the quantities of inputs. The measures would then be logically consistent though their usefulness for the analysis of economic problems would certainly be open to question.

REPLY

GARSTON AND WORTON

It surprises us that Professor Gort has found sufficient substance in our passing reference to the Canadian work on historical capital-output ratios to regard it as an endorsement of the perpetual inventory method of estimating fixed capital stocks. We can, however, admit that if it had been appropriate to pursue this question in the paper, our position would have been basically sympathetic. The fact that the main thrust of official

[2] This approach has been taken in a recent paper by Z. Griliches and D. W. Jorgenson, "Sources of Measured Productivity Change: Capital Input," *American Economic Review,* May 1966.

effort in Canada and the U.S. has been, and will probably continue to be, through the perpetual inventory method, must be a prime consideration in any realistic assessment of the possibilities in this field.

In both countries, some of the most fundamental criticisms of the validity of the method have been acknowledged by the use of alternative assumptions as to economic service lives, retirement patterns, and so on. The results so far are necessarily crude and tentative, but most users would surely agree that if the basic data are relatively satisfactory and if the estimating processes are consistent and can be accepted as reasonable, then fairly reliable and analytically useful stock estimates can be produced.

On the problem of adjusting real-output measures for quality change, we remain unrepentant, in spite of Professor Gort's amusing *reductio ad absurdum* of our proposals. Undoubtedly we were arguing in our "thick-skinned" capacity, although a respectable "thin-skinned" case could be made if space permitted. Let us merely repeat that we wish to close some of the more obvious loopholes in our present measurement procedures which have resulted in a failure to capture the effects of changes in the characteristics of the flow of real goods and services. Partly this can be done within the scope of the average-unit-value deflation approach if sufficiently fine detail is available in the source material. However, our main concern is to see much greater emphasis placed in the future within DBS (Dominion Bureau of Statistics) on the deflation of value data by industrially classified selling- and purchase-price indexes, adjusted for quality according to the convention described.

In this kind of price index, the transactions unit is the product itself and not the service it provides. Thus, if an automobile tire lasts longer, the price quotation cannot be directly adjusted to take account of this increase in the store of services, even if this could be unequivocally assessed, because it is tires and not tire-miles which are priced in the market place. Hence, it seems to us that the most feasible "thick-skinned" way of measuring the difference in quality arising out of changes in the characteristics of a product is by the comparison of their relative costs, whether by the limited and arbitrary conventions commonly in use, or by the more sophisticated technique of regression analysis.

In our proposals for the treatment of interest and rents, we can appreciate as keenly as Professor Gort the very far-reaching and possibly awkward implications for the rest of the system. However, what has prompted us to rush in where angels fear to tread is the feeling that all of us, angels and lesser breeds, may be accepting too complacently the widening "credibility gap" between the national accounts treatment of these income flows and economic reality in the business sector. The growing importance of the financial intermediaries indicates very strongly to us the need for a revival of the discussion of these problems and for a solution that follows natural accounting practices.

The implications for the personal and government sectors of the proposed treatment of interest and rents do not seem to us difficult to deal with in principle or practice. The effects on the financial-flows accounts would almost certainly be beneficial in that changes in a sector's aggregate balance sheet could be related more meaningfully to changes in its investment income. The invariance argument is by no means one-sided and cannot, in our opinion, be reconciled very well with the concept of the *total activity* of an industrial establishment which Canadian real-output measures will eventually reflect. In this context, the differences between debt financing and equity financing are more important than their similarities. Interest is an intermediate cost involving a mandatory obligation to outsiders, whereas dividends are the discretionary distribution of a residual return to owned capital.

We would agree with much of what Professor Gort says regarding factor-cost–market-price measures but we must take exception to at least two points. In the case of international comparisons, it should be noted that many countries use the factor-cost concept, indeed, most European SNA countries utilize it. Of course this difficult matter is now under consideration by the U.N. Statistical Commission and by a number of countries, including Canada, and it may thus be premature to say too much more about it at this time.

While it is true that deflated values for individual commodities will move similarly (assuming properly matched price indexes are available) whether valued inclusive or exclusive of indirect taxes levied at the industry level, this is not necessarily so of any combination of commodities unless indirect taxes as a percentage of market value are similar for all commodities, or all commodities move similarly. These conditions are not met with in Canada at either the commodity group or industry levels. Thus the question of reliability of the factor-cost industry measures, when viewed in the light of industry of origin measure uses, has never been seriously questioned in Canada.

Finally, a further comment on the company-establishment unit classification problem might be useful. In Canada there are substantial differences in the industrial distribution of gross domestic product at factor cost when this distribution is based on establishment data instead of company data. Even a rough comparison of the Canadian data for a weight-base year such as 1949 (bearing in mind that the main component, salaries and wages, is on an establishment basis in both distributions) will indicate the possible range of difference. For example forestry in that year was affected by about 20 per cent, while mining differed by 10 per cent. Other industries were affected by a lesser percentage with manufacturing affected by only 2 per cent. However, within manufacturing some individual industries would be substantially different. Vertical integration by companies across industrial lines in Canada is thus considered to be important and is subject to continual change.

Index